Principles of

ELECTRICITY

AND

MAGNETISM

This book is in the

ADDISON-WESLEY SERIES IN PHYSICS

	Gaussian	*Heaviside-Lorentz*	*Rationalized mks*
Lorentz force equation	$\mathbf{F} = q\left(\mathbf{E} + \dfrac{1}{c}\mathbf{v} \times \mathbf{B}\right)$	$\mathbf{F} = q\left(\mathbf{E} + \dfrac{1}{c}\mathbf{v} \times \mathbf{B}\right)$	$\mathbf{F} = q(\mathbf{E} + \mathbf{v} \times \mathbf{B})$
Maxwell's field relations	$\mathbf{D} = \mathbf{E} + 4\pi\mathbf{P}$ $\mathbf{B} = \mathbf{H} + 4\pi\mathbf{M}$	$\mathbf{D} = \mathbf{E} + \mathbf{P}$ $\mathbf{B} = \mathbf{H} + \mathbf{M}$	$\mathbf{D} = \epsilon_0\mathbf{E} + \mathbf{P}$ $\mathbf{B} = \mu_0\mathbf{H} + \mathfrak{M}$
First	$\boldsymbol{\nabla} \cdot \mathbf{D} = 4\pi\rho$	$\boldsymbol{\nabla} \cdot \mathbf{D} = \rho$	$\boldsymbol{\nabla} \cdot \mathbf{D} = \rho$
Second	$\boldsymbol{\nabla} \cdot \mathbf{B} = 0$	$\boldsymbol{\nabla} \cdot \mathbf{B} = 0$	$\boldsymbol{\nabla} \cdot \mathbf{B} = 0$
Third	$\boldsymbol{\nabla} \times \mathbf{E} = -\dfrac{1}{c}\dot{\mathbf{B}}$	$\boldsymbol{\nabla} \times \mathbf{E} = -\dfrac{1}{c}\dot{\mathbf{B}}$	$\boldsymbol{\nabla} \times \mathbf{E} = -\dot{\mathbf{B}}$
Fourth	$\boldsymbol{\nabla} \times \mathbf{H} = \dfrac{1}{c}(4\pi\mathbf{J} + \dot{\mathbf{D}})$	$\boldsymbol{\nabla} \times \mathbf{H} = \dfrac{1}{c}(\mathbf{J} + \dot{\mathbf{D}})$	$\boldsymbol{\nabla} \times \mathbf{H} = \mathbf{J} + \dot{\mathbf{D}}$
Poynting vector	$\mathbf{S} = \dfrac{c}{4\pi}\mathbf{E} \times \mathbf{H}$	$\mathbf{S} = c\mathbf{E} \times \mathbf{H}$	$\mathbf{S} = \mathbf{E} \times \mathbf{H}$

Principles of
ELECTRICITY
and
MAGNETISM

by

EMERSON M. PUGH

Department of Physics, Carnegie Institute of Technology

and

EMERSON W. PUGH

International Business Machines Research Laboratory

ADDISON-WESLEY PUBLISHING COMPANY, INC.

READING, MASSACHUSETTS, U.S.A.

LONDON, ENGLAND

PREFACE

This book is designed to provide an understanding of the principles of Electricity and Magnetism which are essential for all individuals in technical fields. These principles are concisely and rigorously contained within Maxwell's four field relations and the Lorentz force-on-a-charge equation. However, to fully appreciate this concise formulation, the student must understand its relationship to the equations that are studied in elementary courses, which are actually more useful in solving many problems. There are two approaches to demonstrating this relationship: either one can assume the validity of Maxwell's relations and the Lorentz equation to derive the less general relations, or one can show how Maxwell's relations arise as a natural extension of the less general equations. The latter procedure is adopted here because years of teaching experience have shown it to be the better one for the majority of students.

The equations of Maxwell and Lorentz are so much more useful when expressed in vector notation that it is desirable to do so even when students have little or no prior knowledge of vectors. For this reason, the principles of vector algebra and calculus are treated simultaneously with elementary electrostatics at the beginning of the book, and then are used throughout the text. This approach has proven very useful whether used as an introduction to vectors and a review of electrostatics, or as an introduction to electrostatics and a review of vectors, or as either an introduction to or a review of both. The rate at which these chapters can be handled, of course, depends on the backgrounds of the students. Interestingly enough, classroom experience indicates that students can learn both the electrostatic principles and the vector notation as rapidly as they can learn electrostatics without the benefit of vectors; and when students already have been introduced to vectors, their use greatly speeds the learning of electrostatics.

Throughout the text, advanced mathematical methods are utilized when they simplify the treatment or make it more rigorous; however, no prior knowledge of mathematics beyond algebra and calculus is assumed. Instead, the additional mathematics such as vectors, complex variables, and line integrals are treated here to the extent necessary for an understanding of the subject matter.

It is impossible to point out all the places where a special effort has been made to simplify difficult concepts. However, special emphasis has been given to the discussions of transmission of energy from an emitter of electromagnetic energy to an absorber, for frequencies that vary from the low frequencies of ordinary power transmission to the ultrahigh frequencies of radar, and we can see why waveguides replace transmission lines as

v

frequencies increase. The electromagnetic fields of an oscillating dipole are expressed in simple and rigorous forms that facilitate the analysis of energy flow both close to and far from the dipole. Physical definitions have been provided for such mathematical operations as the gradient, the divergence, the curl, and the line integral that facilitate an understanding of the mathematical proofs.

In general, fundamental principles are illustrated throughout by applications to suitable devices. Practical devices have been used wherever possible, but suitability has been determined more by their usefulness in illustrating the principles than by their usefulness in laboratories or industry. In order to avoid confusing basic principles with device considerations, other important practical devices are treated only in the problems, where rather complete discussions can be found. However, the galvanometer is treated in considerable detail, both because it is important in many applications and because it provides illustrations for several fundamental principles.

Amperian currents rather than the magnetic-pole concepts have been used in discussing the source of magnetic fields. This choice was dictated by the wealth of experimental evidence which indicates that **B** and **E** are the most basic of the four electromagnetic-field vectors. The magnetic-dipole concept, however, is derived from Amperian-current considerations and is used to demonstrate the symmetry between the electrostatic and magnetostatic formalisms. This justifies the use of the dipole concept in the discussion of the properties of magnetic materials, thereby simplifying the solution of some problems.

The following comments may help to determine how this text can be used in various courses:

For a two-semester course: This book is designed primarily for such a course and it should be possible for the student to become familiar with practically all the material, with adequate time to solve enough problems so that he learns to use the basic concepts. Many of these problems provide much more than a simple drill, since they frequently contain concepts that could have been contained in the text if it had not been desirable to keep the text brief and more readable. Because each section is designed to build onto the preceding one, it is recommended that they be studied in the order of presentation whenever circumstances permit.

When a laboratory course is given concurrently: If a laboratory is run concurrently with the course work, it may be desirable to begin immediately with some discussion of direct- and alternating-current circuits. This can be accomplished by studying Sections 6–7, 6–8, 6–9, and 6–10 on direct-current circuits, followed by Section 4–8 on complex variables and Sections 10–1 through 10–9 on alternating-current circuits. The discussion of the galvanometer in Section 7–8 may also be included. The rest of the material should then be presented in the same order as in the text. *For a one-semester course:* In many schools, curricular limitations make it impossible to devote two semesters to this subject. Obviously, some important material must be omitted in a single-semester course. Such a course should present concepts that are of immediate use and that provide a sound basis for future study. Maxwell's relations are so important to this basis that they should be studied immediately rather than devoting time, as has been done in many single-semester courses, to the review of elementary relations. A suitable one-semester course can be obtained from this text for students with better-than-average background by careful selection of topics and by spending less time on problems than is anticipated in a two-semester course. A skeleton course complete enough to retain continuity may omit Chapters 6 and 10 on direct- and alternating-current circuits as well as Sections 4–5 through 4–11, Sections 5–6, 5–8, 5–9, 7–8, 9–10, 11–3, and 11–5 through 11–8. All discussions and problems involving coordinate systems other than those with rectangular and spherical coordinates, together with the discussion of anisotropic crystals, could be omitted. How many of the above sections would actually have to be eliminated in a one-semester course will depend upon the academic background of the students in the course, especially upon their background in mathematics, and upon the depth of the coverage that is desired.

ACKNOWLEDGMENTS

Students in the classes of 1955 through 1960, who majored in physics at the Carnegie Institute of Technology, have contributed much to the development of this text. In particular, the last two of these classes, who used the book in lithographed form, provided useful suggestions and constructive criticism. George Lang, who taught from these notes, contributed a few of the problems and gave us many helpful suggestions. We are indebted to Mary Haber and Margaret Young for sacrificing some of their vacation time to type and proofread the manuscript.

February 1960   E.M.P.
                                                            E.W.P.

CONTENTS

CHAPTER 1. SYSTEMS OF UNITS 1

1–1 The original cgs systems of units 3
1–2 The gaussian system of units 5
1–3 Rationalization 6
1–4 The rationalized mks system of units 7
1–5 Legal definitions for the mks units 8

CHAPTER 2. VECTOR MATHEMATICS FOR ELECTROSTATIC FIELDS . . 13

2–1 The vector notation 13
2–2 Vector addition and subtraction 14
2–3 Unit vectors and rectangular components 16
2–4 Coordinate systems 17
2–5 Electrostatic fields 20
2–6 Dipole fields 22
2–7 Fields by direct integration 24
2–8 Scalar or dot product of vectors 28
2–9 Line element 30
2–10 Line integral 31
2–11 Electrostatic potentials 32
2–12 Partial differentiation 35
2–13 Gradient of potential 37
2–14 Vector or cross product of vectors 40
2–15 Identities in vector algebra 44

CHAPTER 3. FUNDAMENTAL THEOREMS OF ELECTROSTATICS WITH
            DIFFERENTIAL OPERATORS 51

3–1 Solid angles 51
3–2 Gauss' law 54
3–3 Divergence of vector fields 60
3–4 The Gauss mathematical theorem 63
3–5 Capacitors and capacitance 65
3–6 Curl of a vector field 66
3–7 Stokes' theorem 70
3–8 The operator del 71

CHAPTER 4. SOLUTION OF ELECTROSTATIC PROBLEMS 81

4–1 Electrostatic solutions with Laplace's equation . . . 82
4–2 Method of images 83
4–3 Uniqueness theorem 88
4–4 Some solutions with spherical coordinates 91
4–5 Some solutions with cylindrical coordinates 96

ix

4–6   Laplace's equation in rectangular coordinates   100
4–7   Infinite series of images   102
4–8   Complex quantities.   104
4–9   Functions of a complex variable for two-dimensional problems .   107
4–10 Some characteristics of electrostatic fields   114
4–11 Eccentric cylinder problems   116

CHAPTER 5.   DIELECTRIC MATERIALS   129

5–1   The atomic structure of matter   129
5–2   Mechanisms of polarization   132
5–3   Maxwell's first relation   137
5–4   Dielectric constants   140
5–5   Boundary conditions with dielectrics   141
5–6   Uniqueness theorem with dielectric materials   144
5–7   Dielectric sphere in a uniform field   147
5–8   Dielectric cylinder in a uniform field.   150
5–9   Microscopic electric fields   151
5–10 Energy relations in static electric fields   154
5–11 Total energy to create static electric fields   159
5–12 Electric dipoles   163

CHAPTER 6.   STEADY CURRENTS   170

6–1   Metallic conductors   170
6–2   Ohm's law   173
6–3   Energy and power conversions   176
6–4   Sources of electric energy and power.   178
6–5   Conservation of charge   183
6–6   Steady current-density solutions   184
6–7   Kirchhoff's laws   189
6–8   Solution of d-c network problems   190
6–9   Direct-current instruments   192
6–10 Routine solution of networks   199

CHAPTER 7.   ELECTROMAGNETIC INDUCTION   209

7–1   Field definitions   209
7–2   Forces on current-carrying wires   213
7–3   Conductors moving in magnetic fields   216
7–4   Maxwell's second relation   220
7–5   Maxwell's third relation   222
7–6   Induced emf's   223
7–7   Electric power conversion   225
7–8   Galvanometers   226

CHAPTER 8.   MAGNETIC FIELDS OF ELECTRIC CURRENTS   241

8–1   The Biot-Savart law   241
8–2   Steady current form of Maxwell's fourth relation   247

8–3   Maxwell's fourth relation   253
8–4   Summary of Maxwell's field relations   254
8–5   General scalar and vector potentials   256
8–6   Low-frequency solutions of the potential equations   257
8–7   Mutual and self-inductance   260
8–8   The standard ampere   266

CHAPTER 9.   MAGNETIC MATERIALS   276

9–1   Magnetic fields due to magnetized materials   277
9–2   Critique of Maxwell's fourth relation   281
9–3   Fields of permanent magnets and electrets   282
9–4   Axial fields of a magnetized cylinder   285
9–5   Boundary-value problems   287
9–6   Ferromagnetic sphere in a uniform field   289
9–7   Measurement of B versus $\mu_0 H$ 292
9–8   Scalar magnetic potentials   296
9–9   Work required to produce magnetic fields   302
9–10 The atomic origin of magnetism   304
9–11 Ferromagnetic materials   308

CHAPTER 10.   ALTERNATING CURRENTS   324

10–1   Differential equation for an a-c series element   325
10–2   Solution of the differential equation with complex variables . .   326
10–3   Steady a-c in a series element.   330
10–4   Kirchhoff's laws for a-c networks.   332
10–5   Admittance, conductance, and susceptance   336
10–6   Analytical and graphical solutions of a-c network problems . .   337
10–7   Nonohmic circuit elements   342
10–8   Alternating-current bridges and other instruments.   346
10–9   Inductive coupling   351

CHAPTER 11.   ELECTROMAGNETIC RADIATION   364

11–1   Wave equations for nonconducting isotropic media   366
11–2   Relationships between electric and magnetic fields in plane waves   369
11–3   Laws of optics   371
11–4   The Poynting vector   377
11–5   Retarded potentials   381
11–6   Radiation from an oscillating dipole   383
11–7   Transmission lines at high frequencies   391
11–8   Waveguides   395

APPENDIX   405

ANSWERS TO SELECTED PROBLEMS   415

INDEX   423

CHAPTER 1

SYSTEMS OF UNITS

Electrostatic forces were observed as early as the time of Homer and probably had been observed throughout the ages. The magnetic forces due to natural permanent magnets also must have been observed in prehistoric times. Nevertheless, it remained for Gilbert, personal physician to Queen Elizabeth in the 16th century, to make the first scientific study of both of these forces.

It is now well known that all matter is made up of elementary particles, most of which carry either a positive or a negative charge. Compared with gravitational forces, the electrostatic forces between these particles are colossal.

With such powerful forces around them, how could the early philosophers have remained so ignorant of their existence? Probably because nature had hidden these forces so effectively by generally providing just as many negative charges (electrons) as there are positive charges of equal magnitude (protons) in each object. Only when this delicate balance is upset can these forces be observed as electrostatic forces.

Coulomb, in 1789, was the first to determine experimentally the fundamental law of attraction and repulsion between localized electrostatic charges. Coulomb expressed this law, which is named after him, in terms of the force F between two point charges of magnitude q and q' respectively. It states that

$$F = k \frac{qq'}{r^2},$$

where r is the distance between the point charges, and k is a constant which in a vacuum depends only on the units used in measuring the q's, r, and F. A positive sign for the product qq' means that the charges are repelled by each other, while a negative sign means they are attracted.

Chemical, mechanical, electric, and magnetic properties of all materials are strongly dependent upon the coulomb forces. However, when fundamental particles like the electron and proton are separated by much less than 10^{-9} meter, as they are within most materials, the laws of interaction are too complex to be easily understood. An understanding of the role played by these coulomb forces in producing the physical and chemical properties of materials has been achieved only since 1927, with the development of quantum mechanics.

1

While the theoretical understanding of electricity and magnetism progressed so rapidly in the 19th century that Maxwell had predicted the existence of electromagnetic waves by 1864, the subject was largely a laboratory curiosity until the latter part of that century. It is true that Morse had invented the telegraph, which was put into operation by several companies as early as 1851, but the general public did not become familiar with the phenomena of electricity until the telephone and electric light brought electric wires into private homes. The first telephone switchboard was established by Bell in New Haven, Connecticut, in 1878 with 21 subscribers, and the first central power station was established by Edison to light 12 blocks of New York City in 1882. Someone in this latter group of customers installed an electric motor to grind coffee, and the electric power industry was born. To be able to charge customers equitably, the electric industry had to adopt a standard system of units for measurement. The system they adopted was called "practical" because the magnitudes for the various units were selected to be more useful in the practical problems of the day than were the cgs units used by scientists. The names of these practical units—ampere, volt, ohm, farad, coulomb, watt, joule, henry, etc.—are now familiar to most people.

In searching for a single system of units that could properly be called "the absolute system," scientists had developed a number of systems all based upon cgs units. Having established a single cgs system for use in mechanics, they had set about extending this system to the more recently discovered laws of electrostatics and magnetostatics. Soon it was discovered that at least two different systems were emerging, each of which had equally good claims to the term "absolute." Most of the textbooks in use between the two World Wars used one cgs system for electrostatics, another cgs system for magnetostatics, and the "practical" system for direct and alternating currents. The multiplicity of systems caused confusion, especially for beginning students. Two additional cgs systems, each attempting to unify the original systems, were developed and used in advanced theoretical texts. It was eventually recognized that there is no single system that properly can be called "absolute."

The arbitrary nature of systems of units can be seen from the development of units in mechanics. All mechanical systems of units have started from Newton's second law, stated as $F = ma$ rather than $F = kma$. In using $F = ma$, the law for gravitational attraction has had to be written as $F = Gmm'/r^2$, where G is neither dimensionless nor unity. There is no reason to consider either of these laws to be more fundamental than the other. If the system had been started from the gravitational law, the laws would have been written as $F = mm'/r^2$ and $F = kma$. Force would then have the dimensions of $(\text{mass/length})^2$, with units of $(\text{gm/cm})^2$. For consistency, the k in Newton's second law then must have the units gm-sec^2/cm^3. This system is just as consistent as the system now in general use. Fortunately, the system chosen for mechanical units appears to provide the simplest calculations in most cases.*

After a thorough study of the problem, a committee† of the American Association of Physics Teachers recommended dropping all of the cgs systems but the gaussian and converting the "practical" system to a rationalized mks system. The decision to retain the gaussian system stemmed from the fact that most of the theoretical papers then in the literature had used either these units or ones that could be easily converted to them. The decision to adopt the mks system stemmed primarily from a study and some suggestions made by Giorgi in 1901. He noted that the practical units had been chosen to have magnitudes which were obtained by multiplying the corresponding magnetic cgs units by powers of ten. Furthermore, these powers of ten were so fortunately chosen that the practical units could fit into a simple, consistent system based upon the meter, kilogram, and second. Other reasons for adopting the mks system were:

(a) Practically all measuring instruments have long been calibrated in practical units (these units have since been accurately defined by international agreements).

(b) The names of the units are well known and are simple to use.

(c) Especially in its rationalized form, the mks system is useful for all types of electric and magnetic problems, including those in advanced theories.

A considerable understanding of the subject combining electricity and magnetism can be obtained by studying the historical development of systems of units.

1-1 The original cgs systems of units. Historically, electrostatics and magnetostatics were studied before current electricity. Knowledge of these phenomena increased rapidly after the demonstration by Coulomb that the forces between static charges and the forces between magnetic poles both followed the inverse-square law. This similarity between the two phenomena made possible the parallel development of the laws of electrostatics and magnetostatics. It also resulted in the simultaneous development of two independent systems of units. Both systems were based upon the centimeter-gram-second system that had become so

---

* An amusing and informative discussion of units has been given by A. G. McNish, *Physics Today*, p. 19 (April 1957).

† *Am. Phys. Teacher* **3**, 90, 1935, and **6**, 144, 1938.

useful in mechanics. In the Coulomb's law equations for the force between two concentrated charges and between two isolated magnetic poles:

$$F = k \frac{qq'}{r^2}, \tag{1-1}$$

$$F = k_m \frac{q_m q'_m}{r^2}, \tag{1-2}$$

the k and k_m were left out, which amounted to assuming that $k = k_m = 1$ and that both constants were dimensionless. With F in dynes and r in centimeters, Eqs. (1-1) and (1-2) provided the means for defining and measuring "unit charges" and "unit poles," respectively.

Precise measurements showed that when the experiments were done in air or any other isotropic medium instead of in a vacuum, the results depended upon this medium. To allow for the effect of the medium, ϵ, the dielectric constant, and μ, the permeability, were placed in the denominators of (1-1) and (1-2) respectively. These quantities were arbitrarily chosen to be dimensionless and to be $\epsilon_v = \mu_v = 1$ in a vacuum. Thus, using $F = qq'/r^2$ as the defining equation, a charge that would repel an equal and like charge with a force of 1 dyne at a distance of 1 cm in a vacuum was defined as a unit charge. The unit magnetic pole was defined from $F = q_m q'_m/r^2$ in the same fashion.

Next, unit electrostatic and unit magnetostatic fields were defined, respectively, as the electric field that would exert one dyne of force per unit charge, and the magnetic field that would exert one dyne of force per unit pole. The defining equations were $E = F/q$ and $H = F/q_m$.

When it was discovered that magnetic fields could be produced by electric currents or by the motion of electric charges, the two systems of units could no longer be considered as independent. Biot and Savart showed that magnetic fields produced by current circuits could be calculated by integrating

$$dH = K_I \frac{I \, dl \sin \theta}{r^2}$$

around the complete electric circuit. It was then realized that this equation made it possible to define a unit current in a fundamental manner by letting K_I be unity and dimensionless. The equation for defining a unit current then became

$$dH = \frac{I \, dl \sin \theta}{r^2}.$$

This unit became the cgs-electromagnetic unit (cgs-emu) of current.

However, the electrostatic system (cgs-esu) provides another very straightforward method of defining a unit current. Since current is merely the flow of electric charges, a unit current can be defined as the current that transports a unit charge past any point in the circuit in one second, $I = dq/dt$. Using the electrostatic unit for the charge, a unit of current was defined and called the cgs-electrostatic unit (cgs-esu) of current. These two units for electric current proved to differ from each other, both in magnitude and in dimensions. In fact, it is quite obvious that one complete set of units can be obtained by starting with Eq. (1–1) and another complete set can be obtained by starting with Eq. (1–2).

Originally, no names were assigned for units either in the cgs-esu or in the cgs-emu, probably because they were presumed to be *the* fundamental units, for which no particular names were needed. This attitude now seems strange since there were, in fact, two complete and different sets of so-called "fundamental" units. Since both systems were cgs units, this caused considerable confusion. In the 1930's before the adoption of the mks system, some of the confusion was alleviated by assigning names to the units in each of the cgs systems. Because the practical units were obtained by multiplying the corresponding units in the cgs-emu system by powers of ten, the cgs-emu system was considered to be the absolute system, whose units should be the absolute ampere, the absolute ohm, etc. The names actually chosen and used for these quantities in the cgs-emu system were the practical units with the prefix *ab*, i.e., abampere, abvolt, abcoulomb, abohm, abfarad, etc. In a similar manner, the cgs-esu units were named statampere, statvolt, statcoulomb, statohm, statfarad, etc.

Long before these names were coined the surprising discovery had been made that the ratio obtained by dividing the quantity measuring a given charge in statcoulombs by the quantity measuring the same charge in abcoulombs was 2.9979×10^{10} cm/sec, which equaled c, the velocity of light, both numerically and dimensionally, within the limits of error of the most accurate measurements. This discovery gave Maxwell the clue for his remarkable theory of electromagnetic fields which led to his electromagnetic theory of light and his prediction of the existence of electromagnetic waves of lower frequencies.

1–2 The gaussian system of units. Gauss had pointed out that the two cgs systems could be made into one system by placing c (the velocity of light) in cm/sec in the denominator of the Biot-Savart law; that is,

$$dH = \frac{I\, dl \sin \theta}{cr^2}.$$

The gaussian system thus developed is the system that is now most commonly used by physicists in their advanced theoretical work. The five elementary equations required for defining this system are listed in the first column

TABLE 1–1

SOME ELEMENTARY DEFINING EQUATIONS

Gaussian	Heaviside-Lorentz	Rationalized mks
$F = \dfrac{q_m q_m'}{r^2}$	$F = \dfrac{q_m q_m'}{4\pi r^2}$	$F = \dfrac{q_m q_m'}{4\pi \mu_0 r^2}$
$H = \dfrac{F}{q_m}$	$H = \dfrac{F}{q_m}$	$H = \dfrac{F}{q_m}$
$dH = \dfrac{I\, dl \sin\theta}{c r^2}$	$dH = \dfrac{I\, dl \sin\theta}{c 4\pi r^2}$	$dH = \dfrac{I\, dl \sin\theta}{4\pi r^2}$
$q = \displaystyle\int I\, dt$	$q = \displaystyle\int I\, dt$	$q = \displaystyle\int I\, dt$
$F = \dfrac{q q'}{r^2}$	$F = \dfrac{q q'}{4\pi r^2}$	$F = \dfrac{q q'}{4\pi \epsilon_0 r^2}$

of Table 1–1. The first two of these equations define unit pole and unit magnetic field as they had been defined in the cgs-emu system, and the last two define unit current and unit charge as they had been defined in the cgs-esu system. The middle equation, from Biot and Savart, accomplishes a unification of the first two with the last two; that is, by the introduction of c into the denominator of this relation dH is expressed in oersteds from the emu system, when I is in statamperes from the esu system. Most of the units in the gaussian system have the prefix *stat*, as statcoulomb, statampere, and statvolt; however, the units of magnetic field are the same as in the cgs-emu; namely, oersteds for H, and gauss for B. It is interesting that these two names are in very common use even though it has often been pointed out that, in these systems, B and H must have the same units, since $B = H + 4\pi M$.

1–3 Rationalization. One further refinement of the gaussian system was introduced independently by Heaviside and Lorentz. This refinement, which is called rationalization, is illustrated by the second column of elementary equations in Table 1–1. The resulting system, called the Heaviside-Lorentz system, is an excellent one. Since no names have been chosen for its units, its adoption at this late date would seem to upset all of the well-established units. Although the advantages to be gained are not sufficient to justify rationalization of the gaussian system, the development was important, for it led to the adoption of the rationalized rather than the unrationalized system of mks units.

The process of rationalization consists in substituting the expression for the area of a sphere, $4\pi r^2$, for the r^2 in the denominator of the first, third, and fifth of the defining equations in Table 1–1. While, at first sight, this appears to make some equations more complex, it does remove the 4π's from equations that are very frequently used in calculations. The net result of rationalization is to simplify the most useful equations. A complete understanding of the advantages and disadvantages of the various systems can be obtained only by studying the subject with each system in mind.

1–4 The rationalized mks system of units. The so-called "absolute" system (cgs-emu) was developed from the first four elementary relations in the first column of Table 1–1, but with the c left out of the denominator of the third relation. This defined I in abamperes and q in abcoulombs. The "practical" units ampere and coulomb were each arbitrarily defined as $1/10$ of the corresponding "absolute" units. The abvolt then was defined by the energy relation 1 abvolt $\times$ 1 abcoulomb = 1 erg, and the "practical" unit, the volt, was arbitrarily defined as 10^8 abvolts. The combined effect of the arbitrary definitions for the coulomb and volt fortunately produced the relation 1 volt $\times$ 1 coulomb = 10^7 erg = 1 joule. Giorgi pointed out that a fundamental system, based upon the standard meter and the standard kilogram, could be devised to include the "practical" units of electricity and magnetism. While the defining equation, $F = ma$, defines the dyne as the unit of force, with m in grams and a in cm/sec^2, it defines a unit of force equal to 10^5 dynes with m in kilograms and a in m/sec^2. In the 1930's this new unit of force was appropriately christened the *newton*. The unit of energy in the mks system then became the newton·meter = 10^5 dynes $\times$ 10^2 cm = 1 joule. Since the "practical" units had been defined from the "absolute" units, using arbitrarily chosen powers of ten, a fundamental system including the "practical" units could be developed from the elementary relations in the third column of Table 1–1 by giving the arbitrary constant μ_0 the correct value. It is easily demonstrated that $\mu_0 = 4\pi 10^{-7}$ is the correct numerical value, where the 4π stems from the decision to rationalize the equations. While μ_0 could be chosen dimensionless, it is much more convenient to assign it the value

$$\mu_0 = 4\pi 10^{-7} \text{ henry/m.}$$

The necessity for introducing μ_0 into the first mks relation and ϵ_0 into the fifth does increase the complexity of the system. However, these constants do take care of all conversions of units. Furthermore, they are related by $\mu_0 \epsilon_0 c^2 = 1$, where c is 2.9979×10^8 m/sec, the velocity of light in vacuums.

Hence

$$\epsilon_0 = \frac{1}{\mu_0 c^2} \cong 8.854 \times 10^{-12} \text{ farad/m.}$$

Appendix I contains a table designed to make the numerical conversions between those units most frequently found in the literature as simple as possible.

The advantages of the mks system over the other two systems can be seen by examining the frontispiece and Table 1–1. The gaussian system is simplest only in the two Coulomb laws and the Biot-Savart law. Although these equations are useful for teaching elementary principles, they are less frequently used in calculations of real problems. The Lorentz force equation, Maxwell's field relations, and the Poynting vector are included in the frontispiece. Although these do require the vector notation, introduced in the next two chapters, and the general principles developed later in the text, it is not necessary to understand these relations to compare the simplicity of their forms in the three systems.

1–5 Legal definitions for the mks units. The five elementary equations of the rationalized mks system that are listed in Table 1–1 could provide the basis for establishing all of the mks units. With μ_0 chosen to be exactly $4\pi 10^{-7}$ henry/m, all units would have their present legal value. However, the Coulomb law for forces between isolated magnetic poles cannot be used for precise measurements or precise definitions. Magnetic poles are always poorly defined and, in fact, are undoubtedly fictitious. Far more precise measurements can be made upon the forces between current-carrying wires. *Since the forces between two circuits carrying the same current can be precisely calculated and precisely measured, these forces are now used to establish a standard ampere as the basic unit for the mks system.* The principles involved in calculating the forces between current circuits are discussed in more detail in Chapter 8. It is sufficient to note here that the magnetic fields calculated from the third equation in the last column of Table 1–1 are proportional to I, but the Lorentz equation for the force on an element of wire must be written $dF = \mu_0 H I \, dl \sin \phi$. These resulting forces are proportional to I^2 but also depend upon the value of μ_0. Thus the magnitudes of all the electric and magnetic units are determined by the arbitrarily chosen constant μ_0. The names of the gaussian and mks units for several quantities are shown in Table 1–2 for easy reference.

In 1908 an International Conference on Electrical Units and Standards met in London and adopted independent definitions for an international ohm, an international ampere, and an international volt. Later, when it became possible to make measurements to five and six significant figures, inconsistencies appeared. In fact, the magnitudes of all these

TABLE 1-2

THE UNITS FOR VARIOUS SYMBOLS

Gaussian	Heaviside-Lorentz	Rationalized mks
q statcoul	these units have no names	q coul
q_m cgs-emu of pole strength		q_m weber
I statamp		I amp
H oersted		H amp/m
B gauss		B weber/m^2
M gauss		M amp/m
$\mathfrak{M} = M$ gauss		$\mathfrak{M} = \mu_0 M$ weber/m^2
E dyne/statcoul or statvolt/cm		E newton/coul or volt/m
D statcoul/cm^2		D coul/m^2
P statcoul/cm^2		P coul/m^2
S erg/(cm^2 sec)		S watt/m^2
ϵ (unitless)		ϵ farad/m
μ (unitless)		μ henry/m
ρ statcoul/cm^3		ρ coul/m^3
J statamp/cm^2		J amp/m^2

international units differed slightly from those obtained from fundamental principles beginning with the units of mass, length, and time. It was soon realized that the electrical units should be legally defined in terms of the well-established units of mass, length, and time. Careful experiments by the national laboratories of major nations were required. These were scheduled for completion by 1940 but were delayed by World War II.

In October 1946 the International Committee on Weights and Measures recommended the following definitions,* which are substantially the same as the definitions that were passed by the Congress of the United States prior to March 1, 1949:

1. *The ampere* (unit of electric current). The ampere is the constant current which, if maintained in two straight parallel conductors of infinite length, of negligible circular sections, and placed 1 meter apart in a vacuum, will produce between these conductors a force equal to 2×10^{-7} newton per meter of length.

---

* National Bureau of Standards Circular 475, p. 36, June 1949.

2. *The volt* (unit of difference of potential and of electromotive force). The volt is the difference of electric potential between two points of a conducting wire carrying a constant current of 1 ampere, when the power dissipated between these points is equal to 1 watt.

3. *The ohm* (unit of electric resistance). The ohm is the electric resistance between two points of a conductor when a constant difference of potential of 1 volt, applied between these two points, produces in this conductor a current of 1 ampere, this conductor not being the seat of any electromotive force.

4. *The coulomb* (unit of quantity of electricity). The coulomb is the quantity of electricity transported in 1 second by a current of 1 ampere.

5. *The farad* (unit of electric capacitance). The farad is the capacitance of a capacitor between the plates of which there appears a difference of potential of 1 volt when it is charged by a quantity of electricity equal to 1 coulomb.

6. *The henry* (unit of electric inductance). The henry is the inductance of a closed circuit in which an electromotive force of 1 volt is produced when the electric current in the circuit varies uniformly at a rate of 1 ampere per second.

7. *The weber* (unit of magnetic flux). The weber is the magnetic flux which, linking a circuit of 1 turn, produces in it an electromotive force of 1 volt as it is reduced to zero at a uniform rate in one second.

Object of these definitions. These definitions are intended solely to fix the magnitude of the units and not the methods to be followed for their practical realization. This realization is effected in accord with the well-known laws of electromagnetism. For example, the definition of the ampere represents only a particular case of the general formula expressing the forces which are developed between conductors carrying electric currents, chosen for the simplicity of its verbal expression. It serves to fix the constants in the general formula which has to be used for the realization of the unit.

$$\frac{1}{4\pi\varepsilon_0} = 9 \times 10^8 \ nt - m^2\big/coul^2$$

Problems

*1-1. Compute the electrostatic force of repulsion between two α-particles at a separation of 10^{-11} cm, and compare with the force of gravitational attraction between them.

Each α-particle has a charge of $+2e$, or $2 \times 1.60 \times 10^{-19}$ coul and a mass (2 protons $+$ 2 neutrons) of $4 \times 1.67 \times 10^{-24}$ gm.

1-2. 6.02×10^{23} atoms of monatomic hydrogen have a mass of one gram. How far would the electron of a hydrogen atom have to be removed from the nucleus for the force of attraction to equal the weight of the atom?

*1-3. Radium decomposes radioactively to form radon (atomic number 86) by emitting an α-particle from its nucleus. (a) What is the force of repulsion between the radon nucleus and the α-particle when the distance between them is 5×10^{-11} cm? (b) What is the acceleration of the α-particle at this distance?

1-4. In the Bohr model of the hydrogen atom, an electron revolves in a circular orbit around a nucleus consisting of a single proton. If the radius of the orbit is 5.28×10^{-9} cm, find the number of revolutions of the electron per second. The force of electrostatic attraction between proton and electron provides the centripetal force.

*1-5. Two charges of $+10^{-9}$ coul each are 8 cm apart in air. Find the magnitude and direction of the force exerted by these charges on a third charge of $+5 \times 10^{-11}$ coul that is 5 cm distant from each of the first two charges.

1-6. Two equal positive point charges are a distance $2a$ apart. Midway between them and normal to the line joining them is a plane. The locus of points where the force on a point charge placed in the plane is a maximum is, by symmetry, a circle. Calculate the radius of this circle.

*1-7. How many excess electrons must be placed on each of two small spheres spaced 3 cm apart if the force of repulsion between the spheres is to be 10^{-19} n?

1-8. Each of two small spheres is positively charged, the combined charge totaling 26 statcoul. What is the charge on each sphere if they are repelled with a force of 3 dynes when placed 4 cm apart?

*1-9. Point charges of 2×10^{-9} coul are situated at each of three corners of a square whose side is 0.20 m. What would be the magnitude and direction of the resultant force on a point charge of -1×10^{-9} coul if it were placed (a) at the center of the square? (b) at the vacant corner of the square?

1-10. Calculate the force exerted on 1 μcoul of positive charge, concentrated at a point, by another equal charge 1 m from it. Make your calculations in cgs-esu and in mks units, leaving ϵ_0 as an unknown quantity in the latter case. Calculate the magnitude of ϵ_0 from these two results.

*1-11. The quantity of an electric charge can be expressed as q_s in statcoulombs or as q_a in abcoulombs. Since these two were defined by different equations they have different dimensions in terms of mass, length, and time (M, L, and T). The first four gaussian equations in Table 1-1, with the c omitted from the Biot-Savart relation, establish the magnitude and dimensions of q_a in abcoulombs. Remembering that force has the dimensions (mass·length/time^2) or the units (gm·cm/sec^2):

---

* Answers to starred problems will be found at back of book.

(a) Determine the units of q_a in gm, cm, and sec, and

(b) the units of q_s in gm, cm, and sec (from the fifth gaussian equation).

(c) Show that the ratio of the two quantities involves a velocity in cm/sec.

(d) Show that the introduction of a velocity into the denominator of the Biot-Savart equation makes the five gaussian equations consistent.

(e) Could this c have been introduced into one of the Coulomb's law equations, instead of into the Biot-Savart relation, to make the five equations consistent dimensionally? Demonstrate your statement.

1–12. In both of the cgs systems the unit of energy is the erg = dyne·cm and in all of the systems the work required to move a charge dq through a potential difference of V is $dW = V\,dq$. From the fact that there are 2.998×10^{10} statamp in 1 abamp, calculate the relation between statvolts and abvolts. Would you expect to find portable instruments in a well-equipped laboratory capable of measuring 1 statvolt and 1 abvolt?

1–13. The expression *electron-volt* is often found in modern magazines. Of what physical quantity is this a unit? Express the electron-volt in terms of the proper mks unit.

CHAPTER 2

VECTOR MATHEMATICS FOR ELECTROSTATIC FIELDS

Coulomb's law for the attraction or repulsion between two point charges was discussed briefly in Chapter 1. When the force on any charge q is due to the nearness of a number of other charges such as q_1, q_2, q_3, etc., the force exerted on q by each of these charges must be calculated separately, since each of these forces usually points in a different direction. The total force on q is the resultant of all these forces and can be obtained by graphical construction, but unless the forces are all in the same plane graphical solutions will be difficult.

Fortunately, rather simple vector algebra and calculus have been invented that are ideally suited for the analytical solutions of the problems involving such forces. Since most of the subject of Electricity and Magnetism deals with forces of one kind or another, in the aggregate time will be saved by spending a little time now to learn these vector methods.

In this and the next chapter the vector rules and operations that will be needed are included. Only the essential operations are presented, and these will be used over and over again in the chapters that follow. The presentation of these vector operations provides an opportunity for reviewing some of the important principles covered in more elementary texts.

2–1 The vector notation. Physical quantities of the simplest type are completely defined by the assignment of a single number combined with the unit of measure. Examples are a mass of 25 lb, a temperature of 53°C, and a pressure of 110 lb/in². These are called *scalar* quantities.

Some other physical quantities can be completely defined only by specifying a direction in addition to the magnitude. These are called *vector* quantities. Examples of vector quantities are a velocity of 25 mi/hr in the northeast direction and a current density of 29 amp/m² to the right and parallel to the surface of a conductor. Such statements are cumbersome. It is much simpler to draw straight lines with lengths proportional to the magnitudes of the quantities and with arrowheads to indicate their directions. For vectors not in a single plane, a three-dimensional coordinate system can be used for drawing these lines in perspective.

Ordinary algebra was invented to deal primarily with scalar quantities. A somewhat similar algebra, vector algebra, is used to deal with vector quantities. Like ordinary algebra, vector algebra makes use of addition, subtraction, and multiplication. A notation is needed to distinguish vectors from scalars. By rather general agreement, vectors are printed in boldface type, while italic type is used for scalars. For example, the symbol **R** designates a vector and R designates its scalar magnitude. The following axioms define the properties of these vectors:

1. Two vectors are equal to each other if they have the same magnitude and point in the same direction. The relative location of the vectors in space does not affect this equality.

2. The multiplication of a vector by a scalar results in a new vector, pointing in the same direction as the original vector and having a magnitude equal to the product of the individual magnitudes. The vector 3**R** is three times as long as the vector **R**, as shown in Fig. 2–1.

FIG. 2–1. Two vectors, **R** and 3**R**.

2–2 Vector addition and subtraction. Suppose a wide river is flowing northward at 3 mi/hr and an outboard motorboat on this river is heading due east at 4 mi/hr with respect to the water. With respect to the land, this boat moves with a velocity equal to the resultant of these two velocities; namely, at 5 mi/hr in the direction 36°52′ north of east. In vector language, the velocity **v** of the boat with respect to the land is the vector sum of the velocity of the river, $\mathbf{v}_R$, and the velocity of the boat with respect to the water, $\mathbf{v}_B$. The vector equation

$$\mathbf{v} = \mathbf{v}_R + \mathbf{v}_B$$

designates that **v** is the resultant or vector sum of $\mathbf{v}_R$ and $\mathbf{v}_B$. *It does not mean that the magnitude v of the vector **v** is equal to the algebraic sum of the magnitudes of the other two vectors;* i.e.,

$$v \neq v_R + v_B.$$

The general definition for the sum of any two vectors, for example **A** and **B**, is shown in Fig. 2–2, where the process of vector addition is illustrated. If **A** and **B** are any two vectors representing physical quantities having the same units and drawn to the same scale, the sum

$$\mathbf{R} = \mathbf{A} + \mathbf{B}$$

is obtained by drawing **B**, using its correct length and direction, with

its tail at the head of **A**. The vector sum **R** is the single vector that can
be drawn from the tail of **A** to the head of **B**. Obviously,

$$\mathbf{A} + \mathbf{B} = \mathbf{B} + \mathbf{A},$$

since the vector **R**, drawn on the left as a solid line in Fig. 2–2, represents the sum of the left side of the equation, while the vector **R** drawn
on the right as a dashed line represents the sum on the right side of this
equation. These two **R**'s are identical, since they point in the same
direction and have the same length.

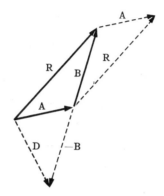

FIG. 2–2. Vector addition and subtraction. The vectors illustrated are
related by $\mathbf{R} = \mathbf{A} + \mathbf{B} = \mathbf{B} + \mathbf{A}$ and $\mathbf{D} = \mathbf{A} - \mathbf{B}$.

Figure 2–2 also illustrates the subtraction of vectors. To subtract
B from **A**, merely add to vector **A** the vector **−B**, which is the same
length as **B** but points in the opposite direction. In Fig. 2–2 the vector

$$\mathbf{D} = \mathbf{A} - \mathbf{B}$$

is the difference between vectors **A** and **B**.

The vector addition of two vectors is easily extended to the addition
of three or any number of vectors. If **C** is a third vector in Fig. 2–2,
the resulting relation,

$$\mathbf{A} + \mathbf{B} + \mathbf{C} = \mathbf{R} + \mathbf{C},$$

contains the sum of just two vectors on the right side of the equation.
Since the sum of two vectors has been defined, this equation defines the
sum of three vectors. Note that **C** does not need to be in the plane determined by **A** and **B**. To obtain the sum

$$\mathbf{S} = \mathbf{A} + \mathbf{B} + \mathbf{C} + \mathbf{D} + \mathbf{E},$$

draw **B** starting with its tail at the head of **A**, then **C** with its tail at the head of **B**, then **D** with its tail at the head of **C**, etc. The vector sum **S** is that single vector that can be drawn from the tail of **A** to the head of **E**. No matter what order is used in adding the five vectors, vector **S** will be found to have the same length and direction.

2–3 Unit vectors and rectangular components. In the previous section vector additions and subtractions were performed graphically. While graphical methods are excellent in learning to visualize the processes, some analytical methods will be needed for obtaining numerical results. This is especially true when the vectors cannot be drawn in the same plane.

Set up a rectangular coordinate system with the x-, y-, and z-axes having their origin at the tail of a vector **A**, as shown in Fig. 2–3. The vector **A** can be thought of as the sum of three vectors: one parallel to the x-axis of length A_x, a second parallel to the y-axis of length A_y, and a third parallel to the z-axis of length A_z, where A_x, A_y, and A_z are the respective rectangular components of **A** along the three axes. It is not correct, however, to write A as the sum of A_x, A_y, and A_z, since these are all scalar quantities for which the correct relation is

$$A^2 = A_x^2 + A_y^2 + A_z^2.$$

To write a vector equation for **A**, three unit vectors **i**, **j**, and **k** are introduced, which respectively point in the positive x-, the positive y-,

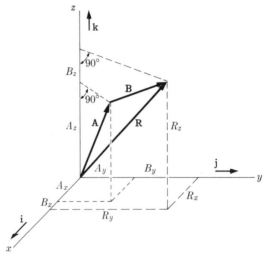

FIG. 2–3. The vectors **R** = **A** + **B** are shown with their x-, y-, and z-components. Note that $A_x + B_x = R_x$, $A_y + B_y = R_y$, and $A_z + B_z = R_z$.

and the positive z-directions. The equation

$$\mathbf{A} = \mathbf{i}A_x + \mathbf{j}A_y + \mathbf{k}A_z$$

then correctly expresses the magnitude and direction of $\mathbf{A}$. The unit vectors $\mathbf{i}$, $\mathbf{j}$, and $\mathbf{k}$ have magnitudes of one, with no dimensions of their own. The rectangular components A_x, A_y, and A_z have the same units or dimensions as A. For example, the velocity of the boat on the river, mentioned at the beginning of Section 2–2, would be written

$$\mathbf{v} = \mathbf{i}(4 \text{ mi/hr}) + \mathbf{j}(3 \text{ mi/hr})$$

if the coordinate x- and y-axes are drawn to point east and north, respectively.

Figure 2–3 also illustrates in rectangular coordinates the vector sum

$$\mathbf{R} = \mathbf{A} + \mathbf{B}.$$

From the diagram it can be seen that the x-component of the resultant vector $\mathbf{R}$ equals the algebraic sum of the x-components of $\mathbf{A}$ and $\mathbf{B}$. The same is true for the other components:

$$R_x = A_x + B_x,$$
$$R_y = A_y + B_y,$$
$$R_z = A_z + B_z.$$

When all the vectors involved are written in terms of the unit vectors $\mathbf{i}$, $\mathbf{j}$, and $\mathbf{k}$, the operations involving addition or subtraction become simple algebraic operations. For example, if

$$\mathbf{R} = \mathbf{A} + \mathbf{B} - \mathbf{C}$$

then

$$\mathbf{R} = \mathbf{i}(A_x + B_x - C_x) + \mathbf{j}(A_y + B_y - C_y) + \mathbf{k}(A_z + B_z - C_z).$$

2–4 Coordinate systems. There are many coordinate systems besides the rectangular x, y, z system just treated. These systems have been invented to simplify the solution of particular problems and, in general, the solution of any problem is simplified by choosing the best coordinates for that problem. The systems most commonly used are the rectangular, the cylindrical, and the spherical coordinate systems, which have many common properties. All the problems in this book can be solved in one of these three systems.

Cylindrical and spherical coordinates. Each of the three coordinate systems employs three coordinates to locate a point in space. In the cylindrical system the coordinates are r, ϕ, and z, which locate the point P as shown in Fig. 2–4. The x-, y-, and z-axes are given to show the rela-

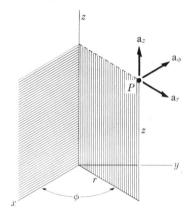

FIG. 2–4. Cylindrical coordinates r, ϕ, and z.

tionships between the two systems. Notice that r and ϕ are measured in the xy-plane. The angle ϕ may be measured from any convenient plane through the z-axis, though in general it is measured from the xz-plane as in Fig. 2–4. In this system three unit vectors, a_r, a_ϕ, and a_z (or k), are defined as follows:

a_r points in the direction in which P moves when r is increased with ϕ and z constant,

a_ϕ points in the direction in which P moves when ϕ is increased with r and z constant,

a_z points in the direction in which P moves when z is increased with r and ϕ constant.

Note that in rectangular coordinates the respective directions of i, j, and k can also be defined, respectively, as the directions in which P moves when only x increases, when only y increases, and when only z increases. Note also that i, j, and k are mutually perpendicular and that a_r, a_ϕ, and a_z are also mutually perpendicular. *Coordinate systems in which the unit vectors are mutually perpendicular are called orthogonal coordinate systems.*

In Fig. 2–5 the point P is located in a spherical coordinate system. In this system the unit vectors are a_R, a_θ, and a_ϕ which point, respectively, in the directions in which P moves on increasing only R, only θ, and only ϕ. These unit vectors are mutually perpendicular, and therefore the system is orthogonal. When there is no likelihood of confusing the unit vectors a_R in spherical coordinates and a_r in cylindrical coordinates, it is common to write the unit-radial vector of spherical coordinates as a_r, also. This then reserves a unit vector a_R which can point in any direction, not necessarily radially.

While the three systems have many similarities, the rectangular system differs markedly from the other two in one respect; namely, its

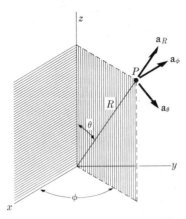

Fig. 2–5. Spherical coordinates R, θ, and ϕ.

unit vectors do not depend on the coordinates, but always point in the same direction. For example, a point may be located uniquely in rectangular coordinates by giving its distance from the origin as

$$\mathbf{R} = \mathbf{i}3\text{ m} + \mathbf{j}4\text{ m} + \mathbf{k}12\text{ m},$$

whereas the corresponding expression in spherical coordinates

$$\mathbf{R} = \mathbf{a}_R 13\text{ m},$$

shows only that the point is 13 m from the origin and does not locate the point uniquely. The uncertainty arises from the fact that the direction of $\mathbf{a}_R$ depends on both θ and ϕ. This uncertainty can hardly be considered a disadvantage, however, since it is a distinct advantage in some problems (for example, when an expression is needed for a general point arbitrarily located on the surface of a sphere).

Vector examples. In Fig. 2–6 a position vector $\mathbf{R}$ and a velocity vector $\mathbf{v}$ are plotted. Since $\mathbf{R}$ is in meters, while $\mathbf{v}$ is in m/sec, these two cannot be added or subtracted. However, diagrams containing vectors representing different kinds of quantities are often very useful. For example, Fig. 2–6 could represent a mass point located in space at P but having a velocity $\mathbf{v}$. The magnitudes and directions of $\mathbf{R}$ and $\mathbf{v}$ have been chosen so that each of them can be expressed in all three coordinate systems with rather simple numbers. The position of P can be expressed by

$$\mathbf{R} = \mathbf{i}3 + \mathbf{j}4 + \mathbf{k}12$$

or

$$\mathbf{R} = \mathbf{a}_r 5 + \mathbf{a}_\phi 0 + \mathbf{a}_z 12$$

or

$$\mathbf{R} = \mathbf{a}_R 13.$$

FIG. 2–6. Vector diagram showing a position vector **R** and a velocity vector **v**. The relations among the three coordinate systems are illustrated.

Likewise, the velocity can be expressed by

$$\mathbf{v} = -\mathbf{i}52 + \mathbf{j}39 - \mathbf{k}156$$

or

$$\mathbf{v} = \mathbf{a}_r0 + \mathbf{a}_\phi65 - \mathbf{a}_z156$$

or

$$\mathbf{v} = -\mathbf{a}_R144 - \mathbf{a}_\theta60 + \mathbf{a}_\phi65.$$

The reader should study these examples carefully to help him in understanding vector expressions. These examples will be used in our study of other vector principles. The study of the electrostatic fields that are produced by distributions of charges can be used to illustrate the usefulness of vector algebra.

2–5 Electrostatic fields. Electrostatic fields are found in the neighborhood of any distribution of electric charges. *The electrostatic field* **E** *at any point is defined by the relation* $\mathbf{E} = \lim_{q\to 0} \mathbf{f}/q$, *where* **f** *is the force that would act on a test charge q if it were placed at that point.* It is necessary to define the field as the limit of the force/charge as the test charge approaches zero only because a finite test charge may change the distribution of neighboring charges, especially if these reside on conductors. The simple definition $\mathbf{E} = \mathbf{f}/q$ is valid for any size of test charge, *provided the charges producing the field are not displaced by the presence of the test charge.* The definition states that the electric field **E** is a vector that points in the same direction as the force vector $\mathbf{f}$ when the test charge q is positive.

If a point charge Q is located at the origin of coordinates in Fig. 2–5 and a test charge q is located at P, Coulomb's law for the force $\mathbf{f}$ on q can be written as

$$\mathbf{F} = \mathbf{a}_r \frac{Qq}{\epsilon_0 4\pi r^2} = \mathbf{a}_r k \frac{Qq}{r^2},$$

where $k = 1/4\pi\epsilon_0 \cong 9 \times 10^9$ n·m^2/coul^2 and $\mathbf{a}_r$ is the unit radial vector in spherical coordinates. The field $\mathbf{E}$ produced at P by the charge Q at the origin is then

$$\mathbf{E} = \mathbf{a}_r k \frac{Q}{r^2}. \tag{2–1}$$

If in addition to Q there are other point charges, the field at P will be the vector sum of the individual vector fields due to each of the charges. To write a general expression for such a field, it is desirable first to write the field at P due to a charge that is not at the origin but is at some general point in space. When the charge Q is not at the origin, the expression for the field at P due to Q is somewhat more easily visualized when it is written in rectangular rather than in spherical coordinates. Rectangular coordinates can be placed so that Q is located at (a, b, c) and the general point P is located at (x, y, z). The distance R between Q and P is then given by $R^2 = (x - a)^2 + (y - b)^2 + (z - c)^2$. A vector drawn from Q to P is expressed by

$$\mathbf{R} = \mathbf{i}(x - a) + \mathbf{j}(y - b) + \mathbf{k}(z - c).$$

A unit vector $\mathbf{a}_R$ parallel to $\mathbf{R}$ can be obtained by dividing $\mathbf{R}$ by its magnitude; i.e.,

$$\mathbf{a}_R = \frac{\mathbf{R}}{R} = \mathbf{i}\frac{x - a}{R} + \mathbf{j}\frac{y - b}{R} + \mathbf{k}\frac{z - c}{R},$$

and the field at P due to the charge Q is then

$$\mathbf{E} = \mathbf{a}_R \frac{kQ}{R^2}.$$

Note the distinction between the unit radial vector $\mathbf{a}_r$ and the more general unit vector $\mathbf{a}_R$.

If a series of n point charges are located with q_1 at (x_1, y_1, z_1), q_2 at (x_2, y_2, z_2), etc., with, finally, q_n at (x_n, y_n, z_n), the electric field $\mathbf{E}$ at P will be given by the vector sum of the electric fields due to the individual charges. Thus

$$\mathbf{E} = k \sum_{i=1}^{i=n} \frac{q_i}{r_i^2} \left[\mathbf{i}\frac{x - x_i}{r_i} + \mathbf{j}\frac{y - y_i}{r_i} + \mathbf{k}\frac{z - z_i}{r_i} \right], \tag{2–2}$$

where

$$r_i = \sqrt{(x - x_i)^2 + (y - y_i)^2 + (z - z_i)^2}.$$

Field calculations. The electric field at all points in space due to any particular distribution of point charges can be calculated by direct substitution into Eq. (2–2). To obtain such a general expression, the point P at which the field is calculated is given the general coordinates (x, y, z). Each of the charges in the distribution contributes one term to the summation; its particular magnitude and its particular coordinates are substituted into that term. If many charges are involved, the expression is too long to be practical. Fortunately, simpler methods can be developed for calculating fields in most actual problems. However, since the simpler methods are based upon the fundamental law expressed by Eq. (2–2), its implications should be mastered. The calculation of the field at some particular point due to two point charges should help to clarify this law.

As an illustration of the use of the general expression, a charge $q_1 = -16 \times 10^{-10}$ coul can be placed at the origin, where $x_1 = y_1 = z_1 = 0$, and another charge $q_2 = 12 \times 10^{-10}$ coul can be placed at the point in the yz-plane where $x_2 = 0$, $y_2 = 3$ m, and $z_2 = 4$ m. The field can then be found at any other point, for example on the z-axis where $x = 0$, $y = 0$, and $z = 4$ m.

$$\mathbf{E} = \frac{9 \times 10^9 (-16 \times 10^{-10})}{4^2} \left[\mathbf{k}\, \frac{4}{4} \right]$$

$$+ \frac{9 \times 10^9 (12 \times 10^{-10})}{3^2} \left[\mathbf{j}\, \frac{0-3}{3} + \mathbf{k}\, \frac{4-4}{3} \right],$$

$$\mathbf{E} = -1.20\mathbf{j} - 0.90\mathbf{k}, \qquad \text{all in n/coul.}$$

The field at a point 4 m above the origin on the z-axis is then 1.50 n/coul pointing in such a direction that its components along the x-, y-, and z-axes are respectively 0, -1.20 n/coul, and -0.90 n/coul. This calculation could have been simplified by choosing either cylindrical or spherical coordinates with the axis of symmetry passing through the two charges.

2–6 Dipole fields. In nature electric charges frequently occur in pairs having equal magnitudes but opposite signs. When a dielectric is brought into an electric field, its electrons do not drift as they do in metals because they are too tightly bound to the nuclei. While they do not drift, they do become displaced so that the center of the cloud of electrons surrounding each nucleus no longer coincides with the center of that nucleus. While the external electric field produced by each atom is zero when these centers coincide, it is not zero when the centers are displaced.

Fig. 2–7. An electric dipole consisting of two charges $+q$ and $-q$ separated by a distance l. The field at P due to the dipole is calculated in the text.

Any pair of equal and opposite charges whose centers are separated constitute a dipole. The most important dipoles have very small separations between two relatively large charges; these will be called *ideal* dipoles. Since ideal dipoles will be encountered frequently, it is desirable to obtain a general expression for the electric fields they produce.

Consider charges $-q$ at the origin and $+q$ on the z-axis at $z = l$, where $l \ll r$, as shown in Fig. 2–7. With complete symmetry about the z-axis, the ϕ coordinate of the spherical coordinates can be ignored. The vector distance to P from $+q$ is $\mathbf{r}_1$ and from $-q$ is $\mathbf{r}$. The electric field at P is then given by

$$\mathbf{E} = \frac{kq\mathbf{r}_1}{r_1^3} - \frac{kq\mathbf{r}}{r^3} = \frac{kq}{r^3}\left[\frac{\mathbf{r}_1 r^3}{r_1^3} - \mathbf{r}\right]. \qquad (2\text{–}3)$$

The first term in the brackets should be converted to the spherical coordinates to obtain a more understandable expression. From Fig. 2–7,

$$\mathbf{r}_1 = \mathbf{r} - \mathbf{1} = \mathbf{r} - \mathbf{k}l$$

and

$$r_1^2 = r^2 + l^2 - 2rl\cos\theta.$$

Hence

$$r_1^{-3} = r^{-3}[1 + (l/r)^2 - 2(l/r)\cos\theta]^{-3/2}.$$

Since $(l/r) \ll 1$, the binomial theorem may be used to expand the expression in brackets into a power series in l/r, in which powers higher than the first can be neglected.   Then

$$\frac{r^3}{r_1^3} = 1 + 3(l/r)\cos\theta.$$

Multiplying this by $r_1 = r - kl$ and again discarding higher terms in l/r gives

$$\frac{r_1 r^3}{r_1^3} = r[1 + 3(l/r)\cos\theta] - kl.$$

But

$$k = a_r \cos\theta - a_\theta \sin\theta$$

and

$$r = a_r r;$$

hence

$$\frac{r_1 r^3}{r_1^3} - r = a_r 2l \cos\theta + a_\theta l \sin\theta.$$

Substituting this into Eq. (2–3) gives the electric field of the ideal dipole:

$$E = \frac{kql}{r^3}(a_r 2\cos\theta + a_\theta \sin\theta).$$

Note that the field produced is proportional to the product of the magnitude of one of the charges and the distance they are separated. *This product ql is called the moment of the dipole*, which will be designated by p. The *ideal dipole field* is then given by

$$E = \frac{p}{4\pi\epsilon_0 r^3}(a_r 2\cos\theta + a_\theta \sin\theta), \tag{2–4}$$

since $k = 1/4\pi\epsilon_0$.

Fields of ideal dipoles vary inversely as the cube of the distance of the observer from the center of the dipole. They are twice as strong on the extension of the dipole axis as on the normal plane that bisects this axis. It will be found that the electric field of an ideal dipole given in Eq. (2–4) can be obtained more easily by first calculating the electrostatic potentials around the dipole. In order to calculate electrostatic potentials, a vector method must be introduced for determining the force required to move a charge in an electrostatic field. This method will utilize the scalar or dot product of vectors.

2–7 Fields by direct integration.   While Eq. (2–2) is useful only for calculating fields due to distributions of point charges, it can be expressed in the form of a vector integral for use in calculating fields due to continuous distributions.   Just as a scalar integral can be considered to constitute an algebraic summation of infinitesimal scalar elements, *a vector*

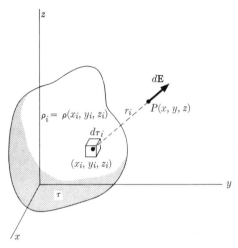

F$_{\text{IG}}$. 2–8. Showing the direction and magnitude of $d\mathbf{E}$, the electric field at P due to the charge in an infinitesimal element of the volume τ.

integral constitutes a vector summation of infinitesimal vector elements. In Fig. 2–8 charges are smoothly distributed within the irregular volume τ, and it is desired to calculate the electric field at the point P whose coordinates are (x, y, z). A small element of volume $d\tau_i$ located at (x_i, y_i, z_i) contains the charge $\rho_i\, d\tau_i$, where ρ_i is the charge density at (x_i, y_i, z_i). If $d\tau_i$ is sufficiently small the field it produces at P can be calculated from Coulomb's law:

$$d\mathbf{E}_i = \mathbf{a}_i k \, \frac{\rho_i\, d\tau_i}{r_i^2}, \tag{2–5}$$

and the total field at P can be obtained by adding vectorially the contributions of all such elements within the volume

$$\mathbf{E} = \int_\tau k \mathbf{a}_i \, \frac{\rho_i\, d\tau_i}{r_i^2}, \tag{2–6}$$

where $\mathbf{a}_i$ is a unit vector directed from (x_i, y_i, z_i) toward (x, y, z), r_i is the distance between these two points, and $d\tau_i$ is the element of volume $dx_i\, dy_i\, dz_i$. Note that during this integration the point P is fixed, so that x, y, and z must be treated as constants. Frequently the process of integration can be simplified by writing the integrand in terms of the unit vectors $\mathbf{i}$, $\mathbf{j}$, and $\mathbf{k}$, which provides three scalar integrals, each multiplied by one of these unit vectors.

This process can be illustrated by calculating the electric field near an infinite plane that has a uniform surface density of charge σ, whose units in the mks system are coul/m^2. Coordinates can be chosen so that the

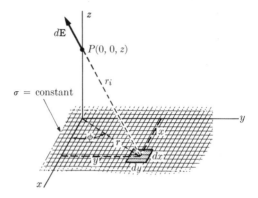

FIG. 2-9.   The direction and magnitude of $d\mathbf{E}$, the electric field at P due to the surface charge in an infinitesimal element of area in the xy-plane.

xy-plane coincides with the charged plane.   Since the charged plane extends to infinity in all directions, the field point P can be placed at z on the z-axis, without loss of generality.   The field at P due to the charge enclosed in the area $dx\,dy$ at the coordinates $(x, y, 0)$, as shown in Fig. 2-9, is

$$d\mathbf{E} = \frac{k\sigma\,dx\,dy}{r_i^2}\left(-\mathbf{i}\,\frac{x}{r_i} - \mathbf{j}\,\frac{y}{r_i} + \mathbf{k}\,\frac{z}{r_i}\right),$$

where

$$r_i^2 = x^2 + y^2 + z^2.$$

A double integration of $d\mathbf{E}$, with x and y each varying from $-\infty$ to ∞, is required to determine $\mathbf{E}$.   Since $\mathbf{i}$, $\mathbf{j}$, and $\mathbf{k}$ are constants, $\mathbf{E}$ can be expressed by three scalar double integrals, each multiplied by a unit vector.   That is,

$$\mathbf{E} = k\sigma\left(-\mathbf{i}\int_{-\infty}^{\infty}\int_{-\infty}^{\infty}\frac{x\,dx\,dy}{r_i^3} - \mathbf{j}\int_{-\infty}^{\infty}\int_{-\infty}^{\infty}\frac{y\,dx\,dy}{r_i^3} + \mathbf{k}\int_{-\infty}^{\infty}\int_{-\infty}^{\infty}\frac{z\,dx\,dy}{r_i^3}\right).$$

$$(2\text{-}7)$$

The first two double integrals are each zero, as should be expected from symmetry considerations, but the third gives

$$\mathbf{E} = \mathbf{k}\,\frac{\sigma}{2\epsilon_0}, \qquad (2\text{-}8)$$

a field which is independent of the coordinates at all points above the charged plane.   Below the plane the field has this same magnitude but is in the $-\mathbf{k}$ direction.

The foregoing calculations may appear artificial, since infinite planes do not exist.   However, Eq. (2-8) is an excellent approximation to the fields at points that are relatively close to a large flat sheet having a uniform surface density of charge. For points less than 0.005 cm from its center, a flat disk of 1-cm diameter can be assumed infinite, unless inaccuracies must be kept below 1%.

Rectangular coordinates are not suitable for the solution of all problems involving vector integrations. When other coordinates are used, the possibility that unit vectors may not be constant during the integration must be carefully considered. The symmetry of the problem of Fig. 2–9 suggests that cylindrical coordinates should be more suitable than the rectangular coordinates. The element of area on the charged plane would then be $ds = r\,d\phi\,dr$ and

$$d\mathbf{E} = \frac{k\sigma r\,d\phi\,dr}{r_i^2}\left(-\mathbf{a}_r\,\frac{r}{r_i} + \mathbf{k}\,\frac{z}{r_i}\right),$$

where

$$r_i^2 = r^2 + z^2.$$

The field at P is then given by

$$\mathbf{E} = k\sigma\left(-\int_0^\infty\int_0^{2\pi}\mathbf{a}_r\,\frac{r^2\,dr\,d\phi}{r_i^3} + \mathbf{k}z\int_0^\infty\int_0^{2\pi}\frac{r\,dr\,d\phi}{r_i^3}\right),$$

where $\mathbf{a}_r$ must remain in the integrand because its direction varies with ϕ, whereas $\mathbf{k}$ can be removed from its integrand, since it is independent of both r and ϕ. The first double integral can be written

$$-\int_0^\infty\frac{r^2\,dr}{r_i^3}\int_0^{2\pi}\mathbf{a}_r\,d\phi,$$

and since

$$\int_0^{2\pi}\mathbf{a}_r\,d\phi = \int_0^{2\pi}(\mathbf{i}\cos\phi + \mathbf{j}\sin\phi)\,d\phi = 0,$$

the first double integral vanishes. The field is then given by the second double integral alone, whose value is the same as the third double integral of Eq. (2–7), namely, $\mathbf{E} = \mathbf{k}(\sigma/2\epsilon_0)$.

It should be noted that $\int_0^{2\pi}\mathbf{a}_r\,d\phi = 0$, whereas $\mathbf{a}_r\int_0^{2\pi}d\phi = 2\pi\mathbf{a}_r$ and is not zero. The vanishing of $\int_0^{2\pi}\mathbf{a}_r\,d\phi$ is easily demonstrated without formal integration by noting that it constitutes a vector sum of coplanar vectors of equal magnitude and, since they are directed uniformly in all radial directions, this sum must be zero. An important corollary is that $\oint d\mathbf{l} = 0$ for any closed path of integration. This can be understood geometrically from the fact that $\int d\mathbf{l}$ over any path represents the vector sum of all displacements included in traversing that path; that is, this integral gives the vector that can be drawn from the point of beginning to the point of ending. When the path is a closed one this vector must be zero. This statement can be proved analytically as follows:

$$\oint d\mathbf{l} = \oint (\mathbf{i}\, dx + \mathbf{j}\, dy + \mathbf{k}\, dz)$$

$$= \mathbf{i} \int_{x_1}^{x_1} dx + \mathbf{j} \int_{y_1}^{y_1} dy + \mathbf{k} \int_{z_1}^{z_1} dz = 0.$$

2–8 Scalar or dot product of vectors. It has been assumed that scalar and vector quantities can be multiplied together to provide new vectors of different lengths. The question arises whether or not an operation involving the multiplication of one vector by another can be defined to yield useful and consistent results. It will be shown that at least two such operations can be defined.

One of the most common operations in physics is to calculate the work done when a given force $\mathbf{F}$ moves a body a given displacement $\mathbf{d}$. If the force is not in the direction of motion, the work done is given by $Fd \cos \widehat{Fd}$. Thus a useful definition for the product of two vectors $\mathbf{A}$ and $\mathbf{B}$ is

$$\mathbf{A} \cdot \mathbf{B} = AB \cos \widehat{AB}. \tag{2–9}$$

This equation defines the operation known either as the dot product or the scalar product, since it gives a scalar quantity and the multiplication is indicated by a dot. The dot distinguishes this from another type of vector multiplication which is indicated by a cross. To determine the usefulness of the dot product it is desirable to investigate (1) the algebraic laws governing dot products of vectors and vector sums, and (2) the geometric and physical properties of these products.

The algebra of dot products. From the definition, $\mathbf{A} \cdot \mathbf{B} = \mathbf{B} \cdot \mathbf{A}$. While this vector operation does commute, the cross product does not. By simple geometry it can be shown that if $\mathbf{S} = \mathbf{D} + \mathbf{E}$, then $\mathbf{R} \cdot \mathbf{S} = \mathbf{R} \cdot \mathbf{D} + \mathbf{R} \cdot \mathbf{E}$. Furthermore, if $\mathbf{R} = \mathbf{A} + \mathbf{B}$,

$$\mathbf{R} \cdot \mathbf{S} = \mathbf{A} \cdot \mathbf{D} + \mathbf{B} \cdot \mathbf{D} + \mathbf{A} \cdot \mathbf{E} + \mathbf{B} \cdot \mathbf{E}, \tag{2–10}$$

which is easily extended to products of the sums of any number of vectors.

Properties of dot products. The definition of the dot product given in Eq. (2–9) indicates that $\mathbf{A} \cdot \mathbf{B} = 0$ if $\mathbf{A}$ and $\mathbf{B}$ are perpendicular, and that $\mathbf{A} \cdot \mathbf{B} = AB$ if they are parallel. These results can be utilized to obtain some useful relations between unit vectors in orthogonal coordinate systems. Since such unit vectors are mutually perpendicular, one unit vector dotted into another is zero unless it is the same unit vector, and then the product is unity. The relations between unit vectors in rectangular coordinates are

$$\mathbf{i} \cdot \mathbf{i} = \mathbf{j} \cdot \mathbf{j} = \mathbf{k} \cdot \mathbf{k} = 1,$$
$$\mathbf{i} \cdot \mathbf{j} = \mathbf{i} \cdot \mathbf{k} = \mathbf{j} \cdot \mathbf{k} = 0;$$

in cylindrical coordinates are

$$\mathbf{a}_r \cdot \mathbf{a}_r = \mathbf{a}_\phi \cdot \mathbf{a}_\phi = \mathbf{k} \cdot \mathbf{k} = 1,$$
$$\mathbf{a}_r \cdot \mathbf{a}_\phi = \mathbf{a}_r \cdot \mathbf{k} = \mathbf{a}_\phi \cdot \mathbf{k} = 0;$$

and in spherical coordinates are

$$\mathbf{a}_r \cdot \mathbf{a}_r = \mathbf{a}_\theta \cdot \mathbf{a}_\theta = \mathbf{a}_\phi \cdot \mathbf{a}_\phi = 1,$$
$$\mathbf{a}_r \cdot \mathbf{a}_a = \mathbf{a}_r \cdot \mathbf{a}_\phi = \mathbf{a}_\theta \cdot \mathbf{a}_\phi = 0.$$

The dot product provides a convenient method for calculating the angle between two vectors or any two directed lines in space. From Eq. (2–9) the angle $\widehat{AB}$ between the positive directions of the vectors **A** and **B** can be obtained by using

$$\cos \widehat{AB} = \frac{\mathbf{A} \cdot \mathbf{B}}{AB}. \tag{2-11}$$

If two vectors **A** and **B** are each written with unit vectors in terms of their components, as illustrated in Section 2–4, their dot product is easily calculated from Eq. (2–10). Nine terms are obtained, but because of the relations between the orthogonal unit vectors all but three of these are zero, and therefore

$$\mathbf{A} \cdot \mathbf{B} = A_x B_x + A_y B_y + A_z B_z. \tag{2-12}$$

The scalar magnitudes for Eq. (2–11) may be calculated from $\mathbf{A} \cdot \mathbf{A} = A^2$ and $\mathbf{B} \cdot \mathbf{B} = B^2$. An important application of this method of calculating angles is the testing of two vectors to determine if they are perpendicular. If neither **A** nor **B** is zero, but $\mathbf{A} \cdot \mathbf{B} = 0$, then **A** and **B** are perpendicular.

Expressions almost identical to Eq. (2–12) may be obtained for cylindrical and spherical coordinates. They are

$$\mathbf{A} \cdot \mathbf{B} = A_r B_r + A_\phi B_\phi + A_z B_z$$

and

$$\mathbf{A} \cdot \mathbf{B} = A_r B_r + A_\theta B_\theta + A_\phi B_\phi.$$

To demonstrate that the dot product between two vectors is independent of the coordinate system, the $\mathbf{R} \cdot \mathbf{v}$ in Fig. 2–6 may be calculated in all three coordinate systems.

In rectangular coordinates,

$$\mathbf{R} \cdot \mathbf{v} = -3 \cdot 52 + 4 \cdot 39 - 12 \cdot 156 = -1872;$$

in cylindrical coordinates,

$$\mathbf{R} \cdot \mathbf{v} = 5 \cdot 0 + 0 \cdot 65 - 12 \cdot 156 = -1872;$$

and in spherical coordinates,

$$\mathbf{R} \cdot \mathbf{v} = -13 \cdot 144 = -1872.$$

The product of the absolute magnitudes of the two vectors is $Rv = 13 \cdot 169 = 2197$, and hence the angle between positive directions of $\mathbf{R}$ and $\mathbf{v}$ is

$$\cos^{-1}(-1872/2197) = 148°34'.$$

Many geometric relations that are in common use can be so easily derived with vector mathematics that they need not be remembered. For example, the expression for r_1 in Fig. 2–7, used in calculating the dipole field, is easily derived. From the diagram,

$$\mathbf{r}_1 = \mathbf{r} - \mathbf{l} \quad \text{and} \quad \mathbf{r}_1 \cdot \mathbf{r}_1 = (\mathbf{r} - \mathbf{l}) \cdot (\mathbf{r} - \mathbf{l});$$

therefore

$$r_1^2 = r^2 + l^2 - 2\mathbf{r} \cdot \mathbf{l} = r^2 + l^2 - 2rl \cos \theta,$$

which is the relation used in Section 2–6.

2–9 Line element. Frequently in physics it is necessary to calculate the work done when a force moves some object along a path in space. In Chapter 1 the potential difference between two points along a wire is defined by the power dissipated by a steady rate of flow of charges between these two points. The wire was not essential to this definition. In general, either positive or negative work is done by an electric field any time a charge moves through it. To calculate this work it is desirable to use a line element $d\mathbf{l}$, which expresses the direction of the displacement of the center of a charge as it moves a short distance through space. In rectangular coordinates this line element is

$$d\mathbf{l} = \mathbf{i}\,dx + \mathbf{j}\,dy + \mathbf{k}\,dz, \tag{2–13}$$

where dx, dy, and dz are the rectangular components of the small displacement. In cylindrical coordinates the line element is

$$d\mathbf{l} = \mathbf{a}_r\,dr + \mathbf{a}_\phi r\,d\phi + \mathbf{k}\,dz.$$

The unit vector $\mathbf{a}_\phi$ is multiplied by $r\,d\phi$ instead of just $d\phi$, because the latter does not give the displacement of the object in length units. From Fig. 2–4 it can be seen that when ϕ increases by $d\phi$ the point P moves the distance $r\,d\phi$. Likewise, from Fig. 2–5 it can be seen that when θ increases by $d\theta$, P moves a distance $r\,d\theta$. Furthermore, when ϕ increases by $d\phi$ in this figure, P moves a distance $r\sin\theta\,d\phi$. In spherical coordinates the line element is then

$$d\mathbf{l} = \mathbf{a}_r\,dr + \mathbf{a}_\theta r\,d\theta + \mathbf{a}_\phi r \sin\theta\,d\phi.$$

2–10 Line integral. When a force $\mathbf{f}$ moves an object a distance $d\mathbf{l}$, the work it does on that object is given by $dW = f\,dl\cos\gamma$, where γ is the angle between $\mathbf{f}$ and $d\mathbf{l}$. The work may be expressed vectorially by $dW = \mathbf{f}\cdot d\mathbf{l}$. Using Eq. (2–12), this can be written $dW = f_x\,dx + f_y\,dy + f_z\,dz$, which contains nothing but scalar quantities. If the force $\mathbf{f}$ moves the object from a point with coordinates (x_1, y_1, z_1) to one with coordinates (x_2, y_2, z_2), the total work done is

$$W = \int_1^2 \mathbf{f}\cdot d\mathbf{l} = \int_{x_1}^{x_2} f_x\,dx + \int_{y_1}^{y_2} f_y\,dy + \int_{z_1}^{z_2} f_z\,dz.$$

In performing the integration with respect to x, for example, the value substituted for f_x must express its value for every point on the path the object travels. This defines the line integral. An example should help clarify the process.

Suppose an object moves in the yz-plane from a point P_1 on the z-axis at $(0, 0, 3)$ to a point P_2 whose coordinates are $(0, 4, 5)$. The work done on this object by a force $\mathbf{f}$ whose value varies from point to point in space in accordance with the relation $\mathbf{f} = \mathbf{i}x + \mathbf{j}z + \mathbf{k}z$ is

$$W = \int_0^0 x\,dx + \int_0^4 z\,dy + \int_3^5 z\,dz.$$

The values for these integrals will depend upon the path traveled from P_1 to P_2, and although there is an infinite number of these paths that could be traveled, calculations for the two paths shown in Fig. 2–10 should clarify the method. The straight line joining the two points directly is expressed analytically by $z = 3 + y/2$. For this path,

$$W = \int_0^4 \frac{6 + y}{2}\,dy + \int_3^5 z\,dz = 24,$$

since $dx = 0$ throughout this path. When the dashed path is followed, the integration must be done in two steps, first over the horizontal and then over the vertical portion. On the horizontal path $z = 3$, independ-

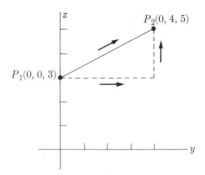

FIG. 2–10. Two of the many possible paths of integration between points P_1 and P_2 are illustrated, one by a dashed line and the other by a solid line.

ently of y, while on the vertical portion $y = 4$, independently of z. The integral then becomes

$$W = \left(\int_0^4 3 \, dy + \int_3^3 3 \, dz \right) + \left(\int_4^4 z \, dy + \int_3^5 z \, dz \right) = 12 + 8 = 20.$$

The work done on the object by **f** depends upon the path traveled in Fig. 2–10, namely, 24 units over the solid line and only 20 units over the dashed line. Since the work done by **f** is not independent of the path, it is called a *nonconservative force*. *By definition, the work done by conservative forces must be independent of the path traveled.*

2–11 Electrostatic potentials. It was pointed out in Section 2–5 that whenever the distribution of charges throughout space is known, the fields can in principle be calculated directly, although the mathematical difficulties are often very great. Usually one does not know the location and value of all charges in space, and therefore more powerful methods for solving electrostatic problems are needed. Even when the charge distributions are known, the fields usually can be computed more easily with potential theory than by the direct summations or integrations of Sections 2–5, 2–6, and 2–7.

In Chapter 4 a general method for solving electrostatic problems is developed. This method is based upon differential equations given by Poisson and Laplace which express the variations of electrostatic potentials with coordinates in space. Two fundamental laws that must be obtained before these equations can be derived are (1) the law stating that in any system of static charges the work done in carrying a test charge around any closed path is zero, and (2) Gauss' law that the electric field **E** can be expressed consistently in terms of the density of electric flux lines. The first of these will now be developed; the second is postponed to Chapter 5.

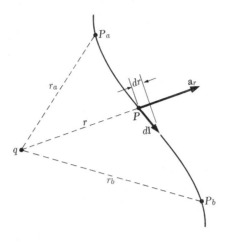

FIG. 2–11. The electric field at point P is given by $\mathbf{E} = k(q/r^2)\mathbf{a}_r$. The difference in potential between points P_a and P_b is calculated in the text by integrating $\mathbf{E} \cdot d\mathbf{l}$ from P_a to P_b.

The work done by the field in moving a test charge q through a distance $d\mathbf{l}$ in an electrostatic field $\mathbf{E}$ is $dW = q\mathbf{E} \cdot d\mathbf{l}$. The difference in potential between the two ends of the element $d\mathbf{l}$ is defined by $-dV = dW/q = \mathbf{E} \cdot d\mathbf{l}$. The negative sign indicates that the field $\mathbf{E}$ points in the direction of decreasing potential. The difference of potential between any two points P_a and P_b is then given by

$$V_a - V_b = \int_{P_a}^{P_b} \mathbf{E} \cdot d\mathbf{l}.$$

Considering only the field due to a single point charge q, the potential difference between points P_a and P_b in Fig. 2–11 can be calculated. The field at any point such as P along the path of integration is given by $(kq/r^2)\mathbf{a}_r$, where $\mathbf{a}_r$ is a unit vector parallel to $\mathbf{r}$ and directed away from q. From the diagram, $dr = \mathbf{a}_r \cdot d\mathbf{l}$ and hence the integral is

$$V_a - V_b = \int_{r_a}^{r_b} \frac{kq}{r^2} \, dr = kq \left(\frac{1}{r_a} - \frac{1}{r_b} \right).$$

Note that it was not necessary to choose a specific path to be able to evaluate this integral. The same value is obtained for every path that can be drawn connecting P_a with P_b. Furthermore, if the integral is evaluated over some path in the opposite direction, from P_b to P_a, an equal but opposite expression is obtained. Obviously, the integral of $\mathbf{E} \cdot d\mathbf{l}$ around any closed circuit must be equal to zero; i.e.,

$$\oint \mathbf{E} \cdot d\mathbf{l} = 0.$$

The difference of potential between P_a and P_b, calculated for the case shown in Fig. 2–12, where there are two point charges q_1 and q_2, is given by

$$V_a - V_b = \int_{P_a}^{P_b} \mathbf{E} \cdot d\mathbf{l} = \int_{P_a}^{P_b} \mathbf{E}_1 \cdot d\mathbf{l} + \int_{P_a}^{P_b} \mathbf{E}_2 \cdot d\mathbf{l}$$

$$= kq_1 \left(\frac{1}{r_{a1}} - \frac{1}{r_{b1}} \right) + kq_2 \left(\frac{1}{r_{a2}} - \frac{1}{r_{b2}} \right), \qquad (2\text{–}14)$$

which is also independent of the path. Obviously, this can be extended to any number of charges, and the work done in moving a test charge around any closed path in a field produced by a system of point charges will be zero. A field is said to be *conservative* when the total work done by it on a small test charge traversing any closed loop is zero. Electrostatic fields are always conservative. In any electrostatic problem it is possible to assign a unique value of potential for every point in space, since the difference of potential between any two points is independent of the path of integration.

Only differences in potentials have been treated thus far, so that some point of reference must be chosen if unambiguous potentials are to be assigned to each point in space. Actually, the point of reference can be chosen quite arbitrarily, although it is common practice to assign zero potential to points at infinity. With this choice, the potential at P_a

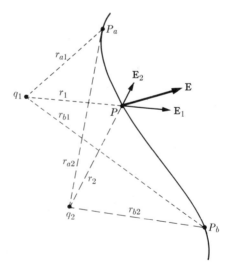

Fig. 2–12. The electric field $\mathbf{E}$ at P is the vector sum of $\mathbf{E}_1$ and $\mathbf{E}_2$, the fields at P due respectively to q_1 only and q_2 only. The difference in potential between points P_a and P_b is calculated by integrating $\mathbf{E} \cdot d\mathbf{l}$ from P_a to P_b.

can be calculated from Eq. (2–14) by placing P_b at infinity, which gives $V_a = kq/r_a$ for Fig. 2–11 and

$$V_a = \frac{kq_1}{r_{a1}} + \frac{kq_2}{r_{a2}}$$

for Fig. 2–12. Since the potentials at a point due to any number of point charges are additive, from Eq. (2–14), the potential at point P due to n point charges $q_1, q_2, \ldots, q_n$ can be expressed as

$$V = \sum_{i=1}^{i=n} \frac{kq_i}{r_i}, \qquad (2\text{--}15)$$

where r_i is the distance of P from the point charge q_i.

Equation (2–15) is useful only for calculating potentials due to distributions of point charges, but, like Eq. (2–2), it can be replaced with an integral for use in calculating potentials due to continuous distributions of charge. Since Eq. (2–15) is a scalar summation, the potential due to continuous distributions of charges can be obtained from the scalar integral

$$V = k \int_\tau \frac{\rho \, d\tau}{r}. \qquad (2\text{--}16)$$

Mathematically, potentials and fields become infinite at each point charge. However, point charges do not exist in nature and all real fields and potentials are finite. Nevertheless, the concept of point charges is a very convenient mathematical fiction, since any collection of charges in a small volume can be treated as a point charge for calculating fields at points at a considerable distance from the center of these charges.

Since potentials are scalar quantities, while the fields are vector quantities, potentials are usually easier to calculate than fields. In Section 2–13 it is shown that once the potential distribution is known, the electric fields can be easily determined. For example, if an electric field $\mathbf{E}$ can be considered uniform and two points are chosen a short distance δd apart on a line parallel to the direction of $\mathbf{E}$, the difference of potential is just $\delta V = -E \delta d$, that is, $E = -\delta V/\delta d$. In fact, for any distribution of potentials, the electric field is just equal to the negative rate of change of potential and its direction is that in which the potential reduces most rapidly.

2–12 Partial differentiation. It is frequently desirable to determine the rate of change of potential in some particular direction. The coordinates should be oriented so that the particular direction is parallel to one coordinate axis. Suppose the potential V is known as a function of the rectangular coordinates. The rate of change of $V = V(x, y, z)$ in the x-direction can be obtained by differentiating V with respect to x, considering both y and z as constants. Such differentiation is called *partial differentiation*, and is designated by $\partial V/\partial x$. As an example, if $V = Axyz + Bz^2$, then, $\partial V/\partial x = Ayz$.

The concept of partial differentiation is so generally useful in physics, mathematics, and other fields that many theorems have been developed for its use. Detailed discussions of partial differentiation and some of these theorems may be found in several texts.* One of these theorems on the *total differential* is presented in this section. An attempt is made to show the plausibility of this relationship, but no rigorous proof is intended.

When V is a function of the coordinates, its value may change from one point in space to another. If the distance between the two points is infinitesimal, the increase in V is given by the total differential. The total differential is defined in rectangular coordinates by

$$dV = \frac{\partial V}{\partial x}\, dx + \frac{\partial V}{\partial y}\, dy + \frac{\partial V}{\partial z}\, dz; \qquad (2\text{–}17)$$

in cylindrical coordinates by

$$dV = \frac{\partial V}{\partial r}\, dr + \frac{\partial V}{\partial \phi}\, d\phi + \frac{\partial V}{\partial z}\, dz; \qquad (2\text{–}18)$$

and in spherical coordinates by

$$dV = \frac{\partial V}{\partial r}\, dr + \frac{\partial V}{\partial \theta}\, d\theta + \frac{\partial V}{\partial \phi}\, d\phi. \qquad (2\text{–}19)$$

The similarity between these equations is obvious, and in fact, the total differential may be expressed by

$$dV = \frac{\partial V}{\partial u}\, du + \frac{\partial V}{\partial v}\, dv + \frac{\partial V}{\partial w}\, dw$$

in any orthogonal system of coordinates in which the coordinates are u, v, and w. These total differential expressions for dV exactly represent the increase in V only when the displacement from the first to the second point is so small that dx, dy, dz; dr, $d\phi$, dz; and dr, $d\theta$, $d\phi$ are infinitesimals. Future discussions will be limited to just these situations. That the dV in these expressions does represent the increase in V under these circum-

---

* W. Kaplan, *Advanced Calculus*, Addison-Wesley Publishing Co., Inc., 1952.
W. T. Martin and E. Reissner, *Elementary Differential Equations*, Chap. 8, Addison-Wesley Publishing Co., Inc., 1956.
M. Morris and O. E. Brown, *Differential Equations*, 2nd ed., Prentice Hall, 1942.

stances is quite plausible. The increase in V if only x changes by dx must be the rate of change with x multiplied by dx; that is, $(\partial V/\partial x)\,dx$. Likewise, the increase in V with a small change in y only is $(\partial V/\partial y)\,dy$, and with a small change in z only is $(\partial V/\partial z)\,dz$. When all three change by dx, dy, and dz, respectively, the total increase is the sum of the separate increases provided these differentials are infinitesimal. Whenever the change in V, due to any term, is a decrease rather than an increase, that term will be negative. The arguments for the other coordinate systems are similar.

2–13 Gradient of potential. It was pointed out in Section 2–11 that the electric field $\mathbf{E}$ is given by the negative rate of change or the negative gradient of potential and that it points in the direction in which the potential reduces most rapidly. This statement is abbreviated to the expression $\mathbf{E} = -\text{grad } V$ or $\mathbf{E} = -\nabla V$. The latter abbreviation suggests that there is an operation that can be performed on the potential function to obtain an expression for the field, and that the nature of this operation should be determined.

To determine the nature of this operation an expression for $\mathbf{E}$ in terms of V and the coordinates is needed. If V increases by dV with an infinitesimal displacement $d\mathbf{l}$, then $\mathbf{E} \cdot d\mathbf{l} = -dV$. This relation can be used to obtain a definition for the gradient of V (∇V) that is valid for any system of coordinates. Such a definition of ∇V, which is invariant to the coordinates, is found in the relation

$$\nabla V \cdot d\mathbf{l} = dV. \qquad (2\text{–}20)$$

The gradient of V, ∇V, is then defined as that vector operation on V that gives the total differential dV when it is dotted into the displacement $d\mathbf{l}$. Obviously, the ∇V thus defined is a vector quantity. To find the expression ∇V in a particular system of coordinates it is only necessary to find the vector expression which, when dotted into the correct expression for $d\mathbf{l}$, gives dV in those coordinates. In rectangular coordinates,

$$d\mathbf{l} = \mathbf{i}\,dx + \mathbf{j}\,dy + \mathbf{k}\,dz$$

and

$$dV = \frac{\partial V}{\partial x}\,dx + \frac{\partial V}{\partial y}\,dy + \frac{\partial V}{\partial z}\,dz.$$

Referring to Eq. (2–8) for dot products in general, it appears that this expression for dV is the dot product of two vectors whose rectangular components are $\partial V/\partial x$, $\partial V/\partial y$, $\partial V/\partial z$ and dx, dy, dz, respectively. Thus the partial derivatives here represent the rectangular components of the vector ∇V. In rectangular components, then,

$$\nabla V = \mathbf{i}\,\frac{\partial V}{\partial x} + \mathbf{j}\,\frac{\partial V}{\partial y} + \mathbf{k}\,\frac{\partial V}{\partial z}\,. \tag{2-21}$$

In cylindrical coordinates, when Eq. (2–20) is compared with

$$d\mathbf{l} = \mathbf{a}_r\,dr + \mathbf{a}_\phi r\,d\phi + \mathbf{k}\,dz$$

and

$$dV = \frac{\partial V}{\partial r}\,dr + \frac{\partial V}{\partial \phi}\,d\phi + \frac{\partial V}{\partial z}\,dz,$$

the resulting expression for ∇V is

$$\nabla V = \mathbf{a}_r\,\frac{\partial V}{\partial r} + \mathbf{a}_\phi\,\frac{1}{r}\,\frac{\partial V}{\partial \phi} + \mathbf{k}\,\frac{\partial V}{\partial z}\,. \tag{2-22}$$

In spherical coordinates,

$$d\mathbf{l} = \mathbf{a}_r\,dr + \mathbf{a}_\theta r\,d\theta + \mathbf{a}_\phi r \sin\theta\,d\phi$$

and

$$dV = \frac{\partial V}{\partial r}\,dr + \frac{\partial V}{\partial \theta}\,d\theta + \frac{\partial V}{\partial \phi}\,d\phi.$$

The vector that can be dotted into $d\mathbf{l}$ to produce dV is

$$\nabla V = \mathbf{a}_r\,\frac{\partial V}{\partial r} + \mathbf{a}_\theta\,\frac{1}{r}\,\frac{\partial V}{\partial \theta} + \mathbf{a}_\phi\,\frac{1}{r\sin\theta}\,\frac{\partial V}{\partial \phi}\,. \tag{2-23}$$

Similarities between these three orthogonal systems should now be fairly obvious. To point out these similarities and to provide general relations valid for any orthogonal system, a general system using the three coordinates u, v, and w can be introduced and the line element can be defined as

$$d\mathbf{l} = \mathbf{a}_u U\,du + \mathbf{a}_v V\,dv + \mathbf{a}_w W\,dw.$$

Here U, V, and W are chosen as in the three familiar systems, so that $U\,du$, $V\,dv$, $W\,dw$ all represent elements of length. To make the result more general, a new differentiable function of coordinates, $\Phi = \Phi(u, v, w)$ can be defined that is not necessarily an electrostatic potential function. Since the total differential is

$$d\Phi = \frac{\partial \Phi}{\partial u}\,du + \frac{\partial \Phi}{\partial v}\,dv + \frac{\partial \Phi}{\partial w}\,dw,$$

the vector that can be dotted into $d\mathbf{l}$ to produce $d\Phi$ is

$$\nabla\Phi = \mathbf{a}_u\,\frac{1}{U}\,\frac{\partial \Phi}{\partial u} + \mathbf{a}_v\,\frac{1}{V}\,\frac{\partial \Phi}{\partial v} + \mathbf{a}_w\,\frac{1}{W}\,\frac{\partial \Phi}{\partial w}\,.$$

This is the general expression for the gradient of Φ in any orthogonal system of coordinates.

Dipole potential and field. The ideal dipole provides an excellent demonstration of the usefulness of potentials in calculating fields. The potential at P in Fig. 2–7 is, from Eq. (2–15),

$$V = kq \left(\frac{1}{r_1} - \frac{1}{r} \right).$$

Since $r_1^2 = r^2 + l^2 - 2rl \cos \theta$ and, when the approximations of Section 2–6 are used, $1/r_1 = (1 + l \cos \theta/r)/r$, the potential of the dipole becomes

$$V = \frac{kql \cos \theta}{r^2}.$$

Since $k = 1/4\pi\epsilon_0$ and $ql = p$,

$$V = \frac{p \cos \theta}{\epsilon_0 4\pi r^2} \tag{2–24}$$

is the potential in spherical coordinates of a dipole whose moment is p. The field is given by

$$\mathbf{E} = -\boldsymbol{\nabla} V = -\left(\mathbf{a}_r \frac{\partial V}{\partial r} + \mathbf{a}_\theta \frac{1}{r} \frac{\partial V}{\partial \theta} \right).$$

Now

$$\frac{\partial V}{\partial r} = -\frac{2kp \cos \theta}{r^3}$$

and

$$\frac{\partial V}{\partial \theta} = -\frac{kp \sin \theta}{r^2},$$

and therefore the dipole field is

$$\mathbf{E} = \frac{p}{\epsilon_0 4\pi r^3} (\mathbf{a}_r 2 \cos \theta + \mathbf{a}_\theta \sin \theta),$$

which is the expression developed in Section 2–6. The expression for the field of an ideal dipole occurs so frequently that it is desirable to define a vector $\mathbf{d}_f$ that might be called the dipole-field vector:

$$\mathbf{d}_f \equiv \mathbf{a}_r 2 \cos \theta + \mathbf{a}_\theta \sin \theta.$$

This dipole-field vector could also be defined by

$$\mathbf{d}_f = -r^3 \boldsymbol{\nabla} \left(\frac{\cos \theta}{r^2} \right).$$

Properties of the gradient. The gradient $\boldsymbol{\nabla} V$ is a vector operation on V (a function of the coordinates) that provides information concerning V in

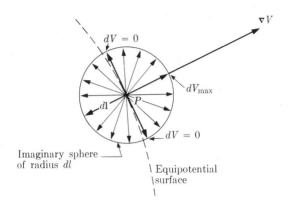

Fig. 2–13. The gradient of V, ∇V, which is defined by $\nabla V \cdot d\mathbf{l} = dV$, is perpendicular to equipotential surfaces and gives the direction and magnitude of the maximum space rate of increase of V.

the neighborhood very close to the general point at which it is evaluated. Defining ∇V by the relation $\nabla V \cdot d\mathbf{l} = dV$ of Eq. (2–20) makes it easy to demonstrate its important properties, namely:

(a) ∇V points in the direction in which V increases most rapidly,

(b) ∇V is everywhere perpendicular to the imaginary surfaces (the equipotentials) on which V is constant, and

(c) the magnitude $|\nabla V|$ is equal to the maximum of the space rate of increase of V.

Now ∇V is a vector that has definite magnitude and direction at P, as shown in Fig. 2–13. On a sphere of infinitesimal radius dl drawn about P the value of V differs from its value at P by an amount dV. According to Eq. (2–20), dV is maximum when $d\mathbf{l}$ is parallel to ∇V and zero when $d\mathbf{l}$ is perpendicular. Therefore V increases most rapidly with displacements parallel to ∇V and stays constant with displacements perpendicular to ∇V, demonstrating properties (a) and (b). When $d\mathbf{l}$ is parallel to ∇V,

$$|\nabla V| = \frac{dV_{\max}}{dl},$$

so that the magnitude of ∇V is the maximum space rate of change of V, demonstrating property (c).

2–14 Vector or cross product of vectors. The dot product of two vectors, which is a scalar quantity, has been defined in Section 2–8, and its usefulness has been demonstrated in Sections 2–9 through 2–13. The defining equation (2–9) uses the cosine of the angle between the vectors. There is also a need, especially in electrodynamics, for a product defined

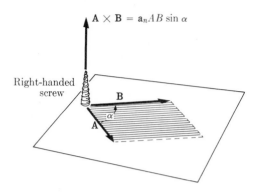

FIG. 2–14. Definition of the vector cross product $\mathbf{A} \times \mathbf{B}$, where $\mathbf{a}_n$ is a unit vector normal to the plane of $\mathbf{A}$ and $\mathbf{B}$.

with the sine instead of the cosine of this angle. Usually, where the product, including the sine, is needed, the result should have both magnitude and direction; i.e., it should be a vector. Consequently, a vector product has been defined that is distinguished from the scalar product by the use of a cross in place of the dot. The definition is

$$\mathbf{A} \times \mathbf{B} = \mathbf{a}_n AB \sin \widehat{AB}, \tag{2–25}$$

where the unit vector $\mathbf{a}_n$ is normal to the plane defined by the vectors $\mathbf{A}$ and $\mathbf{B}$, as shown in Fig. 2–14. The direction of $\mathbf{a}_n$ is the direction in which a right-handed screw would move if it were forced through the plane by rotating it in the direction in which $\mathbf{A}$ would have to rotate to become parallel to $\mathbf{B}$ and point in the same direction. In Fig. 2–14 $\mathbf{a}_n$ points upward, since the screw proceeds in that direction. However, for the product $\mathbf{B} \times \mathbf{A}$, the screw must rotate in the opposite direction and $\mathbf{a}_n$ would then point downward. Obviously,

$$\mathbf{B} \times \mathbf{A} = -\mathbf{A} \times \mathbf{B} \tag{2–26}$$

and the order in which the vectors are written is very important. This constitutes one of the important differences between the cross and the dot products, since with the dot product the vectors may be written in any order.

If $\mathbf{A}$ and $\mathbf{B}$ in Fig. 2–14 have units of length, $\mathbf{A} \times \mathbf{B}$ is numerically equal to the area of the parallelogram (shaded in the figure) that is defined by the vectors $\mathbf{A}$ and $\mathbf{B}$. This product then suggests that an area sometimes may be considered to be a vector quantity. An excellent example is that of a tank filled with gas at high pressure. The force acting on a small area δs of the tank surface is $\delta \mathbf{f} = p\,\delta \mathbf{s}$, where the vector direction is assigned to $\delta \mathbf{s}$, since the pressure p is a scalar quantity. While the direction of the area vector represented by $\mathbf{A} \times \mathbf{B}$ is well defined, ordinarily when areas are used as vectors, rules must be invented for determining their directions. The rule to be used for the direction of the $\delta \mathbf{s}$ of the surface of the gas tank is one that is quite generally used when closed surfaces are involved, namely, $\delta \mathbf{s}$ is parallel to the outward drawn normal.

Simple geometry shows that if $\mathbf{S} = \mathbf{D} + \mathbf{E}$, then $\mathbf{R} \times \mathbf{S} = \mathbf{R} \times \mathbf{D} + \mathbf{R} \times \mathbf{E}$. Furthermore, if $\mathbf{R} = \mathbf{A} + \mathbf{B}$, then

$$\mathbf{R} \times \mathbf{S} = \mathbf{A} \times \mathbf{D} + \mathbf{B} \times \mathbf{D} + \mathbf{A} \times \mathbf{E} + \mathbf{B} \times \mathbf{E}, \qquad (2\text{--}27)$$

which is easily extended to the cross products of the sums of any number of vectors. *It is very important here to maintain the correct order for writing the vectors.* Equation (2–27) makes it possible to obtain relations for the analytical calculation of cross products when the vectors are written with components and unit vectors. The cross products of unit vectors will be needed. In rectangular coordinates,

$$\mathbf{i} \times \mathbf{i} = \mathbf{j} \times \mathbf{j} = \mathbf{k} \times \mathbf{k} = 0; \qquad (2\text{--}28)$$

$$\mathbf{i} \times \mathbf{j} = \mathbf{k}, \quad \mathbf{j} \times \mathbf{k} = \mathbf{i}, \quad \mathbf{k} \times \mathbf{i} = \mathbf{j},$$
$$\mathbf{j} \times \mathbf{i} = -\mathbf{k}, \quad \mathbf{k} \times \mathbf{j} = -\mathbf{i}, \quad \mathbf{i} \times \mathbf{k} = -\mathbf{j}. \qquad (2\text{--}29)$$

An analytical expression for $\mathbf{A} \times \mathbf{B}$ can be obtained from Eq. (2–27). There will be nine terms, but three of these are zero because of Eq. (2–28). The remaining terms are conveniently written in the form of a determinant:

$$\mathbf{A} \times \mathbf{B} = \begin{vmatrix} \mathbf{i} & \mathbf{j} & \mathbf{k} \\ A_x & A_y & A_z \\ B_x & B_y & B_z \end{vmatrix}. \qquad (2\text{--}30)$$

The relations between unit vectors shown in Eq. (2–29) resulted from choosing a right-handed coordinate system. If the x- and y-axes were interchanged in Fig. 2–3, these relations would become $\mathbf{i} \times \mathbf{j} = -\mathbf{k}$, etc., and the system would be called left-handed. The other orthogonal systems have also been chosen to be right-handed. Hence, in cylindrical coordinates, $\mathbf{a}_r \times \mathbf{a}_\phi = \mathbf{k}$, $\mathbf{a}_\phi \times \mathbf{k} = \mathbf{a}_r$, etc., and in spherical coordinates $\mathbf{a}_r \times \mathbf{a}_\theta = \mathbf{a}_\phi$, $\mathbf{a}_\theta \times \mathbf{a}_\phi = \mathbf{a}_r$, etc.

The usefulness of the cross product can best be shown by examples. Several of the following examples are also useful for reviewing elementary principles.

Angular momentum and torque. In Fig. 2–6 an example was given of a mass point moving near the origin of coordinates. Its angular momentum about the origin is $m\mathbf{R} \times \mathbf{v}$, if m is the mass of the point. The vector $\mathbf{R} \times \mathbf{v}$ is parallel to the instantaneous axis of rotation and in the direction a right-handed screw would move with this rotation. Since the numerical magnitudes and directions of both vectors are given, the cross product can be obtained numerically. In fact, this could be obtained by using any of the three coordinate systems in which these vectors are given. The cylindrical coordinates seem the simplest here. The cross product in cylindrical coordinates is given by a determinant similar to that of Eq. (2–30). To simplify this determinant, factor 13 m/sec out of **v** and 1 m out of **R**:

$$\mathbf{R} \times \mathbf{v} = \begin{vmatrix} \mathbf{a}_r & \mathbf{a}_\phi & \mathbf{k} \\ 5 & 0 & 12 \\ 0 & 5 & -12 \end{vmatrix} 13 \text{ m}^2/\text{sec},$$

or $\mathbf{R} \times \mathbf{v} = (-60\mathbf{a}_r + 60\mathbf{a}_\phi + 25\mathbf{k})13 \text{ m}^2/\text{sec}$, which represents a vector of magnitude 1150 m²/sec, pointing 6°48′ above the xy-plane and 135° + 53°8′ = 188°8′ from the positive x-axis. When this is computed in rectangular coordinates, the result is

$$\mathbf{R} \times \mathbf{v} = (-84\mathbf{i} - 12\mathbf{j} + 25\mathbf{k})13\text{m}^2/\text{sec},$$

which is a vector having the same magnitude and direction as the result using cylindrical coordinates.

Force on current in a magnetic field. In elementary texts the force acting on an element of wire of length dl carrying a current is usually given by $df = BI \, dl \sin \theta$, where θ and the direction df must be separately specified. When this is written in vector notation as $d\mathbf{f} = I \, d\mathbf{l} \times \mathbf{B}$, where $d\mathbf{l}$ points in the direction of the current, no further specification is required. With **I**, $d\mathbf{l}$, and **B** in amperes, meters, and webers/m² respectively, $d\mathbf{f}$ is in newtons. This law is treated in more detail in Chapter 7.

Biot-Savart law. The law for the magnetic field dH produced by an electric current I in an element of wire dl is often written as

$$dH = \frac{I \, dl \sin \theta}{4\pi r^2},$$

where r is the distance measured from the element to the point where the field is being calculated. The angle θ and the direction of dH must be separately specified. In vector notation this is written as

$$d\mathbf{H} = \frac{I \, d\mathbf{l} \times \mathbf{a}_r}{4\pi r^2}$$

and no additional specification is needed. The writing of such equations in vector notation usually eliminates the need for diagrams and written explanations. A more detailed discussion of this law will be found in Chapter 8.

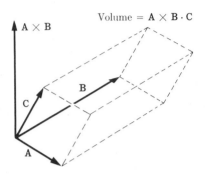

Fig. 2–15. The volume represented by the triple scalar product $\mathbf{A} \times \mathbf{B} \cdot \mathbf{C}$.

2–15 Identities in vector algebra. Dot and cross products between two vectors have been discussed. Often in the course of some derivation or other mathematical exercise, products between more than two vectors arise. There are just two possible types of products involving three vectors, namely, $(\mathbf{A} \times \mathbf{B}) \cdot \mathbf{C}$ and $(\mathbf{A} \times \mathbf{B}) \times \mathbf{C}$.

Triple scalar product. The first of these triple products is usually written $\mathbf{A} \times \mathbf{B} \cdot \mathbf{C}$ without the enclosures, since the expression would be meaningless with parentheses around $\mathbf{B} \cdot \mathbf{C}$. From Fig. 2–14, $\mathbf{A} \times \mathbf{B}$ has a magnitude equal to the shaded area and is perpendicular to it (vertical in the diagram). Dotting this into $\mathbf{C}$ multiplies this area by the vertical component of $\mathbf{C}$, which gives the volume of the parallelepiped shown in Fig. 2–15. Obviously, $\mathbf{B} \times \mathbf{C} \cdot \mathbf{A}$ and $\mathbf{B} \cdot \mathbf{C} \times \mathbf{A}$ give this same volume, and the dot and cross can be interchanged at will. However, the sign of the product is reversed by interchanging any two of the vectors, such as $\mathbf{B} \cdot \mathbf{C} \times \mathbf{A} = -\mathbf{B} \cdot \mathbf{A} \times \mathbf{C}$, but is not changed so long as the three vectors are kept in cyclic order. A convenient expression is

$$\mathbf{A} \times \mathbf{B} \cdot \mathbf{C} = \begin{vmatrix} A_x & A_y & A_z \\ B_x & B_y & B_z \\ C_x & C_y & C_z \end{vmatrix}.$$

Triple vector product. The product $(\mathbf{A} \times \mathbf{B}) \times \mathbf{C}$ is a vector in the plane determined by $\mathbf{A}$ and $\mathbf{B}$, the vectors in the parentheses. This can be seen from Fig. 2–15. The $\mathbf{A} \times \mathbf{B}$ vector is perpendicular to the $\mathbf{AB}$ plane, but the cross product of $\mathbf{C}$ with this is perpendicular to both $\mathbf{A} \times \mathbf{B}$ and $\mathbf{C}$, which puts it right back into the $\mathbf{AB}$ plane. If $\mathbf{A}$ and $\mathbf{B}$ are finite and are not parallel, any vector in the $\mathbf{AB}$ plane can be expressed by $k_1 \mathbf{A} + k_2 \mathbf{B}$, where k_1 and k_2 are scalar constants, properly determined. The correct expression is

$$(\mathbf{A} \times \mathbf{B}) \times \mathbf{C} = \mathbf{B}(\mathbf{A} \cdot \mathbf{C}) - \mathbf{A}(\mathbf{B} \cdot \mathbf{C}),$$

as is easily verified by writing each vector in terms of its components and the unit vectors, and then carrying out the indicated operations. If the parentheses enclose $\mathbf{B} \times \mathbf{C}$, this operation is performed first, the final product is in the $\mathbf{BC}$ plane, and the expression becomes

$$\mathbf{A} \times (\mathbf{B} \times \mathbf{C}) = \mathbf{B}(\mathbf{A} \cdot \mathbf{C}) - \mathbf{C}(\mathbf{A} \cdot \mathbf{B}).$$

Both of these equations have two terms on the right, each consisting of one vector from the parentheses on the left multiplied by the dot product of the other two vectors. These two terms on the right have opposite signs, but the positive sign is associated with the vector from the middle of the original expression on the left.

PROBLEMS

*2-1. The unit vector $\mathbf{a}_r$ in Fig. 2-6 can be expressed in terms of the unit vectors $\mathbf{i}$, $\mathbf{j}$, and $\mathbf{k}$ of the rectangular coordinate system as

$$\mathbf{a}_r = \mathbf{i}3/5 + \mathbf{j}4/5 + \mathbf{k}0.$$

(a) Write each of the unit vectors, $\mathbf{a}_R$, $\mathbf{a}_\theta$, and $\mathbf{a}_\phi$, of the spherical coordinate system in that figure in terms of $\mathbf{i}$, $\mathbf{j}$, and $\mathbf{k}$.

(b) Write each of the unit vectors, $\mathbf{a}_r$, $\mathbf{a}_\phi$, and $\mathbf{k}$ of the cylindrical coordinate system in that figure in terms of $\mathbf{i}$, $\mathbf{j}$, and $\mathbf{k}$.

2-2. A vector like the $\mathbf{v}$ in Fig. 2-6 can be written in spherical coordinates as $\mathbf{v} = \mathbf{a}_R v_R + \mathbf{a}_\theta v_\theta + \mathbf{a}_\phi v_\phi$. (a) Show that the magnitudes of v_R, v_θ, and v_ϕ can be obtained from the dot products $\mathbf{a}_R \cdot \mathbf{v}$, $\mathbf{a}_\theta \cdot \mathbf{v}$, and $\mathbf{a}_\phi \cdot \mathbf{v}$ respectively. (b) Show that the magnitudes of v_r, v_ϕ, and v_z, in a similar expression for $\mathbf{v}$ in cylindrical coordinates, can be obtained from the dot products $\mathbf{a}_r \cdot \mathbf{v}$, $\mathbf{a}_\phi \cdot \mathbf{v}$, and $\mathbf{k} \cdot \mathbf{v}$ respectively.

2-3. The expression for $\mathbf{v}$ in terms of the unit vectors $\mathbf{i}$, $\mathbf{j}$, and $\mathbf{k}$ in the latter part of Section 2-4 can be checked easily by referring to Fig. 2-6.

(a) Use this expression and the relations derived in Problems 2-1(a) and 2-2(a) to determine the magnitudes of v_R, v_θ, and v_ϕ in that figure. Check these with the values used in the expressions for $\mathbf{v}$ in Section 2-4.

(b) Follow the procedure outlined in (a) to determine the magnitudes of v_r, v_ϕ, and v_z for the cylindrical components of the $\mathbf{v}$ in Fig. 2-6. Check these with the values used in the expressions for $\mathbf{v}$ in Section 2-4.

(c) Use the procedures of (a) and (b) to determine the magnitudes of the components of the vector $\mathbf{R}$ in Fig. 2-6 and check these with the expressions for $\mathbf{R}$ in Section 2-4.

*2-4. In Section 2-5 a charge of -16×10^{-10} coul is placed at $(0, 0, 0)$ in a rectangular coordinate system, another charge of 12×10^{-10} coul is placed at $(0, 3\ \mathrm{m}, 4\ \mathrm{m})$, and the electric field $\mathbf{E}$ produced by these charges, at the point P, which has the coordinates $(0, 0, 4\ \mathrm{m})$, is calculated.

---

* Answers to starred problems will be found at back of book.

(a) Draw a diagram showing these charges in the yz-plane and show the field $\mathbf{E}$ with its rectangular components.

(b) Calculate the field at $(0, 6\text{ m}, 8\text{ m})$ due to these two charges and show this field, with its rectangular components, in your diagram of part (a).

(c) Write an expression for the $\mathbf{E}$ at the general point (x, y, z) due to these two charges.

*2–5. An ideal dipole, having the dipole moment $p = 24\pi\epsilon_0$, is at the origin of a rectangular coordinate system and is pointing in the positive y-direction. Draw this in the first quadrant of the yz-plane. Draw arcs of two circles of radii 1 m and 2 m. Using an appropriate scale factor, draw vectors representing the direction and magnitude of the electric field due to the dipole at points on each of these two circles where $\theta = 0°$, $30°$, $60°$, and $90°$.

2–6. A small object carrying a charge of -5×10^{-9} coul experiences a downward force of 20×10^{-9} n when placed at a certain point in an electric field. (a) What is the electric intensity at the point? (b) What would be the magnitude and direction of the force acting on an α-particle placed at the point?

*2–7. What must be the charge on a particle of mass 2 gm for it to remain stationary in space when placed in a downward directed electric field of intensity 500 n/coul?

2–8. In a rectangular coordinate system a charge of 25×10^{-9} coul is placed at the origin of coordinates, and a charge of -25×10^{-9} coul is placed at the point $x = 6\text{ m}$, $y = 0$. What is the electric intensity at (a) $x = 3\text{ m}$, $y = 0$; (b) $x = 3\text{ m}$, $y = 4\text{ m}$?

*2–9. A charge of 16×10^{-9} coul is fixed at the origin of coordinates, a second charge of unknown magnitude is at $x = 3\text{ m}$, $y = 0$, and a third charge of 12×10^{-9} coul is at $x = 6\text{ m}$, $y = 0$. What is the magnitude of the unknown charge if the resultant field at $x = 8\text{ m}$, $y = 0$ is 20.25 n/coul directed to the right?

*2–10. A ring of radius 10 cm has a positive charge q of 5×10^{-9} coul. (a) Compute the electric intensity at points on the axis of the ring, at distances from its center of 0, 5, 8, 10, and 15 cm. Show the results in a graph. (b) In terms of the radius R of the ring, at what axial distance from the center of a charged ring is the electric intensity a maximum? Compare with the graph in part (a).

2–11. Determine the potential at the center of the square and the vacant corner for the charge distribution of Problem 1–9.

*2–12. The potential at a certain distance from a point charge is 600 volts, and the electric field is 200 n/coul. (a) What is the distance to the point charge? (b) What is the magnitude of the charge?

*2–13. Two point charges whose magnitudes are $+20 \times 10^{-9}$ coul and -12×10^{-9} coul are separated by a distance of 5 cm. An electron is released from rest between the two charges, 1 cm from the negative charge, and moves along the line connecting the two charges. What is its velocity when it is 1 cm from the positive charge?

*2–14. A thin metallic ring describes a circle in the xz-plane of a rectangular coordinate system. It has a radius of 10 cm, its axis coincides with the y-axis, and it is uniformly charged with 2.6×10^{-8} coul of electric charge.

(a) Calculate the difference between the potential at the origin and at the point on the y-axis where $y = 24$ cm.

(b) Calculate and plot the potential along the y-axis as a function of y.

(c) Calculate and plot the velocity of a proton that has been projected in the positive direction along the y-axis and has arrived at $y = 24$ cm with the velocity 10^6 m/sec.

2–15. Most commercial capacitors consist of conducting sheets so close together that the electric fields between these sheets can be closely approximated by assuming the conductors to be infinite planes parallel to each other. Fields can be much more simply calculated near an infinite plane than near a finite plane. From the expression for the field of a charged plane of infinite extent, find the fields due to two such planes when they are parallel and uniformly charged with $+\sigma$ and $-\sigma$ surface densities, respectively, (a) between the planes, and (b) outside the space between the planes. Are these fields uniform?

*2–16. Assume that the charged plane of Fig. 2–9 is not infinite but is a disk of radius a about the z-axis. (a) Calculate $\mathbf{E}$ at P. (b) Calculate the percent error involved in using Eq. (2–14) when $a \gg z$.

2–17. Two disks, each like that of Problem 2–16, are parallel and are separated a distance $d \cong a$. They are charged to uniform surface densities of σ on the upper and $-\sigma$ on the lower disk and the positively charged disk coincides with the xy-plane. (a) Calculate $\mathbf{E}$ at a point on the axis above both disks. (b) Simplify the expression from part (a) for $z \gg a$ and compare the result with the expression for the field of an ideal dipole.

*2–18. An infinitely long wire coinciding with the z-axis has a uniform charge λ in coul/m. (a) Find the expression for $\mathbf{E}$ in cylindrical coordinates at points in the xy-plane. (b) Find $\mathbf{E}$ at these same points due only to the charge along the positive z-axis, that is, assuming that there is no charge along the negative z-axis.

2–19. Demonstrate geometrically the correctness of the relation

$$\mathbf{R} \times \mathbf{S} = \mathbf{R} \times \mathbf{D} + \mathbf{R} \times \mathbf{E}$$

when

$$\mathbf{S} = \mathbf{D} + \mathbf{E}.$$

2–20. Show geometrically that if $\mathbf{S} = \mathbf{D} + \mathbf{E}$, then $\mathbf{R} \cdot \mathbf{S} = \mathbf{R} \cdot \mathbf{D} + \mathbf{R} \cdot \mathbf{E}$.

*2–21. Two vectors are defined as follows: $\mathbf{A} = \mathbf{i}4 + \mathbf{j}3 + \mathbf{k}12$ and $\mathbf{B} = \mathbf{i}12 - \mathbf{j}4 - \mathbf{k}3$. Calculate (a) $\mathbf{S} = \mathbf{A} + \mathbf{B}$, (b) $\mathbf{D} = \mathbf{A} - \mathbf{B}$, (c) $P = \mathbf{A} \cdot \mathbf{B}$, and (d) $\mathbf{C} = \mathbf{A} \times \mathbf{B}$. (e) Find the angle between $\mathbf{A}$ and $\mathbf{B}$.

*2–22. Using vector operations: (a) Calculate the angles that the vector $\mathbf{A} = \mathbf{i}3 + \mathbf{j}4 + \mathbf{k}12$ makes with the x-, y-, and z-axes respectively. (b) Calculate the angle that $\mathbf{A}$ of part (a) makes with $\mathbf{B} = \mathbf{i}4 + \mathbf{j}12 + \mathbf{k}3$ and draw the diagram.

*2–23. The direction of a vector in space can be expressed in terms of the cosines of the angles it makes with the three rectangular coordinate axes x, y, and z. These are called the "direction cosines" of the vector. Using vector operations, find the angle between vectors $\mathbf{A}$ and $\mathbf{B}$ whose respective direction cosines are l_1, m_1, n_1, and l_2, m_2, n_2.

2-24. Integrate $\oint \mathbf{A} \cdot d\mathbf{l}$ for $\mathbf{A} = \mathbf{i}y - \mathbf{j}x$ around a closed rectangle whose corners are at the following (x, y) coordinates: $(0, 0)$, $(a, 0)$, (a, b), and $(0, b)$.

*2-25. Expressed in cylindrical coordinates, the force on a very small object is $\mathbf{f} = A\mathbf{a}_\phi/r$. Find the work done in moving this object around the following closed paths:

(a) A circle of radius a about the origin in the xy-plane.

(b) A composite path of four parts, namely, (1) the arc of a circle of radius a with ϕ increasing from 0 to π, (2) the radial line at $\phi = \pi$ extending from $r = a$ to $r = b$ (with $b > a$), (3) the arc of a circle of radius b with ϕ increasing from π to 2π, and (4) the radial line at $\phi = 2\pi$ extending from $r = b$ to $r = a$.

(c) The same path as in (b) for parts 1, 2, and 4, but with part 3 being that arc of a circle of radius b for which ϕ decreases from π to 0.

*2-26. The force acting on a small object that is restrained to move in the xy-plane is $\mathbf{F} = \mathbf{i}y^2 + \mathbf{j}4x$. Calculate the work that must be done on this object to cause it to move through the origin from $(4, -4)$ to $(4, 4)$ along the parabola $y^2 = 4x$ and then back to the starting point along the straight line joining the points.

2-27. Two point charges, each of magnitude q, are placed at $y = b$ and $y = -b$. (a) Find the field $\mathbf{E}$ at $(x = x, y = 0)$. (b) Find the work required to move a small charge q' from $x = 10b$ to $x = b$.

*2-28. Calculate the electric fields in the two regions where the following are the potential distributions:

$$\text{(a)} \quad V = x^3 + 3x^2y + 2y^2z,$$

$$\text{(b)} \quad V = (x - 3)(y - 4) + 5.$$

In both of these potential fields, locate the points where $\mathbf{E} = 0$.

2-29. Write $\mathbf{A}$, $\mathbf{B}$, and $\mathbf{C}$ in rectangular components with unit vectors and demonstrate by direct multiplication that (a) $\mathbf{A} \times \mathbf{B} \cdot \mathbf{C} =$ the volume of the parallelepiped of Fig. 2–15, and that (b) $\mathbf{A} \times (\mathbf{B} \times \mathbf{C}) = \mathbf{B}(\mathbf{A} \cdot \mathbf{C}) - \mathbf{C}(\mathbf{A} \cdot \mathbf{B})$.

2-30. As is mentioned in Problem 2–15, it is often mathematically convenient to deal with charged sheets of infinite extent or charged wires of infinite length, even though such devices cannot exist. When Eq. (2–16) is used to calculate potentials due to these devices, the results may be infinite. It is more realistic in such cases to give these devices constant though very large dimensions, so that the potentials remain finite. Assume that there is a uniform distribution of electrostatic charges, given by λ in coul/m, along the z-axis from $z = -Z$ to $z = Z$.

(a) By direct integration determine the electric field $\mathbf{E}$ at the point P, where in cylindrical coordinates $z = 0$ and $r = r$.

(b) By direct integration determine the potential V at P.

(c) Simplify the expressions for $\mathbf{E}$ and V by assuming that $Z \gg r$.

(d) Show that the simplified expression for $\mathbf{E}$ can be obtained directly from the simplified expression for V.

*2-31. Consider a charged filament like the one described in Problem 2–30, which extends only from $z = 0$ to $z = Z$. (a) By direct integration determine $\mathbf{E}$ at P, where $z = 0$ and $r = r$. (b) By direct integration determine V at P.

(c) Simplify the expressions for $\mathbf{E}$ and V by assuming that $Z \gg r$. (d) Show that the simplified expression for $\mathbf{E}$ *cannot be obtained* from the simplified expression for V. Explain why $\mathbf{E}$ cannot be obtained here from the V of part (b), although in Problem 2–30 $\mathbf{E}$ could be obtained from the V of part (b) there.

2–32. For the charged filament of Problem 2–31, which extends only along the positive z-axis, obtain a potential function from which the $\mathbf{E}$ at P can be obtained. Demonstrate that the $\mathbf{E}$ of part (c) of that problem can be obtained from your expression for V.

*2–33. Two point charges Q and $-q$, where $Q > q > 0$, are located on a z-axis which is the axis of symmetry of a spherical coordinate system. Charge Q is at $z = d$ and charge $-q$ is at $z = b$, where $d/b = (Q/q)^2$. Find the equation for the closed surface where the potential is zero, in terms of r and θ.

2–34. Figure 2–16 shows a geometrical situation commonly encountered in electrostatics. A point charge, a dipole, or other collections of charges may be at P_1 with rectangular coordinates (a, b, c) so that $r_1^2 = a^2 + b^2 + c^2$. The general point at which potentials or fields are to be calculated has the coordinates (x, y, z) or (r, θ, ϕ), so that $r^2 = x^2 + y^2 + z^2$. The vector distance from P_1 to P is $\mathbf{R}$ and $R^2 = (x - a)^2 + (y - b)^2 + (z - c)^2$.

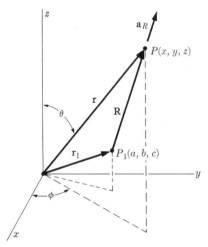

Fig. 2–16. Geometrical relations for calculating fields or potentials at a general point P due to charges located at P_1.

(a) Using vector algebra, show that since $\mathbf{R} = \mathbf{r} - \mathbf{r}_1$ from the diagram, $R^2 = r^2 + r_1^2 - 2\mathbf{r} \cdot \mathbf{r}_1$.

(b) Suppose that $V = R$ and calculate ∇V, first using rectangular coordinates, and second using spherical coordinates. Express these results in terms of the unit vector $\mathbf{a}_R$.

(c) Show that if $V = 1/R$, $\nabla V = -\nabla R/R^2$.

*2–35. Two point charges $+4q$ and $-q$ are separated a distance l. (a) Find the position of the equilibrium point where the electric field is zero. (b) Find the potential at the equilibrium point. (c) Show that the equipotential surface that passes through the equilibrium point consists of two completely closed surfaces, one inside the other and contacting it only at the equilibrium point. [*Hint:* With the origin at charge $-q$ spherical coordinates can be used to calculate where this equipotential cuts the axis. To determine where it cuts the basal plane that passes through $-q$, the origin may be shifted to the location of the $+4q$ charge to allow the solution to be obtained in terms of trigonometric functions.]

*2–36. To help you to understand the potential field near the charges of Problem 2–35, draw additional equipotentials on the diagram. Of special interest are the equipotentials $V = 0$, $V = (1/4\pi\epsilon_0)(2q/3l)$, and the two closed but separated surfaces on which $V = (1/4\pi\epsilon_0)(3q/2l)$. These surfaces can be roughly drawn by calculating three or four well-chosen points. Probably the simplest procedure is to write an expression for potentials on the basal plane, which can be plotted to obtain graphical solutions.

CHAPTER 3

FUNDAMENTAL THEOREMS OF
ELECTROSTATICS WITH DIFFERENTIAL OPERATORS

There are many scientific and practical applications for electrostatic phenomena relating to conductors and insulators shaped into a multitude of geometrical forms. These phenomena may involve charges, fields, potentials, forces, torques, and capacitances. A general method for calculating the relationships between these various quantities for all geometrical configurations is presented in Chapter 4. Briefly stated, the method is to find a solution of a differential equation, known as Laplace's equation, which satisfies the boundary conditions. The fundamental principles needed for this general method are presented in this chapter. All of the principles are here specifically related to electrostatic problems; however, the method is actually applicable to the solution of problems in several other fields of physics, for example in current electricity, in heat flow, and in hydrodynamics.

The general method is based upon a simple physical concept that is often used, without proof, in elementary texts on electric and magnetic fields. This concept is that *continuous flux lines can be drawn in empty space so that, at every point in this space, the density and the direction of these lines represent the intensity and the direction of the field.* The concept is usually extended with some modification to include spaces that are not empty but do contain materials.

It is easy to show that this concept is valid for describing the electrostatic field due to a single isolated point charge q. Imagine radial lines drawn uniformly in all directions from the point charge. If the total number of lines drawn is q/ϵ_0, the density of lines passing through an imaginary sphere surrounding the point is found by dividing the total number of lines by the area of the sphere. For a sphere of any radius r the area is $4\pi r^2$. Thus the density of lines at the surface is just $q/\epsilon_0 4\pi r^2$, which is numerically equal to the electric field at the surface of the sphere. In agreement with Coulomb's law, the density of lines varies with the inverse square of the distance from the point charge and thus the concept is valid for a single isolated point charge. To show that it is valid in general for multitudes of point charges with various distributions, it is desirable to make use of the concept of solid angles.

3–1 Solid angles. To define a plane angle, a circle of radius r is drawn about the apex as the center. The angle in radians is the ratio l/r, where

l is the length of the arc subtending the angle. This definition is useful because l/r is independent of the radius of the circle. A similar procedure is used to define a solid angle. A typical solid angle is indicated by the irregular cone shown in Fig. 3–1. When two spheres of radii r_1 and r_2 are drawn with centers at the apex of this cone, areas s_1 and s_2 are inscribed by the cone on the surfaces of the respective spheres. Since these surfaces are proportional to the squares of the respective radii, the dimensionless ratio $s_1/r_1^2 = s_2/r_2^2 = \omega$ is independent of the size of the sphere and is used to define the solid angle of the cone. *Steradian* is the name given to one unit solid angle. *A steradian is the solid angle subtended at the center of a sphere of one meter radius by an area of one square meter on its surface.* An increase of the area inscribed on a given sphere indicates a proportionate increase in the solid angle, and a total solid angle inscribes the total surface area of $4\pi r^2$. The total solid angle is then 4π steradians, in the same sense as the total plane angle is 2π radians. However, it is often convenient to think of solid angles that exceed 4π steradians, just as it is often convenient to think of plane angles that exceed 2π radians.

Elemental solid angles. In defining solid angles, areas inscribed on the surface of a specially located sphere were utilized. It is often desirable to express solid angles in terms of areas inscribed on very irregular surfaces. Since potatoes have such irregular shapes, they are ideal for visualizing general volumes and general surfaces. If, as in Fig. 3–2, a point O is chosen anywhere inside such a potato, an element of the skin area ds will subtend at O an element of solid angle $d\omega$. By definition, $d\omega = ds_n/r^2$, where r is the distance from O to the center of ds and ds_n is the area inscribed by this elemental solid angle on the surface of a sphere of radius r drawn about O as a center. When ds is sufficiently small, $ds_n = ds \cos \theta$, which can be written as $ds_n = \mathbf{a}_r \cdot d\mathbf{s}$ by defining the element of area on this closed surface as a vector $d\mathbf{s}$ directed along the outward drawn normal. The expression for the elemental solid angle then becomes

$$d\omega = \mathbf{a}_r \cdot \frac{d\mathbf{s}}{r^2}, \tag{3-1}$$

Note that if this is integrated over the whole surface of the potato the result must be 4π:

$$\int_s \mathbf{a}_r \cdot \frac{d\mathbf{s}}{r^2} = 4\pi. \tag{3-2}$$

An expression for the solid angle of a right circular cone in terms of its apex angle is often needed. This can be obtained by integrating Eq. (3–1) over the circular cap of the sphere shown in Fig. 3–3. Using spherical coordinates, the surface element is $(r\,d\theta)(r \sin \theta\,d\phi) = \mathbf{a}_r \cdot d\mathbf{s}$.

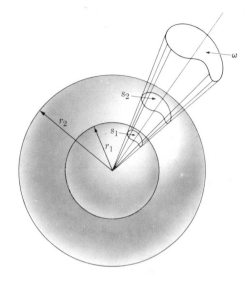

Fig. 3–1. The solid angle subtended by areas s_1, s_2 on two
concentric spheres.

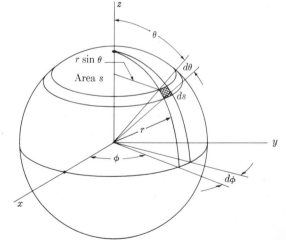

Fig. 3–2. An illustration of the elemental
solid angle $d\omega = ds_n/r^2$ subtended by the area
$d\mathbf{s}$ on the surface of a potato.

Fig. 3–3. An illustration
showing how the solid angle
of a right conical section is
obtained from an integration
of the elemental solid angle
ds/r^2.

The elemental solid angle then is $d\omega = \mathbf{a}_r \cdot d\mathbf{s}/r^2 = \sin\theta\, d\theta\, d\phi$, and the solid angle subtended by the circular cap becomes

$$\omega = \int_0^\theta \sin\theta\, d\theta \int_0^{2\pi} d\phi = 2\pi(1 - \cos\theta). \qquad (3\text{-}3)$$

3-2 Gauss' law. The basis for the mathematical solutions of electrostatic problems is Gauss' law. This law states that the total flux out of any closed surface is proportional to the total charge enclosed by that surface.

At the center of ds in Fig. 3–2 a point charge q at point O produces an electrostatic field $\mathbf{E} = \mathbf{a}_r q/\epsilon_0 4\pi r^2$, which is the average field over ds, when ds is infinitesimal. The electric flux through the element $d\Phi = E_n\, ds$, where E_n is the component of $\mathbf{E}$ normal to the surface, can be written as $d\Phi = E\cos\theta\, ds = \mathbf{E}\cdot d\mathbf{s} = \mathbf{a}_r \cdot d\mathbf{s}\, q/\epsilon_0 4\pi r^2$. From Eq. (3–2), the total flux out of the closed surface due to q is then

$$\Phi = \int_s \frac{q\mathbf{a}_r \cdot d\mathbf{s}}{\epsilon_0 4\pi r^2} = \frac{q}{\epsilon_0}. \qquad (3\text{-}4)$$

While this proves the law for a single charge q at any point O inside a closed surface of any shape, more general situations must be investigated.

Many point charges in space. Consider the more general case shown in Fig. 3–4, where q_1 and q_2 are two charges of any magnitude at any two

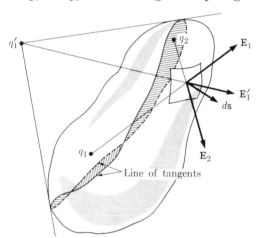

Fig. 3–4. An element of area ds is shown on the surface of a general volume shaped like a potato. Vectors $\mathbf{E}_1$, $\mathbf{E}_2$, and $\mathbf{E}_1'$ represent fields at the element due to q_1, q_2, and q_1', respectively. Since the solid angles subtended by the portions of the potato to the right and left of the line of tangents are equal, all flux entering the left side of the potato from q_1' leaves on the right side.

points inside the closed surface and q_1' is another such charge outside
this surface. The field at the surface element due to these three charges
is the vector sum of the separate fields due to each of the charges,
$\mathbf{E} = \mathbf{E}_1 + \mathbf{E}_2 + \mathbf{E}_1'$. The total flux out of the closed surface is then

$$\Phi = \int_s \mathbf{E} \cdot ds = \int_s \mathbf{E}_1 \cdot ds + \int_s \mathbf{E}_2 \cdot ds + \int_s \mathbf{E}_1' \cdot ds.$$

From Eq. (3–4) the first two integrals give q_1/ϵ_0 and q_2/ϵ_0 respectively,
but the third integral must be considered separately. Note that the
solid angle subtended by the closed surface is 4π for both q_1 and q_2, while
straight lines drawn from q_1' tangent to the closed surface describe a solid
angle ω' that is less than 4π. The points of tangency make a line dividing
the closed surface into two sheets. Over the sheet farther from q_1',

$$\int \mathbf{E}_1' \cdot ds = \frac{q_1'\omega'}{4\pi\epsilon_0},$$

while over the sheet closer to q_1',

$$\int \mathbf{E}_1' \cdot ds = -\frac{q_1'\omega'}{4\pi\epsilon_0},$$

which is negative because $\mathbf{E}_1'$ is directed inward at all points on this
nearer sheet. Therefore,

$$\int_s \mathbf{E}_1' \cdot ds = \frac{(\omega' - \omega')q_1'}{4\pi\epsilon_0} = 0.$$

No charge located outside a closed surface can contribute to the net
flux emanating from that closed surface. Obviously, if there are charges
$q_1, q_2, \ldots, q_n$ inside and charges $q_1', q_2', \ldots, q_m'$ outside any closed surface,
the net flux out of that surface is

$$\Phi = \int_s \mathbf{E} \cdot ds = \sum_1^n \frac{q_i}{\epsilon_0},$$

which is the mathematical statement of Gauss' law.

Usually, the presence of charges in space is evident only because some
of the objects in the space have either more or less electrons than they
have protons. Such conditions are most simply characterized by a density
distribution of charges, symbolized by ρ, in units of coul/m³. The summation of charges is then expressed best by an integral. Gauss' law becomes

$$\int_s \epsilon_0 \mathbf{E} \cdot ds = \int_\tau \rho \, d\tau, \tag{3–5}$$

where τ must be the total volume enclosed by the closed surface s. Charges
outside of s do not contribute to the integral.

Actually, Eq. (3–5) is the more general expression, since the density ρ at any point is defined by

$$\rho = \lim_{\Delta\tau\to 0} \frac{\sum_i q_i}{\Delta\tau},$$

where the q_i's represent all positive and negative charges in $\Delta\tau$. As $\Delta\tau$ approaches zero, it is assumed that ρ will approach some fixed value that is dependent upon the location in space. In physical problems, it is convenient to think of the volume becoming small but still remaining finite. This avoids the violent fluctuations in ρ that would occur if the elemental volume decreased beyond the point where it contains only two or three atoms. The reduction of $\Delta\tau$ should be stopped before noticeable fluctuations are produced. This small but finite volume may be referred to as a *physical point*. A physical point might be 10^{-21} m^3 or smaller, since a volume this small would still contain over 10^8 atoms in a solid or 10^5 atoms in air at atmospheric pressure.

Because mathematical operations on continuous functions are simpler than on discontinuous quantities like point charges, charge distributions are represented by a density function wherever possible.

Flux lines and field intensities. The fact that electric field intensities at all points in space can be represented by the densities of continuous flux lines can now be proved. For this proof, groups of positive charges or individual positive charges can be surrounded by closed equipotential surfaces, so that no positive charge exists in the remaining space not enclosed by an equipotential surface. It was proven in Section 2–13 that such surfaces are everywhere perpendicular to the electric field **E**, and according to Gauss' law of Eq. (3–5), the electric field lines of flux must start from positive charges and must end on negative charges. An extremely large number of flux lines can be drawn parallel to the electric field throughout the intervening space in such a manner that, where they start from each element of an equipotential surface surrounding positive charges, the density of the lines is proportional to the field at that element. Starting flux lines in this manner guarantees that their densities are proportional to the fields on these particular equipotential surfaces, but it remains to be shown that this proportionality exists at all locations in space.

As shown in Fig. 3–5, on one of these initial equipotential surfaces where the field is $\mathbf{E}_1$ over a small area A_1, a point P_1 can be chosen for constructing a tube which is generated by the lines of flux passing through the periphery of the surface A_1 and progressing to a point P_2 where the field is $\mathbf{E}_2$. Constructing a new surface of area A_2 perpendicular to the lines of flux at this point produces a closed surface containing no charge. According to Gauss' law, the net flux out of this enclosure must be zero. Since the flux lines are parallel to the curved surface between

FIG. 3–5.   Tube of flux lines between points P_1 and P_2. The flux through A_1 equals the flux through A_2, and the fields $\mathbf{E}_1$ and $\mathbf{E}_2$ are equal to the total flux lines divided by the areas A_1 and A_2, respectively.

the two areas A_1 and A_2, no flux lines can enter or leave through the curved surface and the total flux entering at P_1 must equal the flux leaving at P_2. Mathematically, $\phi = E_1 A_1 = E_2 A_2$, the field at P_1 is $E_1 = \phi/A_1$, and at P_2 is $E_2 = \phi/A_2$, which shows that the density of the flux lines does represent the strength of the field at the points P_1 and P_2. Since all the intervening space can be filled with such tubes of flux, the same relationships must hold everywhere. This establishes the validity of the physical picture for all electrostatic fields.

Gauss' law calculations of symmetrical fields.   There are a number of problems in electrostatics which can be solved easily by the direct application of Gauss' law. These problems have symmetry such that imaginary closed surfaces can be drawn with shapes such that $\mathbf{E}$ is known to be constant and normal to some surfaces but parallel to all other surfaces. Over the former surfaces the integral can be written $\int \mathbf{E} \cdot d\mathbf{s} = E \int ds$, whereas over the latter surfaces $\int \mathbf{E} \cdot d\mathbf{s} = 0$, so that E can be evaluated. The problem concerning the tube of flux in Fig. 3–5 is of this type.

The tube of force closed at the ends by A_1 and A_2 constitutes the imaginary closed surface, and the vector fields at P_1 and P_2 are uniform and perpendicular to the surfaces A_1 and A_2. The integral $\int_s \mathbf{E} \cdot d\mathbf{s} = 0$ over the long curved portions between these two areas because $\mathbf{E}$ is perpendicular to $d\mathbf{s}$ everywhere on this part of the surface.

This method can be used to calculate the field near a large plane with a uniform density of surface charge. Consider that the charged plane coincides with the xy-plane, has dimensions great enough to be considered infinite in the x- and y-directions, and has a uniform areal density σ_t. The problem is to find the field due to this distribution of charges at a point P whose distance from the plane is z. Since the plane is infinite, any such point must have a field directed parallel to the z-axis. A right circular cylinder may be constructed extending from $-z$ to $+z$ with its axis parallel to the z-axis and with these ends closed by small circular disks of area A. This closed surface s, which is often called a gaussian surface or a pillbox, encloses a total charge of $\sigma_t A$, and from Gauss' law

$\int_s \mathbf{E} \cdot d\mathbf{s} = \sigma_t A / \epsilon_0$. Considering σ_t to be positive, the field is upward at $+z$ and downward at $-z$, but the magnitudes are equal by symmetry and each is directed out of the closed cylindrical surface, so that over the two end disks $\int \mathbf{E} \cdot d\mathbf{s} = E \int ds = E 2A$. Since the fields are parallel to the cylindrical surface, this surface contributes nothing to the integral and hence $2EA = \sigma_t A / \epsilon_0$ or $E = \sigma_t / 2\epsilon_0$. Therefore the magnitude of the field at P is independent of its position, although this can be strictly true only so long as the plane is truly infinite. However, even when such a plane is finite, the expression $E = \sigma_t / 2\epsilon_0$ is a very accurate approximation for points close to the plane.

Another important problem is that of calculating the field near the surface of a conductor in terms of the density σ of its surface charge. The important relation for conductors is

$$\sigma = \epsilon_0 E,$$

which can be demonstrated by means of Gauss' law. It is first necessary to realize that practically all real surfaces appear flat when the observation points are close enough. Even the sharp point of a needle is rounded under a microscope and would appear flat if it could be observed from a point within 10^{-8} meter. A small cylindrical pillbox can be constructed with one disk-shaped end (of small area A) inside the conductor and the other outside, with both parallel to the surface of the conductor. The charge enclosed by this pillbox is σA. Since there is no field in the conductor, $\int \mathbf{E} \cdot d\mathbf{s} = 0$ over the surface of the pillbox inside the conductor. The surface of the conductor is an equipotential surface and the field just outside must, therefore, be normal to the surface, so that $\int \mathbf{E} \cdot d\mathbf{s} = 0$ over the cylindrical sides of the pillbox. Since the field E is normal to the outer disk and is uniform when A is taken very small, Gauss' law gives $\sigma A = \epsilon_0 E A$ or

$$\sigma = \epsilon_0 E = -\epsilon_0 \frac{\partial v}{\partial n}, \tag{3-6}$$

where n is the normal distance from the conducting surface.

The field near a thin charged sheet of infinite extent has been shown to be $E = \sigma_t / 2\epsilon_0$, where σ_t is the total charge density. If the thin sheet is a conductor, one-half the charge would be on each side of the sheet and the surface charge density on either surface would then be $\sigma = \sigma_t / 2$, which makes the last two field calculations consistent.

It is left as an exercise to show that the field around a very long straight wire, charged to a uniform density of charge λ, is $E = \lambda / 2\pi\epsilon_0 r$ and that the field around a uniformly charged sphere is given by $E = q / 4\pi\epsilon_0 r^2$. In other words, Gauss' law shows that with plane symmetry the field is independent of the distance, with cylindrical symmetry it varies inversely as the first power of the distance, and with spherical symmetry it varies inversely as the square of the distance.

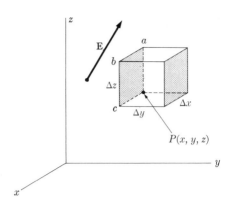

FIG. 3-6. Volume element in rectangular coordinates.

Differential form of Gauss' law. In the integral form the usefulness of Gauss' law for solving electrostatic problems is strictly limited to very simple geometries. On the other hand, the number of problems in electrostatics that need to be solved is essentially infinite because the number of possible distributions of charges and possible shapes and locations of conductors or other materials is infinite. Gauss' law can be modified to solve many of these by exact mathematical methods and many others by approximate methods. This involves developing a differential equation by applying Gauss' law to a small elemental volume in space.

In rectangular coordinates the elemental volume is a rectangular parallelepiped at the point x, y, z, whose dimensions are Δx, Δy, and Δz. Let us apply Gauss' law to this closed surface as shown in Fig. 3-6. The closed surface consists of six rectangles, two of area $\Delta x\,\Delta y$, two of area $\Delta y\,\Delta z$, and two of area $\Delta z\,\Delta x$. Assume that the field in this volume element is a function of the coordinates x, y, and z. According to Gauss' law, the total flux out of this volume is $(\rho/\epsilon_0)(\Delta x\,\Delta y\,\Delta z)$, where ρ is the average density of charge within the volume. The flux out of the shaded rectangle on the left is $-E_y\,\Delta x\,\Delta z$ and the flux out of the shaded rectangle on the right is $E_y\,\Delta x\,\Delta z + (\partial/\partial y)(E_y\,\Delta x\,\Delta z)\,\Delta y$, provided Δx, Δy, and Δz are infinitesimal, and the net flux out of these two shaded rectangles is $(\partial E_y/\partial y)(\Delta x\,\Delta y\,\Delta z)$, since Δx and Δz are independent of y. By symmetry, the net flux out of the other pairs of surfaces is given by $(\partial E_x/\partial x)(\Delta x\,\Delta y\,\Delta z)$ and $(\partial E_z/\partial z)\,(\Delta x\,\Delta y\,\Delta z)$, respectively. The net flux out of this volume element is the sum of these three terms. Equating this sum to $\rho\,\Delta x\,\Delta y\,\Delta z/\epsilon_0$ and dividing both sides by the volume $(\Delta x\,\Delta y\,\Delta z)$ results in

$$\frac{\partial E_x}{\partial x} + \frac{\partial E_y}{\partial y} + \frac{\partial E_z}{\partial z} = \frac{\rho}{\epsilon_0}.$$

The terms on the left side of this equation occur so frequently in physical and mathematical theories that they have been given the name *divergence* of **E**, which is usually written as $\nabla \cdot \mathbf{E}$. Gauss' law for an elementary volume is then given by the differential relation

$$\nabla \cdot \mathbf{E} = \frac{\rho}{\epsilon_0}. \tag{3-7}$$

Notice that $\nabla \cdot \mathbf{E}$ expresses the flux out of the volume element per unit volume. Wherever there is a distribution of charges of density ρ, the divergence of **E** is proportional to ρ. Furthermore, when there are no charges in a given space, the right side becomes zero and the expression states that the flux out of the elemental volume is equal to the flux into that volume.

3–3 Divergence of vector fields. The divergence is a mathematical operation that can be applied to any vector function of coordinates. The general definition of the divergence of any vector such as **A** is

$$\operatorname{div} \mathbf{A} = \nabla \cdot \mathbf{A} = \lim_{\Delta\tau \to 0} \frac{\int_s \mathbf{A} \cdot d\mathbf{s}}{\Delta\tau}, \tag{3-8}$$

where $\Delta\tau$ is the value of the elemental volume. This definition of divergence is independent of the system of coordinates used.

The general definition can be used to find the expression for divergence in cylindrical coordinates by constructing a volume element as shown in Fig. 3–7, using the system of coordinates introduced in Fig. 2–4. In cylindrical coordinates, the sides of the elemental volume are of length Δr, $r\,\Delta\phi$, and Δz. The integral $\int \mathbf{A} \cdot d\mathbf{s}$ taken over the shaded surface on the left is $-A_r r\,\Delta\phi\,\Delta z$ and the integral over the shaded surface on the

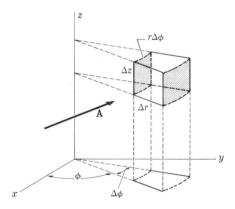

FIG. 3–7. Volume element in cylindrical coordinates.

right is $A_r r \, \Delta\phi \, \Delta z + (\partial/\partial r)(A_r r \, \Delta\phi \, \Delta z) \, \Delta r$. Hence the integral over these two shaded surfaces gives $(\partial(rA_r)/\partial r) \, \Delta r \, \Delta\phi \, \Delta z$ and by symmetry the integrals over the other pairs of surfaces yield

$$\frac{\partial}{\partial\phi} (A_\phi \, \Delta r \, \Delta z) \, \Delta\phi = \frac{\partial A_\phi}{\partial\phi} \, \Delta r \, \Delta\phi \, \Delta z$$

and

$$\frac{\partial}{\partial z} (A_z r \, \Delta\phi \, \Delta r) \, \Delta z = \frac{\partial A_z}{\partial z} r \, \Delta r \, \Delta\phi \, \Delta z$$

respectively. From Eq. (3–8),

$$\nabla \cdot \mathbf{A} = \frac{1}{r \, \Delta r \, \Delta\phi \, \Delta z}$$

$$\times \left[\frac{\partial}{\partial r} (rA_r) \, \Delta r \, \Delta\phi \, \Delta z + \frac{\partial A_\phi}{\partial\phi} \, \Delta r \, \Delta\phi \, \Delta z + \frac{\partial A_z}{\partial z} r \, \Delta r \, \Delta\phi \, \Delta z \right],$$

which reduces to

$$\nabla \cdot \mathbf{A} = \frac{1}{r} \frac{\partial(rA_r)}{\partial r} + \frac{1}{r} \frac{\partial A_\phi}{\partial\phi} + \frac{\partial A_z}{\partial z}, \tag{3–9}$$

which is the expression for the divergence of any vector $\mathbf{A}$ in cylindrical coordinates. This calculation of the divergence of $\mathbf{A}$ in cylindrical coordinates follows the pattern used for the calculation in rectangular coordinates. In each case the volume element has six surfaces over which $\int \mathbf{A} \cdot d\mathbf{s}$ must be evaluated. These are separated into three pairs, each pair of surfaces being perpendicular to one of the three unit vectors. The flux into the element through the first surface of any pair is almost equal to the flux out of the other surface. In any one pair of surfaces, the net flux out of the elemental volume through the two surfaces is just the increase in flux passing through the second surface over that passing through the first. In Fig. 3–7 the flux through the first surface at r and perpendicular to $\mathbf{a}_r$ is $\Phi_r = A_r r \, \Delta\phi \, \Delta z$. The net flux out of the element due to the two surfaces perpendicular to $\mathbf{a}_r$ is just the increase in the flux passing through the second surface, at $r + \Delta r$, over that through the first surface; that is,

$$\frac{\partial\Phi_r}{\partial r} \, \Delta r = \frac{\partial}{\partial r} (A_r r \, \Delta\phi \, \Delta z) \, \Delta r.$$

Repeating this procedure with the surface pairs perpendicular to $\mathbf{a}_\phi$ and $\mathbf{a}_z$ gives three expressions, and the divergence is obtained by adding these three and dividing by the volume of the element.

The procedure is best illustrated by calculating the divergence in general orthogonal coordinates. Table 3–1 can be used to convert any expression given in general orthogonal coordinates to the correct expres-

TABLE 3–1

MULTIPLIERS AND UNIT VECTORS FOR
ORTHOGONAL COORDINATE SYSTEMS

	Coordinates	Multipliers	Unit vectors
General	u $\quad v$ $\quad w$	U $\quad V$ $\quad W$	$\mathbf{a}_u$ $\quad \mathbf{a}_v$ $\quad \mathbf{a}_w$
Rectangular	x $\quad y$ $\quad z$	1 $\quad 1$ $\quad 1$	$\mathbf{i}$ $\quad \mathbf{j}$ $\quad \mathbf{k}$
Cylindrical	r $\quad \phi$ $\quad z$	1 $\quad r$ $\quad 1$	$\mathbf{a}_r$ $\quad \mathbf{a}_\phi$ $\quad \mathbf{a}_z$
Spherical	r $\quad \theta$ $\quad \phi$	1 $\quad r$ $\quad r\sin\theta$	$\mathbf{a}_r$ $\quad \mathbf{a}_\theta$ $\quad \mathbf{a}_\phi$

sion in any of the specific orthogonal coordinate systems. There are many other orthogonal systems that could be included in this table.

If the three orthogonal coordinates are u, v, and w, and the unit vectors in these three directions are $\mathbf{a}_u$, $\mathbf{a}_v$, and $\mathbf{a}_w$, any displacement in such a system of coordinates can be written as $d\mathbf{l} = \mathbf{a}_u U\, du + \mathbf{a}_v V\, dv + \mathbf{a}_w W\, dw$, where U, V, and W are the quantities which must multiply du, dv, and dw to determine linear distances in the directions $\mathbf{a}_u$, $\mathbf{a}_v$, and $\mathbf{a}_w$, respectively. For example, in rectangular coordinates, U, V, and W are unity and dimensionless, while u, v, and w are x, y, and z. In the cylindrical coordinates just described, $U = 1$, $V = r$, and $W = 1$, and $u = r, v = \phi$, and $w = z$. The elemental volume for these general coordinates is shown in Fig. 3–8.

Now consider the pair of surfaces perpendicular to $\mathbf{a}_v$, shaded in the figure. The flux through the surface at v is $\Phi_v = A_v U\, \Delta u\, W\, \Delta w$, and the net flux out through these two surfaces is

$$\frac{\partial \phi_v}{\partial v}\, \Delta v = \frac{\partial}{\partial v}\, (A_v U\, \Delta u\, W\, \Delta w)\, \Delta v.$$

The net flux out through the pair of surfaces perpendicular to $\mathbf{a}_w$ can be obtained by cyclic substitution; that is, by changing u to v, v to w, w to u, U to V, V to W, W to U, etc. A second cyclic substitution gives the net flux out through the pair of surfaces perpendicular to $\mathbf{a}_u$. The divergence then is obtained by adding these three expressions and dividing by the volume $\Delta\tau = UVW\, \Delta u\, \Delta v\, \Delta w$. Since Δu, Δv, and Δw are independent of the coordinates, the final expression is

$$\mathbf{\nabla} \cdot \mathbf{A} = \frac{1}{UVW}\left[\frac{\partial}{\partial u}\,(VWA_u) + \frac{\partial}{\partial v}\,(WUA_v) + \frac{\partial}{\partial w}\,(UVA_w)\right].$$

This general expression for the divergence of $\mathbf{A}$ is easily translated into a specific expression for any orthogonal coordinate system. The problems

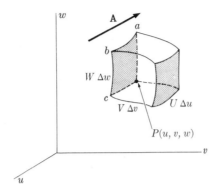

FIG. 3–8. Volume element in general orthogonal coordinates.

in this text can be solved by use of rectangular, cylindrical, or spherical coordinates. For convenience, Table 3–1 contains definitions of the quantities needed for these three coordinate systems in terms of the symbols of the general coordinates. The spherical coordinates used in this text are shown in Fig. 2–5.

3–4 The Gauss mathematical theorem. Gauss' law in integral form, $\int_s \epsilon_0 \mathbf{E} \cdot d\mathbf{s} = \int_\tau \rho \, d\tau$, is given in Eq. (3–5) and in differential form, $\nabla \cdot \mathbf{E} = \rho/\epsilon_0$, in Eq. (3–7). If the differential form is substituted into the integral form, we obtain

$$\int_s \mathbf{E} \cdot d\mathbf{s} = \int_\tau \nabla \cdot \mathbf{E} \, d\tau.$$

This purely mathematical relation is called Gauss' theorem, and since it is true for any vector function of position in space provided that function is continuous and differentiable, it may be written as

$$\int_s \mathbf{A} \cdot d\mathbf{s} = \int_\tau \nabla \cdot \mathbf{A} \, d\tau,$$

where $\mathbf{A}$ is any such function of the coordinates. Although the statements above do not constitute a rigorous proof of this theorem, the general definition for divergence given in Eq. (3–8) makes it possible to provide a simple direct proof.

A perfectly general volume, illustrated by the potato shape of Fig. 3–2, which is surrounded by a closed surface like the skin of the potato can be considered stationary in a vector field $\mathbf{A}$. A symbol ψ can then be defined by $\int_s \mathbf{A} \cdot d\mathbf{s} = \psi$ when the integral is taken over the entire closed surface. A very sharp knife cutting through the volume without disturbing the positions of the parts will produce two volumes with the two added surfaces k and k'. Whatever flux passes out of one volume through k passes into the other volume through k' and integration over all the surfaces of both volumes then gives

$$\int \mathbf{A} \cdot d\mathbf{s} = \int_s \mathbf{A} \cdot d\mathbf{s} + \int_k \mathbf{A} \cdot d\mathbf{s} + \int_{k'} \mathbf{A} \cdot d\mathbf{s} = \psi,$$

since the integral over k' cancels that over k.

More elements of volume and more surfaces can be created by slicing through the potato in various directions with this sharp knife. The new surfaces are always created in pairs such that the integral $\int \mathbf{A} \cdot d\mathbf{s}$ over one surface of the pair cancels this integral over the other. Specifically, the volume may be divided up into a large number of very small volume elements. The defining Eq. (3–8) for divergence then may be applied separately to each of these elemental volumes and the results added. Each volume element inside the potato has six surfaces, but each of these six surfaces can be paired with an adjacent surface of some other volume element. Adding the right sides of Eq. (3–8) for all of the volume elements amounts to integrating $\int \mathbf{A} \cdot d\mathbf{s}$ over all of the surfaces. Since the integrals over the pairs of surfaces cancel, the only surface integrals that contribute to the final result are those over the skin of the original potato. The sum of all terms on the right side of Eq. (3–8) then gives $\int_s \mathbf{A} \cdot d\mathbf{s} = \psi$, which is equal to the sum of terms on the left side of Eq. (3–8) for all of the volume elements. In the limit as $\Delta\tau$ approaches zero, this sum, $\sum_i \nabla \cdot \mathbf{A}_i \, \Delta\tau_i = \psi$, becomes $\psi = \int_\tau \nabla \cdot \mathbf{A} \, d\tau$. Therefore Gauss' mathematical theorem

$$\int_\tau \nabla \cdot \mathbf{A} \, d\tau = \int_s \mathbf{A} \cdot d\mathbf{s} \qquad (3\text{–}10)$$

is true for any volume τ enclosed by a surface s in a region where $\mathbf{A}$ is some continuous and differentiable vector function of the coordinates. This theorem is very useful for transforming certain volume integrals into surface integrals and vice versa.

Poisson's and Laplace's equations. Gauss' law, developed directly from Coulomb's law of forces between static charges, has the integral form

$$\int_s \mathbf{E} \cdot d\mathbf{s} = \int_\tau \frac{\rho}{\epsilon_0} \, d\tau$$

of Eq. (3–5) and the differential form

$$\nabla \cdot \mathbf{E} = \frac{\rho}{\epsilon_0}$$

of Eq. (3–7). The integral form states that the flux out of any closed volume equals the enclosed charges divided by ϵ_0. The differential form makes the same statement for a small element of volume, although here both sides of the equation are divided by the volume of the element. Equation (3–7) can be derived directly from Eq. (3–5) by using Gauss' mathematical theorem, which allows Eq. (3–5) to be written as

$$\int_s \mathbf{E} \cdot d\mathbf{s} = \int_\tau \mathbf{\nabla} \cdot \mathbf{E} \, d\tau = \int_\tau \frac{\rho}{\epsilon_0} \, d\tau.$$

Since this relation is true for any arbitrary volume τ, it is true when τ shrinks to the dimensions of a physical point, where the integrands of the volume integrals become constant and $\mathbf{\nabla} \cdot \mathbf{E} = \rho/\epsilon_0$.

It was shown in Sections 2–11 and 2–13 that any electrostatic field can be expressed as the gradient of a potential, that is, $\mathbf{E} = -\mathbf{\nabla} V$.

Substituting this into Eq. (3–7) gives the important relation, first developed by Poisson,

$$\mathbf{\nabla} \cdot \mathbf{\nabla} V = -\frac{\rho}{\epsilon_0}. \tag{3–11}$$

The operator relation $\mathbf{\nabla} \cdot \mathbf{\nabla} V$, which is usually written as $\nabla^2 V$, is just the divergence of the gradient of V.

Laplace, investigating special situations in free space where $\rho = 0$, obtained the form of this equation,

$$\nabla^2 V = 0, \tag{3–12}$$

that has been given his name, and provided many useful solutions for electrostatic problems.

3–5 Capacitors and capacitance. The useful devices produced by placing two conductors close to but insulated from each other, which were originally called condensers, are now designated by the more consistent name *capacitor*. In use, a charge is moved from one conductor of the capacitor to the other, to give a charge $-q$ to one and q to the other, and to produce a potential difference V between the two conductors. When these conductors are separated in a vacuum, in air, or by most of the insulations that are used in such devices, the ratio q/V, designated by C, is constant. Originally C was called the capacity of the condenser but recently C has been given the more consistent designation of the *capacitance* of the *capacitor*. While in commercial capacitors the two conductors are usually placed close together to produce a relatively large capacitance, any two conductors insulated from each other constitute a capacitor whose capacitance can be determined by measuring both q and V. In many cases, when the two conductors and their separation follow a regular geometric pattern, the capacitance can also be calculated. The simplest capacitor, which is very often used, consists of two parallel plates, each of area A, separated by a small distance d. With the charge q on one plate and $-q$ on the other, the electric field is uniform between the plates, except near the edges of the plates, and is given by Eq. (3–6) as

$$E = \frac{\sigma}{\epsilon_0} = \frac{q}{\epsilon_0 A} \cdot$$

With this uniform field between the plates the potential difference is simply $V = Ed = qd/\epsilon_0 A$, and the capacitance is

$$C = \frac{q}{V} = \frac{\epsilon_0 A}{d},$$

provided the nonuniformity at the edges of the plates can be ignored. In this simple capacitor the capacitance is proportional to A and inversely proportional to d.

Capacitance of isolated conductors. It is sometimes desirable to determine the capacitance of a single isolated conductor. The electric flux lines that leave a positively charged conductor must, by Gauss' law, end on an equal negative charge. Usually the flux lines from a single charged conductor end on the walls of the laboratory or on nearby conductors, but if the charged conductor could be truly isolated, these flux lines would extend to infinity. The capacitance of an isolated conductor may be defined as the capacitance of a capacitor, which consists of the conductor surrounded by a hollow conducting sphere of infinite radius. Since the potential at infinity is zero by definition, the infinite conducting sphere is not essential in the definition. *The capacitance of an isolated conductor is the ratio of its charge divided by its potential.*

The potential of any isolated sphere of radius a and charge q is given by

$$V = \int_{r=a}^{r=\infty} \mathbf{E} \cdot d\mathbf{l} = \int_{a}^{\infty} \frac{q \, dr}{4\pi\epsilon_0 r^2} = \frac{q}{4\pi\epsilon_0 a} \cdot$$

Therefore the capacitance of an isolated sphere is

$$C = \frac{q}{V} = 4\pi\epsilon_0 a,$$

where a is the radius of the sphere.

3–6 Curl of a vector field. In Section 2–11 it is shown that the line integral around any closed path is everywhere zero in an electrostatic field:

$$\oint \mathbf{E} \cdot d\mathbf{l} = 0,$$

which proves that electrostatic fields are conservative and that $\mathbf{E}$ in static fields can be written as the gradient of a potential function. There are many other fields that can be expressed as gradients of potential func-

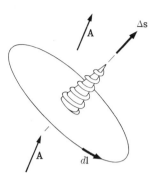

Fig. 3–9. In the defining equation for the curl, Eq. (3–13), the positive direction for Δs is chosen to be the direction in which a right-handed screw would move if rotated in direction $d\mathbf{l}$.

tions because they are conservative. A simpler method for determining whether or not a field is conservative is provided by a vector operator known as the *curl*. Whenever the curl of a vector field is zero, the field is conservative and can be expressed as the gradient of some potential function. The testing of vector fields to determine whether they are conservative is one of the very important uses of the curl operator, but it is by no means its only important use. For example, the curl is used later to obtain a very simple differential expression for the magnetic field in the vicinity of electric currents.

The curl of any vector function of coordinates such as **A** is symbolized by $\nabla \times \mathbf{A}$, which is also a vector. The definition, which is independent of the coordinate system chosen, involves line integration around an element of area Δs oriented arbitrarily in space. The curl of **A**, $\nabla \times \mathbf{A}$, is then defined by the relation

$$\lim_{\Delta s \to 0} (\nabla \times \mathbf{A}) \cdot \Delta \mathbf{s} = \lim_{\Delta s \to 0} \oint \mathbf{A} \cdot d\mathbf{l}, \qquad (3\text{–}13)$$

where the positive direction of Δs is the direction the right-handed screw in Fig. 3–9 would progress if it were rotated in the positive direction of $d\mathbf{l}$.

To specify the direction and magnitude of any vector it is best to determine its components in three coordinate directions. For example, in rectangular coordinates the vector **A** is completely defined by $\mathbf{A} = \mathbf{i}A_x + \mathbf{j}A_y + \mathbf{k}A_z$. From the definition of the curl in Eq. (3–13), its components in any coordinate system can be calculated. In rectangular coordinates the x-component of the curl is calculated by orienting the arbitrary surface Δs perpendicular to the x-axis to make the vector Δs parallel to the x-axis. The right side of Eq. (3–13) always gives the component of $\nabla \times \mathbf{A}$ parallel to Δs.

Curl in rectangular coordinates. To obtain the expression for $\nabla \times \mathbf{A}$ in rectangular coordinates, it is necessary to choose three elements of area, each perpendicular to one of the coordinate axes. The volume element shown in Fig. 3–6 has six faces from which three area elements can be chosen. The shaded surface on the left is perpendicular to the y-axis and can be used to obtain the y-component of $\nabla \times \mathbf{A}$. Using this surface, the left side of Eq. (3–13) is

$$(\nabla \times \mathbf{A}) \cdot \Delta \mathbf{s} = (\nabla \times \mathbf{A})_y \, \Delta s_y = (\nabla \times \mathbf{A})_y \, \Delta x \, \Delta z,$$

and the right side is obtained by integrating around the rectangle from P to a to b to c and back to P. Integrations along these four straight lines provide the four terms

$$A_z \, \Delta z, \quad \left(A_x + \frac{\partial A_x}{\partial z} \, \Delta z \right) \Delta x, \quad \left(A_z + \frac{\partial A_z}{\partial x} \, \Delta x \right) (-\Delta z),$$

and

$$A_x(-\Delta x).$$

When these are added, all but two of the terms cancel, leaving

$$(\nabla \times \mathbf{A})_y \, \Delta x \, \Delta z = \left(\frac{\partial A_x}{\partial z} - \frac{\partial A_z}{\partial x} \right) \Delta x \, \Delta z,$$

or

$$(\nabla \times \mathbf{A})_y = \frac{\partial A_x}{\partial z} - \frac{\partial A_z}{\partial x}.$$

Because of the symmetry of the coordinates, the z- and x-components can be obtained by the cyclic substitutions of z for y, x for z, and y for x, giving

$$(\nabla \times \mathbf{A})_z = \frac{\partial A_y}{\partial x} - \frac{\partial A_x}{\partial y},$$

$$(\nabla \times \mathbf{A})_x = \frac{\partial A_z}{\partial y} - \frac{\partial A_y}{\partial z},$$

and the curl of $\mathbf{A}$ in rectangular coordinates becomes

$$\nabla \times \mathbf{A} = \mathbf{i} \left(\frac{\partial A_z}{\partial y} - \frac{\partial A_y}{\partial z} \right) + \mathbf{j} \left(\frac{\partial A_x}{\partial z} - \frac{\partial A_z}{\partial x} \right) + \mathbf{k} \left(\frac{\partial A_y}{\partial x} - \frac{\partial A_x}{\partial y} \right). \tag{3–14}$$

It is convenient to write this as a determinant:

$$\nabla \times \mathbf{A} = \begin{vmatrix} \mathbf{i} & \mathbf{j} & \mathbf{k} \\ \dfrac{\partial}{\partial x} & \dfrac{\partial}{\partial y} & \dfrac{\partial}{\partial z} \\ A_x & A_y & A_z \end{vmatrix}. \tag{3–15}$$

Unlike the ordinary determinant, this is valid only when expanded in terms of the top row.

Curl in general orthogonal coordinates. An expression for the curl in each coordinate system will be needed. Table 3–1 makes it easy to convert mathematical expressions in general coordinates into any of the other three systems, making it necessary only to obtain the expression for the curl in general coordinates. The volume element in Fig. 3–8 has six surfaces, three of which can be used to obtain the three components that are needed. In fact, it is necessary to use only one surface to determine one of the components, since the other two can be obtained by cyclic substitution.

The shaded surface on the left can be chosen to obtain the v-component of the curl in general coordinates. Following the method used in calculating the y-component in rectangular coordinates, the line integral on the left in Eq. (3–13) should be taken from P to a to b to c and back to P. When this integral was evaluated around the rectangle in Fig. 3–6, the integral along ab almost cancelled that along cP, and the integral along bc almost cancelled that along Pa. The only terms remaining in rectangular coordinates, after the four line integrals were added, were the ones giving the change in magnitude of the integral from cP to ab, $(\partial/\partial z)(A_x \, \Delta x) \, \Delta z$, and from Pa to bc, $-(\partial/\partial x)(A_z \, \Delta z) \, \Delta x$. Because of the direction of the integration, the latter term has a negative sign. A similar type of cancellation takes place for general orthogonal coordinates when integrating along the path $Pabc$ around the shaded surface of Fig. 3–8. The integral along Pa is $A_w W \, \Delta w$, which is equal and opposite to that along bc except for the small variation given by

$$- \left(\frac{\partial}{\partial u} \right) (A_w W \, \Delta w) \, \Delta u.$$

In the same way, the integrals along ab and cP cancel except for the small variation

$$\left(\frac{\partial}{\partial w} \right) (A_u U \, \Delta u) \, \Delta w.$$

For the shaded surface of the general coordinates, $Pabc$ in Fig. 3–8, the curl defining Eq. (3–13) becomes

$$(\mathbf{\nabla} \times \mathbf{A})_v U \, \Delta u \, W \, \Delta w = \left[\frac{\partial}{\partial w} (UA_u) - \frac{\partial}{\partial u} (WA_w) \right] \Delta u \, \Delta w,$$

or

$$(\mathbf{\nabla} \times \mathbf{A})_v = \frac{1}{UW} \left[\frac{\partial}{\partial w} (UA_u) - \frac{\partial}{\partial u} (WA_w) \right],$$

which is the v-component of the curl of $\mathbf{A}$. The other two components can be obtained from this by the cyclic substitution of v for u, w for v, u for w, V for U, W for V, and U for W. The curl is then given by the vector sum of these components, each multiplied by its appropriate unit vector. It is conveniently given by the determinant form

$$\nabla \times \mathbf{A} = \frac{1}{UVW} \begin{vmatrix} U\mathbf{a}_u & V\mathbf{a}_v & W\mathbf{a}_w \\ \dfrac{\partial}{\partial u} & \dfrac{\partial}{\partial v} & \dfrac{\partial}{\partial w} \\ UA_u & VA_v & WA_w \end{vmatrix}, \qquad (3\text{--}16)$$

which again must be expanded in terms of the top row to give meaningful results.

The physical interpretation of the divergence is easy to understand, but the physical meaning of the curl is more difficult. Using an imaginary disk of small area Δs, the curl defining Eq. (3–13) can be integrated around its periphery to give the component of the curl of $\mathbf{A}$ perpendicular to the surface of the disk. The direction of the curl of $\mathbf{A}$ could be obtained by changing the orientation of the disk until this integral is maximum. When the integral is maximum $\Delta \mathbf{s}$ points in the direction of $\nabla \times \mathbf{A}$. In other words, the curl of $\mathbf{A}$ points in that direction in space which maximizes the line integral of $\mathbf{A}$ around a small surface normal to it.

3–7 Stokes' theorem. In Section 3–3, by using an infinitesimal volume element, the divergence is defined as a point function. It is then shown in Section 3–4 that the two sides of the defining equation (3–8) could be integrated over a finite volume to obtain the mathematical theorem of Gauss that is applicable to any volume. A very similar procedure is possible with the equation that defines the curl. By using an infinitesimal surface element, the curl is defined as a point function in Eq. (3–13). Integration of the two sides of this equation over a finite surface of general shape gives Stokes' theorem. Just as Gauss' theorem is useful for transforming volume integrals into surface integrals and vice versa, Stokes' theorem is useful for transforming surface integrals into line integrals and vice versa.

To demonstrate Stokes' theorem, an irregular surface like that shown in Fig. 3–10 can be used to represent a general shape of surface that is not necessarily in one plane. This surface can be divided into a large number of small four-sided elements of surface somewhat like those shown as rectangles in Fig. 3–10. These surface elements can be made small enough so that Eq. (3–13), defining the curl, can be applied to each of them. If the right-hand side of Eq. (3–13) is applied to two adjacent elements, the common boundary will be traversed twice in opposite directions by the line integral. Thus the integrals along this common

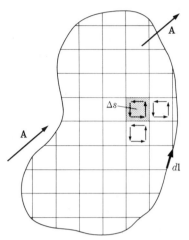

Fig. 3–10. Line integral of **A** is taken counterclockwise around element of area Δs. When this result is added to adjoining elements, the contributions along adjacent boundaries cancel, leaving only the contribution from the outside boundary.

boundary cancel each other, and only the integral around the periphery of the combined surfaces remains. If another adjacent surface element is added, the integrals along the common boundary again cancel. The process is repeated as each adjacent element is added until only the integral around the periphery of the general surface remains. Therefore, when the two sides of Eq. (3–13) are integrated over the whole surface shown in Fig. 3–10, the right side becomes just $\oint \mathbf{A} \cdot d\mathbf{l}$, integrated all around the periphery. The integration of the left side gives just $\int_s \mathbf{\nabla} \times \mathbf{A} \cdot d\mathbf{s}$, which must be integrated over the entire surface s, and the final result is

$$\int_s \mathbf{\nabla} \times \mathbf{A} \cdot d\mathbf{s} = \oint \mathbf{A} \cdot d\mathbf{l}, \qquad (3\text{–}17)$$

which is Stokes' mathematical theorem for transforming line to surface integrals and surface to line integrals.

When $\mathbf{\nabla} \times \mathbf{A}$ is zero everywhere, both sides of Eq. (3–17) are zero. Since the line integral of $\mathbf{A} \cdot d\mathbf{l}$ around any closed path is zero, the vector field **A** is conservative and can be expressed as the gradient of some potential function. The condition $\mathbf{\nabla} \times \mathbf{A} = 0$ is both necessary and sufficient for determining that **A** constitutes a conservative field.

3–8 The operator del. Three differential operations involving scalar and vector quantities have been defined and some of their uses have been explained. The definitions of these operations, called the gradient, the divergence, and the curl, were each made independent of the system of coordinates used. The brief symbols $\mathbf{\nabla}V$, $\mathbf{\nabla} \cdot \mathbf{A}$, and $\mathbf{\nabla} \times \mathbf{A}$ that were introduced to identify the operations appear, at first glance, to be completely unrelated to the defining relations. However, the operations suggested by the symbols can be used to obtain the correct expressions, provided the symbol ∇, called *del*, is treated as a differentiating vector operator,

$$\nabla = \mathbf{i}\,\frac{\partial}{\partial x} + \mathbf{j}\,\frac{\partial}{\partial y} + \mathbf{k}\,\frac{\partial}{\partial z},$$

in rectangular coordinates. The gradient of V is then

$$\text{del } V = \nabla V = \left(\mathbf{i}\,\frac{\partial}{\partial x} + \mathbf{j}\,\frac{\partial}{\partial y} + \mathbf{k}\,\frac{\partial}{\partial z}\right) V$$

or

$$\nabla V = \mathbf{i}\,\frac{\partial V}{\partial x} + \mathbf{j}\,\frac{\partial V}{\partial y} + \mathbf{k}\,\frac{\partial V}{\partial z}.$$

The dot product $\nabla \cdot \mathbf{A}$ would be

$$\frac{\partial A_x}{\partial x} + \frac{\partial A_y}{\partial y} + \frac{\partial A_z}{\partial z},$$

which is the divergence in rectangular coordinates. Likewise, the cross product of del with $\mathbf{A}$, $\nabla \times \mathbf{A}$, gives Eq. (3–14), the curl in rectangular coordinates.

This formal interpretation of the operator del provides expressions for gradient, divergence, and curl in rectangular coordinates as easily as they can be obtained from their general definitions. In most coordinate systems, however, these expressions can be obtained much more easily from the general definitions.

A more precise interpretation of the operator del must be used with cylindrical, spherical, or general coordinates than was required with the rectangular coordinates. Care must be taken to see that this differential operator differentiates everything to its right. In cylindrical coordinates,

$$\nabla = \mathbf{a}_r\,\frac{\partial}{\partial r} + \mathbf{a}_\phi\,\frac{1}{r}\,\frac{\partial}{\partial \phi} + \mathbf{k}\,\frac{\partial}{\partial z}, \tag{3–18}$$

and to obtain the divergence of $\mathbf{A}$, a formal expansion of $\nabla \cdot \mathbf{A}$, can be made to obtain

$$\nabla \cdot \mathbf{A} = \mathbf{a}_r\,\frac{\partial}{\partial r} \cdot \mathbf{a}_r A_r + \mathbf{a}_r\,\frac{\partial}{\partial r} \cdot \mathbf{a}_\phi A_\phi + \mathbf{a}_r\,\frac{\partial}{\partial r} \cdot \mathbf{k} A_z$$

$$+ \mathbf{a}_\phi\,\frac{1}{r}\,\frac{\partial}{\partial \phi} \cdot \mathbf{a}_r A_r + \mathbf{a}_\phi\,\frac{1}{r}\,\frac{\partial}{\partial \phi} \cdot \mathbf{a}_\phi A_\phi + \mathbf{a}_\phi\,\frac{1}{r}\,\frac{\partial}{\partial \phi} \cdot \mathbf{k} A_z$$

$$+ \mathbf{k}\,\frac{\partial}{\partial z} \cdot \mathbf{a}_r A_r + \mathbf{k}\,\frac{\partial}{\partial z} \cdot \mathbf{a}_\phi A_\phi + \mathbf{k}\,\frac{\partial}{\partial z} \cdot \mathbf{k} A_z.$$

This expression is written with nine terms, but it actually contains eighteen, since each term may be expanded into two. For example,

$$\mathbf{a}_r \frac{\partial}{\partial r} \cdot \mathbf{a}_r A_r = \mathbf{a}_r \cdot \mathbf{a}_r \frac{\partial A_r}{\partial r} + \mathbf{a}_r A_r \cdot \frac{\partial \mathbf{a}_r}{\partial r}.$$

Simplification or elimination of these terms may be accomplished, using the relations

$$\mathbf{a}_r \cdot \mathbf{a}_r = \mathbf{a}_\phi \cdot \mathbf{a}_\phi = \mathbf{k} \cdot \mathbf{k} = 1,$$

$$\mathbf{a}_r \cdot \mathbf{a}_\phi = \mathbf{a}_r \cdot \mathbf{k} = \mathbf{a}_\phi \cdot \mathbf{k} = 0,$$

as well as the relations

$$\frac{\partial \mathbf{a}_r}{\partial r} = 0, \qquad \frac{\partial \mathbf{a}_\phi}{\partial r} = 0, \qquad \frac{\partial \mathbf{k}}{\partial r} = 0;$$

$$\frac{\partial \mathbf{a}_r}{\partial \phi} = \mathbf{a}_\phi, \qquad \frac{\partial \mathbf{a}_\phi}{\partial \phi} = -\mathbf{a}_r, \qquad \frac{\partial \mathbf{k}}{\partial \phi} = 0;$$

$$\frac{\partial \mathbf{a}_r}{\partial z} = 0, \qquad \frac{\partial \mathbf{a}_\phi}{\partial z} = 0, \qquad \frac{\partial \mathbf{k}}{\partial z} = 0.$$

The change in direction of $\mathbf{a}_r$ and $\mathbf{a}_\phi$ resulting from a change in ϕ may be seen from an examination of Fig. 3–11. For example, the change in $\mathbf{a}_\phi$ resulting from an incremental increase $\Delta\phi$ in ϕ is a vector pointing in the

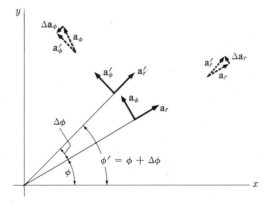

FIG. 3–11. Diagram illustrates why an increase of $\Delta\phi$ in the angle ϕ of cylindrical coordinates results in the following changes in the unit vectors:

$$\Delta \mathbf{a}_\phi = \frac{\partial \mathbf{a}_\phi}{\partial \phi} \Delta\phi = -\mathbf{a}_r \Delta\phi \qquad \text{and} \qquad \Delta \mathbf{a}_r = \frac{\partial \mathbf{a}_r}{\partial \phi} \Delta\phi = \mathbf{a}_\phi \Delta\phi.$$

negative $\mathbf{a}_r$ direction, which is just $-\mathbf{a}_r\,\Delta\phi$. Application of these relations reduces the 18-term expression to

$$\mathbf{\nabla}\cdot\mathbf{A} = \frac{\partial A_r}{\partial r} + 0 + 0$$

$$+ \frac{1}{r}\,A_r + \frac{1}{r}\,\frac{\partial A_\phi}{\partial\phi} + 0$$

$$+ 0 + 0 + \frac{\partial A_z}{\partial z}.$$

This is frequently written as

$$\mathbf{\nabla}\cdot\mathbf{A} = \frac{1}{r}\,\frac{\partial}{\partial r}\,(rA_r) + \frac{1}{r}\,\frac{\partial A_\phi}{\partial\phi} + \frac{\partial A_z}{\partial z}, \qquad (3\text{-}19)$$

in agreement with Eq. (3-9), which was obtained more simply from the fundamental definition of the divergence.

In a similar manner, the curl or Laplacian may be obtained in cylindrical or spherical coordinates. It must be remembered, of course, that the order of operators in an equation must be maintained. These operations can become involved, as the foregoing example illustrates. The operations were simple in rectangular coordinates because the unit vectors are constant in direction as well as in magnitude. The operations are complicated in cylindrical and spherical coordinates because the unit vectors are not constant in direction.

It is recommended that the del operator nomenclature be considered as a memory device and as an abbreviated notation for expressing the quantities formally defined in Sections 2-13, 3-3, and 3-6. Vector operations involving del are given below in various coordinate systems for convenient reference.

Rectangular coordinates

$$\mathbf{\nabla}\psi = \mathbf{i}\,\frac{\partial\psi}{\partial x} + \mathbf{j}\,\frac{\partial\psi}{\partial y} + \mathbf{k}\,\frac{\partial\psi}{\partial z}.$$

$$\mathbf{\nabla}\cdot\mathbf{A} = \frac{\partial A_x}{\partial x} + \frac{\partial A_y}{\partial y} + \frac{\partial A_z}{\partial z}.$$

$$\mathbf{\nabla}\times\mathbf{A} = \mathbf{i}\left(\frac{\partial A_z}{\partial y} - \frac{\partial A_y}{\partial z}\right) + \mathbf{j}\left(\frac{\partial A_x}{\partial z} - \frac{\partial A_z}{\partial x}\right) + \mathbf{k}\left(\frac{\partial A_y}{\partial x} - \frac{\partial A_x}{\partial y}\right).$$

$$\nabla^2\psi = \frac{\partial^2\psi}{\partial x^2} + \frac{\partial^2\psi}{\partial y^2} + \frac{\partial^2\psi}{\partial z^2}.$$

Cylindrical coordinates

$$\nabla\psi = \mathbf{a}_r \frac{\partial\psi}{\partial r} + \mathbf{a}_\phi \frac{1}{r}\frac{\partial\psi}{\partial\phi} + \mathbf{k}\frac{\partial\psi}{\partial z}.$$

$$\nabla\cdot\mathbf{A} = \frac{1}{r}\frac{\partial}{\partial r}(rA_r) + \frac{1}{r}\frac{\partial A_\phi}{\partial\phi} + \frac{\partial A_z}{\partial z}.$$

$$\nabla\times\mathbf{A} = \mathbf{a}_r\left[\frac{1}{r}\frac{\partial A_z}{\partial\phi} - \frac{\partial A_\phi}{\partial z}\right] + \mathbf{a}_\phi\left[\frac{\partial A_r}{\partial z} - \frac{\partial A_z}{\partial r}\right]$$

$$+ \mathbf{k}\left[\frac{1}{r}\frac{\partial}{\partial r}(rA_\phi) - \frac{1}{r}\frac{\partial A_r}{\partial\phi}\right].$$

$$\nabla^2\psi = \frac{1}{r}\frac{\partial}{\partial r}\left(r\frac{\partial\psi}{\partial r}\right) + \frac{1}{r^2}\frac{\partial^2\psi}{\partial\phi^2} + \frac{\partial^2\psi}{\partial z^2}.$$

Spherical coordinates

$$\nabla\psi = \mathbf{a}_r\frac{\partial\psi}{\partial r} + \mathbf{a}_\theta\frac{1}{r}\frac{\partial\psi}{\partial\theta} + \mathbf{a}_\phi\frac{1}{r\sin\theta}\frac{\partial\psi}{\partial\phi}.$$

$$\nabla\cdot\mathbf{A} = \frac{1}{r^2}\frac{\partial}{\partial r}(r^2A_r) + \frac{1}{r\sin\theta}\frac{\partial}{\partial\theta}(A_\theta\sin\theta) + \frac{1}{r\sin\theta}\frac{\partial A_\phi}{\partial\phi}.$$

$$\nabla\times\mathbf{A} = \mathbf{a}_r\frac{1}{r\sin\theta}\left[\frac{\partial}{\partial\theta}(A_\phi\sin\theta) - \frac{\partial A_\theta}{\partial\phi}\right]$$

$$+ \mathbf{a}_\theta\frac{1}{r}\left[\frac{1}{\sin\theta}\frac{\partial A_r}{\partial\phi} - \frac{\partial}{\partial r}(rA_\phi)\right] + \mathbf{a}_\phi\frac{1}{r}\left[\frac{\partial}{\partial r}(rA_\theta) - \frac{\partial A_r}{\partial\theta}\right].$$

$$\nabla^2\psi = \frac{1}{r^2}\frac{\partial}{\partial r}\left(r^2\frac{\partial\psi}{\partial r}\right) + \frac{1}{r^2\sin\theta}\frac{\partial}{\partial\theta}\left(\sin\theta\frac{\partial\psi}{\partial\theta}\right) + \frac{1}{r^2\sin^2\theta}\frac{\partial^2\psi}{\partial\phi^2}.$$

General orthogonal coordinates

$$\nabla\psi = \mathbf{a}_u\frac{1}{U}\frac{\partial\psi}{\partial u} + \mathbf{a}_v\frac{1}{V}\frac{\partial\psi}{\partial v} + \mathbf{a}_w\frac{1}{W}\frac{\partial\psi}{\partial w}.$$

$$\nabla\cdot\mathbf{A} = \frac{1}{UVW}\left[\frac{\partial}{\partial u}(VWA_u) + \frac{\partial}{\partial v}(WUA_v) + \frac{\partial}{\partial w}(UVA_w)\right].$$

$$\nabla\times\mathbf{A} = \mathbf{a}_u\frac{1}{VW}\left[\frac{\partial}{\partial v}(WA_w) - \frac{\partial}{\partial w}(VA_v)\right]$$

$$+ \mathbf{a}_v\frac{1}{WU}\left[\frac{\partial}{\partial w}(UA_u) - \frac{\partial}{\partial u}(WA_w)\right]$$

$$+ \mathbf{a}_w\frac{1}{UV}\left[\frac{\partial}{\partial u}(VA_v) - \frac{\partial}{\partial v}(UA_u)\right].$$

$$\nabla^2 \psi = \frac{1}{UVW} \left[\frac{\partial}{\partial u} \left(\frac{VW}{U} \frac{\partial \psi}{\partial u} \right) + \frac{\partial}{\partial v} \left(\frac{WU}{V} \frac{\partial \psi}{\partial v} \right) + \frac{\partial}{\partial w} \left(\frac{UV}{W} \frac{\partial \psi}{\partial w} \right) \right].$$

Operator identities. There are a number of vector identities that are useful in electromagnetic theories. For convenience, the most useful of those involving differentiation are listed here. No derivation is given for any of these equations because they are all easily proved by expanding them into components in any of the coordinate systems. Since vector equations are independent of the coordinate system in which they are expressed, the equations can be verified in rectangular coordinates. The proof of any of the following relations, by expanding them into their rectangular components, constitutes a revealing exercise. The reader should perform each proof sometime before he has occasion to use the relation.

$$\nabla \cdot (\psi \mathbf{A}) = \psi \nabla \cdot \mathbf{A} + \mathbf{A} \cdot \nabla \psi, \tag{3-20}$$

$$\nabla \times (\psi \mathbf{A}) = \psi \nabla \times \mathbf{A} - \mathbf{A} \times \nabla \psi, \tag{3-21}$$

$$\nabla \cdot (\mathbf{A} \times \mathbf{B}) = \mathbf{B} \cdot \nabla \times \mathbf{A} - \mathbf{A} \cdot \nabla \times \mathbf{B}, \tag{3-22}$$

$$\nabla \cdot (\nabla \times \mathbf{A}) = 0, \tag{3-23}$$

$$\nabla \times (\nabla \times \mathbf{A}) = \nabla (\nabla \cdot \mathbf{A}) - \nabla^2 \mathbf{A}, \tag{3-24}$$

where $\nabla^2 \mathbf{A} = \mathbf{i} \nabla^2 A_x + \mathbf{j} \nabla^2 A_y + \mathbf{k} \nabla^2 A_z$ by definition.

$$\nabla \cdot (\psi \nabla \psi) = (\nabla \psi)^2 + \psi \nabla^2 \psi, \tag{3-25}$$

$$\nabla \times (\nabla \psi) = 0. \tag{3-26}$$

For these equations $\mathbf{A}$ and $\mathbf{B}$ must be vector functions of the coordinates and ψ must be a scalar function of the coordinates, with finite first and second derivatives.

PROBLEMS

*3-1. How many excess electrons must be added to an isolated spherical conductor 10 cm in diameter to produce a field just outside the surface whose intensity is 1.3×10^{-3} n/coul?

3-2. A uniformly charged conducting sphere of 0.4 m diameter has a surface charge density of $8\,\mu$coul/m^2. What is the total number of lines of force leaving the surface of the sphere?

*3-3. The charge density on the surface of a conducting sphere is 8.85×10^{-7} coul/m^2, and the electric intensity 2 m from the surface of the sphere is 3.6×10^4 n/coul. Determine the radius of the sphere.

3-4. A small sphere of mass 0.2 gm hangs by a thread between two parallel vertical plates 5 cm apart. The sphere holds a charge of 6×10^{-9} coul. What difference of potential between the plates will cause the thread to assume an angle of 30° with the vertical?

*3-5. Two hollow concentric spherical conductors have radii of 2 cm and 4 cm respectively. The inner sphere carries a charge of 12×10^{-9} coul, the outer 20×10^{-9} coul. Determine the potential at the following distances from the center: 5 cm, 4 cm, 3 cm, 2 cm, and 1 cm.

3-6. The two spheres of Problem 3-5 are connected by a conductor, which is then removed. What is the potential at the same points?

*3-7. The plates of a parallel-plate capacitor are 5 mm apart and 2 m^2 in area. The plates are in vacuum. A potential difference of 10,000 volts is applied across the capacitor. Compute (a) the capacitance, (b) the charge on each plate, and (c) the electric intensity in the space between them.

3-8. Three capacitors have the capacitances C_1, C_2, and C_3 respectively. Prove that (a) when they are connected in parallel the combined capacitance is $C_p = C_1 + C_2 + C_3$, and (b) when they are connected in series the combined capacitance C_s is given by $1/C_s = 1/C_1 + 1/C_2 + 1/C_3$.

*3-9. A 1-μf capacitor and a 2-μf capacitor are connected in series across a 1200-volt supply line. (a) Find the charge on each capacitor and the voltage across each. (b) The charged capacitors are disconnected from the line and from each other, and reconnected with terminals of like sign together. Find the final charge on each and the voltage across each.

3-10. A 1-μf capacitor and a 2-μf capacitor are connected in parallel across a 1200-volt supply line. (a) Find the charge on each capacitor and the voltage across each. (b) The charged capacitors are then disconnected from the line and from each other, and reconnected with terminals of unlike sign together. Find the final charge on each and the voltage across each.

*3-11. In Fig. 3-12, each capacitance $C_3 = 3\,\mu$f and each capacitance $C_2 = 2\,\mu$f. (a) Compute the equivalent capacitance of the network between points a and b.

FIGURE 3-12.

---

*Answers to starred problems will be found at back of book.

(b) Compute the charge on each of the capacitors nearest a and b, when $V_{ab} = 900$ volts. (c) With 900 volts across a and b, compute V_{cd}.

3–12. Two conductors that form a capacitor consist of concentric spherical shells of radii a and b, where $b > a$ and the space between the spheres is evacuated. With the outer sphere grounded and with a charge Q on the inner sphere, calculate (a) the electric field between the spheres, using Gauss' law, (b) the potential difference between the spheres, and (c) the capacitance of the system. (d) Show that if $d = b - a$, where $d \ll b$, the parallel-plate relation for capacitance, $C = \epsilon_0 A/d$, is valid.

*3–13. A solid sphere of radius a has a volume charge of uniform density ρ. Obtain expressions for both $\mathbf{E}$ and V where $r < a$ and where $r > a$. Plot these expressions as a function of r.

3–14. Two conductors that form a capacitor consist of concentric cylindrical shells of radii a and b and of length L, where $L \gg b > a$. As shown in Fig. 3–13, the outer cylinder consists of three sections insulated from each other. While each of the three sections is charged to the potential V, the charge Q measured as it flows through the instrument G resides only on the central section of length l. The two outer sections, called "guard rings," serve to keep the field inside the central section radial, as it would be if the cylinders were all of infinite length. With the space between cylinders evacuated, calculate (a) both $\mathbf{E}$ and V between cylinders in the center, and (b) the capacitance of the central cylinder with respect to the inner cylinder.

FIGURE 3–13.

*3–15. A solid cylinder of radius a and of infinite length has a volume charge of uniform density ρ. Obtain expressions for both $\mathbf{E}$ and V as functions of r where $r < a$ and where $r > a$. Plot these expressions.

3–16. Two point charges $+4q$ and $-q$ are separated a distance l. Due to these charges the field is zero at an equilibrium point on the extension of a straight line through the two charges, the axis of symmetry. Many lines of flux leave the $+4q$ charge but one group of these follows curved paths to this equilibrium point. Draw the diagram. Choose one of this latter group of lines and calculate the angle it makes with the axis of symmetry just as it leaves the $+4q$ charge.

*3-17. Calculate the angle that the flux line chosen in Problem 3-16 makes with the axis of symmetry as it passes through the plane that is perpendicular to the axis through the charge $-q$.

3-18. Charges are symmetrically distributed about the origin of spherical coordinates so that $\rho = \rho_0(e^{-ar^2}/r)$. Find the electric field.

*3-19. A thick spherical shell between $r = a$ and $r = b$ contains a body charge given by $\rho = \rho_0 e^{ar^3}$. The remaining space $r < a$ and $r > b$ is a vacuum. Calculate $\mathbf{E}$ within this shell.

*3-20. (a) A spherical shell (that need not be metallic) has a uniform surface density of charge σ but has no charge inside it. Use Gauss' law to prove that the field inside is everywhere zero. (b) A hollow cube that is not metallic has a uniform surface density of charge σ but has no charge inside it. Can you use Gauss' law as in part (a) to prove that the field inside is everywhere zero? Discuss any important differences between parts (a) and (b).

3-21. Test whether or not the following fields are conservative. If they are conservative, determine the distribution of charge density ρ required to produce these fields:

(a) $\mathbf{E} = \mathbf{i}x^2 + \mathbf{j}yz^2 + \mathbf{k}y^2z$,
(b) $\mathbf{E} = \mathbf{i}(x^2 - y^2) - \mathbf{j}2xy + \mathbf{k}4$.

*3-22. Determine the charge distribution required in regions where the potentials are given by the following expressions:

In cylindrical coordinates:

(a) r^{-1}
(b) $\ln r$
(c) $r^n \cos n\phi$
(d) $r^2(3 \cos^2 \phi - 1)$

In spherical coordinates:

(e) r^{-1}
(f) $\ln r$
(g) $r^n \cos n\theta$
(h) $r^2(3 \cos^2 \theta - 1)$

3-23. Find the electric fields in spaces where there are the following potential distributions:

(a) $V = \ln \dfrac{r + A}{r - A}$ (cyl. coord.)

(b) $V = \dfrac{\cos \theta \sin \phi}{r^2}$ (sph. coord.)

(c) $V = \dfrac{qe^{-r/a}}{4\pi \epsilon_0 r}$ (sph. coord.)

*3-24. The following are expressions for fields (not necessarily electrostatic) in rectangular coordinates. Determine whether or not each of these can be expressed as a gradient of a potential function. For each field that can be so expressed, determine whether or not the potential function would satisfy Laplace's equation, $\nabla^2 V = 0$:

(a) $\mathbf{A} = \mathbf{i}x + \mathbf{j}y + \mathbf{k}z$,
(b) $\mathbf{A} = \mathbf{i}y + \mathbf{j}z + \mathbf{k}x$,

(c) $\mathbf{A} = \mathbf{i}yz + \mathbf{j}zx + \mathbf{k}xy$,
(d) $\mathbf{A} = \mathbf{i}xy + \mathbf{j}yz + \mathbf{k}zx$.

*3–25. The magnetic field due to a certain distribution of currents is given by $\mathbf{H} = \mathbf{a}_\phi A e^{-r}/r$ in cylindrical coordinates. Test whether or not this field is conservative.

3–26. A new mathematical operation can often be best understood by applying it to simple problems for which the answer is known. The velocity and acceleration of a point moving at constant speed in a circle are well known, but their calculation can be used to illustrate the differentiation of unit vectors. Express the position of a point in cylindrical coordinates by $\mathbf{R} = \mathbf{a}_r b$, where $b = $ constant and $\partial\phi/\partial t = \omega$, a constant. Calculate $\mathbf{v} = \partial\mathbf{R}/\partial t$ and $\mathbf{a} = \partial^2\mathbf{R}/\partial t^2$ and express the latter in terms of $\mathbf{R}$.

Use rectangular coordinates in Problems 3–27 through 3–33:

3–27. Prove Eq. (3–20).

3–28. Prove Eq. (3–21).

3–29. Prove Eq. (3–22).

3–30. Prove Eq. (3–23).

3–31. Prove Eq. (3–24).

3–32. Prove Eq. (3–25).

3–33. Prove Eq. (3–26).

CHAPTER 4

SOLUTION OF ELECTROSTATIC PROBLEMS

In solving electrostatic problems, any one or several of the following quantities may be known or desired: charges, fields, potentials, forces, torques, and capacitances. All of these quantities can be calculated when the distribution of potentials is known. In particular, when expressions for V in terms of the coordinates have been obtained, such quantities are easily calculated.

Poisson's equation $\nabla^2 V = -\rho/\epsilon_0$, which follows directly from Gauss' law, provides the differential equation needed for obtaining such expressions for V. In the great majority of problems it is sufficient to obtain expressions for V only in those regions where $\rho = 0$. This is fortunate, since there are many more methods of solution available for Laplace's form of the equation, $\nabla^2 V = 0$, than for Poisson's more general form. It will be shown that a problem in electrostatics is solved when a solution of Laplace's equation has been found to satisfy the particular boundary conditions of the problem.

Because the number of solutions of Laplace's equation is unlimited, the task of finding the one solution satisfying the conditions of a particular problem may be arduous. For this reason, many types of solutions have been cataloged and special procedures have been developed for obtaining solutions for particular kinds of problems. Some of these special methods are so neat that it is easy to forget that they do, in fact, follow a more general procedure.

Some knowledge of the characteristics of materials is needed for the solution of any electrostatic problem. Consequently a fairly extensive discussion of the electric properties of insulators and conductors is given in the next chapters. For the problems treated in this chapter it is necessary to know only a few properties of metallic conductors. Like all materials in the solid state, metals consist of individual atomic nuclei, arranged in geometric patterns called lattices and surrounded by rapidly moving electrons. In the neutral or uncharged state there are as many electrons as there are protons in all of the atoms. Since electrons and protons have charges that are equal but of opposite sign, these materials normally produce no external electric fields. In metals a few electrons are free to drift quite easily through the lattice. In fact, electrons continue to drift toward surfaces of a metal until they have set up fields that exactly cancel the fields due to external charges. Thus there are never any electric fields in the interior of metals after static conditions have been established. Since there are no internal fields, there can be no potential differences within a metal and its potential must be constant.

4–1 Electrostatic solutions with Laplace's equation.   The general method for solving problems by means of Laplace's equation can be understood best by considering some specific examples. A concentrated charge placed near a flat surface of a massive piece of metal is attracted toward that surface by the induced charge of opposite sign that collects on it. Situations that are more or less accurately described by this statement occur so frequently that it is desirable to be able to determine the magnitude of this attractive force. For example, when the metallic filament or cathode in a vacuum tube is heated, some electrons receive sufficient kinetic energy to escape from the surface. For a theoretical analysis of this phenomenon, the energy required for this escape must be known. The primary force opposing the escape is the attraction due to induced charges. Because the metal is made up of individual atoms arranged in a geometrical pattern called a lattice, the calculation of the attractive force near the surface is very complex. With an electron at greater distances, perhaps beyond ten lattice spacings, the surface may be treated as a plane. For relatively large distances the curvature of the surface may become important, but at such distances the force is so small that it can be neglected.

As originally stated, the problem of calculating the force on a concentrated charge near a plane surface of massive metal could be calculated by the integration methods of Section 2–7 if the distribution of the induced charge on the surface were known, but this distribution is not stated directly in the problem. However, when the potential distribution in a region, including both the concentrated charge and the metallic surface, is known, the density of the induced charge can be calculated. In fact, the force on the concentrated charge and its potential energy can then be calculated directly. Laplace's equation $\nabla^2 V = 0$ is ideally suited for determining the distribution of V in such situations. The general procedure for solving problems with Laplace's equation follows:

1. The region in which the potential must be known should be determined. This region then should be made part of a closed space, completely devoid of charges and completely surrounded by boundaries on which either V or $\partial V/\partial n$ can be specified.
2. The values of V or $\partial V/\partial n$ should be specified on every portion of the boundaries to provide the necessary boundary conditions.
3. A solution of $\nabla^2 V = 0$ should be found that is finite and continuous throughout the bounded space and that also satisfies all of the boundary conditions. Any solution that meets these requirements is the correct and the only solution, as is demonstrated in Section 4–3.

As stated, the real problem involves a concentrated charge near a very large surface. However, only negligible errors are introduced by assuming the plane to be infinite and the charge to be concentrated at a point, to simplify the analysis. The surface may be assumed horizontal, coinciding with the $z = 0$ plane and having zero potential. The zero potential on this surface may be achieved either with a grounded sheet of metal or with a massive metal that fills all space where z is negative. To complete the picture, a point charge q is located on the z-axis at a distance h above this plane.

Following the three steps of the general procedure, the force on q and its potential energy could be uniquely determined if the potential V could be completely specified in its neighborhood. However, to completely determine V, a closed space is needed on whose boundaries V is known. Now $V = 0$ over all the plane and over an imaginary hemispherical surface of infinite radius drawn about the origin. Since the potentials are known on these surfaces, they can constitute the outer boundaries of our closed space. This space can be made free of charge by surrounding q with an imaginary sphere of infinitesimal radius δ, on which the potential must approach $q/4\pi\epsilon_0\delta$ as $\delta \to 0$. This tiny sphere constitutes the inner boundary of the closed space, inside of which $\nabla^2 V$ is everywhere zero.

4–2 Method of images. The next step in the general procedure is to find a solution of $\nabla^2 V = 0$ that will satisfy the foregoing boundary conditions. If this were a problem that had never been solved, this step would require some ingenuity. A study of the solutions that have been obtained is essential, however, for developing the necessary ingenuity.

The plane attracts q downward. If the plane were replaced by a point charge of opposite sign located directly below q, the force would be in the same direction. Furthermore, if this charge had the magnitude $-q$ and were located on the z-axis a distance h below the $z = 0$ plane as shown in Fig. 4–1, the potential of this plane due to these two charges would be zero. Since the two charges are finite, the potential at infinity would also be zero. In addition, the $-q$ charge would be too far from the $+q$ charge to affect the potential on the inner boundary when δ is made sufficiently small. The potential distribution within the bounded space due to these two charges, as calculated from Eq. (2–15), is

$$V = \frac{q}{4\pi\epsilon_0[(z - h)^2 + r^2]^{1/2}} + \frac{-q}{4\pi\epsilon_0[(z + h)^2 + r^2]^{1/2}}. \quad (4\text{--}1)$$

This expression does satisfy all of the boundary conditions, namely, $V = 0$ when $z = 0$, $z = \infty$, or $r = \infty$, and $V = q/4\pi\epsilon_0\delta$ when δ is very small. As can be readily checked by direct differentiation, Eq. (4–1) also satisfies $\nabla^2 V = 0$ throughout the bounded region and is therefore the correct expression for the potential. The first term gives the potential due to q, and the second term, which will be designated by V', gives the potential due to the induced charge distribution on the metallic surface.

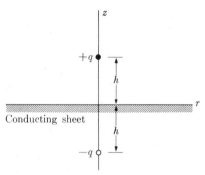

FIG. 4–1. The potential above the conducting sheet due to $+q$ and the conducting sheet is identical to that produced by $+q$ and the image charge $-q$ in the absence of the sheet.

This procedure for determining potentials is called the method of images, because $-q$ is placed at the location where the optical image of q would be in the metallic surface acting as a mirror. The procedure of satisfying boundary conditions by placing imaginary point charges outside the bounded space is called the method of images, whether or not these charges represent optical images. Image charges must not be placed inside the bounded regions, because V then becomes infinite at such points, so that $\nabla^2 V = 0$ cannot then be satisfied throughout the bounded region.

The force on q is given by $\mathbf{F} = -q\nabla V'$, where $\nabla V'$ must be evaluated at the point $r = 0$ and $z = h$, where q is located. This force can also be calculated directly from the Coulomb's law attraction of $-q$ for q, which is

$$F = \frac{-q^2}{4\pi\epsilon_0(2h)^2}. \qquad (4-2)$$

For an electron ten lattice spacings $(3.6 \times 10^{-10}\,\text{m})$ from a copper surface, this so-called image force is

$$F = \frac{-e^2}{4\pi\epsilon_0(2h)^2} = 4.4 \times 10^{-10}\,\text{newton},$$

which would result in the relatively large acceleration of $4.9 \times 10^{20}\,\text{m/sec}^2$. Since this image force is an important factor in confining electrons within conductors, it is discussed in more detail in Chapter 6.

The charge distribution on the metallic surface can also be calculated directly from Eq. (4–1). The density of surface charge, derived from Gauss' law, is just $\sigma = \epsilon_0 E = -\epsilon_0\, \partial v/\partial n$ evaluated near the surface of the conductor at $z = 0$. The surface-charge density on the plane is then

$$\sigma = \frac{-qh}{2\pi(h^2 + r^2)^{3/2}},$$

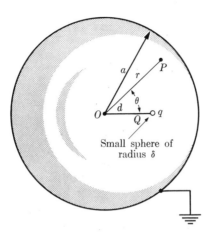

Fig. 4–2. Diagram illustrating the location of a point charge inside a hollow conducting sphere.

which has its maximum directly below the point charge where $r = 0$.

Many other problems can be solved by the image method. There is one that is especially useful for demonstrating the general procedure and that also provides a good example for the proof of the uniqueness theorem given in the next section. This problem calls for the calculation of the force acting on a charged particle somewhere inside a hollow conducting sphere that is connected to ground. A sphere of inner radius a and containing a point charge q located at a distance d from the center O is shown in Fig. 4–2.

Following the general procedure, an expression is needed for the potentials in the region containing q. For the bounded space in which $\nabla^2 V = 0$, that region between an imaginary sphere of very small radius δ about q and the inner surface of the conducting sphere should be selected. No information is available and none is desired concerning the space outside, since the conducting sphere acts as a perfect shield. Using the spherical coordinates shown in the diagram, the outer boundary condition is that $V = 0$ where $r = a$, and the inner boundary condition is that $V = q/4\pi\epsilon_0\delta$ as δ approaches zero.

An expression for V that satisfies $\nabla^2 V = 0$ throughout the bounded space and that also fits these boundary conditions is needed. Expressions for the potentials of point charges always satisfy $\nabla^2 V = 0$ except at the charged points. This statement should be obvious from the fact that the Laplace equation was derived from Coulomb's law, but it can be demonstrated by direct differentiation of Eq. (2–15).

In the actual problem, charges induced on the inner surface of the sphere attract q to the right. Symmetry considerations suggest that this

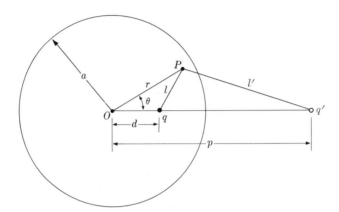

FIG. 4–3. A point charge q and its image q' produce the same potential in the region bounded by $r = a$ as would be produced by q and the hollow conducting sphere of Fig. 4–2.

effect could be produced by replacing the sphere with one or more image charges on the extension of the radial line through q. Since the simplest of the promising solutions should be tried first, just one image charge q' at the distance $p > a$ from O will be tried, as shown in Fig. 4–3. If q' is to replace the electron distribution on the sphere, it must combine with q to produce zero potential on the imaginary sphere of radius a shown in Fig. 4–3. According to Eq. (2–15), the potential inside the sphere is

$$V = \frac{1}{4\pi\epsilon_0}\left(\frac{q}{l} + \frac{q'}{l'}\right),$$

which will be zero on the inner surface if

$$\frac{q}{l} + \frac{q'}{l'} = 0 \qquad (4\text{–}3)$$

for all values of θ when $r = a$.

Now when $r = a$,

$$l^2 = a^2 + d^2 - 2ad\cos\theta$$

and

$$l'^2 = p^2 + a^2 - 2pa\cos\theta,$$

and these can be written

$$l = a\sqrt{1 + (d/a)^2 - 2(d/a)\cos\theta}$$

and

$$l' = p\sqrt{1 + (a/p)^2 - 2(a/p)\cos\theta}.$$

By substituting the latter relations into Eq. (4–3) and setting $d/a = a/p$,

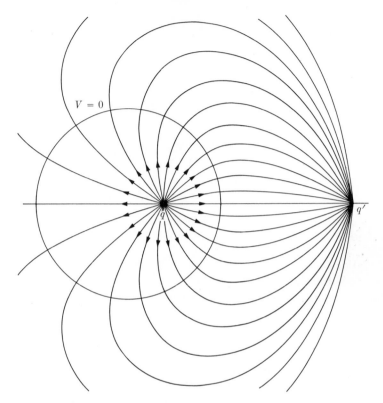

FIG. 4–4. Graph showing the lines of flux caused by the two point charges q and q' of Fig. 4–3.

the radicals containing θ can be factored out to leave

$$\frac{q'}{p} = -\frac{q}{a}.$$

The two charges shown in Fig. 4–3, q at the distance d from O and $q' = -qp/a$ at the distance $p = a^2/d$ from O, do combine to produce zero potential at all points on the imaginary sphere of radius a. The inner boundary condition is automatically satisfied, since q is the only charge in or near this tiny sphere. The potential due to q and q' of Fig. 4–3 is

$$V = \frac{q}{4\pi\epsilon_0}\left[\frac{1}{\sqrt{r^2 + d^2 - 2rd\cos\theta}} - \frac{p/a}{\sqrt{p^2 + r^2 - 2pr\cos\theta}}\right],$$

which gives the fields throughout space for this imaginary situation, as shown in Fig. 4–4. In the real problem the potentials and fields are known

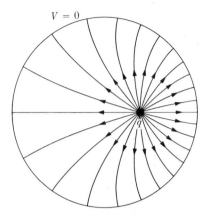

$V = 0$

FIG. 4–5. Graph showing the lines of flux caused by the point charge q and the charge it induces on the hollow conducting sphere of Fig. 4–2.

only inside the sphere, as shown in Fig. 4–5, but these fields are identical to those inside the sphere of Fig. 4–4. Again the force on q is easily calculated from the Coulomb attraction of q', which is

$$F = \frac{qq'}{4\pi\epsilon_0(p - d)^2} = \frac{-q^2ad}{4\pi\epsilon_0(a^2 - d^2)^2} \cdot$$

In this problem the sphere was grounded, and this allowed opposite charges to flow in from the earth. If it were not grounded, then the charge distributing itself over the surface of the sphere would have to come from the sphere itself, not from the ground. The potential would still be constant over the surface of the sphere, but not zero. This problem can be solved by superposing a uniform charge over the outside surface.

4–3 Uniqueness theorem. In the two problems that were solved by the method of images, it was assumed that any single-valued and continuous function V of the coordinates that is a solution of $\nabla^2 V = 0$ throughout a bounded space and that also gives the correct potentials on the boundaries of this space gives the correct potentials throughout. The question arises as to whether there can be two or more functions that each satisfy all of these conditions for a given problem. To investigate the uniqueness of such solutions, let it be assumed that there are two single-valued and continuous functions, V_1 and V_2, each of which satisfies $\nabla^2 V = 0$ throughout the bounded space and each of which gives correct values either for V or $\partial V/\partial n$, the normal component of ∇V on all the boundaries. To facilitate the investigation, two new functions of the coordinates should be defined; namely, the scalar function $\phi = V_1 - V_2$ and the vector function $\phi\nabla\phi$. These functions are chosen because the original assumptions now ensure that $\nabla^2\phi = \nabla^2V_1 - \nabla^2V_2 = 0$ throughout the bounded space and that

$$\phi\frac{\partial\phi}{\partial n} = (V_1 - V_2)\left(\frac{\partial V_1}{\partial n} - \frac{\partial V_2}{\partial n}\right) = 0$$

on all boundaries, since either $V_1 = V_2$ or $\partial V_1/\partial n = \partial V_2/\partial n$ on all these boundaries. According to Gauss' theorem,

$$\int_\tau \nabla \cdot \phi\nabla\phi \, d\tau = \int_s \phi\nabla\phi \cdot d\mathbf{s}, \qquad (4\text{--}4)$$

where τ represents the volume of the bounded space and s represents the total area of its boundaries. The integral on the right is zero because $\phi\nabla\phi = 0$ at all points on the boundary over which this integral is to be evaluated, and therefore the volume integral on the left is also zero. According to the vector identity of Eq. (3–25),

$$\nabla \cdot (\phi\nabla\phi) = \phi\nabla^2\phi + (\nabla\phi)^2$$

and

$$\int_\tau \nabla \cdot (\phi\nabla\phi) \, d\tau = \int_\tau \phi\nabla^2\phi \, d\tau + \int_\tau (\nabla\phi)^2 \, d\tau = 0.$$

Since $\nabla^2\phi = 0$ throughout the bounded space,

$$\int_\tau (\nabla\phi)^2 \, d\tau = 0.$$

The integrand

$$(\nabla\phi)^2 = \nabla\phi \cdot \nabla\phi = \left(\frac{\partial\phi}{\partial x}\right)^2 + \left(\frac{\partial\phi}{\partial y}\right)^2 + \left(\frac{\partial\phi}{\partial z}\right)^2$$

cannot be negative at any point, since each of the three rectangular terms, being squared, must either be positive or zero. For the integral to be zero, the integrand then must be zero throughout τ; that is,

$$\left(\frac{\partial\phi}{\partial x}\right)^2 + \left(\frac{\partial\phi}{\partial y}\right)^2 + \left(\frac{\partial\phi}{\partial z}\right)^2 = 0$$

and

$$\frac{\partial\phi}{\partial x} = \frac{\partial\phi}{\partial y} = \frac{\partial\phi}{\partial z} = 0$$

throughout the bounded space. Since this requires ϕ to be constant, the two solutions can differ only by a constant. Whenever V is specified on any boundary, $\phi = 0$ on the boundary and ϕ must be zero throughout the bounded space. Within the volume τ, then, $V_1 = V_2$ everywhere and the assumption that two different solutions could satisfy the required conditions has led to an absurdity. Any single-valued and continuous function that satisfies $\nabla^2 V = 0$ throughout the bounded space and also gives the correct V or $\partial V/\partial n$ on the boundaries of that space constitutes the solution of that problem.

Frequently, problems are encountered in which part of the boundary of the closed space is a conducting surface s_0 on which neither V nor $\partial V/\partial n$ can be uniquely specified. If this surface is that of a conductor wholly inside the region of interest, it is sufficient to specify the total charge on this conductor and that the potential on this surface is constant. For example, in the image solutions of the previous section the charge q might reside on a small but finite conducting sphere. Since both the potential and the fields near its surface depend upon the surrounding charges as well as upon q, neither V nor $\partial V/\partial n$ can be uniquely specified until the problem is solved. However, by Gauss' law,

$$- \int_{s_0} \nabla V \cdot d\mathbf{s} = \frac{q}{\epsilon_0},$$

and on a conductor $V = $ constant. Hence

$$\int_{s_0} \phi \nabla \phi \cdot d\mathbf{s} = (V_1 - V_2) \left[\int_{s_0} \nabla V_2 \cdot d\mathbf{s} - \int_{s_0} \nabla V_1 \cdot d\mathbf{s} \right]$$

$$= \frac{(V_1 - V_2)(q_2 - q_1)}{\epsilon_0} = 0,$$

and the integral on the right in Eq. (4–4) is still zero provided q is specified so that $q_1 = q_2$. Therefore a solution of Laplace's equation is unique if it satisfies at least one of the following conditions on each part of the surface bounding its closed region: (a) the surface potential V can be specified, (b) the normal component of the field given by $\partial V/\partial n$ can be specified, (c) the surface is an equipotential surface that completely surrounds a specified charge. Since it is desirable to have many solutions from which to choose, Laplace's equation has been the subject of much intensive study. Solutions are available for almost every conceivable geometry, and general methods have been developed for building solutions that will fit particular situations. One of the most useful theorems for this purpose is the one stating that *the sum of any number of individual solutions is itself a solution*, for if

$$V = V_1 + V_2 + \cdots + V_n$$

is the sum of n solutions, then

$$\nabla^2 V = \nabla^2 V_1 + \nabla^2 V_2 + \cdots + \nabla^2 V_n = 0.$$

The mathematical developments involving Laplace's equation are so extensive that a comprehensive treatment of any portion would be out of place here. Before outlining some general procedures in rectangular coordinates, it is desirable to derive a few more useful solutions and to demonstrate the methods for applying these to important physical problems.

4–4 Some solutions with spherical coordinates. When a problem has boundaries that are readily expressed in spherical coordinates, Laplace's equation may be written as

$$\nabla^2 V = \frac{1}{r^2} \frac{\partial}{\partial r} \left(r^2 \frac{\partial V}{\partial r} \right) + \frac{1}{r^2 \sin \theta} \frac{\partial}{\partial \theta} \left(\sin \theta \frac{\partial V}{\partial \theta} \right)$$

$$+ \frac{1}{r^2 \sin^2 \theta} \frac{\partial^2 V}{\partial \phi^2} = 0.$$

Many solutions of this equation are available.* The discussion here will be confined to those problems of this type that have symmetry about an axis, such that V is independent of ϕ. The equation then becomes

$$\frac{\partial}{\partial r} \left(r^2 \frac{\partial V}{\partial r} \right) + \frac{1}{\sin \theta} \frac{\partial}{\partial \theta} \left(\sin \theta \frac{\partial V}{\partial \theta} \right) = 0. \tag{4–5}$$

Solutions of this equation can be obtained by assuming that the variables can be separated and the potential can be written as $V = R(r)P(\theta)$, where R and P, respectively, are functions of r only and θ only. Substituting this value of V into Eq. (4–5), we obtain

$$P \frac{\partial}{\partial r} \left(r^2 \frac{\partial R}{\partial r} \right) + \frac{R}{\sin \theta} \frac{\partial}{\partial \theta} \left(\sin \theta \frac{\partial P}{\partial \theta} \right) = 0,$$

and division by RP gives

$$\frac{1}{R} \frac{\partial}{\partial r} \left(r^2 \frac{\partial R}{\partial r} \right) + \frac{1}{P \sin \theta} \frac{\partial}{\partial \theta} \left(\sin \theta \frac{\partial P}{\partial \theta} \right) = 0, \tag{4–6}$$

in which the first term is a function of r only and the second term is a function of θ only. Since variation of r can affect only the first term and variation of θ can affect only the second, each term must be constant, that is,

$$\frac{1}{R} \frac{d}{dr} \left(r^2 \frac{dR}{dr} \right) = K \tag{4–7}$$

---

* T. M. MacRobert, *Spherical Harmonics*, E. P. Dutton and Co., New York. E. Jahnke and F. Emde, *Tables of Functions with Formulae and Curves*, Dover Publications (1943).

and

$$\frac{1}{P \sin \theta} \frac{d}{d\theta} \left(\sin \theta \frac{dP}{d\theta} \right) = -K. \qquad (4\text{--}8)$$

Each equation, being a function of only one independent variable, is written as an ordinary differential equation. Under the assumption that V can be expressed as a power series in r, we should try $R = r^n$. Substitution in Eq. (4–7) then yields

$$n(n + 1) = K.$$

Substitution of $R = r^{-(n+1)}$ yields the same value for K and provides a second solution. Actually, this value for K must be chosen to keep P finite when $\theta = 0$. The solution of a second order differential equation is then

$$R_n = A_n r^n + B_n r^{-(n+1)}, \qquad (4\text{--}9)$$

where R_n is the general solution for Eq. (4–7) for a particular value of n, and A_n and B_n are arbitrary constants. Since the original Eq. (4–6) is valid for any positive integer from zero to infinity, a general solution consists of the sum of the $R_n P_n$ terms, and

$$V = \sum_{n=0}^{n=\infty} R_n P_n,$$

where P_n is the solution of Eq. (4–8) for a particular value of n. This equation may be written as

$$\frac{1}{P_n \sin \theta} \frac{d}{d\theta} \left(\sin \theta \frac{dP_n}{d\theta} \right) + n(n + 1) = 0,$$

and by setting $\mu = \cos \theta$ and $d\mu = -\sin \theta \, d\theta$, it becomes

$$\frac{d}{d\mu} \left[(1 - \mu^2) \frac{dP_n}{d\mu} \right] + n(n + 1)P_n = 0, \qquad (4\text{--}10)$$

which is called Legendre's equation. Of the two solutions of this equation for the individual values of n, only one is finite for $\theta = 0$ and $\theta = \pi$. These finite solutions are called Legendre polynomials.

It will be sufficient here to show how the first three polynomials are obtained. When $n = 0$, then $P_0 =$ a constant obviously satisfies the equation. When $n = 1$, the equation becomes

$$\frac{d}{d\mu} \left[(1 - \mu^2) \frac{dP_1}{d\mu} \right] + 2P_1 = 0,$$

TABLE 4–1

A SHORT TABLE OF LEGENDRE POLYNOMIALS

$$P_0 = 1$$
$$P_1 = \mu$$
$$P_2 = (1/2)(3\mu^2 - 1)$$
$$P_3 = (1/2)(5\mu^3 - 3\mu)$$
$$P_4 = (1/8)(35\mu^4 - 30\mu^2 + 3)$$
$$P_5 = (1/8)(63\mu^5 - 70\mu^3 + 15\mu)$$
$$P_6 = (1/16)(231\mu^6 - 315\mu^4 + 105\mu^2 - 5)$$
$$P_7 = (1/16)(429\mu^7 - 693\mu^5 + 315\mu^3 - 35\mu)$$

which is satisfied by $P_1 = B\mu$. When $n = 2$, the equation becomes

$$\frac{d}{d\mu}\left[(1 - \mu^2)\frac{dP_2}{d\mu}\right] + 6P_2 = 0,$$

which is satisfied by $P_2 = C(3\mu^2 - 1)$. It is conventional to normalize the P's by making them unity whenever $\mu = 1$, which determines the constants A, B, C, etc. The first eight Legendre polynomials are listed in Table 4–1.

The solution for Eq. (4–6) can now be written in the following form as an infinite series in which each individual term is also a solution:

$$V = \sum_{n=0}^{n=\infty}\left(A_n r^n + \frac{B_n}{r^{n+1}}\right)P_n. \tag{4–11}$$

Conducting sphere in a uniform field. Between two plates of a parallel-plate capacitor the electric field is generally quite uniform for all points that are not too close to the edges of the plates. Figure 4–6(a) shows lines of electric field between two conducting planes on each of which z is constant. A small conducting sphere placed between these plates will distort these field lines as shown in Fig. 4–6(b). A calculation of the distortion in the field produced by such a sphere can be useful in many problems. If the sphere is not large enough to significantly affect the distribution of charges on the conducting planes, this problem can be solved easily by means of Eq. (4–11). It is convenient to assume that the field is produced by one infinite conducting plane at $z = -Z$ with the potential $E_0 Z$, and another at $z = Z$ with the potential $-E_0 Z$, where $Z \gg a$. Before the sphere was introduced, the potential distribution between these planes was given by $V = -E_0 z$ or, in the spherical coordinates of Fig. 4–6(b),

$$V = -E_0 r \cos\theta.$$

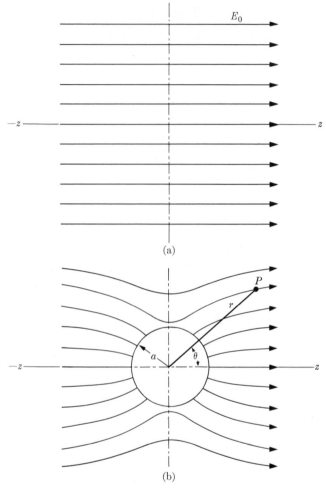

(a)

(b)

FIG. 4-6 (a) Uniform field E_0 pointing in the z-direction. (b) Distortion of field lines due to the presence of a conducting sphere. Point P is an arbitrary location in space which may be located with the spherical coordinates r and θ, since the field is independent of ϕ.

The placing of the sphere with its center at the origin, as shown in Fig. 4-6(b), has created a space in which $\nabla^2 V = 0$ between the surface of the sphere at $r = a$ and the infinite plates. By symmetry, the conducting sphere must have zero potential, and the boundary conditions become

$$V = 0 \qquad \text{at} \qquad r = a$$

and

$$V = -E_0 r \cos \theta \qquad \text{wherever} \qquad r \gg a.$$

The second relation sets up the condition that the field shall not be distorted at great distances from the sphere. If a solution of Laplace's equation can be found that fits both of these boundary conditions, it is the only solution.

In examining the Legendre polynomials of Table 4–1, it appears that only the solutions for $n = 0$ and $n = 1$ can be expected to fit the boundary conditions, since all the other solutions contain higher powers of $\mu = \cos\theta$, which do not appear in the boundary conditions. Combining the first two Legendre polynomials with the corresponding terms from Eq. (4–9), we find that the expression for the potential becomes

$$V = A_0 + \frac{B_0}{r} + A_1 r \cos\theta + \frac{B_1}{r^2} \cos\theta.$$

Substitution into this equation of the boundary conditions as $r \to \infty$ yields

$$V = -E_0 r \cos\theta = A_0 + A_1 r \cos\theta$$

and, since this must be true for all values of θ, $A_0 = 0$ and $A_1 = -E_0$. At the surface of the sphere where $r = a$, $V = 0$, and therefore

$$0 = \frac{B_0}{a} - E_0 a \cos\theta + \frac{B_1}{a^2} \cos\theta,$$

which can be true for all values of θ only if $B_0 = 0$ and $B_1 = E_0 a^3$. Hence the solution to this problem is

$$V = -E_0 r \cos\theta + \frac{E_0 a^3}{r^2} \cos\theta.$$

The field may be calculated directly from this potential:

$$\mathbf{E} = -\boldsymbol{\nabla} V = \left(E_0 \cos\theta + 2\frac{E_0 a^3}{r^3} \cos\theta \right) \mathbf{a}_r$$

$$+ \left(-E_0 \sin\theta + \frac{E_0 a^3}{r^3} \sin\theta \right) \mathbf{a}_\theta,$$

which can be expressed as

$$\mathbf{E} = E_0 \mathbf{k} + \frac{E_0 a^3}{r^3} (\mathbf{a}_r\, 2 \cos\theta + \mathbf{a}_\theta \sin\theta). \tag{4–12}$$

It is interesting to compare this field expression with that due to a dipole, in Eq. (2–4), since this can be divided into the sum of the original uniform field plus the field of a dipole located at the origin, with a dipole moment of $4\pi\epsilon_0 a^3 E_0$. The dipole moment is proportional to the external field E_0 and to the volume of the sphere.

4–5 Some solutions with cylindrical coordinates. When the electrostatic problem exhibits cylindrical symmetry, Laplace's equation may be written in cylindrical coordinates:

$$\nabla^2 V = \frac{1}{r}\frac{\partial}{\partial r}\left(r\frac{\partial V}{\partial r}\right) + \frac{1}{r^2}\frac{\partial^2 V}{\partial \phi^2} + \frac{\partial^2 V}{\partial z^2} = 0.$$

Only those problems where V is independent of z will be considered here, so the equation becomes

$$\nabla^2 V = r\frac{\partial}{\partial r}\left(r\frac{\partial V}{\partial r}\right) + \frac{\partial^2 V}{\partial \phi^2} = 0.$$

If the variables are separable, the function $V = R(r)C(\phi)$ is a solution. Its substitution into the differential equation produces the relation

$$\frac{r}{R}\frac{\partial}{\partial r}\left(r\frac{\partial R}{\partial r}\right) + \frac{1}{C}\frac{\partial^2 C}{\partial \phi^2} = 0 \qquad (4\text{--}13)$$

after division by RC. Since the first and second terms are respectively functions of r only and ϕ only, each term must be constant. As in the solution of Eq. (4–6), these constants can be determined by assuming $R = r^n$, the substitution of which gives the two ordinary differential equations

$$\frac{r}{R_n}\frac{d}{dr}\left(r\frac{dR_n}{dr}\right) = n^2 \qquad (4\text{--}14)$$

and

$$\frac{1}{C_n}\frac{d^2 C_n}{d\phi^2} = -n^2. \qquad (4\text{--}15)$$

The first is satisfied by either r^n or r^{-n} for R_n and the second is satisfied by either $\sin n\phi$ or $\cos n\phi$ for C_n, where n must be a positive integer if C_n is to be single-valued. A general solution for Eq. (4–13) must include

$$V = \sum_{n=1}^{n=\infty} (A_n r^n + B_n r^{-n})\cos n\phi \qquad (4\text{--}16)$$

and

$$V = \sum_{n=1}^{n=\infty} (A_n r^n + B_n r^{-n})\sin n\phi.$$

The summations do not include $n = 0$ because when $n = 0$ Eq. (4–14) can be integrated directly to give

$$R_0 = \ln r/a.$$

TABLE 4–2

CYLINDRICAL SOLUTIONS TO LAPLACE'S EQUATION

$n = 0$	$V = \ln r$	
$n = +1$	$V = r \cos \phi,$	$V = r \sin \phi$
$n = -1$	$V = \dfrac{1}{r} \cos \phi,$	$V = \dfrac{1}{r} \sin \phi$
$n = +2$	$V = r^2 \cos 2\phi,$	$V = r^2 \sin 2\phi$
$n = -2$	$V = \dfrac{1}{r^2} \cos 2\phi,$	$V = \dfrac{1}{r^2} \sin 2\phi$
$\vdots$		

Table 4–2 lists individual solutions* of Eq. (4–13). These same solutions can also be obtained by means of the complex variable procedure of the next section.

Conducting cylinder in a uniform field. A conducting cylinder with its axis perpendicular to a uniform electric field causes distortions in that field similar to those caused by the conducting sphere discussed in the previous section. For example, a very long, fine copper wire stretched midway between two large plates of a parallel-plate capacitor will cause distortions in the field near the wire, like those shown in Fig. 4–7(b). The solutions of $\nabla^2 V = 0$ obtained in this section can be used to calculate the field around such a cylinder. Sufficient accuracy can be achieved by assuming that the capacitor plates are infinite and widely separated. The uniform field shown in Fig. 4–7(a) before the cylinder is introduced can be produced by one infinite conducting plane at $x = -X$ with the potential $E_0 X$ and another at $x = X$ with the potential $-E_0 X$, where $X \gg a$. The potential of the uniform field is then

$$V = -E_0 x = -E_0 r \cos \phi$$

in the cylindrical coordinates of Fig. 4–7(b). With the cylinder in place, $\nabla^2 V = 0$ in the space between the planes and the cylinder.

If the cylindrical axis coincides with the z-axis, the boundary conditions are

$$V = 0 \quad \text{at} \quad r = a$$

and

$$V = -E_0 r \cos \phi \quad \text{wherever} \quad r \gg a.$$

---

* A more detailed discussion of these solutions may be found by looking up Bessel functions in mathematics texts such as W. Kaplan, *Advanced Calculus*, Addison-Wesley Publishing Co., Inc., 1952, and J. D. Murnaghan, *Introduction to Applied Mathematics*, John Wiley and Sons, Inc., 1948.

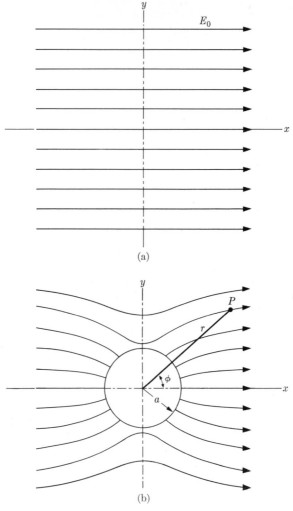

FIG. 4–7. (a) Uniform field E_0 pointing in the x-direction. (b) Distortion of field lines due to the presence of a conducting cylinder. The problem is independent of z, so that an arbitrary point in space may be located with the coordinates r and ϕ.

Since $\cos \phi$ is the only function of ϕ in these boundary conditions, the solution may be assumed to be

$$V = Ar \cos \phi + \frac{B \cos \phi}{r}.$$

Substitution of the boundary conditions at $r \gg a$ gives

$$V = Ar \cos \phi = -E_0 r \cos \phi, \quad \text{or} \quad A = -E_0,$$

and substitution of the boundary conditions at $r = a$ gives

$$V = -E_0 a \cos \phi + \frac{B \cos \phi}{a} = 0, \quad \text{or} \quad B = E_0 a^2.$$

Hence the solution is

$$V = -E_0 r \cos \phi + E_0 a^2 \frac{\cos \phi}{r}. \tag{4–17}$$

The field, determined directly from Eq. (4–17), is

$$\mathbf{E} = -\boldsymbol{\nabla} V = \left(E_0 \cos \phi + E_0 \frac{a^2}{r^2} \cos \phi \right) \mathbf{a}_r$$

$$+ \left(-E_0 \sin \phi + E_0 \frac{a^2}{r^2} \sin \phi \right) \mathbf{a}_\phi,$$

which may be written in the form

$$\mathbf{E} = E_0 \mathbf{i} + E_0 \frac{a^2}{r^2} (\mathbf{a}_r \cos \phi + \mathbf{a}_\phi \sin \phi). \tag{4–18}$$

The first term is just the uniform field that existed in the absence of the cylinder, while the second term is the field due to the cylinder. Figure 4–7(b) shows the field lines obtained from Eq. (4–18). It is interesting to note that on the surface of the cylinder where $r = a$, the field is $2E_0$ at $\phi = 0$ or π, and zero at $\phi = \pi/2$ or $3\pi/2$. The latter result should have been expected, since the tangential component of $\mathbf{E}$ must be zero.

The distribution of potential expressed by Eq. (4–17) is an exact solution only for an infinitely long conducting cylinder perpendicular to a uniform field extending throughout all space. Since these conditions cannot be achieved physically, Eq. (4–17) is not an exact expression for any real problem, although it may often express the potentials to accuracies as great or greater than can be determined by the best measuring techniques.

In all the problems thus far solved by means of Laplace's equation, geometrical and physical reasoning has been used as a guide for guessing the correct solutions, with the knowledge that none but the correct solutions would fit the boundary conditions. More mathematical methods are available. The next section gives a very brief outline of a general method for fitting solutions of Laplace's equation in rectangular coordinates to reasonable boundary conditions. However, the reader faced with difficult problems of this type should consult more advanced texts.

4–6 Laplace's equation in rectangular coordinates. In rectangular coordinates Laplace's equation is

$$\nabla^2 V = \frac{\partial^2 V}{\partial x^2} + \frac{\partial^2 V}{\partial y^2} + \frac{\partial^2 V}{\partial z^2} = 0. \tag{4–19}$$

This partial differential equation can be reduced to three ordinary differential equations by assuming a solution of the form $V = XYZ$, where X, Y, and Z are respectively functions of x only, of y only, and of z only. Substitution of this general solution gives

$$YZ \frac{\partial^2 X}{\partial x^2} + XZ \frac{\partial^2 Y}{\partial y^2} + XY \frac{\partial^2 Z}{\partial z^2} = 0,$$

which can be divided by XYZ to give

$$\frac{1}{X} \frac{\partial^2 X}{\partial x^2} + \frac{1}{Y} \frac{\partial^2 Y}{\partial y^2} + \frac{1}{Z} \frac{\partial^2 Z}{\partial z^2} = 0.$$

Because term one is a function of x, term two is a function of y, and term three is a function of z only, each of the three terms must be constant, and each can then be written in the form of an ordinary differential equation:

$$\frac{1}{X} \frac{d^2 X}{dx^2} = \alpha^2, \qquad \frac{1}{Y} \frac{d^2 Y}{dy^2} = \beta^2, \qquad \frac{1}{Z} \frac{d^2 Z}{dz^2} = \gamma^2, \tag{4–20}$$

where $\alpha^2 + \beta^2 + \gamma^2 = 0$.

Two-dimensional illustration. The procedure is most easily illustrated in two dimensions, although the extension to three-dimensional problems follows essentially the same pattern. If all functions are independent of z, the last constant is zero and $\beta^2 = -\alpha^2$. The general solutions for the first two equations are

$$X = A \cos \beta x + B \sin \beta x$$

and

$$Y = Ce^{\beta y} + De^{-\beta y}.$$

While the solution for Y has a form that is different from that for X, the roles of x and y obviously can be interchanged to fit specific boundary conditions. When the individual terms in a summation are all solutions of Laplace's equation, the summation is also a solution. Hence a general solution can be written as

$$V = \sum_n (A_n \cos \beta_n x + B_n \sin \beta_n x)(C_n e^{\beta_n y} + D_n e^{-\beta_n y}), \tag{4–21}$$

with constants to be determined from the boundary conditions. The procedures for evaluating these constants are best illustrated by a specific example.

Evaluation of constants. The infinitely long rectangular tube shown in Fig. 4–8 is well suited to illustrate the general method for obtaining solutions of Laplace's equation. In the figure, three sides have the potential zero, while the fourth side has the potential $V = f(x)$. The solution of this specific problem actually gives the solution for the more general problem, where V is specified as some function not equal to zero on each of the four boundaries. The solution for such a general problem is just the sum of the solutions for four specific problems like the one considered here.

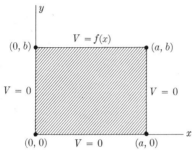

Fig. 4–8. A rectangular tube, infinite in the z-direction, with potentials specified on each boundary.

The general solution of Eq. (4–21) will give $V = 0$ on the right and left boundaries in Fig. 4–8 if each $A_n = 0$ and $\alpha_n = n\pi/a$, where n is any positive integer from 0 to ∞. The condition that $V = 0$ along the x-axis boundary requires that $D_n = -C_n$, and the y-dependent part of the general solution then becomes $Y_n = 2C_n \sinh n\pi y/a$. Since now the B_n's provide the necessary constants, the constants C_n can be chosen to make each $Y_n = 1$ along the upper boundary where $y = b$; that is, a convenient choice is

$$Y_n = \frac{\sinh (n\pi/a)y}{\sinh (n\pi/a)b},$$

which does equal unity where $y = b$. Along the upper boundary, then,

$$V = \sum_n B_n \sin \frac{n\pi}{a} x = f(x). \qquad (4\text{–}22)$$

The theory of Fourier's series shows that the B_n's can be found for any given $f(x)$. To find B_n, multiply Eq. (4–22) by $\sin(m\pi/a)x$, with m an integer, and integrate the resulting relations from $x = 0$ to $x = a$:

$$\sum B_n \int_0^a \sin \frac{n\pi}{a} x \sin \frac{m\pi}{a} x \, dx = \int_0^a \sin \frac{m\pi}{a} x f(x) \, dx.$$

The integral on the left is zero when $m \neq n$, but equals $a/2$ when $m = n$. Therefore

$$B_n = \frac{2}{a} \int_0^a \sin \frac{n\pi}{a} x f(x) \, dx,$$

and in principle each B_n can be determined by evaluating this integral, once the form of $f(x)$ is known.

To illustrate the evaluation of the constants B_n, a constant $f(x) = f_0$ can be chosen. Then

$$B_n = \frac{2f_0}{a} \int_0^a \sin \frac{n\pi x}{a} \, dx$$

or

$$B_n = \frac{2f_0}{a} \left[-\frac{a}{n\pi} \cos \frac{n\pi x}{a} \right]_0^a,$$

which gives $B_n = 0$ for even values of n but gives $B_n = 4f_0/n\pi$ for all odd values of n. The potential inside the rectangle of Fig. 4–8 is then

$$V = \sum_{n=1,3,5,\ldots}^{\infty} \frac{4f_0}{n\pi} \sin \frac{n\pi x}{a} \frac{\sinh (n\pi y/a)}{\sinh (n\pi b/a)}.$$

The techniques illustrated in the foregoing development provide general methods for solving Laplace's equation in rectangular coordinates. Similar methods are available for solving this equation in other coordinate systems.

4–7 Infinite series of images. The problems solved in Section 4–2 to illustrate the method of images were chosen from problems that require only a few images. Some useful problems require an infinite series of images, which produce potentials containing an infinite series of terms. Such potential expressions can be especially useful when the series converges rapidly. A capacitor consisting of a conducting sphere near a large conducting plane is an example of a useful geometry that can be solved with an infinite series of images.

In developing this series it is instructive, first, to consider the plane in Fig. 4–9 to be far from the sphere. The potential near the sphere is then given by an image solution with a single charge q at its center. The value of q can be obtained from the expression for the potential at the

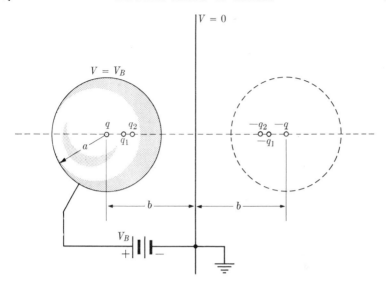

FIG. 4–9. Capacitor consisting of a conducting sphere near an infinite plane.

surface of the sphere, namely,

$$V_B = \frac{q}{4\pi\epsilon_0 a}.$$

The capacitance of this isolated sphere is then $C = q/V_B = 4\pi\epsilon_0 a$.

Sphere and plane. As the conducting plane is brought nearer to the sphere, a charge of opposite sign appears on this plane and tends to reduce the potential of the sphere. With a constant voltage battery connected between the sphere and the plane, the potential of the sphere is kept constant by the additional charge it receives from the battery. If the final charge on the sphere is $Q > q$, the capacitance of the system is

$$C = \frac{Q}{V_B} = \frac{Q}{q}\, 4\pi\epsilon_0 a.$$

This depends upon the ratio Q/q, which can be obtained from the solution of the problem that involves an infinite series of image charges. From the uniqueness theorem, any system of point charges (inside the sphere or to the right of the plane) that produces $V = 0$ on the plane and $V = V_B$ on the surface of the sphere constitutes the correct solution. The six charges shown in Fig. 4–9 can be used to demonstrate how these boundary conditions are satisfied by an infinite series of charges.

Charge q alone produces $V = V_B$ on the surface of the sphere *but does not produce $V = 0$ on the plane.* Adding $-q$ at the distance b behind the plane produces $V = 0$ on the plane but destroys the constant potential on the surface of the sphere. Using the principles developed in Section 4-2 and Fig. 4-3, the potential produced on the surface of the sphere by $-q$ can be cancelled by placing an image charge $q_1 = (a/2b)q$ at the distance $d_1 = a^2/2b$ to the right of the center. Now, however, q_1 disturbs the $V = 0$ on the plane but, since q_1 is smaller than q, the discrepancy is not nearly as large as it was with q alone. A charge $-q_1$ can be introduced to the right of the plane to restore its potential to zero. Then the introduction of a charge $q_2 = q_1 a/(2b - d_1)$ at the distance $d_2 = a^2/(2b - d_1)$ to the right of the center of the sphere restores the potential of the surface of the sphere to V_B. Continuing this process creates an infinite series of charges ($q > q_1 > q_2 > q_3$, etc.) that can be shown to produce potentials expressed by an infinite series that converges rapidly with reasonable values for a and b. The total charge on the sphere is the sum of the image charges in it; that is,

$$Q = q + q_1 + q_2 + q_3 + \cdots$$

and, if $a/2b = \beta$, this can be written as

$$Q = q(1 + \beta + \beta^2 + \beta^3 + 2\beta^4 + 3\beta^5 + \cdots).$$

The capacitance of the system is then

$$C = 4\pi\epsilon_0 a(1 + \beta + \beta^2 + \beta^3 + 2\beta^4 + 3\beta^5 + \cdots). \tag{4-23}$$

Two spheres. This series of images can be used to calculate the capacitance of two metallic spheres each of radius a and with centers separated the distance $2b$. Since the sphere shown dotted on the right in Fig. 4–9 would have the potential $-V_B$, the capacitance would be given by

$$C = \frac{Q}{2V_B} = 2\pi\epsilon_0 a(1 + \beta + \beta^2 + \cdots).$$

Cylinder and plane. Situations occur frequently that can be closely approximated by a capacitor consisting of an infinitely long cylinder with its axis parallel to an infinite conducting plane. This problem is similar to that of the conducting sphere near an infinite plane that we have just treated. The image solution of this problem does not involve an infinite series, because the required potentials can be exactly reproduced with just two infinitely long but uniformly charged filaments. This image solution is left as an exercise. In Section 4–11 a solution involving complex variables is developed that includes this problem as one of its interesting applications.

4-8 Complex quantities. Complex numbers and complex variables are useful in solving many different kinds of physical problems. Here they are useful for finding solutions of Laplace's equation, especially for those two-dimensional problems in which the potentials can be considered to be independent of z. Complex quantities are especially useful for analyzing the properties of vectors that are confined to one plane. Historically, the vector analysis presented in Chapters 2 and 3 was developed in the 1880's by J. W. Gibbs from quaternions, which had been developed by W. R. Hamilton and others in their attempt to extend the vector properties of complex quantities to three-dimensional situations.

Complex numbers are algebraic sums of imaginary numbers and the real numbers that are the ordinary algebraic numbers. Imaginary numbers are real numbers multiplied by the symbol j, where j is defined by $j^2 = -1$. The number $3 + 4j$ is a complex number. The vector characteristics of these numbers stem from the properties they exhibit when they are plotted in what is called a complex plane. A complex plane, shown in Fig. 4–10, is defined by two rectangular coordinate axes in which the real parts of the complex numbers are plotted along the horizontal axis (usually the x-axis), while the imaginary parts are plotted along the vertical axis (usually the y-axis). Points located in this plane represent complex numbers whose absolute magnitudes are defined as the real distances of these points from the origin. The absolute magnitude of $3 + 4j$ is 5, and it is represented by a vector from the origin which is 5 units long and makes an angle of $\tan^{-1} 4/3$ with the real axis.

In the complex plane, the number $+1$ is represented by a vector of unit length making an angle zero with the real axis. Multiplication of this number by j gives the complex number $+j$, which amounts to a 90° rotation about the origin of the original vector. Multiplying again by j produces -1, which amounts to another 90° rotation of this unit vector. In fact, the multiplication of any complex number by j produces a 90°

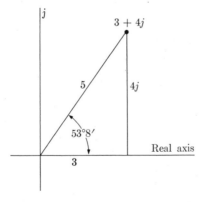

FIG. 4–10. A plot of the complex number $3 + 4j$ in the complex plane. Its absolute value is 5.

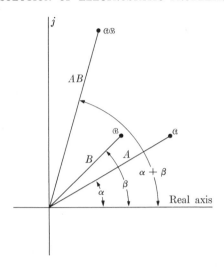

Fig. 4–11. Plots in the complex plane of the complex numbers

$$\alpha = A(\cos \alpha + j \sin \alpha) \qquad \text{and} \qquad \mathfrak{B} = B(\cos \beta + j \sin \beta),$$

together with their product $\alpha\mathfrak{B} = AB[\cos (\beta + \alpha) + j \sin (\beta + \alpha)]$.

rotation without changing the absolute magnitude of the original number. This general property of numbers plotted in complex planes will be found to be particularly useful in the a-c circuit analysis of Chapter 10.

The product of any two complex numbers is another complex number, whose vector representation makes an angle with the real axis that is the sum of the angles made by the original two vectors. Any complex number can be written as $\alpha = A(\cos \alpha + j \sin \alpha)$, where A is its absolute magnitude and α is the angle it makes with the real axis. When two complex numbers are written as $\alpha = A (\cos \alpha + j \sin \alpha)$ and $\mathfrak{B} = B (\cos \beta + j \sin \beta)$, their product, as shown in Fig. 4–11, is

$$\alpha\mathfrak{B} = AB (\cos \alpha + j \sin \alpha) (\cos \beta + j \sin \beta)$$

$$= AB [(\cos \alpha \cos \beta - \sin \alpha \sin \beta) + j (\sin \alpha \cos \beta + \cos \alpha \sin \beta)]$$

$$= AB [\cos (\alpha + \beta) + j \sin (\alpha + \beta)],$$

which proves the statement. This proof is even more obvious when exponential expressions are used.

The exponential form for the complex number α is

$$\alpha = Ae^{j\alpha}.$$

To demonstrate this, $e^{j\alpha}$ can be expanded into a series in powers of α:

$$e^{j\alpha} = 1 + j\alpha - \frac{\alpha^2}{2!} - j\frac{\alpha^3}{3!} + \frac{\alpha^4}{4!} + j\frac{\alpha^5}{5!} - \cdots,$$

and these terms may be rearranged as follows:

$$e^{j\alpha} = \left[1 - \frac{\alpha^2}{2!} + \frac{\alpha^4}{4!} - \cdots\right] + j\left[\alpha - \frac{\alpha^3}{3!} + \frac{\alpha^5}{5!} - \cdots\right].$$

The first brackets contain the power series expansion for $\cos \alpha$, and the second that for $\sin \alpha$. Hence

$$e^{j\alpha} = \cos \alpha + j \sin \alpha$$

and because this represents a dimensionless vector of unit magnitude making an angle α with the positive real axis it is called a unit vector. Now the product of the complex vectors $\mathfrak{a}$ and $\mathfrak{B}$ can be written as

$$\mathfrak{a}\mathfrak{B} = (Ae^{j\alpha})(Be^{j\beta}) = ABe^{j(\alpha+\beta)},$$

which is identical to the result previously obtained by use of trigonometric identities. In general, multiplication of a complex vector $\mathfrak{C} = Ce^{j\gamma}$ by a unit vector $e^{j\theta}$ results in a rotation of the first vector through an angle θ without changing its length:

$$e^{j\theta}\mathfrak{C} = e^{j\theta}Ce^{j\gamma} = Ce^{j(\theta+\gamma)}.$$

Complex conjugate. In the algebraic manipulation of expressions containing complex quantities it is frequently desirable to introduce a new complex quantity, which is called the complex conjugate of some quantity in these expressions. The *complex conjugate* of the quantity $\mathfrak{a} = a + jb$ is designated by $\mathfrak{a}^*$ and is defined by

$$\mathfrak{a}^* = a - jb.$$

The complex conjugate of any complex quantity is obtained by changing the sign of every j that appears in the expression for the original quantity. Complex conjugates have many properties, but two of the most important are that the product of the original quantity with its conjugate is real, and the sum of the original and its conjugate is real; for example,

$$\mathfrak{a}\mathfrak{a}^* = a^2 + b^2 \quad \text{and} \quad \mathfrak{a} + \mathfrak{a}^* = 2a.$$

4–9 Functions of a complex variable for two-dimensional problems. All real problems in electrostatics have geometries that are three-dimensional. However, a very large number of these problems can be approximated with great accuracy by using two-dimensional or even one-dimensional models. In this use of the word "dimensional" it is customary to think in terms of rectangular coordinates, in which a function independent or almost independent of one of the three coordinates may be treated as two-dimensional and a function almost independent of two coordinates may be treated as one-dimensional. A problem to be solved in two dimensions can be drawn on flat paper or on a blackboard, but every mark on the paper represents a physical item extending to infinity on each side of the paper: circles represent cylinders, straight lines represent flat sheets, and dots represent filaments, all of infinite length.

For two-dimensional problems there is a very general method for finding solutions of Laplace's equation which involves the use of a complex variable. Two different potential functions, $G(x, y)$ and $H(x, y)$, which are related to some analytic function ϕ of $Z = x + jy$ by the equation

$$G + jH = \phi(Z), \tag{4-24}$$

will be considered. Whenever two potential functions are related to each other in this manner, each one is necessarily a solution of Laplace's equation, and the two have certain reciprocal properties that will be demonstrated.

To show that both G and H satisfy Laplace's equation, it will first be demonstrated that $\phi(Z)$ is always a solution. The relations $\partial Z/\partial x = 1$ and $\partial Z/\partial y = j$ follow directly from the definition of Z. With these relations it is easily shown that

$$\frac{\partial \phi}{\partial x} = \frac{\partial \phi}{\partial Z} \frac{\partial Z}{\partial x} = \phi' \quad \text{and} \quad \frac{\partial^2 \phi}{\partial x^2} = \frac{\partial \phi'}{\partial Z} \frac{\partial Z}{\partial x} = \phi'',$$

as well as

$$\frac{\partial \phi}{\partial y} = \frac{\partial \phi}{\partial Z} \frac{\partial Z}{\partial y} = j\phi' \quad \text{and} \quad \frac{\partial^2 \phi}{\partial y^2} = j \frac{\partial \phi'}{\partial Z} \frac{\partial Z}{\partial y} = -\phi'',$$

where ϕ' and ϕ'' are defined by

$$\phi' = \frac{\partial \phi}{\partial Z} \quad \text{and} \quad \phi'' = \frac{\partial^2 \phi}{\partial Z^2} = \frac{\partial \phi'}{\partial Z}.$$

Adding

$$\frac{\partial^2 \phi}{\partial x^2} = \phi'' \quad \text{to} \quad \frac{\partial^2 \phi}{\partial y^2} = -\phi''$$

results in

$$\frac{\partial^2 \phi}{\partial x^2} + \frac{\partial^2 \phi}{\partial y^2} = 0,$$

which is just Laplace's equation for ϕ in two dimensions. Applying this to Eq. (4–24) gives

$$\nabla^2 \phi = \nabla^2 G + j\nabla^2 H = 0,$$

which can be true only if $\nabla^2 G$ and $\nabla^2 H$ each equal zero, that is, only if G and H are each solutions of Laplace's equation. This proof that G and H are solutions of Laplace's equation is valid everywhere in space where the first and second derivatives of G and H exist, but not where either function approaches infinity, as is illustrated in the next section.

Solutions for the two-dimensional Laplace equation can be obtained by selecting any analytic functions of the variable Z, each of which will produce two real solutions G and H.

The simplest function of Z is just $bZ = bx + jby$, from which two simple functions, $G = bx$ and $H = by$, are obtained. Obviously, G represents the potential for a uniform field of magnitude $-b$ in the x-direction, whereas H represents a uniform field of magnitude $-b$ in the y-direction. Another simple function is $\phi(Z) = bZ^2 = b(x^2 - y^2) + j(2bxy)$, which gives $G = b(x^2 - y^2)$ and $H = 2bxy$. If G is chosen for the potential function, the potential distribution can be illustrated by giving G various constant values and plotting the equipotential surfaces obtained from these relations. The result is a family of hyperbolas. When the H function is treated in the same manner, a second family of hyperbolas results, and the lines of $H = $ constant cut each of the $G = $ constant curves in such a manner that all intersections are at right angles, as shown in Fig. 4-12. When one set of curves cuts another set of curves in this manner, the two sets are said to be *orthogonal*. It should be noted that the G and H functions for $\phi(Z) = bZ$ are also orthogonal. This behavior will be shown to be general for all G and H functions that can be obtained from $\phi(Z)$.

To show this, ϕ can be differentiated with respect to x and y separately, to yield

$$\frac{\partial \phi}{\partial x} = \frac{\partial G}{\partial x} + j\,\frac{\partial H}{\partial x} = \phi'$$

and

$$\frac{\partial \phi}{\partial y} = \frac{\partial G}{\partial y} + j\,\frac{\partial H}{\partial y} = j\phi',$$

from which it can be seen that

$$j\,\frac{\partial G}{\partial x} - \frac{\partial H}{\partial x} = \frac{\partial G}{\partial y} + j\,\frac{\partial H}{\partial y}.$$

Equating the real and imaginary parts, we find

$$-\frac{\partial H}{\partial x} = \frac{\partial G}{\partial y} \tag{4-25}$$

and

$$\frac{\partial G}{\partial x} = \frac{\partial H}{\partial y}, \tag{4-26}$$

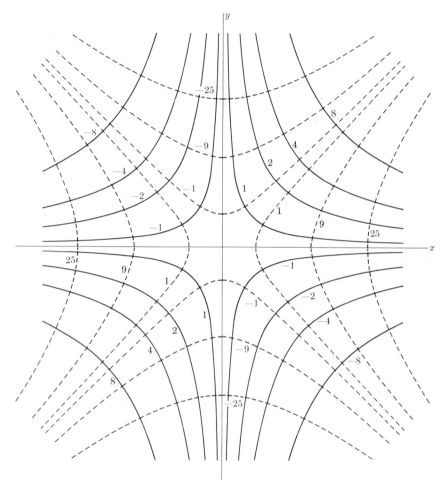

Fig. 4–12. Graph of $G/b = (x^2 - y^2) =$ constant and $H/2b = xy =$ constant. G/b is represented by dashed lines and $H/2b$ is represented by solid lines. The constant values selected for G/b and $H/2b$ are indicated on the curves.

which are called the Cauchy-Riemann relations. The foregoing analysis assumed that $\phi(Z)$ was analytic. Actually, these relations provide a test as to whether or not a given $\phi(Z)$ is analytic. In regions where the Cauchy-Riemann relations are satisfied and where G, H, and their first derivatives are continuous, $\phi(Z)$ is analytic. Multiplying Eqs. (4–25) and (4–26) together and transposing, we obtain

$$\frac{\partial G}{\partial x}\frac{\partial H}{\partial x} + \frac{\partial G}{\partial y}\frac{\partial H}{\partial y} = 0, \qquad (4\text{–}27)$$

which is just $\nabla G \cdot \nabla H = 0$. Whenever the dot product of two nonzero

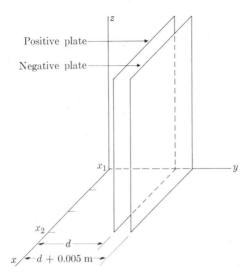

Fig. 4–13. Two parallel conducting plates charged to a potential difference of 100 volts are located perpendicular to the y-axis, as shown.

vectors is zero, the two vectors are at right angles; therefore the gradients of G and H are perpendicular to each other at all points. Since the gradients are always perpendicular to their equipotential surfaces, the equipotential surfaces of G and H must intersect each other at right angles.

These two functions exhibit another useful relationship at all points; namely, $|\nabla G| = |\nabla H|$, which follows immediately from the Cauchy-Riemann relations. Upon squaring and adding Eqs. (4–25) and (4–26), we obtain

$$\left(\frac{\partial G}{\partial x}\right)^2 + \left(\frac{\partial G}{\partial y}\right)^2 = \left(\frac{\partial H}{\partial x}\right)^2 + \left(\frac{\partial H}{\partial y}\right)^2.$$

This may be rewritten as

$$|\nabla G|^2 = |\nabla H|^2, \tag{4-28}$$

which is true only if $|\nabla G| = |\nabla H|$. Equations (4–27) and (4–28) are both very useful in solving two-dimensional problems involving Laplace's equation.

As a simple illustration, consider two large, parallel conducting plates with a difference in potential of 100 volts. The plates may be perpendicular to the y-axis and cut this axis at $y = d$ and $y = d + 0.005$ m, so that they are 0.005 m apart, with the positive plate at $y = d$, as shown in Fig. 4–13. In the space between these plates $\nabla^2 V = 0$ and the potential can be represented by the solution of Laplace's equation, $H = by$. The boundary condition at the positive plate gives

$$H_+ = 100 \text{ volts} + V_0 = bd$$

and that at the negative plate gives

$$H_- = V_0 = b(d + 0.005 \text{ m}),$$

where V_0 is introduced because the absolute potential of the plates was not specified. Subtraction yields

$$100 \text{ volts} = -(0.005 \text{ m})b, \quad \text{or} \quad b = -20{,}000 \text{ volts/m}.$$

The potential between the plates is $V = H = -(20{,}000 \text{ volts/m})y$, the electric field in the space is $\mathbf{E} = -\nabla V = \mathbf{j}\, 20{,}000 \text{ volts/m}$, and the charge density on the positive plate is

$$\sigma = \epsilon_0 E = \epsilon_0\, 20{,}000 \text{ volts/m} = 0.18\,\mu\text{coul/m}^2.$$

In practical cases the plates of the capacitor are never infinite, and it is often desirable to obtain the approximate value of the total charge on one of the plates. For example, if the plates extend from $x_1 = 0$ to $x_2 = 0.3$ m in the x-direction, and from $z_1 = 0$ to $z_2 = 1.0$ m in the z-direction, the total charge on the positive plate is approximately $0.18\,\mu\text{coul/m}^2 \times 0.3 \text{ m}^2 = 0.054\,\mu\text{coul}$. The actual charge is less than this, because the charge density is somewhat lower near the edges. The same value for the charge could have been obtained from the difference between the G's at the two edges of the positive plate, that is, $\epsilon_0(G_2 - G_1) = (bx_2 - bx_1)\epsilon_0 = 0.3b\epsilon_0 = 0.054\,\mu\text{coul}$. This procedure for calculating charges* follows directly from the relations between G and H. Since $\sigma = \epsilon_0 E_n$ and $|\mathbf{E}| = |\nabla H| = |\nabla G|$ is constant between x_1 and x_2 in this problem, the areal density of charge is

$$\sigma = \epsilon_0|\nabla G| = \epsilon_0 \left| \frac{G_2 - G_1}{x_2 - x_1} \right|,$$

where G_1 and G_2 are the values of G at x_1 and x_2, respectively. Therefore the charge per meter of distance in the z-direction is

$$\lambda = \sigma(x_2 - x_1) = \epsilon_0(G_2 - G_1).$$

This method is too complex for so simple a problem, but with a more complex $\phi(Z)$, this relation, which has general validity, is very useful.

---

* An ambiguity in the signs of λ, σ, and q is inherent in calculations of their magnitudes on surfaces of conductors that coincide with equipotential surfaces determined mathematically. When charges are positive with the bulk of the conductor on one side of the equipotential, they are negative with the bulk of the conductor on the other side. The expression $\sigma = \epsilon_0 E_n = -\epsilon_0\,\partial V/\partial n$ from Eq. (3-6) is not ambiguous.

FIG. 4–14. Lines of constant G and H between two curved cylindrical sheets S_1 and S_2.

For this demonstration a general problem like that shown in Fig. 4–14 should be considered, where the curved cylindrical sheets S_1 and S_2 extend to plus and minus infinity in the z-direction. These sheets are charged to potentials of H_1 and H_2, respectively, and it is desired to find the charge per unit length residing on the region of S_1 that extends from P_1 to P_2. The charge per unit area is $\sigma = \epsilon_0 E_1$, where $\mathbf{E}_1 = -\nabla H_1$ is the field evaluated along the surface S_1. The charge per unit length between P_1 and P_2 is given by

$$\lambda = \int_{P_1}^{P_2} \sigma \, dl = \int_{P_1}^{P_2} \epsilon_0 |\nabla H_1| \, dl,$$

since the element of area ds, being one meter long, is equal to the element of length dl. Using the relation $|\nabla H| = |\nabla G|$, the equation for λ becomes

$$\lambda = \int_{P_1}^{P_2} \epsilon_0 |\nabla G| \, dl,$$

and if ∇G points in the direction $d\mathbf{l}$, the quantity $|\nabla G| \, dl = \nabla G \cdot d\mathbf{l} = dG$. The integral then becomes

$$\lambda = \int_{G_1}^{G_2} \epsilon_0 \, dG = \epsilon_0 (G_2 - G_1),$$

where G_1 and G_2 are the values of G at P_1 and P_2, respectively.

Since the potential difference between the sheets is given by $H_2 - H_1$ and since the charge per unit length on S_1 between P_1 and P_2 is given by $\epsilon_0(G_2 - G_1)$, a general relation for the capacitance per unit length of this capacitor is

$$C_l = \frac{\epsilon_0(G_2 - G_1)}{H_2 - H_1}. \qquad (4\text{--}29)$$

4–10 Some characteristics of electrostatic fields. There are some characteristics of all electrostatic fields that are most easily visualized in two dimensions. For example, the characteristics of all equilibrium points in electrostatic fields are clearly shown in Fig. 4–12.

Earnshaw's theorem. If the solid lines in Fig. 4–12 represent equipotential surfaces, the electric field is zero at the origin. A test charge placed at this point would be in equilibrium, but not in stable equilibrium. While the zero potential of this point is a minimum with respect to quadrants 1 and 3, it is a maximum with respect to quadrants 2 and 4. Such points have been given the descriptive name "saddlepoints." A theorem by Earnshaw states that *all equilibrium points in electrostatic fields are saddlepoints.* This is easily visualized by noting that if the point is surrounded by a small closed surface, the net flux out of it must be zero by Gauss' law; that is, field lines that enter through one portion of the surface must leave through some other portion. While there is no field and therefore no force on a test charge placed exactly at the equilibrium point, there is a force on it when it is slightly displaced. This force tends to carry the test charge away from that region rather than to restore it to the equilibrium position. *Charges cannot be in stable equilibrium in electrostatic fields.* The characteristic pattern for flux lines near equilibrium points is shown in Fig. 4–15, where the field is produced by two conducting sheets made to coincide with the two hyperbolic curves, marked 4 in Fig. 4–12, and maintained at the same positive potential. While this two-dimensional equilibrium point is the infinite line representing the z-axis, in real three-dimensional situations equilibrium points are always mathematical points.

Guard rings. A simple capacitor consists of two conducting surfaces insulated from each other, so that they may have different potentials in a static field. If the two surfaces are made to coincide with any two of the equipotentials that have different numbers in Fig. 4–12, the capacitance can be calculated by means of Eq. (4–29). The mathematical expressions for the shapes of the two conducting surfaces must be known if the capacitance is to be calculated exactly. The mathematical expressions defining the surfaces plotted in Fig. 4–12 extend to infinity, as do many such expressions. It is impossible to build capacitors with conducting sheets extending to infinity as required by these expressions. Further-

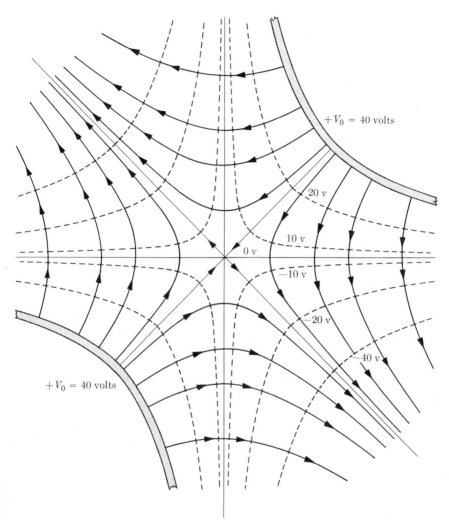

Fig. 4–15. Typical electrostatic field lines and equipotential surfaces near an equilibrium point. Potentials always have "saddlepoint" characteristics in these regions.

more, the calculated capacitance is usually infinite for two such complete sheets. Finite sections of these surfaces can be made to have finite capacitances, but the calculations cannot be accurate because of edge effects.

A technique for eliminating most of the inaccuracies caused by edge effects, called the "guard-ring technique," has been developed. As shown in Fig. 4–14, that section of surface S_1 between P_1 and P_2 and extending one meter in the z-direction has been chosen for one conductor of a capacitor. A fine saw cut separates this section and keeps it insulated from the rest of S_1, whose shape conforms to the mathematical expression for some distance beyond the cut. Connections are shown in Fig. 4–14 for producing a single potential on all of S_1, while measuring only that charge that flows to the isolated section. It is not necessary to physically separate the section of S_2 between P_3 and P_4, since its charge is automatically equal and opposite to that on S_1 between P_1 and P_2. The portion of S_1 outside the saw cut is called a "guard ring," because in the earliest applications of this technique, this portion, whose only function is to control the potential distribution, was in the shape of a ring. A guard ring of this design is shown in Fig. 3–13 for Problem 3–14.

4–11 Eccentric cylinder problems. While only a few of the thousands of known solutions of Laplace's equation can be presented here, there is one more function of $Z = x + jy$ that should be presented, because it provides solutions for many practical problems. It is

$$F(Z) = A \ln \frac{Z + s}{Z - s}. \tag{4–30}$$

To obtain functions useful for solving problems this expression should be separated into its real and imaginary parts and plotted in the complex plane, as shown in Fig. 4–16. The numerator is given by the line O_1P, since

$$Z + s = (x + s) + jy = r_1 e^{j\theta_1},$$

and the denominator is given by the line O_2P, since

$$Z - s = (x - s) + jy = r_2 e^{j\theta_2}.$$

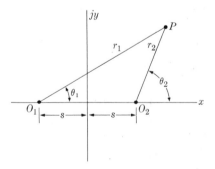

FIG. 4–16. Plot in complex plane of $r_1 e^{j\theta_1} = Z + s$ and $r_2 e^{j\theta_2} = Z - s$. This plot is useful in interpreting the function $\phi(Z) = A \ln [(Z + s)/(Z - s)]$.

The function then can be written as

$$F(Z) = A \ln \frac{r_1 e^{j\theta_1}}{r_2 e^{j\theta_2}} = A \ln (r_1/r_2) - jA(\theta_2 - \theta_1).$$

This function of Z has thus provided the two functions

$$G = A \ln (r_1/r_2) \quad \text{and} \quad H = -A(\theta_2 - \theta_1),$$

where either G or H can be used as potential functions.

When G is taken to be the potential function, families of equipotentials are obtained by setting G equal to a series of different constant values. It is convenient to determine these constant values for G by defining $r_1/r_2 = m$ and $G = A \ln m$, where each value of m determines a particular potential surface. This method of choosing the constant G's is used to facilitate the remaining analysis. Expressions for the equipotential surfaces can be obtained from

$$m^2 = \frac{r_1^2}{r_2^2} = \frac{(x+s)^2 + y^2}{(x-s)^2 + y^2}. \tag{4-31}$$

Multiplying by the denominator, expanding, collecting terms, and dividing by $(m^2 - 1)$, we obtain

$$x^2 - 2\left(\frac{m^2 + 1}{m^2 - 1}\right)xs + s^2 + y^2 = 0,$$

which can be written

$$\left(x - \frac{m^2 + 1}{m^2 - 1} s\right)^2 + y^2 = \left(\frac{2ms}{m^2 - 1}\right)^2, \tag{4-32}$$

as can be verified by expanding both sides. A series of equipotential surfaces can be obtained by plotting Eq. (4–30) with a series of values for m, and each of these equipotentials will be a circle of radius $2ms/(m^2 - 1)$ with its center at $x = (m^2 + 1)s/(m^2 - 1)$. The potential of each circle is then obtained from $G = A \ln m$.

In Fig. 4–17 circles have been plotted for $m = 0$, 1/4, 1/3, 1/2, 1, 2, 3, 4, and ∞. The circles for $m = 0$ and $m = \infty$ have zero radii with centers at $(-s, 0)$ and $(s, 0)$, respectively. These two points, marked O_1 and O_2 in Fig. 4–16, are called singular points or poles, because their potentials are $-\infty$ and ∞. For $m = 1$ the circle has infinite radius and is just the median plane through $x = 0$, as can be seen from the fact that, in Fig. 4–16, $r_1 = r_2$ for all points on the median plane where $m = r_1/r_2 = 1$. Mathematically, all traces in the xy-plane represent surfaces extending to infinity in the positive and negative z-directions, and each circle represents an infinitely long cylinder.

The surfaces for different constant values of H are sections of cylinders with circular arc traces in the xy-plane, with centers on the y-axis. Each circular arc extends from O_1 to O_2, as shown by the dashed curves in Fig. 4–17. Proof that these arcs of circles do represent constant values of H in the xy-plane is readily obtained from Fig. 4–18. Now $H = -A(\theta_2 - \theta_1) = -A\phi$, where $\phi = \theta_2 - \theta_1$ is the angle between PO_1 and PO_2. From a well-known theorem in geometry, the angle between $P'O_1$ and $P'O_2$ is also ϕ, provided P' is a point on the circle passing through P, O_1, and O_2. This curve of constant $H = -A\phi$ extends only from O_1 through P' and P to O_2. The remainder of each circle represents another curve of constant H for which $H = -A\phi'$ and $\phi' = \pi - \phi$.

To illustrate the use of these solutions, the capacitance per meter, C_l, can be calculated for an infinitely long copper cylinder of 3-cm radius whose axis is parallel to an infinite conducting plane and 5 cm from it. The expression for the plane is given by $m = 1$ and, since $G = A \ln m$, the potential of the plane is zero. If the electrical connections in a real situation do not produce zero potential on the plane, *the constant potential of the plane can be added to all of the potentials* calculated here. Adding a constant to all of the potentials in any system does not affect capacitances or any of the fields.

To satisfy the boundary conditions of this problem, it is necessary to find the values of m and s required to provide a circle of radius 0.03 m, having its center 0.05 m from the median plane in Fig. 4–17. The two equations needed for calculating this m and this s can be obtained from Eq. (4–32). They are

$$\frac{m^2 + 1}{m^2 - 1} s = 0.05$$

and

$$\frac{2m}{m^2 - 1} s = 0.03.$$

Dividing the first equation by the second and simplifying, we obtain

$$3m^2 - 10m + 3 = 0,$$

from which $m = 3$ or $1/3$, which shows that a solution can be taken from either side of the median plane in Fig. 4–17. Taking $m = 3$, the potential difference between the cylinder and the plane is $G_2 - G_1 = A (\ln 3 - \ln 1) = A \ln 3$, where A is a constant to be determined by the actual potential difference that is maintained between the cylinder and plane. The absolute value of the total charge per unit length in the

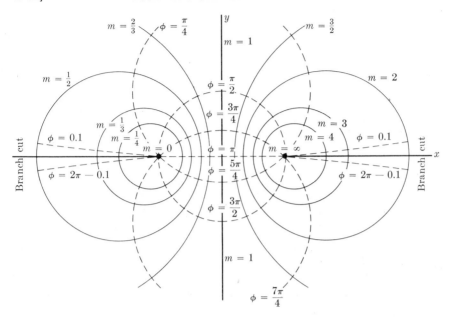

FIG. 4–17. The function $F(Z) = A \ln [(Z + s)/(Z - s)]$ may be separated into its real and imaginary parts, $G = A \ln m$ and $H = -A\phi$. Dashed lines indicate curves for constant H, while solid lines are curves for constant G.

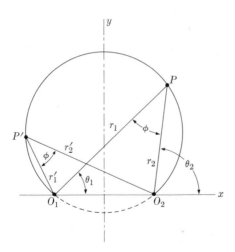

FIG. 4–18. Arcs of circles passing through O_1 and O_2 represent curves of constant H. This fact is illustrated by the figure, since the angle ϕ enclosed by O_1PO_2 is independent of the location of P on the solid portion of the circle, and $H = -A\phi$.

z-direction on the cylinder is obtained by integrating the charge per unit area, σ, all around the cylinder. The integration may start from the x-axis on the right in Fig. 4–17 and progress counterclockwise around the cylinder and back to the starting point. The integration is as follows:

$$\lambda = \oint \sigma \, dl = \oint \epsilon_0 E \, dl = \oint \epsilon_0 |\nabla G| \, dl = \oint \epsilon_0 |\nabla H| \, dl$$

$$= \int_H^{H'} \epsilon_0 \, dH = \epsilon_0 (H' - H) = \epsilon_0 2\pi A, \qquad (4\text{–}33)$$

since $H = -A\phi$ and $-\phi$ ranges from 0 to 2π. The charge per unit length on the cylinder is therefore $\epsilon_0 2\pi A$. The function H has the same range of values along the plane (the y-axis), so that integration along the plane yields the same result. The capacitance per unit length is then

$$C_l = \frac{\epsilon_0 (H_2 - H_1)}{G_2 - G_1} = \frac{2\pi\epsilon_0}{\ln 3}.$$

This is only one of the many problems that can be solved with this function of Z. For example, for two copper cylinders having this same 3-cm radius, with axes parallel and 10 cm apart, the capacitance per meter of length is

$$C_l = \frac{2\pi\epsilon_0}{\ln 3 - \ln 1/3} = \frac{\pi\epsilon_0}{\ln 3}.$$

The capacitance between two cylinders, one inside the other but eccentric, can also be calculated by means of these procedures.

In Chapter 8 it will be shown that the H function gives magnetic potentials of the magnetic fields due to a transmission line consisting of parallel wires carrying currents in opposite directions. Many other applications for these functions should occur to the reader.

Solutions with specified cylinders. Any problem like the foregoing that involves a cylinder near a plane is easily solved, because $m = 1$ for a plane and it is necessary only to find m for the cylinder. Other problems that can be solved with this complex function may be more difficult, because both of the m's may need to be determined from the geometry. While this is simple in principle, common techniques for determining these m's often result in fourth-order equations that must be solved. Fortunately, the m's can be determined without solving fourth-order equations.

As a general problem of this type, consider two cylinders, of radii a and b, with distance d between their centers. Designating the m's for the cylinders by m_a and m_b respectively, the unknown quantities are m_a, m_b, and the s in Eq. (4–32). This equation shows that the given geometrical quantities can be expressed by the following three equations:

$$a = \frac{2m_a s}{m_a^2 - 1},$$

$$b = \frac{2m_b s}{m_b^2 - 1},$$

and

$$d = d_a - d_b = \frac{m_b^2 + 1}{m_b^2 - 1} s - \frac{m_a^2 + 1}{m_a^2 - 1} s.$$

Since the first two equations are easily solved for m_a and m_b in terms of s, it is desirable to first solve the last equation for s. It is easy to show that $d_a^2 = s^2 + a^2$ and $d_b^2 = s^2 + b^2$. The last equation can then be written as

$$d = \sqrt{s^2 + b^2} - \sqrt{s^2 + a^2}.$$

By defining $d/a = D$, $b/a = B$, and $s/a = S$ this can be simplified to

$$D = \sqrt{S^2 + B^2} - \sqrt{S^2 + 1},$$

which can be written as

$$2\sqrt{(S^2 + 1)(S^2 + B^2)} = B^2 + 2S^2 + 1 - D^2.$$

Finally, this can be squared and solved for S^2 to give

$$S^2 = \left(\frac{B^2 - D^2 - 1}{2D}\right)^2 - 1. \tag{4–34}$$

When a problem is stated in terms of a, b, and d, s can be obtained from Eq. (4–34) and m_a and m_b can then be obtained from the first two of the original three simultaneous equations.

For the common problem in which $b > a$ and $(b + a) > d$, the solution can be obtained either with both m's greater than one or with both less than one. The expressions for the m's are

$$m_a = \sqrt{S^2 + 1} \pm S$$

and

$$m_b = \sqrt{(S/B)^2 + 1} \pm S/B.$$

Singular points, or poles. As pointed out, the function

$$F(Z) = A \ln \frac{Z + s}{Z - s} = A \ln \frac{r_2}{r_1} - jA(\theta_2 - \theta_1)$$

has two singular points (poles), at $r_1 = 0$ and at $r_2 = 0$, where the potential $G = \ln (r_2/r_1)$ is infinite. At such points neither Laplace's equation nor the Cauchy-Riemann relations are valid. In particular, when there are singular points where G becomes infinite, the integral $\oint \nabla H \cdot d\mathbf{l}$ is zero only when the path of integration does not make a loop around any of these poles. This can be seen from Stokes' theorem:

$$\oint \nabla H \cdot d\mathbf{l} = \int_s \nabla \times \nabla H \cdot d\mathbf{s},$$

where the integral on the right is identically zero only where H is differentiable, not where it is discontinuous, as at the poles. In complex variable analysis it is shown that $\oint \nabla H \cdot d\mathbf{l} = \pm 2\pi A$ whenever the path of integration does make a loop around a pole. A region can be defined in which $\oint \nabla H \cdot d\mathbf{l} = 0$ everywhere by making a cut along any line joining the poles and prohibiting the paths of integration from crossing this cut. In Fig. 4–17 this effect is achieved by making cuts to infinity along the x-axis from each pole. The function H is therefore multiple-valued. This last relation has been used, in fact, in obtaining Eq. (4–33), the charge per unit of length on a cylinder. This mathematical property of functions containing singular points will be found to be very valuable when magnetic fields due to electric currents are studied in Chapter 8.

REFERENCES

JEANS, J. H., *The Mathematical Theory of Electricity and Magnetism*, Cambridge University Press, 1925.

MAXWELL, J. C., *Electricity and Magnetism, Vol. I*, Clarendon Press, 1953.

PANOFSKY and PHILLIPS, *Classical Electricity and Magnetism*, Addison-Wesley Publishing Company, Inc., 1955.

PIPES, L. A., *Applied Mathematics for Engineers and Physicists*, McGraw-Hill Book Co., Inc., 1946.

SMYTHE, W. R., *Static and Dynamic Electricity*, McGraw-Hill Book Co., Inc., 1939.

Problems

*4–1. The charge q near the infinite conducting plane in Fig. 4–1 induces on that plane a surface density of charge which depends upon the radial distance from the z-axis. (a) Derive an expression for the total induced charge within a circle of radius r. (b) Let θ be an angle, with its apex at q, between the negative z-axis and any point on the circle of radius r. For the circle that encloses the total charge $-q/2$, calculate $\tan \theta$. (c) Determine the value of θ for the circle that encloses $-0.9q$.

4–2. Show by direct differentiation that $\nabla^2 V = 0$ for the V given in Eq. (4–1). If there are any points in space where this relation does not hold, explain the apparent discrepancy.

4–3. (a) Calculate the field $\mathbf{E} = -\boldsymbol{\nabla} V$ directly from the value of V in Eq. (4–1). (b) Calculate the value of $\mathbf{E}$ just above the conducting plane, from the expression obtained in (a). (c) Calculate the value of $\mathbf{E}$ just above the conducting plane, by adding vectorially the fields due to q and its image. Compare this with the field obtained in (b).

*4–4. Remembering that the image charge in Fig. 4–1 does not exist and that the actual fields are due to q and the induced charge, obtain an expression for the field below the surface of the plane.

*4–5. Obtain an expression for σ, the density of the charge induced on the inner surface of the hollow sphere of Fig. 4–2, in terms of q, a, d, and θ.

4–6. Find the density of the charge induced on the surface of the sphere in Fig. 4–6(b) in terms of E_0, a, and θ.

4–7. Equation (2–15) expresses the distribution of potential due to any distribution of point charges. (a) Show by direct differentiation that $\nabla^2 V = 0$ for this distribution. (b) Are there any regions where $\nabla^2 V = 0$ is not satisfied? Identify any such regions and explain the physical meaning of the existence of these regions.

*4–8. The total charge associated with each atomic nucleus is given accurately by $q_n = Z \times 1.6021 \times 10^{-19}$ coul, where Z is the atomic number. Rather recently the radii of these nuclei have been measured with inaccuracies somewhat less than 10%. The result is expressed by $r_n \cong A^{1/3} \times 1.2 \times 10^{-15}$ m, where A is the number of nucleons for all of the common nuclei except the proton, whose radius is 0.7×10^{-15} m. For most of the lighter nuclei $A = 2Z$, and even for the heaviest nuclei $2Z \lesssim A < 2.6Z$. These facts suggest that the positive charges in most nuclei are rather uniformly distributed throughout their volumes. For the purpose of calculation, assume that the nuclei are spheres with uniform charge distributions and that the inverse-square law is valid to the smallest distances.

(a) Calculate the charge densities of the nuclei in which $A = 2Z$ and compare the result with the charge density in the proton. (b) Calculate the potential distribution inside and outside such a nucleus that is far removed from all other charges. (c) Calculate the maximum potential in volts for such isolated nuclei and compare this result with the maximum potential for an isolated proton.

---

* Answers to starred problems will be found at back of book.

4–9. When a finite quantity of charges $\sum q$ (all of the same sign) are grouped together in a finite region, the potential at large distances due to these charges can be shown to approach $V = \sum q/4\pi\epsilon_0 r$, where the large distance r is measured from the interior of the region. Since the magnitude of this potential is decreased by adding charges of opposite sign to the region, the potential due to any finite group of mixed charges must decrease with distance at least as rapidly as $1/r$. Show that for finite charges in a finite region $\int_s V \nabla V \cdot d\mathbf{s}$ approaches zero as r approaches infinity.

4–10. There are many problems in electrostatics in which the charge density is not zero throughout the region of interest. In those special cases in which the charge distribution $\rho = \rho(x, y, z)$ is known throughout the bounded region, (a) show that the uniqueness theorem holds for solutions of $\nabla^2 V = -\rho/\epsilon_0$, and (b) show also that the function $V = V_p + \sum_l V_l$ is a solution of Poisson's equation if V_p is a solution of this equation and the V_l's are each solutions of Laplace's equation.

*4–11. The integral $V = \int_\tau \rho \, d\tau/4\pi\epsilon_0 r$ is a general solution of $\nabla^2 V = -\rho/\epsilon_0$ that can be combined with solutions of $\nabla^2 V = 0$ to satisfy specific boundary conditions whenever the function $\rho = \rho(x, y, z)$ is known throughout the bounded region. Consider a nonconducting sphere of radius a to be placed inside a hollow conducting sphere of inner radius b, where the distance between the centers of the spheres is h. With the conducting sphere connected to ground, (a) find the potential distributions inside the two spheres when the inner sphere has a uniform surface charge density σ, and (b) find the potential distribution inside the two spheres when the inner sphere has a uniform volume charge density ρ.

4–12. A solid metallic sphere of radius a is connected to ground by a long fine wire that maintains its potential at zero, and a point charge q is placed a distance $p > a$ from its center. (a) Find the expression for V in terms of spherical coordinates having their origin at the center of the sphere. (b) Find an expression for σ, the density of charge on the surface of the sphere. (c) Find the force on q due to the charged sphere. (d) Would any of the foregoing results be different if the sphere were hollow rather than solid?

*4–13. In Problem 4–12 assume that the conducting sphere was not connected to ground but was isolated so that it was neutral before the charge q was placed at the distance p from its center. For this new situation obtain the results called for in parts (a), (b), (c), and (d) of Problem 4–12. In addition, (e) find the potential of the sphere, and (f) show that $l/p = (1 - \lambda^2)^{1/3}$, where l is the distance from q to the $\sigma = 0$ points on the sphere and $\lambda = a/p$.

4–14. As in the problem discussed in Section 4–2, a hollow spherical shell of metal has external and internal radii b and a, respectively, and has a point charge q at a distance $d < a$ from its center. How would the solution given there be modified if, instead of being connected to ground, the sphere had been isolated and neutral before q was introduced? (a) Find the modified expressions for V both inside and outside the sphere. (b) Find new expressions for σ on both the inside and outside surfaces. (c) Find the new force on q due to these surface charges.

*4–15. Two semi-infinite conducting planes are perpendicular to each other and are joined along the z-axis from $z = -\infty$ to $z = \infty$. These planes extend from $x = 0$ to $x = \infty$ in the xz-plane, from $y = 0$ to $y = \infty$ in the yz-plane, and are connected to ground. A point charge q is located at the (x, y, z) coordinates $(a, b, 0)$. Find expressions for (a) the charge distribution on the yz-plane, and (b) the force acting on the point charge q.

4–16. One excellent method for checking the correctness of complicated solutions is to determine whether they provide correct results in limiting situations that have been calculated by other methods. Show that the image solution of Fig. 4–3 approaches the image solution of Fig. 4–1 when q approaches very close to the surface of the sphere, without coming into contact with it.

4–17. In Section 4–2 the potentials near a conducting sphere in a uniform field are calculated. A uniform field at the origin of coordinates could be created by placing very large point charges far from the origin, so that the relations obtained in Problem 4–12 could be used. Suppose a uniform field to be created by placing one point charge $+q$ at $z = -p$ and another point charge $-q$ at $z = +p$, where the magnitude of q depends upon p in such a manner as to make $q/4\pi\epsilon_0 p^2 = E_0/2$ a constant. Show that the potentials near a conducting sphere centered at the origin in this uniform field can be obtained from those calculated in Problem 4–12(a).

*4–18. A horizontal metallic surface in the xy-plane is grounded and is so large that it can be considered infinite. An ideal dipole of moment $\mathbf{p}$ is located on the z-axis at $z = h$ and points in the xz-plane at the angle β with the z-axis. Find expressions in cylindrical coordinates for the potential V above the plane and for the surface charge density σ on the plane, (a) when $\beta = 0°$, and (b) when $\beta = 90°$.

*4–19. A positive point charge q placed outside an insulated metallic sphere is attracted toward the sphere. If a is the radius of the sphere and d is the distance of q from its center, find the net charge Q on the sphere that is required to cancel the attraction and produce zero force on q.

4–20. Suppose the point charge q, inside the hollow conducting sphere of Fig. 4–2, is replaced by an ideal dipole of moment $\mathbf{p}$. Find expressions for V inside the sphere and for σ on the inside surface of the sphere, (a) when $\mathbf{p}$ is directed upward perpendicular to OQ, and (b) when $\mathbf{p}$ is directed to the right parallel to OQ.

*4–21. A plane metallic surface is horizontal, is connected to ground, and is so large as to be considered infinite. An infinitely long filament that is a distance h from the plane and parallel to it carries a uniform linear charge density λ. Employ an image solution to find (a) the charge density on the plane, and (b) the force per unit length on the charged filament.

4–22. A hollow conducting cylinder of internal radius a is infinitely long and is connected to earth. A very fine wire, charged to λ in coul/m, is stretched parallel to the cylindrical axis but is a distance h, in meters, from this axis. Find the force per meter of length on the wire.

*4–23. A nonconducting spherical shell of radius a has a potential distribution on its surface that is given by $V = A \cos \theta$ in spherical coordinates. (a) Find the potential inside this sphere.   (b) Find the potential outside this sphere. (c) Find the charge density σ on the surface of this sphere.

4-24. A metallic sphere of radius a is suspended in a perfect vacuum. Draw a straight line from its center at O to a point M which is d meters from O. Place a dipole of moment $\mathbf{p}$ at M perpendicular to OM. For the plane defined by $\mathbf{p}$ and OM:

(a) Calculate a general expression for V outside the sphere, in terms of p, a, d, and the coordinates r and θ, measured from O and the line OM respectively.

(b) Obtain a general expression for the R-component of field E_R, and

(c) show that the density of charge induced on the surface of the sphere in this plane is given by

$$\sigma = \frac{-p \sin \theta}{\tau_s} \left[\frac{\gamma^3 (1 - \gamma^2)}{(1 + \gamma^2 - 2\gamma \cos \theta)^{5/2}} \right],$$

where $\gamma = a/d$ and $\tau_s = 4\pi a^3/3$, the volume of the sphere.

[*Note.* The expressions for the potential and the field are much simpler when written in terms of symbols like r, which is the distance from M to the field point, since r is easily defined in terms of a, d, R, and θ.]

*4-25. The distance between the centers of two metallic spheres, each of radius a, is d. If the total charges on these spheres are Q and $-Q$ respectively, (a) calculate the electric field at the point midway between them, and (b) calculate the difference of potential between the two spheres.

4-26. Find the potential distribution inside the rectangular pipe shown in Fig. 4-8 when the same three sides have the potential $V = 0$ while the fourth side has the potential $f(x) = e^{x/a}$.

*4-27. A two-dimensional capacitor is constructed as shown in Fig. 4-19. The conducting sheet that is connected to the positive terminal of the battery coincides with the mathematical surface given by $x^3 - 3xy^2 = A^3$, where A^3 is a positive constant, and the conducting sheet connected to the negative terminal coincides with $x^3 - 3xy^2 = 0$. The portion of this latter sheet that is connected through G is electrically isolated from the remainder by small breaks at (X, Y) and $(X, -Y)$.

(a) For the capacitor that is determined by the charge that would flow through G on charging, find the capacitance per unit length in terms of A, X, and Y.

(b) Find the charge density on the positive sheet where it cuts the x-axis at $x = A$.

(c) Find the charge density on the isolated V-shaped section as a function of x and find the total charge on this section.

*4-28. In some problems it has been assumed that a fine wire, used to assure that two conductors have the same potential in a static field, would not otherwise disturb the potentials of the field. Such a wire would disturb the potentials if and only if it has charges distributed on it. The magnitude of the disturbance caused by a fine wire can be estimated by solving a concentric cylinder problem with a constant potential difference between the cylinders. Keeping the radius of the outer cylinder constant at b, determine how the charge density λ on the inner cylinder varies as its radius r approaches zero.

FIGURE 4–19.

*4–29. A capacitor consists of two infinitely long conducting cylinders having different axes, one inside the other. Its geometry and dimensions are such that the complex function of Section 4–9 can be used for the analysis. The values of m for the outer and inner cylinders are 3 and 4, respectively. Calculate (a) the capacitance C_l per meter of length, and (b) the dimensions and eccentricity of the cylinders. (c) Can the inside and outside radii of each cylinder be determined in meters, from the information given here? (d) Can you draw any general conclusions concerning the dependence of C_l upon the absolute dimensions of two-dimensional capacitors?

4–30. To draw a family of eccentric circles like those shown in Fig. 4–17, some method for determining the radius a and the distance d of the center of each circle from the median plane is needed.

(a) Prove that $s^2 + a^2 = d^2$, where s is the distance of either pole from the median plane.

(b) A construction circle of radius s can be drawn about the origin, through which all the eccentric circles must pass. A good distribution of these eccentric circles is obtained by marking equidistant points on one quadrant of the construction circle and then drawing one eccentric circle through each of these points. To draw the circle passing through one of these points, designated by P, connect P with the origin O by a straight line making the angle β with the x-axis. Show that the radius a of this eccentric circle is the length of the straight line drawn from P to the x-axis perpendicular to OP. Show also that this determines the center of this eccentric circle.

(c) Show that the value of m for this eccentric circle is given by $m = \csc \beta \pm \operatorname{ctn} \beta$.

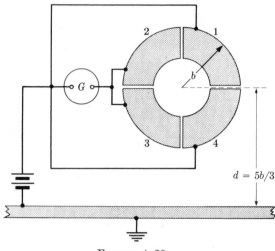

$$d = 5b/3$$

FIGURE 4–20.

(d) Show that the two values for m (m_1 and m_2) given by the equation in (c), correspond to equal cylinders symmetrically spaced on opposite sides of the median plane. Show also that $m_1 m_2 = 1$.

*4–31. Figure 4–20 shows a capacitor consisting of an infinite conducting plane and an infinitely long cylinder. The cylinder has been cut into four quadrants, 1, 2, 3, and 4, which, although insulated from one another, can be connected electrically in any desired manner. The diagram shows quadrants 1 and 4 connected as "guard rings," so that only those charges flowing to quadrants 2 and 3 are measured by G. Neglecting the widths of the saw cuts, calculate the capacitance (a) when quadrants 1 and 4 are the guard rings (as shown), and (b) when quadrants 1 and 2 are the guard rings.

Lines of electric field flux extend from each quadrant to that portion of the plane on which an equal and opposite charge resides. (c) Determine the region on the plane where the flux lines from quadrant 3 terminate.

4–32. A transmission line consists of two copper cylinders of radius a, with their centers separated a distance D. Find the capacitance per meter, C_l.

*4–33. Capacitors like the concentric-cylinder capacitor of Fig. 3–13 have been constructed as standards. How much error would be produced by an error of $d = a\,\delta$ in centering the cylinders, where a is the radius of the inner cylinder and $\delta \ll 1$ is a dimensionless fraction. Assume the inner radius of the outer cylinder to be b.

4–34. Show that the results obtained in Problems 4–21 and 4–22 by image methods can be obtained by the use of complex variables.

*4–35. Solve Problem 4–21 when the charged filament is replaced by an infinitely long metallic cylinder of radius a having the uniform linear charge density λ, where $d > a$ is the distance between the center of the cylinder and the plane.

CHAPTER 5

DIELECTRIC MATERIALS

A perfect dielectric is a material whose internal electric charges are so tightly bound that no electric current can be conducted through it. It is therefore a perfect insulator. While perfect dielectrics do not exist in nature, the properties of real dielectrics are best understood in terms of the properties of perfect dielectrics. Also, many insulating materials have conductivities at room temperature which are less than 10^{-20} of the conductivity of copper, and such conductivities may be treated as zero for most purposes.

While the electric charges are not free to move through these materials, the positive and negative charges may be displaced relative to each other in the presence of an electric field. If a knowledge of the exact displacement of each charged particle were necessary for the solution of electrostatic problems involving dielectrics, such solutions would be impossible. Fortunately, the fields in and around a dielectric may be treated as though they originate from a continuum of charge rather than from individual charges, provided the dielectric is sufficiently extensive to contain a large number of charges. This size limitation has little practical significance, since a solid particle as small as 10^{-3} mm on a side contains more than 10^{12} charged particles.

While a knowledge of the electronic structure of matter is not necessary for the solution of most practical problems involving dielectrics, some knowledge is indispensable for the solution of more sophisticated problems in solid-state physics. Since this also provides a better understanding of the macroscopic properties of dielectrics, a brief introduction to the structure of solids is presented in this chapter.

5–1 The atomic structure of matter. The planetary model of an atom in which negatively charged electrons circle about a very heavy, positively charged nucleus was proposed by Rutherford in 1911 to explain the scattering of alpha particles passing through matter. The predominant small-angle scattering was attributed to numerous collisions with the light electrons, while the occasional large-angle scattering was attributed to very heavy, positively charged nuclei of small diameter. The large-angle nuclear scattering was well described by the Coulomb inverse square law down to distances as small as 10^{-15} m, and so it was assumed that the nuclei were no larger than this.

Bohr-Sommerfeld model of the atom. By 1916 the Bohr-Sommerfeld model of the atom had been developed, in which the planetary electrons are confined to move in well-defined elliptical orbits whose ellipticities and distances from the nucleus are specified by certain quantum conditions. The total energy of an orbital electron is the sum of its potential energy, due to the coulomb attraction to the nucleus, and its kinetic energy, associated with the angular velocity required to keep the electron from spiraling into the nucleus. A major assumption of this model is that electrons circling the nucleus in the specified orbits, or "shells," lose no energy and hence are able to remain in the orbit indefinitely. This is in direct contradiction to classical electromagnetic theory, in which any accelerating charged particle emits energy in the form of electromagnetic radiation, as will be shown in Chapter 11.

It is assumed that energy may be emitted by orbital electrons only in discrete amounts in the process of dropping from one atomic shell to a lower-energy shell. Quantum rules specify the number of electrons which may occupy a given shell, so that, in general, the lower-energy orbits are filled and electrons from higher orbits are unable to make the transition. If the orbital electrons are thermally excited, or otherwise caused to jump from lower shells to higher shells, they may then spontaneously drop back to the lower-energy shell and emit electromagnetic radiation with a characteristic frequency. This frequency is determined by the quantum condition

$$W = hf,$$

where W is the energy difference between the shells, $h = 6.625 \times 10^{-34}$ joule·sec is Planck's constant, and f is the frequency of the radiation. Selecting the electron orbits to obey the condition that the angular momentum has values of $nh/2\pi$, where n may have values of 1, 2, 3, ..., ensures that the theoretically predicted frequencies for radiation resulting from the transition of electrons from one shell to a lower shell will be in excellent agreement with the characteristic atomic spectra. Furthermore, the successive filling of the atomic shells, in accordance with the specified quantum conditions, results in the same periodicity as is exhibited by the periodic table.

Since its conception, the Bohr-Sommerfeld model of the atom has explained so much experimental data that its usefulness as a model is no longer questioned. However, the explanation of some experimental results has had to wait for the development of wave-mechanical calculations.

Wave mechanics. According to the wave-mechanical calculations first proposed by Schroedinger in 1926, an electron cannot be located at an exact point in space, but must be represented by a probability distribution. The quantity actually calculated, known as a wave function, is a function of the coordinates x, y, and z, and is frequently represented by the Greek letter ψ. The probability of an electron being at any point in space is given by the value of $|\psi|^2$ at that point, where $|\psi|$ is the absolute value of the complex wave function. The most probable location for the electron corresponds to the point or curve in space where $|\psi|^2$ is maximum. Since the probability of a given electron being somewhere in space is necessarily unity, the wave function must also have the property that

$$\iiint |\psi|^2 \, dx \, dy \, dz = 1$$

when the integration is performed over all space.

Wave-mechanical solutions are undertaken because they yield results not obtainable by classical models or by the semiclassical quantum model of Bohr and Sommerfeld. For those problems where the classical or semi-classical quantum models are adequate, however, the wave-mechanical calculations must yield essentially the same results. It should not be surprising, therefore, that many features of the Bohr-Sommerfeld model of the atom can be derived directly from wave mechanics. A calculation of the electron wave functions for various atoms, for example, reveals that the locus of the maximum value for $|\psi|^2$ is essentially the same as in the electron orbits proposed by Bohr and Sommerfeld.

For problems in which the simple atomic model gives basically the same results as wave mechanics, it is convenient to talk in terms of the simple model because it is easier to visualize than are the abstract wave functions. A general understanding of the properties of dielectrics can be obtained from the simple atomic model even though the details of the interactions between the atoms and electrons can be explained only in terms of wave-mechanical calculations. Even in semiclassical discussions, however, the orbital electrons are often referred to as the electron cloud or charged cloud, in recognition of the fact that the spatial locations of electrons are known only in terms of a probability distribution.

Solid materials. In any solid material the atoms are regularly spaced with respect to each other in a geometric pattern which is characteristic of the material and which is referred to as its crystal structure or crystal lattice. The electronic orbits of the atoms in a solid are very little changed from those of free atoms, with the exception of the outermost orbits, where large perturbations are produced by the proximity of neighboring atoms. In some materials, notably metals, the perturbations are of such form that the electrons in outer orbits become free to wander through the lattice. Such materials are referred to as conductors. In most solids, however, all electrons are relatively tightly bound to their atomic nuclei located on the lattice sites and are thus unable to conduct electric current. These solids are known as insulators or dielectrics.

The binding in these materials may be divided somewhat crudely into two types, *covalent* and *ionic*. In the first case the coulomb force between a positive nucleus and its orbital electrons is sufficiently strong that the number of electrons orbiting each nucleus in the solid is the same as for the free atom. Each atom is therefore electrically neutral, and the binding energy between atoms is of a quantum-mechanical origin. This type of bonding frequently occurs between identical atoms in a solid or between different elements found near the center of the periodic table. Some typical examples are diamond, sulfur, germanium, indium antimanide, and silicon carbide.

In an ionic bond, the quantum forces, which tend to give lower energies for completely filled electron shells, fill the outer shell of one atom by removing electrons from the slightly filled outer shell of a neighboring atom. The atom which gains the extra electron or electrons becomes a negative ion, while the neighboring atom becomes a positive ion. The binding energy between the ions is then supplied primarily by the coulomb attraction. Ionic bonding frequently occurs between two atoms when one has a nearly filled outer shell while the other has a nearly empty outer shell. Some examples of this ionic bonding are sodium chloride, lithium fluoride, silver chloride, magnesium oxide, and calcium oxide.

5–2 Mechanisms of polarization. Regardless of which type of bonding dominates in a given crystal, the gross charge distribution within the lattice will be the same. Positive nuclei will be regularly spaced throughout the lattice, and the electrons will also be regularly distributed, with a much greater concentration near each nucleus than in the intervening regions. The application of an electric field will displace the electrons surrounding each nucleus a very small distance opposite to the field, so that each nucleus and its electron cloud form a small electric dipole. The displacement produced by a given field depends upon the binding energy between the electron cloud and the nucleus and is a characteristic of the particular dielectric.

In ionic crystals a second form of polarization takes place simultaneously with electron displacement, in which each positively charged ion, made up of the nucleus and its surrounding electron cloud, is displaced in the direction of the field, while the negatively charged ions are displaced in the opposite direction. The magnitude of this effect and its importance relative to electron displacement varies from one crystal to another.

A third mechanism of polarization can occur in a few materials that contain permanent electric dipoles. In the absence of any externally applied electric field, these dipoles are randomly oriented throughout the crystal by thermal vibrations of the lattice, so that there is no net polarization. An externally applied electric field causes polarization by creating a greater alignment parallel to the field. The origin of these internal dipoles is in the nonsymmetrical quantum-mechanical bonding forces which occasionally occur between two or more atoms. A very familiar

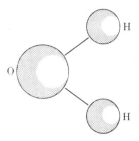

FIG. 5-1. The nonsymmetrical structure of the dipolar water molecule gives rise to a concentration of positive charge to the side of the oxygen atom where the two hydrogen atoms are bonded.

example of this is the water molecule, whose molecular structure is illustrated in Fig. 5-1. The nonsymmetrical location of the positively charged hydrogen ions produces a dipole moment pointing to the right in this figure. The resulting molecule is said to be polar, since it exhibits the properties of a small electric dipole.

Polarization and polarizability. A substance is said to be polarized when the vector sum of all the dipole moments within it is greater than zero. It would be meaningless to define the polarization at mathematical points within a material. However, *polarization at a physical point is defined as the vector sum of the dipole moments per unit volume within the space defined by this physical point.* This polarization is designated by **P**, and it is a vector function of the coordinates. Whenever **P** is directly proportional to the average electric field **E**, within the physical point, the ratio $P/\epsilon_0 E = \chi$ is called the polarizability. The field's tendency to create dipoles is opposed by quantum-mechanical forces, while its tendency to line up permanent dipole moments is opposed by heat vibrations. The latter type of polarization is, therefore, strongly dependent upon temperature, while the former is almost independent of temperature.

Determination of the mechanism of polarization. The temperature dependence of the polarizability originating from permanent dipoles is used to distinguish it from that of electronic or ionic origin. This dependency is well described by the Langevin-Debye equation for the polarizability,

$$\chi = \frac{C}{T},$$

where T is the absolute temperature and C is a constant dependent upon the material.

Further evidence as to the origin of electric polarization in a given substance can be obtained from its response to variations in the frequency of an alternating electric field applied to it. The frequency dependence of a dielectric which has dipolar, ionic, and electric charge displacement

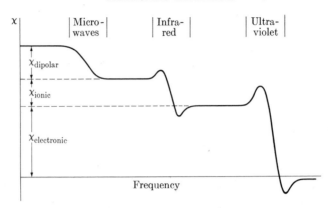

FIG. 5-2. Schematic frequency dependence of the several contributions to the polarizability. (After Charles Kittel, *Introduction to Solid State Physics*, 2nd ed., John Wiley & Sons, Inc., 1956.)

for electric field frequencies below the microwave region is represented in Fig. 5-2. Above the microwave region, the permanent electric dipoles do not have time to orient themselves relative to the field, and their contribution disappears. Above the infrared region, the ionic contribution drops out; and finally, for frequencies higher than those of ultraviolet light, the orbital contribution vanishes. Just before vanishing, the orbital and ionic contributions each pass through a resonance which results in the rapid fluctuations shown in the figure.

The usual method of measuring the polarizability of a dielectric is to compare the capacitance of a capacitor containing the substance with that when it is evacuated. The ratio of these two capacitances determines the polarizability. The capacitance is usually obtained by placing the capacitor in a resonant circuit in a manner which is described in more detail in the chapter on alternating currents. At microwave frequencies and above, measurements utilize a relationship between the index of refraction for electromagnetic radiations and the polarizability of the material. As is shown in Chapter 11, the index of refraction is proportional to the square root of the polarizability at high frequencies.

Static polarization. The exact mechanism of the polarization is important in some applications because it governs the temperature dependence and frequency response of the dielectric; and it is, of course, important in any detailed study of the structure of the material. However, the gross effect of the polarization is independent of the mechanism for static fields and for alternating fields up to frequencies near a million cycles per second.

To understand this effect, some more detailed definitions are needed. A polarization model will be utilized in which the negatively charged cloud surrounding each nucleus is shifted relative to it. Consider the two-

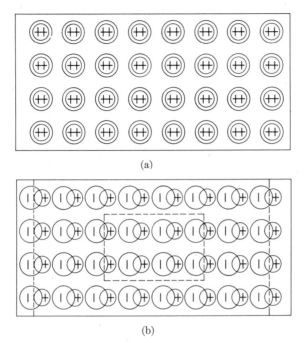

(a)

(b)

FIG. 5–3. (a) A bar of nonpolar dielectric in the absence of electric fields, in which the negative electron clouds neutralize the positive charge of each nucleus. (b) The same dielectric uniformly polarized toward the right. The centers of the electron clouds have shifted equal distances to the left, leaving excess plus charges on the right end and excess negative charges on the left end, with the interior still neutral.

dimensional representation of atoms in a solid bar, in Fig. 5–3. In the absence of an electric field the negatively charged cloud and the positively charged nucleus have the same center for each atom, as shown in Fig. 5–3(a). With the application of a field $\mathbf{E}$, Fig. 5–3(b), the negatively charged cloud shifts opposite to the field by an amount which will be designated by $-\mathbf{R}$. It is actually more convenient to think of the positive nucleus as being moved a distance $\mathbf{R}$ with the field.

Assume for the moment that the charge displacements are the same for each atom or, in other words, that the polarization is uniform throughout the bar. The interior of the bar retains its electric neutrality, since the negative charge that moved into any volume is just offset by the negative charge that moved out of this volume, provided the volume is large compared with an atomic volume. This is illustrated by the dashed rectangle in Fig. 5–3(b), which contains an equal number of positive and negative charges. Electric neutrality is not maintained, however, on the ends of the bar, where there were no charges of opposite sign available to cancel the displaced charges. If σ_p is the areal charge density induced on the right-hand surface, the total charge there is $\sigma_p A$, where A is the cross-sectional area. An equal but opposite charge $-\sigma_p A$ resides on the left.

The charge on the ends is independent of the length of the bar and the total dipole moment of the bar is given by the product of one charge times the distance of separation of the charges, $\sigma_p A l$. If ρ_1 represents the number of displaceable charges per unit volume and R is the average of their displacements, then $\sigma_p = \rho_1 R$, and the total dipole moment is $\rho_1 R A l$, which is proportional to the volume. The polarization at every point in the bar can be written in vector notation as

$$\mathbf{P} = \rho_1 \mathbf{R}, \qquad (5\text{-}1)$$

which is a general relation even for nonuniform polarizations. When the polarization is perpendicular to a surface of the dielectric, as it is at the ends of the bar in Fig. 5-3, the surface density of polarization charges σ_p is equal to $\mathbf{P}$. In any case, in fact, $\sigma_p = P_n$, where P_n is the component of $\mathbf{P}$ normal to the surface of the dielectric. For those materials in which $\mathbf{R}$ is proportional to the average electric field within each physical point, the constant of proportionality is $\chi\epsilon_0/\rho_1$, and the polarization can be expressed in its usual form as

$$\mathbf{P} = \chi\epsilon_0\mathbf{E}. \qquad (5\text{-}2)$$

Values of χ, which is called the polarizability or the electric susceptibility of the material, that have been determined electrostatically at room temperatures are given in Table 5-1 for a few substances.

TABLE 5-1

POLARIZABILITIES OF SOME SUBSTANCES

Helium	0.0000684
Oxygen	0.000523
Water	79.0
Quartz	3.3
Sulfur	3.0

The magnitude of the average displacement $\mathbf{R}$ can be obtained from the special case of pure dry sulfur, which is an excellent insulator. It has 16 electrons per atom, of which 4 are much less tightly bound to the nucleus than are the remaining 12. Since the number of sulfur atoms per cubic meter is 3.8×10^{28}, the density of the 4 displaceable negative charges is 15×10^{28} electrons/m³ or -24×10^9 coul/m³. The displacement of this density of negative charges against the field is equivalent to a displacement of $\rho_1 = 24 \times 10^9$ coul/m³ with the field. If the bar in Fig. 5-3 were composed of sulfur and the average internal fields throughout the bar could be maintained at 1000 volts/m, the polarization given by Eq. (5–2) would be

$$P = 3.0 \times 8.85 \times 10^{-12} \times 1000 = 26.6 \times 10^{-9} \text{ coul/m}^2.$$

Using Eq. (5–1), the relative displacement of the electronic cloud from the nucleus then would be 1.1×10^{-18} m, which is less than a thousandth of the nuclear diameter. Nevertheless, this small displacement of the relatively large density of charges would produce a surface-charge density of magnitude 26.6×10^{-9} coul/m^2 or 16.5×10^{10} electrons/m^2 on each end of the bar.

These calculations and conclusions are based upon a bar of homogeneous dielectric material that is assumed to be uniformly polarized. In practice it is difficult to achieve this uniformity even when the material is homogeneous. The presence of charges on the end surfaces tends to depolarize regions near these surfaces. Often the material is not homogeneous, and its polarizability varies from point to point. Such inhomogeneities usually result in polarization charges being distributed throughout the volume of the material. The volume density of polarization charge will be designated by ρ_p. Note that ρ_p will always be much smaller than ρ_1, since ρ_p is obtained from the algebraic sum of two nearly equal and opposite densities of magnitude ρ_1. The polarization charge density ρ_p can be observed experimentally but ρ_1 cannot. The quantity ρ_1 has been introduced only as an aid to analysis, and will be abandoned as soon as general relations have been established.

5–3 Maxwell's first relation. To investigate the magnitude of ρ_p, it is necessary to calculate the difference between the charge moving into and out of a small elementary volume like any one of those shown in Figs. 3–6, 3–7, or 3–8. For simplicity, the volume in rectangular coordinates shown in Fig. 5–4 will be used. The charge moving in through the shaded surface on the left is $\rho_1 R_y \, \Delta x \, \Delta z$, and that moving out through the shaded surface on the right is

$$+\rho_1 R_y \, \Delta x \, \Delta z + \left(\frac{\partial}{\partial y}\right)(\rho_1 R_y \, \Delta x \, \Delta z)\, \Delta y.$$

The net charge remaining in the element due to this process is the charge entering one side minus the charge leaving the other, or

$$-\left(\frac{\partial}{\partial y}\right)(\rho_1 R_y \, \Delta x \, \Delta z)\, \Delta y.$$

The elementary volume has three such pairs of surfaces, and the net charge remaining inside, due to the charges moving through all six surfaces, is

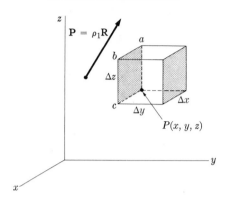

FIG. 5–4. On polarization of a dielectric, the charge moving into and out of an elementary volume leaves a net charge density of $\rho_p = -\nabla \cdot \mathbf{P}$.

just the sum of three expressions similar to this one. The net charge remaining inside is then

$$\left[-\frac{\partial}{\partial y}(\rho_1 R_y) - \frac{\partial}{\partial z}(\rho_1 R_z) - \frac{\partial}{\partial x}(\rho_1 R_x) \right] \Delta x \, \Delta y \, \Delta z.$$

In this expression, $(\partial/\partial y)(\rho_1 R_y \, \Delta x \, \Delta z) \, \Delta y$ has been written as

$$\left(\frac{\partial}{\partial y} \right)(\rho_1 R_y) \, \Delta x \, \Delta y \, \Delta z$$

because

$$\left(\frac{\partial}{\partial y} \right)(\Delta x \, \Delta z) = 0.$$

A similar situation obtains for the other two partial derivatives.

The polarization charge density at the physical point defined by this elemental volume is obtained by dividing this expression by $\Delta x \, \Delta y \, \Delta z$. The resulting expression may be written in vector notation as

$$\rho_p = -\nabla \cdot (\rho_1 \mathbf{R}) = -\nabla \cdot \mathbf{P}, \tag{5–3}$$

which is the same equation that would have been obtained by using the general volume element of Fig. 3–8 instead of that of Fig. 5–4.

In Section 3–2 a general expression, Eq. (3–5), was developed in which ρ expressed the charge density obtained by dividing the algebraic sum of all the charges in a volume element by its volume. However, the polarization charges are harder to measure than are the net charges on charged dielectrics or charges that move through conductors. Therefore the total charge density, which will now be designated by ρ_t, is usually divided into two parts, $\rho_t = \rho_p + \rho$, where ρ_p is the polarization charge density and

ρ includes all the charges that are not specifically polarization charges. The charges included in ρ are frequently called the "real" charges. With this modification the differential form of Gauss' law found in Eq. (3–7) can be written as

$$\boldsymbol{\nabla} \cdot \epsilon_0 \mathbf{E} = \rho_t = \rho_p + \rho.$$

Substituting the expression for ρ_p from Eq. (5–3) and transposing, we obtain

$$\boldsymbol{\nabla} \cdot (\epsilon_0 \mathbf{E} + \mathbf{P}) = \rho$$

or

$$\boldsymbol{\nabla} \cdot \mathbf{D} = \rho, \tag{5–4}$$

where $\mathbf{D}$ is defined by

$$\mathbf{D} = \epsilon_0 \mathbf{E} + \mathbf{P}. \tag{5–5}$$

This defines a new vector function of the coordinates that is called the *displacement vector* $\mathbf{D}$, which was introduced by Maxwell. Equation (5–4) is called *Maxwell's first field relation* in differential form. This can be integrated over any general volume τ surrounded by a closed surface s, to give

$$\int_\tau \rho \, d\tau = \int_\tau \boldsymbol{\nabla} \cdot \mathbf{D} \, d\tau = \int_s \mathbf{D} \cdot d\mathbf{s},$$

using the divergence theorem. *The integral form of Maxwell's first relation* is usually written as

$$\int_s \mathbf{D} \cdot d\mathbf{s} = \int_\tau \rho \, d\tau. \tag{5–6}$$

Physically, both forms of this relation state that the net flux of $\mathbf{D}$ out of any volume is equal to the algebraic sum of the "real" charges within that volume, no matter how large or small the volume.

The vectors $\mathbf{D}$ and $\mathbf{P}$ are defined only at physical points and are very useful for dealing with real materials. It would be meaningless to define them at mathematical points. On the other hand, an electric field can, in principle, be defined at a mathematical point as the limit of the force per unit test charge, as the test charge at this point approaches zero. However, to be consistent the vector $\mathbf{E}$ in Eq. (5–5) should be defined at a physical point. *Unless otherwise specified, the* $\mathbf{E}$ *used in this text will be defined as the volume average throughout a physical point of the electric fields defined at mathematical points, for fields that can be derived from Coulomb's inverse square law.* This ignores quantum-mechanical forces that may be involved, for example, in chemical reactions that take place in an electrolytic cell. This definition ensures that $\mathbf{E}$ represents a conservative field in all static cases. As will be shown in Chapter 7, it also ensures that $\mathbf{E}$ is conservative, in general, so long as there are no magnetic fields in the neighborhood that are changing with time.

5–4 Dielectric constants. In general, all solids consist of crystals that are somewhat more easily polarized in one direction than in another; that is, they are not isotropic.* Usually, in such materials **P** is not parallel to **E**, and therefore **D** is not parallel to either **P** or **E**. Such effects are most important in single crystals of those substances that are strongly anisotropic. In many substances the differences in polarizabilities from one direction to another are small and, furthermore, most solids are made up of a multitude of randomly oriented small crystals. Therefore the majority of ordinary dielectrics can be treated as isotropic materials in which **P** is proportional to **E** and also parallel to it. This condition was tacitly assumed when Eq. (5–2) was written. When Eq. (5–2) and Eq. (5–5) are combined, we have

$$\mathbf{D} = \epsilon_0\mathbf{E} + \epsilon_0\chi\mathbf{E} = \epsilon_0(1 + \chi)\mathbf{E},$$

which can be written as

$$\mathbf{D} = K\epsilon_0\mathbf{E} = \epsilon\mathbf{E}, \tag{5–7}$$

by defining $K = 1 + \chi$ and $\epsilon = K\epsilon_0$. The constant K is usually called the "dielectric constant" of the isotropic material and ϵ is the permittivity.

Anisotropic crystals. Dielectric constants cannot be expressed as simply as in Eq. (5–7) for anisotropic single crystals or for groups of such crystals that are preferentially oriented. In these cases, the general expression† for **D** is given by

$$D_x = \epsilon_{11}E_x + \epsilon_{12}E_y + \epsilon_{13}E_z,$$

$$D_y = \epsilon_{21}E_x + \epsilon_{22}E_y + \epsilon_{23}E_z,$$

$$D_z = \epsilon_{31}E_x + \epsilon_{32}E_y + \epsilon_{33}E_z,$$

where the nine dielectric constants can be reduced to six by means of the relations $\epsilon_{12} = \epsilon_{21}$, $\epsilon_{13} = \epsilon_{31}$, and $\epsilon_{23} = \epsilon_{32}$, which can be proved. These general expressions for the rectangular components of **D** also hold for isotropic substances, where $\epsilon_{11} = \epsilon_{22} = \epsilon_{33} = \epsilon$ and the remaining constants are zero. Substances may be nearly isotropic in static or low-frequency electric fields and may become strongly anisotropic at high frequencies. For example, the anisotropic nature of quartz crystals at optical frequencies‡ is responsible for the double refraction and the polarization phenomena these crystals exhibit in visible light.

---

* In addition to anisotropy, some substances show hysteresis effects. That is, when they have been polarized by an electric field, they may retain some polarization even after the field is removed.

† Georg Joos, *Theoretical Physics*, 1st ed., pp. 330–362, G. E. Stechert and Company, New York, 1934.

‡ Jenkins and White, *Fundamentals of Optics*, 3rd ed., pp. 535–553, McGraw-Hill Book Company, New York, 1957.

In general, liquids are isotropic at all frequencies, but some liquids can be made anisotropic to high-frequency fields by application of either a steady electric field or a steady magnetic field. The anisotropy to visible light produced by steady electric fields is called the Kerr effect, and that produced by steady magnetic fields is called the Faraday effect. Such effects are also exhibited by some solids.

Whenever the dielectric constants for an anisotropic material are true constants, independent of the magnitude or direction of $\mathbf{E}$, the analysis can be somewhat simplified in special cases. For example, when a capacitor containing such a dielectric is being charged, the field at any point in the dielectric changes its magnitude but not its direction, so that $\mathbf{E} = \gamma \mathbf{E}_f$, where $\mathbf{E}_f$ is the final field at this point and γ varies from zero to unity during the charging. At the same time, the value of $\mathbf{D}$ at any point is given by $\mathbf{D} = \gamma \mathbf{D}_f$, where $\mathbf{D}_f$ is the final value of $\mathbf{D}$ at this point. Thus the angle between $\mathbf{D}$ and $\mathbf{E}$ remains constant throughout the charging process. This simplifying relation is used for the discussion of energy relations in Section 5-10.

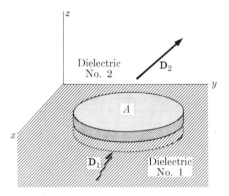

FIG. 5-5. Gaussian pillbox with its lower half in dielectric No. 1 and its upper half in dielectric No. 2.

5-5 Boundary conditions with dielectrics. In order to solve electrostatic problems involving dielectric materials, the boundary conditions between two different dielectrics or between a dielectric and a metal must be obtained. A very small cylindrical pillbox can be constructed as shown in Fig. 5-5, with one of the flat circular surfaces in dielectric No. 1 and the other in dielectric No. 2, both being very close to the bounding surface represented by the xy-plane.

The displacement vector $\mathbf{D}$ may be represented by $\mathbf{D}_1$ and $\mathbf{D}_2$ in the two media, and their respective components normal to the bounding surface may be represented by D_{1n} and D_{2n}. The boundary conditions can then be obtained by applying Eq. (5-6),

$$\int_s \mathbf{D} \cdot d\mathbf{s} = \int_\tau \rho \, d\tau,$$

to this pillbox, where the integral on the right is zero because there are no real charges inside the pillbox. By making the area of the cylindrical surface very small compared with the two flat circular surfaces, the contribution to the integral on the left from the cylindrical surface can be made as negligibly small as desired. The only contributions then will come from the two flat surfaces, each of area A. These areas too may be made so small that $\mathbf{D}$ is constant over them, so that the left integral of Eq. (5-6) gives

$$-D_{1n}A + D_{2n}A = 0,$$

and the boundary condition becomes

$$D_{1n} = D_{2n}. \tag{5-8}$$

Another boundary condition may be obtained from the fact that $\mathbf{E}$ is conservative, so that $\oint \mathbf{E} \cdot d\mathbf{l} = 0$ for any closed curve that can be drawn in an electrostatic field. A closed rectangular loop can be chosen as shown in Fig. 5-6, where $b \gg a$, although b may be made so small that the field in each medium may be considered uniform over the parts of the path that lie in it. With these assumptions the normal and tangential components of the electric field $\mathbf{E}_1$ in dielectric No. 1 can be designated E_{1n} and E_{1t}, while the corresponding components of $\mathbf{E}_2$ can be designated by E_{2n} and E_{2t}. Starting from the upper right corner and progressing counterclockwise, the line integral is

$$-E_{2t}b - E_{2n}a - E_{1n}a + E_{1t}b + E_{1n}a + E_{2n}a = 0,$$

which gives

$$E_{2t} = E_{1t}. \tag{5-9}$$

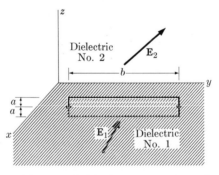

FIG. 5-6. Rectangular path for the line integration $\oint \mathbf{E} \cdot d\mathbf{l} = 0$, with half of the path in each of the adjoining dielectrics.

Equations (5–8) and (5–9) provide the boundary conditions needed for solving problems involving interfaces between two dielectrics.

In the special case where the boundary is between a conductor and a dielectric, **E** is zero everywhere in the conductor. Therefore, since $E_t = 0$ in the metal, it is necessarily zero in the dielectric also. While $E_n = 0$ in the metal, it is not zero in the dielectric, because a real charge resides at the bounding surface of the metal. From the Maxwell relation it can be seen that if D_n is the component of **D** in the dielectric normal to the conducting surface, then

$$D_n = \sigma, \tag{5–10}$$

where σ is the surface density of charge on the conductor. Typical fields near boundaries between different kinds of media are shown in Fig. 5–7. On crossing the boundary separating the two isotropic dielectrics of Fig. 5–7(a) the field changes direction toward the normal, because dielectric No. 1 has been assumed to have greater polarizability than dielectric No. 2. The fields **D** and **E** remain parallel to each other in each isotropic medium,

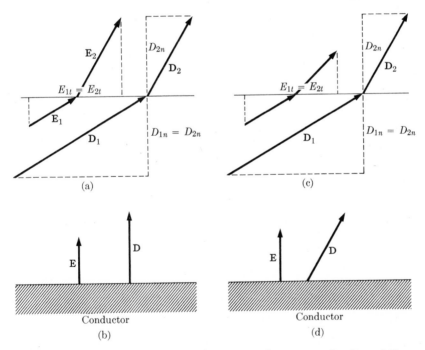

FIG. 5–7. Electric vectors at a surface separating two media: **D** and **E** are parallel in linear isotropic media but not in anisotropic media. The **E** vector is always perpendicular to a conducting surface. (a) Isotropic to isotropic dielectric media. (b) Conductor to isotropic dielectric medium. (c) Isotropic to anisotropic dielectric media. (d) Conductor to anisotropic dielectric medium.

while $D_{n1} = D_{n2}$ and $E_{t1} = E_{t2}$. At the boundary between a conductor and the isotropic dielectric of Fig. 5–7(b), **D** and **E** must both be normal to the surface, because they must be parallel and $E_t = 0$. In this case the conductor has a surface density of charge $\sigma = D$. At the boundary between the isotropic and the anisotropic dielectric shown in Fig. 5–7(c), **D** and **E** are parallel in the first dielectric but not in the second. Their directions and magnitudes must be such as to satisfy both boundary conditions; namely, $D_{1n} = D_{2n}$ and $E_{1t} = E_{2t}$. Finally, at the boundary between a conductor and the nonisotropic dielectric, illustrated in Fig. 5–7(d), **E** must be normal because $E_t = 0$, but **D** may be at some angle to the surface, since it is only necessary that $D_n = \sigma$.

These conditions also may be used to show that the surface density of polarization charge is given by $\sigma_p = P_n$, where P_n is the component of **P** parallel to the outward-drawn normal to the surface. It is simpler to integrate Eq. (5–3) directly over the volume of the pillbox in Fig. 5–5, to obtain

$$\int_\tau \rho_p \, d\tau = -\int_\tau \mathbf{\nabla} \cdot \mathbf{P} \, d\tau = -\int_s \mathbf{P} \cdot d\mathbf{s}.$$

Again making the cylindrical surfaces small compared with A and making A small enough so that the fields are uniform over the flat surfaces, this relation becomes $\sigma_p A = (P_{1n} - P_{2n})A$, or

$$\sigma_p = P_{1n} - P_{2n},$$

for the net polarization-charge density on the surface of separation. If dielectric No. 2 is replaced with a vacuum, the relation becomes

$$\sigma_p = P_n.$$

5–6 Uniqueness theorem with dielectric materials. Problems involving stationary groups of charges and charged conductors in empty space have been discussed in Chapter 4, where the uniqueness of the solutions for these problems has also been treated. In most of the real problems in electrostatics, the spaces are not empty but contain one or more dielectric materials. The introduction of dielectric materials into these problems necessarily modifies the problem-solving procedures, which in turn requires a reappraisal of the uniqueness of the resulting solutions. A perfectly general discussion would need to consider anisotropic and non-homogeneous dielectric materials, which may also exhibit hysteresis effects. However, the little that can be gained from maintaining such perfect generality does not justify the additional complications that would be introduced. For practical purposes it is sufficient to consider two homogeneous and isotropic materials with different dielectric constants occupying a closed space which is surrounded by some surface with known boundary conditions. For this discussion an air space or an empty space may be considered to be one of the dielectrics.

Figure 5–8 shows two dielectric materials, with dielectric constants K_1 and K_2, occupying a closed space on the surface of which the boundary conditions are known. The outer surface in contact with dielectric No. 1 is designated by s_1, that in contact with dielectric No. 2 is designated by s_2, and the common surface separating the two is designated by s_c. The two dielectrics occupy volumes τ_1 and τ_2 respectively. If the boundaries have been chosen so that $\rho = 0$ in both τ_1 and τ_2,

$$\mathbf{\nabla} \cdot \mathbf{D} = \mathbf{\nabla} \cdot (-\epsilon \mathbf{\nabla} V) = 0$$

throughout both regions, including the common boundary s_c. However, since ϵ changes abruptly at this boundary, $\nabla^2 V \neq 0$ on s_c, although $\nabla^2 V = 0$ in both τ_1 and τ_2. It is usually necessary to obtain one mathematical expression V_1 for the potentials in τ_1 and another expression V_2 for the potentials in τ_2. The boundary conditions on s_1 and s_2 must be satisfied by V_1 and V_2 respectively, and the boundary conditions developed in the last section must be satisfied along s_c by the two functions together. Following a procedure similar to that of Section 4–3, it will be assumed that two other functions of the coordinates, V_1' and V_2', meet these requirements and that two new functions $\phi_1 = V_1 - V_1'$ and $\phi_2 = V_2 - V_2'$ can be defined.

Throughout dielectric No. 1, $\nabla^2 V_1 = \nabla^2 V_1' = 0$ and hence $\nabla^2 \phi_1 = 0$. Likewise, throughout dielectric No. 2, $\nabla^2 V_2 = \nabla^2 V_2' = 0$, and hence $\nabla^2 \phi_2 = 0$. On s_1 either $\phi_1 = 0$ or $\mathbf{\nabla}\phi_1 \cdot d\mathbf{s} = (\mathbf{\nabla} V_1 - \mathbf{\nabla} V_1') \cdot d\mathbf{s} = 0$, while on s_2 either $\phi_2 = 0$ or $\mathbf{\nabla}\phi_2 \cdot d\mathbf{s} = (\mathbf{\nabla} V_2 - \mathbf{\nabla} V_2') \cdot d\mathbf{s} = 0$. On

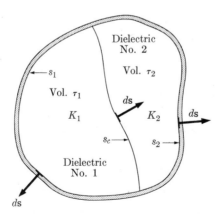

Fig. 5–8. Two linear dielectrics in a volume of general shape which is enclosed by a surface on which the electrostatic boundary conditions are known.

the common boundary, $V_1 = V_2$, $V_1' = V_2'$, and the normal components of $\mathbf{D}$ are continuous.

Considering dielectric No. 1 first, Gauss' theorem can be written as

$$\int_{s_1} \phi_1 \nabla \phi_1 \cdot d\mathbf{s} + \int_{s_c} \phi_1 \nabla \phi_1 \cdot d\mathbf{s} = \int_{\tau_1} \nabla \cdot (\phi_1 \nabla \phi_1) \, d\tau,$$

and because of the boundary conditions on s_1 the first integral is zero. Furthermore, the volume integral on the right can be written as

$$\int_{\tau_1} \nabla \cdot (\phi_1 \nabla \phi_1) \, d\tau = \int_{\tau_1} \phi_1 \nabla^2 \phi_1 \, d\tau + \int_{\tau_1} (\nabla \phi_1)^2 \, d\tau,$$

where the first integral on the right is zero because $\nabla^2 \phi_1 = 0$ throughout τ_1. The Gauss' theorem expression then reduces to

$$\int_{s_c} \phi_1 \nabla \phi_1 \cdot d\mathbf{s} = \int_{\tau_1} (\nabla \phi_1)^2 \, d\tau. \tag{5-11}$$

The analysis for the space inside τ_2 is similar to that just given for τ_1, but the $d\mathbf{s}$ in Gauss' theorem is conventionally chosen as positive along the outward-drawn normal of any closed space. If $d\mathbf{s}$ is chosen as pointing to the right along the surface s_c, as shown in Fig. 5–8, to keep the same element of area for both integrations, it will point into rather than out of τ_2, so that the surface integral for ϕ_2 must be given a negative sign:

$$-\int_{s_c} \phi_2 \nabla \phi_2 \cdot d\mathbf{s} = \int_{\tau_2} (\nabla \phi_2)^2 \, d\tau. \tag{5-12}$$

Multiplying Eq. (5–11) by K_1, Eq. (5–12) by K_2, and adding the two, we obtain

$$\int_{s_c} (\phi_1 K_1 \nabla \phi_1 - \phi_2 K_2 \nabla \phi_2) \cdot d\mathbf{s} = \int_{\tau_1} K_1 (\nabla \phi_1)^2 \, d\tau$$

$$+ \int_{\tau_2} K_2 (\nabla \phi_2)^2 \, d\tau. \tag{5-13}$$

Now since $V_1 = V_2$ and $V_1' = V_2'$ along the common boundary s_c, then $\phi_1 = \phi_2$ along s_c, so that ϕ_1 and ϕ_2 can be factored out of the integrand of the surface integral. Furthermore, the continuity of D_n along this boundary guarantees that

$$K_1 \nabla \phi_1 \cdot d\mathbf{s} - K_2 \nabla \phi_2 \cdot d\mathbf{s} = 0$$

along s_c, so that the surface integral of Eq. (5–13) is zero. Now $(\nabla \phi_1)^2$ is either positive or zero throughout τ_1 and $(\nabla \phi_2)^2$ is either positive or zero throughout τ_2, so that the two remaining integrals of Eq. (5–13) are separately zero. Following the arguments given in Section 4–3, these integrals can be zero only if ϕ_1 is constant in τ_1 and ϕ_2 is constant in τ_2, but since $\phi_1 = 0$ on s_1 and $\phi_2 = 0$ on s_2, ϕ_1 must be zero throughout τ_1 and ϕ_2 must be zero throughout τ_2. Thus the assumption that more than one set of solutions can be found to satisfy the conditions of the problem has led to absurdity, and any set of solutions that does satisfy all of the conditions is unique.

5-7 Dielectric sphere in a uniform field. A sphere made from a homogeneous and isotropic dielectric becomes polarized in an electric field. The effects produced by placing such a sphere in a uniform field are readily calculated with the assumption that $\mathbf{D} = \epsilon\mathbf{E}$ and $\epsilon = K\epsilon_0$ for the material of the sphere.

The origin of spherical coordinates can be placed at the center of this sphere of radius a, with the positive z-axis pointing in the direction of the field. Since there will be fields inside as well as outside the dielectric sphere, the potential inside will be designated by V_i and that outside by V_o. For values of r between zero and a, $\nabla^2 V_i = 0$, and for r between a and infinity, $\nabla^2 V_o = 0$. The boundary conditions at $r = a$, given by Eqs. (5-8) and (5-9) respectively, are

$$-\epsilon\frac{\partial V_i}{\partial r} = -\epsilon_0\frac{\partial V_o}{\partial r} \tag{5-14}$$

and

$$-\frac{\partial V_i}{\partial \theta} = -\frac{\partial V_o}{\partial \theta}. \tag{5-15}$$

An outer boundary for the region can be chosen where $r \gg a$, sufficiently far from the sphere to make its influence on the uniform field negligible. On this outer boundary, then,

$$V_o = -E_0 z = -E_0 r \cos\theta. \tag{5-16}$$

As in the conducting sphere problem of Section 4-4, symmetry suggests that the following solutions of Laplace's equation should fit the boundary conditions:

$$V_o = A_0 + \frac{B_0}{r} + A_1 r \cos\theta + \frac{B_1}{r^2}\cos\theta$$

and

$$V_i = C + Fr\cos\theta.$$

No terms with r in the denominator are included in V_i, because these would be infinite at $r = 0$. The boundary condition, Eq. (5-16), at $r \gg a$ gives

$$A_0 + A_1 r \cos\theta = -E_0 r \cos\theta,$$

and since this must hold for all values of θ, $A_1 = -E_0$ and $A_0 = 0$.

The other two boundary conditions are more easily satisfied if these constants are introduced immediately, to give

$$V_o = \frac{B_0}{r} - E_0 r \cos\theta + \frac{B_1}{r^2}\cos\theta.$$

The conditions at the sphere's surface are satisfied by performing the differentiations of Eqs. (5–14) and (5–15) and then substituting $r = a$ into the equations that are obtained. Equation (5–14), after dividing through by ϵ_0, becomes

$$\frac{B_0}{a^2} + E_0\cos\theta + \frac{2B_1}{a^3}\cos\theta = -KF\cos\theta$$

and Eq. (5–15) becomes

$$-E_0 a\sin\theta + \frac{B_1}{a^2}\sin\theta = Fa\sin\theta.$$

The fact that these equations must be valid for all values of θ requires that

$$B_0 = 0,$$

$$E_0 + \frac{2B_1}{a^3} = -KF \quad \text{and} \quad -E_0 a + \frac{B_1}{a^2} = Fa.$$

The two remaining unknowns, B_1 and F, can now be obtained from the last two equations, from which

$$B_1 = E_0 a^3 \frac{K-1}{K+2} \quad \text{and} \quad F = -E_0\frac{3}{K+2}.$$

The two potentials can now be written as

$$V_o = -E_0 r\cos\theta + E_0 a^3 \frac{K-1}{K+2}\frac{\cos\theta}{r^2} \tag{5–17a}$$

and

$$V_i = -E_0\frac{3}{K+2}r\cos\theta. \tag{5–17b}$$

Since these satisfy Laplace's equation and the boundary conditions, they are the correct solutions. The potential V_o shows that the field outside the sphere is the sum of the original uniform field plus the field of an ideal dipole at the origin. From Eq. (2–24), the equivalent dipole moment is

$$p = \epsilon_0 E_0 4\pi a^3 \frac{K-1}{K+2}. \tag{5–18}$$

It is interesting that the equivalent dipole moment is proportional to the applied field and to the volume of the sphere, as was the case for the conducting sphere in Section 4–4.

The external and internal fields can be obtained from the gradients of the potentials of Eqs. (5–17a) and (5–17b). The external field is

$$\mathbf{E} = -\boldsymbol{\nabla} V_o = E_0 \mathbf{k} + E_0 \frac{K-1}{K+2} \frac{a^3}{r^3} [\mathbf{a}_r \, 2 \cos \theta + \mathbf{a}_\theta \sin \theta]$$

or

$$\mathbf{E} = E_0 \mathbf{k} + E_0 \frac{K-1}{K+2} \frac{a^3}{r^3} \mathbf{d}_f,$$

and the internal field is

$$\mathbf{E}_i = -\boldsymbol{\nabla} V_i = E_0 \frac{3}{K+2} \mathbf{k}. \tag{5–19}$$

The field inside the sphere is a uniform field smaller than E_0, since $K > 1$. Expressions for the displacement vector outside and inside the sphere may be obtained by multiplying $\mathbf{E}$ by ϵ_0 and $\mathbf{E}_i$ by $K\epsilon_0$. This gives

$$\mathbf{D} = D_0 \mathbf{k} + D_0 \frac{K-1}{K+2} \frac{a^3}{r^3} [\mathbf{a}_r \, 2 \cos \theta + \mathbf{a}_\theta \sin \theta]$$

and

$$\mathbf{D}_i = E_0 \epsilon_0 \frac{3K}{K+2} \mathbf{k}.$$

Since K is greater than unity in a dielectric medium, D_i is greater than the applied displacement D_0, while E_i is less than the applied field E_0, as shown in Fig. 5–9. Physically, the internal reduction in $\mathbf{E}$ is caused by

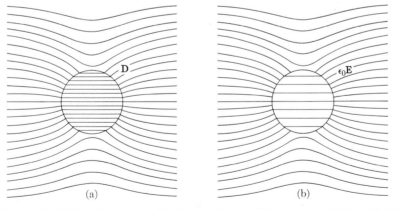

FIG. 5–9. Dielectric sphere with $K = 6$ in a uniform electric field. (a) The **D** lines are continuous and have greatly increased density inside the sphere. (b) Outside the sphere $\epsilon_0\mathbf{E} = \mathbf{D}$, but inside the sphere $\epsilon_0\mathbf{E}$ is considerably reduced by the polarization charges on the surface.

the polarization surface charge induced on the sphere, which opposes the applied field. The increase in **D** results from the requirement that lines of **D** be continuous throughout space when no real charge is present. With the external **D** lines converging on the sphere, the **D** lines within the sphere must be more dense.

A check on the foregoing results can be obtained by substituting $K = \infty$, which will be found to give the relations obtained in Section 4–4 for a conducting sphere in a uniform field. In purely static fields conductors behave like dielectrics with an infinite dielectric constant. A further check is obtained by substituting, for a vacuum, the value of $K = 1$, which makes the effect due to the sphere disappear. Checks of this sort are invaluable for eliminating mistakes in calculations.

5–8 Dielectric cylinder in a uniform field. An infinitely long right-circular cylinder, placed with its axis perpendicular to a uniform electric field, modifies that field in much the same way as does the sphere of the last section. If the cylinder has radius a and is made of the same homogeneous and isotropic dielectric as was the sphere, the modification of the field will be qualitatively the same though numerically different. The z-axis of the coordinate system may be set to coincide with the cylindrical axis, while the x-axis is set to point in the direction of the uniform field whose strength is E_0. With these choices, the usual cylindrical coordinates of Fig. 2–4 can be used, as they were for the conducting cylinder problem of Section 4–5.

The solution for this problem follows the form used in the previous section. The boundary condition equations at $r = a$ are similar to Eqs. (5–14) and (5–15):

$$-\epsilon \frac{\partial V_i}{\partial r} = -\epsilon_0 \frac{\partial V_o}{\partial r}$$

and

$$-\frac{\partial V_i}{\partial \phi} = -\frac{\partial V_o}{\partial \phi}.$$

The boundary condition equation at $r \gg a$ is similar to Eq. (5–16):

$$V_o = -E_0 x = -E_0 r \cos \phi.$$

From the cylindrical harmonics of Table 4–2, the following potential representations are chosen as being most likely to fit the boundary conditions:

$$V_o = Ar \cos \phi + \frac{B \cos \phi}{r}$$

and

$$V_i = Cr \cos \phi.$$

No terms with r raised to negative exponents are used for V_i because they become infinite at $r = 0$. Terms of the form $\sin n\phi$ or $\cos n\phi$ (where $n > 1$), as well as the $\ln r$ term, have been omitted because the boundary condition equation at $r \gg a$ does not suggest the need for these terms. If such terms were included in the potential expressions now, later work would prove their coefficients to be zero.

Application of the boundary condition equations to the assumed solutions gives

$$A = -E_0, \qquad B = \frac{K-1}{K+1} a^2 E_0, \qquad \text{and} \qquad C = -\frac{2E_0}{K+1}.$$

Thus the boundary conditions are satisfied by the assumed solutions that also satisfy Laplace's equation, and are, therefore, the correct solutions. The potentials then are

$$V_o = -E_0 r \cos\phi + \frac{(K-1)a^2 E_0}{(K+1)r} \cos\phi$$

and

$$V_i = -\frac{2}{K+1} E_0 r \cos\phi = -\frac{2E_0 x}{K+1}.$$

The external and internal fields can be obtained from the gradients of these potentials. The external field is

$$\mathbf{E} = E_0 \mathbf{i} + E_0 \frac{K-1}{K+1} \frac{a^2}{r^2} (\mathbf{a}_r \cos\phi + \mathbf{a}_\phi \sin\phi)$$

and the internal field is

$$\mathbf{E}_i = E_0 \frac{2}{K+1} \mathbf{i}.$$

It is left as an exercise to obtain the displacement vector and to compare these results with those for the conducting cylinder in Section 4–5.

5–9 Microscopic electric fields. All discussions thus far have utilized the concept of average fields rather than considering the complex subject of fields near individual atoms. A detailed treatment of this subject is necessarily beyond the scope of this text; however, the nature of such fields can be determined for crystal lattices with cubic symmetry.

Consider a dielectric material which completely fills the space between the two parallel plates of a capacitor, as shown in Fig. 5–10. The macroscopic field in the dielectric is $\mathbf{E}$ but it is desired to find the microscopic field $\mathbf{E}_a$ that acts on an individual atom. The exact form of $\mathbf{E}_a$ depends upon the electric fields of the surrounding polarized atoms, being the vector sum of $\mathbf{E}$ and the fields due to all the atoms within the capacitor. In calculating the magnitude of this field it is desirable to choose an atom

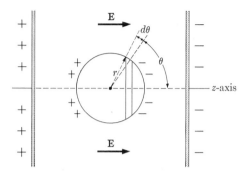

Fig. 5–10. Fictitious hollowed-out sphere of radius r is shown centered about an atom in the dielectric. The size of the sphere is greatly exaggerated.

near the center of the dielectric and to draw an imaginary sphere around this atom to separate the distant atoms from the near neighbors. The sphere drawn in Fig. 5–10 is greatly exaggerated, since it is necessary only that r be large compared with the distance between atoms. The atoms outside the sphere can be treated as a continuum, while the atoms inside the sphere must be treated individually.

The field acting on the central atom can then be expressed by

$$\mathbf{E}_a = \mathbf{E}_1 + \mathbf{E}_2,$$

where $\mathbf{E}_1$ is the field in the fictitious hollow sphere of radius r due to the external field $\mathbf{E}$ and the surrounding polarized dielectric, and $\mathbf{E}_2$ is the sum of the dipole fields of all the atoms within the sphere. If a real spherical cavity were introduced into the dielectric, the polarization of the atoms remaining near the cavity would be distorted. Since no real cavity exists, the calculation of the field inside the fictitious cavity must be based upon a uniform polarization for all atoms. With the field and the polarization directed to the right in Fig. 5–10, the inner surface of the spherical cavity has the polarization charge density $\sigma_p = P_n = -P \cos \theta$. The field at the center of this cavity due to this charge density can be obtained by writing the field due to the ring element of charge, shown in the diagram, and integrating over the surface of the sphere from $\theta = 0$ to $\theta = \pi$. Since the field due to the ring element is along the z-axis, it is given by

$$dE_p = \frac{\sigma_p 2\pi r^2 \sin\theta\, d\theta}{4\pi\epsilon_0 r^2}.$$

Substituting $\sigma_p = -P \cos\theta$, simplifying, and integrating, we obtain

$$E_p = -\frac{P}{2\epsilon_0} \int_0^\pi \cos^2\theta \sin\theta\, d\theta = \frac{P}{3\epsilon_0}.$$

The field $\mathbf{E}_1$ is the sum of the applied field due to the charged capacitor and the field due to the distant atomic dipoles; that is,

$$\mathbf{E}_1 = \mathbf{E} + \frac{\mathbf{P}}{3\epsilon_0}.$$

To this must be added the field $\mathbf{E}_2$, due to the atomic dipoles within the fictitious sphere.

The electric potential due to these atoms may be written from Eq. (2–24) as

$$V = \sum_i \frac{p_i \cos \theta_i}{4\pi\epsilon_0 r_i^2}$$

$$= \frac{p}{4\pi\epsilon_0} \sum_i \frac{z_i}{(x_i^2 + y_i^2 + z_i^2)^{3/2}},$$

where the sum is taken over all atoms within the sphere and each atom is assumed to be polarized by the same amount, p. The z-component of $\mathbf{E}_2$ is given by

$$E_{2z} = -\frac{\partial V}{\partial z}$$

$$= \frac{p}{4\pi\epsilon_0} \sum_i \frac{3z_i^2 r_i - r_i^3}{r_i^6}.$$

This is zero in a cubic-crystal lattice because, by symmetry,

$$\sum_i \frac{x_i^2}{r_i^5} = \sum_i \frac{y_i^2}{r_i^5} = \sum_i \frac{z_i^2}{r_i^5}$$

and therefore

$$\sum_i \frac{r_i^3}{r_i^6} = \sum_i \frac{3z_i^2 r_i}{r_i^6}.$$

The x- and y-components are

$$E_{2x} = -3 \sum_i x_i z_i r_i^{-5} \quad \text{and} \quad E_{2y} = -3 \sum_i y_i z_i r_i^{-5},$$

which are also zero because in a cubic lattice there is a negative value corresponding to each positive value for x, y, or z, so that the sum over all values of the products $x_i z_i$ and $y_i z_i$ must be zero.

The microscopic field on an individual atom in a crystal lattice with cubic symmetry has thus been shown to be

$$\mathbf{E}_a = \mathbf{E}_1 = \mathbf{E} + \frac{\mathbf{P}}{3\epsilon_0},$$

where $\mathbf{E}$ is the uniform macroscopic field through the dielectric. This simple calculation shows that the polarizability of individual atoms is somewhat less than that of the bulk material, since $\mathbf{E}_a$ is larger than $\mathbf{E}$. This result is important in the study of the electronic properties of solids. In particular, it can be shown that lack of cubic symmetry in many dielectrics results in a nonzero value for $\mathbf{E}_2$ and a corresponding nonlinear or even nonisotropic enhancement of the polarization of the material. Some properties of nonlinear and nonisotropic dielectrics are discussed in Sections 5–5 and 5–12.

5–10 Energy relations in static electric fields. As in all other branches of physics, energy relations in electrostatics constitute a powerful tool for solving many problems. It is, therefore, desirable to obtain an energy expression to describe any general configuration of charges and dielectrics in space. For most purposes, an expression for the energy required to produce a given change in the charge distribution or in the geometry is sufficient. A general expression for the energy required to change electric and magnetic fields as a function of time and coordinates will be discussed in Chapter 11; this section treats only the energies required to make slow changes in electrostatic configurations. However, these results will be useful for establishing the more general case.

A basic concept which is to be demonstrated is that the work required to make changes in electrostatic situations can be expressed in terms of the changing electric fields, thus strongly suggesting that all electrostatic energy resides in the electric field. This concept is a great aid to visualization of energy problems, especially in electromagnetic waves, and it does not lead to inconsistencies. Before treating the most general case, the charging of a simple capacitor will be discussed.

Work done in charging capacitors. The simplest capacitor is one with two parallel plates of metal of the same area A, placed very close together compared with their linear dimensions. The region between the plates may either be evacuated or filled with a homogeneous medium, not necessarily isotropic. Ignoring the region near the edges of the plates, the electric field $\mathbf{E}$ between the plates is uniform and is perpendicular to their surfaces. If d is the separation and V is the potential difference between the plates, $V = Ed$. The facing surfaces of the plates have uniform charge densities σ on the one with higher potential, and $-\sigma$ on the other, and from Eq. (5–10) the normal component of $\mathbf{D}$ is $D_n = \sigma$. If a very small charge δq is transported from the plate with lower potential to the one with higher potential, the work done by the battery or other device affecting the transfer is $\delta W = V \, \delta q$. Since $q = A\sigma$, so that $\delta q = A \, \delta\sigma = A \, \delta D_n$, the work done can be stated as

$$\delta W = A \, d \, E \, \delta D_n.$$

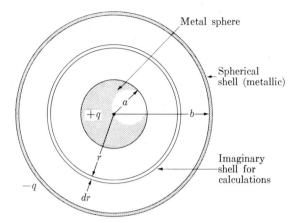

FIG. 5–11. Concentric-sphere capacitor containing a dielectric medium whose properties vary only with the radius.

The volume of the space occupied by these uniform fields is $\tau = A\,d$ and hence

$$\delta W = \tau E\,\delta D_n = \tau \mathbf{E} \cdot \delta \mathbf{D}.$$

The work done in charging this simple capacitor has been expressed in terms of the fields and the total volume occupied by them. For this special case, the increase in electrostatic work per unit volume is given by $\mathbf{E} \cdot \delta \mathbf{D}$.

This expression is true also in the more complicated case of charging a spherical capacitor. Such a capacitor may consist of a conducting sphere of radius a, concentrically surrounded by a conducting spherical shell of inner radius b. The space between the spheres may be filled either with a homogeneous dielectric or with one whose properties vary only with the radius. Rather than calculating the work done in the same manner as for the parallel-plate capacitor, the work can be calculated from the expression

$$\delta W = \int \mathbf{E} \cdot \delta \mathbf{D}\,d\tau$$

to see if it leads to inconsistencies.

The diagram of Fig. 5–11 shows a thin spherical shell of radius r and thickness dr which can be used as a general volume element $d\tau = 4\pi r^2\,dr$, since the fields and the dielectric properties depend only upon r. Applying Gauss' law to the space surrounded by the volume element gives $q = 4\pi r^2 D_n$, which leads directly to $\delta D_n = \delta q/4\pi r^2$, and since $\mathbf{E}$ is necessarily normal to this equipotential surface, the expression for the work done becomes simply

$$\delta W = \int_{r=a}^{r=b} E\,\frac{\delta q}{4\pi r^2}\,4\pi r^2\,dr,$$

which reduces to

$$\delta W = \delta q \int_{r=a}^{r=b} E \, dr = \delta q \, V,$$

where V is the potential difference between the metallic spheres. Since this is just the expression for the work done in transporting a charge δq across a potential difference of V, no inconsistency has resulted from using the assumed expression for work done in terms of the fields.

Note that this development is valid when the outside sphere is made very large; that is, it is valid when $b \to \infty$ and the sphere of radius a becomes an isolated and charged sphere. In this case, the total work required to transfer δq from infinity to the charged sphere is obtained by integrating $\int \mathbf{E} \cdot \delta \mathbf{D} \, d\tau$ from $r = a$ to $r \to \infty$. The development is also valid when the inner radius a is reduced to very small though finite dimensions. However, when the radius is reduced to the dimensions of an atomic nucleus, $\mathbf{P}$ becomes meaningless, and $\mathbf{D}$ becomes $\epsilon_0 \mathbf{E}$.

These examples suggest that the work done in creating certain electrostatic configurations can be calculated on the assumption that all electrostatic energy resides in the field and that the work required to increase the fields at any point is given by $\mathbf{E} \cdot \delta \mathbf{D}$. To prove that this is true in all cases requires a more general treatment.

Work done in arbitrary field configurations. The general problem in electrostatics involves conductors of various shapes and sizes, immersed in nonhomogeneous and nonisotropic media and carrying arbitrary charges. Such a situation is shown in Fig. 5–12, where two metallic conductors a and b of potentials of V_a and V_b, respectively, are shown in a dielectric medium. The surfaces of the conductors necessarily constitute equipotential surfaces, and other equipotential surfaces such as V_1, V_2, V_3, V_4, and V_5 are indicated by their traces in the plane of the diagram. While inhomogeneities and anisotropies in the media affect the configuration of the equipotential lines, the only requirement for the proof is that such equipotential lines do exist.

The equipotential surfaces indicated in Fig. 5–12 represent a typical example of such surfaces near conductors with charges of different magnitude and the same sign. Each conductor has equipotential surfaces like V_5 that surround it alone. Other surfaces, like V_1, V_2, and V_3, surround both conductors. The surface V_4 represents the transition surface between those that surround only one and those that surround both conductors. It consists of two envelopes, one surrounding a and the other surrounding b, that meet at a single point where the field is zero. An infinitesimal test charge would be in equilibrium at such a point, but it could not be in stable equilibrium.

With positive charges on a and b, potentials higher than V_4 are found inside both of the envelopes that form the V_4 equipotential surface. Since

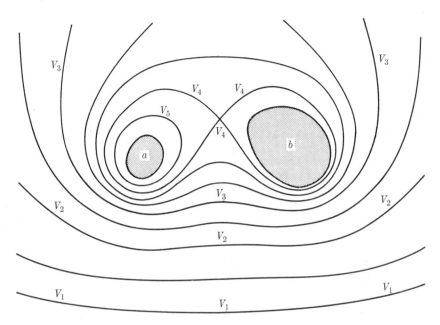

Fig. 5–12. Two charged conductors of irregular shape surrounded by un-determined dielectrics. Equipotential surfaces are indicated by the lines of their intersections with the plane of the paper.

potentials lower than V_4 are found outside these envelopes, the point where the two envelopes are in contact is called a saddlepoint. If the un-equal charges on a and b were of opposite sign, one of the envelopes of the transition surface V_4 would surround the smaller charge but the other envelope would surround both charges, as is shown in the figure accompanying the answer to Problem 2–36. These two envelopes would still meet at a saddlepoint having the characteristics shown in Fig. 4–15. (Saddlepoints were discussed in Section 4–10.)

It is desirable to calculate the energy required to produce infinitesimal increases in the magnitudes of the charges from q_a to $q_a + \delta q_a$ on a and from q_b to $q_b + \delta q_b$ on b. This can be done in two steps, namely, by first calculating the work to transport $\delta q_a + \delta q_b$ from infinity to the surface V_4 and by then calculating the work to transport δq_a from V_4 to a and δq_b from V_4 to b. The total work done is

$$\delta W = V_a\, \delta q_a + V_b\, \delta q_b,$$

which may be written in the form

$$\delta W = V_4\, (\delta q_a + \delta q_b) + (V_a - V_4)\, \delta q_a + (V_b - V_4)\, \delta q_b.$$

The first term on the right of this equation is the work done in bringing δq_a and δq_b from infinity to the potential surface V_4, while the second and third terms represent the work done in bringing δq_a and δq_b from potential V_4 to V_a and V_b, respectively. These three terms are now to be expressed as integrals containing the quantities $\mathbf{E}$ and $\delta \mathbf{D}$.

Consider some equipotential surface with $0 < V < V_4$ such that the surface completely surrounds conductors a and b. Since the total change in the charge within that surface is $\delta q_a + \delta q_b$, Gauss' law requires that

$$\delta q_a + \delta q_b = \int_{s_4} \delta \mathbf{D} \cdot d\mathbf{s},$$

where the subscripts signify that the integral is to be evaluated over a surface that surrounds both conductors. The potential V_4 may be expressed as

$$\int_{V=0}^{V=V_4} -\mathbf{E} \cdot d\mathbf{l} = \int_{V=V_4}^{V=0} \mathbf{E} \cdot d\mathbf{l}$$

integrated along any path from the surface on which $V = V_4$ to a surface at infinity on which $V = 0$. Thus

$$V_4 (\delta q_a + \delta q_b) = \int_{V=V_4}^{V=0} \mathbf{E} \cdot d\mathbf{l} \int_{s_{ab}} \mathbf{D} \cdot d\mathbf{s}$$

$$= \int_{V=V_4}^{V=0} \int_{s_{ab}} (\mathbf{E} \cdot \delta \mathbf{D}) \, d\mathbf{l} \cdot d\mathbf{s},$$

since $\mathbf{E}$ and $d\mathbf{s}$ are parallel, so that $(\mathbf{E} \cdot d\mathbf{l})(d\mathbf{s} \cdot \delta \mathbf{D}) = (d\mathbf{s} \cdot d\mathbf{l})(\mathbf{E} \cdot \delta \mathbf{D})$. Furthermore,

$$\int_{V=V_4}^{V=0} \int_{s_{ab}} d\mathbf{s} \cdot d\mathbf{l}$$

gives the volume of space outside the surface V_4. Hence

$$V_4 (\delta q_a + \delta q_b) = \int_{V=V_4}^{V=0} \int_{s_{ab}} \mathbf{E} \cdot \delta \mathbf{D} \, d\tau.$$

Similarly, it can be shown that

$$(V_a - V_4) \delta q_a = \int_{V=V_a}^{V=V_4} \int_{s_a} \mathbf{E} \cdot \delta \mathbf{D} \, d\tau$$

and

$$(V_b - V_4) \delta q_b = \int_{V=V_b}^{V=V_4} \int_{s_b} \mathbf{E} \cdot \delta \mathbf{D} \, d\tau.$$

These three double integrations effectively constitute an integration of

$\mathbf{E} \cdot \delta\mathbf{D}$ over all space, since $\mathbf{E} = 0$ inside the conductors. It has now been shown that, for any two conductors in a dielectric medium,

$$V_a \, \delta q_a + V_b \, \delta q_b = \int \mathbf{E} \cdot \delta\mathbf{D} \, d\tau,$$

and the extension to an arbitrary number of conductors is obvious. This constitutes a derivation of the relation

$$\delta W = \int \mathbf{E} \cdot \delta\mathbf{D} \, d\tau \tag{5–20}$$

for a general electrostatic configuration. Further discussion will be simplified by considering energies and fields only at some physical point in space where the work per unit volume required to increase the field by an infinitesimal $d\mathbf{D}$ is given by

$$dw = \mathbf{E} \cdot d\mathbf{D}. \tag{5–21}$$

Further simplification can be achieved by assuming a homogeneous material between the two plates of a parallel-plate capacitor to maintain control over the direction and magnitude of $\mathbf{E}$. Generality can be achieved by allowing the homogeneous medium to have any conceivable properties and to have crystal axes oriented in any direction.

5–11 Total energy to create static electric fields. The total energy required to create a field at a point can be obtained directly by integrating Eq. (5–21):

$$w = \int_0^D \mathbf{E} \cdot d\mathbf{D} \tag{5–22}$$

where it is assumed that $\mathbf{D} = 0$ initially. The actual integration can be performed, however, only if the functional relationship between $\mathbf{D}$ and $\mathbf{E}$ is known.

Linear isotropic dielectrics. In the special case where the dielectric is linear and isotropic at a given point, so that $\mathbf{D} = K\epsilon_0\mathbf{E}$, with K being a true constant for the material, the volume density of energy required to produce the field may be expressed by

$$w = \int_0^E K\epsilon_0 E \, dE = \tfrac{1}{2}K\epsilon_0 E^2, \tag{5–23}$$

where $K > 1$ in dielectric materials and $K = 1$ in a vacuum. In a non-homogeneous material, K will have different values at different points, but if K is independent of $\mathbf{E}$, as is assumed here, all the energy of Eq. (5–23) is recovered when $\mathbf{E}$ goes to zero. The constancy of K implies that the forces opposing charge displacement in the dielectric are of the "elastic" type, in which displacements are directly proportional to the field.

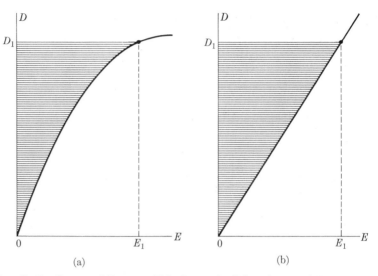

(a)   (b)

FIG. 5–13. Curves of D versus E for isotropic dielectric materials. The shaded areas represent the work per volume required to produce the displacement D_1 (a) in nonlinear materials and (b) in linear materials.

Of special interest is the fact that energy exists in the field even in a vacuum, where $K = 1$. It is frequently desired to determine the *additional* energy required to create a field due to the presence of a linear and isotropic dielectric material. This so-called *intrinsic energy* is just the total energy minus the energy that would exist in the absence of the dielectric,

$$w_{\text{int}} = \tfrac{1}{2}(K - 1)\epsilon_0 E^2 = \tfrac{1}{2}\chi\epsilon_0 E^2.$$

Nonlinear isotropic dielectrics. A nonlinear dielectric is one in which the polarizabilities change with changing electric field. Frequently, a dielectric will exhibit rather large polarizations in weak fields, although larger fields do not produce proportionately larger polarizations. The polarization then is said to saturate at these higher fields. A typical curve of D versus E for such a material is shown in Fig. 5–13(a). The volume density of work done in increasing D from 0 to D_1 is given by Eq. (5–22) as

$$w = \int_0^{D_1} E \, dD,$$

where the vector notation is omitted because **D**, **E**, and d**D** are always parallel in an isotropic medium between parallel plates. The integral of $E \, dD$ from 0 to D_1 for this material is the shaded area to the left of the curve. The curve for a linear dielectric having the same values of E_1 and D_1 is shown in Fig. 5–13(b), where the work required to produce the field

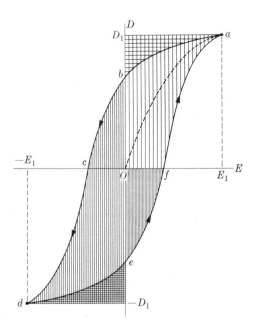

Fig. 5-14. Hysteresis loop for isotropic ferroelectric materials. Areas representing the volume density of work done on the materials are shaded vertically, while horizontal shading indicates the volume energy regained.

is represented by the shaded area to the left of the curve. In this example, the volume density of energy required to produce the fields D_1 and E_1 is considerably larger in the linear dielectric than for the nonlinear example of Fig. 5–13(a), which points up the fact that Eq. (5–23) is applicable only when the polarizability is independent of the field. The difference between these two energy densities is due to the action of nonelastic forces within the material.

Hysteresis effects. Many nonlinear dielectric materials exhibit hysteresis effects, as shown in Fig. 5–14; that is, after being initially polarized to a value D_1 in a field E_1, a residual polarization represented by point b remains even after E has been decreased to zero. Increasing the electric field in the reverse direction finally reduces D to zero at point c, and when the field becomes $-E_1$ the displacement becomes $-D_1$, as indicated by the point d which is equivalent to point a in the first quadrant. As the field is slowly* reversed again, this time from $-E_1$ to E_1, the displacement takes on values from points d to e to f and returns to D_1 at point a. As

---

* For these statements to be true the field changes must be slow enough for any heat energy released within the material to be dissipated. If the temperature increases, the properties of the dielectric usually change.

the field E is repeatedly reversed from $+E_1$ to $-E_1$ and back again, the value of D traces out the hysteresis loop of Fig. 5–14.

The hysteresis effect is caused by irreversible polarization effects within the material which dissipate energy in the form of heat. This loss of energy can be calculated by evaluating Eq. (5–21) over one complete cycle. The integral of $E\,dD$ evaluated from f to a gives the area in the first quadrant enclosed by curves connecting the points f, a, D_1, and O, which is represented by vertical shading. In going from a to b, E is positive but dD is negative, so that the resulting area represented by horizontal shading lines in the first quadrant must be subtracted from the first area obtained. The net area after this subtraction is just the area enclosed by the hysteresis loop in the first quadrant. In the second quadrant both E and dD are negative, so that the resulting area represented by vertical shading must be added to the area already obtained. After the integrations from c to d, d to e, and e to f have been performed and added to the previous results, the total area will be just the area enclosed by the complete hysteresis loop. The total volume density of energy in joules/m^3 dissipated within the material is therefore given by the area enclosed by the hysteresis loop in the D versus E coordinate axes, with D in coul/m^2 and E in volts/m.

Dielectric materials exhibiting hysteresis effects are known as *ferroelectric materials*, because their polarization versus electric field curves are so much like the magnetization versus magnetic field curves of ferromagnetic materials like iron. These materials usually have a rather complex chemical formula and crystalline structure, as for example Rochelle salt, $NaK(C_4H_4O_6)\cdot4H_2O$, and barium titanate, $BaTiO_3$. Interest in these materials has developed only in recent years, while interest in ferromagnetism has existed for centuries. Because a great deal more is known about ferromagnetic than ferroelectric materials, a detailed study of hysteresis effects will be postponed until the study of magnetic materials in Chapter 9.

Linear anisotropic dielectrics. Materials that polarize more easily in some directions than in others are anisotropic. Such materials were discussed briefly in Section 5–4, where the nine dielectric constants were defined. While these many constants are important in high-frequency fields, electrostatic problems can usually be solved by more simple methods. If the space between the plates of a parallel-plate capacitor is filled with a homogeneous but anisotropic dielectric material, the boundary conditions require that the $\mathbf{E}$ vector be normal to the plates, although the $\mathbf{P}$ and $\mathbf{D}$ vectors are usually directed at angles to the normal. At any point the final fields can be designated by $\mathbf{E}_f$, $\mathbf{P}_f$, and $\mathbf{D}_f$, and since $\mathbf{E}$ does not change direction, it can be written as $\mathbf{E} = \gamma\mathbf{E}_f$, where γ increases from zero to unity during the charging process. With linear dielectrics the other two fields also can be written as $\mathbf{P} = \gamma\mathbf{P}_f$ and $\mathbf{D} = \gamma\mathbf{D}_f$. When γ increases by an infinitesimal $d\gamma$, $\mathbf{D}$ increases by $d\mathbf{D} = \mathbf{D}_f \, d\gamma$ and the work per unit volume required to produce this increase is given by

$$dw = \mathbf{E} \cdot d\mathbf{D} = \mathbf{E}_f \cdot \mathbf{D}_f \gamma \, d\gamma.$$

Integration gives

$$w = \int_0^1 \mathbf{E}_f \cdot \mathbf{D}_f \gamma \, d\gamma = \frac{\mathbf{E}_f \cdot \mathbf{D}_f}{2}, \qquad (5\text{–}24)$$

which is a general expression for the work required to set up the fields $\mathbf{E}_f$ and $\mathbf{D}_f$ in any linear dielectric, since it includes Eq. (5–23) as a special case. The energy represented by Eq. (5–24) is all recovered when a capacitor with a dielectric material that polarizes linearly is slowly discharged. Further study shows that the energy given by Eq. (5–24) can be identified as the "free energy" for thermodynamic studies.

5–12 Electric dipoles. Ferroelectric materials having D versus E curves like the one shown in Fig. 5–13 remain polarized after the external field is removed, in somewhat the same way that a permanent magnet remains magnetized. The condition is usually so unstable that this polarization does not last long.

Electrets. More or less permanent polarization can be produced in certain waxes by first melting and then freezing them in a strong electric field. The permanent dipoles become oriented in the molten state and this orientation becomes frozen in on solidification. These permanently polarized objects are the electric equivalent of the permanent magnet, and are called *electrets*.

The electric field produced by an electret is the vector sum of the fields produced by all of the individual dipoles, which is just the field of a dipole of larger dimensions. For example, suppose a cylindrical rod of dielectric material is uniformly polarized parallel to its axis. The effects of all the internal charges cancel and the field is just that produced by the polarization charges appearing on the two end surfaces. The electric field and potential at a considerable distance from this rod are very closely approximated by Eqs. (2–4) and (2–24), but near such large dipoles the potential must be calculated from

$$V = \int_\tau \frac{\rho_p \, d\tau}{4\pi\epsilon_0 r}$$

integrated over the dipole, where $\rho_p = -\boldsymbol{\nabla} \cdot \mathbf{P}$ is the actual distribution of polarization charges and r is the distance of $d\tau$ from the general field point.

Dipoles in electric fields experience forces and torques that can be calculated from $\mathbf{F} = \int_\tau \mathbf{E}\rho_p \, d\tau$, where $\mathbf{E}$ is the field at $d\tau$ that is obtained

by ignoring the field of the dipole itself. These forces and torques can
also be calculated from the energy of the dipole in the field, $U = \int_\tau V\rho_p \, d\tau$,
where V is the potential at $d\tau$, and the potential of the dipole is ignored.
Here the dipole is considered rigid and the energy required to create it is
not included. In the special case where large "point" charges, q and $-q$,
are separated a very small distance l, so that the dipole moment $\mathbf{p} = q\mathbf{l}$
is finite, the potential at $-q$ may be V while that at $+q$ is $V + \delta V$. The
energy of the dipole is then

$$U = q(V + \delta V) - qV = q \, \delta V.$$

When l is very small

$$\delta V = \boldsymbol{\nabla} V \cdot \mathbf{l},$$

and then

$$U = \boldsymbol{\nabla} V \cdot q\mathbf{l} = -\mathbf{E} \cdot \mathbf{p} = -Ep \cos \theta, \tag{5-25}$$

where θ is the angle between $\mathbf{E}$ and $\mathbf{p}$. If the torque on the dipole is L, the
work required to produce an infinitesimal rotation $d\theta$ is

$$-L \, d\theta = \left(\frac{\partial U}{\partial \theta}\right) d\theta,$$

or

$$L = -\frac{\partial U}{\partial \theta} = -Ep \sin \theta. \tag{5-26}$$

This same expression is obtained from a consideration of the forces on the
individual charges shown in Fig. 5–15, where the force $\mathbf{E}q$, parallel to the
field, is separated a perpendicular distance $l \sin \theta$ from an equal but opposite force. The torque due to this couple is $(-Eq)(l \sin \theta) = -Ep \sin \theta$,
which may also be expressed by $\mathbf{L} = \mathbf{p} \times \mathbf{E}$. In a uniform field the two
forces are exactly equal and opposite, leaving no net force on the dipole.

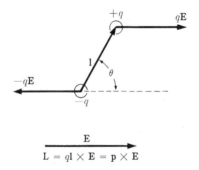

FIG. 5–15. A small electric dipole in a uniform field, showing that the torque
is $\mathbf{L} = \mathbf{p} \times \mathbf{E}$.

In a nonuniform field, however, these forces are not equal and opposite and there is a net force. This is best calculated from the energy of the dipole. If $\mathbf{F}$ is the force exerted by the field on the dipole, the work required to move the dipole an infinitesimal distance $d\mathbf{l}$ is

$$-\mathbf{F} \cdot d\mathbf{l} = dU = \nabla U \cdot d\mathbf{l},$$

or

$$\mathbf{F} = -\nabla U = \nabla(\mathbf{E} \cdot \mathbf{p}). \tag{5-27}$$

Since $\mathbf{p}$ is constant, this force is proportional to the gradient of the component of $\mathbf{E}$ that is parallel to the positive direction of $\mathbf{p}$. The force points in the direction in which this component of $\mathbf{E}$ increases most rapidly.

PROBLEMS

5-1. Two oppositely charged conducting plates, having numerically equal quantities of charge per unit area, are separated by a dielectric 5 mm thick, of dielectric constant 3. The resultant electric intensity in the dielectric is 10^6 volts/m. Compute (a) the free charge per unit area on the conducting plates, (b) the induced charge per unit area on the surfaces of the dielectric.

*5-2. The paper dielectric in a paper and foil capacitor is 0.005 cm thick. Its dielectric constant is 2.5 and its dielectric strength is 50×10^6 volts/m. (a) What area of paper, and of tinfoil, is required for a 0.1-μf capacitor? (b) If the electric intensity in the paper is not to exceed one-half the dielectric strength, what is the maximum potential difference that can be applied across the capacitor?

5-3. The capacitance of a variable radio capacitor can be changed from 50 $\mu\mu$f to 950 $\mu\mu$f by turning the dial from 0° to 180°. With the dial set at 180° the capacitor is connected to a 400-volt battery. After charging, the capacitor is disconnected from the battery and the dial is turned to 0°. (a) What is the charge on the capacitor? (b) What is the potential difference across the capacitor when the dial reads 0°? (c) What is the energy of the capacitor in this position? (d) How much work is required to turn the dial, if friction is neglected?

*5-4. An air capacitor, consisting of two closely spaced parallel plates, has a capacitance of 1000 $\mu\mu$f. The charge on each plate is 1 μcoul. (a) What is the potential difference between the plates? (b) If the charge is kept constant, what will be the potential difference between the plates if the separation is doubled? (c) How much work is required to double the separation?

5-5. A 20-μf capacitor is charged to a potential difference of 1000 volts. The terminals of the charged capacitor are then connected to those of an uncharged

---

* Answers to starred problems will be found at back of book.

5-μf capacitor. Compute (a) the original charge of the system, (b) the final potential difference across each capacitor, (c) the final energy of the system, and (d) the decrease in energy when the capacitors are connected.

5-6. A vacuum triode may be idealized as follows. A plane surface (the cathode) emits electrons with negligible initial velocities. Parallel to the cathode and 3 mm away from it is an open grid of fine wire at a potential of 18 volts above the cathode. A second plane surface (the anode) is 12 mm beyond the grid and is at a potential of 15 volts above the cathode. Assume that the plane of the grid is an equipotential surface, and that the potential gradients between cathode and grid, and between grid and anode, are uniform. Assume also that the structure of the grid is sufficiently open for electrons to pass through it freely. (a) Draw a diagram of potential *vs.* distance, along a line from cathode to anode. (b) With what velocity will electrons strike the anode? (c) If the anode is made 18 volts negative with respect to the cathode, how far will electrons travel beyond the grid?

*5-7. A capacitor consists of two parallel plates of area 25 cm^2 separated a distance of 0.2 cm. The material between the plates has a dielectric constant of 5. The plates of the capacitor are connected to a 300-volt battery. (a) What is the capacitance of the capacitor? (b) What is the charge on either plate? (c) What is the energy in the charged capacitor?

5-8. The plates of a parallel-plate capacitor in vacuum have charges $+Q$ and $-Q$ and the distance between the plates is x. The plates are disconnected from the charging voltage and pulled apart a short distance dx. (a) What is the change dC in the capacitance of the capacitor? (b) What is the change dW in its energy? (c) Equate the work $F\,dx$ to the increase in energy dW and find the force of attraction F between the plates. (d) Explain why F is not equal to QE, where E is the electric intensity between the plates.

*5-9. Calculate the radius of the first Bohr orbit of the hydrogen atom, by equating the Coulomb force between the electron and the nucleus to the centripetal force. Using the quantum condition that the angular momentum is $h/2\pi$, show that this radius is approximately one-half angstrom.

5-10. A very simple calculation for the binding energy per molecule of an NaCl crystal assumes that the total energy arises from the Coulomb attraction between the Na$^+$ ion and the nearest Cl$^-$ ion. Using the known ionic separation of 2.81×10^{-10} m, show that this simple calculation gives a result close to 2/3 of the measured value of 12.8×10^{-19} joule/molecule.

*5-11. A conducting sphere of radius a is surrounded by a dielectric of inner radius a and outer radius b whose dielectric constant is K. Consider four different field points: (1) just inside the dielectric at r slightly greater than a, (2) inside the dielectric at r slightly less than b, (3) just outside the dielectric at r slightly greater than b, and (4) at some general point a distance r from the center of the sphere where $r > b$.

(a) At each of these four points, calculate the displacement $\mathbf{D}$, the electric field $\mathbf{E}$, the polarization $\mathbf{P}$, and the potential V, when q is the charge on the sphere. (b) Plot V and E versus r.

5-12. (a) Calculate σ_p on the inner and outer surfaces of the dielectric shell in Problem 5-11. (b) Show that the field $\mathbf{E}$ inside this dielectric shell can be calculated from two points of view, namely, from $\mathbf{E} = \mathbf{D}/K\epsilon_0$ or from the knowledge of the magnitude and location of the polarization charges, otherwise ignoring the presence of the dielectric.

*5-13. Assume that the dielectric surrounding the charged sphere in Problem 5-11 has a dielectric constant given by $K = 4e^{-[(r/a)-1]^2}$. (a) Calculate $\mathbf{D}$, $\mathbf{P}$, $\mathbf{E}$, and ρ_p as functions of r inside the dielectric. (b) Calculate the total polarization volume charge if $b = 2a$, and compare this with the algebraic sum of the polarization surface charges on the inner and outer surfaces. (c) Plot ρ_p versus r.

5-14. Assume that the dielectric constant in Problem 5-11 has the radial variation given by $K = f(r)$ and calculate $\mathbf{D}$, $\mathbf{P}$, $\mathbf{E}$, and ρ_p as functions of r inside the dielectric.

*5-15 (a) Calculate the capacitance of a capacitor consisting of concentric metallic spheres, with the space between filled with a dielectric of dielectric constant K. Assume that the space has inner and outer radii a and b, respectively. (b) Let $b - a = d$ remain constant while b and a increase so that $b \gg d$. Calculate the approximate capacitance in terms of the area of the sphere, $A = 4\pi b^2$, and compare your expression with that for a parallel-plate capacitor.

5-16. (a) Calculate the capacitance of a capacitor made up of concentric metallic cylinders insulated from each other by a material whose dielectric constant is K. The outer radius of the inner cylinder is a, the inner radius of the outer cylinder is b, and the length of these cylinders is l, where $l \gg (b - a)$. (b) Find the capacitance of this same capacitor when the insulator fills only part of the space between the two concentric cylinders extending from $r = a$ to $r = \sqrt{ab}$.

*5-17. One of the boundary conditions at the interface between two dielectric materials is $D_{1n} - D_{2n} = 0$, as is proved in Section 5-5. Use this same method to find the value of $E_{1n} - E_{2n}$ in terms of the components of the $\mathbf{P}$'s.

5-18. One of the boundary conditions at the interface between two dielectric materials is $E_{1t} - E_{2t} = 0$, as is proved in Section 5-5. Use this same method to find the value of $D_{1t} - D_{2t}$ in terms of the components of the $\mathbf{P}$'s.

*5-19. Assume that both of the dielectrics in Fig. 5-6 are isotropic and homogeneous, with dielectric constants K_1 and K_2, respectively. For points very near the interface between the two, calculate the angle θ_2 between the field $\mathbf{E}_2$ and the z-axis, when the field $\mathbf{E}_1$ is directed at the angle θ_1 to the z-axis.

5-20. Calculate σ_p on the surfaces of (a) the sphere of Section 5-7, and (b) the cylinder of Section 5-8. Compare these results when $K \to \infty$ with the values for σ on the surfaces of conductors of the same shape.

*5-21. As an aid to the understanding of electric and magnetic fields inside materials, Kelvin invented two imaginary cavities: a thin needle-shaped cavity cut parallel to the field, and a thin disklike cavity cut perpendicular to the field. For homogeneous and isotropic materials, (a) prove that in the first cavity the field $E_c = E$, while in the second cavity $E_c = D/\epsilon_0$. (b) Find the field E_c in a spherical cavity of radius a, and in a cylindrical cavity of radius a whose axis is perpendicular to the field.

5-22. Write expressions for $\mathbf{E}$ and $\mathbf{P}$ inside and for $\mathbf{E}$ outside the dielectric sphere of Section 5–7 and the dielectric cylinder of Section 5–8. Compare these expressions as $K \to \infty$ with the corresponding expressions for conductors of the same shape.

*5–23. As has been pointed out, a charged particle is attracted toward a nearby conducting surface by the charge it induces upon that surface. Likewise, such a particle is attracted toward a nearby dielectric surface. To estimate this latter attraction, assume a point charge $+q$ on the z-axis at $z = h$ in space that is otherwise empty wherever z is positive but is filled with a homogeneous and isotropic dielectric of constant K wherever z is negative.

(a) Show that the potential V_o for the region where z is positive is given by placing an image charge q' at $z = -h$, while the potential V_i for the region where z is negative is obtained by replacing the $+q$ charge with an image q'' at $z = h$.

(b) Calculate the image charges q' and q''.

(c) Calculate the force on the $+q$ charge.

(d) Calculate σ_p on the surface of the dielectric in the xy-plane as a function of $r = \sqrt{x^2 + y^2}$.

(e) Calculate the total polarization charge on the xy-plane.

5–24. Replace the point charge in Problem 5–23 with an ideal dipole of moment $\mathbf{p}$, directed at an angle β to the positive z-axis. (a) Determine the locations and magnitudes of the images required to calculate V_o wherever z is positive and V_i wherever z is negative. (b) Calculate the torque acting on the original dipole. (c) Calculate the force acting on the original dipole.

*5–25. Replace the point charge in Problem 5–23 with an infinitely long filament that has a uniform charge per unit length λ, where this filament is parallel to the x-axis and passes through $z = h$. Find (a) the force per unit length on the filament, and (b) the value of σ_p on the xy-plane.

5–26. Suppose that a certain wax for making electrets can retain a uniform polarization $\mathbf{P}$, parallel to the axis, when this wax is formed into a right-circular cylinder of radius a and length $l \gg a$. Calculate the direction and magnitude of the electric fields due to such a cylinder (a) at the center of the cylinder, and (b) at two points on the axis near the positively charged end, one just inside and the other just outside the wax cylinder.

*5–27. According to relativity theory, the total energy of a particle cannot exceed mc^2, where m is the rest mass. Hence for an isolated charged particle the electrostatic energy, which depends upon its radius, must be less than mc^2. This sets a minimum for the radii of the elementary charged particles. Calculate the minimum radii for the following particles: (a) the proton, (b) the nucleus of an atom having Z protons and Z neutrons, and (c) the electron. Compare these radii with the recently measured radii of the proton (0.7×10^{-15} m) and the atomic nuclei ($1.2A^{1/3} \times 10^{-15}$ m), for which the number of nucleons is $A = 2Z$.

5–28. Problems 2–35 and 2–36 call for the calculation of equipotential surfaces near two point charges of $+4q$ and $-q$ that are l meters apart. The potential surfaces are altered very little by assuming that these point charges reside on conducting spheres both of radius $a \cong l/20$. Calculate within 1% the work required to add δq to each conducting sphere by bringing these infinitesimal charges from an infinite distance.

*5-29. A certain parallel-plate capacitor consists of two metal disks, each of radius a, which are separated by the distance d. Assume that $d \ll a$, so that the electric field can be considered to be confined to the evacuated space between the plates. (a) With a charge of $+q$ on one plate and $-q$ on the other, calculate the electrostatic energy of the charged capacitor. (b) From the work required to increase the plate separation from d to $d + \delta d$, where $\delta d \ll d$ and q remains constant, calculate the electrostatic force on the positively charged plate. (c) Instead of keeping q constant, assume that the separation of the plates is increased from d to $d + \delta d$ while the plates are kept at constant potentials by being connected to the terminals of a storage battery. How does the work done in this case compare with that calculated in (b)? If the results are different, account for this difference.

5-30. A region containing many small conducting spheres in an electric field acts like a dielectric, since the spheres become induced dipoles. (a) Calculate the effective dielectric constant for the following geometrical arrangement, assuming that the field around each sphere is not affected significantly by the presence of the other spheres. Consider a simple cubic lattice; i.e., a space completely filled with imaginary cubes having edges in common, each of which is $4a$ in length. Further, assume that metallic spheres, each of radius a, are located with their centers at each corner. (b) Correct your calculation by taking account of the fields of the surrounding dipoles, including those of the distant spheres.

CHAPTER 6

STEADY CURRENTS

Electric currents may exist in any medium in which electric charges are free to migrate. Ionized gases and ionic liquids, as well as many solid materials, are good conductors. The fundamental principles governing conductivity apply equally well to all conductors; however, in this chapter special attention is given to solid conductors because of their greater practical importance.

The crystal structure and distribution of electrons within a solid conductor are similar to those of nonconductors as described in Chapter 5. The basic difference is that all electrons in nonconductors are tightly bound to their respective nuclei, while in conducting materials a few electrons from the outer atomic shells are free to wander through the crystal. These electrons are referred to as "free electrons" or, more properly, as conduction electrons because they transport electric current through the solid.

6-1 **Metallic conductors.** The number of conduction electrons per atom in a metal depends on the electronic structure of the atoms and on the degree of perturbation of the outer electron shells when the atoms are placed in the crystal lattice. An examination of the periodic table reveals that the elements Li, Na, K, Cu, Rb, Ag, Cs, and Au have completely filled inner shells, with only one additional electron in the outer shell. In these simple metals one would expect intuitively that the one outer electron would become a conduction electron in the metallic solid. That the number of conduction electrons per atom is approximately one in these metals has been verified experimentally by Hall measurements of the type described in Chapter 7. Intuitive estimates of the number of conduction electrons in other metals are less likely to be correct, since most metals have (on the average) a fractional number of conduction electrons per atom. The transition elements Ni, Co, Pd, Rh, and most of their alloys, for example, each have approximately 0.6 conduction electrons per atom. The number of current carriers per atom in metals is always of the order of magnitude of one, while in semiconductors it is very much lower, being of the order of 10^{-9} in germanium at room temperature. The very small number of carriers in semiconductors results in interesting electrical properties, some of which are discussed in later chapters.

Thermal vibrations within a metal keep the conduction electrons constantly moving through the lattice, with velocities as high as 10^6 m/sec even at room temperature. Since this motion is random, it does not give rise to a net electric current. Application of an electric field results in a slower drift velocity superimposed upon these random thermal velocities in a direction opposite to the electric field. The resulting electric current, by convention, is taken to be in the direction of the field.

With conduction electrons moving so rapidly through the metal at all times, it is logical to inquire what prevents them from continuing their motion out into space and thus escaping from the metal. A simple calculation of the electrostatic forces acting on an escaping electron quickly reveals why this does not take place. Assume that an electron has escaped from the plane surface of a metal by a distance x, as illustrated in Fig. 6-1. Then, using an image solution of the type discussed in Section 4-2, the electron is attracted back to the surface of the metal by the force

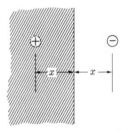

$$F = \frac{e^2}{4\pi\epsilon_0(2x)^2},$$

that is, its electric potential energy relative to the outside world is given by

$$V = -\frac{e^2}{16\pi\epsilon_0 x}. \quad (6-1)$$

FIG. 6-1. The image force is largely responsible for the attraction of an electron back toward the metallic surface from which it has escaped.

According to this equation, the work required to remove an electron would be infinite, because $V \rightarrow \infty$ as $x \rightarrow 0$. Actually, Eq. (6-1) is accurate only for distances large compared with the lattice spacings or for distances large compared with 10^{-9} m. For regions closer to the metal than this, the surface may no longer be treated as a continuum of charge but, instead, individual electronic interaction must be considered. An exact solution would require quantum mechanics; however, a better approximation can be obtained by adding an experimentally determined constant to the denominator of Eq. (6-1). The potential energy function for the electrons then becomes

$$V = \frac{e^2}{16\pi\epsilon_0 x + (e^2/W)}, \quad (6-2)$$

where W is known as the work function and is obviously the work required to remove an electron from $x = 0$ to $x \rightarrow \infty$.

When the temperature of the metal is increased, some electrons may receive enough energy to penetrate the potential barrier into space. This is called thermionic emission and accounts for the electrons emitted from the heated cathode of an electronic vacuum tube. A fairly accurate theoretical equation for thermionic emission has been calculated by Richardson and Dushman, using Fermi-Dirac statistics. Their equation is

$$J = AT^2 \exp(-W/kT),$$

where J is the emitted current density, T is the temperature of the metal in degrees Kelvin, and k is the Boltzmann constant, 1.38×10^{-23} joule/deg. Some experimentally determined values for A and W are $A = 32 \times 10^4$ amp/m^2 deg^2 and $W = 8.5 \times 10^{-19}$ joule in platinum, and $A = 75 \times 10^4$ amp/m^2 deg^2 and $W = 7.1 \times 10^{-19}$ joule in tungsten. The energy required for an electron to be emitted from the surface is decreased when the metal is charged to a negative potential; this type of emission is called the Schottky effect.

The electronic forces responsible for preventing the escape of electrons from the surface of a metal are also responsible for making the ensemble of conduction electrons behave as a very slightly compressible fluid. A bunching of electrons within a metal creates strong electric forces which tend to smooth out the distribution. Some appreciation of the magnitude of the potential that is generated by small changes in electron concentrations can be obtained from the fact that a copper sphere 0.1 m in diameter becomes charged to 1000 volts when only 10^{-15} of its conduction electrons are removed.

This fundamental property of conduction electrons in metals is responsible for the hydraulic analogy which likens steady electric currents in wires to the flow of water through gravel-filled pipes. When properly used, this analogy is an excellent one, although recently it has fallen into disfavor because it has been so frequently misused. All analogies necessarily have limited applicability and the use of any analogy without pointing out its limitations is likely to lead to misconceptions. An excellent feature of the analogy is the similarity between potentials and pressures, since, with steady flow, potential differences and pressure differences are both scalar functions of the coordinates. Furthermore, pressure differences can be defined by the work per unit volume done on the water flowing between two pressures, just as potential differences are defined by the work per unit charge done on the charges flowing between two points. Serious limitations do show up, however, when the flow is intermittent or alternating, since there are no good counterparts in the hydraulic analogy for the phenomena of the charging of capacitors or of the magnetic fields associated with currents.

6–2 Ohm's law. When the potential difference across a conductor is V and the current through the conductor is I, the ratio

$$R = \frac{V}{I} \qquad (6\text{–}3)$$

defines the resistance R of the conductor. Ohm's law states that this ratio is independent of the magnitudes and directions of V and I and depends only upon the physical properties and the geometry of the conductor. Conductors for which this law is accurate are called ohmic conductors and all others are called nonohmic. This law is quite accurate for most metals under standard conditions, and it is valid for most conductors and semiconductors within certain limitations. One rather obvious limitation is that the conduction electrons cannot move with a velocity greater than the velocity of light. This is no practical limitation in copper, which has one conduction electron per atom or about 10^{29} per cubic meter, but in germanium, with as few as 10^{19} conduction electrons per cubic meter, this limitation can be important. The current density in any material can be expressed by $\mathbf{J} = -nNe\mathbf{v}$, where N is the number of atoms per unit volume, n is the number of conduction electrons per atom, e is the charge on an electron, and $\mathbf{v}$ is the average drift velocity. Using $nN = 10^{19}$, $e = -1.6 \times 10^{-19}$, and $v = 3 \times 10^{8}$ (all in mks units), a maximum current density of 5×10^{8} amp/m^2 is obtained for germanium. Thus, regardless of the potential applied to a germanium wire with 0.1 mm^2 cross section, no more than a 50-amp current can be generated. In actual fact, the limiting current is considerably lower than this; at high voltages breakdown in the crystal occurs, freeing more electrons to conduct current. These considerations are mentioned here to point up the fact that the ohmic behavior of materials should not be taken for granted. All materials fail to be ohmic under some conditions and some materials are ohmic only under very limited conditions. Some special examples of nonohmic materials are discussed in a later chapter.

In metallic conductors, where Ohm's law is particularly accurate, the law can be obtained by elementary considerations of the forces on free electrons. Newton's law alone would predict an unlimited velocity increase for conduction electrons under the influence of an electric field. A damping term is needed and is physically reasonable in view of the interaction between the electrons and the crystal lattice. Assuming this damping to be proportional to the velocity (a friction-type damping), the equation of motion becomes

$$e\mathbf{E} = m\,\frac{d\mathbf{v}}{dt} + \frac{m}{t_r}\,\mathbf{v}, \qquad (6\text{–}4)$$

where m/t_r is the damping constant, e is the charge on an electron, and $\mathbf{v}$ is a drift velocity superimposed on the random thermal velocities. The solution of this differential equation is

$$\mathbf{v} = \frac{et_r}{m}\, \mathbf{E}[1 - \exp\,(-t/t_r)] \tag{6-5}$$

and the reason for using the symbol t_r in the damping parameter becomes evident, since it represents a relaxation time. For times long compared with t_r, the drift velocity is simply $\mathbf{v} = (et_r/m)\mathbf{E}$, and the current density is

$$\mathbf{J} = nNe\mathbf{v} = \frac{nNe^2 t_r}{m}\,\mathbf{E}. \tag{6-6}$$

Making the substitution $\rho = m/nNe^2 t_r$, the above equation reduces to

$$\mathbf{E} = \rho\mathbf{J}, \tag{6-7}$$

which is the most general form of Ohm's law. For the simple case of a linear conductor of length l and cross-sectional area A, Eq. (6–7) becomes $V = IR$, where $R = \rho l/A$, $I = JA$, and $V = El$.

Because of the relationship between t_r and ρ, it is possible to determine the value for t_r in Eq. (6–5). Using values for copper of $m = 0.9 \times 10^{-30}$ kgm, $e = 1.6 \times 10^{-19}$ coul, $\rho = 1.7 \times 10^{-8}$ ohm·m, $n = 1$ electron/atom, and $N = (6.025 \times 10^{23}$ atoms/mole$) \times (1/63.5$ mole/gm$) \times (8.89 \times 10^6$ gm/m$^3) = 8.5 \times 10^{28}$ atoms/m^3, a relaxation time of $t_r \cong 2 \times 10^{-14}$ sec is obtained. This indicates that the momentum of the conduction electrons should not cause them to lag the applied voltage except at very high frequencies approaching that of visible light, and it is experimentally well substantiated that energy losses in waveguides may be calculated accurately using the assumption that $t_r \ll 1/f$ for frequencies as high as $f = 10^{10}$ cycles/sec or more.

The damping parameter introduced in Eq. (6–4) has been justified on the classical basis of interactions between the conduction electrons and the positive nuclei of the metallic crystal. Even in an absolutely perfect single crystal with no imperfections, no impurities, and no thermal vibrations, the drift velocity of conduction electrons would be retarded by continual collisions with the nuclei of the lattice. In this respect, wave mechanics is in direct contradiction with classical mechanics.

A wave-mechanical calculation treats the crystal lattice as a periodic potential function with the periodicity of the lattice spacings. No damping of the motion of the conduction electrons is obtained so long as this potential remains strictly periodic. However, at temperatures above absolute zero, the thermal vibrations of the crystal destroy the periodicity and a finite resistance results. A theoretical calculation of the temperature variation for a pure metal has been made by Gruneisen and its re-

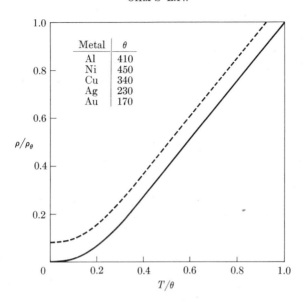

FIG. 6–2. The solid line is Gruneisen's calculation for the variation of resistivity with temperature, in which θ is the Debye temperature and ρ_θ is the resistivity of the metal at the Debye temperature. The dashed curve, which is a plot of ρ for Cu + 0.2% Ni divided by ρ_θ for pure Cu, illustrates Matthiessen's rule. Representative values of θ obtained from specific heat measurements are listed in the figure.

sult is plotted in Fig. 6–2. The constant θ is the characteristic Debye temperature of the material and may be determined by specific heat measurements, while ρ_θ is the resistivity of the metal at its Debye temperature. At high temperatures the resistivity is proportional to T, and at low temperatures it is proportional to T^5. Some experimentally determined values of θ for various metals are listed on the curve. This curve is in excellent agreement with experimental observations on many metals.

For metals containing a small amount of impurity, a modification to Gruneisen's curve must be made. This modification, which is known as Matthiessen's rule, states that the scattering of conduction electrons by impurity atoms is temperature-independent, so that the total resistivity of the material may be expressed by

$$\rho \text{ (total)} = \rho \text{ (Gruneisen)} + \rho \text{ (impurity)},$$

where ρ (impurity) is a temperature-independent resistivity due to impurity scattering. The change in resistivity for copper with 0.2% nickel is illustrated by the dashed curve in Fig. 6–2. In commercially pure metals, the small number of impurities present has little effect on the resistivity at room temperature, amounting to 0.1% to 1.0%. The effect does become important, however, at low temperatures where the resistivity of pure metals approaches zero.

Because of the almost linear change of resistivity with temperature near room temperature, it is possible to express this variation by

$$\rho(t) = \rho(20°C)[1 + \alpha(t - 20)]. \qquad (6\text{-}8)$$

Room-temperature resistivities of some common materials are listed in Table 6–1, along with their temperature coefficients. Impurity scattering in Cu can be increased by adding more Ni until ρ (impurity) becomes the dominant term, but Matthiessen's rule becomes less and less accurate. Certain alloys of Cu and Ni have been used in making resistors for measuring instruments because of their relatively high resistivities and low temperature coefficients.

The temperature coefficients for nonmetals are typically larger than those for metals and are of opposite sign, as indicated by the nonmetals in Table 6–1. To understand this, consider the expression for resistivity as obtained for metallic conduction,

$$\rho = \frac{m}{nNe^2t_r}.$$

This expression is just as applicable for semiconductors as it is for metals and, as in metals, t_r decreases with increasing temperatures. However, in semiconductors the conductivity is limited more by the small number of current carriers than by the size of t_r. Some electrons which are bound to lattice sites at low temperatures are freed at higher temperatures by thermal vibrations of the lattice. Thus the decreasing resistivity with increasing temperature in nonmetals reflects an increase in the number of current carriers rather than a change in the relaxation time.

6–3 Energy and power conversions. Motions of charges in electric fields usually result in conversions of energy from one form to another. A charged particle in free space loses or gains kinetic energy. Conduction electrons within a conductor gain energy, which is transmitted to the atoms on lattice sites as thermal vibrations. The work done by an electric field on a charge moving through it is given by

$$W = \int \mathbf{F} \cdot d\mathbf{l} = \int q\mathbf{E} \cdot d\mathbf{l},$$

integrated over the path of the moving charge, q. For a charge moving with the field the integrand is positive, showing that the electric field energy is being converted to some other form. However, for a charge moving in the opposite direction the integrand is negative, and the energy conversion is reversed.

TABLE 6–1

RESISTIVITIES AND TEMPERATURE COEFFICIENTS OF SOME COMMON
MATERIALS AT ROOM TEMPERATURES

Element	Resistivity, ohm·m	Temperature coefficient per C°	Alloy or compound	Resistivity, ohm·m	Temperature coefficient per C°
Silver	1.6×10^{-8}	3.75×10^{-3}	Constantan 45%Ni–55%Cu	49×10^{-8}	0.5×10^{-5}
Gold	2.2×10^{-8}	3.4×10^{-3}	Nichrome, Ni-Cr-Fe	112×10^{-8}	40.0×10^{-5}
Copper	1.7×10^{-8}	4.1×10^{-3}			
Aluminum	2.7×10^{-8}	4.0×10^{-3}	Bakelite	10^{10}	-0.06
Tungsten	5.3×10^{-8}	4.7×10^{-3}	Glass	10^{12}	-0.07
Nickel	6.9×10^{-8}	3.4×10^{-3}			
Carbon	3.5×10^{-3}	-0.03	Mica	10^{15}	-0.07
Sulfur	10^{15}				

The power being delivered to a charge moving with the velocity **v** is given by

$$p = q\mathbf{E} \cdot \mathbf{v},$$

and the total power being delivered to all the charges in an element of volume $d\tau$ is

$$dP = \sum p_i = \sum q_i \mathbf{E}_i \cdot \mathbf{v}_i,$$

where the sum is performed over all the charges in the volume element. When this expression is applied to conduction electrons in a volume small enough so that they all have the same drift velocity and are all acted upon by the same field **E**, the above equation becomes

$$dP = Nne\mathbf{E} \cdot \mathbf{v}\, d\tau,$$

where N is the number of atoms per unit volume and n is the average number of conduction electrons per atom. Using the expression $\mathbf{J} = Nne\mathbf{v}$ for current density, the power delivered to an element of volume may be expressed as

$$dP = \mathbf{E} \cdot \mathbf{J}\, d\tau. \tag{6–9}$$

A positive sign again indicates that electric power is being converted to some other form. The total electric power being converted within any volume τ is

$$P = \int_\tau \mathbf{E} \cdot \mathbf{J}\, d\tau. \tag{6–10}$$

Joulean heat. The current density in an ohmic conductor is $\mathbf{J} = \mathbf{E}/\rho$, provided the conductor is isotropic. According to Eq. (6–10) the power converted into heat within a volume τ of such a conductor is

$$P = \int_\tau \rho \mathbf{J} \cdot \mathbf{J}\, d\tau = \int_\tau J^2 \rho\, d\tau, \tag{6–11}$$

and the heat produced within this volume is called joulean heat. In any single conductor carrying a current I, imaginary surfaces can be drawn perpendicular to **J** so that $I = \int_s J\, ds$. Then, if $d\tau = ds\, dl$, with dl measured parallel to **J**, Eq. (6–10) becomes

$$P = \int_s J\, ds \int_l E\, dl = IV = I^2 R, \tag{6–12}$$

when IR from Ohm's law is substituted for V. Equation (6–12) is the well-known relation for joule heating in an ohmic resistor.

6–4 Sources of electric energy and power. Electromagnetic generators with rotating armatures, storage batteries and other chemical cells, thermocouples, and the so-called static generators that include the Van

FIG. 6–3. A Van de Graaff generator projecting positively charged particles down an evacuated tube from C to O.

de Graaff generator are all capable of converting some other form of energy into electric energy. Each of these devices can be made to produce steady currents in networks of conductors. To do so, they must continually convert some form of energy to electric energy to balance the electric energy which is continually being converted back to some other form of energy, for example to heat within the conductors or to mechanical energy by the motors. The integral of Eq. (6–10) is therefore negative when performed over just the volume occupied by one of these devices. However, there may be regions within these devices where the integrand is positive, i.e., where the energy conversions proceed in the opposite direction, for example the joulean heat produced in the windings of an electromagnetic generator or the mechanical energy delivered to that portion of the belt of a Van de Graaff generator that carries a small residual charge out of the charge-collecting sphere.

Van de Graaff generator. The Van de Graaff generator is ideal for illustrating these power conversions. As shown in Fig. 6–3, this device consists of a conveyor belt of insulating material, which can be operated mechanically to transport charges to a conducting sphere against the forces of a strong electric field. Since very large potential differences can be obtained with this device, it is commonly used for accelerating elementary charged particles for scientific experiments. In the figure it is assumed that a steady stream of positively charged particles is projected down the evacuated tube from C to O, arriving at O with relatively large kinetic energies.

The fine needlepoints at A are connected to ground through a low-voltage source. Depending on the polarity of this source, electrons will either be sprayed onto the belt from the points or be withdrawn from the belt by the points. This latter case is electrically equivalent to spraying positive charges onto the belt. With mechanical power turning the lower pulley clockwise, this positive charge is carried up to the insulated metallic sphere. The appearance of positive charges on the sphere means that electrons have been withdrawn from the sphere through the needlepoints at B, and sprayed onto the belt. These partially neutralize the belt's positive charge, but complete neutralization does not occur because electrons move across the gap only while the field between the belt and the points is sufficiently strong. Although a background of positive charges remains on the belt, the number of electrons removed per second from the belt at A, under steady-state conditions, equals the number returned per second to the belt at B. For this condition to be maintained, there must be an equal current from the sphere to ground, consisting of positively charged particles proceeding down the tube from C to O, plus some leakage currents through imperfect insulation.

The background charge remaining on the belt absorbs some energy from the field on the downward motion of the belt but returns this energy as it travels upward. Only the additional charges added at A and removed at B absorb net energy from the belt. Neglecting the losses due to leakage currents, this energy reappears as kinetic energy of the accelerated particles. The power being delivered to the belt can be calculated from Eq. (6–10). On the upward-moving portion of the belt $\mathbf{E} \cdot \mathbf{J}\, d\tau = -EI_t\, dl$, which is negative because $\mathbf{E}$ and $\mathbf{J}$ are oppositely directed, while on the downward-moving portion $\mathbf{E} \cdot \mathbf{J}\, d\tau = EI_r\, dl$, which is positive because $\mathbf{E}$ and $\mathbf{J}$ are in the same direction. The currents are defined by $I_t = I + I_r$, where I_t is the total current directed upward on the left and I_r is the residual current carried by the background charges remaining on the belt after it passes B. The net power delivered to the belt is

$$P = -\int_A^B EI_t\, dl + \int_B^A EI_r\, dl$$

$$= -I\int_A^B E\, dl - I_r\int_A^B E\, dl + I_r\int_B^A E\, dl,$$

which may be written in vector notation as

$$P = I\int_A^B \mathbf{E} \cdot d\mathbf{l} + I_r\oint \mathbf{E} \cdot d\mathbf{l} = -I\mathcal{E},$$

where in this case

$$-\int_A^B \mathbf{E} \cdot d\mathbf{l} = \mathcal{E}$$

is the emf of the device and

$$\oint \mathbf{E} \cdot d\mathbf{l} = 0$$

when integrated around the path of the belt in this electrostatic field.

Storage batteries and other chemical cells. When a battery is supplying a steady current for a network of conductors, the current in the battery is directed from the terminal of low potential to that of high potential. Chemical forces are responsible for moving the charges against the internal electrostatic field, and in doing this work, chemical energy is converted to electric energy. It is possible to reverse the direction of electric current in any chemical cell by sufficiently increasing the electric potential by means of an external emf. The increased electrostatic potential is then strong enough to cause a net flow of charge against the chemical forces, and electric energy is converted to chemical energy. Chemical energy created in a dry cell in this manner is not in a form that can be recovered by reversing the current, but in a storage battery the process is almost completely reversible for moderate currents. When electric charges are forced to flow against the chemical forces, electric energy is converted to chemical energy and the battery is said to be charging. The battery is said to be discharging when this chemical energy is converted to electric energy by forcing an electric current through an external circuit.

Thermocouples. The simplest thermocouple consists of a wire of one metal with its ends joined to those of a wire of some other metal to form a closed loop. In general, if the two junctions are maintained at different temperatures there will be a current in the loop that depends upon the nature of the two metals and the temperatures of the two junctions. Such thermocouples can be used to maintain steady currents in a network of resistors by cutting one of the wires of the simple loop into two parts and joining the resulting loose ends to the network.

If there are temperature differences throughout the network there may be many thermocouples to consider. However, if all but the original two junctions are maintained at a single temperature, these original junctions will provide the only emf and it will depend upon the nature of the original two metals and the temperatures of the two original junctions. Heat energy is then continually absorbed at the hotter of these two junctions and converted into electric energy. However, electric energy is also continually converted back into heat at the colder of these two junctions, and this heat must be continuously removed from the cold junction if its low temperature is to be maintained. The fact that some electric energy must be converted back to heat at the cold junction makes this device similar to all other heat engines in that only a fraction of the heat energy supplied can be converted to other forms of useful energy. If an external emf is used to drive current in the opposite direction through the thermocouple, a "heat-pump" action can be produced, absorbing some heat at the cold junction and releasing a greater quantity of heat at the hot junction. Unfortunately, the magnitudes of the emf's available from such junctions are so low that they are not yet practical for power applications in general. Thus far these devices have been found to be most useful for measuring temperatures at otherwise inaccessible locations.

Electromagnetic generators. Electric dynamos and other direct-current electromagnetic generators are discussed in detail in Chapter 7. In a dynamo, wire windings on a rotor are mechanically caused to revolve in the presence of a steady magnetic field. The conduction electrons in the windings experience a force, of electromagnetic origin, parallel to the wire, and an emf is produced. This emf is proportional to the speed of the rotor and the strength of the magnetic field. If the rotor windings are connected to an external circuit, charges will flow through the circuit, with a resultant dissipation of electric power. This electric power is supplied by the mechanical power used to turn the rotor. The greater the electric power produced, the more mechanical power must be supplied.

Because of frictional losses and electric losses within the windings of the generator, the mechanical power used must always be greater than the electric power produced. The resistive losses within the rotor windings are proportional to the square of the rotor current, and so are much smaller when little or no current is being drawn by the external circuit. The emf of a generator is defined as the limit of the voltage across the terminals of the rotor as the rotor current approaches zero. Briefly stated, *the emf of a device is defined as the open-circuit potential difference across its output terminals.* While the emf of a device can also be defined in terms of the amount of power it converts to or from the electric form, this definition in terms of potential difference is just as fundamental and is more easily applied.

While a measurement of the zero-current voltage is practical for batteries and thermocouples, it is not practical for most electromagnetic generators. Most dynamos, for example, utilize the magnetic field of an electromagnet powered by the dynamo's current output. Thus with zero current through the rotor, there would be zero emf. The emf of such generators may be measured, however, by supplying current to the electromagnet from an external source.

The power converted to electric power from some other form determines the emf of each of these devices. The emf of a device is given by the ratio of the power converted, to the current through the device, provided this power includes that which may be immediately converted to heat by the internal resistance of the device. In a single closed loop consisting, for example, of resistors all in series and these in series with a source of steady current,

$$\oint \mathbf{E} \cdot d\mathbf{l} = 0,$$

which is valid for steady conditions where neither electric nor magnetic fields vary with time. This integral can be separated into two parts; first, the integral through the resistors in series, where

$$\int \mathbf{E} \cdot d\mathbf{l} = \int \rho \mathbf{J} \cdot d\mathbf{l} = \int A\mathbf{J} \cdot \frac{\rho \, d\mathbf{l}}{A} = I R_1 + I R_2 + \cdots = \sum_j I R_j,$$

and second, that through the source of emf, where

$$\int \mathbf{E} \cdot d\mathbf{l} = -\varepsilon$$

for a source with no internal resistance, but

$$-\varepsilon + I R_i$$

for one with the internal resistance R_i.

6–5 Conservation of charge. One of the best-established laws of nature is that electric charge is always conserved. The net charge flowing per second into any arbitrary volume τ through its bounding surface s equals the rate of increase of charge in that volume. Mathematically, this means that

$$-\int_s \mathbf{J} \cdot d\mathbf{s} = \int_\tau \frac{\partial \rho}{\partial t} \, d\tau, \qquad (6\text{--}13)$$

where $\mathbf{J}$ is the current density in coul/m^2 sec and ρ is the charge density in coul/m^3. Gauss' theorem can be used to transform the surface integral into a volume integral:

$$-\int_\tau \boldsymbol{\nabla} \cdot \mathbf{J} \, d\tau = \int_\tau \frac{\partial \rho}{\partial t} \, d\tau.$$

Since τ is an arbitrary volume, the integrands of these two-volume integrals can be equated to give

$$\boldsymbol{\nabla} \cdot \mathbf{J} + \frac{\partial \rho}{\partial t} = 0, \qquad (6\text{--}14)$$

which is usually referred to as the conservation of charge equation. Because of its importance it will be referred to many times throughout this text.

6–6 Steady current-density solutions.   When current densities in a region are steady there can be no time-dependent change in the charge densities and Eq. (6–14) for the conservation of charge becomes $\nabla \cdot \mathbf{J} = 0$. With isotropic resistors obeying Ohm's law, $\mathbf{J}\rho = -\nabla V$ and the equation becomes

$$\nabla^2 V = 0.$$

Problems involving steady currents then can be solved by means of Laplace's equation, by the methods discussed in Chapters 4 and 5.

The procedure can be demonstrated with the problem shown in Fig. 6–4, in which a difference of potential V_B is maintained between the outer cylinder of copper and the inner cylinder of nickel by the porous washer on the left that is saturated with an electrolyte. The nickel, electrolyte, and copper thus constitute a chemical cell. The washer on the right can be a semiconductor like carbon, but the problem will first be solved for the case with no current by assuming the washer to be a perfect dielectric with a large dielectric constant $K > 30$. The resistances of the metal cylinders and the chemical cell are of no importance for the dielectric problem, and they can be ignored relative to the semiconductor resistance if t, a, b, and $c - b$ do not differ by more than a factor of 10.

The space inside the dielectric washer can be considered two-dimensional because the fringing flux of $\mathbf{D}$ existing in the space to the right of the dielectric is small enough to be ignored with this large dielectric constant. With the nickel cylinder at one potential and the copper cylinder at another, lines of electric flux pass between the two cylinders. By the symmetry of the problem, these must be radial lines drawn perpendicular to both cylinders, and the density of these lines must decrease as $1/r$ between the cylinders. A potential function is to be found whose gradient has the

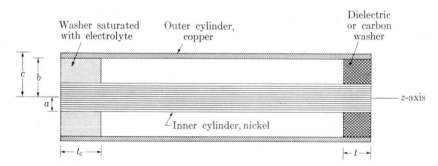

Fig. 6–4. Concentric cylinders of nickel and copper form an electrochemical cell with the electrolyte at the left of this diagram. These cylinders also constitute a transmission line for either the capacitor or the resistor found at the right of the diagram.

form of $1/r$. Such a potential is represented by

$$V = G \ln r,$$

which is readily shown to satisfy Laplace's equation. To be the correct solution, it must also satisfy the boundary conditions $V = V_{Ni}$ at $r = a$ and $V = V_{Cu}$ at $r = b$. These conditions yield two equations:

$$V_{Ni} = G \ln a$$

and

$$V_{Cu} = G \ln b,$$

from which $V_B = V_{Cu} - V_{Ni} = G \ln b/a$ and

$$V = \frac{V_B \ln r}{\ln b/a}.$$

The field in the dielectric is then

$$\mathbf{E} = -\boldsymbol{\nabla} V = -\frac{V_B \mathbf{a}_r}{r \ln b/a},$$

and the charge densities on those surfaces of the nickel and copper cylinders that are in contact with the dielectric are

$$\sigma_{Ni} = \epsilon E_{Ni} = \frac{\epsilon V_B}{a \ln b/a}$$

and

$$\sigma_{Cu} = -\epsilon E_{Cu} = -\frac{\epsilon V_B}{b \ln b/a}$$

respectively. Since the magnitude of the charge where either cylinder is in contact with the dielectric is $2\pi t \epsilon V_B / \ln (b/a)$, the capacitance of this section is given by

$$C = \frac{q}{V_B} = \frac{2\pi \epsilon t}{\ln b/a}.$$

If the dielectric is now replaced with a carbon washer of identical shape, the region where $\nabla^2 V = 0$ and its boundary conditions remain the same. The potential distribution in the washer is still

$$V = \frac{V_B \ln r}{\ln b/a}$$

and the field is still

$$\mathbf{E} = -\frac{V_B \mathbf{a}_r}{r \ln b/a}.$$

However, there is now a current density $\mathbf{J} = \mathbf{E}/\rho$, and the total current through the washer can be obtained by integrating over either metallic surface in contact with the washer to obtain

$$I = \int \mathbf{J} \cdot d\mathbf{s} = \frac{V_B 2\pi t}{\rho \ln b/a}.$$

The resistance of the washer is then

$$R = \frac{V_B}{I} = \frac{\rho \ln b/a}{2\pi t}.$$

For this geometry the product $RC = \rho\epsilon$, although the accuracy of this expression depends upon the accuracies of the individual expressions for R and C. The expression for R cannot be mathematically exact unless ρ for the air space is infinitely larger than that for carbon. Likewise, the calculation for C could be mathematically exact only if K for the dielectric were infinitely larger than that for the air space. Since the ratio of resistivities will be near 10^{18}, the expression for R is sufficiently accurate for all purposes. However, the ratio of the dielectric constants will seldom be as large as 30, so that the expression for C is much less accurate. The error in the product stems from the fact that the potential distributions are not quite the same in the dielectric washer as in the carbon washer.

The expression $RC = \rho\epsilon$ can be shown to have general validity only when the potential distribution in an isotropic and linear dielectric is identical with that in the same shape of semiconductor, which is both isotropic and ohmic. The chief advantage of the similarities in the expressions for these two types of problems lies in the fact that a current problem can sometimes be solved by electrostatic methods, using assumptions that would be unrealistic for the electrostatic problem but not for the current problem. For example, to correlate the Hall effects of ferromagnetic materials with their magnetic properties,* it was desirable to make simultaneous measurements of the Hall emf, the magnetic fields, and the magnetization within a rectangular bar of iron. For the magnetic measurements the fields should be parallel to a long bar, but high current densities perpendicular to these fields were needed. Figure 6–5 shows how a high current density was achieved, perpendicular to the length of the bar and constant along the line HH'. A relatively large current I entered the bar through the copper wedge in contact with its upper surface, spread out through the bar, and left it through the copper wedge contacting the bottom surface. In the neighborhood of the line HH', this produced a relatively large and fairly uniform current density,

---

* Emerson M. Pugh, "Hall Effect and the Magnetic Properties of Some Ferromagnetic Materials," *Phys. Rev.* **36**, 1505 (1930), Fig. 1.

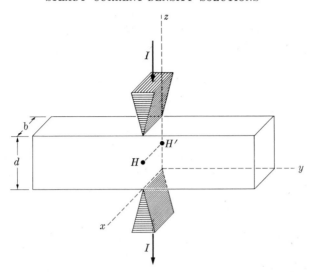

Fig. 6–5. A rectangular bar of ferromagnetic metal designed for measuring its Hall effect and its magnetic properties simultaneously. The sample current I passes through the bar from the upper to the lower copper wedge.

whose magnitude had to be calculated accurately. Since $\mathbf{E} = -\nabla V$ in an electrostatic field and $\mathbf{J} = -\nabla V/\rho$ in this situation, the problem could be solved if $\mathbf{E}$ could be determined for some fictitious electrostatic problem with the same boundary conditions on V and ∇V.

The actual current density pattern is two-dimensional in the bar, with the wedge contacts acting as source and sink. Electrostatically, these contacts can be simulated by charged filaments of infinite length. If the bar also is assumed to be infinitely long, the boundary conditions require that ∇V be parallel to the y-axis along both the upper and the lower surfaces of the bar, where $\mathbf{J}$ must parallel the surface. These boundary conditions can be satisfied easily for an electrostatic problem with an infinite series of equally charged filaments each infinitely long; that is, with filaments parallel to the x-axis, through $z = 0$, $\pm d$, $\pm 2d$, $\pm \cdots$ $\pm nd \pm \cdots$, where the filaments must be positively charged when n is odd and negatively charged when n is even. This infinite array of image filaments is symmetrically spaced above and below the xy-plane, in which one negatively charged filament passes through the origin. Symmetry requires that everywhere in this xy-plane the field $\mathbf{E}$ is directed parallel to the y-axis toward this negative filament. Since it is infinite, the array is also symmetrical about a parallel plane through the positive filament at $z = d$. Fields in this plane are parallel to it but directed away from the positive filament. These images then guarantee that currents based upon them will be properly directed. To find the magnitudes of the current densities, the effective charge per unit length, q_l, of the filaments must be determined. It is not difficult to show that $q_l = \rho \epsilon I_l$, where $I_l = I/b$ is the current per unit length through one of the wedge contacts.

From this set of image charges the field $\mathbf{E}$ at HH' can be written as an infinite series that fortunately converges quite rapidly, and from the limit of its convergence it can be shown that the current density at HH' is just $J = I/bd$. This solves the problem, since J can be determined from the easily measured quantities I, b, and d.

For a bar of finite length the problem can be solved by extending the pattern of image filaments throughout space, as shown in Fig. 6–6, where the pattern extends to infinity in both the y- and z-directions. Because they are two-dimensional, these problems can also be solved by means of complex variables.

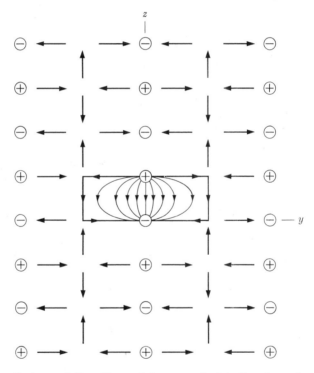

FIG. 6–6. System of line filament images, electrically charged, that are required to produce the electric fields found in the iron bar of Fig. 6–5. The current densities in this bar are parallel and proportional to these fields. The filaments are infinitely long and the array extends to infinity in the y- and z-directions.

6-7 Kirchhoff's laws. Kirchhoff stated two laws, both of which are indispensable for solving problems concerning d-c currents in networks of conductors. When the extremely low compressibility of the "fluid" of conduction electrons in metals is considered, the first law seems so obvious for steady currents that it hardly needs to be stated. These laws are:

1. The algebraic sum of the n charges flowing out of any junction is zero; that is, if I_1, I_2, I_3, ..., I_n are the currents out of a junction, then

$$\sum_{i=1}^{i=n} I_i = 0. \tag{6-15}$$

2. For any closed loop that can be drawn in a network, the algebraic sum of current through each resistor times its resistance for all of the resistors in a closed loop is equal to the algebraic sum of all the emf's encountered in traversing this loop. This may be expressed mathematically as

$$\sum_j I_j R_j = \sum_j \mathcal{E}_j. \tag{6-16}$$

The first law can be proved mathematically from the conservation of charge, Eq. (6-13):

$$\int_s \mathbf{J} \cdot d\mathbf{s} = -\int_\tau \frac{\partial \rho}{\partial t} \, d\tau.$$

The junction should be surrounded by some imaginary surface s enclosing a volume τ, as shown in Fig. 6-7. Under steady conditions the volume integral is zero and the surface integral gives Eq. (6-15).

The second law can be demonstrated by following the procedure of Section 6-4, where the integral

$$\oint \mathbf{E} \cdot d\mathbf{l} = 0$$

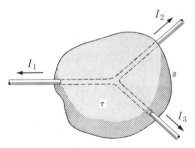

FIG. 6-7. Currents I_1, I_2, and I_3 leaving a junction enclosed within an arbitrary volume. Kirchhoff's first law that $I_1 + I_2 + I_3 = 0$ can be proved by applying Gauss' law $\int_s \mathbf{J} \cdot d\mathbf{s}$ to the bounding surface s.

around the enclosed loop of a network was divided into two integrals: (1) through all the resistors but excluding all sources of emf to obtain

$$\int \rho \mathbf{J} \cdot d\mathbf{l} = \sum_j I_j R_j,$$

and (2) through all of the sources of emf in the loop to obtain

$$\int \mathbf{E} \cdot d\mathbf{l} = \sum_j (-\mathcal{E}_j + I_j R_{ij}),$$

where R_{ij} represents the internal resistance of the source whose emf is $\mathcal{E}_j$. Therefore

$$\sum_j I_j(R_j + R_{ij}) = \sum_j \mathcal{E}_j,$$

which can be written simply as

$$\sum_j I_j R_j = \sum_j \mathcal{E}_j,$$

provided the internal resistance of each source is added to the resistance of the series segment of the network in which it resides.

6–8 Solution of d-c network problems. The solution of d-c problems involving networks of resistors connected together usually can be simplified by first calculating the equivalent resistance of some of the combinations of resistors. Whenever a group of resistors within a larger network is connected to that network by just two wires, this group can be replaced by a single resistor without affecting the rest of the network. The resistance of the single resistor required to replace the group is called its equivalent resistance. For example, in Fig. 6–8 the group of resistors enclosed by the smaller of the dashed-line rectangles can be replaced by a single resistor without affecting the currents in the rest of the network. Furthermore, the group enclosed by the larger dashed rectangle also can be replaced without changing the current through the battery.

When resistors are connected in series in a d-c circuit, there is the same current I in each and the difference of potential across the group is the sum of the differences of potential across the separate wires. If R_1, R_2, ..., R_n are the resistances of resistors connected in series and R_s is their equivalent resistance, then, from Eq. (6–16),

$$IR_s = IR_1 + IR_2 + \cdots + IR_n$$

and

$$R_s = R_1 + R_2 + \cdots + R_n.$$

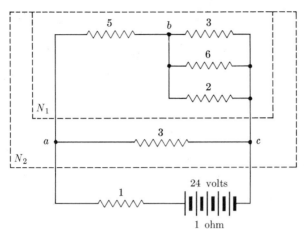

FIG. 6–8. A direct-current circuit which is completely solvable by the effective resistance method.

When a group of resistors are joined so that one end of each is connected to one common junction while the other end of each is connected to another, the resistors are in parallel and the potential difference V is the same across all resistors. However, there are different currents, I_1, I_2, I_3, etc., through each resistor, so that the total current, according to Eq. (6–15), is $I_p = I_1 + I_2 + \cdots + I_n$. Defining R_p as the equivalent resistance of these resistors in parallel, this becomes

$$\frac{V}{R_p} = \frac{V}{R_1} + \frac{V}{R_2} + \cdots + \frac{V}{R_n}$$

and

$$\frac{1}{R_p} = \frac{1}{R_1} + \frac{1}{R_2} + \cdots + \frac{1}{R_n}. \qquad (6\text{–}17)$$

The network problem of Fig. 6–8 is easily solved by the method of equivalent resistances. The equivalent resistance of the three resistors connected in parallel between b and c, by Eq. (6–17), is just 1 ohm. Since this is in series with a 5-ohm resistor, the equivalent resistance of the group enclosed by the small rectangle is 6 ohms. The effective resistance within the large rectangle between a and c is just 2 ohms, since the 6-ohm resistance in the small rectangle and the 3-ohm resistor are in parallel. The network then becomes a simple series circuit containing an emf of 24 volts and a total resistance of $2 + 1 + 1 = 4$ ohms, which gives a current through the battery of 6 amp. The current through any separate series segment can now be determined by simple applications of these two laws. For example, since the voltage drop from a to c is 6 amp $\times$ 2 ohms = 12 volts, the current through the middle 3-ohm re-

sistor is 12 volts/3 ohms = 4 amp, and that through the 5-ohm resistor
is 6 amp − 4 amp = 2 amp.

Complex networks. The simple network of Fig. 6–8 has been reduced
by the method of equivalent resistances to a problem in a single unknown
current. With many networks, there will be more than one unknown
current after all possible equivalent resistances have been calculated. In
general, there will be one unknown current for every remaining series
branch. If N is the number of unknowns, it will be necessary to obtain
N independent equations from Kirchhoff's two laws for the solution. Since
Kirchhoff's junction equation (6–15) is very simple, the number of unknowns can be decreased conveniently by writing results from each junction equation directly on the network diagram. For example, at a junction like that in Fig. 6–7, the unknown I_3 can be eliminated by writing
instead $-(I_1 + I_2)$. At each junction one unknown current can be
eliminated, although the equation for the last junction considered is
never independent of the rest. If J is the number of junctions, the number
of unknowns can usually be reduced to $N - J + 1$. This number of
equations must be obtained by applying Kirchhoff's closed loop equation
(6–16) to $(N - J + 1)$ closed loops. Each branch of the network must
be included in at least one loop equation. These general methods for
solving network problems are demonstrated in the next section by solution of the potentiometer and the Wheatstone bridge problems.

6–9 Direct-current instruments. Many of the instruments for measuring properties of d-c networks employ some form of the d'Arsonval
galvanometer, whose characteristics are treated more extensively in the
next chapter. A schematic drawing of one type of these galvanometers,
which is made portable by supporting the coil assembly with its pointer
in jeweled bearings, is shown in Fig. 6–9. Current through the coil, in
the nearly constant magnetic field, causes it to turn against the restoring
torque of a coiled spring, not shown in the diagram. If the instrument
is well designed the deflection of the pointer from zero to full scale is
proportional to the current in the coil. As it stands, such an instrument
will measure currents up to its capacity, which may be 10^{-3} amp, although
these instruments have been built to give full-scale deflections with
only 5×10^{-6} amp. It is neither feasible nor desirable to construct
galvanometer coils to carry very much larger currents.

The laws of equivalent resistances presented in the previous section
make it possible to combine resistors with galvanometers to make instruments for the direct reading of wide ranges of currents, and of potential
differences. By adding a dry cell, resistance can also be read directly.
For precision measurements, resistors are needed with accurately known
resistances that remain constant over reasonable ranges of temperature

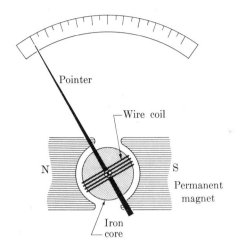

Pointer

Wire coil

N   S

Permanent magnet

Iron core

FIG. 6–9. Schematic drawing of a galvanometer pivoted in jeweled bearings.

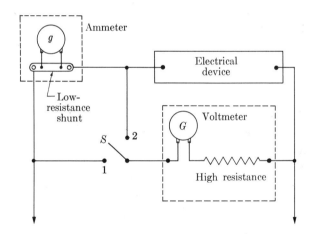

Ammeter

Electrical device

Low-resistance shunt

Voltmeter

High resistance

FIG. 6–10. A diagram to show how resistors are combined with a sensitive pivot-type galvanometer to produce either an ammeter or a voltmeter. It also shows two ways for connecting these instruments to measure the current through and the potential difference across an electrical device.

and for a considerable time. Fortunately, resistors are available that satisfy these requirements reasonably well.

Ammeters and voltmeters. An ammeter connected in series to measure the current through some electrical device is shown in Fig. 6–10. It consists of a galvanometer whose coil resistance is R_g connected in parallel with a resistor or shunt often of very low resistance R_p, because it must carry a large fraction of the current being measured. The equivalent resistance of the ammeter is

$$R_A = \frac{R_p R_g}{R_g + R_p}$$

and, if I_g is the current in the coil, the total current through the ammeter is

$$I = \left(\frac{R_p + R_g}{R_p}\right) I_g.$$

For galvanometer scales calibrated in terms of I_g, the ratio inside the parentheses provides the factor for determining I. It is desirable for R_A to be small compared with the resistances in series with it, for otherwise the ammeter causes too much disturbance to the circuit into which it is connected.

The voltmeter consists of one of these same sensitive galvanometers of resistance R_G, connected in series with a resistor having a very high resistance R_S. The potential difference measured by this voltmeter is the difference of potential across its terminals:

$$V = (R_S + R_G)I_G.$$

Because V is proportional to I_G, it is also proportional to the deflection. The total resistance of the voltmeter,

$$R_V = R_S + R_G,$$

should be very large, to avoid disturbing the circuits into which it is connected.

When these instruments are connected into networks to determine currents or potential differences, they become part of the network and alter its characteristics. To obtain precision results the networks must be analyzed with their measuring instruments in place. For example, two ways are shown in Fig. 6–10 for connecting the ammeter and voltmeter to obtain the current through the device and the potential difference across it. If I_1 and V_1 are the readings of the instruments when S is switched to contact 1 and I_2 and V_2 are these readings with S at contact 2, the following equations can be shown to give I, the current through the device, and V, the potential difference across it:

With S at 1,

$$I = I_1 \quad \text{and} \quad V = V_1\left(\frac{R}{R_A + R}\right),$$

and with S at 2,

$$I = I_2\left(\frac{R_V}{R + R_V}\right) \quad \text{and} \quad V = V_2.$$

Which connection is best depends upon the relative values of the resistances involved. A good rule is that 1 is best when $R/(R_A + R) \cong 1$ and 2 is best when $R_V/(R + R_V) \cong 1$.

Multiple-purpose meters. Meters for measuring both current and voltage may be purchased under various trade names. These instruments contain one galvanometer and several resistors that can be switched into series or into parallel with the galvanometer. Those of high resistance provide for measurements of several ranges of voltage, while those of low resistance provide for measurements of several ranges of current. Frequently these instruments also contain a battery which may be switched into series with the galvanometer. Its readings will then be inversely proportional to the resistance included in the circuit. With the use of proper calibrating resistors within the instrument, it can be adjusted to read the value of any resistance connected between its terminals.

The major advantage of the instruments discussed in this section is that they give rapid, direct readings of the desired quantity. In some applications, however, their precision is not good enough. The current drawn from the circuit to produce the galvanometer deflection is the major source of error in some applications; but even when this is not a serious problem, there is still the limitation in the accuracy with which a scale may be read. For applications in which considerable accuracy is required a null reading instrument is superior to a deflection instrument. Many circuits have been devised for specific applications,* but those most commonly used are the potentiometer and the Wheatstone bridge.

Potentiometer. The basic circuit for the potentiometer is shown in Fig. 6–11. The zigzag line from b to c represents a resistance wire of uniform cross section and total resistance R. The arrow touching the

Fig. 6–11. Slidewire potentiometer with current designations suitable for easy solution of the circuit.

---

* For a discussion of several such circuits, see W. C. Michels, *Advanced Electrical Measurements*, D. Van Nostrand Co., Inc., 1957.

line at point a represents a sliding electric contact that divides R into two portions, R_x and $R - R_x$. The unknown difference of potential, V_u, that is to be measured is connected in series with a galvanometer as shown. By sliding the contact a along the resistance R, the galvanometer deflection may be reduced to zero and the instrument is then said to be balanced. This determines the value of V_u when no current is passing through it, as can be shown by solving the circuit as a network problem.

This problem fortunately provides an excellent illustration of the methods outlined in the previous section. The number of series branches is $N = 3$, but two junctions reduce the required number of unknown currents to $N - J + 1 = 2$. The directions for the unknown currents may be chosen arbitrarily, since, when the assigned direction is wrong, the solution will give the correct magnitude but with a minus sign. The current I_g through the galvanometer is of primary interest; its direction is designated by the arrow in Fig. 6–11. The other unknown current will be designated by I and chosen to pass through the potentiometer battery labeled V. The current equation for either junction now shows that the current through R_x is $I + I_g$. The two independent equations that are required can be obtained from the closed loop containing V_u, G, and R_x, and the closed loop containing V and R. If we let R_g be the internal resistance of the galvanometer, the resulting equations are

$$I_g R_g + (I + I_g) R_x = V_u$$

and

$$(I + I_g) R_x + I(R - R_x) = V.$$

These may be rewritten as

$$I_g (R_g + R_x) + I R_x = V_u$$

and

$$I_g R_x + I R = V,$$

and an immediate solution is found by the determinant method:

$$I_g = \frac{\begin{vmatrix} V_u & R_x \\ V & R \end{vmatrix}}{\begin{vmatrix} R_g + R_x & R_x \\ R_x & R \end{vmatrix}} = \frac{R V_u - V R_x}{R R_g + R_x(R - R_x)}. \qquad (6\text{--}18)$$

To obtain the unknown potential difference V_u, the bridge is balanced by adjusting R_x until $I_g = 0$. If I_g is set equal to zero in Eq. (6–18) the following simple relation is obtained:

$$V_u = V \frac{R_x}{R}. \qquad (6\text{--}19)$$

This suggests that the accuracy of the unknown voltage V_u is determined by the accuracy of V, R_x, and R, and that this accuracy is independent of R_g. This is not quite true. The accuracy with which the potentiometer can be balanced depends upon how much current I_g is required to visibly deflect the galvanometer. For maximum accuracy a high-sensitivity galvanometer is desirable; it is also desirable to have R_g small, since by Eq. (6–18) this greatly affects the value of I_g for a given unbalance. Most potentiometers are provided with an extra resistance to be connected in series with R_g to reduce sensitivity until a rough balance is obtained. The extra resistance is then removed for greater accuracy.

In the foregoing discussion it has been assumed that V and R are constant and known. In practice, a standard cell, whose emf V_s is accurately known from a Bureau of Standards certificate, is used for comparison. This cell is substituted into the circuit of Fig. 6–11 in place of the unknown V_u. Now if the galvanometer reads zero when R_x has been changed to R_s, the expression for V_s is $V_s = V(R_s/R)$. Division into Eq. (6–19) then yields

$$V_u = V_s \frac{R_x}{R_s},$$

which gives the unknown voltage in terms of the voltage of the standard cell and the ratio between two resistances.

Wheatstone bridge. Electrical measurements quite generally involve the comparison of the quantity to be measured with a standard. In principle, all electrical measurements can be made directly from the mechanical units of length, mass, and time, but such measurements are made by the Bureau of Standards in setting up their master standards. The standards used in other laboratories have been standardized by comparison with a master standard.

The Wheatstone bridge shown in Fig. 6–12, or some modification of this bridge,* is commonly used for the accurate comparison of unknown resistances with some standard designated by R_s. Like the potentiometer, the Wheatstone bridge employs the galvanometer as a null-reading instrument only.

The function of the galvanometer is to indicate when the circuits are balanced, so that there is no current in it. A great advantage of null methods is that they do not require a calibrated galvanometer. From Fig. 6–12 the requirement that there is no current in the galvanometer imposes two conditions on the circuit: first, the difference of potential between b and c is zero; and second, there is a single current I_s through ab and bd, and another single current I_R through ac and cd. From this analysis, elementary texts show that $R_x = R_s(1 - n)/n$. While this

---

* W. C. Michels, *Advanced Electrical Measurements*, D. Van Nostrand Co. Inc., 1957.

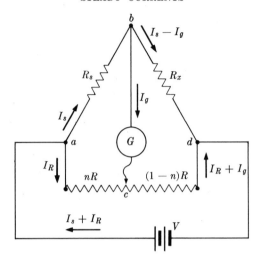

Fig. 6–12. Slidewire Wheatstone bridge with current designations suitable for easy solution of the circuit.

is the correct relation for a balanced bridge, it provides no information concerning the accuracy with which this balance can be obtained.

An expression for the current I_g through the galvanometer is needed to determine the accuracies obtainable with a Wheatstone bridge. Such an expression can be obtained by the methods outlined in the previous section. Since the bridge network has six series branches and four junctions, the number of unknown currents can be reduced to $N - J + 1 = 6 - 4 + 1 = 3$. In Fig. 6–12, currents I_g, I_s, and I_R have been assumed through G, R_s, and nR respectively, while junction equations have been used to determine the values of the currents in the remaining branches. The three unknown currents I_s, I_R, and I_g can be found from three independent equations for three closed loops such as $abca$, $bdcb$, and $acdVa$. The three equations obtained from these loops can be solved for I_g by means of determinants.

Although the result is complicated,* it can be considerably simplified and made more meaningful by assuming that only a small unbalance is produced by increasing the resistance in the R_x branch from $R_s(1 - n)/n$ to $R_s(1 + \delta)(1 - n)/n$, where $\delta \ll 1$. The solution resulting from this approximation is

$$I_g = \frac{n \, V \delta}{R_s + nR + R_g/(1 - n)}. \tag{6–20}$$

Study of this relation shows that best results are obtained when all of the five branches have nearly equal resistances.

---

* The general solution may be found in L. Page and N. I. Adams, *Principles of Electricity*, D. Van Nostrand Co., Inc., 2nd ed., pp. 169–172, 1949.

6–10 Routine solution of networks. The solution of d-c networks can be reduced to a routine procedure that includes some automatic checks on the correctness of the equations. The procedure can be illustrated with either the circuit of Fig. 6–11 or that of 6–12, but the symmetry of the resultant equations can be seen more easily with the circuit parameters shown in Fig. 6–13, which is essentially the same network as that in Fig. 6–12. Since there must be three unknown currents, the three currents I_1, I_2, and I_3 can be assumed to circulate in the three loops of the network as shown. Loop equations are then written for each of the three loops, in which the resistances are collected with each current that they multiply. This gives

$$I_1(R_1 + R_5 + R_3) - I_2 R_5 - I_3 R_3 = 0,$$

$$-I_1 R_5 + I_2(R_2 + R_4 + R_5) - I_3 R_4 = 0,$$

$$-I_1 R_3 - I_2 R_4 + I_3(R + R_3 + R_4) = V,$$

which show a characteristic symmetry that helps to avoid blunders. The solution of these equations for any of the three unknown currents can be written as the ratio obtained by dividing one third-order determinant by another. The determinant for the denominator of this ratio, which is the same for each of these solutions, is given by

$$\begin{vmatrix} (R_1 + R_5 + R_3) & -R_5 & -R_3 \\ -R_5 & (R_2 + R_4 + R_5) & -R_4 \\ -R_3 & -R_4 & (R + R_3 + R_4) \end{vmatrix},$$

which is symmetric about the diagonal. The numerator for calculating I_1, I_2, or I_3 is obtained from this determinant by replacing column 1,

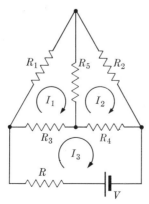

FIG. 6–13. Typical network, showing how the routine method of solution can be applied.

column 2, or column 3, respectively, in this determinant with the terms on the right of the original three equations. With experience it is not necessary to write the separate equations, since the determinant for the denominator can be written directly from the diagram and the determinants for the numerators can be constructed directly from this denominator.

This system of solution may have one disadvantage if only the galvanometer current of Fig. 6–12 is desired. With the routine solution, $I_g = I_1 - I_2$ can be obtained from the two separate solutions for I_1 and I_2, while with the system of solution used in the previous section I_g was obtained directly from only one solution. However, the advantages in using a routine system with automatic checks on the correctness of the solutions will usually outweigh this apparent advantage in having to solve for only one of the unknowns.

Actually, an additional check can be introduced, if the network is such that it can be drawn on a flat surface with no intersecting branches. In the determinant of the denominator, all of the off-diagonal terms can be made negative by choosing loop currents that are either all clockwise, as in Fig. 6–13, or all counterclockwise.

PROBLEMS

6–1. A 660-watt electric iron is plugged into a 110-volt outlet. Calculate the number of electrons per second passing through the iron.

*6–2. One of the coils which energizes the magnet for the C.I.T. cyclotron at Saxonburg, Pa. has the dimensions given in Fig. 6–14, where the dimensions refer to the outer edges of the copper. The coil lies in a plane which is perpendicular to the cylindrical axis of symmetry, as shown in the diagram. The coil is made of 24 turns of copper conductor having a cross section 51 cm in height (the full height of the coil) and 3.4 cm in width (the direction of the coil radius). A space of 0.4 cm between each of the turns is occupied by some insulation and the channels for the cooling oil which flows upward between the turns. In operation, the coil carries a direct current of 20,000 amp, and the temperatures of the cooling oil are 25°C as it enters and 30°C as it leaves the coil. (a) What is the resistance of this coil in operation and what voltage is required to operate it? (b) If the oil has a specific heat of 0.5 cal/gm·C°, how much must flow through the coil? State the approximations you use, and indicate the approximate accuracy of your answer.

Axis of symmetry

FIGURE 6–14

6–3. A 100-volt d-c generator with 1 ohm internal resistance is used to charge a 66-volt storage battery with 2 ohms internal resistance. A 5-ohm rheostat is connected in series with these two to control the charging current. (a) Find the power delivered by the generator. (b) Find the heat loss in each part of the circuit. (c) Find the chemical energy stored in the battery during 3 hr of charging.

6–4. Two of the currents and all of the resistances of a certain network are shown in Fig. 6–15. Batteries A and B have negligible internal resistance. (a) Find the current through the 10-ohm resistor. (b) Find the power delivered to the 3-ohm resistor. In what form does this energy appear? (c) Find the emf's $\mathcal{E}_A$ and $\mathcal{E}_B$ of the two batteries. (d) Find the power delivered to battery B. In what form does this energy appear?

FIGURE 6–15

---

* Answers to starred problems will be found at back of book.

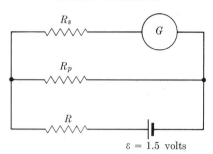

$\varepsilon = 1.5$ volts

FIGURE 6-16

FIGURE 6-17

*6-5. The emf of a dry cell measured 1.56 volts on a potentiometer and 1.24 volts on a voltmeter of resistance 300 ohms. What is the internal resistance of the cell?

6-6. A suspended-coil wall galvanometer G is connected in the circuit shown in Fig. 6-16 with a dry cell, a fixed resistor $R = 10^5$ ohms, and two dial-decade resistors R_s and R_p. When $R_s = 0$ and $R_p = 25$ ohms, G deflects 15 cm. When $R_s = 70$ ohms and $R_p = 50$ ohms, G deflects 20 cm. Find the galvanometer resistance R_G and its sensitivity in amp/mm deflection.

*6-7. A certain simple potentiometer like that shown in Fig. 6-11 has movable contacts at both a and b. Contact a has 15 positions, each 10 ohms apart. Contact b moves on a slidewire having 11 ohms total resistance. The maximum resistance of R_x is thus 161 ohms. The slidewire is divided into 220 divisions but the settings can be estimated to 1/5 of a division. When a dry cell with $V = 1.5$ volts is used, the total resistance is adjusted to $R = 1500$ ohms. (a) To what accuracy can an unknown voltage of approximately 0.0012 volt be measured with this instrument? (b) If the only available galvanometer has a sensitivity of 5×10^{-6} amp/cm and a resistance of 200 ohms, with what accuracy can the unknown voltage of (a) be determined? Deflections of 0.1 mm are just observable. (c) Suppose an unknown emf (~ 0.0012 volt) with an internal resistance of 500 ohms is being measured, using the galvanometer described in (b). With what accuracy can this voltage be read?

6-8. In Fig. 6-17 the numbers give the resistances in ohms of the resistors under them. Calculate (a) the current through the battery whose emf is 60 volts, (b) the current through the 6-ohm resistor between b and c, and (c) the actual potentials at a and b.

6-9. A flexible cable for conducting electricity consists of N strands of copper wire, each of which has the cross-sectional area a in m^2 and the length l in meters. The strands are insulated from each other except at the two ends, where they are all connected. (a) Calculate the effective resistance of this cable in terms of N, a, l, and ρ_{Cu}. (b) The actual length of this flexible cable is only $L = 0.95l$, because the individual strands are wound spirally. Consider a solid copper wire designed to have the same resistance with *the same length L* as this flexible cable. Calculate the ratio τ_s/τ_0, where τ_s = volume of copper in the strands and τ_0 = volume of copper in the solid wire.

*6-10. A simple series circuit consists of an 18-volt battery with an internal resistance of 0.1 ohm in series with two resistors whose resistances 0.4 ohm and 6.0 ohms are independent of temperature or current. A semiconductor, whose resistance in ohms is given by $R = \sqrt{18/I}$, where I is the current through it in amperes, is connected across the 6-ohm resistor. Calculate I.

*6-11. Because the crystal structures of Cu and Ni are so nearly identical, one would expect the mobilities of the free electrons in the two materials to be similar. Mobility is defined by $\mu = \sigma/Nne$, where σ is the conductivity, N is the number of atom/m^3, n is the number of conduction electrons per atom, and e is the electronic charge. Calculate μ_{Cu}/μ_{Ni} at room temperature and give a qualitative explanation of its value. Problem 6-12 shows that this ratio must be considered to be an average value.

*6-12. There is some evidence that the ferromagnetic nature of nickel affects the scattering of conduction electrons in such a manner that half of these have far more mobility than the other half. Calculate the ratio of the mobilities of the conduction electrons of copper to the mobility of the more mobile half of the conduction electrons in Ni on the assumption that these more mobile conduction electrons in nickel have 10 times the mobility of the other half. [*Hint.* The conduction by the two groups of conduction electrons can be treated as though they constitute parallel circuits.]

6-13. Early strings of Christmas tree lights had eight bulbs in series connected across 110 volts. With filaments at high temperatures these bulbs burned out frequently. Some individuals found that when two strings were connected in series the bulbs were bright enough and lasted almost indefinitely. On the assumption that the resistances of the bulbs remain the same, compare the watts output for each bulb on the string of eight with that for each bulb on the string of sixteen and also compare the total power used by these two strings. Actually, the power used by the string of sixteen is much greater and the bulbs are much brighter than this simple calculation indicates. Explain why these statements are true.

6-14. The power source for a research magnet on the third floor of a laboratory is a d-c generator located in the basement 300 ft away (this distance is the length of the conduit necessary to carry the wires). The generator terminal potential difference may be regulated between 200 and 300 volts, and the mag-

(a)   (b)

(c)

FIGURE 6–18

net, which has a total resistance of 0.50 ohm, may need up to 250 volts across its terminals. Make a recommendation as to the material and size of wire to be used to connect the magnet to the generator.

*6–15. For pumping water, 2500 watts of power must be transmitted to a motor from a generator 1000 m away. The transmission line, consisting of two copper wires of equal diameter, should not dissipate more than 6% of the power delivered to the motor. (a) Calculate the minimum diameter of the copper wires if the motor requires 110 volts across its terminals. (b) Calculate the minimum diameter of the copper wires if the motor requires 240 volts across its terminals. (c) What voltage must be generated in each case?

*6–16. Figure 6–18(a) shows a cross section of a coil of wire on a spool, whose shape and size are limited by the magnet for which it is designed. In Chapter 9 it is shown that the effectiveness of such a coil depends upon the number of its ampere-turns, which is limited by the rate heat can be lost from its surfaces. Would many turns of fine wire be superior to fewer turns of larger wire? (a) Calculate the number of ampere-turns as a function of the spool dimensions $(a, b, \text{ and } l)$, the wire diameter d, the space factor k, and the power P dissipated. The space factor k is the ratio of the volume of copper in the coil to the volume of the space occupied by the coil. (b) Does the equation obtained in (a) suggest the diameter of the wire that should be used?

*6–17. A large number N of identical storage cells is available, each with emf $\mathcal{E}$ and internal resistance r, to furnish the current for an electromagnet having a resistance R.

(a) Calculate the current in the winding when the N cells are connected into p parallel strings, each having s cells in series.

(b) Determine the relationship between R, p, N, and r for maximum current.

(c) If $R = 0.5$ ohm, $\mathcal{E} = 2.2$ volts, $r = 0.1$ ohm, and $N = 36$, what value of p would you choose to obtain maximum current? Designate this value as p_m.

(d) Calculate the current, using $p = p_m$, $p = p_m + 1$, and $p = p_m - 1$.

(e) Calculate the current per cell for each case in (d) and state whether this information should influence your choice of p.

*6–18. For finding the current density distributions in the very long bar of ferromagnetic material shown in Fig. 6–5, a method is outlined in the text for using an electrostatic solution involving an infinite series of imaginary line charges. (a) Calculate the charge per unit length λ required for these line charges in terms of I, ρ, and b, which are respectively the current through the bar, its resistivity, and its width. (b) Write the expression as an infinite series for the current density J along line HH' through the middle of a very long bar. (c) Show that J approaches I/ab.

6–19. Two identical stainless steel spheres of radius a buried deep in the ground are separated by the distance $l \gg a$. By means of insulated wires connected to each sphere a difference of potential V is maintained between them. Assuming the earth to have a uniform resistivity ρ, calculate the resistance between the two spheres. The expression for R should contain l, to show how large l must be before its magnitude can be neglected.

6–20. A stainless steel sphere of radius a is buried in ground having a uniform resistivity ρ, near a very large sheet of stainless steel. If the normal distance between the center of the sphere and the plane is $l/2$, the resistance can be expressed in terms of an infinite series containing increasing powers of a/l. Calculate this resistance, retaining terms in the series up to $(a/l)^2$.

*6–21. Calculate the resistance between the two spheres of Problem 6–19, retaining terms in the series up to $(a/l)^3$.

*6–22. Suppose that the very large sheet of stainless steel in Problem 6–20 is bent at right angles, so that one part coincides with the xy-plane while the other part coincides with the xz-plane. Find the resistance between this bent sheet and a stainless steel sphere of radius a which is buried at the distance $l/2$ from each of the planes, assuming that $a \ll l$.

*6–23. A certain d-c transmission line consists of two large copper wires of radius a, nickel-plated to reduce corrosion. These are buried in the ground a distance $2s$ apart. (a) Assuming that the ground has a uniform resistivity $\rho \gg \rho_{Cu}$, calculate the conductance per meter of length between the wires. (b) Assuming that the potential difference between the wires is a constant V, calculate the power lost in heating the ground when the length of the line is l.

6–24. The spiral copper winding shown in Fig. 6–18(b) has advantages over the more conventional wire winding shown at (a) in that figure. When a fixed number of ampere-turns NI must be crowded into the space shown, the design in (b) provides less heat loss than the design in (a) and this heat loss is more easily dissipated.

(a) Calculate the resistance per turn of the spiral if the copper sheet has a thickness t.

(b) Calculate the total resistance of a spiral of N turns that will fill the space shown if the insulation between sheets makes the space factor k the same as that in Problem 6–16. This resistance should be expressed in terms of N, a, b, l, k, and ρ_{Cu}.

(c) With a fixed power input P, calculate the ratio of the ampere-turns produced by the designs of Fig. 6–18(a) and (b). Calculate the numerical ratio for $b = 1.8a$.

[Note. The design of Fig. 6–18(b) has the disadvantages of being much harder to fabricate and of requiring a power source with a high current capacity and a low emf.]

*6–25. Magnetic fields of electromagnets like those shown in Fig. 6–18 depend strongly upon the number of ampere-turns that can be passed through the space between the pole piece and the base. In the (c) part of the figure is a design of spiral copper winding that has less resistance per turn than does the spiral design in (b). With this design more ampere-turns are produced with the same power and the joulean heat is more easily dissipated than with either of the coils shown at (a) or (b). (a) Using the design and dimensions shown in (c) of Fig. 6–18, calculate the resistance per turn for copper sheet of thickness t. (b) Suppose the three coil designs shown in Fig. 6–18 are being considered for use in the iron frame of the magnet shown there. With constant power, calculate the ratios of the ampere-turns for the designs of (b) and (c), each versus that for the design in (a).

6–26. When the Wheatstone bridge of Fig. 6–12 is balanced $R_x = R_s(1 - n)/n$. Prove that when this bridge is unbalanced by increasing R_x to $R_s(1 + \delta)(1 - n)/n$, the current through the galvanometer is given by Eq. (6–20), assuming that $\delta \ll 1$.

6–27. One method for measuring the resistance of a galvanometer is known as Kelvin's method. The galvanometer whose resistance R_g is to be measured replaces R_x in the Wheatstone bridge shown in Fig. 6–12, while G is replaced by a circuit-closing key. How should such a bridge be balanced? Calculate R_g if the bridge balances with $R_s = 200$ ohms and with $n = 0.65$.

*6–28. Many modern experiments require large electromagnets with constant magnetizing currents. Direct connection to d-c power lines causes too much fluctuation. Storage batteries are better, but they must be monitored constantly because their voltages drift lower as they become discharged. The so-called floating-battery circuit, shown in Fig. 6–19, provides a remarkably constant current with a relatively small storage battery. Find an expression for the fractional variation in magnet current, $\delta I_m/I_m$, in terms of the circuit constants, and the fractional variation in the line voltage, $\delta V/V$. Discuss the case where the time average of the current through the battery is zero, so that V_B remains constant. (Actually storage batteries require a very small charging current I_c to keep their emf's constant. Best regulation is obtained when the average battery current is I_c.) State the circuit constants needed for best regu-

FIGURE 6–19

FIGURE 6–20

lation and decide whether these constants are practical. Regulation will be improved by the inductance of the magnet that is ignored here.

6–29. An electromagnet has two coils, each with 1 ohm resistance, that can be connected either in series or in parallel. It is desired that each coil carry an 85-amp current that is as steady as possible. Direct current lines with either 220 volts or 110 volts are available but each has a 2% voltage fluctuation. Two storage batteries are available, each with 88 volts emf and 0.044 ohm internal resistance. (a) Design two different floating-battery circuits like the one shown in Fig. 6–19, one for use when coils are in series and the other for the parallel connection. Determine the values of the resistances needed in R and R_1 for each design. (b) Calculate the fractional fluctuations in I_m when the coils and the batteries are used in series. (c) Calculate the fractional fluctuations in I_m when the coils and the batteries are used in parallel.

*6–30. A machine called a dynamo, which is designed to operate as a d-c motor, can usually be used as a d-c generator. Suppose that two identical dynamos, G and M, are used as a generator and a motor respectively, to transport power from a gasoline engine to a distant water pump. As shown in Fig. 6–20, the direct current generated by G flows to and from M along two wires which constitute the transmission line. The dynamos have wire-wound armatures that rotate between poles of electromagnets. Assume that in each dynamo an emf is generated that is proportional to the rate of rotation of the armature, i.e., 0.1 volt per rev/min. Since this can be true only if the field is constant, it will be assumed that the electromagnet is saturated as long as the current in its windings exceeds 0.8 amp. (Actually it is impossible to maintain a constant field with this simple arrangement. The current through the armature affects the field and must be compensated to achieve a constant field.) Each field winding has 100 ohms resistance and is connected directly across the dynamo terminals, as shown in Fig. 6–20. Suppose that the armature of G rotates at 1200 rev/min and that of M at 1000 rev/min. Calculate (a) the currents through the field windings and through the armatures of G and M, (b) the power delivered by the gasoline motor to the generator and the power delivered to the water pump, if all mechanical losses can be neglected, and (c) the over-all efficiency in transmitting power from gasoline motor to water pump, neglecting all mechanical losses.

6–31. When an electric motor drives a water pump, the current through its armature may be nearly proportional to the vertical height h (meters) to which the water is being pumped. Use the equipment and connections of Problem 6–30 and assume that the motor's armature current must be $I_m = 1.5h$. Consider one case where water must be pumped 8 m and another where it must be pumped 16 m. A governor on the gasoline motor controls the flow of gasoline to keep the generator rotating at a constant speed of 1200 rev/min. For each of the two heights to which water is to be pumped, calculate the following: (a) the current through the motor, I_m, (b) I_1 and I_2, (c) the back emf and the speed of rotation of the motor, (d) the total mechanical power delivered to the pump by the motor, and (e) the mechanical power that must be delivered to the generator. (f) If the volume of water pumped per second is proportional to the speed of the pump, compare the volume of water that can be pumped to the two different heights. Calculate the number of cubic meters per second pumped to 8 m if all mechanical losses can be neglected.

CHAPTER 7

ELECTROMAGNETIC INDUCTION

Both magnetic and electrostatic phenomena were observed by ancient man, as is evidenced by references to these phenomena in some of the earliest writings. Discussions of the properties of natural magnets are found in the writings of Thales of Miletus (600 B.C.), Socrates, and Plato. However, knowledge of magnetism was still only qualitative in 1600 A.D. when Gilbert summarized the known facts in his *De Magnete*.

Quantitative studies did not begin until the demonstration by Coulomb in 1785 that the forces between magnetic poles obeyed an inverse-square law. It was soon discovered that magnetic poles were unlike electric charges, in that poles could not be isolated. Furthermore, in 1820 Oersted established a relationship between moving charges and magnetism when he discovered that a compass needle could be deflected by an electric current. These facts stimulated Ampere to devise a theory which presumed that the magnetic properties of all materials were due to the circulation of submicroscopic electric currents. It is now well established that most, if not all, of these magnetic properties are due to such currents. These currents, now called "amperian currents," consist chiefly of electrons spinning about an axis or orbiting about the positively charged nuclei.

The observed magnetic forces can now be ascribed solely to forces between charges in motion. The magnetic fields produced by moving charges will be treated in Chapter 8; the forces on charges moving through magnetic fields are discussed here. Thus magnetic fields are defined here in terms of the forces on moving charges.

7–1 Field definitions. Electric charges moving through magnetic fields experience forces in addition to the electric field force expressed by $\mathbf{F} = q\mathbf{E}$. The total force acting on a charge in the presence of both electric and magnetic fields is given by the Lorentz force-on-a-charge equation

$$\mathbf{F} = q(\mathbf{E} + \mathbf{v} \times \mathbf{B}), \qquad (7\text{--}1)$$

where $\mathbf{B}$ is a vector field referred to as the magnetic induction and $\mathbf{v}$ is the velocity of the charge q moving through the field.

Equation (7–1) was originally a generalization of the empirical law governing the force on current-carrying wires in magnetic fields. This generalization has now been justified by many experiments involving charged particles and has been shown to be consistent with other theoretical considerations. It is, therefore, accepted as the fundamental law from

which other relations can be derived and serves as a convenient definition
of both **E** and **B** when written in the form

$$\mathbf{E} + \mathbf{v} \times \mathbf{B} = \lim_{q \to 0} \frac{\mathbf{F}}{q} \cdot \tag{7-2}$$

Here q is the magnitude of a small test charge in coulombs, **F** is the force
on the charge in newtons, and **v** is the velocity of the charge in meters per
second. By making $\mathbf{v} = 0$, Eq. (7-2) defines **E** in volts per meter, and with
E determined, the charge can be given a convenient velocity to define **B**.
Just as electric flux lines can be drawn to represent electric fields, magnetic flux lines can be drawn to represent magnetic fields. Maxwell's
second relation, which will be introduced in Section 7-4, shows that the
intensity and the direction of the **B** field at every point in space can be
represented by the density and direction, respectively, of continuous flux
lines. *The mks unit for* **B**, *therefore, is expressed in weber/m^2, and the mks
unit of magnetic flux is the weber.* It is shown in Section 7-3 that this
definition leads to practical methods for measuring **B** in terms of emf's
induced in search coils.

Considerable confusion may result from any attempt to apply Eq. (7-1)
or (7-2) to coordinate systems other than those fixed to the earth. For
example, a charge moving through a large uniform magnetic field in the
absence of an electric field experiences a force $q\mathbf{v} \times \mathbf{B}$; however, if a new
coordinate system is chosen in which the charge is at rest, then in the new
system $\mathbf{v} = 0$, and no force would appear to be acting on q. This dilemma
can be resolved by making the correct relativistic transformation from the
laboratory system to a system moving with the charge. An observer in
such a system would measure an electric field having the magnitude
$\mathbf{v} \times \mathbf{B}$. Relativistic transformations are beyond the scope of this book,
but can be found in more advanced texts.*

All treatments in this book assume that the observer is in the laboratory
coordinate system. Actually the relations obtained are valid whenever all
the phenomena involved are referred to a coordinate system in which the
observer is at rest. Many devices and experiments make use of the forces
described by Eq. (7-1). The cyclotron and Hall effect are chosen as two
illustrations of the use of this equation; other illustrations may be found
among the problems.

Cyclotron. A cyclotron consists of two copper dees, labeled D_1 and D_2
in Fig. 7-1, placed between two flat pole faces of a very large electromagnet. The two dees could be made by constructing a giant copper pill-

---

* See, for example, Panofsky and Phillips, *Classical Electricity and Magnetism*, Addison-Wesley Publishing Co., Reading, Mass., 1955, or Abraham and
Becker, *Classical Electricity and Magnetism*, Blackie and Son Ltd., London,
1937.

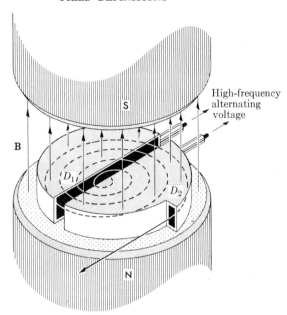

FIG. 7-1. Copper dees for a cyclotron. The dashed line indicates the path of a proton being accelerated to high energies. The uniform magnetic field **B** between the large poles of an electromagnet makes the proton travel arcs of circles within the dees.

box and then halving it with a plane cut that includes the central axis. The two dees are then enclosed in an evacuated container to allow free motion of the charged particles.

A beam of protons or other charged particles is injected into one dee near the axis, with its velocity parallel to the faces of the dees. Within a dee $E = 0$, and each particle in the beam travels in a circular arc under the influence of the force $q\mathbf{v} \times \mathbf{B}$. Since this force is perpendicular to $\mathbf{v}$, the magnitude of $\mathbf{v}$ does not change, and the kinetic energy of the particle remains constant as it traverses its path inside either dee. By equating the Lorentz force qvB to the centrifugal force mv^2/r, the radius of the path of the particle is found to be proportional to v, that is, $r = mv/qB$. The time required for a particle to complete one revolution is $t_r = 2\pi r/v = 2\pi m/qB$, which is independent of both r and v. A potential difference between the dees is caused to alternate at a frequency of $f_r = 1/t_r = qB/2\pi m$, so that those particles that happen to arrive at the separation between the dees when the potential difference is a maximum in the direction that will increase their velocities complete the next half revolution in time to emerge from this dee just when the potential difference is maximum in the opposite direction. Each time such a particle passes across the separation, its energy is increased by qV_m, which is evidenced by an increase in both velocity and path radius. The maximum velocity obtained, v_m, depends upon the maximum radius r_m available within the uniform field, and is given by $v_m = r_m qB/m$. A localized field, either electric or magnetic, is usually provided to cause the beam of charged particles to emerge along a predetermined path, shown near D_2 in the diagram.

This calculation is valid only for velocities that are small compared with the velocity of light, because of the relativistic increase in the mass of the particle as it approaches the velocity of light. Higher velocities and higher energies can, however, be achieved by properly controlling either the frequency or the field. The pole pieces at the Carnegie Institute of Technology Research Center are about 12 ft in diameter and produce a field of approximately 2 weber/m². Since protons in this cyclotron reach one-tenth of the velocity of light on paths only one foot in diameter, the larger diameters are utilized by accurately controlling the frequency of the potential applied across the dees. With this modification, protons can be given energies up to $4 \cdot 10^8$ electron-volts, and such a cyclotron is called a synchrocyclotron.

Hall effect. When a conductor is placed in a magnetic field with a current that is perpendicular to the field, a voltage is induced across the conductor, perpendicular to both the current and the magnetic field. This voltage, known as the Hall voltage, is rather simply explained by means of Eq. (7–1).

A conductor of length l, width w, and thickness t oriented with respect to the xyz-axes as shown in Fig. 7–2 may carry an electric current in the x-direction through a magnetic field directed along the z-axis. The force on the conduction electrons in such a conductor is given by Eq. (7–1). Under steady-state conditions it is impossible for electrons to move in the

Fig. 7–2. Hall effect sample, a thin rectangular strip (length l, width w, thickness t) in the xy-plane with field **B** parallel to the z-axis. A potentiometer connected to the probes measures the Hall voltage.

y-direction, so that the net force in that direction must be zero. Equation (7–1) then reduces to

$$F_y = 0 = q(E_y - v_x B_z),$$

where v_x is the average velocity of the conduction electrons flowing opposite to the current. If N is the number of conduction electrons per cubic meter and e is the charge on an electron, the current is given by

$$I_x = Nev_xwt,$$

where e and v_x are both negative for electronic conduction. The potential difference across the width of the conductor is $V_y = E_yw$; therefore the expression for the force in the y-direction reduces to

$$F_y = 0 = e\left(\frac{V_y}{w} - \frac{I_x}{Newt} B_z\right)$$

or

$$\frac{V_yt}{I_xB_z} = \frac{1}{Ne}.$$

This expression for the Hall voltage V_y gives the number of conduction electrons per cubic meter in terms of easily measurable quantities. In view of the grossly oversimplified assumptions used in deriving this relation, it is surprising that it quite accurately predicts the Hall voltages observed in many metallic elements and in many semiconductors. As should be expected from their position in the periodic table, the following metals exhibit Hall voltages which indicate that each has approximately one conduction electron for every atom in the solid: Na, K, Cu, Ag, and Au. Semiconductors, on the other hand, have been shown to have a very small fraction of one conduction electron per atom.

The theoretical basis for the success of the classical expression for the Hall emf lies in the fact that the quantum-mechanical expression reduces to the classical one in the special case of a nearly empty conduction band. Interestingly enough, for the case of a nearly full band the quantum-mechanical expression still reduces to the classical one except for a change in sign. This has given rise to the statement that conduction in some materials is by positively charged carriers or, equivalently, that it is due to "hole conduction." Because the Hall emf indicates the number of conduction electrons in materials, it has become a powerful tool in the study of the electronic structure of solids.

7–2 Forces on current-carrying wires. The total force acting on a current-carrying wire can be thought of as the sum of the forces acting on all of the current carried within the wire. Consider a small element of wire of length dl carrying the current I, in which ρ is the density of conduction carriers (negative for electrons), v is the average velocity of the carriers in the direction $d\mathbf{l}$, and A is the cross-sectional area of the wire perpendicular to $d\mathbf{l}$. The total conduction charge in the element is given by $\rho A\,dl$, so that the $q\mathbf{v}$ needed for Eq. (7–1) is $q\mathbf{v} = \rho A v\,d\mathbf{l} = I\,d\mathbf{l}$. In the usual case in which the net charge on the wire is zero, there is no force on the wire due to $\mathbf{E}$. Equation (7–1) then gives the expression for the force acting on an element of wire carrying a current:

$$d\mathbf{F} = I\,d\mathbf{l} \times \mathbf{B}. \qquad (7\text{–}3)$$

The force $d\mathbf{F}$ on each element is perpendicular to both $\mathbf{B}$ and $d\mathbf{l}$. The total force on a long wire can be obtained by integrating Eq. (7–3) over the length of it. In dealing with wires, it is best to let $d\mathbf{l}$ indicate the direction of the current instead of I, since total current is not a vector, as is illustrated by the fact that the total current I through a surface s of any shape is given by

$$I = \int_{s} \mathbf{J} \cdot d\mathbf{s}.$$

Any volume element $d\tau$ in which there is a current density $\mathbf{J}$ and a magnetic field $\mathbf{B}$ is acted on by a force $d\mathbf{F}$, obtained directly from Eq. (7–1):

$$d\mathbf{F} = \rho\,d\tau\,\mathbf{v} \times \mathbf{B} = \mathbf{J} \times \mathbf{B}\,d\tau. \qquad (7\text{–}4)$$

This equation readily reduces to Eq. (7–3) for the case of an element of wire of length $d\mathbf{l}$.

Torques on plane current-carrying loops. The windings for electric motors often consist of many individual coils of wire, each of which approximates a plane loop of wire carrying current in a closed path. Simple discussions of galvanometer characteristics usually treat the galvanometer coil as a plane loop. Even electrons moving in orbits about their nuclei can be treated as closed current loops for many purposes. When the current is the same at all points on the loop and the magnetic field is uniform, the loop experiences a torque but no net force.

In calculating the torque on the current loop, the shape of the loop will be assumed arbitrary, although confined to some plane in space and residing in a uniform field directed at any angle. The analysis is facilitated by drawing a rectangular coordinate system, as shown in Fig. 7–3, with its origin coinciding with the center of area of the loop, its xy-plane coinciding with the plane of the loop, and with the magnetic field $\mathbf{B}$ in the yz-plane. The force on the element $d\mathbf{l}$ is then

$$
\begin{aligned}
d\mathbf{F} &= I\,d\mathbf{l} \times \mathbf{B} \\
&= I(\mathbf{i}\,dx + \mathbf{j}\,dy) \times (\mathbf{j}B_y + \mathbf{k}B_z) \\
&= I(\mathbf{i}B_z\,dy - \mathbf{j}B_z\,dx + \mathbf{k}B_y\,dx).
\end{aligned}
$$

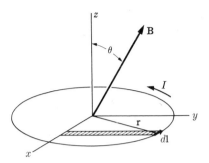

Fig. 7–3. Current-carrying loop of wire in the xy-plane experiences a torque about the x-axis in the uniform $\mathbf{B}$ field.

With $\mathbf{B}$ constant, the net force on the rigid loop is zero because $\oint dx = \oint dy = \oint dz = 0$. This can be obtained more directly from

$$\mathbf{F} = \oint I\, d\mathbf{l} \times \mathbf{B} = -I\mathbf{B} \times \oint d\mathbf{l},$$

where $\oint d\mathbf{l}$ is zero, since it is a vector sum representing the net displacement of a point traveling once around the closed path and returning to its starting point.

The total torque acting on this rigid loop is obtained by calculating moments of force about the origin for all of the elements in the loop and obtaining their vector sum. From Section 2–14, the moment of force acting on a typical element may be expressed by

$$d\mathbf{L} = \mathbf{r} \times d\mathbf{F} = I\mathbf{r} \times (d\mathbf{l} \times \mathbf{B})$$

$$= I[d\mathbf{l}(\mathbf{r} \cdot \mathbf{B}) - \mathbf{B}(\mathbf{r} \cdot d\mathbf{l})].$$

By introducing $\mathbf{r} = \mathbf{i}x + \mathbf{j}y$ and $B_x = 0$, the two terms in the brackets can be expanded into

$$\mathbf{B}(\mathbf{r} \cdot d\mathbf{l}) = \mathbf{B}(x\, dx + y\, dy)$$

and

$$d\mathbf{l}(\mathbf{r} \cdot \mathbf{B}) = B_y(\mathbf{i}y\, dx + \mathbf{j}y\, dy),$$

thus giving a total of four terms. Three of these terms make no contribution to the torque, since $\oint x\, dx = \oint y\, dy = 0$ around any closed loop. The remaining term is the area integral $\oint y\, dx$, which can be evaluated from its value in each of the four quadrants. In the first two quadrants y is positive and dx is negative, so that the integration of the element of area shown in Fig. 7–3 for that part of the loop lying to the right of the x-axis is just the negative of the area between the curve and the x-axis. In the third and fourth quadrants y is negative and dx is positive, so that completion of the integration yields the negative of the total area of the loop.

Representing this area by A, we find

$$\mathbf{L} = \oint i I B_y y \, dx = i I B_y \oint y \, dx = -i I A B_y,$$

a torque that can be written as

$$\mathbf{L} = -i p'_m B \sin \theta = \mathbf{p}'_m \times \mathbf{B}, \qquad (7\text{--}5)$$

where by definition* $\mathbf{p}'_m = \mathbf{k} I A$. Equation (7–5) is then identical in form to the torque that would act on a true magnetic dipole of moment $\mathbf{p}'_m$ in a magnetic field $\mathbf{B}$. This results in the very useful concept that *closed current loops act like magnetic dipoles in respect to the torques they experience in a magnetic field.*

7–3 Conductors moving in magnetic fields. When conductors move in magnetic fields, emf's are generated and electric currents are produced in closed circuits to which they are connected. The power required to produce these currents comes from the mechanical power needed to move the conductors through the magnetic fields. The law of conservation of energy requires that the current produced by this motion be in such a direction as to give rise to forces opposing the motion.

Lenz' law. A more general statement applicable to all magnetic induction processes was given by Lenz. It states that *an induced emf is directed so as to tend to oppose the cause producing it.* If the moving conductors are not connected to closed circuits there will be no current and no opposition; however, the emf's are always directed so that if a current exists there will be opposition.

Electric dynamos. Simple d-c motors and generators have such similar constructions that they can be used interchangeably, and they are both frequently referred to as dynamos. Coils of insulated wire wound on an iron core make up the rotor or armature that rotates in a constant magnetic field between the poles of an electromagnet. An old style machine with coils wound around a hollow iron core is illustrated schematically in Fig. 7–4. The principles involved are essentially the same as for more modern machines, which are somewhat more difficult to illustrate clearly. Details of the wiring are shown only for the top half of the rotor, and the pole pieces and collector brushes are shown disassembled for clarity.

The armature coil consists of a single wire wrapped many times around the hollow armature, but each loop of the coil is connected electrically to armature segments, as shown in the figure. As the armature rotates, these segments make electrical contact only at the sides, where they slide

---

* Later in this text it will be found convenient to define a magnetic dipole moment by $\mathbf{p}_m = \mu_0 \mathbf{p}'_m$.

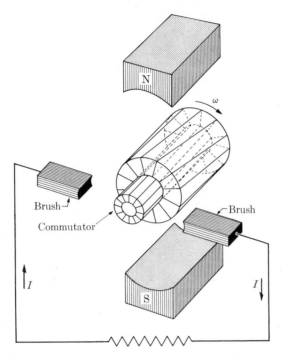

Fig. 7–4. Electric dynamo (d-c generator or motor) with a hollow cylindrical iron core for a rotor. For clarity, the poles are separated from the rotor and the brushes are separated from the commutator.

by the collector brushes. In effect, these brushes produce two parallel circuits, one consisting of the coils on top that are connected in series and are moving to the right, and the other consisting of the coils on the bottom that also are connected in series but are moving to the left.

As the outer wires of the coils pass the north pole, the electrons within these wires experience a force $\mathbf{F} = q\mathbf{v} \times \mathbf{B}$, where $\mathbf{v}$ is the velocity of the wire. Since it is perpendicular to $\mathbf{B}$ and to the motion of the wire, this force causes a drift of the conduction electrons toward the commutator segments, producing a positive current in the opposite direction, as indicated in Fig. 7–4. The inner wires of the coils are so effectively shielded from the magnetic field by the iron core that they do not contribute significantly to the induction process. The conduction electrons in those outer wires that are passing the south pole are directed away from the commutator segments and constitute a current that also is directed toward the brush on the right. The upper and lower circuits then contribute equally to the current in the external circuit. The direct current produced by such a dynamo would contain a small a-c ripple caused by the changing conditions as the brushes slip from one commutator segment to another.

It is easily verified that the dynamo will act as a motor when current is forced through the windings by an external circuit. It is necessary only to consider the torques exerted on the closed current-carrying loops of wire in a magnetic field, as derived in Section 7–2.

Simple linear generator. Rather than analyze the dynamo in more detail, it is more instructive to study the emf induced in a single conductor consisting of a straight metal rod moving through a uniform magnetic field with constant velocity **v**. Such a rod is shown moving along two frictionless metal rails in Fig. 7–5. Each of the charges in the rod experiences a force $q(\mathbf{v} \times \mathbf{B})$, but only the conduction electrons are free to drift through the rod. These electrons drift until sufficient charges have accumulated near the ends of the rod (or onto the rails in the figure) to set up an electric field **E** that counteracts the magnetic force. Positive charges appear on rail 1 and negative charges on rail 2. Because the electric field between the rails cancels the magnetic force on the charges in the rod, $\mathbf{F} = e(\mathbf{E} + \mathbf{v} \times \mathbf{B}) = 0$ when the conduction electrons stop drifting. The emf induced in the moving rod is the open-circuit difference of potential between the rails, which can be measured by connecting a voltmeter with extremely high resistance across the rails, as shown in Fig. 7–5. Upon integrating over the length of the moving conductor from the positive to the negative rail or terminal, we find that the emf is given by

$$\mathcal{E} = \int \mathbf{E} \cdot d\mathbf{l} = - \int \mathbf{B} \cdot \mathbf{v} \times d\mathbf{l}.$$

For the constant conditions shown in Fig. 7–5 and with **B**, **v**, and **l** mutually perpendicular, $\mathcal{E} = Blv$, which is a familiar expression found in elementary texts. For the more general conditions shown in the figure,

$$\mathcal{E} = -\mathbf{B} \cdot \mathbf{v} \times \mathbf{l} = -\mathbf{B} \cdot \frac{d\mathbf{s}}{dt} = -\frac{d\phi}{dt},$$

where ϕ is the total flux of **B** passing through the closed circuit.

In general, $d\mathcal{E} = -\mathbf{B} \cdot \mathbf{v} \times d\mathbf{l}$ gives the emf induced in any small element of wire that moves through a field of intensity **B** with velocity **v**. As can be seen from Fig. 7–6, the area swept per second by the element of wire is $\mathbf{v} \times d\mathbf{l}$ and the flux through this swept area is $\mathbf{B} \cdot \mathbf{v} \times d\mathbf{l}$. Consequently, the emf induced in any closed circuit in motion in a magnetic field is given by

$$\mathcal{E} = - \oint \mathbf{B} \cdot \mathbf{v} \times d\mathbf{l}, \tag{7–6}$$

which is just $-d\phi/dt$ when only wires are moving. Whenever the motion of a closed circuit in a fixed magnetic field consists only of the motion of some or all of the insulated wires that make up that circuit, the induced emf is given by $\mathcal{E} = -d\phi/dt$.

Fig. 7-5. Simple linear generator—a conducting rod sliding with velocity **v** along conducting rails in a uniform magnetic field **B**.

Fig. 7-6. Element of wire $d\mathbf{l}$ moving with velocity **v** and sweeping magnetic flux at the rate of $\mathbf{B} \cdot d\mathbf{l} \times \mathbf{v}$ per second.

Measurement of **B**.   A very common method of measuring magnetic induction is the search-coil method, which utilizes the principles of Eq. (7-6). A coil is wound with N turns of wire, each enclosing a well-defined area such that the vector sum of these areas is $N\mathbf{s}$, and this vector also defines the axis of the coil. The coil is placed in the field with its axis parallel to that component of **B** which is to be measured. The coil is connected in series with some device for measuring the total charge that flows through the circuit, such as the ballistic galvanometer or fluxmeter we shall discuss in Section 7-8. When the search coil is rapidly removed from the field to a region where **B** is zero, the resulting emf induced in the coil causes a transient current through the instrument which results in the passage of a total charge q that is proportional to the flux originally threading the coil. This can be readily demonstrated by using the fact that the emf's induced in the N turns are additive, so that

$$\varepsilon = -N \frac{d\phi}{dt}.$$

The total charge flowing through the circuit is then

$$q = \int \frac{dq}{dt} \, dt = \int \frac{\varepsilon}{R} \, dt = -\frac{N}{R} \int \frac{d\phi}{dt} \, dt = -\frac{N\phi}{R},$$

where R is the total resistance of the circuit. The total flux through the coil was

$$\phi = \int_s \mathbf{B} \cdot d\mathbf{s} = \mathbf{B}_a \cdot \mathbf{s}$$

where $\mathbf{B}_a$ is the average value of $\mathbf{B}$ within the coil before it was removed. In principle, $\mathbf{B}$ at a point can be approximated to any desired accuracy by making coils with smaller areas $\mathbf{s}$. Each observation of this sort determines the component of $\mathbf{B}$ that is parallel to the coil axis just before the coil is removed from the field. If the direction as well as the magnitude of $\mathbf{B}$ is to be determined, observations must be taken for three mutually perpendicular directions.

The technique described gives the fundamental principle, although many modifications are possible. For example, the flux through the coil can be changed from ϕ to 0 by merely rotating the coil 90° whenever the direction of $\mathbf{B}$ is known. Another modification rotates the coil at a constant angular velocity and measures the alternating voltage produced. It is easy to show that when the axis of rotation is perpendicular to the field $B = \varepsilon_m/\omega N s$, where ε_m is the maximum emf in volts and ω is the angular velocity of the coil in radians per second.

7–4 Maxwell's second relation. The method of measuring $\mathbf{B}$ makes it easy to determine values for this vector near electric currents or inside and around magnetized materials. For example, the average direction and magnitude of $\mathbf{B}$ at the center of a permanent bar magnet can be determined by winding a search coil about the middle of the bar, connecting it to a fluxmeter, and then slipping it off the bar. The large deflection that results shows that the magnitude of $\mathbf{B}$ is quite large inside the magnet and that it points towards the positive end (usually designated as the north or north-seeking pole). The complete pattern of $\mathbf{B}$ values in and around bar magnets has been determined by techniques of this sort. The lines, or tubes, of flux pass through the bar from points near the negative end and pass out into space at points near the positive end. In the surrounding space they follow curved paths from the positive to the negative end, and are continuous throughout space, with no beginning and no ending. Many experiments have shown that this pattern is typical of magnetic induction fields from all conceivable sources, and that the lines of magnetic induction are everywhere continuous, having no points of origin or termination.

The situation is correctly expressed by Maxwell's second relation in integral form:

$$\int_s \mathbf{B} \cdot d\mathbf{s} = 0, \tag{7–7}$$

where s is a completely closed surface surrounding a volume τ of perfectly general shape and location. The differential form of Maxwell's second relation is obtained by using the Gauss mathematical theorem to transform the surface integral of Eq. (7–7) into a volume integral:

$$\int_s \mathbf{B} \cdot d\mathbf{s} = \int_\tau \mathbf{\nabla} \cdot \mathbf{B} \, d\tau = 0,$$

and since this is a general relation for all volumes,

$$\mathbf{\nabla} \cdot \mathbf{B} = 0, \tag{7–8}$$

which is the differential form of Maxwell's second relation. This relation shows that the **B** fields can always be represented by continuous lines of magnetic flux, as is pointed out in Section 7–1. In Section 3–2 the integral form of Gauss' law,

$$\epsilon_0 \int_s \mathbf{E} \cdot d\mathbf{s} = \int_\tau \rho \, d\tau,$$

was applied to the typical tube of flux shown in Fig. 3–5 to show that electric flux originates on positive charges and ends on negative charges. When the arguments presented there are applied with Eq. (7–7) to the magnetic case, it is found that the magnetic flux must be continuous throughout space, since there are no real magnetic poles to provide either a source or a sink.

This experimental evidence for Maxwell's second relation can hardly be regarded as a formal proof but, strictly speaking, there is no formal proof for any of Maxwell's field relations. As with most of the fundamental laws of nature, the validity of these laws rests on the fact that their predictions agree with the results of carefully performed experiments. Since the results of most experiments have been checked with more elementary and possibly less fundamental relations, it is important to determine how closely the predictions of the elementary relations agree with those of Maxwell's relations. It is therefore demonstrated in Section 8–1 that Maxwell's second relation can be obtained directly from the Biot-Savart law provided it is assumed that all magnetic fields, including those due to magnetized materials, are generated by the flow of electric charges in closed paths.

7-5 Maxwell's third relation. One method described in the previous section for measuring the magnetic induction inside a permanent bar magnet consists of measuring the charge induced to flow through a coil when the coil is slipped off the magnet. If, instead, the coil is held fixed and the magnet is removed from the coil, the charge that flows through the meter is $q = N\phi/R$, as before, where ϕ is the flux passing through the coil before the magnet is removed. The correspondence between these cases was first observed by Faraday, and the equation

$$\mathcal{E} = -N \frac{d\phi}{dt}, \qquad (7\text{--}9)$$

which expresses the induced emf at any instant of time for either case in terms of the rate of change of flux passing through the coil, is known as Faraday's law. It is adequate for analyzing the emf's induced in nearly all applications.

It should be noted, however, that there is a basic difference between the two experiments. With the observer in the laboratory coordinate system, the first case constitutes a coil moving in a time-independent field, while the second case constitutes a stationary coil in a field that changes with time. While Eq. (7–9) can usually be used to describe either case, occasionally a problem arises which suggests the need for caution. The homopolar generator discussed in the following section represents such a problem. Equation (7–9) is, however, always valid when applied to stationary circuits in time-dependent magnetic fields.

Recognizing this limitation to Faraday's law, it is possible to use it to obtain a more general expression, known as Maxwell's third relation. Note that the magnetic flux ϕ through a closed loop of wire is equal to the flux through any imaginary surface s whose periphery coincides with the wire. If **B** is the field at the element $d\mathbf{s}$ of this surface, then

$$\phi = \int_s \mathbf{B} \cdot d\mathbf{s}.$$

The emf induced in a stationary circuit is given by Faraday's law:

$$\mathcal{E} = -\frac{d\phi}{dt} = -\int \dot{\mathbf{B}} \cdot d\mathbf{s},$$

where $\dot{\mathbf{B}} = \partial \mathbf{B}/\partial t$. The current induced in the wire loop alters the value of **B**, but the equation is valid so long as **B** represents the resultant field due to all causes. The fact that charges do flow in the wire indicates that there must be an electric field. For conduction along fine wires of cross section a in series,

$$\mathcal{E} = \int i \, dR = \int Ja \, \frac{\rho \, dl}{a} = \int J\rho \, dl,$$

which is consistent with the more general expression

$$\mathcal{E} = \oint \rho \mathbf{J} \cdot d\mathbf{l} = \oint \mathbf{E} \cdot d\mathbf{l}$$

integrated around the circuit. The line integral for the induced electric field is seen to be independent of the value of ρ and is valid for any closed path whether or not wires are present. Combining the two expressions for $\mathcal{E}$, we find that

$$\oint \mathbf{E} \cdot d\mathbf{l} = -\int_s \dot{\mathbf{B}} \cdot d\mathbf{s}, \tag{7–10}$$

which has general validity and is called Maxwell's third relation in integral form. The differential form of Maxwell's third relation is obtained by using Stokes' theorem to transform the line integral into a surface integral; that is,

$$\oint \mathbf{E} \cdot d\mathbf{l} = \int_s \boldsymbol{\nabla} \times \mathbf{E} \cdot d\mathbf{s} = -\int_s \dot{\mathbf{B}} \cdot d\mathbf{s}.$$

Since s represents any general surface, the integrands of the two surface integrals must be equal, and therefore

$$\boldsymbol{\nabla} \times \mathbf{E} = -\dot{\mathbf{B}}. \tag{7–11}$$

Because $\boldsymbol{\nabla} \times \mathbf{E} \neq 0$ wherever $\mathbf{B}$ changes with time, the electric field is not in general conservative, and it cannot be expressed as the gradient of a scalar potential. However, it is shown in Section 8–5 that $\mathbf{E}$ can be expressed in terms of a scalar and a vector potential. Note that $\mathbf{E}$ is a conservative field and can be expressed as the gradient of a scalar potential wherever $\dot{\mathbf{B}} = 0$.

7–6 Induced emf's. The third field relation of Maxwell, given in integral form by Eq. (7–10) and in differential form by Eq. (7–11), applies specifically to changing fields in stationary circuits. For the special case in which a circuit encloses a plane area $\mathbf{A}$ in a uniform magnetic field $\mathbf{B}$, where it is assumed that both $\mathbf{A}$ and $\mathbf{B}$ may be time-dependent, Faraday's law gives the correct result and may be written as

$$\mathcal{E} = -\frac{d\phi}{dt} = -\frac{d}{dt} (\mathbf{B} \cdot \mathbf{A})$$

or

$$\mathcal{E} = -\mathbf{A} \cdot \frac{d\mathbf{B}}{dt} - \mathbf{B} \cdot \frac{d\mathbf{A}}{dt}.$$

The first term could be obtained from the direct application of Eq. (7–10) and the second term could be obtained from the force-on-a-charge equation, as was done in Section 7–3. Faraday's law, however, is not adequate for all situations, as is illustrated by the following discussion of a homopolar generator.

Consider a flat disk of copper mounted on an axle so that it can be turned by mechanical power, and assume that some means can be devised for making good electric contact between the periphery of this rotating disk, shown in Fig. 7–7, and the fixed copper ring surrounding it. The ring is assumed to be so thick that its electrical resistance is negligible compared with that of the resistor R through which it is electrically connected to the axle of the disk. If the disk is now caused to rotate in a uniform magnetic field **B** which is perpendicular to its surface, an emf is induced which produces a current through the resistor R even though the total magnetic flux through the closed circuit remains strictly constant.

Although Eq. (7–9) predicts a zero emf in this situation, Eq. (7–6) predicts an emf of $B\omega r^2/2$, where B is the external field, and ω is the angular velocity of the disk and r its radius. The following is a general expression for analyzing emf's induced in all situations in our laboratory coordinates:

$$\mathcal{E} = -\int_s \dot{\mathbf{B}} \cdot d\mathbf{s} - \oint \mathbf{B} \cdot \mathbf{v} \times d\mathbf{l}, \qquad (7\text{–}12)$$

where the surface integral must be evaluated over a surface bounded by the circuit and the line integral must be evaluated around the closed

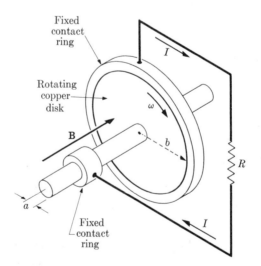

Fig. 7–7. Homopolar generator—a copper disk rotating in a uniform magnetic field. The heavy-copper contact ring assures that the induced current is radial.

circuit. Equation (7–12) should be used whenever there is doubt about the applicability of Faraday's equation. Equation (7–12) is equivalent to Eq. (7–9) whenever the latter is valid.

7–7 Electric power conversion. Probably the most important single aspect of electromagnetic phenomena is the ease with which electromagnetic energy is converted into other forms of energy and vice versa. The fundamental relation needed for these conversions can be obtained from consideration of the power delivered to a charge q by the electric and magnetic fields in which it resides. If $\mathbf{F}$ is the force on q and $\mathbf{v}$ is its velocity, the power delivered is

$$P = \mathbf{F} \cdot \mathbf{v} = q(\mathbf{E} + \mathbf{v} \times \mathbf{B}) \cdot \mathbf{v}$$

or

$$P = q\mathbf{E} \cdot \mathbf{v}, \tag{7–13}$$

since $\mathbf{v} \times \mathbf{B} \cdot \mathbf{v} = 0$. In terms of electric currents, the volume density of power delivered to a charge density ρ moving with velocity $\mathbf{v}$ is

$$p = \mathbf{f} \cdot \mathbf{v} = \rho\mathbf{v} \cdot \mathbf{E} = \mathbf{J} \cdot \mathbf{E}, \tag{7–14}$$

where $\mathbf{J}$ is the current density. These two equations, which were derived and used in Chapter 6 for steady-state conditions, have here been shown to have general validity. Wherever these expressions differ from zero, conversions of power are taking place between electrical and other forms of energy. Where the sign of the product is positive, electric power is converted to other forms. Where this sign is negative, the conversion proceeds in the opposite direction. Two dynamos similar to the one pictured in Fig. 7–4 are often connected by a transmission line. The armature of one may be rotated by a steam or gasoline engine to generate power, which is carried by the electric current in the line to the other dynamo acting as a motor. Charges are made to flow opposite to the force of the electric field in the generator but not in the motor. In principle, two Faraday disks like the one in Fig. 7–7 can be used for this purpose, and because the detailed analysis is easier with the disks, we shall consider such a system.

In Fig. 7–8 the disk on the left generates power for the motor disk on the right. From Eq. (7–12), the emf of either disk rotating at ω radians per second is

$$\mathcal{E} = \int_a^b B\omega r \, dr = \tfrac{1}{2}B\omega(b^2 - a^2).$$

If the total resistance of the two wires of the transmission line is R_l and the internal resistance of each disk is R_i, the current I is given by

$$I(R_l + 2R_i) = \mathcal{E}_1 - \mathcal{E}_2.$$

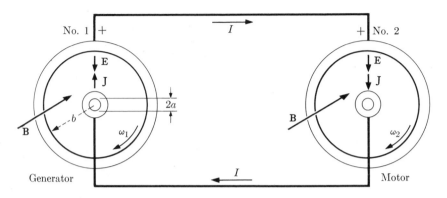

FIG. 7–8. Homopolar generator supplying power through a transmission line to a homopolar motor.

Multiplying through by I to obtain the power relations, we obtain

$$I^2 R_l + I^2 R_i + I^2 R_i = \mathcal{E}_1 I - \mathcal{E}_2 I.$$

The five terms taken in order represent (1) the heat loss in the line, (2) the heat loss in disk No. 1, (3) the heat loss in disk No. 2, (4) the total power generated by disk No. 1, and (5) the electric power converted into mechanical power in disk No. 2 to overcome the torque due to friction and the mechanical load. A heavier load slows the rotation of the motor disk and reduces its back emf $\mathcal{E}_2$. If $\mathcal{E}_1$ is maintained constant, this reduction in $\mathcal{E}_2$ increases I and therefore the product $\mathcal{E}_2 I$ increases, since $I = (\mathcal{E}_1 - \mathcal{E}_2)/(R_l + 2R_i)$. The total electric power delivered by No. 1 to the rest of the circuit, $\mathcal{E}_1 I - I^2 R_i$, can be obtained by integrating $-\int \mathbf{E} \cdot \mathbf{J} \, d\tau$ over its disk, since $\mathbf{E}$ and $\mathbf{J}$ are there oppositely directed. Furthermore, the total power converted into mechanical energy and heat in No. 2, $\mathcal{E}_2 I + I^2 R_i$, is obtained by integrating $\int \mathbf{E} \cdot \mathbf{J} \, d\tau$ over its disk, where $\mathbf{E}$ and $\mathbf{J}$ are parallel.

7–8 Galvanometers. The moving-coil galvanometer, whose essential features are shown in Fig. 7–9, has been so improved in design and construction that it has practically replaced all other types of galvanometers. It has become an essential component in a multitude of instruments designed to measure or detect a great variety of physical quantities. For example, it is an important component in instruments for measuring currents from 10^{-11} amp to 10^6 amp, potential differences from 10^{-8} v to 10^6 v, magnetic fluxes from 10^{-6} weber/m² to 10^4 weber/m², etc.

Usually the coil of a galvanometer is held in its zero position by elastic forces. In a good portable instrument the coil may be mounted in jeweled bearings and held in its zero position by spiral springs that also serve to connect the coil to external circuits. A less portable instrument may have

Fig. 7–9. Coil with angular position indicator for a typical moving-coil galvanometer. The magnetic flux through this coil is given by $\phi = \phi_m(\theta - \theta_0)$.

the coil suspended between two taut metal filaments that supply the elastic torque and also provide the conducting leads. The most sensitive galvanometers are not portable. Their coils are suspended by single metallic filaments that are made very long and thin to reduce the restoring torque. This single filament provides one conducting lead to the coil, but two are needed. The second lead is usually a light metal ribbon that contributes very little to the restoring torque on the coil.

For observing angular positions of the coils, metal pointers are rigidly attached to the coil in most portable instruments, while light mirrors are fastened to the coils of the more sensitive instruments. For these latter instruments many unique optical devices have been devised and are being used for determining angular deflections with great accuracy.

The circuit shown in Fig. 7–10 is adequate for representing most circuits that might be connected to a galvanometer. The resistance R_g includes that of the galvanometer and any control resistors connected in series with it, while R includes the internal and external resistances associated with the source of emf. Effects produced by eliminating the shunt can be determined by merely making $R_s = \infty$.

In writing the differential equation for the galvanometer, use will be made of the relation derived in Section 7–2 for the torque on a closed loop of wire. The geometry of the permanent magnet is so designed that the flux lines are nearly radial for all angles within the allowed coil deflection, so that the magnitude of the torque applied to the coil is always $NiAB$, where N is the number of turns in the coil, i is the instantaneous current through the coil, A is its area, and B is the field of the permanent magnet. Referring to Fig. 7–10, the current through the coil can be

Fig. 7–10. Typical circuit connected to a galvanometer. Variations in R_s and R_g provide flexible controls of the sensitivity and damping characteristics.

expressed as the sum of the current through the coil induced by the source of emf plus the current through the coil induced by the motion of the galvanometer coil through the field B. The expression is

$$i = i_e + i_c = \frac{\mathcal{E}}{R_e} + \frac{\mathcal{E}_c}{R_c},$$

where i_e and i_c both represent currents through the galvanometer coil and the effective resistances R_e and R_c defined by this equation can be shown to be

$$R_e = R + R_g + \frac{R_g R}{R_s} \qquad (7\text{-}15)$$

and

$$R_c = R_g + \frac{R_s R}{R_s + R} \qquad (7\text{-}16)$$

by using simple circuit analysis like that presented in Section 6–8. By defining $\phi_m = BA$, the differential equation for the rotation of the galvanometer coil through an angle θ is found to be

$$G \frac{d^2\theta}{dt^2} + 2G\alpha' \frac{d\theta}{dt} + k\theta = N\phi_m \left(\frac{\mathcal{E}}{R_e} + \frac{\mathcal{E}_c}{R_c} \right), \qquad (7\text{-}17)$$

where G is the axial moment of inertia of the coil, k is the spring constant, and $2G\alpha'$ is a convenient expression for the damping constant. If the coil is in equilibrium when $\theta = \theta_0$ and if the flux through it is zero in this position, then at the deflection angle θ this flux is given by $\phi = \phi_m(\theta - \theta_0)$. As the coil swings it produces the emf

$$\mathcal{E}_c = -N \frac{d\phi}{dt} = -N\phi_m \frac{d\theta}{dt},$$

and the differential equation of motion may then be rewritten as

$$\frac{d^2\theta}{dt^2} + 2\alpha \frac{d\theta}{dt} + \omega_0^2 \theta = S\mathcal{E}, \qquad (7\text{-}18)$$

where $\alpha = \alpha' + N^2\phi_m^2/2GR_c$, $\omega_0^2 = k/G$, and $S = N\phi_m/GR_e$. The general solution for this second-order differential equation with constant coefficients is the particular integral plus the complementary function. The particular integral θ_p depends on the time-dependent nature of $\mathcal{E}$, while the complementary function θ_c does not. The solution for θ_c is defined as the general solution for the differential equation with the right side set equal to zero. This solution may be obtained by trying a solution of the form $\theta = e^{\mathcal{D}t}$, from which

$$\mathcal{D}^2 + 2\alpha\mathcal{D} + \omega_0^2 = 0.$$

This quadratic equation yields the two solutions

$$\mathcal{D}_1 = -\alpha + \sqrt{\alpha^2 - \omega_0^2} \quad \text{and} \quad \mathcal{D}_2 = -\alpha - \sqrt{\alpha^2 - \omega_0^2}. \qquad (7\text{–}19)$$

Since the solution for a second-order differential equation must have two arbitrary constants, the solution is

$$\theta_c = \mathcal{C}e^{\mathcal{D}_1 t} + \mathcal{B}e^{\mathcal{D}_2 t}, \qquad (7\text{–}20)$$

where each of the constants $\mathcal{C}$, $\mathcal{B}$, $\mathcal{D}_1$, and $\mathcal{D}_2$ may be complex. The nature of θ_c depends upon whether $\sqrt{\alpha^2 - \omega_0^2}$ is real or imaginary.

Underdamped galvanometer. When the radical in Eq. (7–19) is imaginary, it can be written as

$$j\sqrt{\omega_0^2 - \alpha^2} = j\beta.$$

Then Eq. (7–20) can be written as

$$\theta_c = Ae^{-\alpha t} \sin(\beta t + \delta), \qquad (7\text{–}21)$$

where β and the arbitrary constants A and δ can be chosen to be real. The resultant oscillatory motion is gradually damped out by the exponential term, as illustrated by curve U in Fig. 7–11. Assuming that α' may be neglected, Eq. (7–18) shows that $\alpha = N^2\phi_m^2/2GR_c$, and the galvanometer is underdamped when

$$R_c > \frac{N^2\phi_m^2}{2G\omega_0}.$$

Overdamped galvanometer. When the radical in Eq. (7–19) is real, it can be written as

$$\sqrt{\alpha^2 - \omega_0^2} = \gamma,$$

and then Eq. (7–20) can be expressed as

$$\theta_c = Be^{-\alpha t} \sinh(\gamma t + \delta), \qquad (7\text{–}22)$$

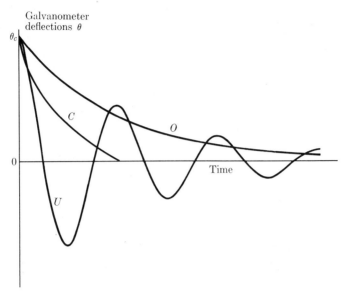

FIG. 7–11.   Curves showing how the deflection θ of a galvanometer coil decays toward zero with different types of damping. The underdamped, overdamped, and critically damped cases are shown by the curves marked U, O, and C, respectively.

where γ and the arbitrary constants B and δ are real. When $\alpha \gg \omega_0$ damping is so complete that not only do no oscillations occur, but it requires a long time for the coil of the galvanometer to reach its equilibrium position. Again assuming α' to be negligible, the galvanometer is overdamped when

$$R_c < \frac{N^2 \phi_m^2}{2G\omega_0}.$$

Critically damped galvanometer. A galvanometer is said to be critically damped when $\alpha = \omega_0$. If α' may be neglected, critical damping can be achieved by making

$$R_c = \frac{N^2 \phi_m^2}{2G\omega_0}.$$

Since critical damping represents the transition between the underdamped and the overdamped conditions, the critically damped expression for θ_c can be obtained by letting either β or γ approach zero. In either case,

$$\theta_c = Ce^{-\alpha t}(t + D), \tag{7–23}$$

where the arbitrary constants C and D are real.

Each of equations (7–21), (7–22), and (7–23) decays exponentially with time, but Eq. (7–23) decays the most rapidly, as can be seen from the plots of these expressions in Fig. 7–11. "Critical-damping resistance," R_x, is defined as the value of R_c for critical damping less the actual resistance of the galvanometer.

Steady-current galvanometer. The general solution of Eq. (7–18) contains a term θ_p that does depend upon $\mathcal{E}$. When a steady potential difference $\mathcal{E} = V$ is supplied by the source in Fig. 7–10, this term is obtained by assuming $\theta_p = K$, which satisfies the differential equation and gives $\omega_0^2 K = SV$, or

$$ K = \frac{\gamma V}{\omega_0^2} = \frac{N \phi_m}{G \omega_0^2} \frac{V}{R_e}. $$

Hence

$$ \theta_p = \frac{N \phi_m}{G \omega_0^2} \frac{V}{R_e} = \frac{N \phi_m}{G \omega_0^2} I_g, $$

where I_g is the final steady current through the galvanometer. The angle θ_p is the steady deflection remaining after θ_c has decayed to zero. The sensitivity of the galvanometer to current depends upon

$$ \frac{\theta_p}{I_g} = \frac{N \phi_m}{G \omega_0^2} = \frac{N \phi_m}{K}. \tag{7-24} $$

Whenever possible, the galvanometer should be used in the critically damped condition, since final deflections are then achieved most rapidly.

Ballistic galvanometer. Galvanometers are often described as ballistic galvanometers when the first throw is being used to determine the total flow of charge, although this term was originally applied only to underdamped galvanometers used in this fashion. If the total flow is completed with sufficient rapidity, the first throw is proportional to the total charge regardless of the nature of the damping. This could be demonstrated by solving the differential equation in two stages. It is simpler, however, to recognize that a brief pulse of current through the coil gives it the angular momentum

$$ G \frac{d\theta}{dt} = \int N \phi_m i \, dt = N \phi_m q. $$

Thereafter the coil deflection is controlled by Eq. (7–18) with $\mathcal{E} = 0$, which means that thereafter $\theta_p = 0$. Since θ_p is zero for the subsequent motion, the expression for θ obtained from Eq. (7–20) is

$$ \theta = \alpha e^{\mathfrak{D}_1 t} + \mathcal{B} e^{\mathfrak{D}_2 t}, $$

regardless of the damping conditions. From the boundary conditions that at $t = 0$, $\theta = 0$ and $d\theta/dt = N\phi_m q/G$, we obtain the two equations

$$0 = \mathfrak{A} + \mathfrak{B} \qquad \text{and} \qquad \frac{N\phi_m q}{G} = \mathfrak{A}\mathfrak{D}_1 + \mathfrak{B}\mathfrak{D}_2.$$

With the values for $\mathfrak{D}_1$ and $\mathfrak{D}_2$ given in Eq. (7–18), these yield

$$\mathfrak{A} = -\mathfrak{B} = \frac{N\phi_m q}{2G\sqrt{\alpha^2 - \omega_0^2}},$$

from which we obtain

$$\theta = \frac{N\phi_m q}{2G\sqrt{\alpha^2 - \omega_0^2}} (e^{\mathfrak{D}_1 t} - e^{\mathfrak{D}_2 t}). \tag{7–25}$$

This general expression takes the form of Eq. (7–20) when $\alpha > \omega_0$, the form of Eq. (7–21) when $\alpha < \omega_0$, and the form of Eq. (7–22) when $\alpha = \omega_0$. In each case the function passes through at least one maximum. If the first maximum occurs at the time $t = t_m$, the first throw deflection is given by

$$\theta_m = \frac{N\phi_m q}{2G\sqrt{\alpha^2 - \omega_0^2}} (e^{\mathfrak{D}_1 t_m} - e^{\mathfrak{D}_2 t_m}). \tag{7–26}$$

If two experiments are performed with the same galvanometer and the same circuit with the same resistances, but with the two different values, q_1 and q_2, for q, then the expressions for the first throws, θ_{m1} and θ_{m2} respectively, will have identical values for N, ϕ_m, α, ω_0, $\mathfrak{D}_1$, $\mathfrak{D}_2$, and t_m. Therefore, in such experiments,

$$\frac{\theta_{m1}}{\theta_{m2}} = \frac{q_1}{q_2}$$

regardless of which type of damping is used. When sufficient sensitivity is available, the critically damped (or just slightly underdamped) galvanometer is the most convenient.

Galvanometer sensitivities. The sensitivity of a galvanometer to steady currents is described best in terms of the ratio θ/I, where θ is the final steady angular deflection produced by a steady current I in the coil. *The sensitivity of a galvanometer to a charge pulse* is described by the ratio θ_i/q, where θ_i is the maximum angular deflection produced by the passage of a pulse of total magnitude q through the coil. Pulse sensitivity, so defined, has meaning only if the source of the pulse has infinite resistance and is connected directly across the coil; e.g., the source may be a capacitor. Otherwise pulse sensitivity should be stated for the galvanometer combined with its circuit. It is left as an exercise to show that current sensitivity and pulse sensitivity are closely related.

Fluxmeter. A fluxmeter consists of a galvanometer in which $k = G\omega_0^2 = 0$ and in which $\alpha' \cong 0$. It can be used to read the change in the magnetic flux that threads through a calibrated search coil, even when this change requires a relatively long time. In operation, the indicator may be first set at zero and the flux change then causes a permanent deflection that is proportional to this flux change. The instrument is equivalent to a thoroughly overdamped galvanometer. In fact, a galvanometer that has a very high current sensitivity can be converted to an excellent fluxmeter by connecting a low-resistance shunt across its terminals.

With the foregoing assumptions, the differential equation can be written as

$$\frac{d^2\theta}{dt^2} + 2\alpha \frac{d\theta}{dt} = SN_s \frac{d\phi}{dt},$$

where N_s is the number of turns in the search coil and $d\phi/dt$ is the rate of change of flux through it. If we let $d^2\theta/dt^2 = d\omega/dt$, this equation can be multiplied by dt and integrated directly; that is

$$\int_0^\infty \frac{d\omega}{dt}\,dt + 2\alpha \int_0^\infty \frac{d\theta}{dt}\,dt = SN_s \int_0^\infty \frac{d\phi}{dt}\,dt,$$

which becomes

$$(\omega_f - \omega_i) + 2\alpha(\theta_f - \theta_i) = SN_s(\phi_f - \phi_i),$$

where the subscripts i and f identify respectively the initial and final values of the quantities. At the start of the experiment ω_i was set equal to zero, and the final angular velocity ω_f must be zero to satisfy the law of conservation of energy. Therefore, from the definitions of symbols given for Eq. (7–18),

$$\phi_f - \phi_i = \frac{2\alpha(\theta_f - \theta_i)}{SN_s} = \frac{R_e N}{R_c N_s} \phi_m(\theta_f - \theta_i),$$

and the total deflection is proportional to the total change in flux through the search coil. It is instructive to note that the value ϕ_f for the final flux through the search coil is usually established before θ and ω reach their final values of θ_f and $\omega_f = 0$, since any residual energy, $\frac{1}{2}G\omega^2$, of the swinging coil must be converted to heat in the resistors.

PROBLEMS

7-1. Figure 7-12 shows a triangular loop of wire in which there is a current of 6 amp. The magnetic intensity $\mathbf{B}$ = 1.1 webers/m^2 is uniform over the triangle and parallel to the side AC, as shown. Find the magnitude and direction of the force acting (a) on the sides AB, BC, and AC. (b) Calculate the dipole moment of the loop and the magnitude and direction of the torque acting on it.

*7-2. Figure 7-13 shows a homopolar motor which consists of a 4-spoked metal wheel free to revolve in a magnetic field which is constant at B = 2.0 webers/m^2 over the spokes and zero over the rim. The spokes sweep out a circle of radius 30 cm and each carries the same outward radial current at all times, because the rim has a much lower resistance than the spokes even though these are negligible compared with R. (a) In which direction will the wheel rotate, in the direction indicated or in the opposite direction? (b) If the friction were truly negligible, what final speed, in radians per second, would the wheel achieve when connected to a storage battery having $\mathcal{E}_B$ = 90 volts and negligible resistance? (c) Calculate the speed of the wheel when the friction and the mechanical load on the motor amounts to 300 watts and R = 6 ohms.

*7-3. The general principles of a d-c dynamo are simplified in Fig. 7-14. Let R = 3 ohms, $\mathcal{E}_B$ = 36 volts, l = 0.9 m, and $\mathbf{B}$ = 1.5 webers/m^2, into and normal to this paper. The mass of the rod is 0.3 kgm. (a) With no friction and no load on the rod, calculate the magnitudes and the directions of its initial acceleration, and its final velocity. (b) If the rod must pull a load requiring a force of 6.2 newtons, what will be its final velocity? (c) If this dynamo is to act as a generator to produce a 3-amp charging current through the battery, in what direction and how fast must the rod be pulled along the rails? (d) How much force is required to maintain this motion? (e) Calculate the electric power delivered by the rod and compare this with the mechanical power delivered to the rod.

7-4. In Fig. 7-15 an electron is projected along the axis midway between the plates of a cathode-ray tube with an initial velocity of 2×10^7 m/sec. Assume that there is a downwardly directed electric field, having the uniform magnitude 20,000 n/coul over 4 cm of the path, but zero over the remaining 12 cm of the path, to the fluorescent screen at F. (a) How far above the axis has the electron moved when it reaches the end of the plates? (b) At what angle with the axis is it moving as it leaves the plates? (c) How far above the axis will it strike the fluorescent screen F?

*7-5. Suppose the potential difference between the spherical terminal of a Van de Graaff generator and the point at which charges are sprayed onto the upward moving belt is 2 million volts. If the belt delivers negative charge to the sphere at the rate of 2×10^{-3} coul/sec, what horsepower must be expended to drive the belt against electrical forces?

7-6. Derive the relations given in Eqs. (7-15) and (7-16) for the effective resistances in the galvanometer circuit of Fig. 7-10.

---

* Answers to starred problems will be found at back of book.

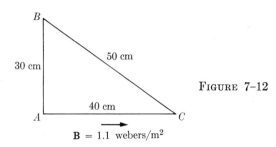

30 cm

50 cm

40 cm

B

A

C

FIGURE 7–12

$\mathbf{B} = 1.1$ webers/m^2

R

V_B

N

S

FIGURE 7–13

Rail

ε_B

×   ×   ×   ×

l B

FIGURE 7–14

R

×   ×   ×   ×

Rail

V_a

c

a b

V

D

E

G

F

FIGURE 7–15

7-7. According to the definition of an emf given in Section 6–4, the Hall effect sample shown in Fig. 7–2 produces an emf $\mathcal{E}_H$ in the circuit connected to the potentiometer. Power will be dissipated in this circuit whenever there is a current I_p through the potentiometer. Show that this dissipated power is $\mathcal{E}_H I_p$ and that this is just equal to the power $\mathcal{E}_H' I$ that must be absorbed from the main circuit by a Hall-effect-induced back emf $\mathcal{E}_H'$.

*7-8. The fact that elementary particles like the electron have magnetic dipole moments and mechanical angular momentum provides qualitative confirmation for the concept that magnetic dipoles may be produced only by electric charges moving in closed paths. However, attempts to construct detailed models that are completely consistent have met with little success. (a) Calculate the dipole moment of a circular disk of radius a and thickness t rotating about its axis with angular velocity ω, assuming a uniform charge density ρ. (b) Calculate the dipole moment of a uniformly charged sphere rotating about a diameter. Assume that the sphere has a uniform charge density ρ, a radius a, and an angular velocity ω.

7-9. In the differential equation (7–18), the constant ω_0 is fixed by the construction of the galvanometer, but α depends upon the resistance of the external circuit. When $\alpha^2 < \omega_0^2$, Eq. (7–19) can be written as $\mathfrak{D}_1 = -\alpha + j\beta$ and $\mathfrak{D}_2 = -\alpha - j\beta$, where β is real. For this case, show that Eq. (7–21) is equivalent to Eq. (7–20) and that A and δ are real if $\mathfrak{B} = \mathfrak{C}^*$, the complex conjugate of $\mathfrak{C}$.

7-10. (a) Show that Eq. (7–21) approaches Eq. (7–23) in the limit as $\beta \to 0$. Calculate C and D in terms of A and δ. (b) Show that Eq. (7–22) approaches Eq. (7–23) in the limit as $\gamma \to 0$. Calculate C and D in terms of B and δ.

*7-11. In 1897 Sir J. J. Thomson proved that the "cathode glow" in evacuated tubes like the one shown in Fig. 7–15 was due to negatively charged "corpuscles" with a constant charge-to-mass ratio e/m. The figure shows his equipment, in which the corpuscles (now called electrons) were accelerated from the cathode c by a large potential difference V_a, between c and a, and collimated into a narrow beam by passing them through slits at a and b. When there were no other fields in the tube, the electrons traveled straight to F, where they caused the glass to fluoresce. To deviate this beam so that it would impinge on a point G, which was a distance d above F, an electric field was produced by applying a potential difference V between the parallel metal plates D and E, whose distance of separation was s. The beam was then brought back to F by applying just the right strength of magnetic field B, perpendicular to both the beam and the electric field. The velocity v of the electrons passing through the slit at b was never as large as one-tenth the velocity of light, so that Newton's laws of mechanics were sufficiently accurate. To simplify calculations it will be assumed that the E and B fields are uniform over the length l of the path of the beam from b to F. The following quantities could be measured: V_a, V, B, l, s, and d.

(a) Calculate the deflection d produced by the electric field alone and state whether e/m can be determined without applying the B field.

(b) Calculate e/m in terms of the measurable quantities. Can e and m be separately determined by this experiment?

(c) Determine maximum values for V_a and V in terms of l, s, and d.

(d) Show that by placing a slit at F this device can be used to select particles with a single velocity v, regardless of the magnitudes of the charges or masses of these particles.

*7–12. Figure 7–16 shows the principle of the Bainbridge mass spectrograph, which he used to determine the masses of the ionized nuclei of the isotopes of several elements. By means of a device similar to that in Fig. 7–15 a narrow beam of isotopes with different masses but with equal charges is projected into the evacuated chamber, shown on the right in the figure in the shape of a half circle. As pointed out in Problem 7–11(d), the isotopes in such a beam all have the same velocity. With a uniform magnetic field B, perpendicular to the paper in the semicircular chamber of the diagram, the isotopes travel different circles and blacken a photographic plate or film fastened to the plane AA'. Assuming that there are uniform electric and magnetic fields E_v and B_v respectively in the velocity selector, calculate (a) the masses of the isotopes in terms of the distances, $d_1, d_2, \ldots$, from the slit of the blackened regions on the photographic plate, and (b) the separations between the traces on the photographic plate due to the tin isotopes with mass numbers 116 and 120, from the trace due to that with mass number 118, which is 75 cm from the slit. (c) Assuming that both B and B_v are approximately 1 weber/m^2, calculate the approximate velocity of the isotopes and the approximate potential difference V applied across the plates of the velocity selector, if these plates are 2 cm apart.

FIGURE 7–16

7–13. In Aston's mass spectrograph the beam of isotopes may have any distribution of velocities, so that no velocity selector is required. This instrument employs electric and magnetic fields, E and B, that are perpendicular to the original beam but are parallel to each other. Set up coordinate axes with a photographic plate in the yz-plane and a beam of positively charged isotopes projected toward this plane parallel to the negative x-axis. If the fields are uniform and parallel to the positive z-axis, the photographic plate will show parabolic traces.

(a) Assuming that the beam enters the uniform fields at $x = x_0$, calculate the equation for these parabolas, for isotopes of mass m and charge e. In this calculation assume that the deflections are so small that the forces on the particles due to the magnetic field can be calculated from their original velocities.

(b) Determine the errors, if any, produced by ignoring velocity components in the y- and z-directions in the expression for the forces on the particles due to the magnetic field.

*7-14. Bohr's original model for the hydrogen atom assumed that an electron of charge e and mass m traveled in a circle of radius a with angular velocity ω around a much heavier nucleus that had a positive charge of the same magnitude e. He assumed that the angular momentum of the electron was quantized, so that $ma^2\omega = nh/2\pi$, where $h/2\pi = 1.05 \times 10^{-27}$ erg·sec $= 1.05 \times 10^{-34}$ joule·sec and $n = 1, 2, 3, \ldots$

(a) Find a in terms of n, h, m, and e.

(b) Find the total energy, W_n (kinetic plus potential), in terms of the same quantities.

(c) According to Bohr's hypothesis, light is emitted by a hydrogen atom whenever the electron falls from an orbit having a large n to one with a smaller n. The frequency f of the light emitted was given by $hf = W_n - W_{n'}$. Determine the frequency and wavelength of the light emitted when the electron falls from the orbit where $n = 4$ to that where $n = 2$. Is this frequency visible to the human eye?

*7-15. As pointed out in Section 7-1, an ordinary cyclotron operating with a constant frequency on the dees cannot accelerate protons to very high energies, because the protons fall out of step at this frequency, when their mass increases as they approach the velocity of light. Higher-energy protons can be obtained by periodically decreasing the frequency on the dees to keep in step with the rotational frequency of groups of protons. With this modification the device becomes a synchrocyclotron. At the synchrocyclotron of the Carnegie Institute of Technology, the maximum radius available to the protons is 1.74 m, where the magnetic field is nearly uniform at approximately $B = 2$ webers/m². The relativistic mass of a particle is given by $m = m_0/\sqrt{1 - \beta^2}$, where $\beta = v/c$, the ratio of the velocity of the particle to the velocity of light, and m_0 is the rest mass of the particle; i.e., m_0 is its mass measured at relatively low velocities. The energy required to accelerate the particle to the velocity v from rest is $(m_0c^2/\sqrt{1 - \beta^2}) - m_0c^2$.

(a) Calculate the frequency of the alternating voltage required between the dees to achieve the initial accelerations. (b) Calculate the velocity of the protons in their outermost circle. (c) What must be the frequency on the dees to keep in step with the protons in this outer circle? (d) Calculate the total increase in the energy of the protons, in electron volts. (e) What modification in the frequency pattern would be required to use deuterons instead of protons?

7-16. Suppose that the rod of the linear dynamo shown in Fig. 7-14 is pulled to the right along the rails at a constant velocity of $v = 2V_B/Bl$. (a) Calculate the magnitude and direction of the current through the battery. (b) Calculate the mechanical power delivered to the rod and show in detail what happens to this power.

*7–17. Suppose that the rod of the linear dynamo shown in Fig. 7–14 is connected to pull a load whose motion is resisted by the force Gv. (a) Calculate the terminal velocity of the rod and the mechanical power it delivers at this terminal velocity. (b) Calculate the power delivered by the battery. What happens to this power?

7–18. In Fig. 7–14 replace the battery with a capacitor of capacitance C, charged to the potential difference V_B. Suppose this charged capacitor is instantaneously connected to the rails at the time $t = 0$. Calculate (a) the final velocity of the rod, and (b) the displacement x of the rod from its initial position, as a function of C, V_B, B, R, m, and t.

*7–19. A single circular loop of wire of radius a and resistance R lies in the xy-plane with its center at the origin. A magnetic field parallel to the z-axis reduces to zero according to the relation $\mathbf{B} = \mathbf{k}B_0 e^{-\alpha t}$. (a) Assuming that R is large, so that the magnetic field of the induced current can be ignored, calculate the current, the charge that has passed any given point on the loop, and the power dissipated as heat. (b) Show that the total charge passing any given point depends only on the total change in flux, and is independent of $f(t)$, where $B = f(t)$, even when R is small.

7–20. Suppose that the magnetic field in Problem 7–19 is constant at $\mathbf{B} = \mathbf{k}B_0$ but the loop rotates about the y-axis at the constant angular velocity ω rad/sec. Using the assumption that R is large, calculate (a) the current, (b) the torque on the loop, and (c) the mechanical power required to rotate the loop. Compare the mechanical power with the rate of heat generation.

*7–21. A thin conducting disk of radius a and thickness h is in a uniform magnetic field that is perpendicular to its surface. The resistivity ρ of the disk is sufficiently large that the magnetic fields due to the induced currents (which are called eddy currents) can be ignored. If the field is given by $B = B_0 \cos \omega t$, (a) find the current density as a function of r and t, and (b) find the power dissipated by the eddy currents as a function of time.

7–22. Integrate the power, Eq. (7–14), over the space occupied by the rotating disk in the homopolar generator of Fig. 7–8. Perform the same integration for the homopolar motor and compare both results with the power relations obtained in the text.

*7–23. The steady current sensitivity of a galvanometer, θ/I, is closely related to its charge-pulse sensitivity, θ_i/q. When a certain sensitive galvanometer had no circuit connected to its terminals, its coil was observed to make ν complete oscillations per second with negligible damping. Its θ_i/q then was determined by discharging a capacitor through its coil. Calculate (a) the steady current sensitivity, and (b) the steady voltage sensitivity, if the coil resistance is R_g.

7–24. The current sensitivity θ/I of a sensitive galvanometer has been determined, where θ is the final steady deflection produced by a steady current through the coil of I. This galvanometer is to be used in the circuit of Fig. 7–10 for measuring the charge from a capacitor as it is discharged through the circuit. The magnitude of the shunt resistance is adjusted to $R_s = R_x$, the critical damping resistance. Calculate the charge sensitivity of the galvanometer circuit to obtain an expression for θ_i/q, where θ_i is the maximum deflection produced when the capacitor discharges the charge q through the circuit.

*7–25. One of the most successful devices for producing high-energy electrons is the betatron invented by D. W. Kerst in 1940. The principle can be understood from Problem 7–19, where the change in flux through a circular loop of wire caused the conduction electrons in the wire to flow around it. If the wire is replaced with an evacuated hollow toroid of larger cross section, free electrons injected into this space can be accelerated to rather large energies by flux changes through the loop that are quite easily achieved. For the device to be successful the electrons must be constrained to move in the evacuated space of the toroid, preferably along the central circle. This is accomplished by maintaining a magnetic field of the required magnitude in the toroid along this central circle. Call the average field inside this circle B_a and the field at the circle itself B_0. Fortunately, if the electrons are at rest when these two magnetic fields start increasing from zero, the electrons can be held to their circular orbit by maintaining the correct constant ratio between B_0 and B_a.

The force on a particle is always given by $\mathbf{F} = d(m\mathbf{v})/dt$, where $m = m_0/\sqrt{1 - \beta^2}$ and $\beta = v/c$.

(a) Calculate the velocity achieved by the electron when the average field inside an orbit of radius R has increased from zero to B_a.

(b) Calculate the radius R' of the circle an electron will travel when it is moving with velocity v perpendicular to a field B_0.

(c) Show that the electron will move in a stable orbit of constant radius $R' = R$ provided that, as the two fields are increased from zero, the ratio $B_a/B_0 = 2$ is maintained.

(d) Suppose that such a machine could be built to maintain the above relations for an orbit of radius 1 m and a final average field within the orbit of 1.6 webers/m^2. What would be the increase in energy of the electrons in electron volts?

7–26. A certain very sensitive galvanometer encounters so little friction that its α' may be neglected. (a) Show that its ω_0 may be obtained by timing the oscillations of its coil on an open circuit. (b) Show that when ω_0 is known the important ratio $N\phi_m/G$ can be obtained by observing the steady deflection produced by a known steady current. (c) With the results obtained in (a) and (b), show that both $N\phi_m$ and G can be obtained by determining the critical damping resistance.

7–27. The galvanometer in Problem 7–26 can be used as a fluxmeter by making R_s, in the circuit of Fig. 7–10, very small compared with its critical damping resistance. (a) Prove this statement. (b) Show that the measurements outlined in (a), (b), and (c) of Problem 7–6 are sufficient for calibrating this fluxmeter, provided all resistances are known.

7–28. A sensitive galvanometer to be used as a fluxmeter is connected with $R_s \ll R_x$ in the circuit of Fig. 7–10. (a) Assume that the magnetic flux in the N_s turns of the search coil follows the relation $\phi = Ae^{-at}(1 - e^{-at})$, where $a = 1/\text{sec}$, and calculate the galvanometer deflection θ as a function of t. (b) Plot both ϕ and θ versus t on the same graph, from $t = 0$ to $t = 5$ sec, choosing constants so that the maximum for each curve exceeds half the available ordinate on your coordinate paper.

CHAPTER 8

MAGNETIC FIELDS OF ELECTRIC CURRENTS

In 1820 Hans C. Oersted made the discovery that an electric current would exert a force on a magnetized needle. Investigations of this phenomenon were quickly started by several scientists, including Dominique Arago and André M. Ampere, who independently magnetized needles by wrapping them with coils of wire carrying electric currents. Ampere's investigations, which were both experimental and mathematical, led him to the concept of magnetic shells which is discussed in Section 9–8. Wilhelm Weber had proposed that the magnetization of iron resulted from the orientation of molecular magnets, and Ampere proposed that the magnetic moment of the molecules might originate in circular electric currents. Consequently, the circulating charges of the atoms and molecules are often referred to as "amperian currents." The mathematical relation between steady currents and the magnetic fields induced by them was first formulated by Biot and Savart.

8–1 The Biot-Savart law. The law formulated by Biot and Savart and listed in Section 2–14 is usually written in vector notation as

$$d\mathbf{B} = \mu_0 \frac{I \, d\mathbf{l} \times \mathbf{a}_r}{4\pi r^2},$$

(8–1)

where $d\mathbf{B}$ is the contribution to the field, at point P in Fig. 8–1(a), that is due to a current I in the wire element $d\mathbf{l}$. The vector distance of P from this element is $\mathbf{r} = r\mathbf{a}_r$. In this form the law cannot be verified experimentally, because it is impossible to isolate an element of wire carrying a steady current to determine its effect upon the field. Steady currents are found only in closed circuits; therefore the magnetic field at any point due to a steady current is the vector sum of the contributions from all parts of the closed circuit. The field at the point P in Fig. 8–1(a) is given by

$$\mathbf{B} = \mu_0 \oint \frac{I \, d\mathbf{l} \times \mathbf{a}_r}{4\pi r^2}$$

(8–2)

integrated over the closed circuit, provided the wire carrying the current I is so fine that its dimensions can be neglected. With finite conductors of various shapes, like those in the circuit of Fig. 8–1(b), the expression is

$$\mathbf{B} = \mu_0 \int \frac{\mathbf{J} \times \mathbf{a}_r \, d\tau}{4\pi r^2}$$

(8–3)

integrated throughout the region where there are currents. The magnetic

(a)   (b)

FIG. 8–1. (a) Current-carrying wire giving rise to a **B** field at P, in accordance with the law of Biot-Savart. (b) Current-carrying loop of finite dimensions.

fields due to many shapes of closed circuits have been calculated by means of Eq. (8–3) and the results have been verified experimentally. The calculated values have agreed so exactly with experiment that the correctness of the integral form of the law for steady currents is no longer questioned.

Fields of circuits with straight wire sections. It is often necessary to calculate magnetic fields due to circuits composed of several straight sections of wire. An expression for the field due to a single section of wire can be used to obtain the total field of a more complex figure by taking the vector sum of the fields produced by the individual straight segments. In Fig. 8–2(a), for example, the field **B** at P due to the current I in the rectangular wire loop is the vector sum of the fields at P due to the four straight sides.

The method for calculating the field caused by a wire segment at an arbitrary point P is illustrated in Fig. 8–2(b). The term $d\mathbf{l} \times \mathbf{a}_r$ in Eq. (8–2) is seen to be directed out of the paper for all values of ϕ and is numerically equal to $dl \sin \theta = dl \cos \phi$. Also from the figure, $r = a \sec \phi$, $l = a \tan \phi$, and $dl = a \sec^2 \phi \, d\phi$, so that the magnitude of **B** at P becomes

$$B = \int_{-\alpha}^{\beta} \frac{\mu_0 I \cos \phi \, d\phi}{4\pi a} = \frac{\mu_0 I}{4\pi a} (\sin \beta + \sin \alpha), \qquad (8\text{–}4)$$

where **B** is a vector directed out of the paper. For the special case of an infinite wire, $\sin \beta = \sin \alpha = 1$ and $B = \mu_0 I / 2\pi a$. Beginning with Eq. (8–4), we can readily verify that the magnitude of **B** at point P in the rectangle is given by

$$B = \frac{\mu_0 I}{4\pi} \sum_{n=1}^{4} \frac{1}{a_n} (\sin \beta_n + \sin \alpha_n),$$

where the a_n's represent the perpendicular distances from P to the respec-

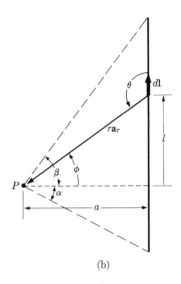

(a)   (b)

Fig. 8-2. (a) Illustration showing angles and lengths needed to calculate **B** at P within a current-carrying rectangular wire loop. (b) Diagram for calculating **B** at P due to the current I in a finite segment of a straight wire.

tive sides and the α_n's and β_n's are the angles indicated in Fig. 8-2(a). For the special case of a point in the center of a square with sides $2a$ in length, this becomes

$$B = \frac{\mu_0 \sqrt{2}\, I}{\pi a}.$$

Axial field of a solenoid. Fairly strong fields may be produced by winding wires in the form of a solenoid, so that the fields due to successive turns are additive. A common type of solenoid, shown in Fig. 8-3, consists of fine insulated wire wound in a tight spiral of one layer. By making the axis of the solenoid coincide with the z-axis and by placing its lower circle an unspecified distance Z above the xy-plane, the calculation of the field at the origin provides an expression for the field at a general point on the axis.

If the winding, starting at the point $(a, 0, Z)$ in rectangular coordinates, proceeds in the direction of increasing ϕ which is also the direction of the current I, the element of length of the wire for the Biot-Savart relation can be expressed in spherical coordinates as $d\mathbf{l} = \mathbf{a}_\phi a\, d\phi$. In these spherical coordinates $\mathbf{a}_r$ points away from the origin, while in the Biot-Savart law it points away from the element. Therefore the equation must be written as

$$d\mathbf{B} = -\mu_0 I\, \frac{d\mathbf{l} \times \mathbf{a}_r}{4\pi r^2} = \mathbf{a}_r \times \mathbf{a}_\phi\, \frac{\mu_0 I a}{4\pi r^2}\, d\phi = -\mathbf{a}_\theta\, \frac{\mu_0 a\, d\phi}{4\pi r^2}. \quad (8\text{-}5)$$

FIG. 8–3. Single-layer cylindrical solenoid. The magnetic field at a general point on the axis is calculated from the Biot-Savart law, by integrating along the wire winding.

The integration must progress along the full length of the wire winding from $\phi = 0$ to $\phi = 2\pi N$, where N is the total number of turns in the length L. If $n = N/L$, the diagram shows that

$$z = Z + \frac{\phi}{2\pi n} = a \operatorname{ctn} \theta,$$

which can be differentiated to give

$$d\phi = 2\pi na \csc^2 \theta \, d\theta.$$

Since $r = a \csc \theta$, Eq. (8–5) becomes

$$d\mathbf{B} = \mathbf{a}_\theta \frac{\mu_0 nI \, d\theta}{2} \tag{8–6}$$

or

$$d\mathbf{B} = (\mathbf{a}_r \cos \theta - \mathbf{a}_z \sin \theta) \frac{\mu_0 nI \, d\theta}{2}.$$

Elements of wire on the two ends of any diameter that is perpendicular through the axis produce radial components of field that cancel each other, although their axial components are all directed upward parallel to the z-axis. Thus each complete turn of wire produces no net radial component. This can be demonstrated by writing $\mathbf{a}_r = \mathbf{i} \cos \phi + \mathbf{j} \sin \phi$ in Eq. (8–5) and integrating. Ignoring the radial components, the field

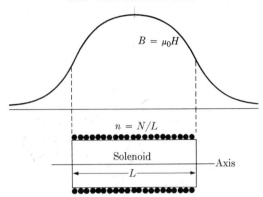

Fig. 8–4. Magnetic fields along the axis of a short solenoid.

at the origin is then given by

$$\mathbf{B} = -\mathbf{a}_z \frac{\mu_0 n I}{2} \int_\alpha^\beta \sin\theta \, d\theta = \mathbf{a}_z \frac{\mu_0 n I}{2} (\cos\beta - \cos\alpha). \qquad (8\text{–}7)$$

The $\mathbf{B}$ field along the axis of a solenoid is shown in Fig. 8–4. The expression for this field has the same mathematical form as the $\mathbf{B}$ field along the axis of the uniformly magnetized cylindrical rod described in Section 9–4, provided the $\mu_0 n I$ is replaced by $\mathfrak{M}$. The field on the axis near the middle of a long solenoid is $B = \mu_0 n I$ because $\alpha = \pi$ and $\beta = 0$. Later in this chapter it is shown that $B = \mu_0 n I$ is the magnitude of the field everywhere inside an infinitely long solenoid.

Maxwell's second relation. The relation $\boldsymbol{\nabla} \cdot \mathbf{B} = 0$ was introduced in Section 7–4 as having been proved experimentally. It is easily shown to be a necessary consequence of the Biot-Savart law when all magnetic fields, including those produced by magnetic polarizations, are presumed to be the result of the motions of elementary charges in free space. Then, from Eq. (8–3), the field at point P in Fig. 8–5 due to steady currents in the volume τ is

$$\mathbf{B} = \mu_0 \int_\tau \frac{\mathbf{J} \times \mathbf{a}_r \, d\tau}{4\pi r^2}.$$

In performing this integration, the coordinates X, Y, and Z are varied to include all of the volume τ, but the position of P remains fixed, with x, y, and z constant. The integration, however, provides an expression for $\mathbf{B}$ at P in terms of x, y, and z, which can be differentiated with respect to these coordinates. Thus, in calculating $\boldsymbol{\nabla} \cdot \mathbf{B}$ the coordinates x, y, and z are treated as the variables. The divergence can be written as

$$\boldsymbol{\nabla} \cdot \mathbf{B} = \boldsymbol{\nabla} \cdot \int_\tau \frac{\mu_0 \mathbf{J} \times \mathbf{a}_r \, d\tau}{4\pi r^2} = \frac{\mu_0}{4\pi} \int_\tau \boldsymbol{\nabla} \cdot \left(\frac{\mathbf{J} \times \mathbf{a}_r}{r^2} \right) d\tau,$$

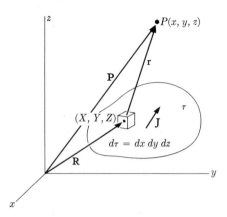

FIG. 8–5. Diagram for using the Biot-Savart law to calculate the **B** field at P due to current densities **J** distributed throughout τ.

where the divergence of the integrand is to be evaluated with **J**, X, Y, and Z held constant, whereas the integration over τ is performed with x, y, and z held constant. Taking the divergence of the integrand, we find

$$\nabla \cdot \left(\frac{\mathbf{J} \times \mathbf{a}_r}{r^2} \right) = \frac{\mathbf{a}_r}{r^2} \cdot \nabla \times \mathbf{J} - \mathbf{J} \cdot \nabla \times \left(\frac{\mathbf{a}_r}{r^2} \right),$$

and since **J** is constant, $\nabla \times \mathbf{J} = 0$. The term $\nabla \times (\mathbf{a}_r/r^2)$ may be evaluated by using

$$\frac{\mathbf{a}_r}{r^2} = \mathbf{i}\left(\frac{x - X}{r^3} \right) + \mathbf{j}\left(\frac{y - Y}{r^3} \right) + \mathbf{k}\left(\frac{z - Z}{r^3} \right),$$

where $r^2 = (x - X)^2 + (y - Y)^2 + (z - Z)^2$. The x-component of $\nabla \times (\mathbf{a}_r/r^2)$ is

$$- \frac{3(y - Y)(z - Z)}{r^5} + \frac{3(z - Z)(y - Y)}{r^5} = 0.$$

The y- and z-components can be obtained from the x-component by cyclic substitution. Since they are also zero, the integrand of the volume integral is zero:

$$\nabla \cdot \mathbf{B} = 0.$$

The Biot-Savart law of Eq. (8–3) that is used in this demonstration is valid only for currents in closed circuits. It will be shown in Section 8–3 that it can be made valid for fluctuating currents in circuits that are not closed by replacing **J** with $\mathbf{J}' = \mathbf{J} + \dot{\mathbf{D}}$.

The substitution of $\mathbf{J}'$ for **J** in the foregoing development does not alter the treatment or the conclusion. While Maxwell's second relation

$\nabla \cdot \mathbf{B} = 0$ has been developed here from the Biot-Savart law, it would be somewhat more logical to assume all of the Maxwell field relations, summarized in Section 8–4, and derive the more elementary relations from them. Maxwell's relations are accepted universally, because predictions based upon them always agree with the results of carefully performed experiments. The procedure of demonstrating Maxwell's relations from elementary concepts is adopted here only because the great majority of students find this procedure to be the more satisfactory.

8–2 Steady current form of Maxwell's fourth relation.   Maxwell's fourth relation contains a new magnetic field vector $\mathbf{H}$ that is very useful for dealing with fields due to magnetized materials. This field $\mathbf{H}$ is called the magnetizing field because the fields tending to orient the atomic current loops or magnetic dipoles can be described in terms of it. In a vacuum, the properties of $\mathbf{H}$ are identical to those of $\mathbf{B}$. In this section the current loops are presumed to be in a vacuum, where $\mathbf{H} = \mathbf{B}/\mu_0$ is an adequate definition for this field. Actually this relationship is quite accurate in air even at atmospheric pressure. As is explained in Section 9–1, when current coils are surrounded by air, this relationship becomes $\mathbf{H} = \mathbf{B}/\mu$, with $\mu \cong 1.000024\,\mu_0$.

The integral form of Maxwell's fourth relation for steady currents gives the value $\oint \mathbf{H} \cdot d\mathbf{l}$ integrated around any closed path in the neighborhood of a closed current loop. This can be obtained by using the Biot-Savart relation

$$d\mathbf{H} = \frac{I}{4\pi}\,\frac{d\mathbf{g} \times \mathbf{a}_r}{r^2} \tag{8–8}$$

to express the field at P in Fig. 8–6 due to the element of wire $d\mathbf{g}$, and then integrating the expression around the current loop. (The element of wire is designated $d\mathbf{g}$ to avoid confusion with the element of length $d\mathbf{l}$ in the line integral for $\mathbf{H}$.)

FIG. 8–6. Current I in a closed loop of wire produces the magnetic field $\mathbf{H}$ at the general point P. The value of $\oint \mathbf{H} \cdot d\mathbf{l}$ around the closed path indicated by arrows can be obtained from a general expression for $\mathbf{H}$.

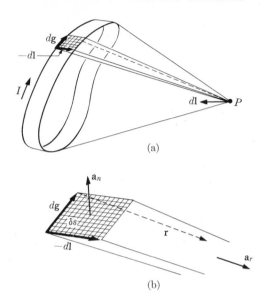

(a)

(b)

Fig. 8–7. Method for evaluating $\oint \mathbf{H} \cdot d\mathbf{l}$ about a current loop. Greater clarity is achieved by displacing the loop by $-d\mathbf{l}$ rather than displacing P by $d\mathbf{l}$.

While the direct integration of $d\mathbf{H}$ around the loop can in principle be accomplished, it is more convenient mathematically to integrate $d\mathbf{H} \cdot d\mathbf{l}$ around this loop, with $d\mathbf{l}$ constant. Integration around the current loop therefore yields

$$\oint d\mathbf{H} \cdot d\mathbf{l} = d\mathbf{l} \cdot \oint d\mathbf{H} = d\mathbf{l} \cdot \mathbf{H}. \tag{8–9}$$

In the diagram of Fig. 8–7(a), every point on the current loop has been displaced a distance $-d\mathbf{l}$ instead of moving P a distance $d\mathbf{l}$. This is done because only relative displacements are important, and because displacement of the loop rather than the point simplifies the analysis. The displacement of the loop produces the ribbonlike surface shown in Fig. 8–7(a) which subtends at P a small solid angle designated by $d\omega$. The crosshatched portion of the ribbon subtends a smaller solid angle $\delta\omega$, and from the magnified drawing of this crosshatched surface in Fig. 8–7(b) its area δs can be seen to be given by

$$-d\mathbf{l} \times d\mathbf{g} = \delta s \mathbf{a}_n,$$

where $\mathbf{a}_n$ is a unit vector directed outward and normal to the surface. From the definition of solid angles,

$$\delta\omega = \frac{-\delta s \mathbf{a}_n \cdot \mathbf{a}_r}{r^2} = \frac{d\mathbf{l} \times d\mathbf{g} \cdot \mathbf{a}_r}{r^2} = \frac{d\mathbf{g} \times \mathbf{a}_r \cdot d\mathbf{l}}{r^2}.$$

Combining this with Eq. (8–8), we find that

$$d\mathbf{H} \cdot d\mathbf{l} = \frac{I}{4\pi} \frac{d\mathbf{g} \times \mathbf{a}_r \cdot d\mathbf{l}}{r^2} = \frac{I}{4\pi} \delta\omega.$$

Both sides of this equation are to be integrated over the ribbonlike surface. The integral of the left side is given in Eq. (8–9), while the integral of $\delta\omega$ merely sums the solid angles subtended by all of the area elements like δs. Therefore the integration yields

$$\mathbf{H} \cdot d\mathbf{l} = \frac{I}{4\pi} d\omega. \tag{8–10}$$

Since ω depends upon the location of P, it is a function of the coordinates of P. With the gradient of ω being defined by $\nabla\omega \cdot d\mathbf{l} = d\omega$, Eq. (8–10) may be written as

$$\mathbf{H} \cdot d\mathbf{l} = \frac{I}{4\pi} \nabla\omega \cdot d\mathbf{l},$$

which makes it possible to express $\mathbf{H}$ as

$$\mathbf{H} = \frac{I}{4\pi} \nabla\omega = -\nabla\left(\frac{-I\omega}{4\pi}\right).$$

From this result it appears that the $\mathbf{H}$ due to a current loop can be expressed as the negative gradient of a scalar magnetic potential, given by

$$\Omega = \frac{-I\omega}{4\pi}. \tag{8–11}$$

The potential Ω, however, is single-valued only where $\oint \mathbf{H} \cdot d\mathbf{l} = 0$, which is true only so long as the path of integration does not pass through the current loop.

Conservative field limitation. Integration of $\mathbf{H} \cdot d\mathbf{l}$ around the path represented by the string of arrows in Fig. 8–8 can be readily accomplished by using Eq. (8–10), and the result of integrating $d\omega$ about this path is graphically shown in the figure. The solid angle ω subtended by point P at any location in space is equal to the heavily shaded area on the unit sphere whose center is at P. As the point is moved counterclockwise along the path shown in this figure the shaded area increases from $\omega = 0$ to $\omega = 4\pi$. Since the integration of $d\omega$ around such a path gives 4π, Eq. (8–10) gives

$$\oint \mathbf{H} \cdot d\mathbf{l} = I. \tag{8–12}$$

Thus the $\mathbf{H}$ magnetic field is not conservative in regions where there are currents. However, a region in which $\mathbf{H}$ is always conservative can be mapped out by merely excluding a part of space occupied by any

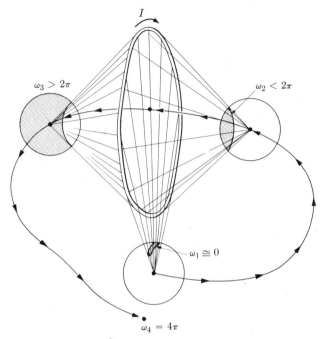

FIG. 8–8. The line integral $\int d\omega$ along the path marked by arrows gives 4π for each time this path threads through the current loop.

sheet having the current loop as its periphery. By preventing paths of integration from looping currents, it can be assured that $\oint \mathbf{H} \cdot d\mathbf{l} = 0$. Equation (8–12) can be further generalized to include the cases where more than one current circuit is looped. For the case shown in Fig. 8–9,

$$\oint \mathbf{H} \cdot d\mathbf{l} = I_1 + I_2$$

and, in general,

$$\oint \mathbf{H} \cdot d\mathbf{l} = \sum_i I_i,$$

where the I_i's represent all the currents looped. The obvious extension from discrete currents to current densities is

$$\oint \mathbf{H} \cdot d\mathbf{l} = \int_s \mathbf{J} \cdot d\mathbf{s}, \tag{8–13}$$

which is the integral form of Maxwell's fourth relation for steady currents, where $\mathbf{J} \cdot d\mathbf{s}$ must be integrated over a surface bounded by the path of integration for $\oint \mathbf{H} \cdot d\mathbf{l}$. The left side of Eq. (8–13) may be transformed into an area integration by Stokes' theorem, Eq. (3–17), with the result

$$\oint \mathbf{H} \cdot d\mathbf{l} = \int_s \nabla \times \mathbf{H} \cdot d\mathbf{s} = \int_s \mathbf{J} \cdot d\mathbf{s}.$$

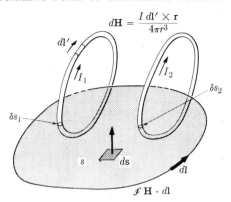

$$dH = \frac{I\,dl' \times r}{4\pi r^3}$$

Fig. 8–9. Integral of $\mathbf{H} \cdot d\mathbf{l}$ about the path indicated yields a value $I_1 + I_2$.

Since the last two integrals are always taken over the same general surface, the integrands must be equal, so that

$$\nabla \times \mathbf{H} = \mathbf{J}. \tag{8–14}$$

This is the differential form of Maxwell's fourth relation for steady currents.

Equations (8–12) and (8–13) are useful for calculating $\mathbf{H}$ in many situations where the necessary symmetry exists. For example, the field near a long straight wire carrying a current I can be calculated by integrating along the circumference of a circle, perpendicular to the wire and centered upon it. On such a circle $\mathbf{H}$ must be tangent to the circle and constant in magnitude. Equation (8–12) gives $H2\pi r = I$ or $H = I/2\pi r$, if r is the radius of the circle.

Symmetrical toroid. One of the simplest and most useful examples is that of calculating H in a symmetrical toroid such as a hoop made of nonmagnetic material formed into a shape similar to that of a bicycle tire and uniformly wound with insulated wire in a tight spiral, as shown in

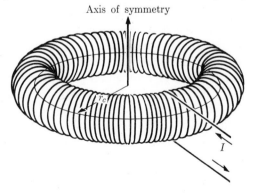

Fig. 8–10. Nonmagnetic toroid surrounded by a wire-wound solenoid.

Fig. 8–10. Since this figure is symmetrical about the central axis corresponding to the axle of the bicycle wheel, any circle drawn about this central axis defines a path on which the field must be constant and directed tangent to the circle unless the circle passes through or too close to the individual turns of wire. On circles passing close to the wires, H fluctuates from turn to turn, but these fluctuations can be reduced by using finer wires more closely wound. All other circles that can be drawn about the central axis either are wholly within the solenoid and loop all of the N turns, or are wholly outside of the solenoid and loop no turns. If the current in the wire is I, then

$$\oint \mathbf{H} \cdot d\mathbf{l} = H2\pi r = NI$$

or

$$H = \frac{NI}{2\pi r}$$

for all points inside the solenoid, where r is the radial distance of the point from the axis of symmetry. Circles outside the solenoid do not loop any turns, so that $H = 0$ everywhere outside the solenoid and all the magnetic field is confined within the solenoid.

If the solenoid is shaped like a fat doughnut with a small hole, the magnitude of $H = NI/2\pi r$ varies considerably within the doughnut. However, when the internal radius of the solenoidal winding is small compared with the radius r_c of its centerline, the field is practically constant and is given by $H \cong NI/2\pi r_c$. The length of this latter solenoid is $L = 2\pi r_c$, and hence

$$H = \frac{NI}{L} = nI,$$

which was given as the expression for the field on the axis of an infinitely long solenoid. Here the expression is shown to be true for all points inside the winding, and is not limited to the axis. Since an infinitely long solenoid cannot be constructed, this constitutes one practical approximation.

Magnetic field of a small loop of current. The magnetic field at a point P that is some distance from a current-carrying loop of wire varies with the coordinates of the point in the same manner as does the field of an ideal electric dipole. When the loop of wire is in a plane, the axis of the effective magnetic dipole is a line perpendicular to the plane through the center of the area A enclosed by the loop. This axial line can be taken as the axis of spherical coordinates with the origin at the center of the area, and the coordinates of P then become r, θ, and ϕ. For values of r large compared with the linear dimensions of the area, i.e., for $r \gg \sqrt{A}$, the field would be independent of ϕ. From Eq. (8–11), the potential due to the loop is then $\Omega = -I\omega/4\pi$, where I is the current in the loop and ω

is the solid angle subtended by A from the point P. When r is large,

$$\omega = -\frac{A \cos \theta}{r^2}$$

and hence

$$\Omega = \frac{IA \cos \theta}{4\pi r^2} \quad \text{and} \quad \mathbf{H} = -\boldsymbol{\nabla}\Omega.$$

These have the same mathematical form as $V = p \cos \theta / \epsilon_0 4\pi r^2$ and $\mathbf{E} = -\boldsymbol{\nabla}V$ for the ideal electric dipole.

8-3 Maxwell's fourth relation. The incompleteness of the Biot-Savart law in its usual form for dealing with fluctuating currents is mentioned in Section 8-1. In the previous section this law is shown to lead directly to Eq. (8-14):

$$\boldsymbol{\nabla} \times \mathbf{H} = \mathbf{J}.$$

That this law is not complete can be seen from the fact that the divergence of the curl of a vector is zero; that is,

$$\boldsymbol{\nabla} \cdot \boldsymbol{\nabla} \times \mathbf{H} = 0$$

but $\boldsymbol{\nabla} \cdot \mathbf{J}$ does not vanish in general, because the conservation of charge relation gives

$$\boldsymbol{\nabla} \cdot \mathbf{J} = -\frac{\partial \rho}{\partial t}.$$

Therefore Eq. (8-14) can be correct only where charge densities do not vary with time.

Maxwell first pointed out this discrepancy and proposed a modification based upon Eq. (5-4). Differentiation of this equation with respect to time yields

$$\frac{\partial}{\partial t} \boldsymbol{\nabla} \cdot \mathbf{D} = \boldsymbol{\nabla} \cdot \dot{\mathbf{D}} = \frac{\partial \rho}{\partial t}$$

and substitution of this into the charge conservation equation gives

$$\boldsymbol{\nabla} \cdot \mathbf{J} + \boldsymbol{\nabla} \cdot \dot{\mathbf{D}} = 0.$$

Equation (8-14) may be made consistent mathematically by the addition of $\dot{\mathbf{D}}$ to the right side, since the divergences of both sides of the equation then become zero. The equation is written as

$$\boldsymbol{\nabla} \times \mathbf{H} = \mathbf{J} + \dot{\mathbf{D}}, \tag{8-15}$$

which is the general differential form of Maxwell's fourth relation. If both sides of the equation are integrated over a surface s and the left side is transformed into a line integral by Stokes' theorem, the general integral form of Maxwell's fourth relation is obtained as

$$\oint \mathbf{H} \cdot d\mathbf{l} = \int_s (\mathbf{J} + \dot{\mathbf{D}}) \cdot d\mathbf{s}. \qquad (8\text{--}16)$$

The displacement vector. Integration of Biot-Savart's equation over completely closed circuits in which there are steady currents gives the correct value for the magnetic field at every point in space. However, it does not give the correct magnetic fields due to fluctuating currents because, according to Eqs. (8–15) and (8–16), not only currents but also time variations in $\mathbf{D}$ produce magnetic fields. Since $\mathbf{J}$ and $\dot{\mathbf{D}}$ perform the same function in this equation and necessarily have the same units, Maxwell presumed that $\dot{\mathbf{D}}$ represented a type of current density. He named this current the "displacement current" and called $\mathbf{D}$ the *displacement vector.*

The nature of this displacement current can be partially visualized by considering what happens in a dielectric material between two capacitor plates. As the capacitor is charged, the electric field between the plates increases, thus increasing the polarization of the dielectric. The shift of positive charges one way and negative charges the other way is equivalent to an electric current, even though the polarization charges never break away from their localized positions within the dielectric. This current density, given by $\partial \mathbf{P}/\partial t = \dot{\mathbf{P}}$, is only part of the displacement current; the total displacement current is defined by

$$\dot{\mathbf{D}} = \epsilon_0 \dot{\mathbf{E}} + \dot{\mathbf{P}}.$$

Therefore, even in a vacuum where no polarization charges exist, there is a displacement current represented by $\epsilon_0 \dot{\mathbf{E}}$, and there is no satisfactory method for visualizing this portion of the displacement current. The best verification of the concept is furnished by the propagation of electromagnetic waves in space as discussed in Chapter 11. It was, in fact, the concept of the displacement vector which first led Maxwell to his prediction of the existence of these waves before they had been discovered experimentally. The fact that oscillating electric fields in a vacuum do produce magnetic fields has been well established.

8–4 Summary of Maxwell's field relations. Some very general relations, known as Maxwell's relations, have been obtained in the foregoing pages as extensions of empirically determined laws. These equations are collected here in their differential and integral forms and renumbered for easy reference:

$$\nabla \cdot \mathbf{D} = \rho, \qquad \int_s \mathbf{D} \cdot d\mathbf{s} = \int_\tau \rho \, d\tau, \qquad \text{(M-1)}$$

$$\nabla \cdot \mathbf{B} = 0, \qquad \int_s \mathbf{B} \cdot d\mathbf{s} = 0, \qquad \text{(M-2)}$$

$$\nabla \times \mathbf{E} = -\dot{\mathbf{B}}, \qquad \oint \mathbf{E} \cdot d\mathbf{l} = -\int_s \dot{\mathbf{B}} \cdot d\mathbf{s}, \qquad \text{(M-3)}$$

$$\nabla \times \mathbf{H} = \mathbf{J} + \dot{\mathbf{D}}, \qquad \oint \mathbf{H} \cdot d\mathbf{l} = \int_s (\mathbf{J} + \dot{\mathbf{D}}) \cdot d\mathbf{s}. \qquad \text{(M-4)}$$

Equation (M-1) is obtained directly from the inverse square law for the force one point charge exerts upon another. The vector $\mathbf{D}$ appears here instead of $\mathbf{E}$ because of the decision to separate the effects due to polarization charges from the effects due to "real" charges, with ρ designating the volume density of "real" charges. Since there are no "real" poles but materials do contain magnetic dipoles that can be aligned in much the same way that electric dipoles are aligned, Eq. (M-2) is similar to Eq. (M-1). The zero on the right in this relation proclaims that isolated magnetic poles do not exist. Equation (M-3) is obtained directly from Faraday's law of induction. The steady-current form of Eq. (M-4) is obtained from Biot-Savart's law, while the addition of the $\dot{\mathbf{D}}$ term is a modification necessitated by the mathematical requirement that $\nabla \cdot (\nabla \times \mathbf{H}) = 0$. These four relations are valid for space containing materials of all kinds, dielectric, conducting, or magnetic, where ρ is the density of the "real" or nonpolarization charges and $\mathbf{J}$ is that part of the total current density that is not responsible for magnetization within materials. This is discussed in detail in Section 9-2.

Maxwell's equations in their differential and integral forms combined with the force-on-a-charge equation constitute a very concise expression of electromagnetic theory. The law for the conservation of charge also is essential, although it need not be stated explicitly, since it can be obtained by combining (M-1) with (M-4). All problems in classical electricity and magnetism can be solved with these equations. This does not, however, destroy the usefulness of the older laws; in fact, one who knew only Maxwell's relations would find it desirable to use them to derive less general relations, such as Biot-Savart's law, for the solution of certain problems.

While the validity of Maxwell's relations for problems already solved by the older laws was readily established, the usefulness of this more general formulation lies in its ability to solve unsolved problems or to predict phenomena as yet unobserved. A crucial test of Maxwell's relations was their prediction of the existence of electromagnetic waves before they had been observed, and the beauty of their formulation cannot be appreciated fully without a study of these phenomena.

8–5 General scalar and vector potentials. The differential equations of Laplace and Poisson have proved to be very useful for solving problems concerning static and steady-state phenomena. However, the general forms for Maxwell's relations show that, in general, neither of these equations can be valid for time-dependent phenomena because neither $\nabla \times \mathbf{E}$ nor $\nabla \times \mathbf{H}$ equals zero. It is desirable, therefore, to investigate the possibility of developing differential equations that are valid in general. The fact that $\nabla \cdot \mathbf{B} = 0$ everywhere suggests that $\mathbf{B}$ can be expressed in terms of a vector potential function $\mathbf{A}$, such that

$$\mathbf{B} = \nabla \times \mathbf{A}, \tag{8-17}$$

since according to Eq. (3–23) the divergence of the curl of a vector is zero. Equation (M–2) then becomes

$$\nabla \cdot \mathbf{B} = \nabla \cdot (\nabla \times \mathbf{A}) = 0$$

and substitution of the time derivative of Eq. (8–17) into Eq. (M–3) yields

$$\nabla \times (\mathbf{E} + \dot{\mathbf{A}}) = 0.$$

This defines a new vector $\mathbf{E} + \dot{\mathbf{A}}$ whose curl is zero, so that it can be expressed as the gradient of a scalar potential:

$$\mathbf{E} + \dot{\mathbf{A}} = -\nabla V. \tag{8-18}$$

It should be noted that the definition of this new scalar potential is consistent with the earlier definition of the scalar potential in which $\mathbf{E} = -\nabla V$ for the steady-state condition in which $\dot{\mathbf{B}} = 0$.

The potential functions contained in Eqs. (8–17) and (8–18) will not be useful for electromagnetic problems unless they can be shown to satisfy the other two Maxwell relations. To check this, Eqs. (M–1) and (M–4) can be written as

$$\nabla \cdot \mathbf{E} = \frac{\rho}{\epsilon} \quad \text{and} \quad \nabla \times \mathbf{B} = \mu\mathbf{J} + \mu\epsilon\dot{\mathbf{E}}$$

respectively. For the relations in this section it is assumed that $\mathbf{D} = \epsilon\mathbf{E}$ and $\mathbf{B} = \mu\mathbf{H}$, where ϵ and μ are true constants. The expressions are then valid in free space or in materials with linear constants. The introduction of the new potentials into the first of these two equations gives

$$\nabla^2 V + \nabla \cdot \dot{\mathbf{A}} = -\frac{\rho}{\epsilon}$$

$$\nabla^2 \mathbf{A} - \mu\epsilon\ddot{\mathbf{A}} = -\mu\mathbf{J} + \nabla(\nabla \cdot \mathbf{A} + \mu\epsilon\dot{V}).$$

Lorentz recognized that these could be reduced to two symmetrical equations, in which V and $\mathbf{A}$ would be separated, by introducing the relation

$$\nabla \cdot \mathbf{A} + \mu\epsilon\dot{V} = 0, \qquad (8\text{-}19)$$

which is called the Lorentz condition. Such a relation is possible because $\mathbf{B} = \nabla \times \mathbf{A}$ does not define $\mathbf{A}$ uniquely. The resulting equations:

$$\nabla^2 V - \mu\epsilon\ddot{V} = -\frac{\rho}{\epsilon}, \qquad (8\text{-}20)$$

$$\nabla^2 \mathbf{A} - \mu\epsilon\ddot{\mathbf{A}} = -\mu\mathbf{J}, \qquad (8\text{-}21)$$

provide general differential equations for the potentials V and $\mathbf{A}$ respectively. While these appear to be independent equations, they must be related by the equation of charge conservation. Substitution of these equations into $\nabla \cdot \mathbf{J} + \partial\rho/\partial t = 0$ yields the wave equation

$$\nabla^2(\nabla \cdot \mathbf{A} + \mu\epsilon\dot{V}) - \mu\epsilon\frac{\partial^2}{\partial t^2}(\nabla \cdot \mathbf{A} + \mu\epsilon\dot{V}) = 0,$$

which obviously is satisfied by the Lorentz condition of Eq. (8–19).

Equation (8–21) can be written as three separate scalar equations, one for each of the three rectangular components of $\mathbf{A}$, each of which is identical in form to Eq. (8–20). Any general solution for Eq. (8–20) then automatically provides a general solution for Eq. (8–21).

8–6 Low-frequency solutions of the potential equations. The differential equation for scalar potential functions, Eq. (8–20), is identical with Poisson's equation whenever $\ddot{V} = 0$, which indicates that it merely gives a more general expression for the potential function that was first introduced for solving static problems. At low frequencies, in fact, the $\mu\epsilon\ddot{V}$ term in Eq. (8–20) and the $\mu\epsilon\ddot{\mathbf{A}}$ term in Eq. (8–21) are so small that they can be neglected. This might be expected from the fact that $\mu_0\epsilon_0 = 1/c^2 \cong 10^{-17} \sec^2/\mathrm{m}^2$, which suggests that $\ddot{V}$ and $\ddot{\mathbf{A}}$ must be quite large before these terms significantly affect the solution of any problem. Since such arguments are by no means conclusive, it is desirable to accept the statement here, with reservations that may be resolved when a particular problem is solved both with the general relations of Eqs. (8–20) and (8–21) and with these relations simplified by setting $\ddot{V} = 0$ and $\ddot{\mathbf{A}} = 0$.

In Section 11–6, the electric and magnetic fields of an oscillating electric dipole are calculated by means of the general differential equations, but the terms are separated in such a manner that those terms that would be obtained from the simplified relations can be identified. The amplitudes of the oscillating electric and magnetic fields of the dipole can be estimated from the g's and h's, respectively, given in that section: g_3 and h_2

give the amplitudes of the important terms obtained by ignoring the $\dot{V}$ and $\ddot{A}$ terms, and g_1, g_2, and h_1 give the amplitudes of the terms added by including the time-derivative terms in the differential equations. Since at low frequencies in any laboratory g_3 is much larger than g_2, which is much larger than g_1, a conservative estimate of the errors caused by the simplifications are obtained by calculating g_2/g_3 and h_1/h_2. When observations are to be made at 60 cycles/sec within 5 meters of the oscillating currents, the fractional errors do not exceed

$$\frac{g_2}{g_3} = \frac{h_1}{h_2} = \frac{2\pi f r}{v} = 6 \cdot 10^{-6}$$

or 6 parts per million. For the errors produced by neglecting $\ddot{V}$ and $\ddot{A}$ to exceed 1% in such a laboratory, the frequencies must exceed 10^5 cycles/sec. Since the amplitudes of the oscillating energies depend upon the squares of the field amplitudes, the errors in the energy amplitudes are much lower. They are approximately

$$\left(\frac{2\pi f r}{v}\right)^2.$$

For low frequencies, then, these two equations can be written as $\nabla^2 V = -\rho/\epsilon$ and $\nabla^2 \mathbf{A} = -\mu \mathbf{J}$, respectively.

The first of these is Poisson's equation, which is strictly valid for static densities of real charges in media where ϵ is a true constant. When the right side is written as $-\rho_t/\epsilon_0$, where $\rho_t = \rho + \rho_p$ is the density of all charges, including those due to polarizations, this equation is valid for all static problems. Such problems are treated in some detail in Chapters 4 and 5. A general solution for the potential at P in Fig. 8–5 is given by

$$V = \int_\tau \frac{\rho \, d\tau}{4\pi r},$$

provided all the real charges lie within τ and all space is filled with a medium whose dielectric constant is ϵ. If in this same figure the real current densities are all confined within τ and all space is filled with a medium where the permeability is μ, a general solution of $\nabla^2 \mathbf{A} = -\mu \mathbf{J}$ is

$$\mathbf{A} = \mathbf{i} \int_\tau \frac{\mu J_x \, d\tau}{4\pi r} + \mathbf{j} \int_\tau \frac{\mu J_y \, d\tau}{4\pi r} + \mathbf{k} \int_\tau \frac{\mu J_z \, d\tau}{4\pi r}$$

or

$$\mathbf{A} = \int_\tau \frac{\mu \mathbf{J} \, d\tau}{4\pi r}. \tag{8–22}$$

For most of the applications the medium will be air, where $\epsilon \cong \epsilon_0$ and $\mu \cong \mu_0$.

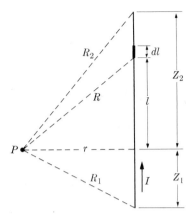

FIG. 8–11. Section of a straight wire carrying a current I parallel to the z-axis, with $Z_1 \gg r$ and $Z_2 \gg r$. The **B** field at P can be obtained from the vector potential.

A vector potential calculation. The use of the vector potential **A** for calculating magnetic fields can be demonstrated with the section of straight wire shown in Fig. 8–11. From Eq. (8–22),

$$\mathbf{A} = \int_{l=-Z_1}^{l=Z_2} \frac{\mu_0 \mathbf{k} I \, dl}{4\pi R},$$

and since r is constant for this integration,

$$\mathbf{A} = \frac{\mu_0 \mathbf{k} I}{4\pi} \int_{l=-Z_1}^{l=Z_2} \frac{dl}{\sqrt{r^2 + l^2}} = \frac{\mu_0 \mathbf{k} I}{4\pi} \{\ln (Z_2 + R_2) - \ln (-Z_1 + R_1)\}.$$

Since

$$(-Z_1 + R_1) = \frac{R_1^2 - Z_1^2}{R_1 + Z_1} = \frac{r^2}{R_1 + Z_1},$$

the vector potential of the current I in this straight wire is

$$\mathbf{A} = \mathbf{k} \frac{\mu_0 I}{4\pi} \{\ln (Z_1 + R_1)(Z_2 + R_2) - 2 \ln r\},$$

which is a vector function parallel to the z-axis. If the wire is very long, so that $Z_1 \gg r$ and $Z_2 \gg r$, then $(Z_1 + R_1)(Z_2 + R_2) \cong 4Z_1 Z_2$ is constant and the **B** field is easily obtained in cylindrical coordinates from the expression

$$\mathbf{B} = \nabla \times \mathbf{A} = -\mathbf{a}_\phi \frac{\partial A_z}{\partial r} = \mathbf{a}_\phi \frac{\mu_0 I}{2\pi r}.$$

This field is the same as that obtained for an infinitely long wire by direct integration of the Biot-Savart law in Section 9–1. In specific problems the use of the vector potential may or may not simplify the calculations, but in general discussions it frequently leads to important simplifications.

8–7 Mutual and self-inductance. When there is a current I_1 in the primary circuit No. 1 of Fig. 8–12, some of the magnetic flux lines that are produced thread through the secondary circuit No. 2. Time changes in I_1 then produce induced voltages in this secondary circuit, the magnitude of which can be written as

$$\mathcal{E}_2 = -\frac{d\phi}{dt} = -M_{12}\frac{dI_1}{dt}, \qquad (8\text{–}23)$$

where ϕ is the magnetic flux threading through the imaginary surface s_2 shown in the diagram and M_{12} is a constant that depends upon the shapes and the relative locations of the two circuits. If the roles of the two circuits are reversed, changes in the current in No. 2 produce induced voltages in No. 1, given by

$$\mathcal{E}_1 = -M_{21}\frac{dI_2}{dt}.$$

The mks unit for mutual inductance is the henry. The mutual inductance between two circuits is one henry when an emf of one volt is induced in one circuit by current changing in the other circuit at the rate of one ampere per second.

The two constants M_{12} and M_{21} are not equal in general, as, for example, when ferromagnetic materials are nearby. However, in the important special cases where μ is constant, the relation

$$M_{12} = M_{21}$$

can be shown to be valid.

FIG. 8–12. Changes in the primary current I_1 produce emf's $\mathcal{E}_2$ in the secondary circuit, given by $\mathcal{E}_2 = M\,dI_1/dt$, where M is the mutual inductance.

In the case where changes in the current I_1 in Fig. 8–12 induce voltages in the second circuit, the magnetic flux through this circuit is given by

$$\phi = \int_{s_2} \mathbf{B} \cdot d\mathbf{s}_2 = \int_{s_2} \nabla \times \mathbf{A} \cdot d\mathbf{s}_2 = \oint_2 \mathbf{A} \cdot d\mathbf{l}_2 \qquad (8\text{–}24)$$

where Stokes' theorem is used to obtain the line integral. According to Eq. (8–22), the vector potential at the element $d\mathbf{l}_2$ is given by

$$\mathbf{A} = \frac{\mu I_1}{4\pi} \oint_1 \frac{d\mathbf{l}_1}{r}, \qquad (8\text{–}25)$$

which must be integrated over the first circuit for each line element $d\mathbf{l}_2$ of the second. Substituting (8–25) in (8–24) gives

$$\phi = \frac{\mu I_1}{4\pi} \oint_2 \oint_1 \frac{d\mathbf{l}_1 \cdot d\mathbf{l}_2}{r},$$

from which

$$\mathcal{E}_2 = -\frac{d\phi}{dt} = -\frac{dI_1}{dt} \frac{\mu}{4\pi} \oint_2 \oint_1 \frac{d\mathbf{l}_1 \cdot d\mathbf{l}_2}{r}$$

and

$$M_{12} = \frac{\mu}{4\pi} \oint_2 \oint_1 \frac{d\mathbf{l}_1 \cdot d\mathbf{l}_2}{r}. \qquad (8\text{–}26)$$

Interchanging the roles of the two circuits merely interchanges the subscripts, which does not alter the value of the double integral. Therefore

$$M_{21} = M_{12} = M$$

and the subscripts can be omitted when μ is constant throughout space.

Circular circuits on the same axis. The mutual inductance of the two circular circuits on the same axis shown in Fig. 8–13 can be calculated by means of Eq. (8–26). The double integral can be obtained by first

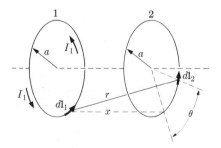

Fig. 8–13. Two circular circuits which are coaxial and have equal radii. When $x \gg a$, the mutual inductance is $M \cong \mu \pi a^4 / 2x^3$.

integrating dl_2 around the second circuit while dl_1 remains fixed, and then integrating dl_1 around the first circuit. Now $dl_1 \cdot dl_2 = dl_1 \, dl_2 \cos \theta$, $r^2 = x^2 + (2a \sin \theta/2)^2$, and $dl_2 = a \, d\theta$. The double integral can then be written as

$$\oint_1 dl_1 \int_0^{2\pi} \frac{a \cos \theta \, d\theta}{r} ,$$

which will give a general relation for any value of the constants. Since the integration is not simple for small values of x, only the case where x is considerably larger than $2a$ will be evaluated. With this simplification, the θ integral becomes

$$\int_0^{2\pi} \frac{a}{x} \left(1 - \frac{2a^2}{x^2} \sin^2 \frac{\theta}{2} + \cdots \right) \cos \theta \, d\theta,$$

which can be evaluated easily in terms of the variable $\theta/2$. The value of this integral is $\pi a^3/x^3$, and the mutual inductance is then given by

$$M = \frac{\mu}{4\pi} \left(\frac{\pi a^3}{x^3} \right) \oint_1 dl_1 = \frac{\mu \pi a^4}{2x^3} ,$$

since $\oint_1 dl_1 = 2\pi a$. This relation for M is much more simply obtained directly from Eq. (8–23) by assuming that when x is large the magnetic field over the second circuit has the uniform value $B = \mu a^2 I_1/2x^3$ as calculated for its center. Therefore

$$-\frac{d\phi}{dt} = -(\pi a^2) \frac{\mu a^2}{2x^3} \frac{dI_1}{dt} = -M_{12} \frac{dI_1}{dt}$$

or

$$M_{12} = \frac{\pi \mu a^4}{2x^3} .$$

Equation (8–26) is useful for making accurate calculations of mutual inductances and for demonstrating the equivalence of the coefficients M_{12} and M_{21}. However, the actual integrations with this equation are usually so complex that simpler methods based directly upon Eq. (8–23) should be used whenever possible.

Self-inductance. When the current I_1 changes in circuit No. 1 of Fig. 8–12, the magnetic flux changes through this circuit as well as through the second circuit. The voltages induced in the first circuit then are said to be self-induced, and the coefficient L_1 in the relation

$$\varepsilon_1 = -L_1 \frac{dI_1}{dt} \tag{8–27}$$

is called its coefficient of self-inductance or merely its self-inductance.

A circuit is said to have one henry of self-inductance when an emf of one volt is induced in this circuit by its current changing at the rate of one amp/sec.

It might be expected that L_1 could be calculated from Eq. (8–26) by integrating both $d\mathbf{l}_1$ and $d\mathbf{l}_2$ over the first circuit. This procedure is valid in principle only when the wire is infinitesimally fine and hence the integral becomes infinite. Actually the self-inductance of any circuit like the ones in Figs. 8–12 and 8–13 is strongly dependent upon the diameter of the wire and would be infinite if the wire could be made infinitesimal.

It is instructive to calculate the self-inductance per meter of length of a long and straight coaxial cable, consisting of a solid inner cylinder of copper of radius a and a thin and hollow copper cylinder of radius $b > a$. From Eq. (8–13), the magnetic field between cylinders is $B = \mu_0 I_1 / 2\pi r$, and the total flux per meter of length is

$$\phi = \int_a^b B_0 \, dr = \frac{\mu_0 I_1}{2\pi} \ln \frac{b}{a},$$

from which

$$L_1 = \frac{\mu_0}{2\pi} \ln \frac{b}{a}.$$

The self-inductance is strongly dependent upon this radius of the inner cylinder, approaching infinity as a approaches zero. In this calculation the magnetic fields within the cylinders have been ignored. This is valid especially for low frequencies and cylinders of small cross section. The internal fields do affect the distributions of current densities in the cylinders, but do not affect the over-all inductance. While the self-inductance of a coil with known geometry can be calculated with relations similar to Eq. (8–26), considerable care is required. If circuits are immersed in a medium having a constant μ, the mutual inductances and the self-inductances depend only upon the geometries of the circuits and this constant μ. When high accuracy is not required, the M's and the L's are more easily calculated from Eqs. (8–23) and (8–27) than from equations like (8–26).

Energy stored in electromagnetic circuits. Work must be done in setting up currents in the circuits shown in Fig. 8–12, in addition to the $\int I^2 R \, dt$ energy loss that is dissipated in heat. This additional work is stored as energy in the field, and whenever μ is constant it may be recovered as the currents decrease to zero. To calculate this magnetic field energy it is desirable to assume that the circuit resistances are negligible. The current in the first circuit then can be increased from zero to I_1 and that in the second circuit can be increased from zero to I_2 by applying the emf's $\mathcal{E}_1'$ and $\mathcal{E}_2'$ to the two circuits respectively, where these emf's are equal and opposite to the emf's induced by the changing flux. The power delivered to circuit No. 1 is $p_1 = \mathcal{E}_1' i_1$ and the energy delivered to it in the time dt is

$$du_1 = p_1\, dt = \mathcal{E}_1' i_1\, dt$$

or

$$du_1 = i_1 \left(L_1 \frac{di_1}{dt} + M \frac{di_2}{dt} \right) dt.$$

Similarly, the energy delivered to circuit No. 2 is

$$du_2 = L_1 i_2\, di_2 + M i_2\, di_1.$$

The total energy delivered to both circuits is the integral of the sum of these two differential energies.

Since $d(i_1 i_2) = i_1\, di_2 + i_2\, di_1$ and $M(i_1\, di_2 + i_2\, di_1) = M\, d(i_1 i_2)$,

$$U = \int (du_1 + du_2) = L_1 \int_0^{I_1} i_1\, di_1 + L_2 \int_0^{I_2} i_2\, di_2 + M \int_0^{I_1 I_2} d(i_1 i_2)$$

and

$$U = \tfrac{1}{2} L_1 I_1^2 + \tfrac{1}{2} L_2 I_2^2 + M I_1 I_2.$$

When the second circuit current I_2 is zero or when the first circuit is alone, this reduces to

$$U = \tfrac{1}{2} L_1 I_1^2$$

and the energy in the field due to a single circuit is $\tfrac{1}{2} L I^2$. When many closed circuits are involved, the energy expression can be expanded into the form

$$U = \tfrac{1}{2} \{ L_1 I_1^2 + M_{12} I_1 I_2 + M_{13} I_1 I_3 + \cdots$$
$$+ M_{12} I_2 I_1 + L_2 I_2^2 + M_{23} I_2 I_3 + \cdots$$
$$+ M_{13} I_3 I_1 + M_{23} I_3 I_2 + L_3 I_3^2 + \cdots \}. \qquad (8\text{--}28)$$

Forces and torques between current circuits. The foregoing energy relation is useful for calculating forces and torques between current circuits. For example, when there are two rigidly shaped circuits in which constant currents are maintained, only the mutual inductance M_{12} in this equation is changed by relative motions between the circuits. An infinitesimal displacement $\delta\mathbf{l}$ of either circuit with respect to the other results in a change of energy which is given by

$$\delta U = I_1 I_2 \nabla M_{12} \cdot \delta\mathbf{l} = I_1 I_2\, \delta M_{12},$$

and this is positive when I_1 and I_2 have the same sign and δM is positive. However, in those cases where I_1 and I_2 do have the same sign, the force acting on either circuit tends to pull it in the direction in which M increases most rapidly. For example, the circular circuits of Fig. 8–13 attract each other whenever their currents are in the same direction, and their mutual inductance obviously would increase if they were to move closer together. When such internal forces move either circuit, external work is performed and at the same time the energy of the system increases. This apparent anomaly can mean only that some source or sources of energy have been ignored. In this case it is the energy that must be supplied to maintain the currents constant.

The flux through the second circuit is

$$\phi_2 = L_2 I_2 + M_{12} I_1$$

and that through the first circuit is

$$\phi_1 = L_1 I_1 + M_{12} I_2.$$

If the second circuit is allowed to move an infinitesimal distance $\delta \mathbf{l}$ closer to the first, it will do an amount of external work given by

$$\delta W = \mathbf{F} \cdot \delta \mathbf{l},$$

where $\mathbf{F}$ is the force on the second circuit due to the first. At the same time the flux changes through both circuits produce induced emf's that must be counteracted if the currents are to remain constant. The emf's required are $\mathcal{E}_1' = d\phi_1/dt$ and $\mathcal{E}_2' = d\phi_2/dt$, and the work done by these emf's is

$$\delta W = (\mathcal{E}_1' I_1 + \mathcal{E}_2' I_2)\, \delta t = 2 I_1 I_2\, \delta M_{12},$$

which must equal the sum of the mechanical work done and the increase in energy. Hence

$$2 I_1 I_2\, \delta M_{12} = \mathbf{F} \cdot \delta \mathbf{l} + I_1 I_2\, \delta M_{12}$$

or

$$\mathbf{F} \cdot \delta \mathbf{l} = I_1 I_2\, \delta M_{12},$$

and the force can be written as

$$\mathbf{F} = \boldsymbol{\nabla} U = I_1 I_2 \boldsymbol{\nabla} M_{12}. \tag{8–29}$$

Similar arguments show that the torque on either of the two rigid circuits, produced by the presence of the other circuit, is

$$\text{Torque} = \frac{\partial U}{\partial \theta} = I_1 I_2 \frac{\partial M_{12}}{\partial \theta}, \tag{8–30}$$

where the partial derivative has the positive sign because, again, energy must be supplied to keep the currents constant.

8–8 The standard ampere. In Chapter 1 it was pointed out that the "practical" units, ampere, volt, ohm, etc., were defined by the arbitrary relations 1 ampere $= 0.1$ abampere, 1 volt $= 10^8$ abvolts, 1 ohm $= 10^9$ abohms, etc., where the prefix ab designates units from the cgs-emu system, which had been called the "absolute system." The cgs-emu system was originally developed from Coulomb's law for forces between isolated magnetic poles. This artificial approach was abandoned when it was realized that the current unit could be established directly from mechanical units by using the forces between current-carrying circuits of known geometry. When the mks system was adopted to include the "practical" units, it was realized that the ampere itself could be established directly from mechanical units. The mks system is now developed from the *standard* ampere, which is defined in terms of forces between current-carrying circuits, and this amounts to defining μ_0 as exactly $4\pi10^{-7}$

Fig. 8–14. Photograph of the ampere balance used in the 1957 establishment of the ampere. (Courtesy of the U.S. Bureau of Standards.)

henry/m. It is possible to construct and position solenoids so accurately that their self-inductances and their mutual inductances can be calculated with no larger error than one part per million. According to Eqs. (8–29) and (8–30), the magnitude of a steady current I can be determined by passing this current through two such solenoids connected in series and measuring either the force or torque on one while the other is held stationary.

Ampere balance. The balance shown in Fig. 8–14 was used by the U. S. Bureau of Standards in 1957 to recheck the value of the standard ampere that had been established with a similar balance in 1942. A small coil, shown above the fixed coil in Fig. 8–15, is suspended from one arm

Fig. 8–15. Photograph showing the construction of the two coils used in the ampere balance shown in Fig. 8–14. Here the smaller coil is shown suspended above the larger coil, although during a standardizing operation it is suspended in the middle of the larger coil. (Courtesy of the U.S. Bureau of Standards.)

of the precision balance at the center of the larger fixed coil. A small break at the center of the fixed coil allows the current in the upper half to be directed opposite to that in the lower. This provides a gradient in the magnetic field of the fixed coil that can be accurately calculated. Since the coils are connected in series, the current has the same magnitude in the suspended coil and in each half of the fixed coil. The weights required to keep the suspended coil balanced at the center determine the magnitude of this current.

The 1957 experiments at the Bureau of Standards also determined the standard ampere by measuring the torque on a small coil suspended in the relatively uniform field of a long solenoid that carried the same current as the small coil. The two measurements agreed to within 5 parts per million, although their average differed from the 1942 results by 10 parts per million. Since it was impossible to preserve a standard ampere, this last comparison had to be made with the substandards of resistance and voltage that had been established by the earlier experiments and preserved at the Bureau. These substandards, the standard cell for constant voltage and the standard resistor for constant resistance, had apparently varied little during the intervening years.

It is not possible to establish substandards for both resistance and voltage with the single experiment that determines the ampere. Either the ohm or the volt must be established independently.

Standard resistors. In principle, the ohm could be established directly from measurements of the heat losses in a resistor when it carries a known current, but calorimetric measurements are far too inaccurate for this purpose. As will be shown in Chapter 10, a sinusoidal current $i = I_m \sin \omega t$ in a pure inductor results in a sinusoidal potential difference

$$v = L \frac{di}{dt} = \omega L I_m \cos \omega t = V_m \cos \omega t,$$

where $V_m/I_m = \omega L$ is called the reactance, in ohms, of the inductor. Since the L for a precisely constructed inductor can be calculated to six significant figures and the frequency $f = \omega/2\pi$ can be determined to even better precision, the reactance of a precision inductor provides an ideal standard for calibrating standard resistors. Several ingenious bridge-type circuits have been devised for comparing such inductive reactances with resistances.

One of the simplest of the bridge-type circuits used for standardizing resistors is the Campbell circuit, which uses the two precision mutual inductances, M_1 and M_2 in Fig. 8–16, instead of a single self-inductance. To obtain a balance, the alternating current through the very sensitive indicating instrument G is reduced to zero by varying both S and the frequency f of the a-c generator that is shown at the left of the diagram.

Fig. 8–16. Campbell bridge-type circuit for calibrating the standard resistance r by comparing it with the geometrical average of the precisely determined mutual inductances M_1 and M_2.

When a balance has been achieved, the unknown resistance r is given by

$$r = 2\pi f \sqrt{\frac{M_1 M_2}{\Re}}, \qquad (8\text{–}31)$$

where the ratio $\Re = R/r$ can be accurately determined in terms of lengths with a Wheatstone bridge. The resistance R is the total resistance of the middle upper loop, including S, and the resistances of the secondary of M_1 and the primary of M_2. The inductances M_1 and M_2 are obtained from bridge-type comparisons with a standard inductor whose mutual inductance has been calculated accurately from its precisely determined dimensions. Analysis of this Campbell bridge shows that it cannot be balanced without ensuring that both

$$(L_1 + L_2)r = M_1 S$$

and the relation given in Eq. (8–31) are satisfied. The proof of these relations is left as a problem at the end of Chapter 10.

Once a circuit of this type has been set up, its operation is sufficiently simple so that it can be used frequently to check the constancy of standard resistors. The Campbell circuit was first used by the British National Physical Laboratory, but somewhat more complex modifications of this circuit are now in use at other standardizing laboratories.

PROBLEMS

*8–1. A long straight wire carries a current of 10 amp along the z-axis, as shown in Fig. 8–17. A uniform magnetic field whose flux density is 10^{-6} w/m^2 is directed parallel to the x-axis. What is the resultant magnetic field at the following points: (a) $x = 0$, $y = 2$ m, (b) $x = 2$ m, $y = 0$, (c) $x = 0$, $y = -0.5$ m?

8–2. Two long straight wires, A and B, are arranged in a vertical plane 10 cm apart as in Fig. 8–18. B carries a current of 6 amp into the plane of the paper. (a) What must be the magnitude and direction of the current in A for the resultant field at point a, 5 cm under A, to be zero? (b) What is then the resultant field at b, 5 cm above B, and at c, 6 cm from A and 8 cm from B?

*8–3. A long straight wire carries a current of 1.5 amp. An electron travels with a velocity of 5×10^6 cm/sec parallel to the wire, 10 cm from it, and in the same direction as the current. What force does the magnetic field of the current exert on the moving electron?

8–4. A closely wound coil has a diameter of 40 cm and carries a current of 2.5 amp. How many turns does it have if the magnetic induction at the center of the coil is 1.26×10^{-4} w/m^2?

*8–5. A solenoid is 10 cm long and is wound with two layers of wire, having an average diameter of 3 cm. The inner layer consists of 50 turns, the outer layer of 40 turns. The current is 3 amp, in the same direction in both layers. What is the magnetic induction at a point near the center of the solenoid?

*8–6. The long straight wire AB in Fig. 8–19 carries a current of 20 amp. The rectangular loop whose long edges are parallel to the wire carries a current of 10 amp. Find the magnitude and direction of the resultant force exerted on the loop by the magnetic field of the wire.

8–7. A solenoid 50 cm long and 8 cm in diameter is wound with 500 turns. A closely wound coil of 20 turns of insulated wire surrounds the solenoid at its midpoint, and the terminals of the coil are connected to a ballistic galvanometer. The combined resistance of coil, galvanometer, and leads is 25 ohms. Find the quantity of charge displaced through the galvanometer when the current in the solenoid is quickly decreased from 3 amp to 1 amp.

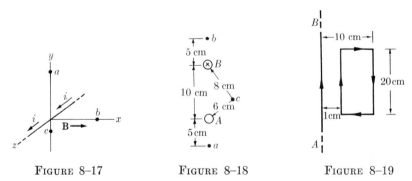

FIGURE 8–17   FIGURE 8–18   FIGURE 8–19

* Answers to starred problems will be found at back of book.

8–8. The wire circuit shown in Fig. 8–20 follows along arcs and chords of a circle whose radius in meters is a. Find the direction and magnitude of the magnetic field produced at the center of this circle by a current of I (amperes) in this circuit.

*8–9. Calculate the mutual inductance between the long straight wire and the rectangular coil shown in Fig. 8–19.

8–10. (a) Directly from the Biot-Savart law, show that the **B** field at the center of a solenoid, whose length L is very small compared with its radius a, is $B = \mu_0 NI/2a$. (b) The **B** field inside a very long solenoid is uniform and is given by $B = \mu_0 NI/L$. Show that the general relation of Eq. (8–7) gives these expressions for the **B** fields at the centers of the very short and the very long solenoids respectively.

*8–11. Figure 8–21 shows a wire carrying a current I in a logarithmic spiral that is given by $r = ae^{-\phi/\pi}$. Find **B** at the origin.

FIGURE 8–20

FIGURE 8–21

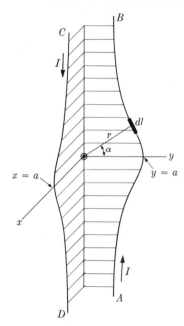

FIGURE 8–22

8–12. In Fig. 8–22 there is a current I upward in the wire from A to B and downward in the wire from C to D. The two wires have symmetrical shapes about the z-axis, AB being in the yz-plane and CD being in the xz-plane. The distance r from the origin of any element dl of either wire is given by $r = a/(1 + \sin^2 \alpha) \cos \alpha$ and each wire extends from $\alpha = -\pi/2$ to $\alpha = \pi/2$. Find $\mathbf{B}$ at the origin.

*8–13. A regular tetrahedron consisting of four equilateral triangles with sides of length a rests on a table. A current I is directed counterclockwise in a wire that coincides with the periphery of the base. Calculate the field $\mathbf{B}$ at the apex.

8–14. In standardizing the ampere in 1957, Driscoll and Cutkosky of the National Bureau of Standards used the balance shown in Figs. 8–14 and 8–15. The small coil was supported by the balance at the middle of the large solenoid, shown mounted below the balance. Since the force on this small coil depends upon the gradient of the field in the solenoid, center taps were provided to direct the current in opposite directions in the upper and lower halves. The exact fields of this solenoid were calculated from formulas developed by Snow. These formulas are too complex to be used here but the magnitude of the force on the small coil can be obtained by assuming that (1) the solenoid is infinitely long with n turns/m and with the current I in opposite directions in the upper and lower halves, and (2) in the space occupied by the small coil, the axial component of the solenoid's magnetic field equals that along its axis.

(a) Calculate $\mathbf{B}$ and ∇B at the center of the solenoid.

(b) Calculate the electromagnetic force on a very short coil of N_2 turns whose centerlines follow paths described by circles of radius a about the axis.

Assume that the small coil is exactly centered at the middle of the solenoid, with the two axes coinciding, and that the small coil carries the same current I as is carried by each half of the solenoid.

(c) Determine the magnitude of this force and the absolute accuracy that would be required in the weighing to establish 1 amp to 5 parts per million.

Assume the following dimensions, which were used in the Bureau of Standards' experiment: n of the solenoid = 1000 turns/m, N_2 = 31 turns in 3.1 cm of length, and a = 14 cm.

8–15. An infinitely long wire of radius a carries a current I. If r is the perpendicular distance of a point P from the center of the wire, the field at P is independent of the size of the wire so long as $a < r$. (a) Prove this statement directly from Eq. (8–3). (b) Prove this statement by means of Eq. (8–12). (c) Find the field inside the wire where $r < a$.

*8–16. Two very long, straight, and parallel filaments of wire carry currents I_1 and I_2 in the same direction. Suppose that they are d meters apart and calculate the force exerted by the first wire on each meter of length of the second. Show from Problem 8–15 that the result will not be changed if the first wire has a finite radius $a_1 \cong d/4$. Would the result be changed if both wires had finite radii, $a_1 \cong a_2 \cong d/4$?

*8–17. In Fig. 6–4, the two concentric cylinders of Cu and Ni (the latter being solid) provide electrodes for the electrolytic cell on the left, whose emf is V_e, and also provide a transmission line for carrying current to the carbon washer on the right. Assume that the resistivity ρ_c of carbon is so much larger than that of any of the rest of the circuit that all the other resistances can be neglected.

(a) Find the current I as a function of V_e, ρ_c, and the dimensions of the cylinders.

(b) Find $\mathbf{E}$ as a function of r for $0 < r < a$; $a < r < b$; $b < r < c$; and $r > c$.

(c) Find $\mathbf{H}$ as a function of r for $0 < r < a$; $a < r < b$; $b < r < c$; and $r > c$, where $\mathbf{H}$ is induced by a current I.

*8–18. Two long, straight wires are parallel and are separated by the distance $2s$. They carry a current I in opposite directions. Draw a diagram, similar to that of Fig. 4–16, of a cross section normal to the wires locating a field point in terms of the coordinates r_1, r_2, θ_1, and θ_2, where r_2 is the distance in this plane of the field point from the center of the wire carrying current into the paper and θ_2 is the angle between r_2 and a line through the centers. The coordinates r_1 and θ_1 are corresponding coordinates measured from the center of the wire carrying current out of the paper. (a) Write an equation in these coordinates for the magnetic potential Ω. (b) Using this potential, calculate $\mathbf{H}$ in the plane of symmetry as a function of y.

*8–19. (a) Show that a general solution can be obtained for Problem 8–18 from the complex-variable solution for eccentric cylinders found in Section 4–11. (b) If each wire has a finite diameter compared with the distance between them, determine whether the periphery of each wire will coincide with a circle in Fig. 4–17 having a constant m or will have its center coincide with a pole where either $m = 0$ or $m = \infty$. If the latter should be true, how would you treat those circles surrounding the poles that are partly inside and partly outside the wires?

8–20. To check the standard ampere determined by the balance in Figs. 8–14 and 8–15, the Bureau of Standards measured the torque on a small coil mounted in the center of a long solenoid, where both coil and solenoid carried the current to be checked. The solenoid had 1000 turns 35 cm in diameter and 1 m long, and the small coil had 110 turns 15 cm in diameter and 11 cm long. (a) Calculate the torque on the coil when it is oriented for maximum torque, with a current of 1 amp. (b) Assuming that the torque can be determined with sufficient accuracy, decide which dimension of the coils is most difficult to determine with the required accuracy.

*8–21. (a) Calculate the approximate self-inductance of the Bureau of Standards' large solenoid described in Problem 8–20, assuming that the uniform field found in very long solenoids exists throughout this solenoid. (b) A better approximation is obtained by assuming the axial component of the internal field to vary as it does along the axis, but having this constant value in each plane normal to the axis. Calculate the self-inductance on this assumption and compare it with the Bureau of Standards' calculation of 103 millihenries.

*8–22. Two toroidal windings, each similar to the one shown in Fig. 8–10, are tightly wound in single layers of wire. They each have the same centerline radius r_c, but the smaller solenoid is wound with an internal radius a and is inside the larger solenoid, which is wound with an internal radius $b > a$. The numbers of the turns on the inner and outer solenoids are N_a and N_b respectively. The inductance of such a device is easily calculated with considerable accuracy, although the device might be difficult to construct accurately. Each of the calculations that follow should be done (1) assuming $r_c \gg b$, and (2) assuming r_c only slightly larger than b. (a) Calculate the self-inductances L_a and L_b for the two solenoids. (b) Calculate the mutual inductance M between the two solenoids.

8–23. Two rigidly mounted circuits have self-inductances L_1 and L_2 and mutual inductance M. Calculate the self-inductances of this system for the circuits connected in series (a) when they are connected so that the magnetic field from the first adds to the field of the second, and (b) when these fields are opposed to each other.

8–24. Suppose the circular circuit on the right in Fig. 8–13 is free to rotate about an axis through one diameter. (a) Calculate M as a function of the angle α through which this circle has been rotated, assuming $X \gg a$. (b) Calculate the force and the torque on the circle at the right if each circle carries the current I in the same direction.

*8–25. The rectangular components of the vector equation $\nabla^2 \mathbf{A} = -\mu \mathbf{J}$ each have the same form as does the scalar equation $\nabla^2 V = -\rho/\epsilon$, which was originally derived from Gauss' law. This law is often used to obtain boundary conditions for solutions of $\nabla^2 V = 0$. (a) Derive an integral equation having the form of Gauss' law, $\epsilon_0 \int_s \mathbf{E} \cdot d\mathbf{s} = \int_\tau \rho \, d\tau$, for the z-component of $\mathbf{A}$. Note that this relation is sufficiently simple to be useful only for components associated with constant unit vectors. (b) Obtain the expression for $\mathbf{A}$ near a long straight wire carrying a current I by using the relation derived in (a) to provide the boundary conditions needed for solving $\nabla^2 \mathbf{A} = 0$.

*8–26. A transmission line consists of two long straight wires d meters apart that carry the current I in opposite directions. (a) Find the expression for $\mathbf{A}$ outside these wires. (b) Calculate $\mathbf{B}$ from $\mathbf{A}$.

*8–27. Currents in a thin spherical shell of radius a produce magnetic fields whose value throughout the interior of the shell is given by $\mathbf{H} = \mathbf{k}G$. (a) Find the distribution of currents in this spherical shell. (b) Find the field outside the shell.

*8–28. A spherical shell of radius a has a uniform surface density of charge σ and is rotating about a vertical axis with the angular velocity ω. (a) Calculate the vector potential $\mathbf{A}$ outside this shell. (b) Calculate $\mathbf{A}$ inside the shell. (c) Calculate $\mathbf{B}$ inside and outside the shell.

CHAPTER 9

MAGNETIC MATERIALS

All materials exhibit magnetic properties, although in some materials these properties are much more pronounced than in others. This magnetic behavior is due to the fact that practically all of the elementary particles of which these materials consist show magnetic dipole moments. In the unmagnetized state these dipoles are oriented so that their moments cancel each other vectorially and thus produce no external magnetic fields. When the materials are placed in a magnetic field, some of these dipoles become preferentially oriented and thus contribute to the external field. In these respects the magnetic behavior of materials is much like the electric behavior of dielectric materials that contain permanent electric dipoles. However, there are many ways in which the magnetic behavior of materials in magnetic fields differs from the electric behavior of dielectric materials in electric fields.

While it is easy to separate positive from negative charges, all attempts to separate positive from negative poles have failed. It is now generally believed that all of the elementary magnetic dipoles consist of circulating charges, e.g., electrons orbiting about a positive nucleus or spinning about an axis. These circulating charges are called amperian currents in honor of André Ampere who first postulated their existence. The fact that current loops exhibit magnetic dipole moments has been demonstrated. In Section 7–2 it was shown that the torque on a current loop in a magnetic field is $L = p'_m \times B$, where the vector p'_m has the magnitude IA and points in the direction of advance of a right-handed screw which is rotated in the direction of the current I. By modifying the definition for the magnetic dipole moment* to

$$p_m = \mu_0 p'_m,$$

a desirable symmetry between electric and magnetic symbols is achieved. The torque on the dipole can then be written as

$$L = p_m \times H,$$

where p_m has the magnitude $p_m = \mu_0 I A$ and $H = B/\mu_0$. Furthermore, in Section 8–2, it was shown that the scalar magnetic potential, produced

---

* In some texts "dipole moment" means p'_m, while in others it means p_m. The latter is preferred here because it retains desirable symmetry in the electric and magnetic equations. The unit of p'_m is amp·m² and of p_m is weber·m.

276

by a current loop at points not too close to it, can be written as

$$\Omega = \frac{p_m \cos \theta}{\mu_0 4\pi r^2}$$

in a system of spherical coordinates having its axis of symmetry coincident with p_m. These two equations have the same mathematical form as do the expressions for the torque on an electric dipole p in an electric field:

$$L = p \times E,$$

and for the scalar electric potential due to such a dipole:

$$V = \frac{p \cos \theta}{\epsilon_0 4\pi r^2}.$$

Thus the two models are mathematically equivalent in macroscopic problems where field observations are not made inside of amperian current loops.

9–1 Magnetic fields due to magnetized materials. The polarization of dielectric materials was shown in Section 5–2 to be caused by the orientation of electric dipoles within the material or by the relative displacement of positive and negative charges with respect to each other. There are no magnetic poles to correspond to electric charges, but the motions of charged particles within materials do effectively create *magnetic dipoles*, whose behavior in magnetic fields is analogous to that of electric dipoles in electric fields. This similarity makes it possible to adopt magnetostatic symbols that correspond to the electrostatic symbols listed in Table 9–1. With the adoption of these symbols, magnetostatic problems can often be solved by substituting the magnetic for the electric symbols in solutions to similar problems dealing with electrostatic phenomena.

Six vector fields. As indicated in Table 9–1, three vectors, D, E, and P, are needed to describe electrostatic fields and three vectors, B, H, and $\mathfrak{M}$, are needed to describe magnetostatic fields. In principle, only one electric and one magnetic vector would be needed if the exact location and motion of all charges were known within the region of interest. Under such circumstances the two vectors E and B would be chosen, since they determine the forces on electric charges. The other four vectors are introduced to facilitate the description of electric and magnetic polarizations, and for this purpose they are absolutely essential, since it is impossible to know the exact location of all charges within real materials.

The mathematical correspondence between B and D for static conditions is evidenced by Maxwell's first and second equations, Eqs. (M–1) and (M–2), which become $\nabla \cdot D = 0$ and $\nabla \cdot B = 0$ when regions are selected where there are no real electric charges, so that $\rho = 0$. The fact that the expression $\nabla \cdot \mathbf{B} = 0$ is a general relation for all space indicates that "real" magnetic poles do not exist. However, materials with permanent electric dipoles that are oriented preferentially produce external electric fields that are identical to the magnetic fields produced by materials with their magnetic dipoles similarly oriented. In Chapter 5 the vector $\mathbf{P}$ is defined as the vector sum at a physical point of the electric dipole moments

TABLE 9–1

MAGNETOSTATIC SYMBOLS THAT CORRESPOND MATHEMATICALLY
TO ELECTROSTATIC SYMBOLS

Electrostatic symbols and units		Corresponding magnetostatic symbols and units	
Electrostatic field	$\mathbf{E}$ volts/m	Magnetizing field	$\mathbf{H}$ amp/m
Electric displacement	$\mathbf{D}$ coul/m^2	Magnetic induction	$\mathbf{B}$ webers/m^2
Electric dipole moment	p coul·m	Magnetic dipole moment	p_m webers·m
Polarization	$\mathbf{P}$ coul/m^2	Magnetization	$\mathfrak{M}$ webers/m^2
Density of "real" charges	ρ coul/m^3	No real poles	
Surface density of "real" charges	σ coul/m^2	No real poles	
Volume density of polarization charges	ρ_p coul/m^3	Volume density of magnetic poles	ρ_m webers/m^3
Surface density of polarization charges	σ_p coul/m^2	Surface density of magnetic poles	σ_m webers/m^2
Electrostatic potential	V volt	Magnetostatic potential	Ω amp
Electric constant, $\epsilon_0 = 1/c^2\mu_0$	ϵ_0 farads/m	Magnetic constant, chosen as $4\pi/10^7$	μ_0 henries/m
Dielectric constant, ϵ/ϵ_0	K	Relative permeability, μ/μ_0	K_m

per unit volume; this suggests a similar definition for a magnetization vector. *The magnetization $\mathfrak{M}$ is defined as the vector sum per unit volume at a physical point of the magnetic dipole moments.* Since **P** has the same units (coul/m^2) as **D**, the magnetization $\mathfrak{M}$ is defined here with the same units (webers/m^2) as **B** to maintain the symmetry. The mathematical definition is

$$\mathfrak{M} = \frac{\sum \mathbf{p}_m}{\tau_0} \qquad (9\text{–}1)$$

summed over all the dipole moments within the volume τ_0 of the physical point.

The fact that **D** is divided into two parts in Eq. (5–5), $\mathbf{D} = \epsilon_0 \mathbf{E} + \mathbf{P}$, suggests that **B** might also be so divided. Experiments have shown the desirability of introducing a vector **H** that can be defined by an expression like

$$\mathbf{B} = \mu_0 \mathbf{H} + \mathfrak{M}. \qquad (9\text{–}2)$$

Many authors write this equation as $\mathbf{B} = \mu_0(\mathbf{H} + \mathbf{M})$ because they believe magnetization should have the same units as **H**. However, this eliminates the symmetry between the magnetic and electric equations, which is important for clarifying the roles of the various vector fields. Equation (9–2) could also be written as $\mathbf{B} = \mathfrak{K} + \mathfrak{M}$ with $\mathfrak{K} = \mu_0 \mathbf{H}$, which is useful for some purposes. For isotropic materials in which the magnetization is proportional to **H**, Eq. (9–2) is usually written as

$$\mathbf{B} = \mu_0 \mathbf{H}(1 + \chi_m) = K_m \mu_0 \mathbf{H} = \mu \mathbf{H},$$

which defines the *magnetic susceptibility as χ_m and the relative permeability as K_m.*

Paramagnetic, diamagnetic, and ferromagnetic materials. Materials are classified magnetically according to their magnetic susceptibilities. These classifications are discussed in more detail in Section 9–10, but they can be briefly defined as follows: In paramagnetic materials $0 < \chi_m < 1$, in diamagnetic materials $0 > \chi_m > -1$, and in ferromagnetic materials χ_m is a multiple-valued function that is usually much greater than one. In attempting to line up the magnetic dipoles in a ferromagnetic material, nonconservative forces are encountered that can result in materials remaining magnetized when either **B** or **H** is zero.

Comparison of magnetic and electric fields. While the fields **E** and **B** can be given definite values at mathematical points in space by making the test charge in the defining Eq. (7–2) a point charge of infinitesimal magnitude, the fields **P** and $\mathfrak{M}$ must be considered to be averages over small volumes. In defining **D** and **H**, with $\mathbf{D} = \epsilon_0 \mathbf{E} + \mathbf{P}$ and $\mathbf{H} = (\mathbf{B} - \mathfrak{M})/\mu_0$, the symbols **E** and **B** should be taken to represent the average values of these fields at physical points. The vectors $\mathbf{D}$ and $\mathbf{H}$ also represent averages over the volumes of physical points. Note that the symbol $\mathbf{H}$ was first introduced in Chapter 8 to represent $\mathbf{H} = \mathbf{B}/\mu_0$ in free space. This relation does not disagree with the definition given here, since $\mathfrak{M} = 0$ in free space, but the definition given here does provide $\mathbf{H}$ with properties that are very different from those of $\mathbf{B}$. To clarify these differences and to demonstrate the usefulness of the newly defined vector $\mathbf{H}$, a mathematical treatment reminiscent of that used in defining $\mathbf{D}$ will be used.

Taking the divergence of both sides of Eq. (9–2) and using Maxwell's second relation produces

$$\nabla \cdot \mathbf{B} = \nabla \cdot \mu_0 \mathbf{H} + \nabla \cdot \mathfrak{M} = 0.$$

While $\nabla \cdot \mathbf{B} = 0$ always, $\nabla \cdot \mu_0 \mathbf{H} = -\nabla \cdot \mathfrak{M}$ and is frequently not zero. Both the $\mathbf{B}$ and the $\mathbf{H}$ fields produced by magnetized materials can be described in terms of equivalent currents, but this process becomes quite complex when the $\mathbf{H}$ fields are described. It is much simpler to describe the $\mathbf{H}$ fields due to magnetized materials in terms of

$$-\nabla \cdot \mathfrak{M} = \rho_m, \tag{9–3}$$

which can be thought of as a volume density of magnetic poles due to the magnetization. This description retains the parallelism between magnetic and electric fields, since $-\nabla \cdot \mathbf{P} = \rho_p$ is the volume density of charges due to polarization. A law similar to the Gauss law for polarization charges can now be obtained by combining Eq. (9–3) with Eq. (9–2) and integrating over an arbitrary volume τ. This gives

$$\int_\tau \nabla \cdot \mu_0 \mathbf{H} \, d\tau = \int_\tau \rho_m \, d\tau$$

or

$$\int_s \mu_0 \mathbf{H} \cdot d\mathbf{s} = \int_\tau \rho_m \, d\tau, \tag{9–4}$$

where s is the closed surface surrounding τ. This is identical in form to the Gauss law that was proved from the inverse-square law for electrostatic fields. Conversely, since an equation like (9–4) holds, the fields due to the poles in the small volume element $d\tau$ must obey the inverse-square law

$$d(\mu_0 \mathbf{H}_m) = \frac{\mathbf{a}_r \rho_m \, d\tau}{4\pi r^2}, \tag{9–5}$$

where $r\mathbf{a}_r$ is the vector distance from the center of the small element to the field point P at which the field is observed. Since here only the fields due to magnetized materials are considered, the subscript m has been introduced to distinguish these fields from those due to the real or non-amperian currents discussed in Chapter 8.

To demonstrate Eq. (9–5), an imaginary sphere of radius r, so that it passes through P, can be drawn about $d\tau$ as a center. With $d\tau$ very small, symmetry requires that the fields at the surface of the sphere be radial and of equal magnitude. Equation (9–4) then becomes $4\pi r^2\, d(\mu_0 H_m) = \rho_m\, d\tau$, which proves the statement in Eq. (9–5). The $\mathbf{H}_m$ field due to magnetized materials then can be calculated from

$$\mathbf{H}_m = \int_\tau \frac{\mathbf{a}_r \rho_m\, d\tau}{\mu_0 4\pi r^2}. \tag{9–6}$$

Conservative magnetic fields. It was proved in Section 2–11 that fields following an inverse-square law like that of Eq. (9–5) are always conservative. Therefore

$$\oint \mathbf{H}_m \cdot d\mathbf{l} = 0 \qquad \text{and} \qquad \nabla \times \mathbf{H}_m = 0,$$

so that $\mathbf{H}_m$ is everywhere conservative. That $\mathbf{B}$ and $\mathfrak{M}$ are not necessarily conservative can be shown by taking the curl of Eq. (9–1), which yields

$$\nabla \times (\mu_0 \mathbf{H}_m) = \nabla \times \mathbf{B} - \nabla \times \mathfrak{M} = 0,$$

from which $\nabla \times \mathbf{B} = \nabla \times \mathfrak{M}$ and $\nabla \times \mathfrak{M}$ does not in general equal zero. For example, at the surface of a magnetized material, the tangential component of $\mathfrak{M}$ is usually finite inside but zero outside the surface, so that $\oint \mathfrak{M} \cdot d\mathbf{l} \neq 0$ along a path traversing regions both inside and outside such surfaces.

It has now been demonstrated that when fields are static and due only to the electric polarization or to the magnetization of materials, $\nabla \cdot \mathbf{D} = 0$, $\nabla \cdot \mathbf{B} = 0$, $\nabla \times \mathbf{E} = 0$, and $\nabla \times \mathbf{H} = 0$, while $\nabla \times \mathbf{D} \neq 0$, $\nabla \times \mathbf{B} \neq 0$, $\nabla \cdot \mathbf{E} \neq 0$, and $\nabla \cdot \mathbf{H} \neq 0$. All these equations follow directly from Maxwell's four field relations, summarized in Section 8–4, provided that the $\mathbf{J}$ in (M–4) includes only the nonamperian currents.

9–2 Critique of Maxwell's fourth relation. In the development of Maxwell's fourth relation in Section 8–3, the definition $\mathbf{H} = \mathbf{B}/\mu_0$ was used, which is the correct definition from the atomic point of view where magnetic materials consist of electric currents circulating in a vacuum. Equation (8–15) then can be written as

$$\nabla \times \mathbf{B}/\mu_0 = \mathbf{J}_t + \dot{\mathbf{D}} = \mathbf{J} + \mathbf{J}_m + \dot{\mathbf{D}}, \tag{9–7}$$

where $\mathbf{J}_t = \mathbf{J} + \mathbf{J}_m$ is the total density of all currents, $\mathbf{J}_m$ is the density of the amperian currents responsible for the magnetization, and $\mathbf{J}$ is the density of the nonamperian currents.

If the view in which $\mathbf{B} = \mu_0 \mathbf{H} + \mathfrak{M}$ is adopted, Eq. (9–7) becomes

$$\nabla \times \mathbf{H} + \nabla \times \mathfrak{M}/\mu_0 = \mathbf{J} + \mathbf{J}_m + \dot{\mathbf{D}},$$

or, since

$$\nabla \times \mathfrak{M} = \mu_0 \mathbf{J}_m, \tag{9–8}$$

the relation designated by (M–4),

$$\nabla \times \mathbf{H} = \mathbf{J} + \dot{\mathbf{D}},$$

is valid, with $\mathbf{J}$ being the density of nonamperian currents and $\mathbf{H}$ being the magnetizing field that is specifically defined in Section 9–1. Thus Maxwell's four field equations summarized in Section 8–4 are valid inside materials, with ρ being the density of the "real" or nonpolarization charges and with $\mathbf{J}$ being the density of the "real" or nonamperian currents. This completes the demonstration that static problems involving magnetic fields due to magnetized materials can be solved with the relations developed for electric fields due to polarized materials.

9–3 Fields of permanent magnets and electrets. To clarify the relations obtained in the previous section, it is desirable to obtain solutions for problems in magnetostatics and electrostatics that have the same geometries. Two right circular cylinders with identical dimensions, one uniformly polarized parallel to the axis and the other uniformly magnetized parallel to the axis, provide an excellent example. The nature of each field can be demonstrated by drawing flux lines having densities proportional to the magnitudes of the fields at each point in space. This requires four diagrams: one each for the $\mathbf{D}$ and the $\mathbf{E}$ field of the electret, and one each for the $\mathbf{B}$ and the $\mathbf{H}$ field of the permanent magnet. Since the geometries are identical and since the $\mathbf{D}$ and the $\mathbf{B}$ fields follow the same mathematical relations, it is possible to choose proportionality factors such that these two fields may be represented by a single set of flux lines, as shown in Fig. 9–1(a). With this choice for the densities of the $\mathbf{D}$ and $\mathbf{B}$ lines, the $\epsilon_0 \mathbf{E}$ and the $\mu_0 \mathbf{H}$ fields can be correctly represented by another set of flux lines, as shown in Fig. 9–1(b).

In this figure the fields can be considered to be due to the polarization charges with the electret and to the poles with the permanent magnet. On the top surface of the electret there is a uniform distribution of charges given by $\sigma_p = P$ and on the top surface of the permanent magnet there is a uniform distribution of poles given by $\sigma_m = \mathfrak{M}$. The charges and poles on the bottom surfaces are equal but opposite in sign. Flux lines of $\epsilon_0 \mathbf{E}$ and $\mu_0 \mathbf{H}$ emerge from the positive surfaces and terminate on the negative surfaces. These fields are conservative, but the divergences are not zero on the flat end surfaces. The $\mathbf{D}$ and $\mathbf{B}$ fields are obtained by adding $\mathbf{P}$

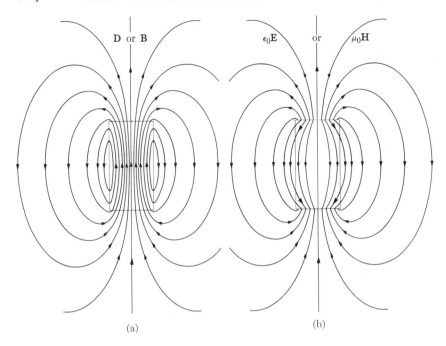

(a)   (b)

FIG. 9-1. The **D** and **B** fields of a cylindrical electret and permanent magnet are shown in (a). To provide direct comparison, the fields $\epsilon_0\mathbf{E}$ and $\mu_0\mathbf{H}$ of these devices are shown in (b).

and $\mathfrak{M}$ respectively to the fields shown in (b). These **D** and **B** lines of flux are continuous throughout space, since the divergences are zero everywhere. However, these fields are not conservative, as is obvious from the fact that $\oint \mathbf{D} \cdot d\mathbf{l} > 0$ and $\oint \mathbf{B} \cdot d\mathbf{l} > 0$ for paths of integration that follow any of the flux lines in the positive direction around the complete circuit. Outside the cylinders, the flux patterns of the (a) and (b) diagrams are identical, since in empty space $\mathbf{D} = \epsilon_0\mathbf{E}$ and $\mathbf{B} = \mu_0\mathbf{H}$.

D *versus* **E** *and* **H** *versus* **B**. In free space **D** and $\epsilon_0\mathbf{E}$ are completely equivalent concepts, as are also **B** and $\mu_0\mathbf{H}$. From the atomic point of view, where fields are created in free space by charges at rest or in motion, there is no need for the **D** and **H** field concepts because all phenomena can, in principle, be accounted for by the **E** and **B** fields alone. The **D** and **H** fields have been invented solely to simplify the analyses of phenomena observed on a macroscopic scale with polarizable and magnetizable materials.

While it has been known for a long time that only one electric and one magnetic field are needed for analyses on the atomic scale, there have been disagreements as to which two of the four fields should be considered fundamental. Actually there has been little or no disagreement with the conclusion that **E** represents a more basic concept than **D**. However, arguments as to whether the **B** or the **H** field is more basic persisted for a long time before experiments of a rather sophisticated nature were able to resolve the issue.

Obviously, magnetic fields vary greatly from point to point within magnetized materials. To decide between **B** and **H**, it is sufficient to determine which of the two best represents the magnetic field averaged over a sufficiently large volume. The difficulty arises from the fact that different types of probes see different average fields. For example, conduction electrons see a much different average magnetic field than do neutrons projected through the material. The problem has been studied by theoretical methods by Wannier,* by measurement of the deflections of cosmic rays passing through iron by Rasetti,† and by measurement of the diffraction of neutrons in magnetic materials by Hughes,‡ and by others. The motions of conduction electrons are strongly affected by the positively charged nuclei and the tightly bound electrons that surround them. Therefore conduction electrons do not move at random through magnetized material and no averages obtained with them should be taken too seriously. However, neutrons and high-speed cosmic-ray particles should pass randomly through these materials, and these experiments do indicate that **B** rather than **H** represents the average field. From the analysis presented in Chapter 8, these particles could see fields that averaged to **B** only by passing in a strictly random fashion through all current loops, including electron orbits and spinning electrons.

The **H** *field.* Since it has been experimentally established that the average magnetic field in a magnetic material is **B**, it is reasonable to question why **H** should be introduced at all. The answer is simply that **H** strongly affects the alignment of the current loops (magnetic dipoles) within the medium. For example, the permanent magnet shown in Fig. 9–1 tends to be demagnetized by its **H** field, which is directed nearly opposite to its magnetization. The **H** field, which is properly designated as *the magnetizing field,* will cause a decrease of magnetization if the magnet is jarred or heated. Note that if **B** were responsible for changing the magnetization, the magnetization described by Fig. 9–1 should increase with jarring rather than decrease. When the magnetic properties of materials are measured, the results are properly plotted as B versus H or $\mathfrak{M}$ versus H.

Probably the simplest methods for distinguishing **H** from **B** in actual experiments are based upon the boundary conditions that are presented in Section 9–5.

---

* G. H. Wannier, *Phys. Rev.* **72**, 305 (1947).

† F. Rasetti, *Phys. Rev.* **66**, 1 (1944).

‡ D. J. Hughes, *Pile Neutron Research,* Addison-Wesley, 1954, especially Sections 11–4 and 10–6.

9-4 Axial fields of a magnetized cylinder. When a cylinder is uniformly magnetized like the one discussed in the previous section, its fields throughout space can be calculated from the principles developed in Section 9-1. Because of the complexity of the general expressions for these fields, it is actually more instructive to calculate the simpler expressions for **H** along the cylindrical axis. Figure 9-2 shows the top and bottom surfaces of a magnetized cylinder, each of radius a. The field **H** at the general point P, which is located on the axis a distance z above the base, may be calculated by integrating over the field contributions arising from the excess magnetic poles residing on the bottom and top surfaces. Since the pole density on the bottom surface is $\sigma_m = -\mathfrak{M}$, the expression for the poles enclosed in a ring of radius r and width dr is given by $dq_m = \sigma_m 2\pi r\, dr = -\mathfrak{M}2\pi r\, dr$. Because of the symmetry of the ring element, all the radial components of the field at P cancel, leaving only the axial components, given by

$$dH_- = \frac{dq_m \cos\theta}{\mu_0 4\pi(z^2 + r^2)} = \frac{-z\mathfrak{M}r\, dr}{2\mu_0(z^2 + r^2)^{3/2}},$$

which is negative because it is directed downward. Integration gives

$$H_- = -\int_0^a \frac{z\mathfrak{M}}{2\mu_0} \frac{r\, dr}{(z^2 + r^2)^{3/2}} = \frac{\mathfrak{M}}{2\mu_0}\left[\frac{z}{(z^2 + r^2)^{1/2}}\right]_0^a$$

or

$$H_- = \frac{\mathfrak{M}}{2\mu_0}(\cos\alpha - 1).$$

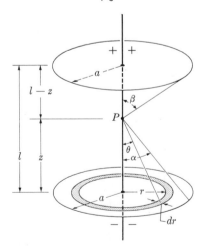

Fig. 9-2. Calculation of the **H** field along the axis of a uniformly magnetized bar of cylindrical shape. This **H** field is due to uniform distributions of poles on the end surfaces.

The total field at P is the sum of the fields due to the positive poles on the top surface and the negative poles on the bottom surface; that is,

$$H = H_+ + H_- = \frac{-\mathfrak{M}}{2\mu_0}(1 - \cos \alpha) - \frac{\mathfrak{M}}{2\mu_0}(1 - \cos \beta)$$

or

$$\mu_0 H = -\mathfrak{M}\left(1 - \frac{\cos \alpha + \cos \beta}{2}\right),$$

which applies only to points on the axis inside the cylinder, where $\mathbf{H}$ is always negative. On the axis above the top surface the positive poles produce a field that is directed upward, although the field due to the bottom surface is still directed downward. *The field on the axis above the cylinder is*

$$\mu_0 H = \mu_0(H_- + H_+) = \frac{-\mathfrak{M}}{2}(1 - \cos \alpha) + \frac{\mathfrak{M}}{2}(1 - \cos \beta)$$

or

$$\mu_0 H = \mathfrak{M}\left(\frac{\cos \alpha - \cos \beta}{2}\right) = B,$$

which is positive, since it is directed upward. Since in free space $\mathbf{B} = \mu_0\mathbf{H}$, this also gives the expression for $\mathbf{B}$ on the axis above the cylinder.

The fields along the axis of a uniformly magnetized cylinder whose length l is four times its radius a are plotted in Fig. 9–3. The $\mathbf{B}$ field is continuous, with a smooth maximum at the center of the cylinder and with no sudden change in value on passing out into empty space. The $\mu_0\mathbf{H}$ field, on the other hand, changes sharply from its negative values within the cylinder to positive values in empty space. The magnitude of this sharp change is just $\mathfrak{M}$, since $\mu_0\mathbf{H} = \mathbf{B} - \mathfrak{M}$ inside and $\mu_0\mathbf{H} = \mathbf{B}$ outside the bar.

It is instructive to note that the $\mathbf{B}$ field due to this uniformly magnetized cylinder is identical throughout space, inside and outside the cylinder, to the $\mathbf{B}$ field produced by the solenoid discussed in Section 8–1. The $\mathbf{B}$ field along the axis in Fig. 9–3 is the same as the $\mathbf{B}$ field along the axis in Fig. 8–4. There is, however, no field in the solenoid to correspond to the $\mathbf{H}$ field in the magnetized cylinder.

In practice it is very hard to produce a uniformly magnetized cylinder like the one assumed in this example, because of the very large demagnetizing fields at the ends of such cylinders. Usually the strong negative $\mathbf{H}$ fields reduce the magnetization near the ends, thus causing the poles on the end surfaces to spread around onto the cylindrical surface that is adjacent to them. A body polarization also may appear near the ends, because $\nabla \cdot \mathfrak{M}$ may not be zero inside the cylinder. The broken lines in Fig. 9–3 show the kinds of fields that may be produced by a real permanent

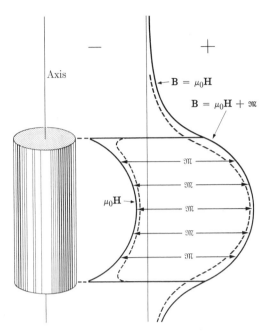

Fig. 9-3. Solid lines indicate the **B** and μ_0**H** fields on the axis of a uniformly magnetized permanent magnet of the cylindrical shape shown. Broken lines indicate the same fields for a real magnet.

magnet. The fact that uniform magnetic fields cannot be produced in magnetizing a cylindrical bar makes it difficult to use them for determining magnetic properties. No exact solution has been obtained for the magnetic fields of a ferromagnetic cylinder of finite length; however, exact solutions can be obtained for ferromagnetic materials formed into spheres or into ellipsoids of revolution.

9–5 Boundary-value problems. The field $\mathbf{H}_m$ due to magnetized materials has been shown to be conservative. Therefore it can always be expressed as $\mathbf{H}_m = -\nabla\Omega$, where Ω is a scalar potential function. Since $\nabla \cdot \mathbf{B} = 0$ everywhere, Laplace's equation

$$\nabla^2\Omega = 0 \qquad (9\text{-}9)$$

is valid in those regions where $\mathbf{B} = \mu_0 K_m \mathbf{H}_m$, with K_m a true constant. This relation is also valid in other regions, for example in regions where the fields and the magnetization are known to be constant. It does not hold, in general, in regions that include surfaces of separation between materials having different magnetic properties. When problems are to be solved for a region containing such surfaces, the region is divided into two or more regions in each of which Laplace's equation can be satisfied. The solutions for Ω for these separate regions must satisfy the boundary conditions along common boundaries. The procedures are essentially the same as were used in Chapter 5 with dielectric materials.

Boundary conditions. The correspondence between $\mathbf{B}$ and $\mathbf{D}$ and between $\mathbf{H}$ and $\mathbf{E}$ makes it possible to write boundary conditions immediately for $\mathbf{B}$ and $\mathbf{H}$ at any surface separating two magnetic materials. From Eqs. (5–8) and (5–9) these are

$$B_{1n} = B_{2n} \qquad (9\text{–}10)$$

and

$$H_{1t} = H_{2t}, \qquad (9\text{–}11)$$

where B_{1n} and B_{2n} are the components of $\mathbf{B}$ normal to the surface between medium 1 and 2, and H_{1t} and H_{2t} are the components of $\mathbf{H}$ tangent to this surface. The proofs of these conditions follow the patterns set in Section 5–5. Applying the integral $\int_s \mathbf{B} \cdot d\mathbf{s} = 0$ to a pillbox like that in Fig. 5–5 gives the first condition, Eq. (9–10), and applying $\oint \mathbf{H} \cdot d\mathbf{l} = 0$ to a closed path like that in Fig. 5–6 gives the second condition, Eq. (9–11).

Spheres and cylinders in uniform fields. While uniform magnetizations cannot be produced in most geometrical shapes, they can be produced rather easily in a few geometries, such as spheres, ellipsoids of revolution, and infinitely long cylinders fashioned of homogeneous and isotropic materials. The axes of the ellipsoids must be parallel to the field, while the axis of the cylinder should be perpendicular to the field.

As an example, assume a sphere of radius a, in which $\mathbf{B} = \mu\mathbf{H}$ with μ a true constant, placed in a uniform field of strength $\mathbf{B}_0 = \mu_0\mathbf{H}_0$ parallel to the z-axis. This problem is mathematically identical to the problem of the dielectric sphere of radius a in which $\mathbf{D} = \epsilon\mathbf{E}$ with ϵ a true constant. The solution for the magnetic problem is obtained directly from the solution for the electric problem found in Section 5–7 by substituting $\mathbf{B}$ for $\mathbf{D}$, $\mathbf{H}$ for $\mathbf{E}$, μ for ϵ, K_m for K, and Ω for V. The internal and external potentials, from Eq. (5–17), are

$$\Omega_i = - \frac{3}{K_m + 2} H_0 z$$

and

$$\Omega_0 = - \left(1 - \frac{K_m - 1}{K_m + 2} \frac{a^3}{r^3} \right) H_0 r \cos \theta.$$

The internal and external fields can be obtained from these potentials or directly from the electrostatic fields given in Section 5–7 for the corresponding problem. The internal fields are

$$\mathbf{H}_i = \frac{3}{K_m + 2} \mathbf{H}_0 = \frac{3}{\chi_m + 3} \mathbf{H}_0, \qquad (9\text{–}12)$$

$$\mathbf{B}_i = \frac{3K_m}{K_m + 2}\,\mathbf{B}_0 = \frac{3(\chi_m + 1)}{(\chi_m + 3)}\,\mathbf{B}_0, \qquad (9\text{-}13)$$

and

$$\mathfrak{M} = \mathbf{B}_i - \mu_0\mathbf{H}_i = \frac{3(K_m - 1)}{(K_m + 2)}\,\mathbf{B}_0 = \frac{3\chi_m}{\chi_m + 3}\,\mathbf{B}_0, \qquad (9\text{-}14)$$

and it is evident that the magnetization is uniform throughout the sphere. In the diamagnetic materials discussed in Section 9–10, $0 > \chi_m > -1$, and the magnetization $\mathfrak{M}$ is opposite in direction to the original field $\mathbf{B}_0$, as can be seen by making χ_m negative in the above equations.

The solution for an infinitely long cylinder made from the same kinds of material and placed with its axis normal to the uniform field $\mathbf{B}_0 = \mu_0\mathbf{H}_0$ can be obtained directly from the equations in Section 5–8. The potentials are

$$\Omega_i = -\frac{2}{K_m + 1}\,H_0 z$$

and

$$\Omega_0 = -\left(1 - \frac{K_m - 1}{K_m + 1}\frac{a^2}{r^2}\right)H_0 r\cos\theta.$$

The internal fields are given by

$$\mathbf{H}_i = \frac{2}{K_m + 1}\,\mathbf{H}_0 = \frac{2}{\chi_m + 2}\,\mathbf{H}_0,$$

$$\mathbf{B}_i = \frac{2K_m}{K_m + 1}\,\mathbf{B}_0 = \frac{2(\chi_m + 1)}{\chi_m + 2}\,\mathbf{B}_0,$$

and

$$\mathfrak{M} = \frac{2(K_m - 1)}{(K_m + 1)}\,\mathbf{B}_0 = \frac{2\chi_m}{\chi_m + 2}\,\mathbf{B}_0,$$

which show that the magnetization is also uniform throughout such a cylinder.

The foregoing solutions are applicable to paramagnetic, diamagnetic, and a few ferromagnetic materials in weak fields. In the next section it is demonstrated that with some modifications these solutions can be applied to any isotropic and homogeneous ferromagnetic material formed into these same shapes.

9–6 Ferromagnetic sphere in a uniform field. Solutions of boundary-value problems for ferromagnetic materials are at least as difficult and usually more difficult than solutions for nonferromagnetic materials. This follows logically from the nonlinear, multivalued nature of the relation between $\mathfrak{M}$ and H, as shown by the typical curve for ferromagnetic materials in Fig. 9–4. However, exact solutions can be obtained in special

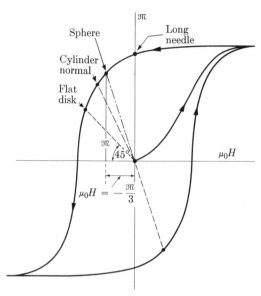

Fig. 9–4. Magnetizations and demagnetizing fields of permanent magnets formed in various shapes from a given material. In each $\mathfrak{M}$ must reduce in value along the second quadrant of the hysteresis loop until the demagnetizing field $\mu_0 H$ is (a) $-\mathfrak{M}/3$ in a sphere, (b) $-\mathfrak{M}/2$ in a cylinder (magnetized normal to its axis), (c) $-\mathfrak{M}$ in a flat plate, but (d) zero in a very long needle.

cases where $\mathfrak{M}$ is uniform throughout the material, as can be achieved with infinite cylinders, spheres, and ellipsoids of revolution.

It should be noted, however, that when nonferromagnetic materials of these shapes are properly oriented in a uniform field, as was done in the last section, the internal magnetization is necessarily uniform, but that for ferromagnetic materials the past history is important. For example, if a sphere is placed in a rather weak uniform field and a permanent magnet is then placed near it to induce nonuniform magnetization, some of the nonuniform magnetization will remain even after the magnet is removed. This is caused by the multivalued nature of most magnetization curves. Similarly, a sphere with nonuniform residual magnetization will retain some of this nonuniform magnetization in the presence of a uniform applied field until the field becomes strong enough to saturate the sample. When $\mu_0 H$ is increased well beyond the values plotted in Fig. 9–4, $\mathfrak{M}$ remains constant at the largest value shown in that figure and the material is said to be saturated. All of the internal dipoles that can be aligned parallel to the applied field are so aligned.

The very special case of a homogeneous, isotropic, ferromagnetic sphere which initially had no magnetization will now be considered. When a uniform magnetic field is superimposed upon this sphere and its magnitude is increased from zero to some final value, the internal magnetization increases but remains uniform throughout the sphere. While the functional relation between H and $\mathfrak{M}$ is not known, it is evident that for a given H the magnetization can be expressed by $\mathfrak{M} = \chi'_m \mu_0 H$, where χ'_m is not a constant susceptibility but rather a field-dependent proportionality factor having a fixed value for the conditions specified. Since for any given field value χ'_m is merely a constant of proportionality, as is χ_m, the solution for a ferromagnetic sphere can be obtained directly from the solution for a nonferromagnetic sphere by substituting χ'_m for χ_m.

Making this substitution in Eqs. (9–12) and (9–13) and multiplying the first equation by μ_0, we obtain

$$\mu_0 \mathbf{H}_i = \mu_0 \mathbf{H}_0 - \frac{\chi'_m}{3} \mu_0 \mathbf{H}_i = \mu_0 \mathbf{H}_0 - \tfrac{1}{3}\mathfrak{M} \qquad (9\text{–}15)$$

and

$$\mathbf{B}_i = \mathbf{B}_0 + \frac{2\chi'_m}{\chi'_m + 3} \mu_0 \mathbf{H}_0 = \mathbf{B}_0 + \tfrac{2}{3}\mathfrak{M} \qquad (9\text{–}16)$$

for the internal fields. Note that the internal $\mu_0 \mathbf{H}_i$ is less than the applied field by $\mathfrak{M}/3$, while the internal $\mathbf{B}_i$ is greater than the applied field by $2\mathfrak{M}/3$. The correctness of these results can be checked by subtracting Eq. (9–15) from (9–16) to obtain

$$\mathbf{B}_i - \mu_0 \mathbf{H}_i = \mathbf{B}_0 - \mu_0 \mathbf{H}_0 + \mathfrak{M},$$

and since $\mathbf{B}_0 = \mu_0 \mathbf{H}_0$, this becomes

$$\mathbf{B}_i = \mu_0 \mathbf{H}_i + \mathfrak{M},$$

which is obviously correct.

Spherical permanent magnet. An interesting case arises when a sphere is first saturated in a strong external field which is then reduced uniformly to zero. This case can be described by setting $\mu_0 \mathbf{H}_0 = \mathbf{B}_0 = 0$ in Eqs. (9–15) and (9–16) to give

$$\mu_0 \mathbf{H}_i = -\tfrac{1}{3}\mathfrak{M}$$

and

$$\mathbf{B}_i = \tfrac{2}{3}\mathfrak{M}.$$

For this case in which the applied field is zero, the ratio between $\mathfrak{M}$ and $\mu_0 H_i$ represented by χ'_m is

$$\chi'_m = \frac{\mathfrak{M}}{\mu_0 H_i} = -3.$$

The two equilibrium positions for the permanent magnetization of such a sphere in a zero field are represented by the intersections of the line of slope -3 with the hysteresis loop in Fig. 9–4. In the more general case of a uniformly magnetized sphere that was not originally saturated, the ratio between $\mathfrak{M}$ and $\mu_0 H_i$ would still be -3, but their magnitudes would be less. It is easily verified that χ'_m is -2 for the case of an infinite cylinder permanently magnetized perpendicular to its axis.

It is evident that good materials for permanent magnets should have very broad, open hysteresis loops like the one in Fig. 9–4, to give as large a residual magnetization as possible. It is also evident that the shape of the magnet is important, since the value of χ'_m is shape-dependent. In general, a long thin rod magnetized *parallel* to its axis maintains its magnetization better than a short stubby one, since $|\chi'_m|$ is larger in the first case.

Demagnetizing factors. For the special geometries studied in this section, with $\mathfrak{M}$ uniform through the sample, the internal field may be expressed by

$$\mu_0 H_i = \mu_0 H_0 - \mu_0 H_d,$$

where H_0 is the uniform applied field and H_d, directed opposite to the applied field, is the field generated by the magnetization of the sample. This quantity $\mu_0 H_d$, which is known as the *demagnetizing field*, is proportional to $\mathfrak{M}$, and may be expressed as

$$\mu_0 H_d = -D\mathfrak{M},$$

where D is known as the *demagnetizing factor*.

Examination of Eq. (9–15) reveals that $D = 1/3$ for a sphere, and the reader may verify that $D = 1/2$ for an infinite cylinder whose axis is perpendicular to the direction of magnetization. The demagnetizing factor D for four different geometries is given by the absolute magnitude of the slopes of the broken lines in Fig. 9–4. The value of D for a flat sheet magnetized perpendicular to its surface is approximately unity, since most of the lines of $\mathbf{H}$ passing from the north poles on one face to the south poles on the other must pass through the sheet. For a long thin rod magnetized parallel to its axis $D \cong 0$, since the north and south poles are relatively weak and relatively far from the center of the rod.

The demagnetizing factor is not an exact concept for shapes in which $\mathfrak{M}$ is not uniform throughout. However, it is convenient in practice to ascribe some average D to various shapes in order to indicate the magnitude of the internal field.

9–7 Measurements of B versus $\mu_0 H$. The demonstration that uniform magnetizations and uniform fields can be produced with particular shapes suggests how such curves can be obtained in the laboratory. Figure 9–5 shows a cross section through the equator of the sphere studied in Section 9–6, in which the fields are perpendicular to the plane of the diagram. Two search coils are shown wound around the sphere, one as close to the equator as possible and the other of somewhat larger diameter. The

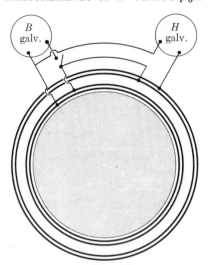

FIG. 9–5. Cross section through the equator of the ferromagnetic sphere of Section 9–6, showing search coils wound to determine changes in B and H. The inner coil alone determines δB, while the inner and outer coils connected in series-opposition determine δH.

inner coil is connected to a fluxmeter to determine changes in the total flux through the sphere, which are expressed by $\delta\phi = \pi a^2 \, \delta B_i$. Successive values of δB_i can be added to determine B_i as the external field is built up in steps from zero. If the outer coil has the same number of turns and is connected in series-opposition with the inner coil, the fluxmeter then reads only the changes in the flux threading between the two coils. The fluxmeter reading then determines changes in $\mu_0 H_i$ because in this annular region the external and internal H fields are equal. Here at the equator, where the fields are tangential to the spherical surface, the boundary conditions require that $H_{0t} = H_{it}$. With one fluxmeter connected to the inner coil and another to the two coils in opposition, B_i versus $\mu_0 H_i$ curves can be determined by combining the results obtained with the incremental changes.

This method of measurement is particularly easy to apply to samples shaped into prolate ellipsoids, because the location of the coils at the equator is less critical than for a sphere. In fact, for this purpose a long cylindrical rod can be used, because it makes an excellent approximation to a prolate ellipsoid and is much easier to fabricate. The errors caused by the lack of uniform magnetization near the ends of the bar can be neglected in sufficiently long rods.

When calculations are to be made with ferromagnetic materials it is essential to have experimentally determined B versus H curves available. The curves should be ones that have been determined under essentially the same conditions as will be experienced in the work being calculated. While there are many different B versus H curves that can be determined for a given ferromagnetic material, there are only three or four types that are of general importance: (1) the virgin curve, (2) the normal magnetization curve, (3) the hysteresis loop approaching saturation on each half-cycle, and (4) some δB versus δH curves at different fixed-field biases. The virgin curve (1) is obtained when the material is first magnetized after having been cooled from above its Curie temperature in a zero magnetic field. This is not nearly as important as the normal magnetization curve (2) that is obtained by a cycling process. In the cycling process the material is first demagnetized by cyclically reversing the applied magnetic field and slowly reducing it. After demagnetization a small field H is applied and reversed several times. One-half the change in magnetic induction produced by reversing H is taken as the value of B to be plotted versus H. When B versus H curves are given without specifying the experimental procedure they are nearly always "normal magnetization" curves. Normal curves for permalloy, iron, and alnico 5 are shown* in Figs. 9–6, 9–7, and 9–8, respectively. Figure 9–7 also illustrates a type (4) curve from which incremental permeabilities can be obtained. At each point on the normal curve a given reduction δH in H produces different changes δB in B. The incremental permeability is defined as $\mu_i = \delta B/\delta H$. In obtaining hysteresis loops like the one for iron shown in Fig. 9–9, the material is usually first magnetized to saturation by some maximum field H_{max}. Changes δB in B are then observed when the field is suddenly

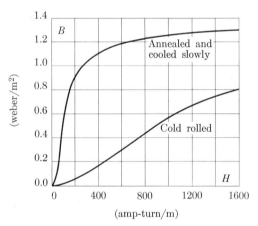

Fig. 9–6. Normal magnetization curve for 70 permalloy (70% Ni, 30% Fe), showing the effect of mechanical and heat treatment.

* Figures 9–6, 9–7, 9–8, and 9–9 are reproduced by permission from R. M. Bozorth, *Ferromagnetism*, D. Van Nostrand, 1951.

FIG. 9–7. Normal magnetization curve for iron. Minor hysteresis loops for small changes δH in H at various points are shown. Values for the incremental permeability $\mu_i = \delta B/\delta H$ at these points are also indicated.

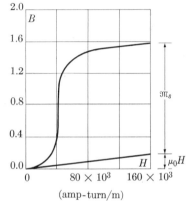

FIG. 9–8. Normal magnetization curve for alnico 5. Since $\mathfrak{M}$ becomes a constant $\mathfrak{M}_s$, the slope at high fields becomes μ_0.

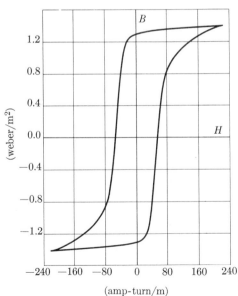

FIG. 9–9. Hysteresis loop for iron.

reduced from H_{max} to H. Values of B corresponding to H are then obtained from $B = B_{max} - \delta B$, where B_{max} is the value of B when $H = H_{max}$.

9–8 Scalar magnetic potentials. In Section 9–1 it was shown that for fields due to magnetized materials

$$\oint \mathbf{H}_m \cdot d\mathbf{l} = 0$$

always, and in Section 8–2 it was shown that for fields due to steady currents

$$\oint \mathbf{H}_c \cdot d\mathbf{l} = \int_s \mathbf{J} \cdot d\mathbf{s} = \sum_i I_i,$$

where $\sum_i I_i$ is the sum of all currents looped by the path of integration. Since the total field is the vector sum $\mathbf{H} = \mathbf{H}_c + \mathbf{H}_m$, due both to currents and to magnetized materials, the equation

$$\oint \mathbf{H} \cdot d\mathbf{l} = \int_s \mathbf{J} \cdot d\mathbf{s} = \sum_i I_i \qquad (9\text{--}17)$$

is the general relation for steady-state conditions. This means that the presence of any ferromagnetic material in the field of a solenoid or other current-carrying circuit does not alter the magnitude of the line integral along any given closed path even though it will usually alter the field at all locations.

Ferromagnetic toroid. If the solenoid shown in Fig. 8–10 is wound around a toroid of homogeneous and isotropic ferromagnetic material, then

$$\oint \mathbf{H} \cdot d\mathbf{l} = NI$$

for every circular path about the axis of symmetry that threads through the N turns of wire each carrying the current I. Symmetry requires that $\mathbf{H}$ be tangential to the path and that its magnitude be the same at all points. Therefore, $H2\pi r = NI$ and

$$H = \frac{NI}{2\pi r},$$

which is independent of the properties of the ferromagnetic material. This result stems from the fact that there are no free magnetic poles; that is, $\nabla \cdot \mathfrak{M} = -\rho_m = 0$ throughout the material. This geometry has been used for some of the most precise determinations of B versus H or $\mathfrak{M}$ versus H curves of materials. The incremental method of the previous section is employed but only one search coil and one fluxmeter are needed, since H is obtained directly from the magnitude of the current and from the geometry. Changes in total flux are easily determined by winding a search

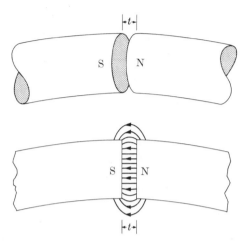

Fig. 9–10. Portion of a ferromagnetic toroid showing a narrow saw cut of width t. The passage of "fringing flux" outside the air gap is shown in the lower cross section.

coil around the toroid and connecting it to a fluxmeter. Subtracting the change in flux due to the change in current determines the change in flux due to the material. Thus δB or $\delta \mathfrak{M}$ is easily determined.

Toroid with thin saw cut. Rather remarkable changes are produced by merely making a saw cut through a toroid normal to the centerline. Integration along the centerline still gives

$$\oint \mathbf{H} \cdot d\mathbf{l} = NI,$$

but the symmetry is destroyed, so that $\mathbf{H}$ is no longer constant along this path. To determine the field as a function of current it is now necessary to invoke Maxwell's second relation, which guarantees the continuity of the $\mathbf{B}$ lines of flux. If the width t of the saw cut is small, most of these flux lines will go across the air gap normal to the surfaces of the gap, although there will be some fringing at the edges, as shown in Fig. 9–10. Aside from this fringing, which may be neglected to a good approximation only when t is very small compared with the internal diameter of the toroid, the rest of the field is still confined to the region inside the solenoid. Thus B along the centerline circle will be practically constant. From previously determined B versus H curves applicable to this material, the value of the internal magnetizing field H_i required to produce a given internal flux B_i along the centerline in the iron can be determined. In the air gap, $K_m \cong 1$, so that $H \cong B_i/\mu_0$ and hence the integral along the centerline is

$$NI = \oint \mathbf{H} \cdot d\mathbf{l} = H_i(2\pi r_c - t) + \frac{B_i t}{\mu_0}.$$

This can be written as

$$NI = H_i 2\pi r_c + \frac{(B_i - \mu_0 H_i)t}{\mu_0}$$

or

$$N(I -. I_0) = \frac{(B_i - \mu_0 H_i)t}{\mu_0},$$

where $H_i 2\pi r_c = N I_0$ is the number of ampere-turns required to produce B_i in the original uncut toroid. Although t was made small, B_i is generally so much larger than $\mu_0 H_i$ that I may need to be considerably larger than I_0. The difference $N(I - I_0)$ expresses the number of ampere-turns required for the air gap, and may be thought of as arising from the need to overcome the demagnetizing field produced by the poles induced on the surface of the cut.

Magnetic "Kirchhoff's laws." The foregoing calculations suggest that magnetic flux in ferromagnetic materials follows laws that are mathematically similar to Kirchhoff's laws for electric current circuits, especially if the great majority of the flux is confined within the ferromagnetic material. From the continuity principle, the flux into any junction of these materials equals the flux out of this junction, or

$$\phi_1 + \phi_2 + \phi_3 + \cdots = 0,$$

which is like the junction relation for currents. Cyclotron magnets and many other electromagnets are often constructed like the one shown in Fig. 9–11. The flux passes upward through the air gap in the center and divides into two equal parts, half returning to the bottom pole through the iron on the right and the other half through that on the left. These two paths for the flux remind one of parallel electric circuits each carrying half the current.

The line integral for any path that threads through the coils wound around the two center poles is

$$\oint \mathbf{H} \cdot d\mathbf{l} = NI,$$

where NI gives the total ampere-turns in these coils. A convenient choice of path follows a line of flux that passes through the center of the bar of iron on the right, as shown by the broken line in Fig. 9–11. Wherever the flux is constant along the length of any iron bar, B is constant and the H required to produce that B is constant. While such ideal conditions are seldom encountered in practice, it is frequently desirable to assume that they do exist, because more accurate assumptions usually lead to very long and laborious calculations.

It can be assumed that the closed flux circuit indicated by the broken line is made up of six sections of lengths l_1, l_2, l_3, l_4, l_5, and l_6 having cross-sectional areas A_1, A_2, A_3, A_4, A_5, and A_6 respectively, and that all the

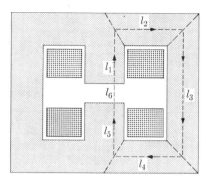

FIG. 9–11. Typical design for an electromagnet in which dotted rectangles represent the coil windings. A path l for magnetic flux is divided into approximate lengths of l_1, l_2, l_3, l_4, and l_5 through the iron and l_6 across the air gap.

flux ϕ passes through sections 1, 5, and 6, while only half, or $\phi/2$, passes through sections 2, 3, and 4. The magnetic induction in each section is then $B_1 = \phi/A_1$, $B_2 = \phi/2A_2$, $B_3 = \phi/2A_3$, $B_4 = \phi/2A_4$, $B_5 = \phi/A_5$, and $B_6 = \phi/A_6$. Often, by construction, sections 1 and 5 are identical and sections 2 and 4 are identical, which simplifies the calculations. The area A_6 of the air gap is not well defined, but it is frequently assumed to be given by $A_6 \cong A_1 = A_5$. The narrower the gap between the pole faces, the better is this approximation. In designing a magnet the value of B that is desired in the air gap is usually known, so that the total flux $\phi = B_6 A_6$ can be determined. This establishes the values for the remaining B's. Curves of B versus H which have been determined experimentally for the materials used in constructing each section should then be consulted to determine the value of H_1 required to produce B_1, of H_2 required to produce B_2, etc. In the air gap, $H_6 = B_6/\mu_0$. The line integral now gives

$$\oint \mathbf{H} \cdot d\mathbf{l} \cong H_6 l_6 + H_1(l_1 + l_5) + H_2(l_2 + l_4) + H_3 l_3 \cong NI,$$

(9–18)

from which the required number of ampere-turns can be determined.

If the magnetic inductance in these materials were proportional to the magnetizing fields, so that B/H were a true constant, Eq. (9–18) could be simplified and made more useful. The quantity

$$Hl = \frac{Bl}{\mu} = \frac{\phi l}{\mu A}$$

could then be written for each bar as

$$Hl = \phi\Re,$$

where $\Re = l/\mu A$ is called the *reluctance* of the bar. Furthermore, NI is usually called the *magnetomotive force* or mmf, and Eq. (9–18) is written

$$\phi_1 \mathfrak{R}_1 + \phi_2 \mathfrak{R}_2 + \phi_3 \mathfrak{R}_3 + \cdots = \text{mmf},$$

where ϕ_1, ϕ_2, ϕ_3, etc. are the fluxes through the respective sections. This relation corresponds to the circuital law for closed electric current circuits given by Kirchhoff. Note that the reluctance equation $\mathfrak{R} = l/\mu A$ is similar to the resistance equation $R = l/\sigma A$, where σ is the conductivity. This suggests why μ has been called permeability. Unfortunately for this type of analysis, $\mu = B/H$ is usually very far from constant, and the procedure is therefore limited to obtaining crude estimates. In general, the procedure outlined in leading up to Eq. (9–18) gives much more accurate results.

Magnetized sheet and its equivalent current. The external fields produced by magnetized materials can always be simulated by current circuits. For example, it is easily demonstrated that the current circuit shown in Fig. 9–12(a) is equivalent to the uniformly magnetized sheet in part (b) of that figure. The potential at P due to the element $d\mathbf{s}$ of the magnetized sheet can be obtained from the expression for the potential of an ideal dipole, provided the linear dimensions of this element are small compared with r. This requires that $r \gg t$ and that $r^2 \gg ds$, which can be satisfied for any value of r provided t and ds are made arbitrarily small. If the magnetic moment per unit area of the magnetized sheet in Fig. 9–13 is p_a, then the moment of the element is $p_a\,d\mathbf{s}$, and the potential $d\Omega$ at P due to this element is

$$d\Omega = \frac{-p_a\,d\mathbf{s} \cdot \mathbf{a}_r}{\mu_0 4\pi r^2} = \frac{-p_a}{4\pi\mu_0}\,d\omega,$$

where the minus sign appears because the magnetization is directed away from P in Fig. 9–13, with the south poles on the side of the sheet nearest P. With p_a constant, integration of this equation over the surface gives

$$\Omega = \frac{-p_a\omega}{4\pi\mu_0}, \tag{9–19}$$

where ω is the solid angle subtended by the whole surface s at P.

The magnetic scalar potential of current loops like the one in Fig. 9–12(a) is given in Eq. (8–11) as

$$\Omega = -\frac{I\omega}{4\pi}.$$

Comparison of these potentials shows that (a) and (b) in Fig. 9–12 are equivalent provided

$$p_a = \mu_0 I. \tag{9–20}$$

This equivalence of the magnetic sheet and the current loop means that

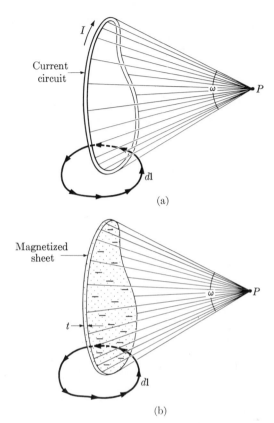

(a)

(b)

Fig. 9–12.   The magnetic scalar potential at P due to the current loop in (a) is identical to that at P due to the uniformly magnetized sheet in (b) and is proportional to the solid angle subtended by the loop area at P. The integral $\oint \mathbf{H} \cdot d\mathbf{l}$ is equal to I for the current loop but is zero for the magnetized sheet.

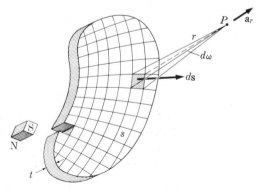

Fig. 9–13.   A small segment $d\mathbf{s}$ of a magnetized sheet gives rise to a magnetic dipole field at P.

they produce identical magnetic fields everywhere except inside the magnetic sheet. Even inside the sheet the **B** fields are identical, but the **H** fields are very different. The line integral $\oint \mathbf{H} \cdot d\mathbf{l}$ can be evaluated over each of the identically shaped paths indicated by arrows in (a) and (b) of Fig. 9–12. Its magnitude is I/μ_0 for the path in (a) and zero for the path in (b). Because the external fields are identical, the two integrals must have the same value over all the path outside the magnetized sheet. Therefore, inside this sheet,

$$\int \mathbf{H} \cdot d\mathbf{l} = -\frac{I}{\mu_0} = H_i t,$$

where $H_i = -I/\mu_0 t$ gives the value of **H** inside the sheet.

Since fields add vectorially, the fields due to any uniformly magnetized object can be analyzed by imagining it to be made up of a stack of many thin sheets, each uniformly magnetized. Since each magnetized sheet in the object can be replaced with a current loop, it is evident that the external field of any uniformly magnetized object can be duplicated by suitably chosen current loops. For example, a current can be chosen for the solenoid of Fig. 8–3 such as to make it nearly equivalent to the uniformly magnetized cylinder of Fig. 9–3. It could be made exactly equivalent if the finite number of turns could be replaced by an infinite number of turns of infinitesimal diameter but carrying the same amp-turns/m.

The interchangeability of the fields of these two devices can be used for making accurate measurements of susceptibility.* A cylindrical specimen in a uniform magnetic field is oscillated in and out of a many-turn search coil connected to a sensitive voltage detector. The magnetic moment of the oscillating sample results in a time variation in flux linkage in the search coil and a corresponding voltage signal. If a fine-wired solenoid is wrapped around the cylinder and the correct current sent through it, then the external field of the sample can be exactly canceled. The voltage detector will read zero when this null condition is achieved, and the magnetization of the sample is calculated from the equivalent current. A major advantage of this system is that the flux linkages between the sample and search coil need not be known.

9–9 Work required to produce magnetic fields. It was shown in Chapter 5 that the work required to produce electrostatic fields is the sum of all the energies needed to produce the fields at each of the physical points involved. To determine the work required to produce the final field $\mathbf{D}_f$ at any point in a dielectric having arbitrary properties, the charging of a

---

* A. Arrott, "Principle for Null Determination of Magnetization," *Rev. Sci. Inst.* **28**, 99–102 (1957).

parallel-plate capacitor homogeneously filled with such a dielectric was studied. This geometry has the advantage that with no restriction placed upon the properties of the dielectric the fields within it are homogeneous at all times and the required work is the same for every physical point. The work per unit volume is

$$w = \int_0^{D_f} \mathbf{E} \cdot d\mathbf{D},$$

and the power per unit volume is

$$p = \mathbf{E} \cdot \dot{\mathbf{D}}.$$

A similar procedure can be adopted for determining the work and the power per unit volume required to produce the final field $\mathbf{B}_f$ in materials having arbitrary magnetic properties. An infinitely long solenoid homogeneously filled with such a magnetic material has the same advantage as had the parallel-plate capacitor. The $\mathbf{B}$ and $\mathbf{H}$ fields are both confined to the inside of such a solenoid and these fields are uniform throughout. To avoid complications with joulean heat in the windings, it is best to ignore their resistance, although in real situations the energy required to produce the joulean heating must be added. Starting with both fields and the current all equal to zero, fields can be produced by increasing the current. If I is the current and n the number of turns per meter, $H = nI$. If the material fills the solenoid and has the cross-sectional area A, a back emf is produced in the winding by the increase in magnetic induction. The emf per meter required to overcome this back emf is

$$\mathcal{E} = n\frac{d\phi}{dt} = nA\dot{B}_a,$$

where B_a is the axial component of $\mathbf{B}$. The power per meter of length is

$$P = \mathcal{E}I = \frac{nA\dot{B}_a H}{n} = A\mathbf{H} \cdot \dot{\mathbf{B}},$$

and the power per unit volume required to produce these fields is

$$p = \mathbf{H} \cdot \dot{\mathbf{B}}. \tag{9–21}$$

The work per unit volume required to produce the final field $\mathbf{B}_f$ is

$$w = \int_0^{B_f} \mathbf{H} \cdot d\mathbf{B}.$$

A numerical value for the work required to produce a given field can be determined only if the relationship between $\mathbf{B}$ and $\mathbf{H}$ is known. This energy is usually not recovered when the magnetization disappears. This is especially true with ferromagnetic materials, for which some B versus H relationships are shown in Figs. 9–6 through 9–9. When a material is taken through a hysteresis loop like that shown in Fig. 9–9, energy is converted into heat, and the amount of heat per unit volume produced each time the cycle is completed is given by the area of the loop shown in the figure. As should be expected, a unit of area on any of these four figures is

$$\frac{\text{amp}}{\text{m}} \cdot \frac{\text{weber}}{\text{m}^2} = \frac{\text{joule}}{\text{m}^3}.$$

Equation (9–21) has been justified here only for the special case of a homogeneously filled solenoid, but more advanced theory indicates that it is a general relationship. Further evidence for its general validity is presented in Chapter 11 in the discussion of the Poynting vector.

9–10 The atomic origin of magnetism. According to the Bohr-Sommerfeld model of the atom, negatively charged electrons circulate about the positively charged nucleus in closed orbits which may be thought of as closed current loops. Because a closed current loop gives rise to a magnetic dipole moment, each orbiting electron should have associated with its motion about the nucleus not only an angular momentum but also a magnetic moment. Each electron also spins rapidly about its own axis (electron spin), giving rise to more angular momentum and another source of magnetic dipole moment. It is well known, however, that there is no net orbital or spin angular momentum associated with completely filled atomic shells. This is because quantum-mechanical rules require that there be just as many electrons rotating clockwise as counterclockwise about the nucleus in a closed shell. The electron spins in a filled shell are similarly required to be oriented in space so that they give no net angular momentum. Just as the angular momentum averages to zero in closed shells, so the current in these closed loops also averages to zero. The angular momentum and magnetic dipole moment of each atom must therefore come only from incompletely filled shells. This has been well verified by experiment.

The gyromagnetic ratio. A very simple relation exists between the dipole moment and the angular momentum of electrons. The dipole moment is $\mu_0 I A$, which reduces to $\mu_0 e \omega r^2/2$, since $A = \pi r^2$ and $I = e(\omega/2\pi)$ for an electron traveling in a circular orbit about a nucleus. Since the angular momentum is $m\omega r^2$, the ratio of magnetic dipole moment to the angular momentum is $\mu_0 e/2m$, which is known as the *gyromagnetic ratio*. (This ratio is more commonly written in gaussian units as $e/2mc$.) The values of angular momentum which an orbital electron may have are 0, $h/2\pi$, $2h/2\pi$, $3h/2\pi$, etc., where h is Planck's constant and equal to $6.62 \cdot 10^{-34}$ joule·sec or $6.62 \cdot 10^{-27}$ erg·sec. The smallest nonzero magnetic moment associated with the orbital motion of an electron is therefore $(\mu_0 e/2m)(h/2\pi)$ in mks units and $(e/2mc)(h/2\pi)$ in gaussian units, and it is known as one *Bohr magneton.*

If the electron were a sphere of negatively charged matter spinning rapidly about its axis, by a similar calculation the same gyromagnetic ratio would be obtained for electron spin as for electron orbital motion. Experimentally, however, the ratio between spin magnetic moment and spin angular momentum is just twice this large, being $\mu_0 e/m$ in mks units and e/mc in gaussian units. This apparent discrepancy has been resolved by relativistic considerations. Since the angular momentum of an electron associated with its spin may have values of plus or minus $h/4\pi$, the magnetic momentum associated with one electron spin is just one Bohr magneton. A general expression for the gyromagnetic ratio can be written as $g\mu_0 e/m$ in mks units and $g(e/2mc)$ in gaussian units, where g, the *magneto-mechanical factor*, is unity for orbital motion and two for electron spin. Thus $1 < g < 2$ when both orbital motion and electron spin contribute to the magnetization.

Experimental verification of these relations was first achieved by Einstein and de Haas in 1915. They suspended a ferromagnetic cylinder in a magnetizing coil by a fine wire, as illustrated in Fig. 9–14. The magnetization of the sample was reversed by reversing the magnetizing field of the coil, and thus a corresponding reversal of angular momentum was produced. The magnetization reversal can be measured by the methods discussed in Section 9–7, and the change in angular momentum can be determined by the resulting rotation of the sample about the vertical axis. Some values of g recently determined by more precise magnetic-resonance techniques are indicated in Table 9–2.

I

FIG. 9–14. The Einstein-de Haas method of measuring gyromagnetic ratios. Current reversal in the magnetizing coil reverses the magnetization and the associated angular momentum in the cylindrical specimen, thus causing the sample to rotate.

The relatively large values of g indicate that the orbital contribution to the total magnetic moment is quite small. This is explained by the fact that the motion of electrons in the unfilled outer shells is sufficiently perturbed by the proximity of the electrons of other atoms so that their angular momentum is reduced almost to zero. Because of the reduction in orbital angular momentum occurring when an atom is situated in a solid crystal, the magnetic moment of many materials is caused almost entirely by electron spin.

TABLE 9-2

EXPERIMENTAL VALUES FOR THE
MAGNETOMECHANICAL FACTOR

Substance	g
Iron	1.93
Cobalt	1.85
Nickel	1.88
Permalloy (FeNi)	1.90
Magnetite (Fe$_3$O$_4$)	1.93

Paramagnetism. In paramagnetic materials the magnetic dipoles associated with the atoms are randomly oriented in the absence of an applied magnetic field. The tendency of these dipoles to align themselves parallel to the applied field is proportional to the strength of the field and may be expressed by

$$\mathfrak{M} = \mu_0 \chi_m \mathbf{H}.$$

The quantity $\mathfrak{M}$ may be written in terms of the dipole moments $\mathbf{p}_i$ of individual atoms as

$$\mathfrak{M} = \frac{1}{\tau} \sum_i \mathbf{p}_i,$$

summed over all atoms in the volume τ.

The tendency of the dipole moments to have random orientation in the absence of an applied field is caused by thermal vibrations. It is therefore not surprising that the ease with which these dipoles can be aligned is inversely proportional to the temperature in most materials, obeying the Curie law

$$\chi_m = \frac{C}{T},$$

where C is the Curie constant and T is the temperature in degrees Kelvin.

Diamagnetism. In many materials the magnetization tends to align itself opposite to the applied field, obeying the same law as do the paramagnetic materials:

$$\mathfrak{M} = \mu_0 \chi_m \mathbf{H},$$

except that χ_m is negative. To understand the negative polarizations of these diamagnetic materials, consider an attempt to set up a magnetic field inside a loop of material with zero resistance. From Lenz' law, the current induced in such a loop will be in the direction to prevent the establishment of the field. The resulting current loop would constitute a magnetic dipole pointing opposite to the applied field, and an array of such loops would behave as a diamagnetic medium. The orbital electrons in completely filled atomic shells behave very much like nonresistive current loops. In the absence of an applied field they have no net magnetic moment. Application of a magnetic field alters their orbits slightly so as to oppose the applied field, and the new orbital motion remains indefinitely until the applied field is again changed. This diamagnetic susceptibility is virtually temperature-independent.

Conduction electrons. Thus far only the diamagnetic contribution of electrons in closed shells and the paramagnetic contribution resulting from the orbital and spin angular momentum of electrons in unfilled shells have been treated. The free electrons in a conduction band, however, make a paramagnetic contribution from their spins and a diamagnetic contribution from their motion through the lattice. While the reader can no doubt think of classical arguments to make these contributions plausible, this is a case where classical considerations fail to give even an approximately correct numerical result. In this case the statistical treatment of quantum mechanics shows the paramagnetic effect to be about twice the diamagnetic effect, and both effects to be almost temperature-independent.

TABLE 9-3

SOME TYPICAL MAGNETIC SUSCEPTIBILITIES
AT ROOM TEMPERATURE

Material	χ_m
Aluminum	$+1.75 \times 10^{-6}$
Copper	-0.76
Lithium	$+1.90$
Sodium	$+0.68$
Uranium	$+4.86$
Graphite	-7.9
Nickel chloride	$+150.$
Sodium chloride	-1.09

Some magnetic susceptibilities. Most materials make both paramagnetic and diamagnetic contributions, and nonferromagnetic materials are classed as *dia-* or *para*magnetic, depending upon which of these contributions is the larger. The magnetic susceptibilities of some typical materials are listed in Table 9–3. While there is considerable variation in the values of susceptibility from one material to another, all values are quite small. In ferromagnetic materials these contributions to the total magnetization can usually be neglected, since they are of the order of one thousand to one million times smaller than the ferromagnetic contribution even in relatively large fields.

9–11 Ferromagnetic materials. Materials that have large magnetizations even in the presence of very weak magnetic fields are called *ferromagnetic*. Only the three elements iron, nickel, and cobalt are ferromagnetic at room temperature and above. Almost all ferromagnetic alloys and compounds contain one or more of these three elements or manganese, which belongs to the same group of transition elements in the periodic table. The ease of magnetization of these materials results from quantum-mechanical forces which tend to align neighboring atomic spins parallel to each other even in the absence of an applied magnetic field. The quantum-mechanical energy reduction associated with the complete alignment of neighboring atomic spins is called the *exchange* energy. The large magnetizations exhibited by ferromagnetic materials have led to a variety of commercial uses for them. It is therefore desirable to study their properties in some detail.

Temperature dependence. The magnetic properties of ferromagnetic materials are strongly temperature-dependent. In the absence of an applied field they exhibit spontaneous magnetization below a temperature T_C known as the Curie temperature, and are strongly paramagnetic above that temperature, with susceptibilities that decrease with increasing temperature. The total ferromagnetic moment itself is temperature-dependent, starting with zero at the Curie temperature and approaching a fixed value asymptotically as the temperature is lowered toward absolute zero. Above the Curie temperature, the susceptibility may be described rather well by the Curie-Weiss law

$$\chi_m = \frac{C}{T - T_C},$$

but there is no simple expression for the variation of spontaneous magnetization below T_C. A typical plot of C/χ_m above T_C is given in Fig. 9–15, as well as a curve showing the spontaneous magnetization $\mathfrak{M}_s$ divided by the spontaneous magnetization at absolute zero, $\mathfrak{M}_0$, for temperatures below T_C. The Curie temperatures for iron, cobalt, nickel, and permalloy are listed in Table 9–4, and from the Curie temperatures, it is evident that these materials have almost as much magnetic moment at room temperature as they have at the low temperatures approaching absolute zero.

Magnetization of metals. The magnetization $\mathfrak{M}_s$ of Co, Ni, and many of their alloys can be understood from a very simple model. All these metals acquire most of their ferromagnetism from the unpaired spins in the partially filled 3d shell. According to Table 9–2 the orbital contribution can be virtually neglected, so that one expects a magnetization contribution of one Bohr magneton for each vacancy in the almost filled 3d shell.

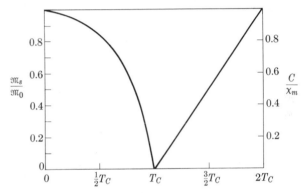

Fig. 9–15. Temperature dependence of some properties of ferromagnetic materials. The dependence of the saturation magnetization is shown up to the Curie point (from $T = 0$ to $T = T_C$) and the dependence of the reciprocal of the paramagnetic susceptibility is shown from $T = T_C$ to $T = 2T_C$. Properties of real materials vary somewhat from these idealized curves. (By permission, from R. M. Bozorth, *Ferromagnetism*, D. Van Nostrand Co., 1951.)

TABLE 9–4

PROPERTIES OF SOME FERROMAGNETIC METALS

	Fe	Co	Ni	Permalloy (80% Ni 20% Fe)
Measured Curie temperature (°K)	1043	1400	631	780
Electrons available for outer shell	8	9	10	9.6
Average number of conduction electrons	0.6	0.6	0.6	0.6
Vacancies in outer shell	2.6	1.6	0.6	1.0
Measured Bohr magnetons per atom	2.2	1.7	0.6	1.0

Examination of the periodic table indicates that after all the lower shells are filled, Co has nine remaining electrons in the outer 3d shell, which has room for a maximum of 10 electrons. Thus there appears to be only one vacancy in this shell; however, it is known experimentally that Co, Ni, and many alloys of these elements have, on the average, 0.6 conduction electron per atom. By placing an average of 0.6 electron per atom into the nonferromagnetic conduction band, there are left 1.6 vacancies on the average in the outer shell of Co, which might be expected to cause ferromagnetism. When the experimentally measured magnetization is converted into magnetization per atom in Bohr magnetons, the result is 1.7. This is quite good agreement for such a simple model. A similar calculation for Ni gives 0.6 vacancy per atom, which corresponds very closely to the 0.6 Bohr magneton per atom determined from its saturation magnetization at low temperatures. While the explanation for the 2.2 Bohr magnetons per atom found in Fe must follow a similar pattern, the details are less certain. However, alloys of Co-Ni and Fe-Ni, which have more electrons per atom than pure Co, do fit the simple picture presented here. For example, the permalloy shown in Table 9–4 has $(8 \times 0.2 + 10 \times 0.8) = 9.6$ electrons per atom available for the outer shells. With 0.6 electron per atom in the conduction band, it has one vacancy per atom, in agreement with the one Bohr magneton per atom found by experiment.

Ferromagnetic domains. The preceding discussion suggests that below its Curie temperature a piece of ferromagnetic material should exhibit a strong magnetic moment even in the absence of an applied magnetic field. However, ferromagnetic materials usually show little or no magnetization until they have been subjected to at least a small magnetic field. This can be understood by considering the classical forces acting between magnetic dipoles. Just a little experience with permanent bar magnets is needed to show that it is difficult to hold a group together with all the north poles pointing in the same direction. Strong forces tend to rotate the magnets so that they lie next to each other in head-to-tail positions. In a ferromagnetic material, the quantum-mechanical forces tending to align the individual atomic dipoles parallel to each other are in competition with these classical forces trying to align them antiparallel. The net result is that up to a certain size bundle of dipoles, the quantum forces hold all the dipoles parallel. Larger pieces of material are divided by classical magnetostatic forces into regions within which all atomic dipoles are parallel to each other while the direction of alignment differs from one region to the next. A region within which all atomic dipoles are aligned parallel is known as a magnetic domain, and the separation between two domains is known as a domain wall. Magnetic domains may have volumes from 10^{-6} cm^3 to 10^{-2} cm^3, therefore bulk materials usually contain millions of domains.

Atomic dipoles have a tendency to align themselves parallel to certain crystalline directions. In the body-centered cubic structure of iron, for example, the dipoles tend to lie parallel to one of the three perpendicular directions defined by the cube edges. These are known as easy directions of magnetization. This anisotropy in the magnetic properties of metallic crystals is caused by a quantum-mechanical coupling between the electron spins and the electrostatic crystalline field. In normal bulk materials, which contain many tiny crystallites joined together in a complex crystal structure, there is some tendency for each crystallite to be a single domain, with its magnetic moment lying parallel to an easy axis. This one-to-one correspondence between domain walls and crystallite boundaries is strongly perturbed, however, by the effects of other energy contributions.

The actual shapes and sizes of magnetic domains can be calculated, in general, only by a process of minimization of the total energy contributed from all causes. Such a calculation would demonstrate the experimentally observed fact that some crystallites contain several domains while some domains contain several crystallites. A detailed study of this problem will not be attempted here. A considerable understanding of the problem can be obtained, however, from the special case of domain walls within a large single crystal.

In the single crystal illustrated in Fig. 9–16(a) all the dipoles are aligned parallel to one easy axis. In Fig. 9–16(b) the magnetostatic energy has been greatly reduced by dividing the crystal into four domains lying in a head-to-tail configuration. The total reduction in energy is not as great as magnetostatic considerations alone would predict, since there is a large energy increase, proportional to the domain wall area, resulting from the quantum-mechanical exchange forces attempting to prevent disalignment between dipoles along the wall.

(a)   (b)   (c)

FIG. 9–16. Domains in a ferromagnetic single crystal. The configuration in (a) produces a large external field and therefore a large magnetostatic energy. The external field and the magnetostatic energy are progressively reduced from (a) to (b) to (c).

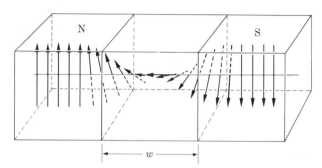

FIG. 9–17. Schematic illustration of variation of magnetic dipole alignment through domain wall of width w.

Domain walls. A domain wall actually consists of a transition region of finite width between two differently directed magnetized domains, with the dipoles becoming more nearly aligned parallel to the second domain as the distance from the first to the second domain is traversed. The change of alignment of the dipoles in a 180° domain wall is illustrated in Fig. 9–17. The quantum exchange energy between two dipoles is proportional to the square of the angle between them. For a 180° wall the energy between two dipoles is approximately $JS^2(\pi/N)^2$, where N is the total number of dipoles lying in a line extending across the width of the wall, J is the exchange energy term, and S is the dipole spin. The total energy of this string of N dipoles is therefore proportional to $1/N$. Minimization of exchange energy would yield an infinitely wide wall; however, this neglects anisotropy and magnetostatic and magnetoelastic energy terms. When these terms are included, a finite wall is obtained, which for iron is about 1000 A. Using $N \cong 300$, the total energy of the wall is then rather well determined from the dominant exchange energy term

$$W = \frac{JS^2\pi^2}{N}.$$

It is found to be about 1 erg/cm^2 or 10^{-3} joule/m^2. A minimization of the sum of the total wall energy and the magnetostatic energy gives a good estimate of the number of walls in a given volume.

If lines of magnetic flux were drawn in Fig. 9–16(a) and (b), it would be apparent that the external field is far more extensive in (a) than in (b), and this necessarily increases the total energy. A further reduction in energy can, therefore, be accomplished by the addition of domains of closure as illustrated in Fig. 9–16(c), where the external field has been virtually eliminated. A low total energy is further maintained by this pattern, since all domains are magnetized parallel to an easy axis.

Actual photographs of a domain pattern similar to that described are shown in Fig. 9–18.   The Bitter technique used for this observation, developed by Francis Bitter in 1931, consists in observing finely divided ferromagnetic particles in a colloidal suspension placed on the polished surface of the crystal under observation.   A microscope cover-glass placed in contact with the colloidal suspension flattens out any surface irregularities and permits good optical observation with a microscope.   The large field gradients in the vicinity of the domain walls are seen to attract the particles in the suspension and thus reveal the domain pattern.   A great variety of domain patterns in many materials have been observed in this manner.*

Fig. 9–18.   Domains of closure in Si-Fe single crystal photographed by Bitter technique.   Arrows illustrate direction of magnetization within individual domains.   The complex treelike domain structure observed in the upper left corner is beyond the scope of this discussion, but further reduces the total energy under some conditions.   (Courtesy of H. J. Williams, Bell Telephone Laboratories, Murray Hill, New Jersey.)

---

* Some of these patterns as well as an excellent review article on magnetic domains may be found in an article by C. Kittel and J. K. Galt, "Solid State Physics," Vol. 3, Academic Press, 437–564, 1956.

Magnetization curves. Interesting changes in domain patterns caused by changes in the applied field have been observed in iron whiskers by De Blois and Graham. These whiskers consist of long, hairlike single crystals whose growth results from the tendency of metallic vapor to condense on the end of a solidified strand rather than on the sides. Since such whiskers are nearly perfect crystals and often show optically perfect faces, they are ideally suited for the study of domain patterns by the Bitter technique. Figure 9–19 shows a sequence of four domain patterns taken for different values of the applied field. A gradual and continuous wall motion occurs as the field is reduced from (a) to (b) and then increased in the reverse direction from (b) to (c). However, a further increase in H from (c) to (d) results in a discontinuous displacement of the walls and a complete change in the domain pattern.

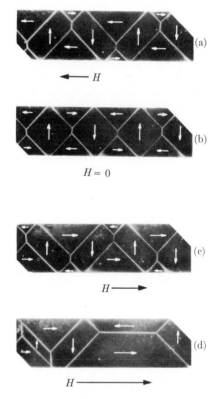

FIG. 9–19. Reversible and irreversible domain wall motion. Walls move smoothly from (a) to (b) to (c) and back, but jump suddenly from (c) to (d) when fields are applied as indicated. Whisker is 50 μ on a side. (Photographs by R. W. DeBlois and C. D. Graham, Jr., *Journal of Applied Physics*, **29**, 936, 1958.)

These changes can be correlated with the typical magnetization curve shown in Fig. 9–20. The initial portion of the curve results from reversible wall motion, as from (b) to (c) in Fig. 9–19, while the steep portion corresponds to discontinuous changes such as occurred from (c) to (d) in Fig. 9–19. As early as 1919, Barkhausen observed discontinuous steps in the steep portion of magnetization curves of small iron wires. These steps, illustrated in the magnified inset of Fig. 9–20, are now referred to as Barkhausen jumps and may be related to discontinuous domain wall displacements. The leveling-off region at the top of the magnetization curve occurs after all domains in the bulk material are magnetized nearly parallel to the field. It is due to a gradual rotation of the magnetization within the domains, tending to arrange it so as to lie more nearly parallel to the magnetizing field.

It should not be surprising that most of the energy loss of the magnetization reversal occurs in the steep portion of the curve where predominantly irreversible wall displacements occur. These irreversible displacements are responsible for the wide area enclosed by a hysteresis loop which is proportional to the energy dissipated in the cycle. In real materials the magnetization curves cannot be broken down into purely irreversible and purely reversible portions; however, the division of the magnetization curve in Fig. 9–20 does illustrate the regions where these processes dominate.

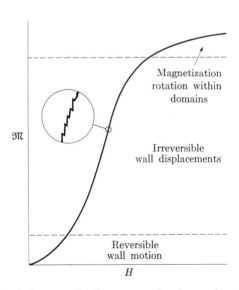

FIG. 9–20. Typical magnetization curve, showing regions in which reversible and irreversible effects dominate.

PROBLEMS

*9–1. A copper wire of radius a carries a steady current i. (a) What is the flux density at a point within the material of the wire, at a distance r from its axis? (b) Find the magnetic energy density at points within a thin cylindrical shell of radius r, thickness dr, and length l. (c) Find the total magnetic energy within a portion of the wire of length l.

9–2. Suppose a cylindrical bar magnet of alnico 5, 1 cm in diameter and 10 cm long, is permanently and uniformly magnetized to an intensity of magnetization of 1.2 w/m². (a) What is the strength of the poles at the ends of the magnet? (b) What is the magnetic moment of the magnet? (c) What is the torque exerted on the magnet when it is suspended in air at right angles to a magnetic field of flux density 1 milliweber/m²? (d) Compare the magnitude of H in the above field with the coercive force of alnico 5.

*9–3. A solenoidal winding of 100 turns of wire is wound on a wooden rod of the same dimensions as the bar magnet in Problem 9–2. What current must be sent through the wire in order that the torque acting on the solenoid in an external field shall equal the torque on the bar magnet?

9–4. Sketch the lines of induction of a diamagnetic sphere in a uniform external field.

*9–5. In Fig. 9–21, a long straight conductor perpendicular to the plane of the paper carries a current I. A bar magnet having point poles of strength q_m at its ends lies in the plane of the paper. (a) What is the magnitude and direction of the magnetic intensity $\mathbf{H}$ at point P? (b) Let the length of the magnet be 8 cm and its pole strength $q_m = 10^{-5}$ weber. Let $a = 6$ cm, $b = 5$ cm, $c = 5$ cm, and let $I = 100$ amp. Find the magnitude of the magnetic intensity $\mathbf{H}$ at point P.

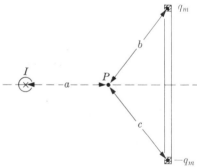

FIGURE 9–21

*9–6. A permanent magnet consists of a right circular cylinder that is uniformly magnetized like the cylinder in Fig. 9–3, but whose length l is large compared with its radius a. Calculate $\mathbf{B}$ and $\mathbf{H}$ for the following points as a function of $\mathfrak{M}$: (a) On the axis outside but very close to the surface that is positively magnetized. (b) On the axis inside but very close to the surface that

* Answers to starred problems will be found at back of book.

is positively magnetized. (c) At the center of the bar on the axis. (d) Near the center of the bar but just outside the lateral surface. (e) Use the relations governing fields on the two sides of a bounding surface to check your results.

9–7. The similarity of the magnetostatic relations with those for electrostatic phenomena suggests that a magnetic pole q_m should experience a force of $q_m\mathbf{H}$ in a magnetic field. Assume the cylinder of Fig. 9–3 placed in a uniform field with the positive direction of its axis at an angle θ to the field. Calculate the torque on the cylinder (a) from the force on the poles q_m and $-q_m$ on the end surfaces, assuming that they can be considered as concentrated at their respective centers, and (b) from the sum of the torques on the individual dipoles of the cylinder.

9–8. The magnetic field near a long straight wire coinciding with the z-axis can be written in cylindrical coordinates as $\mathbf{H} = \mathbf{a}_\phi I/2\pi r$. Place the center of the magnetized cylinder of Fig. 9–3 a distance r from the wire, where r is quite large compared with the length of the cylinder, with its axis parallel to $\mathbf{a}_\phi$. Calculate the net force on the cylinder.

*9–9. In Problems 9–7(a) and 9–8 the properties of a magnetized cylinder have been described in terms of point poles concentrated at the centers of the end surfaces. How well does such a description approximate the fields produced by this cylinder? Calculate the percent errors in using this point of view for finding $\mathbf{H}$ (a) at the center of the cylinder of Fig. 9–3 where $l = 4a$, and (b) at a point on its axis $10l$ above its top surface.

[*Note.* The description of real cylinders that are permanently magnetized in terms of two point poles is usually less accurate than it is for these uniformly magnetized cylinders. In real magnets the point poles must be considered concentrated some distance in from the ends.]

*9–10. A small cylinder of length $l = 10a$, made of alnico 5 and uniformly magnetized to 0.8 w/m², is fastened with its axis horizontal. An identical magnet constrained to remain directly above and parallel to the first magnet is caused to float in this position by the mutual repulsive forces. At what height does this magnet float if the specific gravity of alnico 5 is 7.3? With these relative dimensions of $l = 10a$, can any two alnico 5 magnets float each other regardless of their actual dimensions? If not, what is the size limitation?

*9–11. Two identical magnets like those of Problem 9–10 are placed as shown in Fig. 9–22, with $l = 2b$ and $d = nb$. Calculate the torque each exerts on the other. Express these in terms of their dipole moments p_m and the distance d.

FIGURE 9–22

*9–12. A ferromagnetic sphere of radius a is permanently magnetized uniformly in the z-direction to a magnetization $\mathfrak{M}$. Suppose this sphere to be surrounded by a mixture of very heavy oil and powdered iron whose relative permeability is $K_m \cong 5$. Further, suppose that this mixture extends to very large r's and does not affect the value of $\mathfrak{M}$ in the sphere. (a) Find the magnetic potentials and the fields inside and outside the sphere in terms of the total dipole moment $p_m = 4\pi a^3 \mathfrak{M}/3$, the K_m, and the spherical coordinates. (b) Actually, if the internal fields are altered by the presence of the permeable mixture, the value of $\mathfrak{M}$ will change. Compare the values of $\mathfrak{M}$ when the sphere is in the mixture with the $\mathfrak{M}$ when the sphere is in a vacuum, assuming that in each case the magnetization is produced by following the hysteresis loop of Fig. 9–9.

9–13. Place a small magnetized cylinder, of the kind illustrated in Fig. 9–3 but with $l = 50a$, in the permeable mixture described in Problem 9–12. Calculate potentials and fields at points where $r \gg l$, in terms of the total dipole moment $p_m = \pi a^2 l \mathfrak{M}$, the K_m, and the spherical coordinates. Can you give a physical explanation for the fields in this case having a different dependence upon K_m than they did in the case of the magnetized sphere of Problem 9–12?

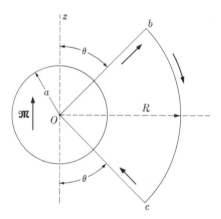

FIGURE 9–23

*9–14. A permanently magnetized sphere is shown in Fig. 9–23. Express the $\mathbf{B}$ and $\mathbf{H}$ fields inside and outside this sphere and use these expressions in calculating

$$\int \mathbf{H} \cdot d\mathbf{l} \quad \text{and} \quad \int \mathbf{B} \cdot d\mathbf{l}$$

for each portion of the closed path $ObcO$. From these parts determine the values of the closed-path line integrals

$$\oint \mathbf{H} \cdot d\mathbf{l} \quad \text{and} \quad \oint \mathbf{B} \cdot d\mathbf{l}.$$

*9–15. Suppose that small cavities have been cut out of a very large ferromagnetic material in which there is a uniform magnetization $\mathfrak{M}$ and a uniform magnetizing field $\mathbf{H}$ that is parallel to $\mathfrak{M}$. Find the fields $B_c = \mu_0 H_c$ inside cavities of the following shapes: (a) a spherical cavity of radius a, (b) a very long and thin cylindrical cavity parallel to $\mathfrak{M}$, (c) a thin disklike cavity perpendicular to $\mathfrak{M}$, and (d) a long cylindrical cavity of radius a with its axis perpendicular to $\mathfrak{M}$.

[*Note*. The cavities (b) and (c) have been imagined by many authors to illustrate the difference between the $\mathbf{H}$ and $\mathbf{B}$ fields respectively in a ferromagnetic medium.]

*9–16. Hall effect measurements on ferromagnetic materials have demonstrated that in such materials the Hall electric field must be written as $E_H = J(R_0 B + R_1 \mathfrak{M})$, where R_0 is the ordinary Hall coefficient whose magnitude is related to the numbers of the conduction carriers, and R_1 is an extraordinary coefficient which is often very large and is always temperature-dependent. Only meager progress has been made on theoretical attempts to understand R_1. To obtain reliable values for R_0, measurements of E_H versus B must be obtained at fields considerably larger than those required to saturate $\mathfrak{M}$. The slope of the E_H/J versus B curve above saturation gives R_0. Unfortunately, the fields that can be produced by electromagnets with cores of iron or other ferromagnetic materials are severely limited by the saturation of these cores. Assuming that the electromagnet produces a uniform field except in the immediate neighborhood of the small sample being measured, calculate the magnitude, B_0, of this uniform field that would be required to produce in a sample of pure iron fields that are at least 1 w/m² greater than would be required to saturate it: (a) if the sample of iron is shaped like that in Fig. 7–2, and (b) if the sample of iron is in the form of a circular cylinder of length l and diameter w whose axis coincides with the x-axis in Fig. 7–2. (c) Discuss the advantages and disadvantages of using samples of the cylindrical rather than the conventional shape.

*9–17. The horizontal component B_H of the earth's magnetic field can be determined with a compass and a magnetized sphere. This experiment, devised years ago, also determines the magnetic moment $P_m = 4\pi a^3 \mathfrak{M}/3$ of the sphere. Place the origin of coordinates at the point where B_H is to be determined, with the x-axis parallel to B_H. The compass needle placed at the origin will point parallel to the x-axis. Place the center of the magnetized sphere on the y-axis at $y = l$ and orient it so that it produces the largest possible deflection θ of the compass.

(a) Calculate the ratio $\mathfrak{R} = P_m/B_H$ in terms of θ and l. (b) Remove the compass and suspend the sphere by a torsionless thread with its center at the origin. A very small angular twist from its equilibrium position will cause the sphere to oscillate in the earth's field with a frequency f that can be measured. Calculate the product $\mathfrak{P} = P_m B_H$ in terms of f, a, and m, where m is the mass of the sphere. Calculate B_H, P_m, and $\mathfrak{M}$ from the equations obtained in (a) and (b), in terms of $\mathfrak{R}$ and $\mathfrak{P}$.

9–18. (a) Use the fields calculated in Problems 9–12(a) and 9–13 for spherical and cylindrical permanent magnets to determine the torque on a small permanent magnet of dipole moment p_t placed at a general point in a spherical coordinate system. Assume that the axis of the small dipole makes an angle

α with the magnetic field in each case. (b) Compare the torques produced by these two shapes of magnet when $K_m > 1$ with those produced when $K_m = 1$.

*9–19. (a) Use the fields calculated in Problems 9–12(a) and 9–13 for spherical and cylindrical permanent magnets to determine the torque on a small circular loop of wire carrying a current I such that its dipole moment is $p_t = \mu_0 I A$, where A is the area enclosed by the circular loop. Place the current loop with its center at a general point in the spherical coordinate system and with its axis making an angle α with the magnetic field at this point. Compare the torques calculated here with the torques on a test magnet calculated in Problem 9–18.

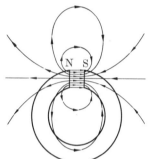

FIGURE 9–24   FIGURE 9–25

9–20. (a) A Rowland ring, shown in Fig. 9–24, has a cross section of 2 cm^2, a mean length of 30 cm, and is wound with 400 turns. Find the current in the winding that is required to set up a flux density of 0.1 w/m^2 in the ring, (1) if the ring is of annealed iron (Table 9–5), (2) if the ring is of silicon steel (Table 9–6). (3) Repeat the computations above if a flux density of 1.2 w/m^2 is desired. (b) Find the current required to establish a flux of 4×10^{-4} weber in the ring if it is of silicon steel. (c) Compute the flux in the ring if the current in the windings is 6 amp.

*9–21. The hysteresis loop of the iron that is formed into a toroid is shown in Fig. 9–9. The surface of the iron has the shape that would be swept out by a circle of small radius a as it moved perpendicular to its plane with its center on a larger circle of radius $r_c > 20a$. An air gap like that shown in Fig. 9–25 is produced in this toroid by sawing out a nearly cylindrical rod of iron of radius a and length $l = 2a$. Assume that the iron is given a uniform magnetization $\mathfrak{M}_i$ parallel to the large circle. Although the iron removed from the toroid cannot be a true cylinder, it may be assumed to be cylindrical for the calculations that follow. Calculate the values of $\mu_0 H$ and B in terms of $\mathfrak{M}_i$ and a at the following points on the large circle: (a) in the middle of the air gap, (b) at one end of the air gap in the air, (c) at the same end of the air gap but just inside the iron, and (d) at a point diametrically opposite the center of the air gap.

9–22. The air gap in the iron toroid described in Problem 9–21 is filled with nickel that saturates in relatively weak fields at $\mathfrak{M}_n = 0.6$ w/m^2. Assuming that the iron is uniformly magnetized, as in Problem 9–21, to $\mathfrak{M}_i = 1.3$ w/m^2,

TABLE 9-5

MAGNETIC PROPERTIES OF ANNEALED IRON

Magnetic intensity	Flux density	Permeability	Magnetization	Relative permeability
H, amp·turns / meter	B, webers / m^2	$\mu = B/H$, henries / meter	$\mathfrak{M} = B - \mu_0 H$, webers / m^2	$K_m = \mu/\mu_0$
0	0	$3{,}100 \times 10^{-7}$	0	250
10	0.0042	4,200	0.0042	330
20	0.010	5,000	0.010	400
40	0.028	7,000	0.028	560
50	0.043	8,600	0.043	680
60	0.095	16,000	0.095	1270
80	0.45	56,000	0.45	4500
100	0.67	67,000	0.67	5300
150	1.01	67,500	1.01	5350
200	1.18	59,000	1.18	4700
500	1.44	28,800	1.44	2300
1,000	1.58	15,800	1.58	1250
10,000	1.72	1,720	1.71	137
100,000	2.26	226	2.13	18
800,000	3.15	39	2.15	3.1

TABLE 9-6

MAGNETIC PROPERTIES OF SILICON STEEL

Magnetic intensity H, amp·turns / meter	Flux density B, webers / m^2
0	0
10	0.050
20	0.15
40	0.43
50	0.54
60	0.62
80	0.74
100	0.83
150	0.98
200	1.07
500	1.27
1,000	1.34
10,000	1.65
100,000	2.02
800,000	2.92

calculate the fields B and $\mu_0 H$ at the points on the large circle specified in (a), (b), (c), and (d) of that problem.

*9–23. A region can be partially shielded from external magnetic fields by surrounding it with a sufficient thickness of high-permeability ferromagnetic material. To determine the effectiveness of such shielding, calculate the field B_i inside a hollow ferromagnetic cylinder when there is an external field B_0 perpendicular to the cylindrical axis. The internal and external radii of the cylinder are a and b respectively and the length of the cylinder is very large compared with either a or b. The relative permeability of the shield is K_m, which may be only 10^3 but can be as large as 10^5 in some new materials, especially in weak fields. This problem can be modified by assuming a hollow sphere instead of a hollow cylinder. The resulting fields have values that do not differ very much from those in the cylinder.

FIGURE 9–26

9–24. The shape and dimensions of the large magnet constructed for the Carnegie Tech cyclotron are shown in Fig. 9–26. The two pole pieces are round and both have the maximum diameter of 164 in. The remainder of the magnetic circuit is made up of rectangular sections whose dimensions perpendicular to the diagram are each 208.7 in. The purest iron available in these sizes, whose magnetic properties are close to those given in Table 9–5, was used. During operation the field at the center is 2.050 w/m² and this falls off linearly with radius to 1.970 w/m² at the radial distance 68.4 in., whence it falls rapidly to zero at 72 in. The coils, which are made of oil-cooled copper straps, are connected in series and carry 21,000 amp. (a) Estimate the total ampere-turns and the number of turns required for this magnet. (b) Assuming that only 10% of the space in the coils is required for insulation and cooling oil, estimate the cross section of the copper straps. (c) What voltage and what power are required for the magnetization?

FIGURE 9-27

*9-25. The two toroids, sections of which are shown in Fig. 9-27, are single-layer compact windings that share the same circle of centers, with the radius r_c. Assume that the small solenoid is wound on a core of the special ferromagnetic alloy *perminvar*, for which $\mu \cong 300\,\mu_0$. Further assume that the radii a and b of the two coils are related by $b^2 = 2a^2$ and that the circle passing through their centers has the radius $r_c \gg b$. (a) Calculate the self-inductances of the two coils, L_a and L_b, and their mutual inductance, M. (b) Calculate L_a, L_b, and M for a situation in which the perminvar fills all the space inside the large as well as the small solenoid.

9-26. Suppose that a current I is sent through the two solenoids of Problem 9-25, which are connected in series aiding. Calculate the electromagnetic energy (a) with the perminvar inside the small solenoid only, and (b) with the perminvar filling all the space inside both the large and small solenoids.

CHAPTER 10

ALTERNATING CURRENTS

Electric currents that oscillate sinusoidally play an important role in modern society. Oscillating currents in homes range from 60 cycles/sec for lights, clocks, washers, and similar appliances to 10^8 cycles/sec for short-wave radio and television. The range of frequencies utilized in military and commercial applications is even broader.

Because of the time dependence of alternating currents, the simple procedures for solving problems involving steady currents are not directly applicable. For example, in the derivation of Kirchhoff's law for junctions, Eq. (6–15), the time derivative in the conservation of charge relation

$$\int_s \mathbf{J} \cdot d\mathbf{s} = - \int_\tau \frac{\partial \rho}{\partial t} \, d\tau$$

was set equal to zero. This is not permissible with alternating currents. Furthermore, in demonstrating Kirchhoff's law for closed circuits, as stated in Eq. (6–16), the electric field was assumed to be conservative, a condition that applies only where $\nabla \times \mathbf{E} = 0$. However, by Maxwell's third relation, $\nabla \times \mathbf{E} = -\dot{\mathbf{B}}$, and $\mathbf{E}$ can be conservative only where $\mathbf{B}$ is independent of time. This can be true only if the current densities are independent of time.

As should be expected, the difficulties encountered in solving network problems increase with increasing frequencies of the oscillations. The disturbing effect of the $\partial \rho / \partial t$ term depends upon the capacitances in the network, and the disturbing effect of the $\dot{\mathbf{B}}$ term depends considerably upon the inductances. Neither of these terms becomes important in simple resistor circuits until fairly high frequencies are reached. However, most circuits utilizing alternating currents employ devices specifically designed to enhance the effect of the $\partial \rho / \partial t$ and $\dot{\mathbf{B}}$ terms. These are called capacitors and inductors, respectively. When these are included in a network, it is necessary to modify the simple techniques used with steady currents even at low frequencies.

A network containing resistors, inductors, and capacitors will be treated as though it contains a number of what are called "series elements," which are defined to consist of a resistor, a capacitor, and an inductor connected in series between two junctions. Since most of the inductance in such an element is in the inductor, all of the inductance L will be considered concentrated in this device. Likewise, the capacitance can be considered to be concentrated in the capacitor. The total resistance of the element, including that of the inductor and of the capacitor, can be considered as concentrated in the resistor.

10–1 Differential equation for an a-c series element. Development of new laws governing a-c networks requires the determination of relationships between potential differences and currents in a single series element like that shown in Fig. 10–1. If all collections of charges are assumed to be negligible except across the capacitor, then currents in R and L at each instant are the same and are equal to $i = dq/dt$. Furthermore, the charge on the left plate of the capacitor is $q = q(t)$ and the charge on the right plate is just $-q$, so that the charge leaving the right plate produces the same current i directed toward the junction b. The time-dependent potential difference across C is $v_C = q/C$ and the potential difference across R is just $v_R = iR = R(dq/dt)$. While it is practically impossible to make an inductor with zero or even negligible resistance, no error is introduced by assuming such a device, provided its actual resistance is included in R. The potential difference across a pure inductor is

$$v_L = L\frac{di}{dt} = L\frac{d^2q}{dt^2}.$$

Assuming that all magnetic field effects due to changing currents are lumped into the inductor, these three potential differences can be added to give the potential difference across the series element,

$$v = v_L + v_R + v_C.$$

This can be written as a differential equation:

$$L\frac{d^2q}{dt^2} + R\frac{dq}{dt} + \frac{q}{C} = v(t). \tag{10–1}$$

Because multiple frequencies associated with nonsinusoidal oscillations tend to introduce undesired power losses in many circuits, alternating currents are usually produced to be as nearly sinusoidal as possible. Also, nonsinusoidal oscillations may be treated as sums of sinusoidal oscillations of different frequencies. For these reasons, the potential difference between a and b in Fig. 10–1 will be assumed to have the form

$$v(t) = V_m \cos \omega t, \tag{10–2}$$

where $\omega = 2\pi f$ and f is the frequency of the oscillations in cycles/sec.

Fɪɢ. 10–1. A series element, basic for all a-c networks, containing inductance L, resistance R, and capacitance C.

Substitution of Eq. (10–2) into Eq. (10–1) gives a simple differential equation which may be solved readily in terms of real quantities. However, later work in a-c circuits will be greatly facilitated by the use of complex quantities; in particular, they will aid the development of graphic and analytic solutions discussed in Section 10–5. The shift to complex notation will therefore be made immediately. Equation (10–2) becomes

$$\mathcal{V}(t) = V_m \,(\cos \omega t + j \sin \omega t) = V_m e^{j\omega t},$$

where $v(t)$ is just the real part of $\mathcal{V}(t)$, and Eq. (10–1) becomes

$$L \frac{d^2 \mathcal{Q}}{dt^2} + R \frac{d\mathcal{Q}}{dt} + \frac{\mathcal{Q}}{C} = \mathcal{V}(t), \qquad (10\text{–}3)$$

where q is the real part of $\mathcal{Q}$.

It can be readily verified that the derivative of a complex number is the sum of the derivatives of the real and imaginary parts, that the integral is the sum of the integrals of the real and imaginary parts, and that the sum of complex numbers is the sum of the real parts plus the sum of the imaginary parts. However, as is shown in Section 4–6, the process of multiplying one complex quantity by another does not provide a simple product of the original real quantities separated from the imaginary quantities. For this reason, complex quantities are not used in Section 10–3 for calculating a-c power.

10–2 Solution of the differential equation with complex variables. Equation (10–3) is an ordinary second-order differential equation with constant coefficients. The general solution for it is the sum of two functions: $\mathcal{Q}_c$, the general solution for Eq. (10–3) with $\mathcal{V}(t) = 0$; and $\mathcal{Q}_p$, some particular integral that satisfies Eq. (10–3) as it is written.

Complementary function. It will now be shown that the first function, called the complementary function, determines the transient phenomena in the series element. The nature of the transient and its rate of decay is determined by the ratio of R to the geometric average of the other two constants, L and $1/C$. It is oscillatory when R is small and monotonic when R is large. The complementary function is found by substituting $\mathcal{Q} = e^{\mathfrak{D}t}$ into Eq. (10–3), with $\mathcal{V}(t) = 0$, to obtain

$$L\mathfrak{D}^2 + R\mathfrak{D} + \frac{1}{C} = 0.$$

The solutions of this quadratic equation in $\mathfrak{D}$ are given by

$$\mathfrak{D} = -\frac{R}{2L} \pm \sqrt{\left(\frac{R}{2L}\right)^2 - \frac{1}{LC}}.$$

When $R/2 > \sqrt{L/C}$, the two solutions can be written as

$$D_1 = -\alpha + \gamma$$

and

$$D_2 = -\alpha - \gamma,$$

where

$$\alpha = \frac{R}{2L} \quad \text{and} \quad \gamma = \sqrt{\left(\frac{R}{2L}\right)^2 - \frac{1}{LC}}.$$

Both terms are real, and $\alpha > \gamma$. When, however, $R/2 < \sqrt{L/C}$, the two solutions can be written as

$$\mathfrak{D}_1 = -\alpha + j\beta$$

and

$$\mathfrak{D}_2 = -\alpha - j\beta,$$

where

$$\beta = \sqrt{\frac{1}{LC} - \left(\frac{R}{2L}\right)^2}$$

is also real.

For large resistances, then, the complementary function is real and can be written as

$$\mathfrak{Q}_C = q_C = Ae^{D_1 t} + Be^{D_2 t}, \tag{10-4}$$

which decays monotonically because both D_1 and D_2 are negative real numbers. For small resistances, the complementary function can be written as

$$\mathfrak{Q}_C = e^{-\alpha t}(\mathfrak{G}_1 e^{-j\beta t} + \mathfrak{G}_2 e^{+j\beta t}).$$

By choosing $\mathfrak{G}_1 = a + jb$ and $\mathfrak{G}_2 = \mathfrak{G}_1^* = a - jb$, this can be transformed into an all real function. Remembering that $e^{j\beta t} = \cos \beta t + j \sin \beta t$ and that $\cos (\beta t - \delta) = \cos \delta \cos \beta t + \sin \delta \sin \beta t$, we can write this function as

$$\mathfrak{Q}_C = q_c = Ke^{-\alpha t} \cos (\beta t - \delta), \tag{10-5}$$

where $K = 2\sqrt{a^2 + b^2}$ and $\delta = \tan^{-1}(b/a)$ are two new arbitrary constants which are real. Actually, Eq. (10-5) could have been assumed directly and then checked to show that it satisfies Eq. (10-3) when the right side is zero. Equation (10-5) is an oscillatory function whose amplitude decays with time.

The arbitrary constants A and B for large resistances or K and δ for small resistances are determined from the initial conditions, that is, from the values of q and dq/dt at $t = 0$. When $v(t)$ is a sinusoidal potential difference determined by an a-c generator, the values of the arbitrary constants are determined by the phase at which the generator is connected or disconnected. If desired, the effects produced by these transients can be minimized by making the changes at predetermined phases. For example, devices have been invented to interrupt large alternating currents at the instant these currents pass through zero, to avoid the disastrous arcs that otherwise would form.

It should be noted that while the solutions obtained thus far apply specifically to the series element shown in Fig. 10–1, the form of the function $v(t)$ has not been specified. These solutions will thus determine the transient currents in such a series element whether the source of potential difference produces sinusoidal potentials, steady potentials, or any other time-dependent potentials.

The rate of decay of these transient terms is important in most applications. With $R/2 > \sqrt{L/C}$, the second term in Eq. (10–3) decays first, since $D_2 = -(\alpha + \gamma)$ is always more negative than $D_1 = -(\alpha - \gamma)$. When $R/2 \gg \sqrt{L/C}$, the first term decays very slowly, but as $R/2 \to \sqrt{L/C}$ the rate of decay approaches $e^{-Rt/2L} = e^{-t/\sqrt{LC}}$, which gives the maximum rate of monotonic decay. With $R/2 < \sqrt{L/C}$, the transient is an oscillation whose amplitude is proportional to $e^{-Rt/2L}$. The transient oscillations continue for a long time with small resistances, but with $R/2 \to \sqrt{L/C}$ the amplitudes approach the decay rate $e^{-t/\sqrt{LC}}$. The most rapid rate of decay is then $e^{-t/\sqrt{LC}}$, when $R/2 = \sqrt{L/C}$, which is called the *critical damping* condition. It is easily shown that as this relation is approached the two forms of the solution, Eqs. (10–4) and (10–5), each approach the relation $Q_C = (F + Gt)e^{-\alpha t}$, which is the solution when the two roots of the quadratic equation in $\mathfrak{D}$ are equal. Figure 10–2 shows the transient time variations in the charge on the capacitor of Fig. 10–1 for the three characteristic damping conditions, namely, (1) overdamped with $R/2 > \sqrt{L/C}$, (2) underdamped with $R/2 < \sqrt{L/C}$, and (3) critically damped with $R/2 = \sqrt{L/C}$.

The complete solution of Eq. (10–3) is

$$Q = Q_C + Q',$$

where Q', the particular integral, is any function that satisfies Eq. (10–3) as it is written. In many a-c networks the transients decay so rapidly that they can be ignored. The particular integral, which determines the quasi steady-state relations, then becomes the more important term.

Particular integral. Assuming that the potential difference impressed across the series element in Fig. 10–1 is the real part of $V_m e^{j\omega t}$, the particular integral of Eq. (10–3) can be obtained by assuming $Q' = \mathfrak{B}e^{j\omega t}$, where $\mathfrak{B}$ is a constant that may need to be complex to provide for a possible difference in phase angle between the oscillating charge and the oscillating potential difference. The effect of a complex $\mathfrak{B}$ on the phase may be seen by writing $\mathfrak{B} = Be^{j\beta}$, so that $\mathfrak{B}e^{j\omega t} = Be^{j(\omega t + \beta)}$.

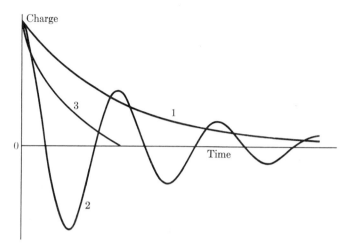

Fig. 10–2. Transient time variations in the charge on a capacitor in a series element for the three characteristic damping conditions: (1) overdamped with $R/2 > \sqrt{L/C}$, (2) underdamped with $R/2 < \sqrt{L/C}$, and (3) critically damped with $R/2 = \sqrt{L/C}$.

Direct substitution into Eq. (10–3) gives

$$\mathfrak{R}j\omega e^{j\omega t}\left[R + j\left(\omega L - \frac{1}{\omega C}\right)\right] = V_m e^{j\omega t}. \tag{10–6}$$

Impedance and reactance. The term in brackets can be written as

$$R + j\left(\omega L - \frac{1}{\omega C}\right) = \mathsf{Z} = Z e^{j\theta}, \tag{10–7}$$

where by definition Z is the *complex impedance* and Z is the *real impedance.* The phase angle θ will be more definitely defined soon. By writing time-dependent current in all portions of the series element as the real part of $\mathfrak{s}' = d\mathfrak{Q}'/dt = \mathfrak{R}j\omega e^{j\omega t}$ and the time-dependent potential difference as the real part of $\mathcal{U}' = V_m e^{j\omega t}$, Eq. (10–6) can be written as

$$\mathfrak{s}'\mathsf{Z} = \mathcal{U}'. \tag{10–8}$$

Equation (10–8) is like the d-c Ohm's law relation $IR = V$, although with a-c each term is complex. The symbols $\mathcal{U}'$ and $\mathfrak{s}'$, whose real parts represent steady sinusoidal oscillations, are primed here to save the unprimed symbols $\mathcal{U}$ and $\mathfrak{s}$ for some time-independent quantities that will be introduced later for network calculations. The fact that Z is, in general, complex means that $\mathfrak{s}'$ is seldom in phase with $\mathcal{U}'$; that is, the time-dependent potential difference and current reach their maxima at different times.

10–3 Steady a-c in a series element. Steady alternating currents in networks are so important that the calculation procedures should be simplified as much as possible. The absolute magnitude of the impedance and the phase relations between the current and voltage can be understood more easily if we write

$$\mathbf{Z} = R + jX = Ze^{j\theta},$$

where

$$Z = \sqrt{R^2 + X^2}, \qquad \theta = \tan^{-1}\frac{X}{R}, \qquad X = \omega L - \frac{1}{\omega C}.$$

The relationships among these quantities are graphically presented in the so-called "impedance triangle" of Fig. 10–3. Here Z is the absolute magnitude of the impedance and θ is the phase angle by which the current maximum lags the voltage maximum. The quantity X is defined as the *reactance* of the series element and can be written as $X = X_L - X_C$, where $X_L = \omega L$ and $X_C = 1/\omega C$ are called the *inductive reactance* and the *capacitive reactance* respectively.

Equation (10–6) can be written as

$$\mathscr{I}' = \frac{V_m}{Z} e^{j(\omega t - \theta)},$$

and since the real part of this complex expression gives the time-dependent values of the actual current,

$$i = \frac{V_m}{Z} \cos(\omega t - \theta).$$

The maximum current in this element is $I_m = V_m/Z$, which shows that the maximum values of current and voltage also obey an Ohm's law type of relation.

Power absorption in a-c series elements. The power being absorbed at any instant by a series element is the product of the instantaneous current

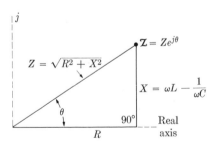

Fig. 10–3. Impedance triangle plotted in a complex plane for a typical series element, in which the magnitudes R, L, and C are lumped into separate devices.

and the instantaneous difference of potential. Since it is the product of the real current and the real voltage that is involved, the product of the complex quantities cannot be used. The time-dependent power absorbed is then

$$p = vi = V_m I_m \cos \omega t \cos (\omega t - \theta),$$

which shows that the element may alternately absorb and emit power to the rest of the circuit to which it is connected. To determine the net power P absorbed by the element, the time average of p must be obtained. Setting $\beta = \omega t$ and $\omega T = 2\pi$, where T is the period of oscillation, we obtain

$$P = \frac{1}{T} \int_0^T p \, dt = \frac{1}{2\pi} \int_0^{2\pi} p \, d\beta$$

and

$$P = \frac{V_m I_m}{2\pi} \left[\cos \theta \int_0^{2\pi} \cos^2 \beta \, d\beta + \sin \theta \int_0^{2\pi} \cos \beta \sin \beta \, d\beta \right].$$

The value of the first integral is π and that of the second is zero. Hence

$$P = \frac{V_m I_m \cos \theta}{2}. \tag{10–9}$$

In its early development, alternating current was used chiefly for lighting, where the incandescent lamp filaments produced elements with nearly pure resistance. In these elements, $X = 0$, $\cos \theta = 1$, and Eq. (10–9) can be written as

$$P_R = \frac{I_m^2 R}{2} \quad \text{or} \quad P_R = \frac{V_m^2}{2R}.$$

When these same filaments were used with d-c, the power was given by

$$P = I^2 R \quad \text{or} \quad P = \frac{V^2}{R}.$$

It was therefore decided to define an "effective current" and an "effective voltage" for a-c networks as $I = I_m/\sqrt{2}$ and $V = V_m/\sqrt{2}$ respectively. These definitions have proved so useful that a-c ammeters and voltmeters are still calibrated to read these "effective" or "root-mean-square" values. It should be noted that this decision made it possible to make filament bulbs whose brightness on 110 volt a-c was identical with their brightness on 110 volt d-c. Equation (10–9) can then be written as

$$P = VI \cos \theta, \tag{10–10}$$

where $\cos \theta$ is called the *power factor*.

Alternating-current resistance. From the impedance triangle of Fig. 10–3, it can be seen that Eq. (10–10) can be written as $P = I^2R$, which shows that all the power absorbed by a simple series element is absorbed in the resistance. However, as will be shown in Section 10–9, nearby circuits may react upon a primary circuit to absorb power from it. In fact, nearby magnetic or conducting materials may absorb power in a similar fashion. This means that circuits measured with a-c often exhibit greater resistance than do the same circuits when measured with d-c. Resistance to a-c is defined by the relation

$$R_{a\text{-}c} = \frac{P}{I^2},$$

which is the resistance that must be used, instead of the d-c resistance, for all a-c network problems. The R in a-c circuit problems must always be understood to mean $R_{a\text{-}c}$, which can be measured with a wattmeter and an ammeter.

10–4 Kirchhoff's laws for a-c networks. By considering each series element to have localized inductance, capacitance, and resistance, Kirchhoff's two laws can be used with small modifications for the time-dependent quantities associated with low-frequency alternating currents. The modified laws are remarkably accurate up to and often beyond 1000 cycles/sec, depending upon the properties of the circuits. The expression "alternating currents," or just a-c, is sufficiently descriptive to distinguish the phenomena in this range of frequencies from those usually designated by "high frequency," where more sophisticated techniques must be employed.

Junctions in a-c networks. Kirchhoff's first law states that the algebraic sum of the steady currents out of any junction is zero. So long as the frequencies are not too high, this law can be extended to the time-dependent values of alternating currents out of any junction; that is,

$$\sum_i i_i(t) = 0.$$

When the time-dependencies of these current functions are sinusoidal, complex variables $\mathcal{I}_i'(t)$ can be chosen whose real parts are equal to these real currents, so that

$$\sum_i \mathcal{I}_i'(t) = 0. \tag{10–11}$$

The usefulness of such complex expressions can be seen from Fig. 10–4, where the currents out of a grounded junction in a balanced three-phase network are shown. The three resistors are identical, and the potential differences between the three power lines and the ground are identical

(a)

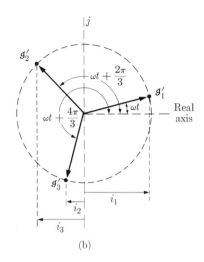

(b)

Fig. 10-4.   (a) A three-phase network connected through three identical resistors to a neutral junction which is connected to ground.   (b) A time-dependent plot in the complex plane of the three currents out of the junction. With the currents in each phase having the same maximum I_m, which is the length of each vector, the algebraic sum of the time-dependent currents $i_1 + i_2 + i_3 = 0$ at every instant and there is no current in the ground connection.

in magnitude but differ in phase.   The currents i_1, i_2, and i_3 in the three resistors are given by the real parts of $\mathcal{I}_1' = I_m e^{j\omega t}$, $\mathcal{I}_2' = I_m e^{j(\omega t + 2\pi/3)}$, $\mathcal{I}_3' = I_m e^{j(\omega t + 4\pi/3)}$ respectively.   Now

$$\mathcal{I}_1' + \mathcal{I}_2' + \mathcal{I}_3' = I_m e^{j\omega t}[e^{j0} + e^{j(2\pi/3)} + e^{j(4\pi/3)}],$$

but the terms in brackets can be written as $1 + (-0.5 + j0.866) + (-0.5 - j0.866) = 0$, which by Eq. (10-8) gives $\mathcal{I}_1' + \mathcal{I}_2' + \mathcal{I}_3' + \mathcal{I}_g' = 0$, if the current in the ground connection is defined as the real part of $\mathcal{I}_g'$. However, $\mathcal{I}_1' + \mathcal{I}_2' + \mathcal{I}_3' = 0$, so that $\mathcal{I}_g' = 0$ and there is no current in the ground connection.

In the diagram of Fig. 10-4(b) the three vectors should be visualized as each rotating about the origin with the constant angular velocity ω rad/sec and thus maintaining their angular separations of 120°.   The projections of these rotating vectors on the horizontal or real axis at any instant gives the currents in the corresponding resistors at that instant. The algebraic sum of these instantaneous currents is always zero because the vector sum of the three vectors is zero.

Provided all the currents in a network have the same frequency, the currents out of any junction can be represented by a vector diagram like that in Fig. 10-4(b), where the vector sum $\sum_i \mathcal{I}_i' = 0$.   The vectors representing currents out of such junctions can be written as $\mathcal{I}'_i = I_{mi}e^{j(\omega t+\theta_i)}$, but the necessity for visualizing all vectors as rotating tends to confuse the relationships between the vectors. The time-dependence is usually eliminated from these vector diagrams by defining time-independent vectors by

$$\mathcal{I}_i = \frac{\mathcal{I}'_i e^{-j\omega t}}{\sqrt{2}} = \frac{I_{mi}}{\sqrt{2}} e^{j\theta_i} = I_i e^{j\theta_i}, \qquad (10\text{--}12)$$

where I_i is the effective value of the ith current. Equation (10–11) then becomes

$$\sum_i \mathcal{I}_i = 0, \qquad (10\text{--}13)$$

which is the time-independent form of Kirchhoff's junction law that is generally used in a-c circuit problems. With this modification, the vector diagram of Fig. 10–4(b) can be drawn as shown in Fig. 10–5(a), where the absolute magnitudes of the vectors represent the effective currents and the angles between the vectors provide the phase angles. *The absolute orientation of such a diagram is entirely arbitrary, and the horizontal components (the real values) have no physical meaning whatsoever.* The vector sum of the vectors shown in Fig. 10–5(a) can be exhibited somewhat more clearly by drawing the vectors head to tail, as shown in Fig. 10–5(b). When such a figure fails to close, the vector sum is the vector distance from the tail of the first to the head of the last. The figure is purposely drawn to show a finite sum which is the negative of $\mathcal{I}_g$, although $\mathcal{I}_g = 0$ in the problem illustrated.

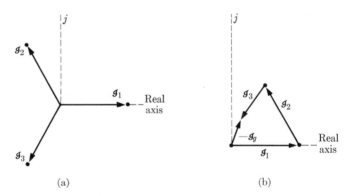

(a)   (b)

FIG. 10–5.   (a) Time-independent vector diagram representing the three currents out of the grounded junction of Fig. 10–4(a). Effective or root-mean-square currents are represented by the lengths of the vectors. (b) The same vectors are plotted to more clearly represent the vector sum $\mathcal{I}_1 + \mathcal{I}_2 + \mathcal{I}_3$, which is here shown to equal a finite $\mathcal{I}_g$, although $\mathcal{I}_g = 0$ in the problem being illustrated.

Closed loops in a-c networks. Kirchhoff's second law for networks of steady currents states that the algebraic sum of the voltage drops around any closed loop equals the algebraic sum of the emf's encountered in traversing that loop. With the inductances concentrated in inductors and with these relatively low frequencies, this law also holds for the time-dependent quantities and can be written as

$$\sum_j v_j(t) = \sum_j e_j(t).$$

Following the procedure used with the current equation, complex functions $\mathcal{G}'_j Z_j$ and $\mathcal{E}'_j$ can be chosen so that their real parts equal v_j and e_j respectively. The foregoing equation then is included in the relation

$$\sum_j \mathcal{G}'_j Z_j = \sum_j \mathcal{E}'_j. \tag{10–14}$$

Still following the procedure used with the current relations, a new complex quantity can be defined as

$$\mathcal{E}_j = \mathcal{E}'_j \frac{e^{-j\omega t}}{\sqrt{2}}.$$

The substitution of this and the current relation into Eq. (10–14) gives

$$\sum_j \mathcal{G}_i Z_i = \sum_j \mathcal{E}_j, \tag{10–15}$$

which is the time-independent form of Kirchhoff's second law for a-c circuits that is usually used.

The significance of Eqs. (10–14) and (10–15) can be demonstrated and a better understanding of Eqs. (10–7) and (10–8) can be obtained by considering the series element of Fig. 10–1. The vector diagrams in Fig. 10–6 are drawn on the assumptions that the potential difference across this element is $\mathcal{V}' = V_m e^{j\omega t}$ and that the current through the inductor, capacitor, and resistor is $\mathcal{G}' = I_m e^{j(\omega t - \theta)}$. Since the complex impedances are $Z_R = R$, $Z_L = jX_L$, and $Z_C = -jX_C$, the time-dependent potential differences are the real parts of

$$\mathcal{V}'_R = \mathcal{G}' R = I_m R e^{j(\omega t - \theta)},$$

$$\mathcal{V}'_L = \mathcal{G}' j X_L = I_m X_L j e^{j(\omega t - \theta)},$$

and

$$\mathcal{V}'_C = -\mathcal{G}' j X_C = -I_m X_C j e^{j(\omega t - \theta)},$$

respectively, and these are plotted in Fig. 10–6(a). The corresponding

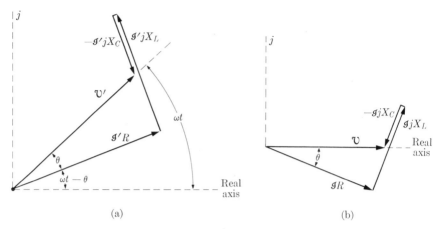

(a)   (b)

FIG. 10–6. Vector diagrams for the potential differences in the series element of Fig. 10–1. In (a) the vectors have lengths corresponding to the maximum potential differences and the projections on the real axis give the true time-dependent values. In (b) the vectors have lengths corresponding to root-mean-square values.

time-independent vectors, which are plotted in Fig. 10–6(b), are

$$\mathcal{V}_R = RIe^{-j\theta}, \quad \mathcal{V}_L = X_L Ije^{-j\theta}, \quad \text{and} \quad \mathcal{V}_C = -X_C Ije^{-j\theta}.$$

They are shorter by the factor $1/\sqrt{2}$ than the time-dependent vectors. In Fig. 10–6(b) all phase angles are related to the phase of the potential difference, which is chosen as the reference vector and is plotted along the real axis, making $\mathcal{V} = V$ and $\mathcal{I} = Ie^{-j\theta}$. If the current had been chosen as the reference vector, the whole diagram would merely have been rotated counterclockwise through the angle θ with $\mathcal{V} = Ve^{j\theta}$ and $\mathcal{I} = I$.

10–5 Admittance, conductance, and susceptance. In solving network problems certain expressions occur so frequently that they have been given special names.

Admittance. The reciprocal of the complex impedance occurs so frequently that it has been named *admittance*. It is defined by

$$\mathcal{Y} = \frac{1}{Z}.$$

Since $\mathcal{Y}$ is a complex quantity, it can be written

$$\mathcal{Y} = G - jB,$$

from which the quantities G and B have been named the *conductance* and the *susceptance* respectively.

Conductance and susceptance. For the typical series element of Fig. 10–1, the conductance is

$$G = \frac{R}{Z^2}$$

and the susceptance is

$$B = \frac{X}{Z^2}.$$

While admittance is a complex number, whose absolute magnitude is

$$|\mathcal{Y}| = \frac{1}{Z},$$

both conductance and susceptance are real quantities. All three quantities have the unit 1/ohm, which is often called the mho. Note that the conductance is the reciprocal of the resistance only when $X = 0$, and the susceptance is the reciprocal of the reactance only when $R = 0$.

10–6 Analytical and graphical solutions of a-c network problems. Equations (10–13) and (10–15) show that a-c network problems can be treated analytically by the methods developed for solving d-c network problems, provided the complex quantities developed in the previous sections are used. Figures 10–5 and 10–6(b) show that the analytical equations with complex quantities can be represented by diagrams in a complex plane. Solutions can thus be obtained graphically as well as analytically. In graphical solutions, effective currents and effective voltages are treated as simple vector quantities and their complex nature is usually ignored. In both the graphical and the analytical solutions, the lengths of the vectors are determined from the effective rather than the maximum values because effective values are obtained directly from the measuring instruments. Using these simple time-independent complex relations, solutions can be obtained for a-c network problems without resorting to the cumbersome time-dependent forms.

Effective impedance. Whenever a group of elements like that in Fig. 10–1 are connected into a network with just two external terminals, the network can be treated as a single series element with some effective impedance. The treatment is essentially the same as that for a d-c network of resistors. Networks that can be divided into groups of elements all in series or all in parallel are relatively simple to calculate.

When the complex impedances $\mathcal{Z}_1$, $\mathcal{Z}_2$, $\mathcal{Z}_3$, etc. are all connected in series, the complex current $\mathcal{I}$ will be the same in all elements, and the complex potential difference across the group will be

$$\mathcal{V}_s = \sum_i \mathcal{I}\mathcal{Z}_i = \mathcal{I}\left(\sum_i R_i + j\sum_i X_i\right).$$

The complex impedance Z_s of elements in series is then

$$Z_s = \sum_i Z_i = \sum_i R_i + j \sum_i X_i. \qquad (10\text{--}16)$$

When such elements are all connected in parallel, the complex potential difference $\mathcal{V}$ across the group is the potential difference across each one, but the complex current through the group is given by

$$\mathcal{I}_p = \sum_i \mathcal{I}_i = \sum_i \frac{\mathcal{V}}{Z_i} = \frac{\mathcal{V}}{Z_p}.$$

The complex impedance Z_p of elements in parallel is given by

$$\frac{1}{Z_p} = \sum_i \frac{1}{Z_i}. \qquad (10\text{--}17)$$

Resonance. A simple series element consisting of some resistance, inductance, and capacitance is resonant (i.e., has minimum impedance) for the case when X_C and X_L are equal. The total series impedance is then given by

$$Z_s = R + j(X_L - X_C) = R.$$

Because $X_C = 1/2\pi f C$ and $X_L = 2\pi f L$, a circuit is resonant only at the frequency expressed by

$$f_r = \frac{1}{2\pi\sqrt{LC}}.$$

Such circuits can be tuned to particular frequencies by varying either the capacitance or the inductance.

A different type of resonant circuit is produced by connecting a capacitor in parallel with an inductor, as shown in Fig. 10–7. The resonant frequency for such parallel circuits depends upon the resistance as well as upon the inductance and capacitance. Whenever the resistance is small enough to be neglected, the resonant frequency is given by $f = 1/2\pi\sqrt{L/C}$ as in the series circuit. A good capacitor usually has negligible resistance, and inductors for resonant circuits are constructed to have as low resistance as possible. The ratio $Q = X_L/R_L$ is taken as one measure of the quality of an inductor for such purposes. If Q is large compared with unity, the circuit shown in Fig. 10–7 has a sharp maximum impedance very near to the frequency for which $X_L = X_C = X_0$. Under these conditions the circuit can be analyzed in a simple and informative manner by defining $r = R_L/X_0$, which is small compared with unity. While Eq. (10–17) could be used, it is at least as simple to calculate the generator current $\mathcal{I} = \mathcal{I}_L + \mathcal{I}_C$ directly.

FIG. 10–7. Parallel resonant circuit which acts as a frequency filter.

The effective emf of the generator is taken to be V and its internal impedance is assumed to be negligible. The capacitor current is

$$\mathscr{I}_C = \frac{V}{-jX_0} = \frac{jV}{X_0}$$

and the current through the inductor is

$$\mathscr{I}_L = \frac{V}{R + jX_0}\left(\frac{R - jX_0}{R - jX_0}\right) = \frac{V(R - jX_0)}{R^2 + X_0^2}.$$

Dividing the numerator and the denominator by X_0^2, the expression for $\mathscr{I}_L$ is obtained:

$$\mathscr{I}_L = \frac{V}{X_0}(r - j)(1 + r^2)^{-1},$$

which can be expanded in increasing powers of r to give

$$\mathscr{I}_L = -\frac{jV}{X_0} + \frac{V}{X_0}[r + (j - r)(r^2 - r^4 + \cdots)],$$

where the first term is much larger than the second. The generator current is then

$$\mathscr{I} = \mathscr{I}_L + \mathscr{I}_C = \frac{V}{X_0}[r + (j - r)(r^2 - r^4 + \cdots)],$$

in which the higher powers of r can be neglected, to yield

$$\mathscr{I} \cong \frac{Vr}{X_0}.$$

The impedance of this parallel network to current through the generator is $Z_p \cong X_0/r$, which can be very large. In fact, if R_L could be reduced to zero, Z_p would become infinite. Such circuits are often used to filter out undesirable frequencies. Compared with the small current in the generator, a relatively large current $I_L \cong I_C = V/X_0$ circulates in the inductor and capacitor.

Early underwater mines of World War II could be detected by low-frequency magnetic fields that would be reflected by their metallic surfaces. Some coils for producing these fields were mounted on rafts, with capacitors designed to produce resonance. When such a raft was dragged behind a boat, the current in the coils could be maintained large enough to produce strong magnetic fields with rather small currents in the wires connecting the generator on the boat to the coils on the raft.

The foregoing problem is an excellent one for illustrating graphical solutions, as shown in Fig. 10–8. Choosing the real axis for the applied voltage V, the currents $\mathcal{I}_L$, $\mathcal{I}_C$ and their sum $\mathcal{I} = \mathcal{I}_C + \mathcal{I}_L$ have been drawn as vectors, whose lengths give the effective values of the currents in the corresponding elements. Since it is 90° ahead of the voltage, $\mathcal{I}_C$ is plotted along the positive j-axis and $\mathcal{I}_L$, which lags the voltage by the angle $\tan^{-1} X_L/R$, is plotted at this angle below the real axis. The generator current $\mathcal{I}$ is shown as the vector sum of the other two. The solid-line solution has been drawn on the assumption that $X_L = X_C = 12R_L/5$, and the broken-line solution is drawn on the assumption that the frequency alone is varied until $Z_C = Z_L$, that is, until $X_C^2 = X_L^2 + R_L^2$. A little study of this diagram reveals that the generator current would be smallest for some solution lying between those represented by the solid and broken lines. The exact solution for minimum generator current can be obtained analytically.

FIG. 10–8. Graphical solutions for the circuit of Fig. 10–7. The solid lines are drawn for $X_L = X_C = 12R_L/5$, while the broken lines are drawn for a variation in frequency that makes $X_C^2 = X_L^2 + R_L^2$.

Routine method for solving networks. The routine method introduced in Section 6–10 for solving d-c networks can be applied profitably for obtaining steady-state solutions with a-c networks. For example, the relations used for solving the network in Fig. 10–7 could have been obtained by assuming that both of the currents $\mathcal{I}$ and $\mathcal{I}_L$ circulate clockwise in the lower and upper loops respectively. A solution for either $\mathcal{I}$ or $\mathcal{I}_L$ could be written as the ratio of two determinants. In either case the determinant in the denominator would be the same and would be symmetrical about a diagonal. Furthermore, since both currents are assumed to circulate in the same direction, all the off-diagonal terms must be negative. This provides two routine checks on the correctness of the denominator determinant. The determinant for the numerator is constructed from the denominator determinant. The procedure can be illustrated by setting up the determinant solution for $\mathcal{I}_L$ as follows.

First, write loop equations for the upper and lower loops respectively, collecting the impedances multiplying each current, that is,

$$\mathcal{I}_L(\mathcal{Z}_L + \mathcal{Z}_C) - \mathcal{I}\mathcal{Z}_C = 0,$$

$$-\mathcal{I}_L\mathcal{Z}_C + \mathcal{I}\mathcal{Z}_C = \mathcal{V},$$

where
$$\mathcal{Z}_L = R_L + jX_L \quad \text{and} \quad \mathcal{Z}_C = -jX_C.$$

Second, write the solution of these equations for $\mathcal{I}_L$ in determinant form, namely,

$$\mathcal{I}_L = \frac{\begin{vmatrix} 0 & -\mathcal{Z}_C \\ \mathcal{V} & +\mathcal{Z}_C \end{vmatrix}}{\begin{vmatrix} (\mathcal{Z}_L + \mathcal{Z}_C) & -\mathcal{Z}_C \\ -\mathcal{Z}_C & +\mathcal{Z}_C \end{vmatrix}} = \frac{\mathcal{V}}{\mathcal{Z}_L}.$$

An outline of this method for solving a-c Wheatstone bridge problems is given in Problem 10–10.

Network theorems. The procedures outlined for solving steady a-c network problems are adequate for solving problems involving combinations of series elements with sources of alternating emf's. However, modern circuits are so complex that it is often desirable to use simplifying theorems. Three of the most useful theorems, therefore, will be stated without proof, though they can be proved with the complex forms of Kirchhoff's laws that have just been developed.

To understand network theorems it is desirable to differentiate between ideal and real generators. Ideal generators are either ideal voltage generators or ideal current generators. The ideal voltage generator maintains a constant-amplitude sinusoidal potential difference across its terminals regardless of the current through it. The ideal current generator maintains a constant-amplitude sinusoidal current regardless of the potential difference across its terminals.

In circuit terminology any source of electrical energy may be called a generator. A real a-c generator can be replaced either by an ideal voltage generator with an internal impedance in series or by an ideal current generator with this same internal impedance in parallel. When generators are shut down the ideal voltage generator must have zero impedance between its terminals, while the ideal current generator must have infinite impedance, amounting to an open circuit between its terminals. The following theorems are probably the most important of the many theorems that are available. These theorems are stated for a-c networks, where they are needed most, but only the obvious modifications are required to make them applicable to d-c networks.

1. *Superposition Theorem.* Any network involving several generators may be solved by considering one of them at a time, with all other ideal generators shut off. The actual complex current in any branch is then the sum of the complex currents produced by each generator, taken one at a time.

2. *Thévenin's Theorem.* Any two-terminal network may be replaced by a single ideal voltage generator in series with an impedance. The value of the generator voltage is given by the open-circuit potential across the terminals of the network. The impedance is that determined by shutting off all ideal generators in the circuit and calculating the impedance of the network.

3. *Norton's Theorem.* Any two-terminal network may be replaced by a single ideal current generator in parallel with an impedance. The generator current is equal to the current when the terminals of the actual network are short-circuited. The impedance has the same value as defined in the previous theorem.

10-7 Nonohmic circuit elements. In previous discussions it has been assumed that the resistances of all resistor elements are independent of the magnitude or direction of the current through them. Such elements, which are called *ohmic* resistors, include metals, many semiconductors, and some liquids. However, many elements used in a-c circuits have resistances that are dependent upon the current or voltage, and these are said to be *nonohmic*. Vacuum tubes used in electronic circuits contain no nonohmic materials, but they are designed and incorporated into circuits so as to behave like nonohmic conductors. The most important natural nonohmic conductors are certain semiconductors, especially germanium, silicon, and copper oxide. It is possible to use metals to make electrical contacts on single crystals of these elements in such a manner as to form *transistors*. Transistors are rapidly replacing vacuum tubes in many electronic devices.

Just a few simple nonohmic devices will be discussed here, to acquaint the reader with the subject. It should be noted that a sinusoidal voltage applied across a nonohmic element usually results in a current with nonsinusoidal waveform, so that the previous mathematical treatments of a-c problems are not valid. Fortunately, however, nonohmic elements are often used in circuits in such a manner that their output is nearly sinusoidal. Even when this is not true, many physical concepts obtained from the sinusoidal solutions are valid even though the detailed solution is not. For detailed discussions of nonohmic elements in circuits, the reader is referred to books on electronics.

Semiconductor metal rectifiers. The high resistance observed in semiconductors is primarily due to the extreme shortage of carriers in their conduction bands rather than to the mobilities of these carriers. In fact, the mobility of conduction electrons in some semiconductors is greater than the mobility of conduction electrons in copper. The junction between a crystal semiconductor and a metal usually offers more resistance to the current in one direction than to that in the other. Some understanding of this phenomenon may be obtained from a somewhat naive explanation for the simplest case. Current directed so that electrons leave the metal and enter the semiconductor may result in increased conductivity due to the increased number of conduction electrons in the semiconductor. Reversal of the current removes electrons from the crystal and thus reduces the conductivity. A detailed explanation can be obtained only by means of quantum-mechanical considerations of electronic energy levels.*

Any combination that presents more resistance to current in one direction than in the other can be used as a rectifier. To be effective, the ratio between the resistances in the two directions should be as great as possible. This ratio varies greatly with the materials used; it is so small for some materials that it can hardly be observed. Some of the most common rectifiers consist of copper oxide with copper contacts and either germanium or silicon single crystals with various metal contacts. A characteristic curve for a copper-oxide rectifier is shown in the graph of current *vs.* voltage in Fig. 10–9. The curve to the right indicates the current through the rectifier when the sinusoidal voltage indicated below the characteristic curve is connected across it. The magnitude of the effective current during one half-cycle may be so much smaller than it is during the other half that it can be neglected.

For many purposes these unidirectional pulses should be closer together.

---

* For a more complete discussion of this phenomenon, see *Electrons and Holes in Semiconductors*, by William Shockley, Van Nostrand, 1950.

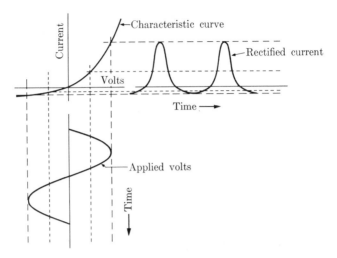

Fig. 10–9. Characteristic curve of a copper-oxide rectifier, showing the form of the rectified current curve when it is connected across a sinusoidal voltage.

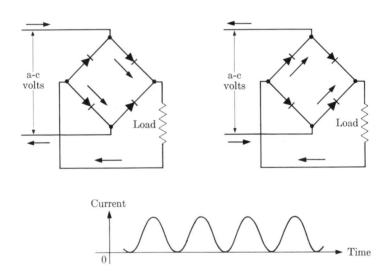

Fig. 10–10. A full-wave rectifying circuit for single-phase a-c. Rectifiers are indicated by —▶︎|— or —|◀︎— , where the first rectifier allows current to pass to the right, and the second one, to the left. Arrows on the circuit at left indicate the direction of the current in the branches for current entering at the top, while those on the right-hand circuit show directions for current entering at the bottom. The current *vs.* time graph indicates that there is a pulsing, unidirectional current through the load when a-c is supplied to the circuit.

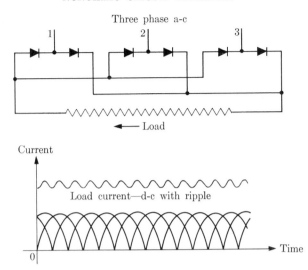

FIG. 10–11. A full-wave rectifying circuit for three-phase a-c is shown at the top. The current through the load is d-c, with a small ripple as indicated in the current *vs.* time graph. The bottom curves represent the three components whose sum is the load current.

A circuit that is frequently used to obtain current during both half-cycles is shown in Fig. 10–10. When a three-phase a-c circuit is available, unidirectional pulses can be spaced even closer together with the circuit shown in Fig. 10–11. The pulses combine to produce a ripple of higher frequency and of relatively small amplitude superimposed upon a steady d-c, as shown in the figure. The amplitude of the ripple can be reduced greatly by passing it through a parallel *L-C* filter like that shown in Fig. 10–7, designed for maximum impedance at the ripple frequency. The inductor coil of this filter should provide very low resistance for the d-c and should provide the large Q required for an effective filter.

Symmetrical nonohmic resistors. In the crystal rectifiers just discussed, the resistance depends upon both the magnitude and the direction of the applied voltage. There are a number of crystals in which the resistance depends only upon the magnitude and not upon the direction of the applied voltage. Of these, thyrite is one of the most useful. It is a black ceramic material formed by heat-treating a mixture of carbon and clay. The characteristic current *vs.* voltage curve for this material is so non-linear that a tenfold increase in the voltage across it may increase the current through it by a factor of 3000. This feature makes it very useful for protecting power lines from lightning or, in fact, any electric equipment from unexpected voltage surges. For example, a large electro-magnet operating on full current has considerable energy stored in its magnetic fields. An accidental breaking of the circuit may produce a high voltage capable of arcing across and destroying the insulation between the magnet coils. A thyrite block placed across the magnet terminals can provide a closed path for the current in the coils, where the stored energy can be dissipated harmlessly. For this purpose a thyrite resistor with the following characteristics can be chosen: across the normal operating voltage its resistance can be large compared with that of the coils, but this resistance will drop rapidly with moderate increases in the voltage.

Resistors sensitive to light and heat. The resistivities of some semiconductors are extremely sensitive to either light or heat. These are very useful for measuring or controlling temperatures on the one hand or light intensities on the other. They are frequently classed as nonohmic, though this classification is not in agreement with our definition. They should be classed as ohmic resistors, whose resistivities are sensitive either to temperature or to light.

Temperature-sensitive resistors are called thermistors. Actually, the metallic filament of a lamp bulb is often used as a thermistor, because its resistance depends so strongly on its temperature. Because of the fineness of these filaments, their temperatures are nearly single-valued functions of the current through them. This makes them act like nonohmic resistors whose resistance depends upon the current. Because carbon has a very high resistivity at low temperatures that decreases rapidly as the temperature increases, it is very useful as an indicating thermometer at low temperatures. For calibration, a carbon resistor may be placed into one arm of a Wheatstone bridge and its resistance at various temperatures recorded. Unknown temperatures can then be determined from its resistance *vs.* temperature curve.

10–8 Alternating-current bridges and other instruments. The Wheatstone and other d-c bridges have their counterparts in several a-c bridges. For example, the bridge shown in Fig. 10–12 is used for the comparison of impedances. When the four impedances have been adjusted so that there is no a-c current through the detector G, the bridge is balanced. Since there is no current through G, there is a single current $\mathcal{I}_1$ through both Z_1 and Z_2, and another single current $\mathcal{I}_2$ through Z_3 and Z_4.

The fact that there is no current through the finite impedance of the detector G then guarantees that the potential drop from b to c is zero. Therefore the potential drop from a to b equals that from a to c, and the potential drop from b to d equals that from c to d:

$$\mathcal{I}_1 Z_1 = \mathcal{I}_2 Z_3$$

and

$$\mathcal{I}_1 Z_2 = \mathcal{I}_2 Z_4.$$

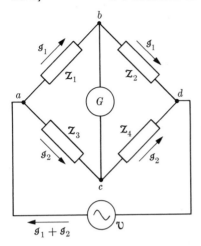

FIG. 10–12. The general form of an a-c bridge shown in the balanced condition.

FIG. 10–13. Bridge for comparing an unknown with a standard inductance.

Dividing the first equation by the second to eliminate $\mathcal{I}_1$ and $\mathcal{I}_2$, we find

$$\frac{\mathcal{Z}_1}{\mathcal{Z}_2} = \frac{\mathcal{Z}_3}{\mathcal{Z}_4}, \tag{10–18}$$

which is an equation that is reminiscent of the d-c Wheatstone bridge relation among four resistances. However, each of the four impedances may contain three elements, R, L, and C, and these twelve different quantities may make a general analysis difficult. The difficulties inherent in a general analysis of a-c bridges has stimulated the design of many different bridges for special purposes. Many of these special bridges use two pure resistance elements to determine unambiguously the ratio between the impedances in the other two arms. While excellent treatments of many bridges can be found in the literature,[*] the important principles can be learned by studying just a few examples.

Inductance bridge. A bridge designed for comparing an unknown inductance with a standard inductance is shown in Fig. 10–13, where the $\mathcal{Z}_3$ and $\mathcal{Z}_4$ of Fig. 10–12 have been replaced by the purely noninductive resistances R_3 and R_4. The standard inductance L_s with its resistance R_s replaces $\mathcal{Z}_1$, and the unknown inductance L_u with its resistance R_u replaces the $\mathcal{Z}_2$ of that figure. It is usually impossible to balance such a bridge by varying only the ratio R_3/R_4. It can be balanced in this way only if $L_u/R_u = L_s/R_s$; that is, if the Q's of the unknown and the standard coils happen to be identical. Ordinarily it will be necessary to

---

[*] L. Page and N. I. Adams, *Principles of Electricity*, 2nd ed., pp. 475–498, Van Nostrand, 1952.

add resistance either to the branch containing the unknown or to the branch containing the standard. Assume that a resistance R_1 should be added to the standard's branch, as shown in Fig. 10–13. Equation (10–18) now gives

$$\frac{R_1 + R_s + jX_s}{R_3} = \frac{R_u + jX_u}{R_4},$$

which provides the two conditions

$$\frac{R_1 + R_s}{R_u} = \frac{R_3}{R_4} \quad \text{and} \quad \frac{R_3}{R_4} = \frac{X_s}{X_u} = \frac{L_s}{L_u},$$

both of which must be satisfied to achieve a balance.

Once this bridge is balanced the value of L_u can be obtained from the second of these relations, but to obtain this balance it is necessary to determine not only the correct ratio R_3/R_4, but also the correct value of R_1 to satisfy the first of these relations. A first approximation to the correct value of R_3/R_4 can be obtained by setting $R_1 = 0$ and determining the value of the ratio that produces the minimum reading on G. With the ratio fixed at this approximate value, d-c is applied to the bridge to determine the value of R_1 required to obtain a balance. Now R_1 is kept at this approximate value and a-c is used to obtain a better value for R_3/R_4. It may be necessary to repeat these procedures several times to achieve a good balance with a-c.

A similar bridge can be used to compare capacitors with a standard. However, when d-c is being used to determine the ratio of the resistances, the capacitors must either be removed or bypassed with a shorting wire.

Frequency bridge. The fact that a series element containing inductance, capacitance, and resistance resonates when $\omega L = 1/\omega C$ can be useful when a bridge for measuring frequencies is to be made. As shown in Fig. 10–14, only one of the four branches contains inductance and capacitance, while the other three contain purely noninductive resistances. Since three of the branches have only pure resistance, the bridge will balance only when the remaining branch has pure resistance. This can be achieved only by making the reactances cancel, as they will when $X_C = X_L$ or when $f = 1/2\pi\sqrt{LC}$. The balancing of the bridge determines the frequency in terms of L and C. Although the frequency is determined independently of the resistances of the branches, the bridge cannot be balanced unless the relation $R_1/R_2 = R_3/R_4$ is satisfied.

For detecting unbalance in bridge circuits using audible frequencies, headphones may be adequate; any device sensitive enough to detect the small currents resulting from an observable unbalance is satisfactory. However, when a current-indicating device is to be used to determine quantitatively the magnitude of the current through it, the requirements

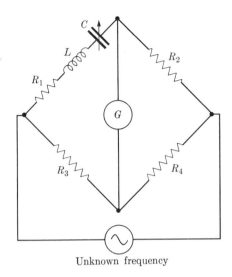

Fig. 10–14. Bridge for measuring sinusoidal frequencies.

on it are more exacting. Direct-reading meters are usually faster than bridges, but are less accurate.

Alternating-current ammeters and voltmeters. Instruments employing a movable coil suspended in the fixed field of a permanent magnet are not directly useful for a-c measurements. The torque on the coil alternates with the current through it and the inertia of the moving system prevents significant deflections. However, by providing a coil assembly with nearly the same mechanical oscillation frequency as the frequency of the alternating current, a sensitive detector for an alternating current of given frequency may be constructed. In such instruments, which are called *vibration* galvanometers, relatively small angular impulses of the right frequency build up resonant vibrations in the coil, whose maximum deflections can then be read.

The fixed permanent magnet design is also used with crystal rectifiers to produce ammeters and voltmeters that are quite satisfactory for alternating currents having wide ranges of amplitude and frequency. These instruments can also be used for measuring voltage or current in d-c circuits, *but the markings on the d-c scales must be different from those on the a-c scales because their calibrations are different.* Figure 10–10 shows a common design for the crystal rectifiers in these instruments in which, however, a moving coil would replace the resistor load. If the ratio of the resistances of these rectifiers for current in the two directions is sufficiently large, the resistance in one direction may be assumed to be zero and in the other infinite. With the design shown in Fig. 10–10, the current through the coil then follows the current vs. time graph in that same figure. If the coil assembly has sufficient inertia to maintain a constant deflection, it will be proportional to the time average of the current in the graph. The time-average and the root-mean-square current are the same for d-c, but with a-c rectified in this fashion, the time-average current is $2I_m/\pi$, while the root-mean-square current is $I_m/\sqrt{2}$, for a current amplitude of I_m. Scale divisions for alternating current must therefore be $2\sqrt{2}/\pi$ times the scale divisions for direct current.

Dynamometers. Devices for measuring alternating current can also be made by replacing the permanent magnet of the galvanometer with a current coil whose magnetic field oscillates with the current. This fixed-field coil is electrically connected in series with the movable coil, so that the instantaneous torque on the latter is proportional to the square of the instantaneous current. The torque is thus unidirectional. The deflections of this instrument, which is called a dynamometer, are proportional to the average of these squares or to the mean square of the current. The chief disadvantage of the dynamometer is that it must have a non-linear scale, which cannot indicate small currents with accuracy.

Wattmeters. The dynamometer type instrument is ideally suited for measuring the average electric power delivered to any device. With the fixed-field coil of a dynamometer connected like an ammeter, in series with the device, and its movable coil connected like a voltmeter, across the terminals of the device, a torque is produced that is proportional to the product of the instantaneous current through the device and the voltage across it. The instantaneous torque is then proportional to the instantaneous power delivered and, with sufficiently high inertia in the moving coil, *there is a steady deflection that is proportional to the average power delivered.* Since this instrument, which is called a wattmeter, indicates the average power, its deflections are proportional to

$$P = VI \cos \theta$$

but not to the product VI. If separate measurements are made of V and I, the lag angle θ can be determined from the wattmeter reading. An important feature of this instrument is that it can be used to measure a-c or d-c with a single calibration.

Wattmeters must be used with great care. It is very easy to burn out one or the other of the wattmeter coils, because the instrument may read zero with either or both of the coils overloaded. This will occur with lag angles of 90°, for which $\cos \theta = 0$. When $\cos \theta = 1$, the reading may be small because the product VI is small, even though either V or I is much too large for its coil. The values of V and I should be determined from separate voltmeter and ammeter readings to assure that neither is too large for its wattmeter coil.

10–9 Inductive coupling. The existence of a time-dependent current in an a-c circuit assures the existence of varying magnetic fields in the neighborhood. If other circuits, magnetic materials, or sizeable conductors are present in these fields, they will interact with the original circuit and change the character of its observable impedance. Usually these interactions absorb some power from the primary circuit. The transfer of power through the secondary winding of a transformer and the heating of a conductor in an induction furnace are familiar examples of such interactions. On the other hand, when a well-designed core of ferromagnetic material is inserted into a choke coil, its inductive reactance can be increased manyfold with little power absorption.

A physical understanding of these phenomena can be obtained by making a careful mathematical study of the inductively coupled circuits shown in Fig. 10–15. The time-dependent currents in the two circuits are the real parts of $\mathcal{I}_1'$ and $\mathcal{I}_2'$. The inductive interactions between the circuits take place through the mutual inductance M between the coils, which have self-inductances of L_1 and L_2. A generator maintains a steadily alternating emf in circuit No. 1 that is the real part of $\mathcal{V}' = V_m e^{j\omega t}$. In the calculations, the total resistance in circuit No. 2 is combined into $R_2 = R_s + R$.

One circuit equation can be written for each closed loop: for the first,

$$R_1 \mathcal{I}_1' + L_1 \frac{d\mathcal{I}_1'}{dt} + M \frac{d\mathcal{I}_2'}{dt} = \mathcal{V}', \tag{10–19}$$

and for the second,

$$R_2 \mathcal{I}_2' + L_2 \frac{d\mathcal{I}_2'}{dt} + M \frac{d\mathcal{I}_1'}{dt} = 0. \tag{10–20}$$

Since only the quasi-steady relations are desired, these can be reduced to algebraic equations by introducing the concepts from Section 10–4

Fig. 10–15. A pair of inductively coupled circuits with the primary circuit No. 1 connected to a source of steadily alternating emf. The total resistance in circuit No. 2 is $R_2 = R_s + R$.

that the time-dependent complex currents and emf in these equations have the form $\mathcal{B}' = \mathcal{B}e^{j\omega t}$, with the time derivatives $\partial\mathcal{B}'/\partial t = j\omega\mathcal{B}$. The resulting equations can be divided through by $\sqrt{2}\,e^{j\omega t}$ to produce the following simultaneous equations in the two unknown complex currents $\mathcal{I}_1$ and $\mathcal{I}_2$:

$$R_1\mathcal{I}_1 + L_1 j\omega\mathcal{I}_1 + Mj\omega\mathcal{I}_2 = \mathcal{V}$$

and

$$R_2\mathcal{I}_2 + L_2 j\omega\mathcal{I}_2 + Mj\omega\mathcal{I}_1 = 0.$$

Solving for $\mathcal{I}_1$, the complex current in the primary circuit can be written as

$$\mathcal{I}_1 = \frac{\mathcal{V}}{Z_e}, \tag{10-21}$$

where

$$Z_e = R_e + jX_e, \tag{10-22}$$

with

$$R_e = R_1 + \frac{R_2 X_m^2}{Z_2^2}, \qquad X_e = X_1 - \frac{X_2 X_m^2}{Z_2^2}, \tag{10-23}$$

and where $X_1 = \omega L_1$, $X_2 = \omega L_2$, $X_m = \omega M$, and $Z_2^2 = R_2^2 + X_2^2$. These are general expressions for the effective resistance, reactance, and impedance of the primary circuit of Fig. 10–15, as modified by the presence of the secondary. Note that if $X_m = 0$, then $R_e = R_1$ and $X_e = X_1$, as should be expected. The effects due to the secondary circuit can be eliminated either by reducing M to zero or by increasing R_2 to infinity, e.g., by opening the secondary circuit.

The power absorbed by the system shown in Fig. 10–15 is

$$P = I_1^2 R_e. \tag{10-24}$$

Study of these relations has proved to be very rewarding in developing physical intuition for work with a-c circuits. Two important cases for such a study now will be presented.

Case I. Ideal transformer. The current, voltage, and power relations in an ideal transformer will be studied as a function of the load on the secondary. The ideal transformer will be defined to have the following characteristics:

(a) It has a closed flux path of ferromagnetic material with a constant permeability high enough to retain all the magnetic flux within its path. In addition, this material has negligible hysteresis and is laminated to have negligible eddy-current losses.

(b) The primary and secondary coils are each wound around the ferromagnetic material so that all of the flux threads through each coil.

For simplicity it will be assumed that the ferromagnetic path has a constant cross section A and length l. For example, if the core of the ideal transformer were the bundle of ferromagnetic wires shown in Fig. 10–16, the length would be $l = 2\pi20$ cm $= 40\pi$ cm and the cross-sectional area would be $A = 10$ cm^2, the sum of the cross-sectional areas of the wires in the bundle.

(c) Since practical considerations limit the size of the coils that can be used, it is convenient to assume that the primary and secondary coils have the same total cross section. Each coil may have either many turns of fine wire or fewer turns of heavier wire, but the relation $N_1a_1 \cong N_2a_2$ is a close approximation, where the primary and secondary coils have N_1 turns of cross section a_1 and N_2 turns of cross section a_2, respectively.

From the characteristics (a) and (b), $L_1 = N_1^2\mu A/l$, $L_2 = N_2^2\mu A/l$, and $M = N_1N_2\mu A/l$, so that $L_1L_2 = M^2$ and $X_1X_2 = X_m^2$. If the wire can be wound so that the average length of the turns in each coil is C, the resistances of the coils are $R_1 = \rho N_1C/a_1$ and $R_s = \rho N_2C/a_2$ respectively, and $R_1 \cong R_sN_1^2/N_2^2 = R_sn^2$, where $n = N_1/N_2$. Then for a given size and shape of coil, both R and L are nearly proportional to N^2 and their ratio is nearly constant. Under the conditions specified, which are often closely approximated in real transformers, $X_1/R_1 = Q = X_2/R_s$, but the R_2 of Eq. (10–23) must be written as $R_2 = R_s + R$, where R is the load on the secondary.

In transformers with ferromagnetic cores, $X_2 \gg R_s$ and $Z_2^2 = X_2^2 + (R_s + R)^2 \cong X_2^2$, so that $X_m^2/Z_2^2 \cong n^2$ *when the load resistance R is small.*

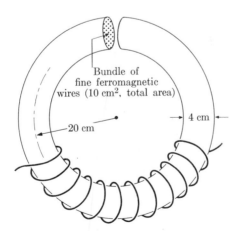

FIG. 10–16. Ferromagnetic core for an ideal transformer, consisting of a bundle of fine insulated wires of material in which μ is large but constant.

With ideal transformers and small load resistances Eqs. (10–22) and (10–23) can be written as

$$R_e \cong R_1 + n^2 R_2$$

and

$$X_e \cong X_1 - n^2 X_2.$$

With small load resistances connected to an ideal transformer, $n^2 X_2 \cong X_1$ and $X_e \cong 0$, which makes the power factor approach unity and makes the load appear to be nearly pure resistance. The power absorbed from a generator maintaining a constant amplitude of potential difference is

$$P = \frac{V^2}{R_1 + n^2 R_2},$$

which becomes $V^2/2R_1$ when R is reduced to zero by shorting the secondary.

On the other hand, when the load resistance R is increased to infinity by opening the secondary circuit, $X_e = X_1$ and the power factor becomes R_1/Z_1, which is very small. The power absorbed is then only $P = V^2 R_1/Z_1^2$. Whenever the load resistance R is large compared with the resistance of the secondary winding R_s, the voltage across R is very nearly $V_L = V(N_2/N_1)$. In real transformers, where hysteresis and eddy-current losses may not be neglected, these power losses decrease the effective inductance and increase the effective resistance.

Case II. Inductive effects of nearby conductors. Any conductor near an a-c circuit reacts to absorb power from that circuit. Because of the many possible shapes and kinds of conductors, the general problem is complex. However, considerable understanding can be gained by calculating the relatively simple case in which a short-circuited coil absorbs power from a coil connected to an alternator. To further simplify the calculations, the coils can be constructed identically and the primary coil connected directly to a constant-amplitude, constant-frequency alternator with negligible impedance. Under these conditions the quantities in Eq. (10–23) have the relations $X_1 = X_2$ and $R_1 = R_2$. To study effects due to changes in the position of the shorted secondary coil, the mutual inductance M or $X_m = \omega M$ can be treated as variable. The effective a-c resistance of the primary is then

$$R_e = R_1\left(1 + \frac{X_m^2}{Z_1^2}\right),$$

and its effective reactance is

$$X_e = X_1\left(1 - \frac{X_m^2}{Z_1^2}\right).$$

When the coils are close together $X_m \rightarrow Z_1$, so that $R_e \rightarrow 2R_1$, $X_e \rightarrow 0$, and the lag angle $\theta \rightarrow 0$. The power loss is large, or nearly $V^2/2R_1$, as in the shorted transformer.

When the coils are far apart $X_m \rightarrow 0$, so that $R_e \rightarrow R_1$, $X_e \rightarrow X_1$, and the lag angle $\theta \rightarrow \tan^{-1}(X_1/R_1)$. The power loss then is only $P = V^2/R_1(Q^2 + 1)$, which is a relatively small quantity when X_1/R_1 is large compared with unity. It should be noted that X_m does not vary linearly with the separation of the coils. In fact, for a secondary coil displaced without rotation along a radial line through the center of the primary, X_m is proportional to $1/r^3$ for $r \gg a$, where a is the radius of the coils.

These illustrations show that the effective a-c resistance of any circuit exceeds its d-c resistance when conducting materials are nearby. As frequencies increase, the effective a-c resistance increases even when there are no power-absorbing materials in the neighborhood. This increase is due to the so-called "skin effect," which causes the current densities to be larger on the surface of a conductor than within the interior. Inductive effects tending to reduce a-c densities have greater magnitudes in the interior than on the surface. Current densities in a solid cylindrical conductor as functions of the frequency and the radial distance from the axis can be calculated with Maxwell's relations, but the results are somewhat complex. It is simpler and quite instructive to show that if a conductor consists of two concentric cylindrical shells that are thin but have the same d-c resistance, the inner cylinder carries the smaller current. This problem is left as an exercise.

PROBLEMS

*10–1. An inductor of reactance 10 ohms and a capacitor of reactance 25 ohms (both measured at 60 cycles/sec) are connected in series with a 10-ohm resistor across a 100-volt (rms), 60-cycle a-c line. (a) Find the voltage across each part of the circuit. (b) What are the expressions for the instantaneous line voltage and line current?

10–2. (a) A pure resistance and a pure inductance are in series across a 100-volt a-c line. An a-c voltmeter gives the same reading whether connected across the resistance or the inductance. What does it read? (b) The magnitudes of the resistance and inductance in part (a) are altered so that a voltmeter across the inductance reads 50 volts. What will the voltmeter read when connected across the resistance?

*10–3. The rms terminal voltage of an a-c generator is 100 volts and the so-called angular frequency $\omega = 2\pi f$ is 500 rad/sec. In series across the generator are a 3-ohm resistor, a 50-μf capacitor, and an inductor whose inductance can be varied from 10 to 80 millihenries. The peak voltage (V_{max}) across the capacitor should not exceed 1200 volts. (a) What is the maximum allowable current in the series circuit? (b) To what value can the inductance be safely increased?

10–4. The reactances of an inductor and a capacitor are equal at a frequency f_0. Show in the same diagram the reactances of the inductor and the capacitor as a function of frequency, over a frequency range from zero to $2f_0$. Show also the reactance of the two in series.

*10–5. An ideal a-c voltage generator is connected to terminals a and b of the simple series element in Fig. 10–1. In terms of R, L, and C, at what frequency will the voltage be maximum (a) across the inductor, and (b) across the capacitor?

10–6. A circuit draws 330 watts from a 110-volt 60-cycle a-c line. The power factor is 0.6 and the current lags the voltage. (a) Find the capacitance of the series capacitor that will result in a power factor of unity. (b) What power will then be drawn from the supply line?

*10–7. When switch S in Fig. 10–17 is closed, the steady current in the battery is 10 amp. (a) Explain how oscillations originate in the L-C circuit when the switch is opened. (b) What is the frequency of the oscillations? (c) What is the maximum potential difference across the capacitor?

*10–8. A 0.01-μf capacitor, a 0.1-henry inductor whose resistance is 1000 ohms, and a switch are connected in a series circuit. The capacitor is initially charged to a potential difference of 400 volts. The switch is then closed. (a) Find the ratio of the oscillation frequency of the circuit to the frequency if the resistance were zero. (b) How much energy is converted to heat in the first complete cycle? (c) How much energy is converted to heat in the complete train of oscillations? (d) What is the maximum additional resistance that can be inserted in the circuit before the discharge becomes nonoscillatory?

10–9. A resistance R and a capacitance C in series are connected across the terminals of an ideal voltage generator which produces the rectangular voltage

---

* Answers to starred problems will be found at back of book.

pulse shown in Fig. 10–18. Take $R = 10^6$ ohms and $C = 0.01\,\mu\text{f}$, and derive expressions giving $q(t)$ and $i(t)$ (a) during the period $0 < t < 0.01$ sec, and (b) when t exceeds 0.01 sec. (c) Plot curves of $q(t)$ and of $i(t)$ versus t.

*10–10. For the calculation of the detector current in an a-c Wheatstone bridge it is desirable to draw the network as it is shown in Fig. 10–19. Since the expression $N - J + 1 = 6 - 4 + 1 = 3$ shows that three unknowns must be considered, the complex currents $\mathcal{I}_1$, $\mathcal{I}_2$, and $\mathcal{I}_3$ can be chosen to circulate in the three loops as shown in the figure.

$$L = 2h, \quad R = 0$$

FIGURE 10–17

FIGURE 10–18

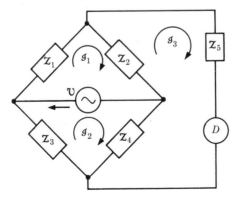

FIGURE 10–19

(a) Use the routine method of solution to show that the current through the detector is given by

$$\mathcal{I}_3 = \mathcal{V}(Z_1 Z_4 - Z_2 Z_3)/\Delta,$$

where the denominator is

$$\Delta = Z_1 Z_2 Z_3 + Z_1 Z_2 Z_4 + Z_1 Z_3 Z_4 + Z_2 Z_3 Z_4 + Z_1 Z_3 Z_5 + Z_1 Z_4 Z_5$$
$$+ Z_2 Z_3 Z_5 + Z_2 Z_4 Z_5.$$

(b) Suppose that Z_4 is the unknown impedance that is to be determined and that $Z_4 = \delta Z$, where $\delta \cong 1$ provides for the inevitable error in the determination of Z_4 due to the lack of sensitivity in the detector. Obtain an expression for δ in terms of the smallest current $|\mathcal{I}_m|$ that is observable in the detector, assuming that each of the remaining Z's is exactly equal to Z.

(c) Make a plot in the complex plane showing those values of δ that cannot be detected, if $|\mathcal{I}_m| = 10\,\mu\text{amp}$, $Z = 300 + 400j$ ohms, and $|\mathcal{V}| = 125$ volts.

10–11. Prove the superposition theorem for a complex network containing at least two generators.

10–12. Assume the validity of Thévenin's theorem and prove Norton's theorem. Show that the impedance in parallel with the ideal current generator must be the same as that in series with the ideal voltage generator. What is the relationship between the generator voltage for Thévenin's theorem and the generator current for Norton's theorem?

10–13. Occasionally another theorem named after Millman is useful. Millman's theorem gives the steady-state voltage at the junction J in Fig. 10–20 as

$$\mathcal{V}_J = \frac{\sum_1^n \mathcal{V}_i \mathcal{Y}_i}{\sum_1^n \mathcal{Y}_i},$$

where all of the $\mathcal{V}$'s are measured from ground potential and where the "black box" may contain any combination of linear elements and generators. Prove this theorem.

10–14. The series element shown in Fig. 10–1 is connected across a storage battery that has the emf V_B and a negligible internal resistance. Assuming

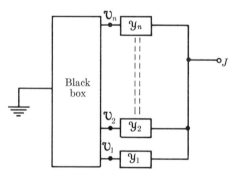

FIGURE 10–20

that a switch provided to complete the circuit is closed at $t = 0$, calculate the charge q on the capacitor as a function of time (a) when $R/2 < \sqrt{L/C}$, and (b) when $R/2 > \sqrt{L/C}$.

*10-15. The a-c generator in Fig. 10-7 is replaced by a storage battery that has negligible internal resistance and the constant emf $\mathcal{E}_B$. A switch has been placed in series with the battery for completing the circuit. If this switch is closed at $t = 0$, calculate the current i through the inductor as a function of time.

*10-16. An a-c generator, in series with a switch for completing the circuit, is connected across the series element of Fig. 10-1. Assume that the generator has negligible impedance and produces a sinusoidal emf with the amplitude V_m and the frequency $f = \omega/2\pi$. Assuming also that $R/2 < \sqrt{L/C}$, calculate the transient current in the element as a function of time, when the switch is closed at two different instants: (a) when the generated emf is maximum, and (b) when the generated emf is zero.

*10-17. A transmission line consists of two straight copper wires that are parallel to each other and have the following dimensions: the radius of each wire is a, the separation between centers is d, and the length of the line is l, where $l \gg d \gg a$. On the assumption that the currents in the two lines are equal throughout their lengths but oppositely directed, calculate (a) the self-inductance L of the line, and (b) the frequency, $f_0 = \omega_0/2\pi$, at which the inductive reactance equals the resistance R of the line. (c) Obtain numerical values for parts (a) and (b), with a line 100 m long consisting of two No. 18 wires 10 cm apart.

10-18. A sinusoidal potential difference of constant amplitude is applied across the series element of Fig. 10-1 at various frequencies from 0 to 500 cycles/sec. The magnitudes of L and C are adjusted so that at 250 cycles/sec $X_L = X_C$. The effective potential difference is 100 volts and $R = 10$ ohms. Plot the effective current I versus the frequency for the two different cases in which X_L at 250 cycles/sec has values such that (a) $Q = X_L/R = 3$, and (b) $Q = X_L/R = 10$.

*10-19. Three wires that are connected to a common junction in an a-c network carry the currents $\mathcal{I}_1$, $\mathcal{I}_2$, and $\mathcal{I}_3$ away from this junction. (a) When the effective values of these currents are 7 amp, 5 amp, and 3 amp, respectively, determine graphically the phase angles of $\mathcal{I}_2$ and $\mathcal{I}_3$ with respect to $\mathcal{I}_1$. (b) From your graphical solution draw a diagram like that in Fig. 10-4(b) to indicate the time-dependent values for these currents. Take the instant of time when $\omega t = 70°$ and show clearly the instantaneous values of the currents in each wire at this instant.

10-20. Two a-c generators are connected in parallel to feed a single load having the complex impedance Z. The two generators have different internal impedances Z_1 and Z_2, and different emf's $\mathcal{V}_1$ and $\mathcal{V}_2$, which are not in phase, although they have the same frequency. (a) Calculate the current $\mathcal{I}$ through the load and $\mathcal{I}_1$ through generator number 1. (b) Determine the numerical values for $\mathcal{I}$ and $\mathcal{I}_1$, for $\mathcal{V}_1 = 120$ v, $\mathcal{V}_2 = 120e^{j\pi/2}$ v, $Z_1 = 1$ ohm, $Z_2 = 2$ ohms, and $Z = (3 + 4j)$ ohms. (c) What fraction of the power lost in Z is generated by generator number 1?

*10–21. Three terminals of a three-phase power line have sinusoidal potentials, with respect to a grounded neutral terminal, of $\mathcal{U}_1$, $\mathcal{U}_2$, and $\mathcal{U}_3$. A junction J *is not grounded*, but is connected to terminal 1 through an impedance Z_1, to terminal 2 through an impedance Z_2, and to terminal 3 through an impedance Z_3.

(a) Calculate the current $\mathcal{I}_1$ through Z_1, assuming that its positive direction is from terminal 1 toward J, and show that

$$\mathcal{I}_1 = \frac{(Z_2 + Z_3)\mathcal{U}_1 - (Z_2\mathcal{U}_3 + Z_3\mathcal{U}_2)}{Z_1Z_2 + Z_1Z_3 + Z_2Z_3}.$$

(b) Calculate the potential $\mathcal{U}_J$ of the junction J.

(c) Obtain the numerical value of $\mathcal{U}_J$ for

$$Z_1 = 10 \text{ ohms}, \quad Z_2 = 11 \text{ ohms}, \quad Z_3 = 9 \text{ ohms},$$

$$\mathcal{U}_1 = 100e^{j2\pi/3} \text{ v}, \quad \mathcal{U}_2 = 100 \text{ v}, \quad \text{and} \quad \mathcal{U}_3 = 100e^{-j2\pi/3} \text{ v}.$$

10–22. In the parallel circuit shown in Fig. 10–7 $X_L = X_C$ when the frequency is given by $f_0 = 1/2\pi\sqrt{1/LC}$, but this frequency does not make the generator current a minimum. Determine the frequency f_r for which the generator current is a minimum.

*10–23. A certain a-c electric clock, designed for 110 volts and 60 cycles/sec, consists of an electromagnet with a toothed steel armature rotating between its poles. While the clock is running, measurements show that $X = \omega L = 3220$ ohms, $R_{\text{a-c}} = 1760$ ohms, and $R_{\text{d-c}} = 760$ ohms, but while its armature is fastened to prevent rotation, measurements show that $X = \omega L = 3330$ ohms, $R_{\text{a-c}} = 1600$ ohms, and $R_{\text{d-c}} = 760$ ohms. Assuming that the power losses in the iron core and in the armature are the same whether or not the armature rotates, calculate (a) the power lost in heating the coil, (b) the power lost in heating the core and armature, and (c) the power used in driving the armature.

10–24. Clocks like the one described in Problem 10–23 make excellent laboratory stopwatches when they are provided with suitable on-off switches. Where these clocks are to be used by students and 110 d-c as well as 110 a-c outlets are available, they should be protected with capacitors connected in series to avoid burning of the wire windings when a d-c outlet is accidentally selected. However, these clocks will not run on less than 0.024 amp and will burn out if the heat loss increases more than 40% over the normal heat loss. (a) What capacitance, connected in series with the clock, will leave the current unchanged? (b) If the only capacitor available has twice the capacitance calculated in (a), what resistance should be added to the system to keep the current constant? (c) How does the power consumption of the original clock compare with the power consumption of the clock as modified in parts (a) and (b) of this problem?

*10–25. The armature of a certain induction motor is a copper "squirrel cage" with no external electric connections. The two poles of the electromagnet have windings connected in series, with a total d-c resistance of 0.5 ohm, across a 200-volt 60-cycle/sec a-c line. Running with no load, this motor draws only 5 amp. However, when it is delivering 3200 watts of mechanical power, it draws 20 amp and a wattmeter shows that the electric power being absorbed is 3600 watts. Find the effective a-c resistance and the effective inductive reactance (a) when the motor is running with no load, and (b) when the motor is driving the 3200-watt mechanical load. [*Note.* It can be assumed that all the heat losses in the motor are proportional to I^2.]

10–26. In October 1957, the Cleveland Electric Illuminating Company announced plans to transmit 335,000 kilowatts at 345,000 volts over 110 miles of line from a coal-powered plant to be built on one bank of the Ohio River, to the city of Cleveland. Transmission losses were to be kept below 3%. While the details were not announced, a study of similar installations suggests the following arrangements: The power will be transmitted over two separate three-phase lines (using six separate conducting cables), with approximately 345,000 volts between the phases. Since commercial loads usually have reactances that are primarily inductive, the power factor at the Cleveland end will be adjusted to near unity by capacitors. The transmission voltage will be achieved by generating 17,500 volts between phases, but this will be stepped up to the transmission voltage by means of transformers. On the basis of these assumptions:

(a) Derive an expression for the cross-sectional area of the cables in terms of V, P, l, ρ, and δ, which are the respective symbols for the voltage between phases, the power transmitted, the length of the transmission line, the resistivity of the cable, and the fractional power loss in the line.

(b) Calculate the diameter of the copper wire required for each of the six wires.

(c) Calculate the sizes of the copper wires that would be required if the transmission voltage must be reduced to 100,000 volts between each of the phases.

(d) Suppose that an inductive power factor of 0.894 is to be corrected to unity by connecting a capacitor between each of the transmission wires. Calculate the capacitance that would be required.

10–27. Replace the load R in Fig. 10–15 with a load of $Z = R + jX$ and show that the phase angle between the current and voltage of the primary is approximately $\tan^{-1} X/R$, with an ideal transformer in which $M^2 = L_1L_2$, $R \gg R_s$, and $\omega L_1/R_1 = \omega L_2/R_s \gg 1$.

*10–28. The full-wave rectifying circuit of Fig. 10–11 is used in a certain experiment to produce a direct current of 2.00 amp through a device having a pure resistance of 100 ohms. The maximum potential of each phase to ground is just 120 volts.

(a) With the device connected as is the load in Fig. 10–11, calculate the maximum, minimum, and average currents through the device.

(b) Calculate the resistance required to reduce the average current to just 2.00 amp.

(c) Assume that half of the resistance calculated in (b) will be in a control rheostat while the other half will be in a circuit like that of Fig. 10–7 for filtering out the ripple. Further, assume that any available inductor will have a Q of 25 on 60 cycles and that the ripple will be sinusoidal with an amplitude that is half the difference between the maximum and the minimum of the curve summing the pulses in Fig. 10–11. Calculate the capacitance needed to make the two reactances of the filter equal for the ripple frequency.

(d) Calculate the amplitude of the current ripple that will pass through the filter as designed in (c). Compare the amplitude of the ripple passing through the filter with the magnitude of the steady current by calculating the ratio of the amplitude to the d-c magnitude.

10–29. Most transformers have closed paths for the magnetic flux inside iron or other ferromagnetic materials. To simplify construction these paths are made rectangular or some other shape that has relatively sharp angles. Calculations for such shapes must take into account the fact that not all the flux is confined to the iron paths. The toroid ring designed by Rowland for precise measurements of magnetic properties is easier to calculate though harder to construct. A special alloy (30% Fe, 25% Co, 45% Ni) called *perminvar* has been developed to have a constant permeability of $\mu = 300 \mu_0$, with negligible hysteresis up to $H = 240$ amp/m. If the core in Fig. 10–16 is made up of many fine wires of this material, insulated to prevent eddy currents, an ideal transformer with negligible core losses can be constructed. In winding insulated copper wire around this core the space factor k, defined in Problem 6–16, can be defined as the ratio of the total copper cross section to the minimum cross section of the coil when this is taken perpendicular to the wires. Assuming that k is 0.7,

(a) calculate the self-inductance L_1 and the resistance R_1 for a coil of N_1 turns whose minimum cross section lies between the radii 18 cm and 17 cm, and

(b) calculate the Q of this coil for a frequency of 60 cycles/sec.

(c) Calculate the number of turns N_1 that must be used in this coil to avoid exceeding the limitation that $H < 240$ amp/m when the coil is connected directly to a 110-volt, 60-cycle/sec line.

(d) Calculate the Q of a secondary coil of N_2 turns whose minimum cross section lies between the radii 17 cm and 16 cm, using the frequency of 60 cycles/sec.

10–30. When the ferromagnetic bundle of wires in Fig. 10–16 is made with the kind of iron that was used in obtaining the hysteresis loop of Fig. 9–9, a sinusoidal potential difference across the coil winding does not produce a truly sinusoidal current in the winding. The nonlinear magnetization curve produces a variable reactance that distorts the current vs. time curve. The problem is complicated further by the fact that magnetization curves vary with the frequency at which they are measured and with the maximum current in the coils. In spite of these difficulties, the curve of Fig. 9–9 can be used to obtain fair approximations for special cases, where the current maxima produce maximum fields of $H_{max} \cong 240$ amp/m and the frequency is 60 cycles/sec or less. For this approximation a constant permeability should be assumed, and this may be chosen as $\mu = B_{max}/H_{max}$ as taken from the curve. Assuming that the iron of Fig. 9–9 is substituted for the perminvar of Problem 10–29:

(a) Calculate N_1 for a primary coil that can be connected directly across a 110-volt and 60-cycle/sec line to produce $H_{max} = 240$ amp/m.

(b) Calculate the d-c resistance of this coil.

(c) Estimate the power loss due to the hysteresis loop plotted in **Fig. 9–9** and determine the resistance that this power loss adds to the d-c resistance of the primary coil.

(d) Determine the a-c resistance of the primary coil, assuming there is no secondary circuit.

*10–31. A long, straight coaxial cable consists of three thin cylindrical shells of copper separated by air. The two inner cylinders, of radii a and $b > a$, are electrically joined at the two ends to constitute one of the conductors in a two-conductor transmission line. The outer cylinder, of radius $c > b$, constitutes the return path. When direct current is used for transmission, the outwardly directed current is equally divided between the two inner cylinders. When alternating current is used for transmission the total effective current $I = I_a + I_b$ is maintained constant, independent of the frequency $f = \omega/2\pi$.

(a) Calculate the ratio I_b/I_a as a function of the frequency, where I_a and I_b are the effective currents in the cylinders of radii a and b respectively. Assume that the resistances per meter of length are R_l, R_l, and $R_l/2$ for the cylinders with the radii a, b, and c respectively.

(b) With d-c transmission the power lost in the two inner cylinders is $P_d = (I/2)^2(R_l + R_l) = I^2 R_l/2$. With a-c transmission, calculate as a function of frequency the power P_a lost in these two cylinders.

(c) Plot I_b/I_a versus f and P_a/P_d versus f, choosing inner cylinders having $a = 1$ cm with 0.04-cm thickness and $b = 2$ cm with 0.02-cm thickness. Use $c = 4$ cm and choose frequencies for plotting that make the inductive effects more important than the d-c resistance.

10–32. The Campbell bridge, which is one of the circuits that has been used at the British National Physical Laboratory for establishing the standard ohm, is shown in Fig. 8–16. The mutual inductances M_1 and M_2 were precisely determined by comparing them with a computable mutual inductor and the ratio $\mathfrak{R} = R/r$ was precisely determined by d-c bridge techniques. Here R is the total resistance in the closed circuit that includes S, the secondary of M_1, and the primary of M_2. By adjusting the alternator frequency, $f = \omega/2\pi$, the current through the galvanometer could be reduced to zero, and then $Rr = \omega^2 M_1 M_2$, or $r = \omega\sqrt{M_1 M_2/\mathfrak{R}}$. Since each quantity on the right was precisely determined from length and time measurements alone, r is established in terms of only these two units. With $\mathcal{J}_G = 0$, show that $Rr = \omega^2 M_1 M_2$ and $(L_1 + L_2)r = M_1 S$.

CHAPTER 11

ELECTROMAGNETIC RADIATION

The publication of Maxwell's *A Dynamical Theory of Electromagnetic Field*, in 1865, unified the various laws of electricity then in existence. All known laws then could be obtained from five fundamental relations, namely, Maxwell's four field equations, Eqs. (M–1), (M–2), (M–3), and (M–4), and the relation for the force on a moving charge, Eq. (7–1). In order to make these five relations consistent mathematically and consistent with the law of conservation of charge, Maxwell had introduced a displacement current. At that time, there were no experiments to justify this concept. However, with the introduction of the displacement current Maxwell's field equations predicted the existence of electromagnetic waves that would propagate through vacuum with a velocity equal to that of light. It was truly amazing that this predicted velocity of propagation, based entirely upon laboratory measurements of electric and magnetic quantities, could be so nearly equal to the measured velocity of light. As measuring accuracies have improved, the two types of measurements have yielded more and more nearly the same results, so that now the two velocities are considered to be identical.* The best value for this velocity is $c = 299{,}792 \pm 2$ km/sec.†

Maxwell's equations also predicted that the velocities of electromagnetic waves through a dielectric would be inversely proportional to the square root of the dielectric constant. Therefore, if light consists of electromagnetic waves, the ratio between refractive indices of two media should equal the square root of the ratio of the dielectric constants. For many materials, such as melted paraffin and certain gases, this relation was fairly accurate. Subsequent researches have shown, however, that complete agreement with this theory is obtained only when the frequency of the waves is considered, since the index of refraction and the dielectric constant both depend upon the frequency used in the measurement. The validity of Maxwell's relations has been verified by so many thousands of experiments that dielectric constants at high frequencies are now commonly obtained from the refractive index, assuming Maxwell's relations to be exact.

---

* A comparison of these results is given by Jenkins and White, *Fundamentals of Optics*, p. 393, McGraw-Hill, 1957.

† An excellent review article by Mulligan and McDonald, *Am. J. Phys.* **25,** 180 (1957), summarizes measurements by Rank and Bennett, Bennett and Plyler, and Blaine and Conner.

Before the publication of Maxwell's theory, a theory for optical phenomena based upon elastic vibration in a kind of solid "aether" had been developed by Huygens, Fresnel, Young, Green, and others. As the studies progressed, the properties that must be assigned to this aether became more and more fantastic. The phenomena of polarized light could be

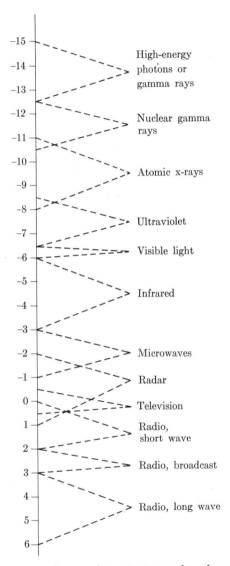

FIG. 11-1. Some names given to important wavelength regions in the continuous spectrum of electromagnetic radiation. The numbers on the vertical axis give the $\log_{10}$ of the wavelength in meters.

explained only if the vibrations in the aether were transverse to the direction of propagation. This seemed to require enormous rigidity in a medium which also must have negligible density and must produce no noticeable drag on planetary motion. The theory that identified light waves as an electromagnetic phenomenon provided an ideal solution for these anomalies.

Maxwell recognized that electromagnetic waves longer than those of visible light should exist, but he doubted that they could be detected. However, between 1885 and 1889, Hertz set up oscillating electric circuits for producing and detecting these waves. He measured their velocity and wavelength and showed that they could be refracted, reflected, diffracted, and polarized much like ordinary light. Hertz' experiments verified the theoretical work of Maxwell. Practical applications followed soon. By 1895 Marconi had demonstrated that these electromagnetic waves could be used for commercial telegraphy, to transmit messages across the Atlantic Ocean without wires.

Modern research has detected and used electromagnetic radiation over a wide range of wavelengths. Approximate ranges of some of these are indicated in Fig. 11–1. It is interesting to note the small portion of this range that is visible to the human eye.

11–1 Wave equations for nonconducting isotropic media. Electromagnetic waves start from regions where there are charges and currents, can pass through regions where there are none, and finally end in regions where again there are charges and currents. The phenomena of wave propagation are simplest in those regions where there are no real charges or currents. The perfectly general case would involve the propagation of waves through regions that are neither isotropic nor homogeneous, but such complexities* should be postponed for later consideration. Here the study will be confined to regions where μ and ϵ can be considered constants, which includes all regions in which the media are homogeneous, isotropic, and have no hysteresis effects; the perfect vacuum is simply a special case.

It will be assumed, then, that $\mu = K_m \mu_0$ and $\epsilon = K \epsilon_0$, where K_m and K are true constants for the media, and that $\rho = 0$ and $\mathbf{J} = 0$. Maxwell's field equations then become

$$\nabla \cdot \mathbf{E} = 0, \tag{11–1}$$

$$\nabla \cdot \mathbf{H} = 0, \tag{11–2}$$

$$\nabla \times \mathbf{E} = -\mu \dot{\mathbf{H}}, \tag{11–3}$$

$$\nabla \times \mathbf{H} = \epsilon \dot{\mathbf{E}}. \tag{11–4}$$

---

* See Chapter XIX in *Theoretical Physics* by Georg Joos, G. E. Stechert, 1934.

From these four equations in two unknowns separate differential equations for **E** and for **H** can be obtained. Equations (11–1) and (11–2) provide no relation between **E** and **H** and no indication of their time-dependence, but Eqs. (11–3) and (11–4) each contain both **E** and **H** and provide a time-dependent relation. Either **E** or **H** can be eliminated from these two relations to obtain a single differential equation with time-dependence. By taking the curl of (11–3) and the time derivative of (11–4), **H** can be eliminated to provide the separate differential equation for **E**:

$$\nabla \times (\nabla \times \mathbf{E}) = -\mu \nabla \times \dot{\mathbf{H}} = -\mu\epsilon\ddot{\mathbf{E}},$$

$$\nabla \times (\nabla \times \mathbf{E}) = -\mu\epsilon\ddot{\mathbf{E}}.$$

Similarly, **E** can be eliminated from (11–3) and (11–4) by taking the curl of (11–4) and the time derivative of (11–3) to obtain $\nabla \times (\nabla \times \mathbf{H}) = -\mu\epsilon\ddot{\mathbf{H}}$.

These expressions can be rendered more useful by using the mathematical identity of Eq. (3–24) to obtain

$$\nabla \times (\nabla \times \mathbf{E}) = \nabla(\nabla \cdot \mathbf{E}) - \nabla^2\mathbf{E} = -\mu\epsilon\ddot{\mathbf{E}},$$

and the introduction of Eq. (11–1) reduces this to $\nabla^2\mathbf{E} = \mu\epsilon\ddot{\mathbf{E}}$, which is a wave equation. Similarly, by using Eq. (11–2) $\nabla^2\mathbf{H} = \mu\epsilon\ddot{\mathbf{H}}$ may be obtained. To see that these are indeed wave equations, consider the special case of a plane wave being propagated along the z-axis. Such a plane wave must be independent of the x- and y-coordinates, so that

$$\frac{\partial \mathbf{E}}{\partial x} = \frac{\partial \mathbf{E}}{\partial y} = 0 \quad \text{and} \quad \frac{\partial \mathbf{H}}{\partial x} = \frac{\partial \mathbf{H}}{\partial y} = 0.$$

The equations then become

$$\frac{\partial^2 \mathbf{E}}{\partial z^2} = \mu\epsilon\ddot{\mathbf{E}} \tag{11-5a}$$

and

$$\frac{\partial^2 \mathbf{H}}{\partial z^2} = \mu\epsilon\ddot{\mathbf{H}}, \tag{11-5b}$$

each of which is a second-order differential equation with two solutions. The two arbitrary vector functions $\mathbf{E} = \mathbf{f}(t - z/v)$ and $\mathbf{E} = \mathbf{F}(t + z/v)$ are both solutions of Eq. (11–5a), as can be demonstrated by direct substitution. Figure 11–2 shows an arbitrarily shaped function of $(t - z/v)$ plotted at time $t = 0$ and again at time $t = T$. It is apparent that in the time T the wave has shifted along the z-axis a distance z_T such that $T = z_T/v$. Such a function, which is independent of x and y, provides a good example of a plane wave of any shape moving with velocity v in the

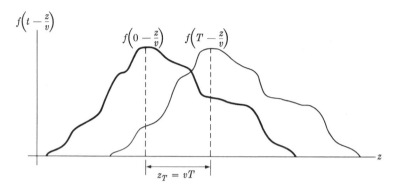

FIG. 11–2. This figure illustrates how a general function of the form $f(t - z/v)$ represents plane waves propagated in the z-direction with velocity v.

positive z-direction. Similarly, any $\mathbf{F}(t + z/v)$ represents a plane wave moving in the negative z-direction. Since any information that can be obtained from waves propagated in the negative z-direction is as easily obtained from waves propagated in the positive z-direction, the functions represented by $\mathbf{F}(t + z/v)$ will be ignored. For waves moving in the positive direction it is desirable to define

$$\mathbf{f}' = \frac{\partial \mathbf{f}}{\partial(t - z/v)} \quad \text{and} \quad \mathbf{f}'' = \frac{\partial^2 \mathbf{f}}{\partial(t - z/v)^2}.$$

Using these definitions, we can write the following partial derivatives:

$$\frac{\partial \mathbf{E}}{\partial z} = -\frac{1}{v}\mathbf{f}', \qquad \frac{\partial \mathbf{E}}{\partial t} = \mathbf{f}',$$

$$\frac{\partial^2 \mathbf{E}}{\partial z^2} = \frac{1}{v^2}\mathbf{f}'', \qquad \frac{\partial^2 \mathbf{E}}{\partial t^2} = \mathbf{f}'',$$

which satisfy (11–5a) if $\mu\epsilon v^2 = 1$ or if

$$v = \frac{1}{\sqrt{\mu\epsilon}} = \frac{1}{\sqrt{K_m K}\,\sqrt{\mu_0\epsilon_0}} = \frac{c}{\sqrt{K_m K}},$$

where the constant c satisfies the relation $\mu_0\epsilon_0 c^2 = 1$. An identical treatment for magnetic waves yields these same relations when we use Eq. (11–5b). Very careful experiments have shown that the c thus defined is accurately equal* to the velocity of light in a vacuum. In most media the product KK_m is greater than one and the wave propagates at a velocity less than c. Since experiments show that K_m is approxi-

---

* Jenkins and White, *Fundamentals of Optics*, p. 393, McGraw-Hill, 1957.

TABLE 11-1

INDEX OF REFRACTION OF SOME GASES COMPARED WITH THE
SQUARE ROOT OF THEIR DIELECTRIC CONSTANTS

Gas	$\sqrt{K}$	Index
Hydrogen	1.000132	1.000138–1.000142
Air	1.000295	1.000293
Carbon monoxide	1.000350	1.000335–1.000340
Carbon dioxide	1.000492	1.000448–1.000454
Nitrous oxide	1.000565	1.000516

mately one when the frequency exceeds $c/0.003$ m, visible light should
have the velocity $v = c/\sqrt{K}$ and the index of refraction should be $\sqrt{K}$.
Table 11-1 compares, for some gases, the $\sqrt{K}$ measured at frequencies
below 3×10^6 cycles/sec with the index of refraction for visible light
($\sim 5 \times 10^{10}$ cycles/sec) traveling through these same gases. Since both
of these quantities vary with the frequency at which they are measured,
the closeness of the agreement is surprising. Similar tables compiled for
solids or liquids do not show such agreements, because the variations
with frequency are more pronounced in these substances.

11-2 Relationships between electric and magnetic fields in plane waves.
To investigate relationships for $\mathbf{E}$ and $\mathbf{H}$ in plane waves, Maxwell's first
equation can be used in the form

$$\frac{\partial E_x}{\partial x} + \frac{\partial E_y}{\partial y} + \frac{\partial E_z}{\partial z} = 0.$$

Since with plane waves propagating in the z-direction $\partial \mathbf{E}/\partial x = \partial \mathbf{E}/\partial y = 0$,
the derivative of each component of $\mathbf{E}$ with respect to x or y is separately
equal to zero, and therefore $\partial E_z/\partial z = 0$. This shows that E_z is either
constant or zero, but the possibility that E_z may be constant merely
means that a static field may exist, which is of no interest in our study
of waves. Therefore, when plane electromagnetic waves are propagated
along the z-axis, $E_z = 0$ and the waves are transverse to the direction of
propagation. A similar argument shows that $H_z = 0$ also, and both of
these field vectors are in a plane perpendicular to the direction of propagation of the wave.

The quantitative relationship between $\mathbf{E}$ and $\mathbf{H}$ can be obtained by
means of (11-3) as follows:

$$\mathbf{\nabla} \times \mathbf{E} = \mathbf{i}\left(\frac{\partial E_z}{\partial y} - \frac{\partial E_y}{\partial z}\right) + \mathbf{j}\left(\frac{\partial E_x}{\partial z} - \frac{\partial E_z}{\partial x}\right) + \mathbf{k}\left(\frac{\partial E_y}{\partial x} - \frac{\partial E_x}{\partial y}\right) = -\mu\dot{\mathbf{H}}$$

and, since $\partial \mathbf{E}/\partial x = 0 = \partial \mathbf{E}/\partial y$,

$$-\mathbf{i}\,\frac{\partial E_y}{\partial z} + \mathbf{j}\,\frac{\partial E_x}{\partial z} = -\mu(\mathbf{i}\dot{H}_x + \mathbf{j}\dot{H}_y + \mathbf{k}\dot{H}_z).$$

Equating components gives

$$-\frac{\partial E_y}{\partial z} = -\mu\dot{H}_x \tag{11-6}$$

and

$$\frac{\partial E_x}{\partial z} = -\mu\dot{H}_y, \tag{11-7}$$

which provide quantitative relationships between $\mathbf{E}$ and $\mathbf{H}$. The following arbitrary functions of $(t - z/v)$ can be chosen for the nonzero components of $\mathbf{E}$ and $\mathbf{H}$:

$$E_x = f\left(t - \frac{z}{v}\right), \qquad E_y = g\left(t - \frac{z}{v}\right),$$

$$H_x = m\left(t - \frac{z}{v}\right), \qquad H_y = n\left(t - \frac{z}{v}\right).$$

Substitution of these functions into Eq. (11–6) gives $(1/v)g' = -\mu m'$ or $g = -\mu v m$, provided that the constant of integration, which has no importance in wave propagation, is neglected. Likewise, Eq. (11–7) gives $-(1/v)f' = -\mu n'$ or $f = \mu v n$. Therefore, since $v = 1/\sqrt{\mu\epsilon}$ and $\mu v = \sqrt{\mu/\epsilon}$, then $g = -\sqrt{\mu/\epsilon}\,m$ and $f = \sqrt{\mu/\epsilon}\,n$, which shows that at any fixed time and fixed location in space the magnetic field is proportional to the electric field and so is in phase with it. Easily remembered expressions for this proportionality are

$$B_y = \frac{E_x}{v} \quad \text{and} \quad B_x = -\frac{E_y}{v}. \tag{11-8}$$

Furthermore, since

$$\mathbf{E} \cdot \mathbf{H} = fm + gn = \left(\sqrt{\frac{\mu}{\epsilon}}\,n\right)m - \left(\sqrt{\frac{\mu}{\epsilon}}\,m\right)n = 0$$

the electric and magnetic vectors are at right angles to each other. *The foregoing relations apply only to plane waves.* The fields $\mathbf{E}$ and $\mathbf{H}$ are not necessarily perpendicular nor are they necessarily transverse to the direction of propagation in other forms of waves.

To further clarify these phenomena, consider the special case of a sinusoidal plane wave that is polarized in the x-direction. In such a wave, $E_y = 0$ and the x-component can be written as $E_x = E_{0x} \sin \omega\,(t - z/v)$. From Eq. (11–8), $H_x = 0$ and $H_y = (E_{0x}/\mu v) \sin \omega(t - z/v)$. These expressions are plotted at $t = 0$ in Fig. 11–3.

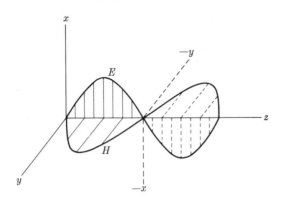

FIG. 11-3. A plane-polarized electromagnetic wave propagating in the z-direction.

11-3 Laws of optics. If light consists of electromagnetic waves, it must be possible to derive the experimentally determined laws of reflection and refraction from the fundamental laws of electricity and magnetism. First, it will be necessary to determine the boundary conditions for electric and magnetic fields at the interface between two media.

Boundary conditions. It has previously been shown for static conditions that the tangential components of $\mathbf{H}$ and $\mathbf{E}$ and the normal components of $\mathbf{B}$ and $\mathbf{D}$ are continuous across the boundary. These conditions were derived by means of the equations $\nabla \times \mathbf{H} = 0$, $\nabla \times \mathbf{E} = 0$, $\nabla \cdot \mathbf{B} = 0$, and $\nabla \cdot \mathbf{D} = 0$ in Sections 5–5 and 9–5, assuming that no real charges existed on the boundary.

Boundary conditions for electromagnetic waves should be derived from the following more general forms of Maxwell's relations, which only assume ρ to be zero:

$$\nabla \cdot \mathbf{D} = 0, \qquad \nabla \cdot \mathbf{B} = 0,$$

$$\nabla \times \mathbf{E} = -\dot{\mathbf{B}}, \qquad \nabla \times \mathbf{H} = \mathbf{J} + \dot{\mathbf{D}}.$$

The divergence equations for $\mathbf{D}$ and $\mathbf{B}$ are the same as the static ones, so that the normal boundary conditions remain unchanged:

$$D_{1n} = D_{2n} \quad \text{and} \quad B_{1n} = B_{2n}. \tag{11-9}$$

The tangential boundary condition for $\mathbf{E}$ may be obtained by applying the integral form of Maxwell's third relation

$$\oint \mathbf{E} \cdot d\mathbf{l} = -\int_s \dot{\mathbf{B}} \cdot d\mathbf{s}$$

to the path illustrated in Fig. 5–6. Starting from the upper left corner and progressing counterclockwise, the left side of the equation becomes

$$-E_{2n}a - E_{1n}a + E_{1t}b + E_{1n}a + E_{2n}a - E_{2t}b$$

and the right side becomes

$$-\overline{B}_n 2ab,$$

where $\overline{B}_n$ is the average normal component of $\dot{B}$ and $2ab$ is the area within the path. If the path is chosen very close to the boundary so that b is much greater than a, all terms containing a or ab may be neglected compared with terms containing b only. The left side of the equation then reduces to $E_{1t} - E_{2t}$, while the right side becomes zero. A similar treatment of the equation containing H yields the same result for H_t, and the tangential boundary conditions on E and H become

$$E_{1t} = E_{2t} \qquad \text{and} \qquad H_{1t} = H_{2t}, \tag{11-10}$$

which are identical with the static conditions.

Snell's law. Application of the above boundary conditions to a plane wave at an interface between two media leads to Snell's law. An expression for a plane wave traveling in an arbitrary direction is needed. A plane wavefront is represented in Fig. 11–4 by sheet W, where the propagation vector $\mathbf{a}$ is a unit vector perpendicular to the sheet. In such a plane wave, the magnitudes of the electric or magnetic fields are the same at every point on sheet W. This condition is satisfied by

$$\mathbf{E} = \mathbf{f}\left(t - \frac{\mathbf{a} \cdot \mathbf{r}}{v}\right) \qquad \text{and} \qquad \mathbf{H} = \mathbf{g}\left(t - \frac{\mathbf{a} \cdot \mathbf{r}}{v}\right),$$

where $\mathbf{a} \cdot \mathbf{r} = r \cos \gamma$ is just the perpendicular distance from the origin to the wavefront and is thus independent of the location on the wave

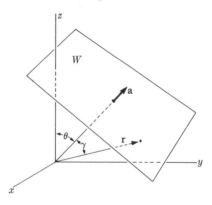

Fig. 11–4. A plane wavefront W, propagating in the $\mathbf{a}$-direction. An arbitrary point on the wavefront is located by $\mathbf{r}$.

as selected by **r**. Just as $\mathbf{f}(t - z/v)$ represents a plane wave traveling in the z-direction, so $\mathbf{f}(t - \mathbf{a} \cdot \mathbf{r}/v)$ represents a plane wave traveling in the **a**-direction. In fact, in the special case where **a** is chosen to be the unit vector in the z-direction, $\mathbf{a} \cdot \mathbf{r}$ reduces to

$$\mathbf{k} \cdot (x\mathbf{i} + y\mathbf{j} + z\mathbf{k}) = z$$

and these equations reduce to the familiar

$$\mathbf{E} = \mathbf{f}\left(t - \frac{z}{v}\right) \quad \text{and} \quad \mathbf{H} = \mathbf{g}\left(t - \frac{z}{v}\right).$$

Snell's law may be demonstrated by assuming the space in Fig. 11–5 to consist of two regions containing different transparent dielectrics separated by an interface that coincides with the xy-plane. The velocity of light in the two dielectrics may be v below the plane where z is negative, and v'' where z is positive. The directions of the incident, reflected, and refracted rays are designated by the unit propagation vectors **a**, **a'**, and **a''**, respectively.

Since monochromatic, polarized light is composed of sinusoidally oscillating electric and magnetic fields, the electric field in the incident wave may be represented by

$$\mathbf{E} = \mathbf{E}_0 \sin \omega \left(t - \frac{\mathbf{a} \cdot \mathbf{r}}{v}\right),$$

while in the reflected and refracted waves it will be represented by

$$\mathbf{E}' = \mathbf{E}'_0 \sin \left\{\omega'\left(t - \frac{\mathbf{a}' \cdot \mathbf{r}}{v}\right) - \delta'\right\}$$

and

$$\mathbf{E}'' = \mathbf{E}''_0 \sin \left\{\omega''\left(t - \frac{\mathbf{a}'' \cdot \mathbf{r}}{v''}\right) - \delta''\right\}.$$

Primes have been added to the ω's to allow for possible changes in frequency, while δ' and δ'' allow for possible phase shifts. The boundary conditions require that the tangential components of the electric and magnetic vectors on one side of the boundary must equal those on the other side. Therefore, at $z = 0$, Eq. (11–10) yields

$$E_x + E'_x = E''_x, \qquad H_x + H'_x = H''_x,$$

and

$$E_y + E'_y = E''_y, \qquad H_y + H'_y = H''_y,$$

(11–11)

and the boundary conditions on **D** and **B** are not needed.

To apply the boundary conditions of Eq. (11–11), the propagation vectors should be expressed in cartesian coordinates. The general expression for a unit vector is

$$\mathbf{i} \sin \theta \cos \phi + \mathbf{j} \sin \theta \sin \phi + \mathbf{k} \cos \theta,$$

where θ and ϕ are the usual spherical coordinates. Without loss of generality, the unit propagation vector for the incident ray may lie wholly within the xz-plane, provided the reflected and refracted rays are free to make any arbitrary angles with respect to this plane.

The condition on the x-components of $\mathbf{E}$ thus results in

$$E_{0x} \sin \omega \left[t - \frac{x \sin \theta + z \cos \theta}{v} \right]$$

$$+ E'_{0x} \sin \left\{ \omega' \left[t - \frac{x \sin \theta' \cos \phi' + y \sin \theta' \sin \phi' + z \cos \theta'}{v} \right] - \delta' \right\}$$

$$= E''_{0x} \sin \left\{ \omega'' \left[t - \frac{x \sin \theta'' \cos \phi'' + y \sin \theta'' \sin \phi'' + z \cos \theta''}{v''} \right] - \delta'' \right\}.$$

For the equations to be satisfied at all times and for all points in the xy-plane, the arguments of the sine functions must be identical (or different by a factor of π, since this affects only the sign of the amplitude). The δ's may, therefore, be 0 or π. The frequency is unchanged, since $\omega = \omega' = \omega''$. Because the sine function of the incident ray is independent of y, the other sine functions must also be independent of y. This requires that $\sin \phi' = \sin \phi'' = 0$. Thus the propagation vectors of the incident, reflected, and refracted rays all lie in the same plane, as illustrated in Fig. 11–5. (Note that requiring $\sin \theta' = \sin \theta'' = 0$ would also satisfy this condition, but this is not an acceptable choice because application to the x-terms would require $\sin \theta = 0$, which is true only if the incident beam strikes the surface perpendicularly.) The condition that the arguments have the same x-dependency requires that $\sin \theta/v = \sin \theta'/v$, which may be satisfied by $\theta = \theta'$ or $\theta = 180° - \theta'$. The latter expression will be selected, since the choice of $\mathbf{a}'$ as the unit propagation vector of the reflected ray requires θ' to be greater than 90°. Examination of Fig. 11–5 reveals that $\theta = 180° - \theta'$ is the familiar law of reflection, more commonly written as $\alpha_1 = \alpha_2$, where $\alpha_1 = \theta$. The x-dependencies further require that $\sin \theta/v = \sin \theta''/v''$, where v and v'' are the velocities of light in the two media. This can be written in the familiar form of Snell's law,

$$n \sin \theta = n'' \sin \theta'',$$

where $n = c/v$, with v being the velocity of light in the medium and c the velocity of light in a vacuum.

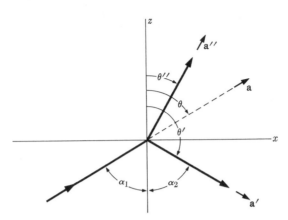

FIG. 11–5. Incident ray lying in the xz-plane impinges on the interface between two media represented by the xy-plane. Directions of incident, reflected, and refracted waves are determined by the unit vectors $\mathbf{a}$, $\mathbf{a}'$, and $\mathbf{a}''$, respectively.

Fresnel's reflection equations. Application of the boundary conditions to both the **H** and **E** vectors can result in a determination of the relative intensities of the reflected and refracted rays. In doing this it is convenient to express the electric and magnetic vectors in two components, E_y and H_y pointing in the y-direction and E_i and H_i lying entirely in the incident xz-plane. All **E** and **H** components must be perpendicular to the direction of propagation of their respective rays. Substitution of the x-component of E_i into Eq. (11–11) gives

$$E_i \cos \theta + E'_i \cos (180° - \theta) = E''_i \cos \theta'',$$

while the y-component condition is unchanged:

$$E_y + E'_y = E''_y.$$

Substitution of the x-component of H_i into Eq. (11–11) gives the same equations except that E is everywhere replaced by H. These equations for H may be expressed in terms of the electric vectors by use of the proportionality between E and H that exists in plane waves. Since $\sqrt{K}$ is approximately equal to the index of refraction and K_m is approximately one, Eq. (11–8) may be rewritten as

$$H_y = \frac{1}{\mu} \frac{E_x}{v} = \sqrt{\frac{K\epsilon_0}{K_m \mu_0}} \, E_x \cong n \sqrt{\frac{\epsilon_0}{\mu_0}} \, E_x.$$

In the present case, where the direction of propagation is not z but some arbitrary direction $\mathbf{a}$, the proportionality exists between H_i and E_y and between H_y and E_i. Thus the boundary conditions on **H** reduce to

$$nE_y \cos \theta + nE'_y \cos (180° - \theta) = n''E''_y \cos \theta''$$

and

$$nE_i + nE'_i = n''E''_i.$$

Snell's law may be used to express n and n'' in terms of θ and θ''. These four equations may then be used to determine the four quantities E'_i, E''_i, E'_y, and E''_y in terms of the incident components E_i and E_y. By liberal application of trigonometric identities, the resulting expressions reduce to the usual form of Fresnel's equations given below:

$$E'_i = E_i \frac{\tan (\theta - \theta'')}{\tan (\theta + \theta'')},$$

$$E'_y = -E_y \frac{\sin (\theta - \theta'')}{\sin (\theta + \theta'')},$$

$$E''_i = 2E_i \frac{\cos \theta \sin \theta''}{\sin (\theta + \theta'') \cos (\theta - \theta'')},$$

$$E''_y = 2E_y \frac{\sin \theta'' \cos \theta}{\sin (\theta + \theta'')}.$$

In the next section it is shown that the energy transmitted by an electromagnetic wave is given by Poynting's vector $\mathbf{S} = \mathbf{E} \times \mathbf{H}$. Using this vector and the proportionality between E and H in plane waves, the relative energy in the reflected and refracted rays for any angle of incidence can be determined from Fresnel's equations.

It is interesting to note that if the angle between the reflected and refracted ray is 90°, that is, $\theta - \theta'' = \pi/2$, then the denominator of the first equation is infinite and E'_i is zero. Light reflected at this angle would have no component of the electric vector in the incident plane. The angle of incidence required for this effect may be expressed in terms of the index of refraction by substituting $\theta - \theta'' = \pi/2$ into Snell's law. The resulting expression,

$$\tan \theta_B = \frac{n''}{n},$$

is known as *Brewster's law*, where θ_B is Brewster's angle. If ordinary light with random planes of polarization strikes an interface with this angle to the normal, the reflected light will be perfectly polarized, with the electric vector perpendicular to the incident plane. This is a standard laboratory technique for producing plane polarized light.

11-4 The Poynting vector. It has now been demonstrated that Maxwell's field equations predict that electromagnetic waves may travel through media or through a vacuum with the same speed as light and that these waves will be governed by the known laws of optics. However, it has not yet been shown that these electromagnetic waves transmit energy, and unless they do, they cannot be detected.

A general expression for the flow of energy into an arbitrary volume τ surrounded by a closed surface s is needed. Any electromagnetic energy that flows into τ through s increases the electric field energy, increases the magnetic field energy, or is converted into other forms of energy. According to Section 9–9, the power per unit volume expended in changing the electric and the magnetic fields is $\mathbf{E} \cdot \dot{\mathbf{D}}$ and $\mathbf{H} \cdot \dot{\mathbf{B}}$ respectively, and according to Section 7–7 the power per unit volume being converted to other forms is $\mathbf{E} \cdot \mathbf{J}$. The power flowing into τ then is obtained by integrating the sum of these three terms over the volume τ; that is,

$$P = \int_\tau (\mathbf{E} \cdot \dot{\mathbf{D}} + \mathbf{H} \cdot \dot{\mathbf{B}} + \mathbf{E} \cdot \mathbf{J})\, d\tau. \qquad (11\text{–}12)$$

This integrand can be simplified and written in terms of a single vector by introducing Maxwell's third and fourth relations, $\dot{\mathbf{B}} = -\nabla \times \mathbf{E}$ and $\dot{\mathbf{D}} + \mathbf{J} = \nabla \times \mathbf{H}$ respectively. The integrand then becomes

$$\mathbf{E} \cdot \nabla \times \mathbf{H} - \mathbf{H} \cdot \nabla \times \mathbf{E} = \nabla \cdot (\mathbf{H} \times \mathbf{E}) = -\nabla \cdot \mathbf{S},$$

where the single vector $\mathbf{S}$, which is called the *Poynting vector* in honor of its inventor, is defined by

$$\mathbf{S} = \mathbf{E} \times \mathbf{H}. \qquad (11\text{–}13)$$

Significantly, $\mathbf{S}$ has the unit watts/m^2, since $\mathbf{E}$ has the unit volts/m and $\mathbf{H}$ has the unit amps/m. The electromagnetic power entering the volume τ through s is

$$-\int_\tau \nabla \cdot \mathbf{S}\, d\tau = -\int_s \mathbf{S} \cdot d\mathbf{s},$$

where the surface integral is obtained by applying Gauss' mathematical theorem. Equation (11–12) then can be written as

$$\int_\tau (\mathbf{E} \cdot \dot{\mathbf{D}} + \mathbf{H} \cdot \dot{\mathbf{B}} + \mathbf{E} \cdot \mathbf{J})\, d\tau + \int_s \mathbf{S} \cdot d\mathbf{s} = 0. \qquad (11\text{–}14)$$

The volume integral gives the total electromagnetic power expended within the volume to change the electric and magnetic fields and to convert electromagnetic energy to other forms. A negative sign for any of these terms indicates that that particular energy conversion is progressing in the opposite direction. The surface integral gives the flux of $\mathbf{S}$ out of the volume.

Obviously, the integral $\int_s \mathbf{S} \cdot d\mathbf{s}$ gives the rate of flow of electromagnetic energy out through the closed surface s. While this does not prove that $\mathbf{S}$ represents the rate of energy flow per unit area at every point in space, the commonly made assumption that $\mathbf{S}$ does indeed represent this rate of energy flow per unit area does not conflict* with experimental facts or other experience. This expression for the Poynting vector should be applied to some simple and familiar situations to gain an understanding of its properties.

Energy flow in electromagnetic waves. Sinusoidal plane waves have been investigated in the previous section and, for a polarized wave, values of $\mathbf{E}$ and $\mathbf{H}$ at $t = 0$ are plotted in Fig. 11–3. The power density propagated by such waves is given by

$$\mathbf{S} = EH\mathbf{k} = \sqrt{\frac{\epsilon}{\mu}} \, E_x^2 \mathbf{k}.$$

For the wave shown in Fig. 11–3,

$$\mathbf{S} = \mathbf{k} \sqrt{\frac{\epsilon}{\mu}} \, E_{0x}^2 \sin^2 \omega \left(t - \frac{z}{v} \right),$$

which pulsates with time at any z, or with z at any time. Its time average at any point in space is given by the integral over a full period from $t = 0$ to $t = T$:

$$p = \frac{1}{T} \int_0^T EH \, dt = \frac{1}{2\pi} \int_0^{2\pi} E_{0x}^2 \sqrt{\frac{\epsilon}{\mu}} \sin^2 \beta \, d\beta,$$

where $\beta = \omega(t - z/v)$. Hence

$$p = \frac{E_{0x}^2 \sqrt{\epsilon/\mu}}{2}$$

represents the time-average power transmitted through a unit area by a plane electromagnetic wave and is proportional to the square of the amplitude. While this expression has been derived for plane polarized light, it can readily be extended, since nonpolarized light consists of many plane polarized waves whose directions of polarization are randomly distributed.

---

* It has been pointed out that when a permanent magnet is placed near a charged capacitor, $\mathbf{S} = \mathbf{E} \times \mathbf{H}$ may have finite values at many points, even though no energy can be detected.

Analysis shows that in all such arrangements $\int_s \mathbf{S} \cdot d\mathbf{s} = 0$ for any closed space that can be chosen, so that the $\mathbf{S}$ field forms closed paths and no energy is absorbed. Energy must be absorbed to be detected.

Chemical cell with $V = G \ln r/a$.　　Carbon washer

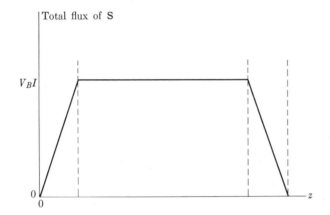

Total flux of S

$V_B I$

0
0

FIG. 11–6. Poynting-vector flux along a d-c transmission line consisting of coaxial cylinders. The Poynting flux builds up linearly in the chemical cell, remains constant in the intervening space, and is absorbed linearly in the carbon washer.

Direct-current energy propagation along a coaxial cable. The simply constructed coaxial transmission line shown in Fig. 11–6 is chosen to demonstrate the role of the Poynting vector in the propagation of energy. The solid inner cylinder of nickel and the hollow outer cylinder of copper provide electrodes for the electrolytic cell on the left and also provide a transmission line, conducting current to the carbon washer on the right. If the cylinders are long but have sufficient cross section that their resistances are negligible, the field **E** in the air space between cylinders will have the same radial dependence as it has in the washer. This is not true of the **E** field in the electrolyte, where chemical forces cause the potential to vary rapidly near each conductor. However, a bimetallic hollow cylinder, with Cu inside and Ni outside, inserted into the electrolyte concentric with the original cylinders would change this potential distribution. In principle it would be possible to insert many such bi-metallic cylinders of different diameters to produce any desired potential distribution. In particular, it could be made to approach the potential distribution in the carbon washer. Such a distribution will be assumed because it greatly simplifies the treatment of the problem. The radial potential distribution throughout the device is then given, in cylindrical coordinates centered on the z-axis, by $V = G \ln r/a$, where G is some constant. Chemical energy is converted to electric energy in the cell and electric energy is converted to thermal energy in the carbon washer. In order to maintain the steady-state conditions assumed for the device, this heat must be removed as rapidly as it is produced.

The electric field at all points between cylinders is $\mathbf{E} = -\nabla V = -\mathbf{a}_r(G/r)$. The steady current I that is directed to the right in the Cu and to the left in the Ni produces a magnetic field that can be calculated from the integral relation

$$\oint \mathbf{H} \cdot d\mathbf{l} = \int_s \mathbf{J} \cdot d\mathbf{s}. \tag{11-15}$$

Convenient surfaces for evaluating these integrals are flat circular disks, each of radius r, centered on and perpendicular to the axis of the device. The line integral then can be evaluated around the periphery and the surface integral can be evaluated over the flat surface. For each of these disks the left side of Eq. (11–15) gives $H2\pi r$, since H is constant everywhere on the periphery. For disks having radii greater than a and less than b and lying between the cell and washer, the surface integral gives I. In this region,

$$\mathbf{H} = -\mathbf{a}_\phi \frac{I}{2\pi r}$$

and

$$\mathbf{S} = \mathbf{a}_r \times \mathbf{a}_\phi \frac{IG}{2\pi r^2} = \mathbf{k} \frac{IG}{2\pi r^2}.$$

It should be noted that $\mathbf{S} = 0$ inside the metal conductors because $\mathbf{E} = 0$, and for $r > c$ it is also zero since $\mathbf{H} = 0$. The expression for the Poynting vector indicates that energy is being propagated parallel to the z-axis and directed from the cell to the washer. The areal density of this propagated power varies with r, but the total flow into the washer can be obtained by integrating over the flat inside surface of the washer; that is,

$$P = \int_s \mathbf{S} \cdot d\mathbf{s} = \int_a^b \frac{IG}{2\pi r^2} 2\pi r \, dr = IG \ln \frac{b}{a},$$

where G must be determined from the boundary conditions. If the potential of the Ni cylinder is zero and that of the Cu cylinder is V_B, the boundary conditions are satisfied by $G = V_B \ln b/a$. The power entering the washer is then

$$P = IV_B,$$

which is also the power leaving the flat inner surface of the electrolytic cell.

Starting from the outside surface of the cell and progressing parallel to the axis, the Poynting vector at each radial distance builds up linearly within the cell and reaches its maximum values at the inner surface. Likewise, each of these Poynting vectors decreases linearly to zero on passing through the carbon washer from its inner to its outer surface. This behavior stems from the fact that $\mathbf{H}$ varies linearly with z inside both the cell and the washer, while $\mathbf{E}$ is independent of z throughout the device. The variation in $\mathbf{H}$ can be shown by applying Eq. (11–15) to one of the imaginary flat disks as it is moved parallel to the axis. The line integral always gives $H2\pi r$, but the values obtained from the surface integrations vary linearly from 0 to I on passing from the outer to the inner surface of the cell or washer. Since the $\mathbf{S}$ for each value of r has the type of z-dependence shown in Fig. 11–6, the total flux of $\mathbf{S}$ also has this z-dependence. It is the curve for the total $\mathbf{S}$ flux that is plotted in Fig. 11–6, since it has the shape that is characteristic of the magnitude of $\mathbf{S}$ at each value of r.

11–5 Retarded potentials. In Section 8–5 the general differential equations for scalar and vector potentials,

$$\nabla^2 V - \mu\epsilon\ddot{V} = -\rho/\epsilon \tag{11–16}$$

and

$$\nabla^2 \mathbf{A} - \mu\epsilon\ddot{\mathbf{A}} = -\mu\mathbf{J}, \tag{11–17}$$

were developed. In electrostatic problems or in any problems where the time derivatives in these equations can be ignored, the scalar potentials were shown to be obtained from

$$V = \frac{1}{4\pi\epsilon} \sum_i \frac{q_i}{r_i}$$

with point charges, or from

$$V = \int_{\tau'} \frac{\rho \, d\tau'}{4\pi\epsilon r}$$

with charges whose distribution function $\rho = \rho(x', y', z')$ is known. When the charge distributions are time-dependent and the time derivatives cannot be ignored, these solutions must be modified.

The time-dependent solution for a distribution of charge will be obtained by calculating the potential δV at the field point P due to the

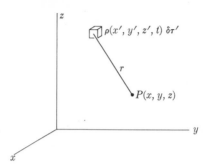

Fig. 11-7. A charge within the volume element $\delta\tau'$ located a distance r from a general point in space.

charge density in the volume element $\delta\tau'$, as illustrated in Fig. 11–7. This potential should depend only on charge density ρ, the time t, and the distance r. Using spherical coordinates with the origin at $\delta\tau'$ and with δV independent of θ and ϕ, the Laplacian can be written as

$$\nabla^2 \, \delta V = \frac{1}{r^2} \frac{\partial}{\partial r} \left(r^2 \frac{\partial \, \delta V}{\partial r} \right).$$

It is desirable to transform this into a function of $r \, \delta V$ by using the relation

$$\nabla^2 \, \delta V = \frac{1}{r} \frac{\partial^2}{\partial r^2} (r \, \delta V).$$

Equation (11–16) for δV at the field point P then becomes

$$\frac{\partial^2}{\partial r^2} (r \, \delta V) - \mu\epsilon \frac{\partial^2}{\partial t^2} (r \, \delta V) = 0,$$

which is a wave equation in the product $r \, \delta V$. Direct substitution shows that $r \, \delta V = f(t - r/v)$, where $v = 1/\sqrt{\mu\epsilon}$, is a solution that represents a wave traveling outward along the radius r. The other solution, $r \, \delta V = g(t + r/v)$, which represents an oppositely directed wave, is not important here.

The function of $(t - r/v)$ must be chosen to give the static potential in the special cases where there is no time-dependence. Thus if the charge density at $\delta\tau'$ is given by $\rho = \rho(x', y', z', t)$, the potential at P due to the volume element $\delta\tau'$ is

$$\partial V = \frac{\rho(x', y', z', t - r/v)}{4\pi\epsilon r} \, \delta\tau',$$

where r again is the distance from $\delta\tau'$ to the field point P shown in

Fig. 11-7. The potential at P due to any distribution of charges is then

$$V = \int_{\tau'} \frac{\rho(x', y', z', t - r/v)}{4\pi\epsilon r} \, d\tau', \qquad (11\text{-}18)$$

which gives solutions for static charge distributions when the dependence on time is set equal to zero, as well as the more general solutions for charge distributions that do change with time. The similarity between Eqs. (11-16) and (11-17) makes it possible to obtain the solution for the vector potential by substituting $\mu\mathbf{J}$ for ρ/ϵ in Eq. (11-18). Thus

$$\mathbf{A} = \int_{\tau'} \frac{\mu\mathbf{J}(x', y', z', t - r/v)}{4\pi r} \, d\tau'. \qquad (11\text{-}19)$$

It should be noted that if a sudden change in the charge or current occurs, its effect will not be noticed at P until the time r/v later. This is physically reasonable if potential is thought of as radiating from the originating charge with a velocity v. Because of the time lag between a given charge distribution in space and the corresponding potential at P, Eqs. (11-18) and (11-19) are said to be equations for *retarded potentials*.

11-6 Radiation from an oscillating dipole. In Section 2-6 the electric field due to a stationary dipole was obtained by calculating the scalar potential V at a general point in space, the electric field being the negative gradient of this potential. However, when the moment of a dipole changes with time, a number of additional complications are introduced. First, since retarded potentials must be used, the phase of the potential depends upon the location of the field point. Second, the electric field is no longer given by the negative gradient of the scalar potential alone, but also involves the vector potential, as indicated by Eq. (8-18), $\mathbf{E} = -\nabla V - \dot{\mathbf{A}}$. Finally, in addition to the electric field, there is a magnetic field generated in accordance with Eq. (8-17), $\mathbf{B} = \nabla \times \mathbf{A}$.

Oscillating dipole potentials. An oscillating dipole is illustrated in Fig. 11-8. It consists of two small metallic spheres with their centers a distance l apart and joined by a conducting wire. It is desired to calculate the potentials at the general field point P located by the spherical coordinates r and θ, where r is chosen to be large compared with l. The potentials and fields must be independent of ϕ because of the symmetry about the axis of the dipole. Assuming that there is a sinusoidal current between the two spheres that is alternately charging and discharging them, the charge on the top sphere can be written as the real part of $+q = q_0 e^{j\omega t}$ and that on the bottom sphere is the real part of $-q = -q_0 e^{j\omega t}$. The current then is the real part of $I = dq/dt = j\omega q_0 e^{j\omega t}$.

The scalar potential may be determined by substituting an expression for the charge density into Eq. (11-18). Since there is no charge in space,

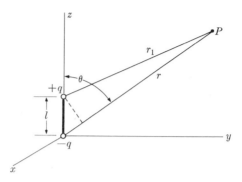

FIG. 11–8. Oscillating electric dipole, where $+q = q_0 \cos \omega t$.

except on the small spheres that are located at the origin and at $z = l$ on the z-axis, the integrand is zero everywhere except over these spheres. If the spheres are very small, r is constant over the sphere at the origin and r_1 is constant over the sphere at $z = l$. Over these spheres the absolute values of $\int \rho \, d\tau' = q_0 e^{j\omega t}$, and therefore the scalar potential is

$$V = \frac{q_0 e^{j\omega(t-r/v)}}{4\pi\epsilon r} - \frac{q_0 e^{j\omega(t-r_1/v)}}{4\pi\epsilon r_1}. \tag{11–20}$$

Because $r \gg l$, $r_1 = r - l \cos \theta$, and Eq. (11–20) may be written as

$$V = \frac{q_0 e^{j\omega(t-r/v)}}{4\pi\epsilon r} \left\{ 1 - \frac{e^{j\omega l(\cos \theta)/v}}{1 - l(\cos \theta)/r} \right\}.$$

The term $\{1 - l\,(\cos\theta)/r\}^{-1}$ may be written as $\{1 + l\,(\cos\theta)/r\}$, by using the first two terms of the binomial expansion, and the term $\exp\{j\omega l\,(\cos\theta)/v\}$ may be expressed by the first two terms of a power series as $1 + j\omega l\,(\cos\theta)/v$, provided that $\omega l/v \ll 1$. This last approximation is applicable provided l is much smaller than the wavelength of the radiation, which is true for many dipoles in nature. Equation (11–20) finally reduces to

$$V = \frac{p_0 e^{j\beta} \cos \theta}{4\pi\epsilon r^2} \left(1 + \frac{j\omega r}{v} \right), \tag{11–21}$$

where $\beta = \omega(t - r/v)$ and $p_0 = q_0 l$, the maximum dipole moment. It is interesting to note that Eq. (11–21) gives the static scalar potential of Eq. (2–24) for the special case where the distance r of the point from the dipole is small compared with the wavelength of the radiation, $\lambda = 2\pi v/\omega$, since the second term in the parentheses is then negligible. Before fields can be calculated, the vector potential as well as this scalar potential is needed.

In determining the vector potential of the dipole, Eq. (11–19) reduces to an integral over the length of the wire between the two spheres, since the current density is zero everywhere else. The expression $\int_{\tau'} \mu \mathbf{J} \, d\tau'$ becomes $\mathbf{k} \int_l \mu I \, dl$, where $\mathbf{k}$ is a unit vector parallel to the z-axis, and the vector potential is given by

$$\mathbf{A} = \mathbf{k} \int_0^l \frac{\mu I(t - r/v)}{4\pi r} \, dl.$$

The value of r in this equation actually ranges from r to r_1 over the length of the wire, but since $r \gg l$ and $r_1 = r - l \cos \theta$, r can be treated as constant and taken outside the integral sign. It is proper to treat r as a constant here because, at any instant, the integrand has the same sign over the length of the dipole; it would not have been satisfactory to treat it as constant in Eq. (11–18), where the integrand would cancel out to this approximation because it has opposite signs over the two spheres. The first nonzero term must be maintained. The resulting expression is

$$\mathbf{A} = \mathbf{k} \frac{\mu}{4\pi r} lI\left(t - \frac{r}{v}\right) = \mathbf{k} \frac{\mu}{4\pi r} lj\omega q_0 e^{\,j\omega(t-r/v)}$$

or

$$\mathbf{A} = \frac{j\omega \mu p_0 e^{j\beta}}{4\pi r} (\mathbf{a}_r \cos \theta - \mathbf{a}_\theta \sin \theta), \qquad (11\text{–}22)$$

since $\mathbf{k} = \mathbf{a}_r \cos \theta - \mathbf{a}_\theta \sin \theta$.

Oscillating dipole fields. The electric and magnetic fields of the oscillating dipole can now be calculated directly from these vector and scalar potentials, using the relations $\mathbf{E} = -\nabla V - \dot{\mathbf{A}}$ and $\mu \mathbf{H} = \nabla \times \mathbf{A}$. In performing these differentiations, the following relations are useful: $\beta = \omega(t - r/v)$, $\partial \beta/\partial r = -\omega/v$, and $\partial \beta/\partial t = \omega$. Since the gradient

$$\nabla V = \mathbf{a}_r \frac{\partial V}{\partial r} + \mathbf{a}_\theta \frac{1}{r} \frac{\partial V}{\partial \theta}$$

has many terms, each component will be calculated separately. The r-component is

$$\frac{\partial V}{\partial r} = \left[\frac{1}{r^2}\left(1 + \frac{j\omega r}{v}\right)\left(-\frac{j\omega}{v}\right) + \left(-\frac{2}{r^3} - \frac{j\omega}{vr^2}\right)\right] e^{j\beta} \frac{p_0 \cos \theta}{4\pi\epsilon},$$

which, on collecting terms, becomes

$$\frac{\partial V}{\partial r} = -\left(\frac{2}{r^3} + \frac{2j\omega}{vr^2} - \frac{\omega^2}{v^2 r}\right) \frac{p_0 \cos \theta}{4\pi\epsilon} e^{j\beta}.$$

The θ-component is

$$\frac{1}{r}\frac{\partial V}{\partial \theta} = -\left(\frac{1}{r^3} + \frac{j\omega}{vr^2}\right)\frac{p_0 \sin \theta}{4\pi\epsilon}e^{j\beta}.$$

Direct differentiation of Eq. (11–22) with respect to time gives the simple relation

$$\dot{\mathbf{A}} = -\frac{\omega^2\mu p_0 e^{j\beta}}{4\pi r}(\mathbf{a}_r \cos \theta - \mathbf{a}_\theta \sin \theta).$$

These expressions for ∇V and $\dot{\mathbf{A}}$ can be combined and the terms with like powers of r collected to give the following expression for $\mathbf{E}$:

$$\mathbf{E} = \frac{p_0 e^{j\beta}}{4\pi\epsilon}\left[-\frac{\omega^2 \sin \theta}{v^2 r}\mathbf{a}_\theta + \left(\frac{j\omega}{vr^2} + \frac{1}{r^3}\right)(\mathbf{a}_r 2 \cos \theta + \mathbf{a}_\theta \sin \theta)\right]. \quad (11\text{–}23)$$

This electric field is made up of terms proportional to $1/r$, $1/r^2$, and $1/r^3$. For static conditions $\omega = 0$ and all but the last terms disappear, with the result

$$\mathbf{E}\text{ (static)} = \frac{p_0}{4\pi\epsilon r^3}(\mathbf{a}_r 2 \cos \theta + \mathbf{a}_\theta \sin \theta).$$

This is the dipole field that was given in Section 2–13, and it falls off rapidly with the distance r from the dipole. At high frequencies and at large distances the first term dominates, since it falls off only as $1/r$ and is proportional to ω^2.

The magnetic field can be obtained directly from the vector potential by means of the defining equation $\mu\mathbf{H} = \nabla \times \mathbf{A}$, which gives

$$\mathbf{H} = \frac{j\omega p_0}{4\pi r^2 \sin \theta}\begin{vmatrix} \mathbf{a}_r & r\mathbf{a}_\theta & r \sin \theta \mathbf{a}_\phi \\ \dfrac{\partial}{\partial r} & \dfrac{\partial}{\partial \theta} & \dfrac{\partial}{\partial \phi} \\ \dfrac{e^{j\beta}\cos \theta}{r} & -e^{j\beta}\sin \theta & 0 \end{vmatrix},$$

which may be reduced to

$$\mathbf{H} = \frac{j\omega p_0 e^{j\beta}}{4\pi}\mathbf{a}_\phi \sin \theta\left(\frac{j\omega}{vr} + \frac{1}{r^2}\right). \quad (11\text{–}24)$$

As should be expected, this expression for the magnetic field approaches zero when $\omega \to 0$, since a static dipole does not produce a magnetic field. However, when ω is finite and $\omega r/v \ll 1$, the second term predominates and we have

$$\mathbf{H}\text{ (low frequency)} = \frac{j\omega q_0 l e^{j\omega t}}{4\pi r^2}\sin \theta \mathbf{a}_\phi.$$

The time-dependent field, which is the real part of this expression, can be written as

$$\mathbf{H} \text{ (low frequency)} = \frac{il \sin \theta}{4\pi r^2} \mathbf{a}_\phi,$$

where $i = -q_0\omega \sin \omega t$ is the time-dependent electric current between the spheres. This last expression could have been obtained directly from the elementary form of the Biot-Savart law. At high frequencies and large distances, the $1/r$ terms are dominant in both the magnetic and electric fields. These terms represent the radiation field in which the $\mathbf{E}$ and $\mathbf{H}$ vectors are in phase and are perpendicular both to each other and to $\mathbf{r}$, the direction of propagation. Thus, at large distances from an oscillating dipole, the radiation field takes on the form of the plane waves discussed in Section 11–2. The lines of electric and magnetic flux shown in Fig. 11–9 are densest in the direction perpendicular to the dipole and drop to zero in the direction of the dipole axis.

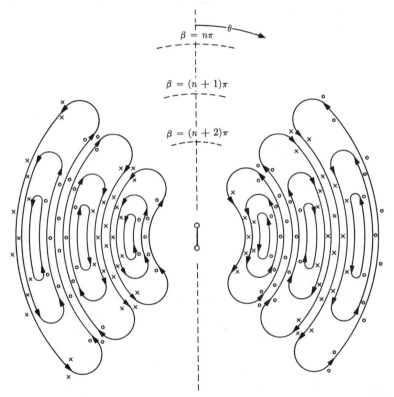

Fig. 11–9. Schematic illustration of the radiation fields from an oscillating dipole. Solid lines represent electric flux, while crosses and circles represent the magnetic flux lines entering and leaving the paper, respectively.

It should be remembered that Maxwell's relations can be satisfied exactly at any point in space only by including all of the terms. For example, the lines of electric flux shown in Fig. 11–9 must include radially directed terms if they are to be continuous, and yet must be zero at $\theta = 0$ and $\theta = \pi$. If the number of closed loops of $\mathbf{E}$ flux shown in the figure is kept constant but their length is increased as they are propagated radially outward, the density of the θ-component falls off as $1/r$, while the density of the r-component falls off as $1/r^2$ and becomes negligible as r becomes very large.

Energy flow from the oscillating dipole. The energy leaving the oscillating dipole per unit of time may be obtained by surrounding the dipole with an imaginary sphere and integrating the normal component of $\mathbf{S} = \mathbf{E} \times \mathbf{H}$ over its surface. As the radius of this imaginary sphere is made arbitrarily large a finite contribution is made only by the $1/r$ terms of $\mathbf{E}$ and $\mathbf{H}$, since the cross product of these terms falls off as $1/r^2$ and the area of the sphere increases as r^2. All other terms of $\mathbf{E}$ and $\mathbf{H}$ fall off more rapidly and become negligible at large distances.

Since the real parts of these $1/r$ terms for $\mathbf{E}$ and $\mathbf{H}$ are

$$\mathbf{E} = -\frac{\omega^2 p_0 \cos \beta}{4\pi v^2} \frac{\sin \theta}{r} \mathbf{a}_\theta$$

and

$$\mathbf{H} = -\frac{\omega^2 p_0 \cos \beta}{4\pi v} \frac{\sin \theta}{r} \mathbf{a}_\phi,$$

the Poynting vector at large distances is

$$\mathbf{S} = \mathbf{E} \times \mathbf{H} = \frac{\omega^4 p_0^2 \cos^2 \beta}{(4\pi)^2 \epsilon v^3} \frac{\sin^2 \theta}{r^2} \mathbf{a}_r$$

and the time average of the Poynting vector is

$$\overline{\mathbf{S}} = \frac{\omega^4 p_0^2}{2(4\pi)^2 \epsilon v^3} \frac{\sin^2 \theta}{r^2} \mathbf{a}_r. \tag{11–25}$$

For many problems, it is more convenient to express Eq. (11–25) in terms of current and wavelength. The effective current is defined as $I = I_0/\sqrt{2}$, where I_0 is the maximum current and $p_0 = I_0 l/\omega$. Furthermore, $\mu \epsilon v^2 = 1$ and $\omega/v = 2\pi/\lambda$, where λ is the wavelength of the electromagnetic wave. Equation (11–25) can then be expressed as

$$\overline{\mathbf{S}} = \sqrt{\frac{\mu}{\epsilon}} \left(\frac{Il}{2\lambda}\right)^2 \frac{\sin^2 \theta}{r^2} \mathbf{a}_r, \tag{11–26}$$

which shows that the radiation is proportional to the square of the current and inversely proportional to the square of the wavelength.

The average power radiated can be found by integrating Eq. (11–26) over a large sphere surrounding the dipole, which yields

$$\overline{P} = \int_s \overline{\mathbf{S}} \cdot d\mathbf{s}$$

$$= \sqrt{\frac{\mu}{\epsilon}} \left(\frac{Il}{2\lambda}\right)^2 \int_0^{2\pi} \int_0^{\pi} \frac{\sin^2 \theta}{r^2} r^2 \sin \theta \, d\phi \, d\theta$$

$$= \sqrt{\frac{\mu}{\epsilon}} \left(\frac{Il}{2\lambda}\right)^2 2\pi \int_0^{\pi} \sin^3 \theta \, d\theta = \frac{2\pi}{3} \sqrt{\frac{\mu}{\epsilon}} \left(\frac{Il}{\lambda}\right)^2,$$

which is the power radiated throughout space that must be supplied to the dipole by some power source if the current oscillations are to be maintained. In addition to this loss by radiation, the power lost in heating conductors is given by $\overline{P} = I^2 R_j$, where R_j may be greater than the d-c resistance $\rho l/A$, because of the tendency for high-frequency currents to concentrate in the outer surface or "skin" of the wire. The total power lost in the dipole is given by

$$\overline{P}_t = \frac{2\pi}{3} \sqrt{\frac{\mu}{\epsilon}} \left(\frac{Il}{\lambda}\right)^2 + I^2 R_j$$

and the effective a-c resistance of the dipole is then $R = \overline{P}_t/I^2$, in ohms.

General energy flow near an oscillating dipole. It has been shown that the only terms of the **E** and **H** fields that contribute significantly to the power radiated are those proportional to $1/r$. To determine what happens to the Poynting vector flux represented by the higher-order terms, every term of the Poynting vector must be investigated. The **E** and **H** fields should be written in their time-dependent form by taking the real parts of the complex expressions in Eqs. (11–23) and (11–24). Since there are five terms in the **E** field and two terms in the **H** field, the Poynting vector **E** × **H** contains ten terms. However, examination of the **E** terms shows that they can be paired off and written as three terms by reintroducing the characteristic dipole-field vector that is defined in Section 2–13 as

$$\mathbf{d}_f \equiv \mathbf{a}_r 2 \cos \theta + \mathbf{a}_\theta \sin \theta.$$

When this simplifying vector is introduced, the electric field of the oscillating dipole can be written as

$$\mathbf{E} = -(\mathbf{a}_\theta g_1 \sin \theta \cos \beta + \mathbf{d}_f g_2 \sin \beta - \mathbf{d}_f g_3 \cos \beta) \quad (11\text{–}27)$$

and its magnetic field can be written as

$$\mathbf{H} = -\mathbf{a}_\phi \sin \theta (h_1 \cos \beta + h_2 \sin \beta), \quad (11\text{–}28)$$

where the g and h constants are defined by

$$g_1 = \frac{p_0\omega^2}{4\pi\epsilon v^2 r}, \qquad g_2 = \frac{p_0\omega}{4\pi\epsilon v r^2}, \qquad g_3 = \frac{p_0}{4\pi\epsilon r^3},$$

and

$$h_1 = \frac{p_0\omega^2}{4\pi v r}, \qquad h_2 = \frac{p_0\omega}{4\pi r^2}.$$

In calculating Poynting vector terms the following cross products are needed: the product $\mathbf{a}_\theta \times \mathbf{a}_\phi = \mathbf{a}_r$ and the product $\mathbf{d}_f \times \mathbf{a}_\phi \equiv \mathbf{d}_s$, which is a newly defined vector that has the value

$$\mathbf{d}_s = \mathbf{a}_r \times \mathbf{a}_\phi 2 \cos\theta + \mathbf{a}_\theta \times \mathbf{a}_\phi \sin\theta$$

or

$$\mathbf{d}_s = -\mathbf{a}_\theta 2 \cos\theta + \mathbf{a}_r \sin\theta.$$

The Poynting vector $\mathbf{S} = \mathbf{E} \times \mathbf{H}$ for the oscillating dipole can now be written:

$$\mathbf{S} = \mathbf{a}_r g_1 h_1 \sin^2\theta \cos^2\beta + \mathbf{a}_r g_1 h_2 \sin^2\theta \sin\beta \cos\beta$$
$$+ \mathbf{d}_s g_2 h_1 \sin\theta \sin\beta \cos\beta + \mathbf{d}_s g_2 h_2 \sin\theta \sin^2\beta$$
$$- \mathbf{d}_s g_3 h_1 \sin\theta \cos^2\beta - \mathbf{d}_s g_3 h_2 \sin\theta \cos\beta \sin\beta,$$

where each of these six terms represents a rate of energy flow. To determine whether there is a net rate of energy flow outward, $\overline{\mathbf{S}}$, the time average of $\mathbf{S}$, must be calculated. If the period of oscillation is T,

$$\overline{\mathbf{S}} = \frac{1}{T}\int_0^T \mathbf{S}\, dt = \frac{1}{2\pi}\int_0^{2\pi} \mathbf{S}\, d\beta,$$

where the integrand consists of the six terms. Three of the six terms may be eliminated immediately by using the relation

$$\frac{1}{2\pi}\int_0^{2\pi} \cos\beta \sin\beta\, d\beta = 0.$$

Cancellation of two of the remaining terms results from

$$\frac{1}{2\pi}\int_0^{2\pi} \cos^2\beta\, d\beta = \frac{1}{2\pi}\int_0^{2\pi} \sin^2\beta\, d\beta = \tfrac{1}{2}$$

together with the relation $g_2 h_2 = g_3 h_1$, which is easily verified. The remaining term, containing $g_1 h_1$, is just the radiation term previously discussed, while the other five terms represent reversible conversions of energy between the electric and magnetic fields.

Some of this local-field energy flow will be absorbed if there are conductors, or dielectric or magnetic materials in the neighborhood of the dipole. Such materials modify the fields so as to cause energy flow to them from the dipole.

The magnetic and electric fields due to a coil of wire in which there is an oscillating current can be calculated with the relations used for the oscillating dipole. As in the oscillating dipole, there are reversible-energy, local-field terms as well as nonreversible-energy radiation terms. Simple examples calculated in Section 10–8 show how nearby conductors, or dielectric or magnetic materials can absorb energy from such oscillating circuits.

Practical antennas. The problem of the simplest of all antennas, the oscillating dipole, has now been solved. The solution applies rather well to any short-wire antenna in which current oscillates in a wire, alternately charging and discharging the ends. It also applies to a radio transmitting antenna consisting of a single wire rising vertically above the ground, provided the antenna is short compared with the wavelength of the radiation. The ground acts as a conducting surface, reflecting the radiation of the wire in such a way that the radiation appears to be coming from a dipole whose bottom end is just as far below the ground as the top of the antenna is above ground. It is known from image solutions that a charge above a conducting surface creates the same field above that surface as would be created by the charge and an oppositely charged image below the surface.

Antennas that are nearly as long as or longer than the wavelength of the transmitted radiation have more complicated solutions. The complication arises from the fact that the current is not uniform along the length of the antenna and the charge is not concentrated at the two ends. Once the current and charge distributions are determined along the length of the wire, the vector and scalar potentials may be found in the same manner as for the oscillating dipole.

A brief treatment of long antennas, loop antennas, and arrays of antennas is given by Harnwell.* For more detailed discussions, books on radio engineering should be consulted.

11–7 Transmission lines at high frequencies. The power required to maintain oscillations in an antenna is usually transported to it by means of transmission lines, or waveguides. The variation of current along a wire as a function of time for high-frequency alternating current is illustrated in Fig. 11–10, with an a-c source located at $x = 0$ supplying the current $I_0 \cos 2\pi ft$. The current maximum from the generator takes a

---

* G. P. Harnwell, *Principles of Electricity and Electromagnetism*, 2nd ed., pp. 599–623, McGraw-Hill, 1949.

Fig. 11–10. The variation of current along a wire as a function of time for high-frequency alternating current.

time t_0 to travel the distance x_0, where $v = x_0/t_0$ is the velocity of propagation of the current. In most cases, this velocity is somewhat less than the velocity of light in a vacuum. Figure 11–10 shows how the current varies sinusoidally along the wire at any instant of time and how it varies sinusoidally with time at any position such as $x = x_0$ along the wire.

The problems arising from such current variations were avoided in Chapter 10 by assuming that the wires in any circuit were much smaller than λ, where $\lambda = v/2\pi f$. Certainly the treatment of Chapter 10 can be used with little error whenever the relation between l, the length of the wires, and f is given by $l \leq v/2000\pi f$. For 60-cycle current, this is true for wires shorter than 800 m, a condition which is easily satisfied. However, for frequencies in the megacycle range used by commercial radio and television stations, the wires in the circuit would have to be shorter than 5 cm.

The simple Kirchhoff's law relations that are based upon $\nabla \cdot \mathbf{J} = 0$ and $\nabla \times \mathbf{E} = 0$ do not hold for these short wavelengths because the current and charge vary along the length of the wire. At these high frequencies energy is carried from point to point by the electric and magnetic fields around the conductor, and may be lost from the system by radiation into space or through energy absorption by nearby materials.

FIG. 11-11. Parallel wires transmitting power from a high-frequency electric generator.

Parallel-wire transmission line. When a high-frequency sinusoidal generator is connected to a long transmission line consisting of two parallel wires with identical characteristics, as shown in Fig. 11-11, the charges and currents have identical magnitudes but opposite signs on the two wires at any given x-coordinate. It can then be assumed that σ is the charge per unit length and i is the current, both being functions of x and t. If c_l is the capacitance per unit length, the potential difference between points a and d is $V = \sigma/c_l$. Furthermore, if l is the self-inductance per unit length, the magnetic flux through the rectangle $abcd$ is $d\phi = il\,dx$. With high frequencies, the analysis requires the use of the time-dependent relations $\mathbf{\nabla}\cdot\mathbf{J} + \partial\rho/\partial t = 0$ and $\mathbf{\nabla}\times\mathbf{E} = -\dot{\mathbf{B}}$, rather than the simpler relations $\mathbf{\nabla}\cdot\mathbf{J} = 0$ and $\mathbf{\nabla}\times\mathbf{E} = 0$ that were used with low frequencies. Integrating the first of these over the volume τ enclosed by the imaginary cylinder shown between a and b in Fig. 11-11 gives

$$\int_\tau \frac{\partial\rho}{\partial t}\,d\tau = -\int_\tau \mathbf{\nabla}\cdot\mathbf{J}\,d\tau = -\int_s \mathbf{J}\cdot d\mathbf{s},$$

where s is the whole surface of the cylinder. The left integral reduces to $(\partial\sigma/\partial t)\,dx$ and the right integral reduces to $i - [i + (\partial i/\partial x)\,dx] = -(\partial i/\partial x)\,dx$, and therefore

$$\frac{\partial\sigma}{\partial t} = -\frac{\partial i}{\partial x}. \tag{11-29}$$

The second fundamental relation should be integrated over the rectangular plane with corners at a, b, c, and d, taking the direction into the paper as positive. This gives

$$-\int_{s'} \dot{\mathbf{B}}\cdot d\mathbf{s'} = \int_{s'} \mathbf{\nabla}\times\mathbf{E}\cdot d\mathbf{s'} = \oint \mathbf{E}\cdot d\mathbf{l}.$$

The left integral reduces to $-d\phi/dt = -(\partial i/\partial t)l\,dx$ and, if the resistance of the wires is negligible, the right integral reduces to

$$\left(V + \frac{\partial V}{\partial x}\,dx\right) - V = \frac{\partial V}{\partial x}\,dx = \frac{1}{c_l}\frac{\partial\sigma}{\partial x}\,dx,$$

so that

$$\frac{1}{c_l} \frac{\partial \sigma}{\partial x} = -l \frac{\partial i}{\partial t}. \tag{11-30}$$

By differentiating Eq. (11–29) with respect to x and Eq. (11–30) with respect to t, the two can be combined to give

$$\frac{\partial^2 i}{\partial x^2} = lc_l \frac{\partial^2 i}{\partial t^2}, \tag{11-31}$$

which is a wave equation having the general solution

$$i = f(x - vt), \tag{11-32}$$

where $v = \sqrt{1/lc_l}$. Since Eqs. (11–29) and (11–30) can be combined to give a similar wave equation for σ, both i and σ are propagated as waves along the wire, as shown in Fig. 11–10. In the development of Eq. (11–30) it has been tacitly assumed that the wavelengths of the oscillations are large compared with the separation of the wires.

By using the complex functions discussed in Section 4–9, the values of l and c_l can be determined with steady-state conditions by finding some function of the complex variable $Z = x + jy$, such as $F(Z) = G + jH$, where either H or G will fit the boundary conditions. It will be assumed that the medium surrounding the wire is a homogeneous one for which $\epsilon = K\epsilon_0$ and $\mu = K_m\mu_0$. According to Eq. (4–29), when the function $H(x, y)$ fits the boundary conditions for the potential, the capacitance per unit length is given by

$$c_l = \frac{\epsilon(G_2 - G_1)}{H_2 - H_1},$$

where the difference of potential between the wires is $H_2 - H_1$ and the charge per unit length is $\epsilon(G_2 - G_1)$. Under these steady-state conditions, the magnetic flux per unit length is given by $\mu(H_2 - H_1)$ and the current is given by $G_2 - G_1$, so that

$$lc_l = \mu\epsilon$$

and the velocity of the waves is $v = \sqrt{1/\mu\epsilon}$, which is the velocity of light in the medium.

The foregoing analysis applies equally well to a transmission line consisting of a coaxial cable, because the values of l and c_l can be obtained in the same fashion. Obviously, any two-conductor line that approximates a two-dimensional geometry can be treated in a similar manner.

The transmission of power along two parallel wires by means of oscillating currents entails certain difficulties: namely, power may be absorbed from such a line by nearby conductors, or dielectrics or magnetic materials; and power is lost by radiation, especially at the higher frequencies. These difficulties are largely eliminated in the coaxial type of transmission line because of the shielding effect of the outer conductor, although power may be lost in the insulation that is used to keep the cylinders separated. Since the power appears to travel in waves through space, being merely guided by the conductors, the question arises as to whether or not the inner cylinder of the coaxial cable could be eliminated. Analysis shows that with frequencies above a minimum whose magnitude depends upon the dimensions of the tube, power can be transmitted very efficiently through hollow conducting tubes that are called *waveguides*.

11-8 Waveguides. Waveguides are frequently constructed so as to confine all electromagnetic radiation within their walls, thus eliminating effects of inductive and capacitive coupling as well as preventing power loss due to radiation. Such a waveguide may consist of a hollow cylinder formed from a highly conducting material such as copper. Electric energy is carried through the tube by electromagnetic waves generated and received at the ends of the tube by antennalike devices. Because electric fields are zero within perfect conductors, the waves are unable to pass through the walls of the guide but are reflected repeatedly until they have traveled the length of the guide.

Even for copper walls which are not "perfect" conductors, the radiation escaping through them is negligible. The amplitude of the electric field penetrating the copper walls decreases with the distance of penetration according to an exponential law. For a plane wave polarized in the x-direction,

$$E_x = E_{0x} e^{-(z/\delta)} \cos \omega \left(t - \frac{z}{\delta \omega} \right),$$

where z is the distance of penetration and

$$\delta = \left(\frac{\lambda_0 \sqrt{\epsilon_0/\mu_0}}{\pi K_m \sigma} \right)^{1/2}$$

is called the skin depth.* In copper, where $K_m = 1$ and $\sigma = 5.8 \times 10^7$ per ohm·m, $\delta = 3.8 \times 10^{-6}\sqrt{\lambda_0}$ and the amplitude of E_x is reduced by a factor of one thousand at 6.9 times the skin depth. This reduction occurs within 0.8×10^{-6} m with a 0.001-m wave and within 0.26×10^{-3} m with a 100-m wave (which is in the broadcast range so that a very thin copper wall will retain most of the radiation). Some power is dissipated by currents induced in the waveguide walls, but this is usually small and is proportional to the skin depth times the frequency. Henceforth, it

---

* A derivation of this may be found in *Principles of Electricity and Electromagnetism* by Harnwell, *op. cit.*, pp. 583–587.

will be assumed that the waveguide walls are perfectly conducting and that the medium is air or vacuum, where the velocity of light is c.

Reflection from an infinite sheet. To gain an understanding of the principles involved in waveguides, the reflection of electromagnetic waves from the surface of a large conducting sheet located in the xz-plane of Fig. 11–12 will be considered. Since the angle of incidence equals the angle of reflection, the angle made by $\mathbf{a}'$ with the z-axis is the negative of the angle made by $\mathbf{a}$, and both rays lie in the yz-plane. It is convenient to express the waves in an exponential form, where the incident and reflected x-components of $\mathbf{E}$ are the real parts of

$$E_x = E_{0x} \exp \{j\omega[t - (-y \sin \theta + z \cos \theta)/c]\}$$

and

$$E'_x = E'_{0x} \exp \{j\omega[t - (y \sin \theta + z \cos \theta)/c]\}.$$

Since the tangential components of $\mathbf{E}$ must be continuous across the boundary and since $\mathbf{E} = 0$ inside the plate, the boundary condition at $y = 0$ is $E_x + E'_x = 0$. This requires that $E_{0x} = -E'_{0x}$, which is equivalent to a 180° phase shift upon reflection. The superposition of the inci-

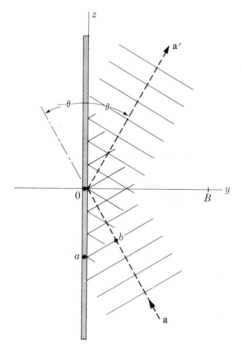

Fig. 11–12. Plane electromagnetic waves reflected from a conducting sheet. The lines perpendicular to the unit propagation vectors represent the positive peaks of the magnetic field.

dent and reflected waves must be done in such a way that the resulting function of y is sinusoidal; this can be accomplished by subtracting E'_x from E_x and dividing by $2j$. The resulting electric field is given by

$$E_{0x} \exp\left[j\omega \left(t - \frac{z}{c} \cos \theta \right) \right] \sin \left(\frac{\omega}{c} y \sin \theta \right), \qquad (11\text{–}33)$$

which represents an electric disturbance traveling along the z-axis parallel to the plates with a velocity $v_p = c/\cos \theta$. This velocity is known as *phase velocity* and clearly is greater than the velocity of light. No violation of relativity occurs here, however, since no signal can be transmitted along the guide with this velocity.

Phase and group velocity. The significance of phase velocity can be understood by studying Fig. 11–12, where an incident ray traveling in the direction **a** is reflected in the direction **a′** by the conducting sheet. The dotted line represents the path of the beam and the solid lines perpendicular to the path represent amplitude maxima of the magnetic field. The points of intersection between the incident maxima and the reflected maxima have twice the amplitude of either beam, and one of these points is indicated by a on the conducting sheet. As the incident ray progresses upward in the z-direction, this double-amplitude maximum reaches the origin in the same time it takes the wave to travel from b to the origin. The velocities of these double-amplitude maxima along the plate are therefore $c/\cos \theta$, which is the phase velocity, since phase velocity is defined as the velocity with which a disturbance in the electromagnetic wave is propagated along the waveguide.

The velocity with which the signal* is propagated along the guide is somewhat slower. It is just the component of the wave velocity parallel to the guide. This velocity, $v_g = c \cos \theta$, is known as group velocity. Group velocity and phase velocity are therefore related in a waveguide by

$$v_g v_p = c^2. \qquad (11\text{–}34)$$

Propagation between parallel plates. In addition to wave propagation in the z-direction, Eq. (11–33) also reveals a standing wave pattern along the y-axis, normal to the plate, having the wavelength $\lambda_n = 2\pi c/\omega \sin \theta = \lambda_c/\sin \theta$, where λ_c is the actual wavelength of the radiation. If a second plate is placed at $y = B$ in Fig. 11–12, then the boundary conditions require that $E_x + E'_x = 0$ at $y = B$. Equation (11–33) immediately gives the condition at $y = B$ that $\sin [(\omega/c)y \sin \theta] = 0$ or $(\omega/c)B \sin \theta =$

---

* A good discussion of waveguides and the velocity with which signals are propagated is given in *Fundamentals of Electric Waves*, by Skilling, Chapter XIII, John Wiley, 1942.

πm, where m is an integer. This may be written as

$$B = \frac{m\lambda_c}{2 \sin \theta} = \frac{1}{2} m\lambda_n.$$

The variation of E_x in the y-direction cannot have arbitrary wavelengths, but only a discrete set.

If a wavelength along the z-axis is defined by the phase velocity as $\lambda_p = v_p/f$, the following relations between λ_p and λ_n may be obtained:

$$1 = \sin^2 \theta + \cos^2 \theta = \frac{\lambda_c^2}{\lambda_p^2} + \frac{\lambda_c^2}{\lambda_n^2}$$

or

$$\frac{1}{\lambda_c^2} = \frac{1}{\lambda_p^2} + \frac{1}{\lambda_n^2}. \tag{11-35}$$

If λ_c is as large as λ_n, then λ_p will be infinite. Since $\lambda_p f = v_p$, this corresponds to an infinite phase velocity, which, according to Eq. (11–34), means that the group velocity is zero and no signal is propagated. The frequency corresponding to $\lambda_c = \lambda_n$ is known as the *cutoff frequency*. For frequencies below the cutoff frequency, λ_c is larger than λ_n and this requires λ_p in Eq. (11–35) to be an imaginary number which may be represented by jR. Substitution of jR for $\lambda_p = 2\pi c/\omega \cos \theta$ in Eq. (11–33) yields

$$E_{0x} e^{j\omega t} e^{-(2\pi z/R)} \sin \left(\frac{\omega}{c} y \sin \theta\right)$$

and all waves with frequencies below the cutoff frequency are attenuated exponentially in the z-direction.

Rectangular waveguide. A common waveguide consists of a hollow rectangular tube which could be represented in Fig. 11–12 by placing conducting plates along the planes defined by $x = 0$ and $x = A$ as well as those already placed at $y = 0$ and $y = B$. Radiation will still propagate in the z-direction, but now restrictions are placed on the waveform in the x- as well as in the y-direction. The following equations may readily be shown to satisfy the boundary conditions on $\mathbf{E}$ at $x = 0, A$ and $y = 0, B$:

$$E_x = E_{0x} \cos \frac{\pi l x}{A} \sin \frac{\pi m y}{B} e^{j(\omega t - z/\lambda_p)},$$

$$E_y = E_{0y} \sin \frac{\pi l x}{A} \cos \frac{\pi m y}{B} e^{j(\omega t - z/\lambda_p)}, \tag{11-36}$$

$$E_z = E_{0z} \sin \frac{\pi l x}{A} \sin \frac{\pi m y}{B} e^{j(\omega t - z/\lambda_p)}.$$

These equations satisfy Maxwell's equations, (11–1), (11–2), (11–3), and (11–4), and the wave equation, Eq. (11–5a).

Application of Eq. (11–3) yields the components of $\mathbf{H}$ for the radiation, and application of Eq. (11–4) to the components of $\mathbf{H}$ returns us to the components of $\mathbf{E}$ given in Eq. (11–36). Application of Eq. (11–1) to Eq. (11–36) gives

$$\left(\frac{\pi l}{A} E_{0x} + \frac{\pi m}{B} E_{0y} + \frac{j}{\lambda_p} E_{0z}\right)\left(\sin\frac{\pi l x}{A} \sin\frac{\pi m y}{B}\right) e^{j(\omega t - z/\lambda_p)} = 0,$$

which places a requirement on the components of $\mathbf{E}$ that is automatically satisfied if either l or m is zero. Where neither l nor m is zero,

$$\frac{\pi l}{A} E_{0x} + \frac{\pi m}{B} E_{0y} + \frac{j}{\lambda_p} E_{0z} = 0.$$

Since the real and imaginary parts must be separately zero, we have

$$\frac{E_{0z}}{\lambda_p} = 0 \quad \text{and} \quad \frac{E_{0x}}{E_{0y}} = -\frac{A m}{B l}$$

for the general case of propagation along the z-axis. The first condition arises from the boundary condition that $E_{0z} = 0$ on the surface of a conducting plate, but it extends this relation throughout the waveguide, so that the E_{0z} components of reflected and incident waves must add up to zero everywhere. The second condition indicates a fixed ratio between the x- and y-components of the electric field, depending upon the dimensions of the guide and the harmonics, l and m, of the radiation. These same conditions may be obtained by applying Eq. (11–2) to Eq. (11–36), which with these restrictions do satisfy Maxwell's equations.

Substitution of the $\mathbf{E}$-components of Eq. (11–36) into Eq. (11–5a) gives

$$\left[-\left(\frac{\pi l}{A}\right)^2 - \left(\frac{\pi m}{B}\right)^2 - \left(\frac{z}{\lambda_p}\right)^2\right] + \frac{\omega^2}{c^2} = 0,$$

which may be written as

$$\left(\frac{z}{\lambda_p}\right)^2 = \left(\frac{2\pi}{\lambda_c}\right)^2 - \left(\frac{\pi l}{A}\right)^2 - \left(\frac{\pi m}{B}\right)^2.$$

This further restriction, arising from the wave equation, indicates that λ_p will be real only if

$$\left(\frac{2}{\lambda_c}\right)^2 > \left(\frac{l}{A}\right)^2 + \left(\frac{m}{B}\right)^2.$$

As in the case of two parallel plates, propagation takes place for real values of λ_p, while imaginary values result in attenuation of the radiation in the z-direction. A rectangular waveguide, therefore, not only transmits electromagnetic radiation without allowing stray fields, but it also acts as a filter, passing only frequencies above the cutoff frequency.

If A is larger than B, the longest wavelength that can be transmitted occurs for $l = 1$ and $m = 0$. This is referred to as the TE_{01} (transverse electric) mode in which $E_x = 0$. Figure 11–13 illustrates the electric and magnetic flux lines for this mode. Visualization of higher transverse electric and transverse magnetic modes is more difficult and is best achieved by a detailed study of the mathematical relations.*

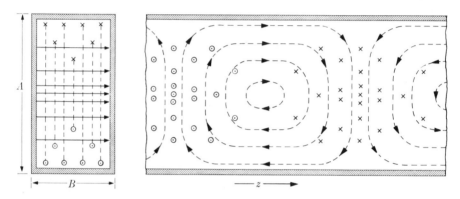

FIG. 11–13. The TE_{01} mode in a rectangular waveguide. Electric flux is represented by solid lines and magnetic flux by dotted lines. The symbol ⊙ represents electric or magnetic flux coming out of the paper, while crosses represent flux entering the paper.

* For a more detailed treatment, see S. Ramo and T. S. Whinnery, *Fields and Waves in Modern Radio*, John Wiley, 1953.

PROBLEMS

*11-1. What is the frequency of electromagnetic waves (in free space) of the following wavelengths: 10^{-8} cm (x-rays), 5×10^{-5} cm (yellow light), 10 cm (microwaves), 300 m (broadcast band)?

11-2. What is the maximum magnetic intensity in a plane radiowave in which the maximum electric intensity is 100 μv/m?

*11-3. The average power radiated by a broadcasting station is 10 kw. Assume the power to be radiated uniformly over the surface of any hemisphere with the station at its center. (a) What is the magnitude of the Poynting vector at points on the surface of a hemisphere 10 km in radius? At this distance, the waves can be considered plane. (b) Find the maximum electric and magnetic intensities at points on this hemispherical surface.

11-4. A radar transmitter emits a uniform conical beam of radiant energy. The solid angle of the cone is 0.01 steradian. The maximum electric intensity at a distance of 1 km from the transmitter is 10 v/m. (a) What is the maximum magnetic intensity? (b) What is the total power in the beam?

*11-5. Assume that a 100-watt incandescent lamp radiates all its energy in a sinusoidal electromagnetic wave, and that the energy is emitted uniformly in all directions. Compute the maximum electric and magnetic intensities at a distance of 2 m from the lamp.

11-6. Pure water has a dielectric constant of 80 in static electric fields but its index of refraction for visible light is 1.33. Calculate the ratio of the static to this high-frequency dielectric constant and account qualitatively for the discrepancy.

11-7. An electric field pulse is described by the relation

$$E_z = \exp[-(vt - y)^{100}].$$

Calculate H and plot E and H versus y at $vt = 0$ and at $vt = 3$.

*11-8. A long cylindrical wire of resistivity ρ and radius a carries a steady current I. Investigate the power carried by the Poynting vector into a finite length l of this wire with the resistance $R = \rho l/\pi a^2$. Choose the z-axis of cylindrical coordinates along the cylindrical axis, positive in the direction of the current.

(a) Calculate E, H, and S at a point P_0, very close to the wire, but where $r > a$.

(b) Draw a cylindrical surface about the wire, of length l and radius r, passing through P_0. Calculate the flux of the Poynting vector S through this cylindrical surface, including the ends, and compare the result with the known value of the power lost in heating this section of wire.

(c) Draw another cylindrical surface wholly within the wire, of length l and radius r, where $r < a$. Again calculate the flux of S through this surface and state how the heat dissipation at points within the wire depends upon the radial distance of these points from the axis.

---

* Answers to starred problems will be found at back of book.

*11–9. Suppose the coaxial cylinders in Fig. 11–6 have the total length $t_c + l + t_R$, where t_c is the length in contact with the cell and t_R is the length in contact with the washer. (a) Find the magnetic field energy U_m stored in the air space. (b) Find the electric field energy U_e stored in the air space and compute the ratio U_m/U_e.

11–10. Coaxial cylinders like those shown in Fig. 11–6 are made very long and the cell is replaced by a sinusoidal generator with the frequency $f = \omega/2\pi$. The space between cylinders is filled with air, and $(b - a) \ll \lambda$ but $l \gg \lambda$, where $\lambda = c/f$ is the wavelength of the electromagnetic waves.

(a) Show that the magnitudes of the electric and magnetic fields are given by the real parts of

$$E_r = \frac{V_m e^{j(\omega t - g z)}}{r \ln b/a} \quad \text{and} \quad H_\phi = \frac{I_m e^{j(\omega t - g z)}}{2\pi r}.$$

(b) Calculate the magnitude and direction of the Poynting vector as a function of cylindrical coordinates.

(c) Calculate the time average of the total Poynting vector flux.

(d) If no power is reflected by the washer, what is the complex impedance of this transmission line?

*11–11. An electromagnetic plane wave, given by $E_y = G \cos \omega(t - z/v)$, strikes a barrier and is reflected as $E'_y = -G \cos \omega(t + z/v)$. (a) Calculate the expression for the standing waves that are produced. (b) Calculate the Poynting vector $\mathbf{S}$ as a function of t and z. (c) Calculate the time average of $\mathbf{S}$.

11–12. A certain oscillating dipole like that in Fig. 11–8 has such a low frequency that the second time derivatives in Eqs. (11–16) and (11–17) can be neglected and the potential equations like Eq. (8–22) are valid.

(a) Calculate V and $\mathbf{A}$ for this dipole, using the simpler expressions.

(b) Calculate $\mathbf{E}$ and $\mathbf{H}$ from these potentials and express them in the forms of Eqs. (11–27) and (11–28), even though there are fewer terms in these simpler expressions.

(c) For both $\mathbf{E}$ and $\mathbf{H}$ calculate the amplitudes of the terms that are missing from the expressions in (b) to the largest amplitudes in these expressions, assuming $f = 10^4$ cycles/sec and $r = 10$ m.

11–13. Calculate the time average of the total power radiated away from the low-frequency dipole, using the simpler field expressions calculated in Problem 11–12(b).

*11–14. Calculate the vector potential $\mathbf{A}$ between the cylinders of the long coaxial line described in Problem 11–10 (a) for direct currents, and (b) for low-frequency sinusoidal oscillations.

11–15. Show that for any two-conductor and two-dimensional transmission line the self-inductance per unit length is given by $l = \mu(G_1 - G_2)/(H_1 - H_2)$, where the G's and H's are obtained from the complex relation $f(Z) = G + jH$. It should be assumed that $G = G_1$ over the first conductor and $G = G_2$ over the second, while $\int_s dH = H_1 - H_2$ when integrated over that part of the surface of either conductor that is in contact with the electromagnetic waves.

*11–16. Assuming that the conductors of the oscillating dipole have negligible resistance, calculate the effective resistance due to the power radiated. This is called the *radiation resistance*.

11-17. A certain broadcasting station radiates 50,000 watts at 10 Mc. If its antenna can be considered to be a dipole of length $l = \lambda/2$, what effective current must it generate?

*11-18. A plane-polarized beam of monochromatic light, directed along the positive y-axis, is represented by $E_z = G \cos \omega(t - y/c)$. An atom located at the origin can be polarized by displacing the center of a single electron through the distance $\mathbf{r}$ from the center of the very massive nucleus, located at the origin. The motion of the electron is given by

$$\frac{d^2\mathbf{r}}{dt^2} + k \frac{d\mathbf{r}}{dt} + \omega_0^2 \mathbf{r} = -e\mathbf{E}/m.$$

(a) Derive an expression for the motion of the electron due to the polarized light.

(b) Write the expression for the oscillating dipole moment of the atom, assuming k to be negligible, and obtain an expression in spherical coordinates for the energy being re-radiated by the atom.

(c) Find the value of k in the differential equation for $\mathbf{r}$, assuming that the only energy loss is that due to the re-radiation (scattering) by the atom.

(d) If ordinary light is scattered along the positive x-axis, does it appear polarized?

11-19. Sunlight is scattered by atoms and molecules in the upper atmosphere. Ordinary light can be considered as a collection of randomly timed pulses with random directions of polarization, perpendicular to the direction of propagation. With light traveling parallel to the y-axis, each pulse contains a long train of waves whose x- and z-components are given by $E_x = G_x \cos \omega(t - y/c)$ and $E_z = G_z \cos \omega(t - y/c)$, where $G^2 = G_x^2 + G_z^2$.

(a) If sunlight parallel to the y-axis strikes the atom described in Problem 11-18, describe the state of polarization, if any, in the light scattered along the positive x-axis.

(b) Determine the frequency-dependence of the scattered light and state which colors should predominate in this light if ω_0 corresponds to ultraviolet frequencies. Do your conclusions agree with observations on light scattered by the sky?

11-20. Show that the three components of Eq. (11-33) do satisfy Maxwell's relations and the boundary conditions.

*11-21. A waveguide consisting of a hollow rectangular conductor has the internal dimensions $a = 5$ cm and $b = 10$ cm. Determine the range of frequencies it can transmit.

11-22. Prove the first two of Fresnel's equations.

11-23. Prove the last two of Fresnel's equations.

11-24. A beam of light is directed perpendicular to the polished surface of glass having the index of refraction n. Calculate the fractions of the light that are reflected and transmitted.

11-25. Show that when a plane electromagnetic wave is incident normally on a plane boundary between two different dielectrics, the rate at which energy leaves the surface in the refracted and reflected beams is equal to the rate at which energy is incident on the surface.

*11–26. What fraction of the energy of a plane electromagnetic wave in air, incident normally on a plane water surface, is reflected if the frequency of the wave is such that the dielectric coefficient of the water is 80? Compare with the fraction reflected if the wave is of visible light, for which the index of refraction of water is 1.33.

*11–27. When a beam of light strikes an interface between air and glass normally, determine any change of phase in the reflected light when the beam progresses (a) from air to glass, and (b) from glass to air.

11–28. A beam of light striking a metal surface exerts a radiation pressure. Calculate this pressure from the force-on-a-charge equation, assuming that plane-polarized and monochromatic light impinges normal to the surface of a conductor having very low resistivity ρ.

11–29. If the incident beam in Fig. 11–13 is in glass of index n and the space above contains air, Snell's law gives $\sin \theta'' = n \sin \theta$. When θ is large enough to make $n \sin \theta > 1$, $\sin \theta'' > 1$, then θ is imaginary and total reflection results. However, some electromagnetic fields in the air are required to satisfy boundary conditions. (a) Show that the boundary conditions can be satisfied for this situation by such fields in the air as that described by

$$ E = M \exp\left[j\omega\left(t - \frac{x \sin \theta''}{c} \right) \right] \exp\left[-\omega_z \frac{\sqrt{n^2 \sin^2 \theta - 1}}{c} \right]. $$

(b) Show that the Poynting vector in this field is directed parallel to the surface.

APPENDIX

APPENDIX

TABLE FOR CONVERSION OF UNITS

This table is designed to make the conversion from one system of units to another as simple and automatic as possible. It contains four columns of units, i.e., mks, gaussian, cgs-esu, and cgs-emu, since practically all published papers on the subject of electricity and magnetism have employed units from one of these four systems.

The only units listed in these columns are those that fit into completely consistent systems of equations. This means that only one unit is mentioned in any square, although in a few instances alternate names for the same unit are listed.

Each row in the table contains equal quantities. For example, 1 coulomb $= 2.998 \times 10^9$ statcoulomb $= 10^{-1}$ abcoulomb. The automatic method for converting a quantity expressed in one system into a proper value expressed in another system has been described by the statement "all conversion factors are unity" when the names of units are treated as algebraic quantities. When it is desired to convert a quantity expressed in one set of units into the same quantity expressed in another set of units, the original quantity is multiplied by ratios, whose values are unity, arranged so that names of units in the denominator cancel the same names in the numerator and leave only the desired names of units. For example, to express the length 20,000 inches in terms of miles,

$$l = 20,000 \, \cancel{in.} \times \frac{1 \, \cancel{ft}}{12 \, \cancel{in.}} \times \frac{1 \, mi}{5280 \, \cancel{ft}} = \frac{20,000}{12 \times 5280} \, mi = 0.317 \, mi.$$

Suppose it is desired to find in farads the capacitance C of a capacitor whose capacitance in the cgs-esu system of units is 1000 statfarads:

$$C = 1000 \, \cancel{statfarads} \frac{1 \, farad}{2.998^2 \times 10^{11} \, \cancel{statfarads}},$$

$$C = 111.2 \times 10^{-11} \, farad.$$

Since 1 farad $= 2.998^2 \times 10^{11}$ statfarads, the ratio

$$\frac{1 \, farad}{2.998^2 \times 10^{11} \, statfarads}$$

is unity. Note that the statfarad in the denominator of the ratio cancels algebraically with the statfarad in the numerator of the given quantity.

TABLE FOR CONVERSION OF UNITS

Unit	mks	gaussian	cgs-esu	cgs-emu
Length	1 meter	100 centimeters	100 centimeters	100 centimeters
Mass	1 kilogram	1000 grams	1000 grams	1000 grams
Force	1 newton	10^5 dynes	10^5 dynes	10^5 dynes
Work, Energy	1 joule	10^7 ergs	10^7 ergs	10^7 ergs
Power	1 watt	10^7 ergs/sec	10^7 ergs/sec	10^7 ergs/sec
Charge	1 coulomb	2.998×10^9 statcoulombs	2.998×10^9 statcoulombs	10^{-1} abcoulomb
Current	1 ampere	2.998×10^9 statampères	2.998×10^9 statampères	10^{-1} abampère
Potential difference	1 volt	$\dfrac{1}{299.8}$ statvolt	$\dfrac{1}{299.8}$ statvolt	10^8 abvolts
Electric field, E	$1 \dfrac{\text{newton}}{\text{coulomb}}$ or $1 \dfrac{\text{volt}}{\text{meter}}$	$\dfrac{1}{2.998 \times 10^4}\dfrac{\text{dyne}}{\text{statcoul}}$ or $\dfrac{\text{statvolt}}{\text{cm}}$	$\dfrac{1}{2.998 \times 10^4}\dfrac{\text{dyne}}{\text{statcoul}}$ or $\dfrac{\text{statvolt}}{\text{cm}}$	$10^6 \dfrac{\text{dynes}}{\text{abcoul}}$ or $\dfrac{\text{abvolts}}{\text{cm}}$
Resistance	1 ohm	$\dfrac{1}{(2.998)^2\,10^{11}}$ statohm	$\dfrac{1}{(2.998)^2\,10^{11}}$ statohm	10^9 abohms

Resistivity	1 ohm·meter	$\dfrac{1}{(2.998)^2\,10^9}$ statohm·cm	$\dfrac{1}{(2.998)^9\,10^9}$ statohm·cm	10^{11} abohms·cm
Capacitance	1 farad	$(2.998)^2\,10^{11}$ statfarads	$(2.998)^2\,10^{11}$ statfarads	$\dfrac{1}{10^9}$ abfarad
Inductance	1 henry	$\dfrac{1}{(2.998)^2\,10^{11}}$ stathenry	$\dfrac{1}{(2.998)^2\,10^{11}}$ stathenry	10^9 abhenries
Magnetic flux density, B	$1\,\dfrac{\text{weber}}{\text{m}^2}$	10^4 gauss	†	10^4 gauss
Magnetic flux, ϕ	1 weber	10^8 maxwells or gauss·cm²	†	10^8 maxwells or gauss·cm²
Magnetic field, H	$1\,\dfrac{\text{ampere}}{\text{meter}}$	$4\pi10^{-3}$ gauss or oersted	†	$4\pi10^{-3}$ gauss or oersted*

* Originally the term gauss was used for both B and H in the gaussian system of units. Some felt, however, that the two quantities should be distinguished from each other and the word oersted was adopted for H only. Since in the gaussian system one always uses the expression $B = H + 4\pi M$, it makes little sense to use different names for the units of B and H.

† These spaces are left blank because, although units for these quantities could be devised in the cgs-esu system, they have not been used.

Actually, it is possible to check many of the numbers in this table by the above-mentioned system. For example, knowing that the electric field in the cgs-emu system of units must be in abvolt per centimeter, one can obtain the number given for this electric field by taking an electric field of one volt per meter and writing it as

$$\frac{1 \text{ volt}}{\text{m}} \times \frac{10^8 \text{ abvolts}}{\text{volt}} \times \frac{1 \text{ m}}{100 \text{ cm}} = 10^6 \frac{\text{abvolts}}{\text{cm}}.$$

Hence, 1 volt/m $= 10^6$ abvolts/cm.

In the mks system there are two constants that occur frequently, neither of which is dimensionless. They are

$$\epsilon_0 = \frac{10^{-9}}{35\pi} \text{ farad/m} \cong 8.85 \times 10^{-2} \text{ farad/m}$$

and

$$\mu_0 = 4\pi \times 10^{-7} \text{ henry/m,}$$

where μ_0 is an exact number by definition. The value of ϵ_0 is obtained from μ_0 and the velocity of light, i.e.,

$$\epsilon_0 = \frac{1}{\mu_0 c^2}, \text{ where } c \text{ is } 2.99792 \pm .00002 \times 10^8 \text{ m/sec.}^*$$

The experimentally determined value of c occurs several places in the table, where it has been rounded off to 2.998×10^8 m/sec.

---

* Rank, Bennett, and Bennett, *Phys. Rev.* **100**, 993, 1955.

NATURAL TRIGONOMETRIC FUNCTIONS

Angle					Angle				
De-gree	Ra-dian	Sine	Co-sine	Tan-gent	De-gree	Ra-dian	Sine	Co-sine	Tan-gent
0°	.000	0.000	1.000	0.000					
1°	.017	.018	1.000	.018	46°	0.803	0.719	0.695	1.036
2°	.035	.035	0.999	.035	47°	.820	.731	.682	1.072
3°	.052	.052	.999	.052	48°	.838	.743	.669	1.111
4°	.070	.070	.998	.070	49°	.855	.755	.656	1.150
5°	.087	.087	.996	.088	50°	.873	.766	.643	1.192
6°	.105	.105	.995	.105	51°	.890	.777	.629	1.235
7°	.122	.122	.993	.123	52°	.908	.788	.616	1.280
8°	.140	.139	.990	.141	53°	.925	.799	.602	1.327
9°	.157	.156	.988	.158	54°	.942	.809	.588	1.376
10°	.175	.174	.985	.176	55°	.960	.819	.574	1.428
11°	.192	.191	.982	.194	56°	.977	.829	.559	1.483
12°	.209	.208	.978	.213	57°	.995	.839	.545	1.540
13°	.227	.225	.974	.231	58°	1.012	.848	.530	1.600
14°	.244	.242	.970	.249	59°	1.030	.857	.515	1.664
15°	.262	.259	.966	.268	60°	1.047	.866	.500	1.732
16°	.279	.276	.961	.287	61°	1.065	.875	.485	1.804
17°	.297	.292	.956	.306	62°	1.082	.883	.470	1.881
18°	.314	.309	.951	.325	63°	1.100	.891	.454	1.963
19°	.332	.326	.946	.344	64°	1.117	.899	.438	2.050
20°	.349	.342	.940	.364	65°	1.134	.906	.423	2.145
21°	.367	.358	.934	.384	66°	1.152	.914	.407	2.246
22°	.384	.375	.927	.404	67°	1.169	.921	.391	2.356
23°	.401	.391	.921	.425	68°	1.187	.927	.375	2.475
24°	419	.407	.914	.445	69°	1.204	.934	.358	2.605
25°	.436	.423	.906	.466	70°	1.222	.940	.342	2.747
26°	.454	.438	.899	.488	71°	1.239	.946	.326	2.904
27°	.471	.454	.891	.510	72°	1.257	.951	.309	3.078
28°	.489	.470	.883	.532	73°	1.274	.956	.292	3.271
29°	.506	.485	.875	.554	74°	1.292	.961	.276	3.487
30°	.524	.500	.866	.577	75°	1.309	.966	.259	3.732
31°	.541	.515	.857	.601	76°	1.326	.970	.242	4.011
32°	.559	.530	.848	.625	77°	1.344	.974	.225	4.331
33°	.576	.545	.839	.649	78°	1.361	.978	.208	4.705
34°	.593	.559	.829	.675	79°	1.379	.982	.191	5.145
35°	.611	.574	.819	.700	80°	1.396	.985	.174	5.671
36°	.628	.588	.809	.727	81°	1.414	.988	.156	6.314
37°	.646	.602	.799	.754	82°	1.431	.990	.139	7.115
38°	.663	.616	.788	.781	83°	1.449	.993	.122	8.144
39°	.681	.629	.777	.810	84°	1.466	.995	.105	9.514
40°	.698	.643	.766	.839	85°	1.484	.996	.087	11.43
41°	.716	.658	.755	.869	86°	1.501	.998	.070	14.30
42°	.733	.669	.743	.900	87°	1.518	.999	.052	19.08
43°	.751	.682	.731	.933	88°	1.536	.999	.035	28.64
44°	.768	.695	.719	.966	89°	1.553	1.000	.018	57.29
45°	.785	.707	.707	1.000	90°	1.571	1.000	.000	∞

COMMON LOGARITHMS

N	0	1	2	3	4	5	6	7	8	9
0	....	0000	3010	4771	6021	6990	7782	8451	9031	9542
1	0000	0414	0792	1139	1461	1761	2041	2304	2553	2788
2	3010	3222	3424	3617	3802	3979	4150	4314	4472	4624
3	4771	4914	5051	5185	5315	5441	5563	5682	5798	5911
4	6021	6128	6232	6335	6435	6532	6628	6721	6812	6902
5	6990	7076	7160	7243	7324	7404	7482	7559	7634	7709
6	7782	7853	7924	7993	8062	8129	8195	8261	8325	8388
7	8451	8513	8573	8633	8692	8751	8808	8865	8921	8976
8	9031	9085	9138	9191	9243	9294	9345	9395	9445	9494
9	9542	9590	9638	9685	9731	9777	9823	9868	9912	9956
10	0000	0043	0086	0128	0170	0212	0253	0294	0334	0374
11	0414	0453	0492	0531	0569	0607	0645	0682	0719	0755
12	0792	0828	0864	0899	0934	0969	1004	1038	1072	1106
13	1139	1173	1206	1239	1271	1303	1335	1367	1399	1430
14	1461	1492	1523	1553	1584	1614	1644	1673	1703	1732
15	1761	1790	1818	1847	1875	1903	1931	1959	1987	2014
16	2041	2068	2095	2122	2148	2175	2201	2227	2253	2279
17	2304	2330	2355	2380	2405	2430	2455	2480	2504	2529
18	2553	2577	2601	2625	2648	2672	2695	2718	2742	2765
19	2788	2810	2833	2856	2878	2900	2923	2945	2967	2989
20	3010	3032	3054	3075	3096	3118	3139	3160	3181	3201
21	3222	3243	3263	3284	3304	3324	3345	3365	3385	3404
22	3424	3444	3464	3483	3502	3522	3541	3560	3579	3598
23	3617	3636	3655	3674	3692	3711	3729	3747	3766	3784
24	3802	3820	3838	3856	3874	3892	3909	3927	3945	3962
25	3979	3997	4014	4031	4048	4065	4082	4099	4116	4133
26	4150	4166	4183	4200	4216	4232	4249	4265	4281	4298
27	4314	4330	4346	4362	4378	4393	4409	4425	4440	4456
28	4472	4487	4502	4518	4533	4548	4564	4579	4594	4609
29	4624	4639	4654	4669	4683	4698	4713	4728	4742	4757
30	4771	4786	4800	4814	4829	4843	4857	4871	4886	4900
31	4914	4928	4942	4955	4969	4983	4997	5011	5024	5038
32	5051	5065	5079	5092	5105	5119	5132	5145	5159	5172
33	5185	5198	5211	5224	5237	5250	5263	5276	5289	5302
34	5315	5328	5340	5353	5366	5378	5391	5403	5416	5428
35	5441	5453	5465	5478	5490	5502	5514	5527	5539	5551
36	5563	5575	5587	5599	5611	5623	5635	5647	5658	5670
37	5682	5694	5705	5717	5729	5740	5752	5763	5775	5786
38	5798	5809	5821	5832	5843	5855	5866	5877	5888	5899
39	5911	5922	5933	5944	5955	5966	5977	5988	5999	6010
40	6021	6031	6042	6053	6064	6075	6085	6096	6107	6117
41	6128	6138	6149	6160	6170	6180	6191	6201	6212	6222
42	6232	6243	6253	6263	6274	6284	6294	6304	6314	6325
43	6335	6345	6355	6365	6375	6385	6395	6405	6415	6425
44	6435	6444	6454	6464	6474	6484	6493	6503	6513	6522
45	6532	6542	6551	6561	6571	6580	6590	6599	6609	6618
46	6628	6637	6646	6656	6665	6675	6684	6693	6702	6712
47	6721	6730	6739	6749	6758	6767	6776	6785	6794	6803
48	6812	6821	6830	6839	6848	6857	6866	6875	6884	6893
49	6902	6911	6920	6928	6937	6946	6955	6964	6972	6981
50	6990	6998	7007	7016	7024	7033	7042	7050	7059	7067
N	0	1	2	3	4	5	6	7	8	9

COMMON LOGARITHMS

N	0	1	2	3	4	5	6	7	8	9
50	6990	6998	7007	7016	7024	7033	7042	7050	7059	7067
51	7076	7084	7093	7101	7110	7118	7126	7135	7143	7152
52	7160	7168	7177	7185	7193	7202	7210	7218	7226	7235
53	7243	7251	7259	7267	7275	7284	7292	7300	7308	7316
54	7324	7332	7340	7348	7356	7364	7372	7380	7388	7396
55	7404	7412	7419	7427	7435	7443	7451	7459	7466	7474
56	7482	7490	7497	7505	7513	7520	7528	7536	7543	7551
57	7559	7566	7574	7582	7589	7597	7604	7612	7619	7627
58	7634	7642	7649	7657	7664	7672	7679	7686	7694	7701
59	7709	7716	7723	7731	7738	7745	7752	7760	7767	7774
60	7782	7789	7796	7803	7810	7818	7825	7832	7839	7846
61	7853	7860	7868	7875	7882	7889	7896	7903	7910	7917
62	7924	7931	7938	7945	7952	7959	7966	7973	7980	7987
63	7993	8000	8007	8014	8021	8028	8035	8041	8048	8055
64	8062	8069	8075	8082	8089	8096	8102	8109	8116	8122
65	8129	8136	8142	8149	8156	8162	8169	8176	8182	8189
66	8195	8202	8209	8215	8222	8228	8235	8241	8248	8254
67	8261	8267	8274	8280	8287	8293	8299	8306	8312	8319
68	8325	8331	8338	8344	8351	8357	8363	8370	8376	8382
69	8388	8395	8401	8407	8414	8420	8426	8432	8439	8445
70	8451	8457	8463	8470	8476	8482	8488	8494	8500	8506
71	8513	8519	8525	8531	8537	8543	8549	8555	8561	8567
72	8573	8579	8585	8591	8597	8603	8609	8615	8621	8627
73	8633	8639	8645	8651	8657	8663	8669	8675	8681	8686
74	8692	8698	8704	8710	8716	8722	8727	8733	8739	8745
75	8751	8756	8762	8768	8774	8779	8785	8791	8797	8802
76	8808	8814	8820	8825	8831	8837	8842	8848	8854	8859
77	8865	8871	8876	8882	8887	8893	8899	8904	8910	8915
78	8921	8927	8932	8938	8943	8949	8954	8960	8965	8971
79	8976	8982	8987	8993	8998	9004	9009	9015	9020	9025
80	9031	9036	9042	9047	9053	9058	9063	9069	9074	9079
81	9085	9090	9096	9101	9106	9112	9117	9122	9128	9133
82	9138	9143	9149	9154	9159	9165	9170	9175	9180	9186
83	9191	9196	9201	9206	9212	9217	9222	9227	9232	9238
84	9243	9248	9253	9258	9263	9269	9274	9279	9284	9289
85	9294	9299	9304	9309	9315	9320	9325	9330	9335	9340
86	9345	9350	9355	9360	9365	9370	9375	9380	9385	9390
87	9395	9400	9405	9410	9415	9420	9425	9430	9435	9440
88	9445	9450	9455	9460	9465	9469	9474	9479	9484	9489
89	9494	9499	9504	9509	9513	9518	9523	9528	9533	9538
90	9542	9547	9552	9557	9562	9566	9571	9576	9581	9586
91	9590	9595	9600	9605	9609	9614	9619	9624	9628	9633
92	9638	9643	9647	9652	9657	9661	9666	9671	9675	9680
93	9685	8689	9694	9699	9703	9708	9713	9717	9722	9727
94	9731	9736	9741	9745	9750	9754	9759	9763	9768	9773
95	9777	9782	9786	9791	9795	9800	9805	9809	9814	9818
96	9823	9827	9832	9836	9841	9845	9850	9854	9859	9863
97	9868	9872	9877	9881	9886	9890	9894	9899	9903	9908
98	9912	9917	9921	9926	9930	9934	9939	9943	9948	9952
99	9956	9961	9965	9969	9974	9978	9983	9987	9991	9996
100	0000	0004	0009	0013	0017	0022	0026	0030	0035	0039
N	0	1	2	3	4	5	6	7	8	9

FUNDAMENTAL CONSTANTS.

Largely based on values in the *American Institute of Physics Handbook* (1957). The probable error for each value has been omitted here; it should properly be considered part of the datum.

Name of Quantity	Symbol	Value
Velocity of light in vacuum	c	2.9979×10^8 m/sec
Charge of electron	q_e	-1.602×10^{-19} coul $=$
		-4.803×10^{-10} statcoul
Rest mass of electron	m_e	9.108×10^{-31} kgm
Ratio of charge to mass of electron	q_e/m_e	1.759×10^{11} coul/kgm $=$
		5.273×10^7 statcoul/gm
Planck's constant	h	6.625×10^{-34} j·sec
Boltzmann's constant	k	1.380×10^{-23} j/°K
Avogadro's number (chemical scale)	N_0	6.023×10^{23} molecules/mole
Universal gas constant (chemical scale)	R	8.314 j/mole·°K
Mechanical equivalent of heat	J	4.185×10^3 j/kcal
Standard atmospheric pressure	1 atm	1.013×10^5 new/m²
Volume of ideal gas at 0°C and 1 atm (chemical scale)		22.415 liter/mole
Absolute zero of temperature	0°K	-273.16°C
Acceleration due to gravity (sea level, at equator)		9.78049 m/sec²
Universal gravitational constant	G	6.673×10^{-11} new·m²/kgm²
Mass of earth	m_E	5.975×10^{24} kgm
Mean radius of earth		6.371×10^6 m $= 3959$ mi
Equatorial radius of earth		6.378×10^6 m $= 3963$ mi
Mean distance from earth to sun	1 AU	1.49×10^{11} m $= 9.29 \times 10^7$ mi
Eccentricity of earth's orbit		0.0167
Mean distance from earth to moon		3.84×10^8 m $\doteq 60$ earth radii
Diameter of sun		1.39×10^9 m $= 8.64 \times 10^5$ mi
Mass of sun	m_S	1.99×10^{30} kgm $= 333,000 \times$ mass of earth
Coulomb's law constant	C	8.98×10^9 new·m²/coul²
Faraday's constant (1 faraday)	F	$96,500$ coul/mole
Mass of neutral hydrogen atom	m_{H^1}	1.008142 amu
Mass of próton	m_p	1.007593 amu
Mass of neutron	m_n	1.008982 amu

FUNDAMENTAL CONSTANTS—*Continued*

Name of Quantity	Symbol	Value
Mass of electron	m_e	5.488×10^{-4} amu
Ratio of mass of proton to mass of electron	m_p/m_e	1836.12
Rydberg constant for nucleus of infinite mass	R_∞	109,737 cm^{-1}
Rydberg constant for hydrogen	R_H	109,678 cm^{-1}
Wien displacement law constant		0.2898 cm·°K

Numerical constants: $\pi = 3.142$; $e = 2.718$; $\sqrt{2} = 1.414$; $\sqrt{3} = 1.732$

PERIODIC TABLE OF THE ELEMENTS

Atomic weights are based on the most recent values adopted by the International Union of Chemistry. (For artificially produced elements, the approximate atomic weight of the most stable isotope is given in brackets.)

Period	Series	I	II	III	IV	V	VI	VII	VIII			O
1	1	1 H 1.0080										2 He 4.003
2	2	3 Li 6.940	4 Be 9.013	5 B 10.82	6 C 12.011	7 N 14.008	8 O 16.0000	9 F 19.00				10 Ne 20.183
3	3	11 Na 22.991	12 Mg 24.32	13 Al 26.98	14 Si 28.09	15 P 30.975	16 S 32.066	17 Cl 35.457				18 A 39.944
4	4	19 K 39.100	20 Ca 40.08	21 Sc 44.96	22 Ti 47.90	23 V 50.95	24 Cr 52.01	25 Mn 54.94	26 Fe 55.85	27 Co 58.94	28 Ni 58.71	
	5	29 Cu 63.54	30 Zn 65.38	31 Ga 69.72	32 Ge 72.60	33 As 74.91	34 Se 78.96	35 Br 79.916				36 Kr 83.80
5	6	37 Rb 85.48	38 Sr 87.63	39 Y 88.92	40 Zr 91.22	41 Nb 92.91	42 Mo 95.95	43 Tc [99]	44 Ru 101.1	45 Rh 102.91	46 Pd 106.4	
	7	47 Ag 107.880	48 Cd 112.41	49 In 114.82	50 Sn 118.70	51 Sb 121.76	52 Te 127.61	53 I 126.91				54 Xe 131.30
6	8	55 Cs 132.91	56 Ba 137.36	57–71 Lanthanide series*	72 Hf 178.50	73 Ta 180.95	74 W 183.86	75 Re 186.22	76 Os 190.2	77 Ir 192.2	78 Pt 195.09	
	9	79 Au 197.0	80 Hg 200.61	81 Tl 204.39	82 Pb 207.21	83 Bi 209.00	84 Po 210	85 At [210]				86 Rn 222
7	10	87 Fr [223]	88 Ra 226.05	89– Actinide series**								

*Lanthanide series:

57 La 138.92	58 Ce 140.13	59 Pr 140.92	60 Nd 144.27	61 Pm [147]	62 Sm 150.35	63 Eu 152.0	64 Gd 157.26	65 Tb 158.93	66 Dy 162.51	67 Ho 164.94	68 Er 167.27	69 Tm 168.94	70 Yb 173.04	71 Lu 174.99

**Actinide series:

89 Ac 227	90 Th 232.05	91 Pa 231	92 U 238.07	93 Np [237]	94 Pu [242]	95 Am [243]	96 Cm [245]	97 Bk [249]	98 Cf [249]	99 E [253]	100 Fm [255]	101 Md [256]	102 No	103

ANSWERS TO SELECTED PROBLEMS

ANSWERS TO SELECTED PROBLEMS

To eliminate ambiguity, and at the same time to save space, the following commonly used conventions have been adopted in these answers:

$$a/b + c \equiv \frac{a}{b} + c, \qquad a/(b + c) \equiv \frac{a}{b + c},$$

and

$$\cos \theta / 4\pi r^2 \sin \beta \equiv \frac{\cos \theta}{4\pi r^2 \sin \beta}.$$

CHAPTER 1

1-1. 0.0918 n, 2.98×10^{-37} n.

1-3. (a) 0.16 n, (b) 2.4×10^{25} m/sec^2.

1-5. 2.16 n. $\times 10^{-7}$

1-7. 625 electrons.

1-9. 9×10^{-7} n along the diagonal, 8.6×10^{-7} n along the diagonal.

1-11. (a) q_a in (gm·cm)$^{1/2}$, (b) q_s in (gm·cm^3)$^{1/2}$/sec.

CHAPTER 2

2-1. (a) $\mathbf{a}_R = \mathbf{i}3/13 + \mathbf{j}4/13 + \mathbf{k}12/13$,
   $\mathbf{a}_\theta = \mathbf{i}36/65 + \mathbf{j}48/65 - \mathbf{k}5/13$,
   $\mathbf{a}_\phi = -\mathbf{i}4/5 + \mathbf{j}3/5$.
   (b) $\mathbf{a}_\phi =$ same as above, $\mathbf{k} = \mathbf{k}$.

2-4. (b) $E_y = 0.173$ n/coul, $E_z = 0.230$ n/coul.
   (c) $E_y = \{3(y - 3)/r_1^3 - 4(z - 4)/r_2^3\}10^{-10}/\pi\epsilon_0$, where $r_1^2 = x^2 + (y - 3)^2 + (z - 4)^2$ and $r_2^2 = x^2 + y^2 + z^2$.

2-5. On the 2-m circle, $E_r = 1.5 \cos \theta$ and $E_\theta = 0.75 \sin \theta$.

2-7. -3.92×10^{-5} coul.

2-9. -25×10^{-9} coul.

2-10. (b) R.

2-12. (a) 3 m, (b) 2×10^{-7} coul.

2-14. (a) 1440 v, (b) $V = 2340/\sqrt{1 + 100z^2}$, (c) $v = 10^4\sqrt{11,440 - 1.6V}$

2-16. (a) $\mathbf{E} = \mathbf{k}\sigma(1 - z/a + z^3/2a^3 - 3z^5/8a^5 + \cdots)/2\epsilon_0$, (b) $(z/a)100\%$.

2-18. (a) $\mathbf{a}_r \lambda/2\pi\epsilon_0 r$, (b) $(\mathbf{a}_r - \mathbf{k})\lambda/4\pi\epsilon_0 r$.

2-21. (c) zero, (d) $\mathbf{i}39 + \mathbf{j}156 - \mathbf{k}52$, (e) $90°$.

2-22. (b) $55°23'$.

2-23. $\cos \theta = l_1 l_2 + m_1 m_2 + n_1 n_2$.

2-25. (a) $2\pi A$, (b) $2\pi A$, (c) zero.

2-26. $256/3$.

2-28. (a) $\mathbf{i}(3x^2 + 6xy) + \mathbf{j}(3x^2 + 4yz) + \mathbf{k}2y^2$ and $\mathbf{i}(y - 4) + \mathbf{j}(x - 3)$.
   (b) On the z-axis and on the line $(3, 4, z)$, respectively.

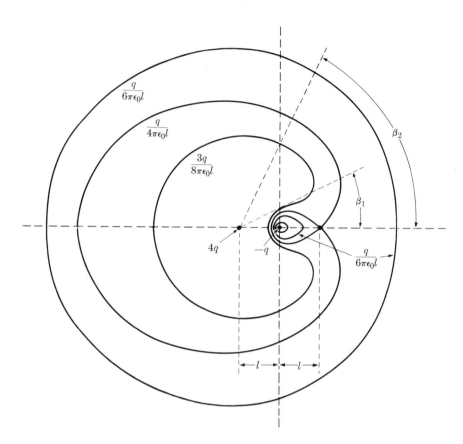

2–31. (a) $\{\mathbf{a}_r Z - \mathbf{a}_z(\sqrt{Z^2 + r^2} - r)\}\lambda/4\pi\epsilon_0 r\sqrt{Z^2 + r^2}$,

(b) $\{\ln(Z + \sqrt{Z^2 + r^2}) - \ln r\}\lambda/4\pi\epsilon_0$.

(d) The point P is sufficiently general for the infinite wire, but not for the half-infinite wire.

2–33. $r = \sqrt{bd}$, a sphere.

2–35. (a) Distant l from $-q$ on the extended centerline.   (b) $q/4\pi\epsilon_0 l$.

(c) Crosses axis at l, $-0.235l$, and $-4.235l$. Angles $\beta_1 = 19°55'$ and $\beta_2 = 70°5'$ (see figure).

2–36. $4q \sin^2 2\beta - q \sin 2\beta - V4\pi\epsilon_0 l = 0$. For $V = 3q/8\pi\epsilon_0 l$, $\beta_1 = 24°18'$ and $\beta_2 = 65°42'$ (see figure).

CHAPTER 3

3–1. 9040 electrons.

3–3. 3 m.

3–5. 5760 v, 7200 v, 8100 v, 9900 v, and 9900 v.

3–7. (a) 0.00354 μf,   (b) 35.4 μcoul,   (c) 20×10^5 n/coul.

3–9. (a) 800 μcoul, 800 v; 800 μcoul, 400 v.

(b) 533 μcoul, 533 v; 1067 μcoul, 533 v.

3–11. (a) 1 μf, (b) 900 μcoul, (c) 100 v.

3–13. $E = \rho r/3\epsilon_0$ and $\rho a^3/3\epsilon_0 r^2$, respectively.

$V = (3a^2 - r^2)\rho/6\epsilon_0$ and $\rho a^3/3\epsilon_0 r$, respectively.

3–15. $E = \rho r/2\epsilon_0$ and $\rho a^2/2\epsilon_0 r$, respectively.

$V = A - \rho r^2/4\epsilon_0$ and $A - (\ln r/a + 1/2)\rho a^2/2\epsilon_0$, respectively.

3–17. 6°58′.

3–19. $(e^{\alpha r^3} - e^{\alpha a^3})\rho_0/3\alpha\epsilon_0 r^2$.

3–20. (b) No, because of the lack of the necessary symmetry. The internal fields are not zero in the cube.

3–24. $\nabla \times \mathbf{A} = 0$ for (a) and (c) but not for (b) or (d). $\nabla^2 V = 0$ for (c) but not for (a).

3–25. $\mathbf{H}$ is not conservative.

CHAPTER 4

4–1. (a) $q(h/(h^2 + r^2)^{1/2} - 1)$, (b) 60°, (c) 84°16′.

4–4. zero.

4–5. $q(d^2 - a^2)/a(a^2 + d^2 - 2ad \cos \theta)^{3/2}$.

4–8. (a) 1.1×10^{25} coul/m^3 for nuclei, 11.1 $\times 10^{25}$ coul/m^3 for proton;

(b) $(3r_n^2 - r^2)\rho/6\epsilon_0$ and $\rho r_n^3/3\epsilon_0 r$; (c) $V_{\max} = \rho r_n^2/2\epsilon_0$.

4–11. Taking the center of the small sphere as the origin of spherical coordinates,

(a) $\sigma a^2(hl - br)/\epsilon_0 hlr$ between spheres and $\sigma a(hl - ba)/\epsilon_0 hl$ inside the small sphere.

(b) $\rho a^3(hl - br)/3\epsilon_0 hlr$ between spheres and $\rho a(3hla^2 - 2ba^2 - hlr^2)/6\epsilon_0 hl$ inside the small sphere. In each case $l^2 = w^2 + r^2 - 2wr \cos \theta$, where $w = (b^2 - h^2)/h$.

4–13. (a) $q(1/l - \lambda/l_1 + \lambda/r)/4\pi\epsilon_0$, where $l^2 = p^2 + r^2 - 2pr \cos \theta$ and $l_1^2 = \lambda^4 p^2 + r^2 - 2\lambda^2 pr \cos \theta$.

(b) $q\{l_a^3 - p^3(1 - \lambda^2)\}/4\pi a p l_a^3$, where $l_a^2 = p^2 + a^2 - 2pa \cos \theta$ and $l_{a1} = \lambda l_a$.

(c) $-q^2\lambda^3(2 - \lambda^2)/(1 - \lambda^2)^2 4\pi\epsilon_0 p^2$. (d) No. (e) $q/4\pi\epsilon_0 p$.

4–15. (a) $qa(r_1^3 - r_2^3)/2\pi r_1^3 r_2^3$, where $r_1^2 = a^2 + (y - b)^2 + z^2$ and $r_2^2 = a^2 + (y + b)^2 + z^2$.

(b) $\dfrac{q^2 a}{16\pi\epsilon_0} \left\{ \dfrac{1}{(a^2 + b^2)^{3/2}} - \dfrac{1}{a^3} \right\}$.

4–18. (a) $\dfrac{4\pi\epsilon_0 V}{p} = \dfrac{z - h}{\{(h - z)^2 + R^2\}^{3/2}} + \dfrac{z + h}{\{(h + z)^2 + R^2\}^{3/2}}$,

$\sigma = -p(R^2 - 2h^2)/2\pi(R^2 + h^2)^{5/2}$.

(b) $\dfrac{4\pi\epsilon_0 V}{pR \cos \phi} = \dfrac{1}{\{(h - z)^2 + R^2\}^{3/2}} - \dfrac{1}{\{(h + z)^2 + R^2\}^{3/2}}$,

$\sigma = 3phR \cos \phi/2\pi(h^2 + R^2)^{5/2}$,

where R, ϕ, and z are the cylindrical coordinates.

4–19. $qap^3/(p^2 - a^2)^2$.

4–21. (a) $-\lambda h/\pi(y^2 + h^2)$, (b) $-\lambda^2/4\pi\epsilon_0 h$.

4-23. (a) $Ar \cos \theta/a$, (b) $Aa^2 \cos \theta/r^2$, (c) $3\epsilon_0 A \cos \theta/a$.

4-25. (a) $2Q(1 + 4\beta^3 + 3\beta^4 - \cdots)/\pi\epsilon_0 d^2$,
    (b) $Q/2\pi\epsilon_0 a(1 + \beta + \beta^2 + \beta^3 + 2\beta^4 + \cdots)$, where $\beta = a/d$.

4-27. (a) $2\epsilon_0(3X^2 Y - Y^3)/A^3$, (b) $3\epsilon_0 V_e/A$, (c) $-4\epsilon_0 V_e x^2/A^3$ and
    $-16\epsilon_0 V_e x^3/3\sqrt{3} \; A^3$.

4-28. $\lambda = 2\pi\epsilon_0 V_c/\ln b/r$. A conducting wire can, in principle, be made so fine
    that its effect upon an electrostatic field can be neglected, since $\lambda \to$ zero
    as $r \to$ zero.

4-29. (a) $2\pi\epsilon_0/\ln 4/3$, (b) $a/s = 8/15$, $b/s = 3/4$, $d_e/s = 7/60$.

4-31. (a) $\pi\epsilon_0/\ln 3$, (b) $4.428\epsilon_0/\ln 3$, (c) $y/b = 8/3$.

4-33. $C_e/C_0 = 1 + \delta^2/2(B^2 - 1) \ln B$, where $B = b/a$.

4-35. (a) $-\lambda s/\pi(y^2 + s^2)$, (b) $-\lambda^2/4\pi\epsilon_0 s$, where $s^2 = d^2 - a^2$.

CHAPTER 5

5-2. (a) $0.226 \, \text{m}^2$, (b) 1250 v.

5-4. (a) 1000 v, (b) 2000 v, (c) 5×10^{-4} joule.

5-7. (a) 5.53×10^{11} f, (b) $0.0166 \, \mu\text{coul}$, (c) 2.49×10^{-6} joule.

5-9. $\epsilon_0 h^2/\pi m e^2$.

5-11. (a) $D = Q/a^2, Q/b^2, Q/b^2, Q/r^2$, where $q = 4\pi Q$.
    $E = Q/\epsilon a^2, Q/\epsilon b^2, Q/\epsilon_0 b^2, Q/\epsilon_0 r^2$, where $\epsilon = K\epsilon_0$.
    $P = Q(K - 1)/Ka^2, Q(K - 1)/Kb^2, 0, 0$.
    $V = Q(1/b + 1/Ka - 1/Kb)/\epsilon_0, Q/\epsilon_0 b, Q/\epsilon_0 b, Q/\epsilon_0 r$.

5-13. (a) D, P, and E are the same as in Problem 5-11.
    $\rho_p = Q(r - a) \exp (r/a - 1)^2/2a^2 r^2$.
    (b) $q(e - 1)/4$.

5-15. (a) $4\pi K\epsilon_0 ab/(b - a)$, (b) $\epsilon A/d$, the same.

5-17. $(P_{2n} - P_{1n})/\epsilon_0$.

5-19. $\text{ctn}^{-1} (K_1 \text{ctn} \theta_1/K_2)$.

5-21. $3KE/(2K + 1)$ in sphere, $2KE/(K + 1)$ in cylinder.

5-23. (b) $q'/q = (1 - K)/(1 + K)$, $q''/q = 2K/(K + 1)$,
    (c) $q^2(K - 1)/(K + 1)16\pi\epsilon_0 h^2$,
    (d) $qh(K - 1)/(K + 1)2\pi(h^2 + r^2)^{3/2}$,
    (e) $q(K - 1)/(K + 1)$.

5-25. (a) $\lambda^2(K - 1)/(K + 1)4\pi\epsilon_0 h$, (b) $-\lambda h/2\pi(K + 1)(x^2 + h^2)$.

5-27. (a) 0.766×10^{-18} m, (b) $0.383Z \times 10^{-18}$ m, (c) 1.40×10^{-15} m.

5-29. (a) $q^2 d/2\pi\epsilon_0 a^2$, (b) $q^2/2\pi\epsilon_0 a^2$, (c) $-q^2 \delta d/2\pi\epsilon_0 a^2$. The work done
    charging the battery is $q^2 \delta d/\pi\epsilon_0 a^2$.

CHAPTER 6

6-2. (a) 3.8×10^{-4} ohm, 7.6 v; (b) 14.3 kgm/sec.

6-5. 77.3 ohms.

6-7. (a) $\pm 10^{-5}$ v, (b) $\pm 10^{-5}$ v, (c) $\pm 3.5 \times 10^{-5}$ v.

6-10. 8.75 amp.

6-11. 2.4.

6-12. 1.34.

6-15. (a) 1.17 cm^2,   (b) 0.246 cm^2,   (c) 116.7 v, 254.2 v.

6-16. (a) $\{Plk(b - a)/(b + a)\pi\rho\}^{1/2}$,   (b) independent of d.

6-17. (a) $s\mathcal{E}/(R + s^2r/N)$ or $s\mathcal{E}/(R + sr/p)$;

    (b) $R = Nr/p^2$;   (c) $p_m = 3$;

    (d) and (e) With $p = 3$, $I = 29.4$ amp or 9.8 amp/cell; but with $p = 4$,

    $I = 27.3$ amp with only 6.8 amp/cell.

6-18. (a) $\lambda = 2I\rho\epsilon_0/b$,

    (b) $J = 4I(1 - 1/3 + 1/5 - 1/7 + 1/9 - \cdots)/\pi bd$.

6-21. $(1 - a/l - a^2/l^2 - a^3/l^3 - 2a^4/l^4 - \cdots)\rho/2\pi a$.

6-22. $(1 - 1.29a/l + \cdots)\rho/4\pi a$.

6-23. (a) $G_l = 2\pi/\rho \ln m$, where $ma = s - \sqrt{s^2 - a^2}$; (b) $P_l = G_lV^2$.

6-25. (a) $2\pi\rho/t \ln 2.49$,   (b) 1.015, 1.26.

6-28. $\delta I_m/I_m = (\delta V/V)R_BV/(R_BV + RV_B)$.

6-30. (a) 1.16 amp, 1.03 amp, 14.5 amp, 12.3 amp;

    (b) 1740 watt, 1230 watt;   (c) 70.7%.

CHAPTER 7

7-2. (b) 500 rad/sec.   (c) Either 333 rad/sec or 667 rad/sec.

7-3. (a) 54 m/sec^2, 26.7 m/sec;   (b) 15.7 m/sec;

    (c) 33.3 m/sec;   (d) 4.05 n;   (e) 135 watts.

7-5. 5.37 hp.

7-8. (a) $\mu_0\pi\rho t\omega a^4/4$,   (b) $\mu_0 4\pi\rho\omega a^5/15$.

7-11. (a) l^2V/V_a4s; no.   (b) $V^2/V_a2B^2s^2$; no.

    (c) 2560 v and 197 v, that is, $m_0v^2/2e$ and svB.

7-12. (a) $BB_ved_i/2E_v$;

    (b) ± 1.27 cm;   (c) 3.06×10^5 m/sec, 6110 v.

7-14. (a) $n^2h^2\epsilon_0/\pi e^2m$,

    (b) $-e^2/8\pi\epsilon_0a$,   (c) ~ 4800 A and visible.

7-15. (a) 30.7×10^6 cycles/sec,   (b) 2.15×10^8 m/sec,

    (c) 19.2×10^6 cycles/sec.

7-17. (a) $v_f = \mathcal{E}_BBl/(B^2l^2 + RG)$, $p_m = Gv_f^2$;   (b) $\mathcal{E}_B(\mathcal{E}_B - Blv_f)/R$.

7-19. (a) $\pi a^2B_0\alpha e^{-\alpha t}/R$, $\pi a^2B_0e^{-\alpha t}/R$.

7-21. (a) $B_0\omega r \sin \omega t/2\rho$,   (b) $(\omega^2B_0^2\pi a^4h/8\rho) \sin^2 \omega t$.

7-23. (a) $\theta_i/q2\pi\nu$,   (b) $\theta/V = \theta_i/q2\pi\nu R_g$.

7-25. (a) $v = G/\sqrt{1 + G^2/c^2}$, where $G = eRB_a/2m_0$;

    (b) $R' = m_0v/eB_0\sqrt{1 - \beta^2}$;

    (c) $v \cong c$, 0.24 billion electron volts.

CHAPTER 8

8-1. (a) zero,   (b) 1.41×10^{-6} w/m^2,

    (c) 3×10^{-6} w/m^2 in the x-direction.

8-3. 2.4×10^{-20} n.

8-5. 3.42×10^{-3} w/m^2.

8-6. 72×10^{-5} n.

8-9. $(\mu_0l/2\pi) \ln b/a$.

8-11. $\mu_0 I(e^2 - 1)/4a$.

8-13. $\mu_0 I/2\sqrt{3}\,\pi a$.

8-16. No.

8-17. (a) $(\mathcal{E}2\pi t/\rho_c)\ln b/a$, (b) 0, $(\mathcal{E}/r)\ln b/a$, 0, 0.

(c) $Ir/2\pi a^2$, $I/2\pi r$, $I(c^2 - r^2)/(c^2 - b^2)2\pi r$, 0.

8-18. (a) $-I(\theta_2 - \theta_1)/2\pi$, (b) $-Is/\pi(s^2 + y^2)$.

8-19. (a) If $2d$ = distance between wire centers, $s^2 = d^2 - a^2$ and the results for Problem 8–18 are correct.

(b) Flux lines follow circles outside the wires but are distorted where they pass through the wires.

8-21. (a) 121 millihenries, (b) 102 millihenries.

8-22. (a) $\mu_0 N_a^2 a^2/2r_c$, $\mu_0 N_b^2 b^2/2r_c$; (b) $\mu_0 N_a N_b a^2/2r_c$. When r_c is not much greater than b, $L_b = (\mu_0 N_b^2 b^2/2r_c)(1 + b^2/4r_c^2 + b^4/8r_c^4 + \cdots)$ and the correction in parentheses is similar for L_a and M, with a replacing b.

8-25. (a) $\displaystyle\int_s \nabla A_z \cdot ds = -\mu \int_\tau J_z \, d\tau$, (b) $\mathbf{A} = -\mathbf{k}(\mu I/2\pi)\ln r/a$.

8-26. (a) $\mathbf{k}(\mu I/2\pi)\ln r_2/r_1$, (b) $(\mu I/\pi r_1^2 r_2^2)[\mathbf{i}2xyd + \mathbf{j}d(d^2 + y^2 - x^2)]$.

8-27. (a) $\mathbf{J} = \mathbf{a}_\phi(3G\sin\theta)/2$ in amp/m, (b) $\mathbf{B}_o = \mathbf{d}_f\mu_0 Ga^3/2r^3$ in w/m^2.

8-28. (a) $\mathbf{a}_\phi\mu_0\omega\sigma a^4\sin\theta/3r^2$, (b) $\mathbf{a}_\phi\mu_0\omega\sigma ar\sin\theta/3$,

(c) $\mathbf{k}2\mu_0\omega\sigma a/3$, $\mathbf{d}_f\mu_0\omega\sigma a^4/3r^3$.

CHAPTER 9

9-1. (a) $\mu_0 Ir/2\pi R^2$, (b) $\mu_0 I^2 r^2/8\pi^2 R^4$, (c) $\mu_0 I^2 l/16\pi$.

9-3. 950 amp.

9-5. (b) $H = 670$ amp/m.

9-6. (a) $\mathbf{a}_z(1 - a^2/2l^2)\mathfrak{M}/2$, $\mathbf{H} = \mathbf{B}/\mu_0$;

(b) $\mathbf{a}_z(1 - a^2/2l^2)\mathfrak{M}/2$, $-\mathbf{a}_z(1 + a^2/2l^2)\mathfrak{M}/2\mu_0$;

(c) $\mathbf{a}_z(1 - 2a^2/l^2)\mathfrak{M}$, $-\mathbf{a}_z 2\mathfrak{M}a^2/\mu_0 l^2$;

(d) $-\mathbf{a}_z 2\mathfrak{M}a^2/l^2$, $\mathbf{H} = \mathbf{B}/\mu_0$.

9-9. (a) 18.3%, (b) 0.01%.

9-10. (a) $0.59\sqrt{a}$ m, (b) $a < 8.7$ cm.

9-11. Torque about the center of mass is $1.67p_m^2/l^4$.

9-12. (a) $\Omega_i = \mathfrak{M}r\cos\theta/\mu_0(2K_m + 1)$, $\Omega_o = \mathfrak{M}a^3\cos\theta/\mu_0(2K_m + 1)r^2$.

(b) In a vacuum, $\mathfrak{M} = 2.1 \times 10^{-4}$ w/m^2; and in the medium, $\mathfrak{M} = 7.7 \times 10^{-4}$ w/m^2.

9-14. $\oint \mathbf{H} \cdot d\mathbf{l} = 0$, $\oint \mathbf{B} \cdot d\mathbf{l} = 3\mathfrak{M}a^3\cos\theta/3R^2$.

9-15. (a) $\mu_0 H + \mathfrak{M}/3$, (b) $\mu_0 H$, (c) $\mu_0 H + \mathfrak{M}$, and (d) $\mu_0 H + \mathfrak{M}/2$.

9-16. (a) 3.15 w/m^2, (b) 2.08 w/m^2.

9-17. (a) $\mathcal{R} = 2\pi\mu_0 l^3\tan\theta$, (b) $\mathcal{P} = \mu_0 8\pi^2 f^2 ma^2/5$,

(c) $B_H = \sqrt{\mathcal{P}/\mathcal{R}}$, $P_m = \sqrt{\mathcal{R}\mathcal{P}}$.

9-19. Torque on loop due to sphere = $\mathbf{a}_p \times \mathbf{d}_f p_m IA3K_m/(2K_m + 1)4\pi r^3$; and due to the needlelike magnet, the torque = $\mathbf{a}_p \times \mathbf{d}_f p_m IA/4\pi r^3$.

9-21. (a) $B = \mu_0 H = 0.293\mathfrak{M}_i$; (b) $B = \mu_0 H = 0.552\mathfrak{M}_i$;

(c) $\mu_0 H = -0.448\mathfrak{M}_i$, $B = 0.552\mathfrak{M}_i$;

(d) $\mu_0 H = -\mathfrak{M}_i a^3/16r_c^3$, $B = \mathfrak{M}_i(1 - a^3/16r_c^3)$.

9–23. $B_i/B_o = 4b^2 K_m/[b^2(K_m + 1)^2 - a^2(K_m - 1)^2]$.

9–25. (a) $L_a = \mu_0 K_m N_a^2 a^2/2r_c$, $M = \mu_0 K_m N_a N_b a^2/2r_c$,
$L_b = \mu_0 N_b^2 (K_m a^2 - a^2 + b^2)/2r_c$;

(b) $L_b = \mu_0 K_m N_b^2 b^2/2r_c$, and L_a and M are the same as in (a).

CHAPTER 10

10–1. (a) 56 v, 139 v, 56 v;
(b) $v = 141 \sin 377t$, $i = 7.84 \sin (377t + \tan^{-1} 1.5)$.

10–3. (a) 21 amp,   (b) 73 millihenries.

10–5. (a) $1/2\pi\sqrt{LC(1 - R^2C/L)}$,
(b) $\sqrt{1 - R^2C/L}\,/2\pi\sqrt{LC}$.

10–7. (b) 39.8 cycles/sec,   (c) 5000 v.

10–8. (a) 0.987,   (b) 6.9×10^{-4} joule,
(c) 8×10^{-4} joule,   (d) 5320 ohms.

10–10. (b) $\delta = 1 + 8|\mathcal{I}_m|\mathcal{Z}/\mathcal{V}$,   (c) $\delta - 1 = 320 \times 10^{-6}e^{j\phi}$, a circle.

10–15. $(1 - e^{-t/R_L C})\mathcal{E}_B/R_L$.

10–16. (a) Assuming the generator voltage to be $v = V_m \cos \omega t$, the transient current is $i_c = K\beta e^{-\alpha t} \cos (\beta t + \delta)$, where $K = V_m \sin \theta/\omega Z \sin \delta$ and $\operatorname{ctn} \delta = (\alpha - \omega \operatorname{ctn} \theta)/\beta$. The symbols Z and θ are defined in Fig. 10–3 and the values of α and β are given in Section 10–2.

(b) Assuming the generator voltage to be $v = V_m \sin \omega t$, the transient current is $i_c = -K_1\beta e^{-\alpha t} \sin (\beta t + \delta_1)$, where $K_1 = V_m \cos \theta/\omega Z \cos \delta_1$, $\tan \delta_1 = (\alpha + \omega \tan \theta)/\beta$, and the symbols α, β, Z, and θ have the same values as given in (a).

10–17. (a) $(\mu_0 l/\pi) \ln \left(\dfrac{d - a}{a} \right)$,   (b) $f_0 = \rho/\pi a^2 \mu_0 \ln \left(\dfrac{d - a}{a} \right)$,
(c) $f_0 = 3.13 \times 10^3$ cycles/sec.

10–19. (a) $\theta_2 - \theta_1 = 158°8'$, $\theta_3 - \theta_1 = 228°11'$;
(b) $i_1 = 3.3$ amp, $i_2 = -4.6$ amp, and $i_3 = 1.3$ amp.

10–21. (b) $\mathcal{V}_J = (\mathcal{V}_1 Z_2 Z_3 + \mathcal{V}_2 Z_1 Z_3 + \mathcal{V}_3 Z_1 Z_2)/(Z_1 Z_2 + Z_1 Z_3 + Z_2 Z_3)$,
(c) $\mathcal{V}_J = -4.85 - j3.18$ v.

10–23. (a) 0.679 watt,   (b) 0.751 watt,   (c) 0.093 watt.

10–25. (a) $R_{\text{a-c}} = 1$ ohm, $X = 40.0$ ohms;
(b) $R_{\text{a-c}} = 9$ ohms, $X = 4.36$ ohms.

10–28. (a) 2.40 amp, 2.078 amp, 2.29 amp;   (b) 14.59 ohms must be added;
(c) $0.202 \, \mu f$;   (d) 19.9×10^{-6} amp or 10^{-5} of the steady 2.00 amp.

10–31. (a) $I_b/I_a = \sqrt{4\pi^2 R_l^2 + \omega^2 \ln^2 (c/a)}/\sqrt{4\pi^2 R_l^2 + \omega^2 \ln^2 (c/b)} = \Re$,
(b) $P_{\text{a-c}} = I^2 R_l(1 + \Re^2)/(1 + \Re)^2$.

CHAPTER 11

11–1. 3×10^{18}, 0.6×10^{15}, 3×10^9, 10^6;   all in cycles/sec.

11–3. (a) 16×10^{-6} watt/m^2;   (b) 0.11 v/m, 2.9×10^{-4} amp/m.

11–5. 38.6 v/m, 0.103 amp/m.

11–8. (a) $\mathbf{k}\rho I/\pi a^2$, $\mathbf{a}_\phi I/2\pi r$, $-\mathbf{a}_r\rho I/2\pi^2 a^2 r$;
  (b) $-I^2 R$, where $R = \rho l/\pi a^2$; (c) $-I^2 R r^2/a^2$.
11–9. (a) $(\mu_0 I^2 l/4\pi) \ln b/a$, (b) $\epsilon_0 V_m^2 \pi l/(\ln b/a)$.
11–11. (a) $\mathbf{j}2G \sin \omega t \sin (\omega z/v)$,
  (b) $\mathbf{k}(4G/\mu v) \sin \omega t \cos \omega t \sin (\omega z/v) \cos (\omega z/v)$, (c) zero.
11–14. (a) $-\mathbf{k}(\mu I_m/2\pi) \ln r/a$,
  (b) $-\mathbf{k}(\mu I_m/2\pi) (\ln r/a) \cos \omega t$.
11–16. $2\pi l^2 \sqrt{\mu}/3\lambda^2 \sqrt{\epsilon}$.
11–18. (a) $z = -eG \cos (\beta + \delta)/m\sqrt{(\omega_0^2 - \omega^2)^2 + \omega^2 k^2}$, where
    $\beta = \omega(t - y/c)$ and $\tan \delta = \omega k/(\omega_0^2 - \omega^2)$;
  (b) $p_0 \cos \beta = e^2 G \cos \beta/m(\omega_0^2 - \omega^2)$ and
    $\overline{S} = \mathbf{a}_r(\omega^4 p_0^2/32\pi^2 \epsilon_0 c^3) \sin^2 \theta/r^2$;
  (c) $k = \mu_0 e^2 \omega^2/6\pi mc$; (d) yes, with $\mathbf{E}$ parallel to the z-axis.
11–21. $f > 1.5 \times 10^9$ cycles/sec.
11–26. 63.6% compared to 2.02% for visible light.
11–27. (a) No phase change, (b) 180° phase change in $\mathbf{E}$.

INDEX

INDEX

Abampere, 5
Abcoulomb, 5
Abfarad, 5
Abohm, 5
Abvolt, 5
Admittance, 336
Alnico 5, magnetization, 295
Alternating current, 324
  ammeters, 349
  bridges, 346
  resistance to, 332
  transients, 327
Alternating-current series element, defined, 324
  differential equation for, 325
Ammeters, a-c, 349
  d-c, 192
Ampere, defined, 266
  legal definition of, 9
Ampere balance, 267
Amperian currents, 241
Antennas, practical, 391
Aston's mass spectrograph, 237
Atomic fields, 152
Atomic structure, 129

Bainbridge mass spectrograph, 237
Ballistic galvanometer, 231
Barkhausen effect, 315
Betatron, 240
B-field, defined, 210
  measurement of, *219*, 293
  of solenoids, 243
  of straight-wire sections, 242
B versus H curves, 295
B versus H, permanent magnets, 282
Biot-Savart law, 241
  field calculations with, 242
Bitter technique, showing domains, 313

Bohr magneton, *305*, 310
Bohr orbits, 166, *238*
Bohr-Sommerfeld atom model, *129*, 304
Boundary conditions, static with dielectrics, 141
  static with magnetic materials, 288
  with time-dependence, 371
Boundary-value problems, rules for solution of, 82
Bozorth, magnetic data, 294, 309
Brewster's angle, 376
Brewster's law, 376
Bridges, Wheatstone, 197
  a-c, 346
Bureau of Standards, legal definitions of units, 8
  standard ampere, 266

Campbell inductance bridge, 269
Capacitance of capacitors, defined, 65
Capacitance, general relation in two dimensions, 114
  of isolated conductors, 66
  of two spheres, 103
Capacitance-resistance relation, 186
Capacitive reactance, 330
Capacitors, 65
Cauchy-Riemann relations, 110
  singular points of, 122
cgs units, 3
Charge conservation relation, 183
Charge density, ρ, defined, 55
  due to polarization, 138
  "real," or nonpolarization, 139
Complementary functions, 326
Complex conjugate, 107
Complex quantities, addition and multiplication of, 105
  exponential forms of, 107

Complex variables, in a-c networks, 326
for eccentric-cylinder problems, 117
as functions for two-dimensional problems, 108
Conductance, general definition of, 336
Conductors, metallic, 170
Conservative fields, electrostatic, 33
magnetostatic, 281
Conservative forces, defined, 32
Conservative H-field limitation, 249
Conversion of units, table for, 405
Coordinate systems, 17
cylindrical, 17
orthogonal, 18
rectangular, 17
spherical, 18
Copper-oxide rectifier, 344
Coulomb's law, vector expression for, 21
vector integration of, 25
Critical damping, in a-c circuits, 328
in galvanometers, 230
Cross product of vectors, defined, 41
properties of, 41
unit vectors, 42
Curie temperature, 309
Curie-Weiss law, 309
Curl, equations derived for rectangular coordinates, 68
in orthogonal coordinates, 70
of a vector field, defined, 66
Current regulation, 206
Cylinders in uniform fields, conducting, 97
dielectric, 150
magnetic, 289
Cylindrical coordinates, 17
Cyclotron, 211
Carnegie Institute of Technology, 201, 238, 322

D-vector, defined, 254
versus $\mathbf{E}$, 282
Damping of galvanometers, 230

d-c energy propagation along a coaxial cable, 379
Debye temperature, 175
Dees, cyclotron, 211
Del operator, mathematical significance of the symbols $\nabla \cdot \mathbf{A}$ and $\nabla \times \mathbf{A}$, 72
a table of its vector operations, 75
Demagnetizing factor, 292
Density of surface charges on conductors, 58
$\mathbf{d}_f$, dipole-field vector, defined, 39, 389
Diamagnetic materials, 279
Diamagnetism, 307
Dielectric boundary conditions, 141
Dielectric constants, anisotropic, 140
isotropic, 140
Dielectric cylinder in a uniform field, 150
Dielectric hysteresis, 161
Dielectric materials, 129
Dielectric sphere in uniform field, 147
Differential equations for scalar and vector potentials, 257
Dipole, electric, 163
electric field of an ideal, 24
energies, 164
general energy flow near an oscillating dipole, 389
ideal, 23
magnetic, 304
magnetic from current loop, 253
oscillating fields, 385
power-flow vector, 390
Dipole moment, alternate units for magnetic current loops, 216, 276
ideal electric, defined, 23, 164
Dipole potentials, electric, 39
magnetic, 249, 253, 277
oscillating, 384
Dipole radiation, 388
Direction cosines, 47
Displacement current, defined, 253
Displacement and real surface densities, 143
Displacement vector, defined, 139

Divergence, of electric fields, 60
general definition of, 60
in rectangular, cylindrical, and orthogonal coordinates, 61
Divergence theorem, 63
Domain walls, 312
Dot product, 28
Dynamometers, 350
Dynamos, electric, 216
Dyne, 7

E-vector, field, defined, 20
versus D, 282
Earnshaw's theorem, 114
Eccentric cylinder problem, complex variables, 117
Effective current for a-c networks, 331
Effective voltage for a-c networks, 331
Einstein–de Haas experiment, 305
Electrets, 163
fields of, 282
Electric dynamo, 217
linear generator, 219
motor, 226
Electric fields, on atoms in a crystal, 151
at a physical point, 139
Electric power, conversion of, 225
Electrostatic fields,
of charge distributions, 25
defined, 20
of an electric dipole, 22, 164
of multiple point charges, 21
of potential distributions, 256
of a uniformly charged plane, 26
Electrostatic-field energy, 154
Electrostatic potentials, defined, 32
of charge distributions, 35
from Laplace's equation, 82 ff.
of multiple point charges, 35
Electronic mobilities in Cu and Ni, 203
Electron spin, 304
Electromotive force, defined, 182
electromagnetically induced, 223
Energy, in electromagnetic circuits, 263

in electromagnetic fields, 377
in electrostatic fields, 154
in magnetostatic fields, 302
Energy conversions in electromagnetic fields, 377
Energy flow, in coaxial cable, 379
in electromagnetic fields, 377
in electromagnetic waves, 378
near an oscillating dipole, 388
Equivalent resistance, 190
Erg, 9
Exchange energy, 308
in domain walls, 312
Extraordinary Hall effect in ferromagnetic materials, 319

Farad, legal definition of, 10
Faraday effect, dielectric, 141
Faraday's law of induced emf's, 222
Fermi-Dirac statistics, 172
Ferroelectric materials, 162
Ferromagnetic domains, 310
Ferromagnetic elements, 310
Ferromagnetic materials, 308
table of properties of, 309
Ferromagnetic sphere in a uniform field, 290
Ferromagnetic toroid, 296
Ferromagnetic transformer cores, 354
Floating battery, 206
Flux, electric, defined, 51
magnetic, defined, 210
Fluxmeter, 233
Flux tubes, 56
Forces, between current circuits, 265
on current circuits in magnetic fields, 213
on dipoles, 165
electrostatic, 21
image, *84*, 171
Lorentz relation for, 209
on magnetized materials, 317
Fourier series, 101
Free energy, in dielectrics, 163
Frequency bridge, 348
Frequency filter, 339

Fresnel's reflection and refraction equations, 375
Full-wave rectifier, 345

Galvanometer, 226
  ballistic and steady-current, 231
  damping characteristics of, 229
  equivalent circuits to, 228
  sensitivity of, 232
  vibration, 349
Gauss, unit defined, 6
Gauss' law, differential form of, 59
  with distributed charges, 55
  proof with point charges, 54
  use in symmetrical problems, 57
Gauss' mathematical theorem, derivation of, 63
Gaussian experiment, 319
Gaussian pillbox, 141
Gaussian system of units, 6
Generator, linear electromagnetic, 217
Giorgi system of units, 7
Gradient, in cylindrical coordinates, 38
  defined, 37
  in orthogonal coordinates, 38
  properties of, 40
  in rectangular coordinates, 38
  in spherical coordinates, 38
Graphical solutions of a-c networks, 337
Group velocity, 397
Gruneisen resistivity curve, 174
Guard-ring technique, 114
Gyromagnetic ratio, 305

Hall effect, 212
  power conversion, 236
  two ferromagnetic constants, 319
Heat, joulean, 178
Heaviside-Lorentz units, 6
Henry, legal definition of, 10
Hertz experiments, 366
H-field, defined, *279*, 247
  from gradient, 249
  importance of, 284
  measurement of, 293

of toroid, 252
versus **B**-field, 282
High-frequency transmission lines, 391
Hole conduction, 213
Homopolar dynamo, 234
Hydraulic analogy, 172
Hysteresis, in dielectrics, 161
  in ferromagnetics, 294

Ideal dipoles, 23
Ideal generators, 341
Ideal transformers, 352
Identities with the del operator, 76
Image force on electrons, 171
Image method, conducting sphere, 86
  dielectric plane, 168
  for electrostatic problems, 83
  infinite series, *102*, 187
Imaginary numbers, 105
Impedance, complex, 329
  effective, 337
  real, 329
Impedance triangle, 330
Impurity atoms in metals, 175
Incremental permeability, 294
Index of refraction, 369
Induced emf's, 223
Inductance bridge, 347
Inductance, mutual and self-, 260
  of solenoids, 274
  of toroidal windings, 274
  of two circular loops, 261
Induction, electromagnetic, 209
Inductive coupling, 351
  power absorption resulting from, 354
Inductive reactance, 330
Inductors, 324
Insulators, 129
Integration of vectors, 25, 31
Intrinsic energy, 160
Instruments, d-c, 192
Iron group of elements and alloys, 308

Joulean heat, 178
Joule, unit defined, 7

Kelvin cavities, 167
Kerr effect, dielectric, 141
Kerst betatron, 240
Kirchhoff's laws,
  for a-c networks, 332
  basic principles for a-c, 324
  complex formulation of, 334
  for d-c networks, 189
  for magnetic circuits, 298

Langevin-Debye polarizability equation, 133
Laplace's equation, 65
  in boundary-value problems, 82
  in cylindrical coordinates, 75
  in orthogonal coordinates, 75
  in rectangular coordinates, 74
  in spherical coordinates, 75
  sum theorem, 90
  uniqueness theorem, 88
Legendre's equation, 92
  table of polynomials, 93
Legal definitions of units, 8
Lenz' law, 216
Light, electromagnetic theory of, 364
Linear charge density, 48
Linear materials, dielectric, 141
  magnetic, 279
Line element, defined, 30
  cylindrical, 38
  orthogonal, 38
  rectangular, 37
  spherical, 38
Line integral, 31
Lorentz condition on scalar and vector
  potentials, 257
Lorentz force relation, 209

Magnetic dipole of current loop, 252
Magnetic fields, work to produce, 303
Magnetic induction, 244
  See also **B**-field
Magnetic materials, 276
Magnetic poles, 316
Magnetic pole density, 280

Magnetic properties of iron and silicon
  steel, tables, 321
Magnetic scalar potential, 249
  of current-carrying loop, 277
Magnetic sheets *versus* current loops, 300
Magnetism, atomic origin, 304
Magnetization curves, 295, 314
Magnetized cylinder, **H**- and **B**-fields, 285
Magnetization, defined, 279
Magneto-mechanical factor, defined
  and table of, 305
Magnetomotive force, 300
Matthiessen's rule, 176
Maxwell's field relations in differential
  and integral form, 255
  first, 137, 139
  second, 220, 246
    proof of, 245
  third, 222
  fourth, critique of, 281
    with steady currents, 247, 249, 251
    with time-dependence, 253
Maxwell's theory of light, 364
Measurements of magnetic fields, 293
Mechanisms of polarization, 132
Metallic conductors, 170
Method of images, 83
  infinite series in, 102
Microscopic fields on atoms, 153
Millman's theorem, 358
Mutual inductance, 260

Networks, routine solutions with a-c, 341, 357
  routine solutions with d-c, 199
Network theorems, 341
Newton, unit of force, 7
Nonconductors, 129
Nonlinear materials, 283
  dielectric, 161
  magnetic, 289
Nonohmic materials, 173
  as circuit elements, 342
  in resistors, 345

Normal magnetization curve, 294
Norton's theorem, 342
Nuclei, 123, 168

Oersted, defined, *6*, 9
Ohm, legal definition of, 10
    standard, 268
Ohmic materials, 173
Ohm's law, 173
    point function, 174
Operator, del, 71
    table of operations with, 75
Operator identities, table of, 76
Optical laws, 371
Orbits, electron, *238*, 166
Ordinary Hall effect in ferromagnetic
    materials, 319
Orthogonal coordinate systems, 18
    table of relations in, 62
    total differential for function V in, 36
Oscillating dipole, 383
    field expressions for, 385
    detailed energy flow near, 389
    potentials, 383
    radiated power from, 389
    radiation resistance of, 389
Overdamped circuits, 329
Overdamped galvanometers, 229

Parallel-plate capacitor, 65, 111
Parallel wires, 116, 128
Paramagnetic materials, 279
Paramagnetism, 306
Partial differentiation, 35
Particular integral for a-c networks,
    328
Permalloy, 294
Permanent magnet fields, 282, 287, 291
Permeability, relative, defined, 279
Perminvar, 323
Phase velocity, 397
Physical point, defined, 56
    of electric fields, 139
    of magnetic fields, 280
    magnetization at, 279
    polarization at, *133*, 279

Plane waves, electric and magnetic
    fields, 369
Point charges, electrostatic fields, 21
Poisson's equation, 81
    derivation of, 64
Polar molecules, 132
Polarizability, defined, 133
    Langevin-Debye equation, 133
    table of, 136
    temperature-dependence of, 133
Polarization, defined, 133
    frequency-dependence of, 133
    mechanism of, 132
    static, 134
    temperature-dependence of, 133
Polarization charges, surface density
    of, 144
    volume density of, 138
Polarized light, 376
Potentials, d-c network, 182
    electrostatic, 32
    general time-dependent scalar and
        vector, 256
    retarded, 381
    scalar, for current loops, 249, 259, 261
    scalar, for magnetic materials, 300
    due to static charge distributions, 35
    vector, 256
Potentiometer, 196
    accuracy of, 202
Power absorption in a-c series ele-
    ments, 331
Power conversion, 225
Power factor, defined, 331
Poynting vector, 377
    in coaxial cable, 379
    derivation of, 377
    near oscillating dipole, 390
    in plane electromagnetic waves, 378
Product of complex quantities, 107
Products of vectors, cross, 40
    dot, 28
    triple scalar, 44
    triple vector, 44

Q-value of an inductor, 353, 359

Quantum mechanics, 171, 304, 307, 308, 311

Radiation from an oscillating dipole, 383
Radiation resistance, 389
Radii of nuclei, *123*, 168
Rationalized units, 6
Reactance, capacitive, 330
  inductive, 330
Rectifiers, 344
Rectifying circuits, full wave, 344
Reflection, electromagnetic waves, 375
  light, 375
  total, 404
Refractive index, 369
Relative permeability, defined, 279
Relativistic mass, 238
Relaxation time, 174
Reluctance, 299
Resistance between concentric cylinders, 186
Resistance-capacitance relation, 186
Resistance, equivalent, 190
  standard, 268
Resistivity, 174
  table of, 177
  temperature-dependence of, 176
Resonance circuits, 338
Retarded potentials, general equations and solutions, 381
Richardson-Dushman equation, 172
Root-mean-square, current, 331
  voltage, 331
Routine solution for a-c networks, 341
Rowland ring, 320
Rutherford scattering, 129

Saddlepoints, 114
Saturation magnetization, 309
Scalar potentials, *see* Potentials
Scattering, of electromagnetic waves by atoms, 403
  of ordinary light, 403
Schottky effect, 172
Search coil, 219
Self-inductance, 262

Semiconductors, 343
  as rectifiers, 343
Series and parallel resistors, 190
Sheet, magnetic, 300
Silicon steel, magnetic properties of, 321
Singular points, in complex variables, 122
Skin depth, 395
Skin effect, 355
Snell's law, 372
Solenoid, 243
Solid angles, defined, 52
  elemental, 52
  of spherical cap, 54
Solids, covalent and ionic binding, 131
Spectrograph, mass, 238
Sphere and plane capacitor, 103
Spheres in uniform fields,
  conducting, in electrostatic fields, 93
  dielectric, in electrostatic fields, 147
  magnetic, in magnetic fields, 288
Spherical coordinates, 17
Spherical permanent magnet, 291
Spin of electron, 304
Spiral windings for electromagnets, 206
Standard ampere, defined, 266
Standard resistor, 268
Statampere, 5
Statcoulomb, 5
Statfarad, 5
Statohm, 5
Statvolt, 5
Steady alternating currents, 329
Steradian, 52
Stokes' theorem, derivation of, 70
Storage batteries, 181
Superposition theorem, 342
Surface charge density on conductors, 58
Susceptance, 336
Susceptibility, magnetic, 279
  table of, 307
Symbols, table comparing magnetostatic with electrostatic, 278
Synchrocyclotron, 238

Temperature-dependence,
  of magnetic susceptibility, 308
  of paramagnetism, 306
  of polarizability, 133
  of resistivity, 179
  of saturation magnetization, 309
Thermistors, 346
Thermocouples, 181
Thévenin's theorem, 342
Thomson's e/m equipment, 236
Three-phase network, 333
Thyrite, 345
Toroid, ferromagnetic, 296
  H-field in, 252
Torques, on current-carrying loops, 214
  on current circuits, 265
Total differential, defined, 36
  in orthogonal systems, 36
Transformer cores, 353
Transient solutions of the series-element differential equation, 327
Transistors, 343
Transmission lines for high frequency, 391
Transmission velocity for high frequencies, 393
Transverse propagation of plane waves, 369
Triode, 166
Triple products of vectors, 44
Two-dimensional problems, complex variables, 108

Underdamped circuits, 329
Underdamped galvanometers, 229
Units, cgs-esu, 5
  cgs-emu, 4
  gaussian, 5
  Heaviside-Lorentz, 6
  legal definitions of, 8
  practical, 2
  rationalized, 6
  rationalized mks, 7
  systems of, 1
  table for conversion of, 405
Unit vectors, cross products, 42

defined, 16
dot products, 29
Uniqueness theorem, for dielectric materials, 144
  for evacuated spaces, 88

Van de Graaff generator, 179
Vector addition and subtraction, 14
Vector diagrams for steady a-c networks, 333
Vector notation, 13
Vector operations with del, table, 74
Vector potential, 256
  low-frequency solutions, 257
  oscillating dipole, 385
Vector unit in rectangular coordinates, 17
Vectors, dot products of, 28
  integration of, 24
Velocity of electromagnetic waves,
  along wires, 394
  compared to light velocity, 364
Vibration galvanometer, 349
Virgin magnetization curve, 294
Volt, legal definition of, 10
Voltmeters, a-c, 349
  d-c, 194

Wattmeters, 350
Wave equations in isotropic dielectrics, 366
Waveguides, 395
  rectangular, 398
Wavelength spectra, 365
Wave mechanics, 130
Weber, legal definition of, 10
  magnetic flux definition of, 210
Wheatstone bridge, 197
Whiskers, magnetic, 314
Work function, 171
Work in charging capacitors, 154
Work per unit volume, to create electrostatic fields, 159
  to polarize linear nonisotropic dielectrics, 163
  to polarize nonlinear dielectrics, 160
  to produce magnetic fields, 303